ADOLESCENT

SUBSTANCE

ABUSE

Etiology, Treatment, and Prevention

Edited by

Gary W. Lawson, PhD
Director
Graduate Studies in Chemical Dependency
School of Human Behavior
United States International University
San Diego, California

Ann W. Lawson, PhD
Associate Professor
Marriage and Family Therapy
School of Human Behavior
United States International University
San Diego, California

AN ASPEN PUBLICATION®
Aspen Publishers, Inc.
Gaithersburg, Maryland
1992

Library of Congress-in-Publication Data

Adolescent substance abuse: etiology, treatment, and prevention/edited by Gary W. Lawson,
Ann W. Lawson
p. cm
Includes bibliographical references and index.
ISBN 0-8342-0254-9
1. Teenagers—Substance use. 2. Alcoholics—Rehabilitation. 3. Narcotic addicts—Rehabilitation.
I. Lawson, Gary. II. Lawson, Ann W.
[DNLM: 1. Substance Abuse—in adolescence. WM 270 A23964]
RJ506.D78A364 1992
362.29'0835—dc20
DNLM/DLC
for Library of Congress
92-11363
CIP

The authors have made every effort to ensure the accuracy of the information herein. However, appropriate information sources should be consulted, especially for new or unfamiliar drugs or procedures. It is the responsibility of every practitioner to evaluate the appropriateness of a particular opinion in the context of actual clinical situations and with due consideration to new developments. Authors, editors, and the publisher cannot be held responsible for any typographical or other errors found in this book.

Editorial Services: Barbara Priest

Library of Congress Catalog Card Number: 92-11363
ISBN: 0-8342-0254-9

Printed in the United States of America

1   2   3   4   5

To today's adolescents who now write papers in school entitled *What I Am Going To Be "If" I Grow Up* from those of us who wrote papers in school entitled *What I Am Going To Be When I Grow Up*—**Good Luck.**

Table of Contents

PART IV   SPECIAL GROUPS

Contributors

David L. Archambault, PhD
Psychologist
Pennhurst Medical Group
Tulsa, Oklahoma

Jacqueline Aroyo, PhD
Staff Psychologist
Child and Family Guidance Services
San Jose, California

Kirt J. Baab, MA
Outreach Counselor
Mental Health Specialist
Fresno, California

Robert E. Banks, PhD
Coordinator
Substance Abuse Counseling Program
Assistant Professor of Psychology
Amarillo College
Amarillo, Texas

Thomas F. Brock, PhD, MFCC
Clinical Director
Park Place Center
Cerritos, California

Patricia Copeland, PhD
Substance Abuse Therapist
San Diego, California

Joy Covert, MS
Director of Counseling, Career, and Health
  Services
Department of Student Affairs
United States International University
San Diego, California

Steven G. Daily, DMin, PhD
Campus Chaplain
Assistant Professor
School of Religion and Education
La Sierra University
Riverside, California

Gayle Dakof, PhD
Deputy Director
Center for Research on Adolescent Drug Abuse
Temple University
Philadelphia, Pennsylvania

Guy Diamond, MA
Post-Doctoral Fellow
Philadelphia Child Guidance Center
Philadelphia, Pennsylvania

James T. Donoghue, MS
Marriage and Family Therapist
Private Practice
Long Beach, California

Jim Foreman, PhD
Senior Intern
Family Service Center
Marine Corps Recruit Depot
San Diego, California

Lewayne D. Gilchrist, PhD
Associate Professor
Associate Dean for Research
School of Social Work
University of Washington
Seattle, Washington

Mary Rogers Gillmore, PhD
Research Assistant Professor
School of Social Work
University of Washington
Seattle, Washington

Audrey Hill, MA
Assistant Professor
School of Social Work
Native Mental Health Consultant
Native Health Services
Laurentian University
Hagersville, Ontario, Canada

Virginia Hill, BA
Director of Social Services
Southern Indian Health Council
Alpine, California

Michelle Holt, ACSW
Supervisor and Consultant
Center for Family Counseling
Oakland, California

Janice Hoshino, MA
Doctoral Candidate
United States International University
Program Administrator
Walden Counseling Services
Outreach Family Counselor
San Diego Service Center for the Blind
San Diego, California

Mary C. Howard, MA
Independent Practitioner
Psychologist
Traveler's & Immigrant's AID of Chicago
Chicago, Illinois

Sophia M. Hyzin, MA
Psychological Intern
Long Beach, California

Divya Kakaiya, PhD
Registered Psychological Assistant
San Diego, California

Tully S. Lale, PhD, CAS
Inpatient Clinical Psychologist
Shasta County Community Mental Health
   Center
Redding, California

Howard A. Liddle, EdD
Professor of Counseling Psychology
Director
Center for Research on Adolescent Drug Abuse
Temple University
Philadelphia, Pennsylvania

Mary Jane Lohr, MS
Project Coordinator
School of Social Work
University of Washington
Seattle, Washington

Merriel F. Mandell, MA, MFCC
Adjunct Faculty
Department of Behavioral Sciences
MiraCosta Community College
Oceanside, California

Christine M. O'Sullivan, PhD
Associate Professor
Alcohol and Drug Abuse Studies
University of South Dakota
Vermillion, South Dakota

Evelyn Palmquist, RN
Marriage, Family, and Child Counselor
Cabrillo Counseling Medical Group
Orange, California

Rick Petosa, PhD, CHES
Associate Professor of Psychology
Ohio State University
Columbus, Ohio

Robert Sanet, OD
Director, San Diego Center for Vision Care
Adjunct Clinical Faculty
Southern California College of Optometry
San Diego, California
Fellow
College of Optometrists in Vision Development

Matthew Selekman, MSW
Clinical Supervisor
MCC Managed Behavioral Care, Inc.
Rosemont, Illinois
Adjunct Faculty
Marriage and Family Therapy Program
Northern Illinois University
DeKalb, Illinois
Lecturer
School of Social Service Administration
University of Chicago
Chicago, Illinois

Shari Shaw, MA, MFCC
Doctoral Candidate
United States International University
San Diego, California

Jeanne Tarter, PhD, RN
Director
Employee Assistance Program
Redlands Medical Group
Redlands, California

David C. Treadway, PhD
Author of *Before It's Too Late: Working with Substance Abuse in the Family* (W.W. Norton, 1989)
Family Therapist in Private Practice
Weston, Massachusetts

Nancy Waite-O'Brien, MA
Psychological Assistant
Psychological Resource Center
Palm Springs, California
Consultant
Betty Ford Center
Rancho Mirage, California

Derek Wangberg, MA
Doctoral Student
Pepperdine University
Malibu, California
Counselor in Private Practice
Santa Ana, California

Michael Watson, MA
Director
Employee Assistance Programs
Oakland, California

Thomas J. Young, PhD
Assistant Professor
Criminal Justice Department
Washburn University
Topeka, Kansas

Preface

Adolescents are our hope for the future. As they mature into adults and assume leadership roles in our society, they will bring with them the values and aspirations that they have accumulated as they grew into adulthood. Unfortunately, the many outstanding young people who will make equally outstanding adults are the forgotten ones. The adolescents who are involved in drugs or in trouble with the law get the headlines. The press has a penchant for reporting almost all of the bad news and almost none of the good news about adolescents. We acknowledge and give credit to all those adolescents who are "making it"—especially the ones who come from disadvantaged families, negative family situations, or repressive personal situations and yet have become contributing members of society. Congratulations to you all!

For the young people who have not fared so well and have become involved in drug abuse or other, equally debilitating situations, we recognize that adolescence is perhaps the most difficult developmental period in a lifetime. It is rivaled only by the final stage of life, very old age. Both adolescence and old age involve an incredible amount of change: physical, emotional, and psychological. Changing social roles, low status, and stress are common to both groups. Many in both groups have turned to the use of chemicals to help them deal with difficult times.

It is to the adolescents who are having more than their share of difficulty getting through this rough period in their lives that this book is dedicated. It is also dedicated to their parents. We are hopeful that this book will provide useful information and ideas for the counselors, schoolteachers, family therapists, psychologists, social workers, probation officers, and others who help troubled adolescents and their families. Perhaps an inquisitive citizen or policymaker will read this book and gain some insight into what social or judicial changes will help to provide adolescents with a better chance for a useful life free of drug abuse and other social ills.

Substance abuse among adolescents is a multifaceted problem that must be approached from many perspectives. The information in this book would have taken a single author years to bring together. The careful selection of a number of qualified individuals to write selected chapters has made it possible to present a great deal of up-to-date information on current research, theory, and practice, however.

We have loosely divided the book into five sections: Etiology, Treatment, Related Problems, Special Groups, and Prevention. Many of these sections are interrelated, because the problems that they address are interrelated. We have tried to include some information that is not generally found in other books on adolescents. For example, gangs, the occult, eating disorders, AIDS, and steroids are topics with which professionals who work with youth today need to be familiar.

It is difficult to work with troubled adolescents on a day-to-day basis. We have applied our clinical experience and knowledge to put together a book that we hope will be helpful to those who work regularly with adolescents. For them and for all our futures, we hope that we have been successful.

Gary W. Lawson
Ann W. Lawson

Part I

Etiology

Why do adolescents engage in substance abuse? Why do they drink alcohol before they reach the legal age? Why do some adolescents experiment with drugs and become addicted while others experiment with little consequence.

In this section of the book we have offered five chapters; each presenting different models of etiology of adolescent substance abuse. Although there are some theoretical overlaps each model has a unique perspective. The first chapter is an overview of a biopsychosocial model. This model integrates the biological or genetic components of etiology with the environmental components of sociocultural and psychological theories. This integrated approach gives a broad picture of the myriad of influences on the development of adolescent substance abuse. Chapter 2 expands this model. It offers important information on why adolescents use drugs, and also addresses the widening scope of the problem. Chapter 3 presents a social learning perspective for etiology, prevention, and treatment. The Social Learning Model is the one accepted by most of the professionals working in the prevention field. Chapter 4 presents an intergenerational family approach to the transmission of substance abuse. It emphasizes the importance of the family in the etiology of adolescent substance abuse, as well as in its treatment and prevention. The final chapter in this section discusses a developmental model based on the work of Erikson. It is an interesting approach to development looking at the interaction between parent and child.

It should be noted that none of these chapters presents the disease model of addiction for adolescents. Although the disease concept of addiction reigns supreme in public opinion as well as in many treatment programs, the disease concept will not be a focus of this book. There are several reasons for this. First, the disease model is not as appropriate for adolescents as it might be for adults. Physical addiction, loss of control, health problems related to alcohol and other drug use, and additional factors used to support the disease concept with adults are often not present in adolescents, thus making it difficult to convince adolescents they have a disease. Therapists who embrace the disease model of etiology limit themselves in their treatment options. Because it is difficult to integrate the disease model and the family systems model, they tend to use family therapy to educate the family about the disease concept instead of working toward a systemic change. If the therapist does not see the family dynamics that caused or perpetuated the substance abuse treatment the success rate will be limited.

There is little if any empirical verification of any of the major aspects of the disease concept for adults or adolescents. Although there are those who argue that the disease model is the only reasonable approach to the problem, we prefer to look at adolescent substance abuse as a *behavior*, and to look at those who are involved in this behavior on a regular basis as having a condition with physical, social, and psychological aspects that need to be addressed in treatment and prevention programs.

This section lays the ground work for a detailed examination of treatment, prevention, and special problems related to adolescent substance abuse. Although they do not reach agreement regarding a single theory of etiology, they do present the reader with alternative views of substance abuse. Those working to treat or prevent adolescent substance abuse need to have a valid theory of its etiology. Developing an understanding of the etiology of adolescent substance abuse makes it easier to treat and prevent. We encourage readers to use the information in this section as well as their personal and clinical experience to organize and conceptualize their own theory of the etiology of adolescent substance abuse. This is helpful as a first step toward developing a personal plan to treat or prevent adolescent substance abuse.

1

A Biopsychosocial Model of Adolescent Substance Abuse

Gary W. Lawson

The only thing more complex than the behavior of someone involved in substance abuse is the behavior of an adolescent. The combination of the two types of behavior almost always defies a rational explanation. Those who have long ago successfully or, maybe, not so successfully (some "recovering adolescents" never quite fully completed the process) passed through adolescence remember this period as one that can be appropriately described by the first line of Dickens' *A Tale of Two Cities*: "It was the best of times and it was the worst of times." Often, what made it the best of times was also what made it the worst of times. Along with the freedom of adolescence comes the responsibility of adulthood. Along with the pleasure of intimate relationships comes the pain caused by the end of those relationships. There are many two-edged swords for adolescents.

Many difficult tasks are associated with adolescence: developing an individual identity, separating from family of origin, establishing new relationships, trying on new values, learning what life is "really" about, becoming self-reliant financially, going to school, getting a job, experimenting with sex or drugs, learning to drive, and perhaps the most difficult task of all—learning to relate on an intimate basis with someone of the opposite sex. As if these developmental tasks were not difficult enough, there are more than a few pitfalls along the way. Raging hormones, body changes (for better or worse), depression, mood swings, pregnancy, sexually transmitted diseases, alcoholic or otherwise dysfunctional parents, peer pressure, illegal drugs, gangs, and religious cults are only a few of these pitfalls; the list is seemingly endless. The world of adolescents in the 1990s is nothing like it was during the late 1950s and 1960s (Taibbi, 1990), and those who passed through adolescence in the earlier "Age of Innocence" and are now working with adolescents must be aware that they cannot fully understand what life is like for adolescents today.

There are a large number of theoretical and research articles that attempt to explain adolescent substance abuse. For example, physiological factors (Goldstein, 1981), behavioral factors (Kandel, 1975), personality characteristics (Mayer & Ligman, 1989), family characteristics (Brook, Lukoff, & Whiteman, 1978), and sociological factors (Brook, Lukoff, & Whiteman, 1981) have all been examined in an effort to understand the etiology of adolescent substance abuse. The substance abuse models fall on a continuum, ranging from simple (Mayer & Ligman, 1989) to very complex and multidimensional (Simons, Conger, & Whitbeck, 1988). Each is useful in helping to identify a piece of the puzzle of the reasons for adolescent substance abuse. Viewed together, however, these models are conflicting, difficult to apply, and confusing, as there is supporting evidence for almost any theoretical model. It is necessary to develop a practical model that is rational and easy to comprehend, that has implications for prevention and treatment, and that takes into account the most important issues in the answer to the question, Why do adolescents abuse substances?

BACKGROUND ISSUES

There are significant differences between society's view of adult substance abuse and its view of adolescent substance abuse. An adult substance abuser has been defined as an individual whose use of a chemical substance (e.g., alcohol) causes continuing difficulties of any kind in that person's life (Lawson, 1989). Almost any adult in a substance abuse treatment program, whether the program involves inpatient or outpatient treatment, falls within this definition. An adolescent, on the other hand, may easily end up in treatment for experimental use of a mind-altering substance, regardless of the personal consequences involved in the use.

Social and economic conditions, parental fears, and the general perception of adolescence as a period of major difficulty all contribute to this response to adolescent substance abuse. Media presentations frequently represent the negative rather than the positive aspects of youth, focusing on youth gangs and their problems, for example, rather than the Future Teachers of America or other positive youth groups. Parents are often frightened by media hype or hospital treatment center advertisements that they have seen on television. Insurance coverage and the parents' willingness to have someone else deal with the "abuser" are also factors. As a result, what may be experimental adolescent behavior becomes a reason to place an adolescent in an inpatient hospital treatment program. Such treatment programs are one of the few large-scale sources of profit for private hospitals. Managers of these programs have become desperate for adolescent admissions because of the vast overbuilding of these facilities that occurred during the 1980s. Thus, adolescent admissions to hospital inpatient units increased from 50,000 in 1984 to 250,000 in 1989 (Wylie, 1990).

This approach raises other questions, however. Does the diagnosis become a self-fulfilling prophecy? Do adolescents become more involved in drugs by identifying themselves with the drug abuser image that they receive as a result of being placed in treatment? Hobbs and Nicholas (1975) suggested that there may be some connection between how adolescents are labeled and how they subsequently behave. The consequences of placing adolescent drug experimenters into drug treatment and labeling them substance abusers should be considered. Just as it is important not to ignore a substance abuse problem, it is important not to overreact.

In a recent longitudinal study, Shedler and Block (1990) found that adolescents who had engaged in some drug experimentation (primarily with marijuana) were the best adjusted in their sample. Adolescents who used drugs frequently were maladjusted and showed a distinct personality syndrome marked by interpersonal alienation, poor impulse control, and emotional distress. Adolescents who had never experimented with any drug by the age of 18 were relatively anxious, emotionally constricted, and lacking in social skills. Psychological differences among frequent drug users, experimenters, and abstainers could be traced to early childhood and were related to the quality of parenting that they received. It has been suggested that certain types of parents tend to raise children who are at high risk for substance abuse (Lawson, Peterson, & Lawson, 1983).

Shedler and Block (1990) concluded that (1) problem drug use is a symptom, not a cause, of personal and social maladjustment, and (2) it is possible to understand the meaning of drug use only in the context of an individual's personality structure and developmental history. In their view, current efforts at drug prevention are misguided to the extent that they focus on symptoms, rather than on the psychological syndrome underlying the drug abuse. Education programs such as the *Just Say No!* program seem to trivialize the factors involved in drug abuse, implicitly denying their depth and pervasiveness. Furthermore, the perception of drug abuse as the result of a "lack of education" diverts attention from the real physiological, psychological, and sociological causes of drug abuse (Shedler & Block, 1990).

ETIOLOGY OF ADOLESCENT SUBSTANCE ABUSE

There is no "typical" substance-abusing adolescent, no specific personality type, family history, socioeconomic situation, or stressful experience that has been found to predict categorically the development of adolescent substance abuse (Lawson, Ellis, & Rivers, 1984). Various physiological, psychological, and sociological factors have been associated with substance abuse; however:

- physiological factors
  1. physical addiction

2. disease or physical disorders
3. related medical problems
4. inherited risk
5. adolescent hormonal factors
6. physical developmental level
7. mental disorders (with physiological cause)

- sociological factors

1. ethnic and cultural differences
2. family background
3. education
4. employment
5. peer relationships
6. school environment

- psychological factors

1. social skills
2. emotional level
3. self-image
4. attitude toward life
5. defense mechanisms
6. developmental level
7. mental obsessions
8. judgment
9. decision-making skills

Physiological Factors

A detailed history of drug and/or alcohol use will help determine if physical addiction is present. An adolescent substance abuser is less likely to be physically addicted than is an adult substance abuser. Addiction-related or physical disorders, including psychopathological problems such a chronic depression, schizophrenia, or other mental disorders, may clearly affect an adolescent's substance abuse.

If there is a history of alcoholism or substance abuse in the parents or grandparents, an adolescent may have a physical predisposition to addiction. There is little or nothing of a physical nature that can be done to reduce this predisposition, but it is useful for the adolescent to be aware of it so that he or she can take precautions to avoid undue risks or psychological and sociological pressures that may lead to substance abuse.

Psychological Factors

Among the major psychological factors involved in substance abuse are emotions and personality. Generally defined as the way in which a person interacts with his or her environment, personality may include the defense mechanisms used and the rules they followed. Psychological factors are often directly related to sociological factors. For example, an adolescent who grows up in a family where there is a great deal of stress may develop certain methods of coping with stress or learn to withdraw from stress altogether. On the other hand, an adolescent who grows up where there is very little stress may not handle stress well at all in later life.

Psychological factors that affect substance abuse include mental obsessions, emotional compulsions, a low self-image, negative attitudes, rigid defense systems, and delusions. Problems may arise in adolescents who have little identification with viable role models; little identification with family; and inadequate interpersonal skills, including communication, cooperation, negotiation, empathy, listening, and sharing. The inability to respond to the limits inherent in a situation (responsibility) and the inability to adapt behavior to a situation constructively in order to meet needs (adaptability) are psychosocial problems. Irresponsibility, refusal to accept consequences of behavior, and scapegoating are all signs of weakness in these areas. Judgment skills are inadequate when the adolescent is unable to recognize, understand, and apply appropriate meanings to relationships. Weaknesses in judgment are expressed as crises in sexual, natural, consumer and drug and alcohol environments and as repetitive self-destructive behavior (Glenn, 1981).

Sociological Factors

The interactions between the adolescent and those around him or her, including family processes with the family of origin, nuclear family, and extended family members, affect an adolescent's substance abuse. The education process or involvement with school is often important to an individual's self-image. Employment history, peer group, and cultural or ethnic background all have an impact on a person's motivation to change offending behavior or to respond to treatment.

Social factors determine not only whether adolescents will drink or use drugs, but also how they will view themselves afterward. In a review of a 33-year prospective study of alcoholism, Vaillant and Milofsky (1982) found that ethnicity (for example, South Europeans are low-risk) and the number of alcoholic relatives were related to the variance in adult alcoholism. Adolescents may differ from adults in their view of substance use or abuse, however. It may be considered "cool" or the accepted norm to use or abuse a substance. Inappropriate or problem use may improve the self-image of the adolescent. Among gang members, for example, the member who can use the most drugs or do the most outrageous thing while "high" on drugs may be one of the most respected. To be "crazy" is to be liked and accepted.

Tarter and Schneider (1976) have identified 14 variables that affect an individual's decision to start, continue, or stop drinking: (1) childhood exposure to alcohol and drinking models, (2) the quantity of alcohol that is considered appropriate or excessive in his or her family, (3) family drinking customs, (4) the type of alcoholic beverage used, (5) levels of inhibition considered safe by the family, (6) the symbolic meaning of alcohol, (7) the family attitude toward public intoxication, (8) the social group associated with drinking, (9) activities associated with drinking, (10) the amount of pressure exerted on the individual to drink and continue drinking, (11) the use of alcohol in social or private context, (12) the individual's mobility in changing drinking preference groups, (13) the permanence of, and (14) the social rewards or punishments for drinking. Four parent types have been associated with an increased risk of substance abuse in their offspring: (1) the alcoholic parent, (2) the teetotaling parent, (3) the overdemanding parent, and (4) the overprotective parent (Lawson et al., 1983).

TREATMENT AND PREVENTION

The primary focus of treatment and prevention is behavior. Whether drug-using behavior or specific behaviors such as gambling or fighting must be treated or prevented, the behavioral situation must be changed.

Three things can change in an individual: behavior, thinking, and feeling. That is, individuals can change their behavior, the way that they think about certain things, or the way that they feel or react emotionally to certain things. Each of these three are interrelated. How individuals think or their attitude is related to how they feel emotionally about a situation or subject and, vice versa, how they behave is definitely related to what they think and how they feel. The goal of a treatment program is to facilitate change in first one and then in all of these areas. The first effort in the treatment of substance-abusing adolescents is usually to change their substance-abusing behavior and then, perhaps, their behavior toward authority figures. This approach may motivate them to change the way that they think about others. For example, they may begin to see their parents as caring about them rather than trying to control them, and this new perception may change the way that they feel about their parents.

Helping an adolescent and his or her family learn all the consequences of drinking, drug use, or specific behavior in question may induce change in the adolescent's behavior. Providing new information may be the simplest way to seek change; it is not always successful, but is effective occasionally. If the adolescent holds the person who is providing the new information in high esteem, the probability of a change is increased. For example, a respected doctor who tells a patient about some major health risk may persuade the patient to change an unhealthful life style. A wife who makes it clear during therapy that she will leave her husband if he drinks again may change his behavior. To avoid making major mistakes in therapy, therapists should find out all that they can about the reasons for their patients' behavior. For example, if aware than an alcoholic is drinking to kill himself (suicide on the installment plan), the therapist can avoid making statements to the patient such as, "If you keep drinking, you are going to die." That may be exactly what the patient wants to hear because he is, in fact, trying to die.

Every adolescent who uses a substance inappropriately has a reason, perhaps many reasons, for the substance abuse. There are also reasons, perhaps just one reason, that will motivate an adolescent to stop using and change the behavior. When many hundreds of recovering alcoholics and drug addicts were asked why they decided to quit using, all of them, even the adolescents, could name something that caused them to change. One adolescent with a history of drug and alcohol abuse who had been sober for 3 years said, "Because my girl friend asked me to." When asked why he had not stopped much earlier when his parents had asked him to, he said, "Because they were the reason I was using. I was angry at them and, I knew my using would hurt them." For this young man, his girl friend's request caused him to change his behavior. Additional therapy around the issues he had with his parents was necessary for him to maintain his sobriety.

For the therapist who works with a substance-abusing adolescent, the task is to find the clues to what will cause change. Such clues are often found in an individual's past. By determining what it was that caused the adolescent to think, feel, or behave in a certain way in the first place, a therapist can plan events in treatment to counteract the reasons for the behavior and to effect change. If the change is to be lasting, the precipitating event or motivation to change must be as powerful or meaningful as the event or events that originally caused the undesirable behavior. For example, adolescents who were adopted may have low self-esteem because they feel that they were unwanted and unloved by their natural parents. It may not be enough for a therapist to say, "I'm sure your natural parents loved you." Actually meeting with their natural parents and learning the reasons behind the adoption may change their thinking and feeling about this significant event in their lives, however. They may come to believe, "I was lovable and my parents loved me, but given the circumstances, they were unable to keep me. So, I'm not unlovable after all."

Treatment planning always includes the family. The events that mold individuals almost always evolve from the family. The inclusion of the family in the treatment and prevention process greatly increases the chances of success (Bernard,

1990; Davis, 1987; Lawson, Peterson, & Lawson, 1983; Stanton & Todd, 1982; Todd & Selekman, 1991).

REFERENCES

Bernard, C. (1990). *Families with an alcoholic member: The invisible patient.* New York: Human Sciences Press.

Brook, J.S., Lukoff, I.F., & Whiteman, M. (1978). Family socialization and adolescent personality and their association with adolescent use of marijuana. *Journal of Genetic Psychology, 133,* 261–271.

Brook, J.S., Lukoff, I.F., & Whiteman, M. (1981). The role of the father in his son's marijuana use. *Journal of Genetic Psychology, 133,* 81–86.

Davis, D. (1987). *Alcoholism treatment: An integrated family and individual approach.* New York: Gardner Press.

Glenn, S. (1981). Directions for the 80's. Paper presented at Nebraska Prevention Center Conference. Omaha, NE.

Goldstein, A. (1981). Endorphins and addiction. In H. Shaffer & M.E. Burglass (Eds.), *Classic contributions in the addictions* (pp. 421–435). New York: Brunner/Mazel.

Hobbs, C.M. & Nicholas, H. (Eds.). (1975). *Issues in the classification of children: A source book on categories, labels and their consequences* (Vols. 1–2). San Francisco: Jossey-Bass.

Kandel, D.B. (1975). Stage of adolescent involvement in drug use. *Science, 190,* 912–914.

Lawson, G. (1989). A rationale for planning treatment and prevention of alcoholism and substance abuse for specific populations. In G. Lawson & A. Lawson (Eds.), *Alcoholism and substance abuse in special populations* (pp. 1–10). Gaithersburg, MD: Aspen Publishers.

Lawson, G., Ellis, D., & Rivers, C. (1984). *Essentials of chemical dependency counseling.* Gaithersburg, MD: Aspen Publishers.

Lawson, G., Peterson, J., & Lawson, A. (1983). *Alcoholism and the family: A guide to treatment and prevention.* Gaithersburg, MD: Aspen Publishers.

Mayer, J.E., & Ligman, J.D. (1989). Personality characteristics of adolescent marijuana users. *Adolescence, 24*(96), 965–975.

Shedler, J., & Block, J. (1990). Adolescent drug use and psychological health: A longitudinal inquiry. *The American Psychologist, 45*(5), 612–630.

Simons, R.L., Conger, R.D., & Whitbeck, L.B. (1988). A multistage social learning model of the influences of family and peers upon adolescent substance abuse. *Journal of Drug Issues, 18*(3), 293–315.

Stanton, M.D., & Todd, T. (1982). *The family therapy of drug abuse and addiction.* New York: Guilford Press.

Taibbi, R. (1990). The uninitiated. *The Family Therapy Networker, 14*(4), 31–35.

Tarter, R.E., & Schneider, D.V. (1976). Models and theories of alcoholism. In R.E. Tarter & A.A. Singleman (Eds.), *Alcoholism: Interdisciplinary approaches to an enduring problem.* Reading, MA: Addison-Wesley.

Todd, T.C., & Selekman, M.D. (1991). *Family therapy approaches with adolescent substance abusers.* Boston: Allyn & Bacon.

Vaillant, G.E., & Milofsky, E.S. (1982). The etiology of alcoholism: A prospective viewpoint. *American Psychologist, 37*(5), 494–503.

Wylie, S.M. (1990). Bounty hunting. *The Family Therapy Networker, 14*(4), 10.

2

Adolescence: A Physiological, Cultural, and Psychological No Man's Land

David L. Archambault

Adolescence is first a matter of biology, that is, an intrinsic developmental process in a strictly physiological sense. It is also a matter of culture; this is where rites of passage, ideals, values, and cultural norms or expectations enter the child's life in a new and more accountable manner. Finally, it is a matter of psychology, insofar as it involves the resolution of internal issues around oneself, one's relationship to others (particularly the opposite sex), and the search for one's place in the world.

Adolescents have special problems in each of these three areas. As a result, they make up a special population with representatives from every other special population. The therapist who works with an adolescent population must be aware of issues that are important to each ethnic, social, and economic group.

Adolescents are individuals in the process of change in every area of life. These changes are not of the adolescents' own choosing, but are forced on them by biology and culture. They must make these changes without regard to how well their environment (e.g., family, education, cultural background) has prepared them for change. Physiologically, their bodies often seem out of control, changing in ways that they do not understand and do not desire (e.g., acne, lumps in the breast, menstruation). Adolescents do not have the experience to know what they are becoming; they are unsure of their worth to others, to society, and to themselves.

Culturally, adolescence is a no man's land. Adolescents find themselves somewhere between the relative safety of childhood, where structure and simplicity were the order of the day, and the unfamiliar complexities and expectations of adulthood. They are no longer accepted as children, but are told (and expected) to act like adults. Yet many of the adult activities that are most visible to adolescents

Source: From *Alcoholism and Substance Abuse in Special Populations* (pp. 223–245) by G.W. Lawson and A.W. Lawson (eds.), 1989, Gaithersburg, MD: Aspen Publishers, Inc. Copyright 1989 by Aspen Publishers, Inc.

and children (e.g., sex, drug and alcohol use) are still considered off limits to adolescents and even punishable. Unless adolescents have been exposed to learning experiences that enable them to be realistic and insightful regarding goals, timetable to development, progress, and relationships with others, they are likely to be dissatisfied with themselves and angry toward those around them and the world in general.

Undoubtedly, some adolescents are well prepared for the transition to adulthood. They have had consistent, culturally appropriate adult models who gave them clear, realistic messages about what to expect from themselves and others. They have been encouraged to set goals and develop the skills needed to achieve those goals. At the same time, they have been encouraged to enjoy their youth and life in general. All things considered, they feel good about themselves and others. They are confident that they can smoothly make the transition to adulthood; indeed, most of the adolescents in this category have had increasing responsibility and achievement as they grew older, so their transition to adulthood is natural and with few surprises.

At the other extreme are adolescents who must sort through almost total chaos and inconsistency to find identity and purpose. Their principal caregivers and role models often provide them with a maze of double messages, hypocrisy, neglect, and abuse (often both physical and mental). These young people and many others who fall between the two extremes may find pleasure or relief from stress or anxiety in a drug that allows them to forget those problems that they are often not responsible for, unable to understand, and unprepared to solve.

WHY DO ADOLESCENTS TAKE DRUGS?

There is no single reason and no list of reasons for drug use that will apply to all adolescents. Drug use results from a complex interaction of genetic endowment, behavior patterns, motives, and social and psychological determinants. Reasons for use may be extremely complex or as simple as availability.

When Segal, Cromer, Stevens, and Wasserman (1982) examined self-reported reasons for drug use among a group of adjudicated juveniles, they found at least three motives for drug use. The first was an expanded awareness/insight motive. Some individuals used drugs because they believed that they could achieve greater understanding about themselves and their environment. The second was a drug effect motive, a desire to produce a "high," a mellowness, an ease with friends, and a feeling of greater creativity. The third motive was to increase activity. Here the goal was to "obtain new and exciting experiences to satisfy curiosity and for the high drug use can bring."

The self-reported reasons in this study indicate that the need to achieve altered states of consciousness is an important element in drug taking. Furthermore, different drugs are used selectively to achieve the desired state of altered consciousness. Marijuana use is associated primarily with a state of mellowness; stimulants, with a desire to increase energy. It seems that expectations associated with the use of certain drugs may help to relieve anxiety or at least cope with it.

Beschner and Friedman (1979) offered several reasons for drug use among adolescents. First, drugs are readily available; second, drugs provide a reliable, quick, easy, and cheap way to feel good; third, drugs offer one way of gaining peer group acceptance, increasingly important as a socializing influence during adolescence; fourth, drugs are used as a coping mechanism to deal with unpleasant feelings and emotions, relieve depression, reduce tension, and cope with pressure.

Relief of Stress

Detained and adjudicated juveniles perceive alcohol as a means to deal with personal needs and problems (Segal et al., 1982). Cahalan, Asin, and Crossley (1969) found that people who are anxious or depressed use alcohol to help with their problems. To some extent, it seems that alcohol has become a self-prescribed tranquilizer for our stressful society. Children see their parents come home from a hard day at work and declare, "I need a drink." Adolescents may have learned early in life that alcohol use has a special function as a means to deal with problems and unpleasant feelings. Beer drinking, in particular, may be seen as a reward for hard work or a means to cool off in hot weather. This could be a result of advertising (e.g., "It's Miller time" or "This Bud's for you for all you do").

Segal and colleagues (1982) found no reports of drinking just to be sociable among adolescents. This finding was in contrast to that indicated in the self-reports of college students (Segal, Huba, & Singer, 1980). Those in the first sample had not arrived at the culturally sanctioned age of alcohol use, however. It is also logical to assume that this was an unusually troubled sample and that alcohol was used as a means to deal with problems. For the troubled adolescent alcohol (or drug) use may be a way to relieve stressful emotions. This type of use simply models the perception of society, which associates drug and alcohol use with mood change.

Both the adolescents and the adults in treatment programs studied by Holland and Griffin (1984) reported growing up in families with many problems. Serious illnesses, usually resulting in unemployment of the main wage earner and the need to go on welfare, were reported by 28% of both groups. Violence was a frequent occurrence in the homes of 57% of the adolescents and 40% of the adults; 40% of the adolescents and 30% of the adults reported being physically abused. Family life seems to have been frequently volatile and unpredictable. These family environments appear poorly structured and lacking in a role model for appropriate parental identification. Feelings of inadequacy are to be expected, as well as poor relationship and communication skills. Peer acceptance, approval, and identification that can be obtained through drug use seems to be a reasonable solution to an intolerable environment.

The type of family environment described by many of the clients in this study supports a modeling effect. Deviant behavior was commonplace in many of the respondents' homes. Adolescents reported a 65% incidence of family drug use, compared to 46% for the adults. Family drinking problems were reported by 61% of the adolescents and 52% of the adults. A family member had an arrest record in 53% of the families of the adolescents and 42% of the families of the adults.

The respondents also scored high on several objective measures of psychological distress. Forty-eight percent of the adolescents and 28% of the adults had received treatment for psychological problems other than drug abuse or alcoholism. Of the adolescents, 20% had received inpatient psychiatric care, and 36% had attempted suicide.

Of this sample, 94% admitted illegal activity other than illegal drug use. The average age of the first illegal activities was 12 for adolescents. Their first arrest took place (on an average) at age 14. For adults, the comparable ages were 16 and 17.7 years. Virtually all measures of criminal activity increased with age.

There may be different motives for drug taking and committing an offense. For instance, criminality may be more related to sociological processes, while drug use could be more significantly related to personality factors and less related to social factors. Treatment would then need to focus on personal development and achieving a positive self-concept along with alternatives to drugs.

Although it may be difficult to accept, there are probably positive reasons that some adolescents use drugs. It may be that, in our society, drug experimentation has become a normal part of growing up, just one component of a rite of passage. Peer acceptance and curiosity can also contribute positive motives for substance use.

Types of Substance Abuse

Beschner and Friedman (1985) separated adolescents' substance abuse into two types. The first type is the experimental situational or recreational user. The second type is the user who has serious personal problems and becomes a compulsive and dedicated user. Beschner noted that this second group composes approximately 5% of those aged 14 to 18; this group has serious drug and drug-related problems and is likely to be the group most in need of treatment.

According to social bond theory, most individuals will deviate from expected behavior if the bonds of conformity are weakened or broken. In fact, the most consistent extralegal factor affecting marijuana use is peer or social support. In testing this theory, Peck (1983) hypothesized that people with large numbers of friends who did not use marijuana would also not use marijuana. Peck found that, of those people who reported having no friends who used marijuana, 95% were non-users themselves. Of those people who reported having only a few friends who smoked marijuana, 66% were non-users. Conversely, of the people who reported that almost all their friends used marijuana, 92% also used marijuana; of those who reported that all their friends smoked marijuana, 96% smoked marijuana. These findings support the hypothesis that people are more likely to behave in accordance with the expectations of their significant others than with the generalized expectations of a society.

These findings also contribute significantly to the understanding of marijuana use by adolescents, whose peer groups are becoming increasingly important and are likely to practice and accept marijuana use.Thus, a non–marijuana-using peer group seems to be crucial to the deterrence of marijuana use. It does not seem unreasonable that these findings would be valid for drug use in general, especially in the early stages of use.

SCOPE OF USE

Traditionally, youth are seen as the key to the successful future of any society. Drug abuse is considered a threat to the healthy development of youth and, therefore, a threat to society. As a result, the greatest focus of recent drug research has been on youth, particularly adolescents, and drug abuse.

"Compared to the heroin addiction epidemic of the 60's and 70's adolescent drug abuse today is more broadly based; it cuts across all socioeconomic strata and involves a wider array of chemical substances" (Beschner & Friedman, 1985). The most often abused drugs by adolescents are tobacco, marijuana, and alcohol. These are often called gateway drugs because their use frequently leads to the use of other drugs.

The National Survey on Drug Abuse in the household population of the United States (Fishburne, Abelson, & Cisin, 1980) produced strong evidence that adolescent substance abuse has increased steadily since the beginning of the survey in 1972. Almost one third of all youth aged 12 to 17 have used marijuana, and more than half of that group have used it within the past 30 days; 10% and 7% of 12- to 17-year-olds have used inhalants and hallucinogens, respectively; approximately 7% have used alcohol; and more than 50% have used tobacco.

According to the Drug Abuse Warning Network System (Glynn, 1981), one third or more of the drug-related emergency room visits in 1980 for marijuana use, phencyclidine (PCP) use, and quaalude use involved youths aged 10 to 19. One quarter of amphetamine-related visits were by youths from this same age group, as were 10% or more of visits due to cocaine, barbiturates, antidepressants, and antianxiety substances.

The University of Michigan's annual survey of high-school seniors (aged 16 to 18) from 1975 to 1981 showed an increased substance use in this age group compared with the youth population in general. The data indicated that 33.37% had used marijuana within the last 30 days, 3.9% had used cocaine within the last 30 days, 10.2% had used stimulants, and 70% had used alcohol. Regarding alcohol use, more than 40% reported binge drinking (five or more drinks in a row) during the 2 weeks prior to the survey.

Seven percent of high-school seniors reported daily use of marijuana (Johnston, Brockman, & O'Malley, 1981). Moreover, 25% of elementary school children feel pressure to try marijuana, beer, wine, and liquor. "Typically, persons who have a degree of experience with marijuana (used more than 10 times) will become involved in the use of another illicit drug" (Beschner & Friedman, 1985, p. 26). For example, alcohol is often used in combination with other drugs, particularly marijuana. Because of this combined usage, it may be misleading to label an adolescent's problem as a drug *or* an alcohol problem. A more realistic approach for most adolescents who enter treatment for substance abuse is a three-part diagnosis of drug, alcohol, and psychological problems (Hubbard, Cavanaugh, Graddock, & Rachel, 1983).

PATTERNS AND CONSEQUENCES OF USE

When Holland and Griffin (1984) compared the patterns and consequences of drug use in adolescent and adult drug treatment clients, they found that adults were more likely to have used cocaine, heroin, and methadone; adolescents were more likely to have used amphetamines, hallucinogens, and marijuana. The average age of onset of drug use was 11.8 years for adolescents and 15.1 years for adults. Most adolescents in treatment had begun using drugs other than alcohol before the seventh grade. Adolescents were equally likely to use other drugs before alcohol as alcohol before other drugs, while adults were more likely to have begun using alcohol. Both adolescents and adults reported using an average of seven drugs other than alcohol. The two groups were similar regarding the number of drug classes used, number of drug classes used regularly, and the highest frequency of use. Adolescents began using a variety of substances earlier than did adults and progressed to regular polydrug use more quickly than did adults. Four of ten (40%) adolescents reported having been physically addicted to drugs. Adults were almost twice as likely to report a physical addiction.

Adolescent self-reported alcohol use was greater than was adult self-reported use. Of the adolescents, 50% described their drinking as frequent or daily, as opposed to 40% of the adults. While 50% of the adolescents rated their drinking a moderate or serious problem, only 34% of the adults did. Adolescents were also more likely to have experienced negative consequences of alcohol use (74% vs. 48%). Holland and Griffin (1984) found that 29% of the adolescents and 23% of the adults had previously received treatment for alcoholism.

The teen-aged driver is responsible for 44% of all fatal crashes at night where alcohol is involved. Drunk driving accidents are the leading cause of death in people aged 16 to 24. Alcohol was found in the blood of 58% of teens killed in traffic accidents, and 43% of those were legally drunk.

Gonzales (1983) used such variables as age at the time of first drink, the place where the first drink was consumed, and parental supervision at the time of the first drink to predict the amount of alcohol consumed and alcohol-related behavioral problems when students were in college. He found that college students who began drinking during their elementary and middle school years had significantly higher levels of use and alcohol-related problems than did those students who started drinking during their high school or college years. Students who had their first drink at a school-related function had a significantly higher incidence of use and related problems than did those students who had their first drink at home or at a bar; in fact, the latter students had a significantly lower incidence of use and related problems than did any of the other groups. Gonzales also found that, although having the first drink with parental knowledge or parental supervision did not significantly predict alcohol use while in college, it did significantly predict the incidence of alcohol-related problems that the students experienced while in college. Students who were introduced to alcohol with parental consent (the majority of this study) experienced significantly fewer behavioral complications from their use of alcohol in college than did those whose parents did not know about their drinking or those who were not sure whether their parents knew about their drinking.

SIGNS OF ABUSE

Although many of the following behaviors are to some extent normal in many adolescents at certain times, frequency of occurrence and clustering of these behaviors are indicative of possible substance abuse and should be investigated:

- changing circle of friends
- undergoing emotional highs and lows
- defying rules and regulations
- showing frustration and giving in to peer pressure
- sleeping more than usual
- giving many excuses for staying out too late

- withdrawing from family functions
- changing to worse physical hygiene
- failing to inform parents of significant school events and social activities
- intercepting the mail
- isolating self (e.g., spending lots of time in own room)
- selling possessions
- playing parents against each other
- undergoing a drastic weight change
- developing a short temper
- adopting a defensive attitude
- coming home drunk or high
- exhibiting abusive behavior

Parents should also be concerned if they notice items missing, such as money or prescription drugs; receive calls from school that their adolescent is missing class or exhibiting abusive behavior; or, of course, find drug paraphernalia. Legal problems should also lead to suspicion.

Classroom signs include

- bloodshot eyes (grass)
- smell
- lack of responsiveness
- truancy
- lots of talk about drugs or alcohol
- absenteeism
- sudden drop in grades
- defensive behavior
- tardiness or leaving the room often
- incomplete assignments
- dress (e.g., roach clips, t-shirts with slogans about drugs)
- verbal abuse toward teachers or classmates
- vandalism
- forged notes from home
- giving in to peer pressure

The list could be endless. Changes from the norm, several behaviors going on at once, and frequency of occurrence are most revealing.

ASSESSMENT OF RISK

Early in treatment, it is important to determine the adolescent's level of risk for substance abuse. In other words, how pervasive in the adolescent's life are those factors which increase the likelihood that he or she will abuse alcohol or drugs? Lawson, Peterson, and Lawson (1983) proposed several questions that aid in determining the level of risk for alcoholism in each of three areas:

1. physiological
   (a) Do you have a parent or grandparent who was or is alcoholic?
   (b) If you have started drinking, are you or were you able to drink larger amounts of alcohol than most of your friends with fewer physical consequences (i.e., hangover)?
   (c) Did you drink large amounts of alcohol from the first time you started drinking?
2. sociological
   (a) Did (do) one or both of your parents have strong religious or moral views against drinking alcohol (or using drugs)?
   (b) Are either of your parents alcoholics?
   (c) Do you come from an ethnic background that has a reputation for a high rate of alcoholism?
   (d) Do you consider your friends to be heavy drinkers?
   (e) Does your social status match your concept of where you feel you should be in society (school, etc.)?
3. psychological
   (a) Did you have a parent who was alcoholic or chemically dependent?
   (b) Were one or both of your parents teetotalers (chose not to drink and condemned those who made a different choice)?
   (c) In your opinion, were your parents overly protective of you?
   (d) Were your parents, in your opinion, overly demanding of you, in words or needs?
   (e) Do you have something to do in life that makes you feel worthwhile (school, sports, hobby, job, etc.)?
   (f) Do you have someone who loves you and someone whom you love?

The questions in these three areas provide a good starting point for the assessment of an adolescent's risks and needs. Assessment is useful only if it in some way affects treatment and thereby benefits the adolescent. If the same treatment or shotgun approach to treatment is used for everyone, assessment is really a pointless procedure. Assessment should explore the adolescent's needs, and treatment should address those specific needs.

Physiological Factors

Virtually every family study of alcoholism has shown that children with alcoholic parents have more problems with alcohol than do children with nonalcoholic parents. Of children who have alcoholic parents, 30% are alcoholic, 40% are moderate drinkers, and 30% are abstainers. Of children whose parents drink moderately, 5% are alcoholics, 85% are moderate drinkers, and 10% are abstainers. Of children whose parents are abstainers, 10% are alcoholics, 50% are moderate drinkers, and 40% are abstainers (Lawson et al., 1983). Although heredity alone has not been shown to cause alcoholism, it does seem to be a significant contributing factor. Heredity and the learning that takes place in the environment created by alcoholic parents accounts for a great deal of the risk of alcoholism in their children.

Normal growth and rapid changes also increase the physiological risk experienced by adolescents. Any condition that threatens the self-image and for which the adolescent is unprepared and unsupported puts the adolescent at risk. Growth makes some adolescents feel awkward. Growing too fast, too slow, or not at all can be equally threatening. Problems with coordination due to growth can have a negative effect on athletic or social (e.g., dancing) skills. Voice changing, rapid skeletal growth, hair on face/chest/genitals, acne, and menstruation are all new experiences for the adolescent. These changes increase the adolescent's awareness of new sexual roles, which can be both exciting and frightening. This is one area that can be hardly overstressed in its effects on a positive self-image.

Sociological Factors

Drug use was at one time (during the 1960s and 1970s) largely associated with the poverty and social deprivation of the inner cities. It is now evident that social deprivation can occur anywhere; it is not restricted to ghetto areas. Moreover, adolescent multiple substance users are found in all socioeconomic levels. "Several high school surveys showed that youthful drug users were more typically from higher socioeconomic classes than non-drug users" (Beschner & Friedman, 1985). Data from household surveys show that white adolescents have a higher lifetime prevalence of illicit drug use than do black or Hispanic youth. They also tend to use a wider variety of substances than do their non-white counterparts and report more drinking and smoking in the month prior to the survey (Beschner & Friedman, 1985).

Schools are an important part of the adolescent's social environment, and drugs have become readily available on many campuses. Drugs are almost sure to be as easily available in upper class urban schools as on inner city campuses. Schools provide an area away from parental supervision where experimentation is accepted by and often encouraged by peers.

Psychological Factors

The family is certainly the crucible of psychological development for adolescents. Those who grow up in homes where education is not valued may see little need to work in school and may receive little encouragement when they do work hard. Schoolwork can have an impact on peer relationships and acceptance or rejection by certain peer groups, however. Adolescents who do poorly in school may not have access to groups that would be a more positive influence. On the other hand, some adolescents are under a great pressure to excel and measure their self-worth solely by achievement (e.g., academic, athletic, musical). This is a precarious position for anyone and creates a great deal of anxiety for which substance abuse may be a coping mechanism or a means to relax.

Pattson, Kessler, and Hondell (1977) found that depressive mood was related to adolescent drug use. Adolescents who use drugs to relieve depression have a particularly high probability of continued drug use when compared to adolescents who use drugs for other reasons. For this group of adolescents, drug use probably has a negative reinforcing effect in that it removes an unpleasant emotion (depression).

> In a study of high school students, drug users were found to have significantly more psychological symptoms—anxiety, obsessive compulsive reactions, hostility reactions, agitation, excitement and violent reactions—and less "maturity" than students who do not use drugs. (Glickman & Utada, 1983, Beschner & Friedman, 1985).

Adolescents in residential treatment often identify difficulty in expressing feelings, boredom, and anger as problems. Adolescents with these problems are psychologically at risk for substance abuse and need treatment that addresses these problems to lower that risk.

Labouvie and McGee (1986) investigated personality variables and their effects on drinking behavior. Adolescents who started drinking early and proceeded quickly to heavier levels of use tended to score lower on achievement, cognitive structure, and harm avoidance than did non-drinking adolescents, while at the same time scoring higher on affiliation, autonomy, exhibitionism, impulsiveness, and play. They were more detached from the adult world and more involved with peer groups or themselves.

Sexual identity is also an important component of the adolescent's psychological health. An adolescent from an alcoholic family or substance-abusing family may not have learned the skills necessary to relate sexually to his or her peers. Such an adolescent is likely to lack confidence and feel unattractive. This can be an especially important issue for adolescents who see sexuality as an integral part of the adult world.

Parental Styles

Parents create a positive or negative environment according to their own learning history and the skills that they acquired from their parents. Parental absence may result in an emotionally unsupportive environment for which drug use may be a coping mechanism.

Parental approaches based on reasoning are generally more successful than are approaches based on strictness of rules and limits. Parental styles that are over- or under-dominating are common in families with substance abuse problems. Lawson and colleagues (1983) found that an alcoholic almost always has at least one parent in one or more of these four identifiable categories: (1) alcoholic, (2) teetotaler, (3) overly demanding, or (4) overly protective.

These parental types are not necessarily pure; a parent or parents may have qualities of more than one type. The common element for all the parental types is that the children do not develop a positive self-image. Even though research shows that parental types are important in the development of alcoholism, it is likely that many other factors also contribute.

The Alcoholic Parent. It is possible for alcoholic parents to foster alcoholism in their children in a variety of ways. Children learn by watching those around them (particularly significant others), and they copy the behavior that they see. If a parent deals with problems or feelings by drinking or using drugs, the child learns that drinking or using drugs is an option in similar situations.

In general, alcoholic parents are in no position to promote the mental and physical health of their children. In their uncomfortable, guilt-ridden state, they are unlikely to have a loving, supporting, meaningful relationship with their children. If there is one nonalcoholic parent in the family, he or she is usually too angry and frustrated to be of much comfort.

Besides the breakdown in parental relationship, many other factors contribute to the high risk of alcoholism in children with alcoholic parents. Disruptions of family rituals (e.g., holidays, dinnertime, weekend) due to drinking, fear, or embarrassment about what will happen when friends come over all contribute to a poor self-image.

The Teetotaler Parent. The term *teetotaler* is used to describe parents who not only have made a decision not to drink, but also condemn those who have made a different choice. These parents feel that drinking is immoral or indecent. The teetotaler is, therefore, different from someone who chooses not to drink, but has a live-and-let-live attitude concerning the choices of others.

Teetotaler parents are characterized by a rigid moralistic approach to life. They give their children black-or-white, right-or-wrong rules that often prove inadequate in a gray world. Intolerance is the attitude toward the world that the children see modeled.

> In short, the teetotaler parent gives the child a set of rules and expectations that are inconsistent with basic human needs and impossible to live by. In turn, the child has the perfect opportunity to graphically show contempt for those rules by abusing alcohol, usually during adolescence or early adulthood. (Lawson et al., 1983)

To further complicate matters, the children usually feel guilty because they cannot live up to their parents' expectations.

The Overly Demanding Parent. Generally, overly demanding parents make their expectations quite clear to their children. The expectations are unrealistic, however. Trying to live vicariously through their children, these parents ask their children to succeed in all the areas in which they wish that they had succeeded (e.g., sports, college, business). Parents who choose careers for their children often fit in this category.

Overly demanding parents may model a degree of success that seems unattainable to a child. The success that they have achieved may have cost them a close relationship with their family, however. Even though their intention is to help their children be happy, the children find it difficult to feel good about themselves when their parents appear to care more about their careers than about their children. This is particularly tragic when the parents believe that what they are doing is for the good of the family. They are only responding to their own significant models and upbringing.

This type of competitive family environment often results in competition among siblings. Furthermore, family rivalry does not necessarily stop with siblings; parents may also compare themselves with one another. "When people compare themselves with someone they see as better, they will perceive themselves as less than they want to be or should be, and their self-image will suffer as a consequence" (Lawson et al., 1983). Sons and daughters of famous people often graphically illustrate these dynamics.

Overly Protective Parents. The child of overly protective parents never has a chance to develop a sense of self-worth and a positive self-image. The child is not given the opportunity to master his or her environment. Children who have no chance to develop the skills needed to master their environment will not have a positive or secure self-image.

Overly protective parents can be the result of two possible dynamics. First, the parents may be overinvested in their children and may be using their children to meet their own ego needs and to attain a sense of self-worth. Second, the parents may be suffering from a reaction formation. The parents may have some doubt that they even really like their children. This thought is so unacceptable that they react by showing their children, as well as the rest of the world, how much they care through their overprotective behavior (Lawson et al., 1983).

"Feel Good" Status

When assessing why an adolescent is using drugs to cope or provide pleasure and excitement in life, therapists often ask the wrong questions. Instead of asking why drug use is so addicting and reinforcing, perhaps they should ask why the adolescent's life is so unreinforcing that he or she is willing to risk it for the opportunity to use drugs. Thus, psychological assessment of risk should look closely at the adolescent's "feel good" status. Until he or she can find a way to meet psychological needs in a more appropriate manner, drug or alcohol abuse is likely to continue.

On a "feel good" scale numbered from 1 to 10, zero being suicidal and 10 being complete ecstasy, the average person probably walks around most of the time feeling like a 6 or 7. Periodically, however, things happen that allow most individuals to jump up the scale to an 8, 9, or even 10. Given this "feel good" status, a drug that enables them to feel like an 8, 9, or 10 is not such a powerful reinforcer because other things enable them to feel very good—at least part of the time. A confused adolescent from a dysfunctional family that offers little emotional support probably feels like a 3, 2, or even a 1. Because of his or her state of deprivation, a drug that enables this individual to feel like an 8 or better is an extremely powerful reinforcer. If this individual has few, if any, alternative behaviors that bring about such good feelings and peace of mind, the drug takes on even greater importance.

TREATMENT

Many clinicians and agencies use current age and primary drug use to describe involvement and select treatment approaches. There is a large body of data, however, that suggest age of onset of use, the number of drugs used, and frequency of use are better indicators of degree of involvement with drugs than type of drugs used. Furthermore, the more frequently drugs are used, the more likely the client is to use a number of drugs. The probability of eventual abstinence decreases as the number of drugs used increases. Treatment should be predicated on these factors as well as current age and primary drug of choice.

There is a service paradox

> in the fact that for some (most?) youth early intervention by service
> workers has been found to increase the probability that the very behav-
> iors one intended to change become stable. This is the source of the
> idea of "radical nonintervention" with its sources in labelling theory.

Some behaviors will vanish if the person is left alone. Certainly, this will not happen in all cases. A chemical dependency therapist must decide whether to intervene or wait, which is possibly a more important decision than the selection of an
intervention approach.

The opportunity to explore and experiment is thought to be crucial to the development of adolescents. Intervention early in the process can prevent an adolescent from coming to terms with the chemicals in his or her own manner. For
example, calling an adolescent an "early-stage drinker" or encouraging the adolescent to see himself or herself as an alcoholic who cannot and never will be able
to drink without losing control over the drinking will certainly threaten the development of a positive self-image. The premature self-definition imposed by treatment prevents the adolescent from becoming who he or she might become. Not
every youth who drinks in a certain way will become an alcoholic. Thus, there is
the paradox that early detection may result in a negative label and self-concept.
On the other hand, it is an unquestionable fact that large numbers of adolescents
abuse chemicals and get into trouble when they do.

There is a solution to this paradox. If treatment meets the need of the individual, the label, if any, should not matter. In fact, it may be possible to provide the
very best treatment without labeling the adolescent. Substance abuse may be an
issue, but it is very likely only one of many issues. Family problems, social and
work skills, impulsiveness, ability to deal with change, sexual identity, and role
models are all issues of potentially equal or greater importance in the treatment
of adolescents.

Few treatment programs in the United States are designed specifically to treat
adolescents.

> Approximately 20.6% of all drug clients in treatment (N = 173,479) are
> 19 years and under. Of the 3,018 substance abuse treatment facilities in
> the National Drug and Alcoholism Treatment Utilization Survey in
> September, 1982, only 155 (5.1%) had adolescents as their main clien-
> tele. (Beschner & Friedman, 1985)

Of the adolescents in treatment, 15.1% enter residential programs. When these
adolescents were compared to those in drug-free outpatient programs, they were
found to be (1) lower in educational level; (2) more likely to have been referred to

treatment by the criminal justice system; (3) more likely to have had previous treatment episodes; and (4) more likely to have been using drugs other than marijuana, such as heroin, other opiates, cocaine, hallucinogens, barbiturates, and inhalants (Beschner & Friedman, 1985).

DeLeon and Deitch (1984) found that, compared to adults, adolescents in treatment had more disorganization in the family, received psychological treatment at an earlier age, and responded more to pressure exerted by family and fear of jail when deciding to stay in treatment. In addition, they found that educational needs and assistance, as well as family support, played a greater role in their treatment.

In studying residential and day treatment programs, Beschner and Friedman found that counselors' attributes were one of the major factors in the effectiveness of the program. Three major attributes were found to be most important, especially in residential settings. "They were: 1) natural ability and ease in relating to adolescents; 2) an ability to project a positive model; and 3) several years of counseling experience" (p. 129). Beschner concluded that alcohol and marijuana use often continues after treatment, indicating that current treatment methods have insufficient impact on adolescent clients. He also concluded that most adolescent clients and their families have multiple social and psychological problems that predate the substance abuse problem. This last conclusion supports the value of family therapy as a crucial part of any treatment program dealing with substance abuse.

In a comparison of drug-free outpatient programs and residential programs, Beschner and Friedman (1985) identified what counselors considered to be the most effective counseling approaches:

1. an understanding and empathetic attitude
2. confronting the client with his/her self-destructive/maladaptive behavior
3. providing emotional support
4. providing practical assistance in solving the client's real-life problems

Evidence regarding the relative effectiveness of any one treatment approach is inconclusive. There is reason to presume that residential drug-free treatment programs are effective with seriously involved drug abusers. "The amount of time spent in a program was found to be a powerful predictor of all post-treatment criterion behaviors for therapeutic community residents, irrespective of age" (Holland & Griffin, 1984).

Because family issues are so pervasively interwoven in all areas, family therapy seems to be the therapy of choice for adolescent substance abuse. The study by Holland and Griffin (1984) showed the high incidence of dysfunctional families among serious drug abusers. Because of their highly dysfunctional nature, some of the families may be unwilling to cooperate. In these cases, family issues and the hurt, anger, and resentment fostered by the family environment should still be major treatment issues. A team of researchers at the University of Miami compared the effectiveness of two family therapy methods in treating young drug abusers: conjoint family therapy and one-person family therapy. The two methods (one involving the entire family, the other working with a single client on family issues) were found to be equally effective in improving family functioning and reducing drug use. This is certainly encouraging research.

PREVENTION

Lawson, Peterson, and Lawson (1983) suggested that the family system should be viewed as the client. They noted that this approach goes beyond a remedy of current substance abuse problems and offers a way to stop the intergeneration cycle of substance abuse by treating the abusers of the future (the children). The impact of a healthy home environment can buttress an adolescent in a relatively sick society. It is much more difficult to counter the effect of a dysfunctional home with school and community programs, although these are also needed.

Primary prevention is intended to prevent a disorder before it occurs. Secondary prevention is an attempt to detect and halt the progress of a disorder early in its development. Therapeutic intervention is then used to restore health and, it is hoped, prevent future problems.

Primary prevention plans have typically had a goal of total abstinence. Informational scare tactics were often used to achieve this goal. Adolescents today, especially those already using drugs, question the credibility of these programs when the information runs counter to their own experience. They may also be unwilling to give up a substance whose use has become a kind of rites of passage to the adult world.

Beschner and Friedman (1986) suggested that a more realistic approach to prevention is to focus on secondary prevention. Because no prevention strategy is likely to stop adolescents from experimenting with drugs or alcohol, Carroll (cited in Beschner & Friedman, 1986) emphasized efforts to disrupt substance abuse behavior before serious damage occurs. Carroll offered three objectives to achieve this secondary prevention: (1) teach adolescents how to identify the early signs of abuse (e.g., how to distinguish between use and abuse); (2) teach adolescents how to assist peers and family members with substance abuse problems by helping them recognize and accept that they have a problem; and (3) teach adolescents where they or their substance-abusing friend or family member can go for help.

Whatever the prevention strategy, it is clear that the perceptual link between chemical use and coping with unpleasant feelings must be broken. Realizing that adolescents use chemicals to feel better as well as "high," therapists must strive to make adolescents feel better through improved family systems, personal and educational achievements, and activities other than drug and alcohol use.

REFERENCES

Beschner, G.M., & Friedman, A.S. (Eds.). (1979). *Youth drug abuse: Problems, issues and treatment.* Lexington, MA: D.C. Heath.

Beschner, G.M., & Friedman, A.S. (1985). Treatment of adolescent drug abusers. *International Journal of the Addictions, 20*(6 & 7), 97–99.

Beschner, G.M. & Friedman, A.S. (Eds.). (1986). *Teen drug abuse.* Lexington, MA: D.C. Heath.

Cahalan, D., Asin, J.H., & Crossley, A. (1969). *American drinking practices* (Monograph of the Ruther Center of Alcohol Studies, No. 6). New Brunswick, NJ: Ruther Center of Alcohol Studies.

DeLeon, G., & Deitch, D. (1984). Treatment of the adolescent abuser in the therapeutic community. In *Treatment services for adolescent drug abusers.* Rockville, MD: National Institute on Drug Abuse.

Fishburne, P.M., Abelson, H.I., & Cisin, I. (1980). *National survey on drug abuse: Main findings, 1979* (Publication No. ADM 80-976). Washington, DC: U.S. Government Printing Office.

Glickman, N., & Utada, A. (1983). *Characteristics of drug users in urban public high schools* (Grant No. HH8 1 D.A. 01657). Rockville, MD: National Institute on Drug Abuse.

Gonzales, G.M. (1983). Time and place of first drinking experience and parental knowledge as predictors of alcohol use and misuse in college. *Journal of Alcohol and Drug Education, 27*(1), 1–13.

Glynn, T.J. (1981). *Adolescent drug abuse: Review of research based preventive intervention efforts.* Rockville, MD: National Institute on Drug Abuse.

Holland, S., & Griffin, A. (1984). Adolescent and adult drug treatment clients: Patterns and consequences of use. *Journal of Psychoactive Drugs, 17*(1).

Hubbard, R.L., Cavanaugh, E.R., Graddock, S.G., & Rachel, J.V. (1983). Characteristics, behaviors and outcomes for youth in TOPS study (Report submitted to NIDA, Contract No. 271-17-3611). Research Triangle Park, NC: Research Triangle Institute.

Johnston, L.D., Brockman, J.G., & O'Malley, P.M. (1981). *Highlights from student drug use in America 1975–1981* (PHHS Publication No. ADM 82-1208). Rockville, MD: National Institute on Drug Abuse.

Labouvie, E.W., & McGee, C.R. (1986). Relations of personality to alcohol and drug use in adolescence. *Journal of Consulting and Clinical Psychology, 54*(36), 289–293.

Lawson, G., Peterson, J., & Lawson, A. (1983). *Alcoholism in the family: A guide to treatment and prevention.* Gaithersburg, MD: Aspen Publishers.

Pattson, S., Kessler, R., & Hondell, D. (1977). Depressive mood and illegal drug use: A longitudinal analysis. *Journal of Genetic Psychology, 131,* 267–289.

Peck, D.G. (1983). Legal and social factors in the deference of adolescent marijuana use. *Journal of Alcohol and Drug Education, 28*(3).

Segal, B., Cromer, F., Stevens, H., & Wasserman, P. (1982). Patterns of reasons for drug use among detained and adjudicated juveniles. *International Journal of The Addictions, 17*(7), 1117–1130.

Segal, B., Huba, G.J., & Singer, J.L. (1980). *Daydreaming and personality: A study of college youth.* Hillsdale, NJ: Lawrence Earlbaum.

3

Adolescent Substance Abuse: A Social Learning Theory Perspective

Mary C. Howard

As 1 of every 6 teen-agers in the United States suffers from a severe addiction problem (Thorne & DeBlassie, 1985), there is no doubt that substance abuse among adolescents is a major concern. Social learning theory is one model that has been used to investigate this problem. Furthermore, the Alcohol, Drug Abuse and Mental Health Administration's Office for Substance Abuse Prevention (OSAP) stated, "Albert Bandura's Social Learning Theory is probably the most widely used among current prevention program planners" (Johnson, Amatetti, Funkhouser, & Johnson, 1988, p. 579). By focusing on the process of modeling and reinforcement, social learning theory is "more explicit about parenting factors which contribute to substance abuse. . . . It predicts a relationship between drug use and participation in a substance using peer group" (Simons, Conger, & Whitbeck, 1988, p. 294). In order to apply this model to adolescent substance abuse, it is necessary to focus on the social aspects of the adolescent substance abuser, that is, the family, peer group, and community/society.

SOCIAL LEARNING THEORY

The basic premise of social learning theory is that behavior is largely acquired and that it takes place as a result of complex relationships between person and environmental influences. In short, social learning theory focuses on the impact of imitation and social rewards on the learning of behavior. As Bandura (1977) wrote,

> Social Learning Theory approaches the explanation of Human Behavior in terms of continuous reciprocal interaction between cognitive, behavioral and environmental determinants. Within the process of reciprocal determinism lies the opportunity for people to influence

29

their destiny as well as the limits of self-direction. This conception of human functioning then neither casts people into the role of powerless objects controlled by environmental forces nor free agents who can become whatever they choose. Both people and their environments are reciprocal determinants of each other. (p. vii)

Social learning theory maintains three basic constructs: observational learning, reinforcement, and definitions/expectancies.

Observational Learning

The process by which an individual makes mental notes of an observed behavior in order to call upon the mental representation for the purposes of imitating the behavior is observational learning. Johnson (1988) referred to this process as differential association; the motivations and techniques for a behavior are associated with a model. Others provide the environment that rewards or punishes the behavior. For instance, a shy adolescent observing his friend who is the life of the party after drinking alcohol may associate being drunk with being popular. Therefore, if the shy teen-ager's desire to be popular is strong, he is likely to model the behavior of his friend and drink at a party. It has been noted that "abstinence from or use of a particular substance is begun and either sustained or terminated through differential association" (Lanza-Kaduce, Akers, Krohn, & Radosevich, 1984, p. 80).

Reinforcement

The manner by which the consequences of a behavior increase, thus determining the likelihood that the behavior will be continued or is repeated, is the reinforcement process. Reinforcement can be either positive (rewards) or negative (elimination of aversive consequence). They differ from punishers in that they increase the probable frequency of a behavior, whereas punishers decrease the probable frequency. In the example given earlier, since the behavior (e.g., getting drunk) is rewarded (e.g., perceived popularity), the probability of the behavior being continued increases. The basic social resources of rewards or punishments encourage use/non-use.

Definitions/Expectancies

Once a behavior has been observed and/or reinforced, it is internalized in the form of a definition that is based on the expectancies perceived. Thus, the definition of a particular behavior shapes the attitudes and expectancies for the behavior. In the aforementioned example, the adolescent's attitude toward the use of alcohol is likely to be permissive because of the modeling and positive reinforcement that he now associates with the behavior of drinking. Since the adolescent has internalized and defined this behavior as good, his attitude and expectancy is that this behavior is good. The more positive the definition of a behavior, the more likely the behavior will be replicated. Through definitions, individuals either condone a behavior, justify the behavior, or endorse the behavior either generally or situationally—all on a selective basis.

MODELING

Bandura (1977) contended that much social learning occurs through casual or direct observation of behavior. He emphasized the role of modeling in the initiation and maintenance of behavior. According to social learning theory, individuals observe behavior from their total environment and tend to model the behaviors that are represented as "normal" (Barnes, Farrell, & Cairns, 1986). For example, the "norm behavior" in attending a baseball game is to eat hot dogs and drink beer. Likewise, if the norm behavior for adolescents at a party is to see how much they can drink, this behavior will be modeled.

Parental Modeling of Substance Use

Parental use of alcohol/drugs is recognized as one of the most important factors in an adolescent's early use of alcohol/drugs and subsequent behavior (Barnes et al., 1986; Brook, Lukoff, & Whiteman, 1978; Morehouse, 1986). Parental patterns of substance abuse are posited to be directly related to substance abuse in adolescents. Data collected from 1,048 adolescents in grades 7 through 12 and from 338 adults from the same school district (although not necessarily the adolescents' parents) who reported having children in the same grades indicated that the patterns of frequent alcohol use were similar between adolescents and adults (30% and 32%, respectively).

When alcohol is readily available, the quantity/frequency of alcohol use by adult models increases; therefore, the usage by their children increases as well (Barnes, 1981). Adolescents whose fathers are heavy drinkers are twice as likely as are other adolescents to be heavy drinkers as well. Those whose parents conform to extreme models of either heavy drinking or abstinence are more likely to abuse substances than are those whose parents are moderate drinkers or model appropriate use (Barnes et al., 1986).

Adolescents who use substances often have at least one parent who is also a substance abuser. Scherer (1973) found a positive relationship between parental alcohol use and adolescent marijuana and lysergic acid diethylamide (LSD) use. In addition, the children of parents who reported high tranquilizer usage reported a similarly high frequency of tranquilizer usage, as well as increased use of marijuana and LSD. Parental modeling of the use of a substance or class of substances consistently influenced the use of that particular substance or class of substances by adolescents. Furthermore, the parental modeling of marijuana use may increase the likelihood that an adolescent will subsequently make a transition from one class of substances to another; hence, alcohol and marijuana continue to be viewed as the "gateway drugs."

Harburg, Davis, and Caplan (1982) stated that adolescent substance abuse not only is the result of imitation, but also, more importantly, is due to the attitudes toward use, established standards, norms, and behavior. For example, adolescents tend to model their perceptions of their parent's drinking habits, usually those of the same sex parent. Parental permissiveness toward drinking and drug use is positively correlated with adolescent substance abuse (Johnson, Shontz, & Locke, 1984; McDermott, 1984; Scherer, 1973).

Parenting Styles

Family socialization and interaction patterns have an impact on adolescent substance abuse. Halebsky (1987) found that strict parenting, inconsistent limit setting, dysfunction, and lack of closeness are all associated with adolescent substance abuse. The amount of structure that the family provides and the degree to which the adolescent accepts the structure influence adolescent marijuana use (Brook et al., 1978). An adolescent is less likely to use marijuana if the mother has an assertive personality, for example. In addition, Barnes, Farrell, and Cairns (1986) found that problem drinking among adolescents increases when maternal support and control decrease, as well as when paternal support decreases, but control increases (findings that are not mutually exclusive). Family closeness also plays a role in determining adolescent substance abuse. Tudor, Petersen, and Elifson (1980) found that adolescents who reported being close to their parents, thus having a high level of parental support and control, were less likely to abuse substances.

Adults are more likely to use ineffective parenting styles if they were raised in a similar situation; they repeat established intergenerational behavioral patterns. Furthermore, Simons, Conger, and Whitbeck (1988) suggested that environmental stress and inadequate coping skills attribute to parental substance abuse.

Coping Skills

Adolescents (and children) learn strategies for coping with stress from their adult caregivers. By way of observation, they learn to make use of alcohol and many other maladaptive behaviors. Their parents, who have learned to escape responsibility by abusing substances, act as responsibility-avoiding models for their children (Akers, 1973; Jurich, Polson, Jurich, & Bates, 1985; Simons et al., 1988).

Parental modeling is of paramount importance in the development of adolescent drinking, as (1) an adolescent's first drink is likely to occur in the home and (2) drinking is symbolically associated with adult behavior (Mayer, 1986; Simons et al., 1988). If a parent repeatedly comes home after a stressful day of work and drinks alcohol to "unwind," the adolescent is likely to perceive this behavior as an acceptable coping skill in dealing with stress. Thus, the attitudes and behaviors of parents regarding alcohol are good predictors of adolescent drinking (Akers, 1973; McDermott, 1984; Needle et al., 1986; Scherer, 1973; Simons et al., 1988).

Similarly, the more a parent's coping style involves other substances, the higher the likelihood that the adolescent will model this same behavior (Simons et al., 1988). For example,

Paula, a housewife, often complained about feelings of anxiety and stress. Her doctor prescribed for her "nerve pills" (Valium) in order to help her relax. She soon became quite dependent on her "nerve pills," stating that they made her feel less depressed and anxious. As a result of the abuse, however, she did not accomplish household chores. Paula and her husband Andrew often argued about money. When Paula became upset after one of these arguments, she ran straight to her bottle of pills and soon after went to sleep. Marsha, their 15-year-old daughter, observed this behavior and began to feel nervous about her parents' problems. She began to have difficulties in school, avoided doing homework, and often skipped her classes. Soon, Marsha began to experiment with her mother's "nerve pills." Enjoying the effects of the pills, Marsha also became dependent and avoided all her responsibilities at school—a behavior modeled by her mother.

Wills and Shiffman (1985) suggested that people use substances for two reasons: (1) to minimize negative mood and (2) to maximize positive mood. They cautioned that the latter depends on an individual's temporary mood state and, possibly, on personality variables. In addition, Wills (1985) noted that stress is a significant predictor of alcohol use, especially in seventh and eighth graders. He found problematic drinking to be related to subjective feelings of stress. Wills surmised that the higher the level of coping, the lower the level of substance use. Moreover, if decision-making skills, cognitive coping skills, and relaxation skills are adequate, the use of substances is likely to decrease, even if the adolescent experiences a high level of stress.

Pentz (1985) focused on two models: a stress coping model and a stress response model. According to the stress coping model, substance use occurs as a coping behavior in reaction to stress. For example, the adolescent who fears social isolation is more likely to engage in drug use to reduce stress. According to the stress response model, stress increases over time because of the substance use. For example, the adolescent who is using drugs as a coping mechanism becomes inhibited from learning or practicing more adaptive, alternate coping behaviors.

Combined Effect of Peer and Parental Modeling

Alcohol use among peers and parents is a predominant predictor for adolescent substance abuse. In their investigation, however, McLaughlin, Baer, Burnside, and Pokorny (1985) could not determine whether adolescents used alcohol after establishing the peer relationship or whether they found peers to share in the alcohol use that they had developed from their parents. Furthermore, the authors cautioned that they could not ascertain whether the adolescent use demonstrated the effects of modeling, whether it was a genetic disposition, or both.

As adolescents begin to form peer groups, they tend to choose friends who have similar interests. For example, adolescent boys who like athletic activities are more likely to become friends with other boys who like athletic activities. In much the same way, adolescents who use substances interact with peers and adults who use the same type of substances (Huba, Wingard, & Bentler, 1979). An adolescent who drinks beer, for example, is more likely to befriend others who drink beer rather than those who "pop pills." On the other hand, adolescents tend to classify substances rather than view them singularly; they may classify beer, marijuana, and cigarettes in the same category, whereas they may place hard liquor, crystal, and heroin in another.

REINFORCEMENT OF LEARNED BEHAVIOR

Using substances can be particularly reinforcing to an adolescent. Because adolescents are likely to learn expectancies about the psychological and behavioral effects of substances through modeling, they may use substances to relax or to cope with stress (Simons et al., 1988).

The anxiety and/or depression that an adolescent experiences may contribute to the reinforcement properties of the substance. For example, an adolescent who lacks social skills may find that a particular substance makes him or her feel less self-conscious. An adolescent with low self-esteem may suddenly feel more confident after smoking marijuana. In these examples, reinforcement is negative; the adolescents are engaging in a behavior (e.g., using a substance) in order to avoid unwanted feelings or behaviors. As modeled within society, adolescents learn to self-medicate their problems. In a 1974 survey, Prendergast found evidence to support this notion, as the use of prescription drugs by fathers correlated with adolescent marijuana use through modeling behavior and self-medication.

In regard to reinforcement, Johnson (1988) found that negative consequences of using substances did not diminish adolescents' subsequent use. This finding appears to contradict the reinforcement properties of social learning theory. Akers (1973) stated that "behavior is strengthened through rewards (positive reinforcement) or weakened (punished) by aversive stimuli (positive punishment) and lack of reward (negative punishment)" (p. 57). Johnson explained that, in the case of adolescent substance abuse, the punishers are short-term and, therefore, ineffective. For example, he claimed that the adolescent's perception of the punisher may not be the same as an adult's perception or that the immediate gratification of substance use may outweigh the occurrence of later punishment (e.g., a hangover). Moreover, Kandel (1980) emphasized that the physiological factors of a drug can be reinforcing, thus contributing to the maintenance of the behavior. In addition, the adolescent may have a hidden motive for using the substances, such as a desire for parental attention. Other social reinforcements also contribute to the maintenance of substance use, such as statements like, "You were so drunk last night that you were wild!"

EXPECTANCY OF BEHAVIOR

As described earlier, behavior is shaped by people's expectations of reward and punishment in a particular situation, which is then ultimately internalized to form an attitude (and definition) regarding the behavior. For example,

> Mark, aged 15, observes that his parents often fight when they are drunk. His father has at times physically hit him when these fights occur. As a result, Mark had developed a negative perception of drunken behavior. His expectation is that a punishment will follow drinking. Therefore, he may develop a negative attitude toward this behavior.

In the complexities of social learning, people distinguish associations, reinforcements, and definitions, and they adjust their behavior accordingly. For instance, an adolescent who becomes violently ill after drinking a bottle of whiskey may perceive the experience as negative, but is unlikely to stop drinking altogether. Rather, he or she is likely to avoid drinking whiskey and to drink another beverage that will provide a more positive experience.

Using data obtained through the Alcohol Expectancy Questionnaire (AEQ) and the Adolescent Alcohol Expectancy Questionnaire (AEQ-A), Brown, Creamer, and Stetson (1987) found that adolescent substance abusers in treatment, particularly those who had an alcohol-abusing parent, expected significantly more reinforcement from alcohol than did their non-abusing peers. These expectations included tension reduction, social changes, enhancement of cognitive and motor performance, increased arousal, and sexual enhancement.

Corcoran and Parker's (1989) examination of the validity and reliability of these measures suggested that the AEQ-A may make it possible to predict an adolescent's drinking status 1 year after the administration of the questionnaire, indicating that there is some stability to alcohol expectancies. The constructs of the AEQ-A measure an adolescent's response to items in terms of how they think alcohol affects the typical or average drinker, however, whereas the AEQ measures the respondent's personal thoughts, feelings, and beliefs regarding alcohol. For instance, an adolescent may respond to one item in reference to her alcoholic father, but respond to another in reference to her friend. This caveat should be considered in the interpretation of the data.

A survey of 1,580 adolescents showed that expectancies as to the effects of alcohol are well developed in adolescents before they begin to drink (Christiansen, Goldman, & Inn, 1982). These expectancies develop primarily through observation of family, peer groups, and the media. Bandura (1977) concurred that mass media convey expectancies, not just to adolescents, but to everyone. He wrote, "Commercials promise that drinking certain beverages . . . will win admiration of attractive people, enhance job performance, bolster positive self-images, actualize individualism and authenticity, tranquilize irritable nerves and arouse affection of spouses" (p. 52). Likewise, DuPont (1987) stated, "Advertising in North America clearly attributes to the social climate of acceptance of such legal drugs as tobacco and alcohol" (p. 501). No wonder there are so many expectancies for drinking alcohol!

DEFINITIONS

According to Bandura (1977) and Akers (1973), a person learns definitions that determine whether behaviors are perceived as good or bad. Since families, peer groups, and society reinforce it socially, adolescent drinking is more than likely to continue. Reinforcements may include concepts such as drinking is good because it makes people like us (positive effect) or drinking makes us forget our troubles (negative reinforcement).

The many individual definitions combine to establish a societal definition or decision. To quote Bandura (1977), "Through such diverse experiences people learn which dimensions are morally relevant and how much weight to attach to them" (p. 46). In defining and differentiating between drugs and alcohol, for example, society has judged the use of drugs to be deviant behavior and the use of alcohol to be socially acceptable, even though social problems do arise from alcohol misuse and abuse.

PREVENTION

Because adolescent drinking and the subsequent display of behavior is viewed more as a functional and "normal" social behavior than a deviant behavior (Perry, 1987), the prevention of adolescent substance abuse has its own challenges. A natural prevention method that reduces the likelihood of adolescent substance abuse is formal group membership, that is, clubs or organizations (Selnow & Crano, 1986). Group membership contributes to the development of character and moral strength that aids adolescents in resisting peer pressure and avoiding ineffective ways of coping with stress. In a New Mexico high school, a prevention program that used student activities, clubs, organizations, and family-oriented programs decreased inhalant use by 12%, depressant use by 18%, stimulant use by 28%, and phencyclidine (PCP) use by 7% among the adolescent population (Lopez, 1987).

Conversely, informal group memberships may have reverse effects. Adolescents who engaged in unstructured peer activities, such as parties, dating, or driving around in a car, were more likely to drink alcohol at an earlier age than were those in formal groups (Kandel, 1980; Margulies, Kessler, & Kandel, 1977). Therefore, it can be assumed that gang membership would have a similar effect and promote the use of substances.

In order to reduce the reinforcing capabilities of substance use, it is necessary to introduce a more effective reinforcer. In other words, an adolescent who abuses substances as a means for coping with depression must acquire a new skill or behavior that will provide greater reinforcement (positive or negative) than does the substance use. For instance, Patton, Kessler, & Kandel (1977) reported that adolescents who experienced depression following marijuana use were more motivated to cease use than were those who reported relief from depression (a negative reinforcer) after smoking marijuana.

Fear of police apprehension and parental discovery have been posited as strong deterrents for psychedelic and narcotic drug use. These negative reinforcers have been shown to be stronger in the cessation of psychedelic and narcotic drug use than the perceived positive reinforcements of the drugs themselves. However, this is not the case with marijuana and alcohol use (Lanza-Kaduce et al., 1984), probably because the use of alcohol and marijuana in this society is considered norm behavior and the use of illicit drugs is considered deviant behavior. Conversely, Johnson (1988) found reinforcement to be a strong influence in marijuana use, but differential association to be a stronger influence in alcohol use.

SOCIAL SKILLS TRAINING AS A PREVENTION TECHNIQUE

Adolescents who demonstrate deficiencies in social skills use substances as a means to escape, relax, avoid, or withdraw from negative situations. In order to overcome these deficiencies, more and more programs in the last decade have been training adolescents in social or interpersonal skills for resisting drug use, sometimes referred to as social competence. Social skills training is an intervention oriented toward the development of specific behavioral skills, such as assertiveness and anger control. Major techniques used in social skills training include modeling, coaching, role playing, instruction, feedback, and alternate coping strategies. Four areas should be included in a program: (1) education about the reasons for substance use, (2) the ways in which role models establish normative behavior, (3) specific behaviors that can be used to resist peer pressure, and (4) learning and development of coping and life skills.

When a social skills training program was introduced during the final stages of treatment in one 10-week program, the group who received the training possessed higher skill levels than did those who had no training (Hawkins, Catalino, Gillmore, & Wells, 1989). In addition, there was a significant reduction in drug use after 1 year of training. This approach has also begun to reduce the onset of smoking by 50% to 70% (Perry, 1987).

After the implementation of a "life skills training" program among 1,200 junior high school students, subjects who participated in the peer-led group experienced a 71% reduction in total marijuana use and an 83% reduction in regular or daily use; modeling, instruction, rehearsal, feedback, homework, and reinforcement techniques were used (Platt & Hermalin, 1989). Likewise, a group of sixth through ninth graders showed a significant decrease in drug behavior after the implementation of a social skills program. It was noted that youths who were assertive and aggressive demonstrated less frequent use/consumption than did other behavioral groups (Platt & Hermalin, 1989).

One component of the life skills or social skills training programs is to increase adolescents' level of "self-efficacy," or their conviction that they can successfully execute a specific behavior (i.e., refusing drugs) to produce a desired outcome. Pentz (1985) noted, "The need to develop self-efficacy and social skills in pro social ways may override an initial interaction to experiment with drugs" (p. 120). Conversely, well-developed drug use behavior may reduce or offset the need to master social competence.

Lied and Marlatt (1975) noted that social problem-solving deficits have been found among youthful heroin addicts. Social problem solving helps adolescents improve the ways in which they think. The primary skills used are cognitive awareness, the capacity to generate alternative solutions, and causal thinking. The better their problem-solving abilities, the less likely they are to use drugs for temporary relief, avoidance, or escape from the world. When Platt and Hermalin

(1989) incorporated social problem solving training in a treatment program for adult methadone and heroin addicts and alcoholics, they found that the skills had been retained after a 1-year period.

REFERENCES

Akers, R. (1973). *Deviant behavior: A social learning approach.* Belmont, CA: Wadsworth.

Bandura, A. (1977). *Social learning theory.* Englewood Cliffs, NJ: Prentice-Hall.

Barnes, G. (1981). Drinking among adolescents: A subculture phenomenon or a model of adult behaviors. *Adolescents, 16*(61), 211–229.

Barnes, G., Farrell, M., & Cairns, A. (1986). Parental socialization factors and adolescent drinking behaviors. *Journal of Marriage and the Family, 48,* 27–36.

Brook, J., Lukoff, I., & Whiteman, M. (1978). Family socialization and adolescent personality and their association with adolescent use of marijuana. *Journal of Genetic Psychology, 133,* 261–271.

Brown, S., Creamer, V., & Stetson, B. (1987). Adolescent alcohol expectancies in relation to personal and parental drinking patterns. *Journal of Abnormal Psychology, 96*(2), 117–121.

Christiansen, B., Goldman, M., & Inn, A. (1982). Development of alcohol related expectancies in adolescents: Separating pharmacological from social learning influences. *Journal of Consulting and Clinical Psychology, 50*(3), 336–344.

Corcoran, K.J., & Parker, P.S. (1989). Some considerations on the reliability and validity of the AEQ-A. *Psychology of Addictive Behaviors, 3*(2), 43–52.

DuPont, R. (1987). Prevention of adolescent chemical dependency. *Pediatric Clinics of North America, 34*(2), 495–505.

Halebsky, M. (1987). Adolescent alcohol and substance abuse: Parent and peer effects. *Adolescence, 22*(88), 961–967.

Harburg, E., Davis, D., & Caplan, R. (1982). Parent and offspring alcohol use. *Journal of Studies on Alcohol, 43*(5), 497–516.

Hawkins, J., Catalino, R., Gillmore, M., & Wells, E. (1989). Skills training for drug abusers: Generalization maintenance, and effects on drug use. *Journal of Consulting and Clinical Psychology, 57,* 559–563.

Huba, G., Wingard, J., & Bentler, P. (1979). Beginning adolescent drug use and peer and adult interaction patterns. *Journal of Consulting and Clinical Psychology, 47*(2), 265–276.

Johnson, E., Amatetti, S., Funkhouser, J., & Johnson, S. (1988). Theories and models supporting prevention approaches to alcohol problems among youth. *Public Health Reports, 103*(6), 578–585.

Johnson, G., Shontz, F., & Locke, T. (1984). Relationships between adolescent drug use and parental drug behavior. *Adolescence, 19*(74), 295–298.

Johnson, V. (1988). Adolescent alcohol and marijuana use: A longitudinal assessment of a social learning perspective. *American Journal of Drug and Alcohol Abuse, 14*(3), 419–439.

Jurich, A., Polson, L., Jurich, J., & Bates, R. (1985). Family factors in the lives of drug users and abusers. *Adolescence, 20*(77), 143–155.

Kandel, D. (1980). Drug and drinking behavior among youth. *Annual Review of Sociology, 6,* 235–285.

Lanza-Kaduce, L., Akers, R., Krohn, M., & Radosevich, M. (1984). Cessation of alcohol and drug use among adolescents: A social learning model. *Deviant Behavior, 5,* 79–96.

Lied, E., & Marlatt, G. (1975). Modeling as a deterrent of alcohol consumption. *Addictive Behaviors, 4,* 47–54.

Lopez, C. (1987). Substance abuse prevention program—Albuquerque, New Mexico. *Journal of the American Medical Association, 258*(22), 3231.

Margulies, R., Kessler, R.C., & Kandel, D.B. (1977). A longitudinal study of the onset of drinking among high school students. *Journal of Studies on Alcohol, 38,* 879–912.

Mayer, J. (1986). Adolescent alcohol misuse: A family systems perspective. In C.M. Felsted (Ed.), *Youth and alcohol abuse* (pp. 52–62). Phoenix: Oryx Press.

McDermott, D. (1984). The relationship of parental drug use and parent's attitude concerning adolescent drug use to adolescent drug use. *Adolescence, 19*(73), 89–96.

McLaughlin, R., Baer, P., Burnside, M., & Pokorny, A. (1985). Psychosocial correlates of alcohol use at two age levels during adolescence. *Journal of Studies on Alcohol, 46,* 212–218.

Morehouse, E. (1986). Working with alcohol-abusing children of alcoholics. In C.M. Felsted (Ed.), *Youth and alcohol abuse* (pp. 129–138). Phoenix: Oryx Press.

Needle, R., McCubbin, H., Wilson, M., Reineck, R., Lazar, A., & Mederer, H. (1986). Interpersonal influences in adolescent drug use—The role of older siblings, parents, and peers. *International Journal of the Addictions, 21*(7), 739–766.

Patton, S., Kessler, R., & Kandel, D. (1977). Depressive mood and adolescent illicit drug use: A longitudinal analysis. *Journal of Genetic Psychology, 131,* 267–289.

Pentz, M.A. (1985). Social competence and self-efficacy as determinants of substance abuse in adolescents. In T. Wills & S. Shiffman (Eds.), *Coping and substance abuse* (pp. 117–139). New York: Academic Press.

Perry, C. (1987). Results of prevention programs with adolescents. *Drug and Alcohol Dependence, 20*(1), 13–19.

Platt, J., & Hermalin, J. (1989). Social skill deficit interventions for substance abusers. *Psychology of Addictive Behaviors, 3*(3), 114–133.

Prendergast, T. (1974). Family characteristics associated with marijuana use among adolescents. *International Journal of the Addictions, 9*(6), 827–839.

Scherer, S. (1973). Self reported parent and child drug use. *British Journal of Addictions, 68,* 363–364.

Selnow, G., & Crano, W. (1986). Formal vs. informal group affiliations: Implications for alcohol and drug use among adolescents. *Journal of Studies on Alcohol, 47*(1), 48–52.

Simons, R., Conger, R., & Whitbeck, L. (1988). A multistage social learning model of the influences of family and peers upon adolescent substance abuse. *Journal of Drug Issues, 18*(3), 293–315.

Thorne, C., & DeBlassie, R. (1985). Adolescent substance abuse. *Adolescence, 20*(78), 341–346.

Tudor, L., Petersen, D., & Elifson, K. (1980). An examination of the relationship between peer and parental influences and adolescent drug use. *Adolescence, 25*(60), 783–789.

Wills, T. (1985). Stress, coping, and tobacco and alcohol use in early adolescence. In T. Wills & S. Shiffman (Eds.), *Coping and substance abuse* (pp. 67–92). New York: Academic Press.

Wills, T., & Shiffman, S. (1985). *Coping and substance abuse.* New York: Academic Press.

4

Intergenerational Alcoholism: The Family Connection

Ann W. Lawson

It is popular to blame adolescent substance abuse on peer pressure or availability of alcohol and other drugs. Although these factors contribute to the problem, adolescents are also greatly influenced by their parents' attitudes, behaviors, values, and teachings. This is not to say that parents are responsible for their children's substance abuse, but family history and dynamics play a major role in the development of chemical dependence in adolescents and, often, their resistance to treatment. Substance abuse, particularly alcoholism, is an intergenerational problem; it occurs in families generation after generation. An understanding of this process can lead to improved treatment and prevention methods to halt the intergenerational spread of addiction in families.

PHYSIOLOGICAL INFLUENCES ON FAMILIAL ALCOHOLISM

Every study of familial alcoholism has shown a higher rate of alcoholism among the relatives of alcoholics than among the general population (Goodwin, 1971). When studying alcoholics in treatment, Winokur and Clayton (1968) found that 28% of the women alcoholics had alcoholic fathers and 12% had alcoholic mothers. The men receiving treatment for alcoholism reported that 21% of their fathers and 3% of their mothers were alcoholics.

In a review of 39 studies of the incidence of familial alcoholism, involving the parents, grandparents, siblings, and children of 6,251 alcoholics and 4,083 nonalcoholics, Cotton (1979) found that an alcoholic was more likely to have a father, mother, or more distant relative who was an alcoholic than was a nonalcoholic. Almost one third of any sample of alcoholics had at least one parent who was an alcoholic, and, in every study of the families of alcoholics and nonalcoholics, the incidence of alcoholism was higher in the families of alcoholics. Two thirds of the studies indicated that at least 25% of the alcoholics had fathers who were alcoholics; the range was 2.5% to 50%. The frequency of reported alcoholism was higher in male relatives than in female relatives, but the fact that alcoholism in women is often hidden may have affected these reports. Cotton also found that women alcoholics are more likely than are men alcoholics to come from families in which excessive drinking had occurred, which may indicate that women are more vulnerable to the familial impact of alcoholism. Midanik (1983) supported this finding when she found that alcoholic women reported more alcoholic and problem drinking in first-degree relatives than did men. This familial transmission also occurred in other subgroups: American Indians, Irish Americans, and whites as opposed to blacks.

These studies indicate that alcoholism runs in families, but they do not answer the important question of whether it is nature or nurture that produces this familial transmission. Because alcoholism does not follow an exact Mendelian mode of inheritance, it is difficult to separate the effects of heredity from the effects of environment in the etiology of alcoholism. Parents produce both the genetic and environmental factors. Researchers have tried to isolate the genetic influences in three types of studies: (1) twin studies, (2) adoption and half-sibling studies, and (3) genetic marker studies.

Twin Studies

In twin studies, researchers examine the genetic component of the transmission of alcoholism by comparing identical with fraternal twins where alcoholism affects at least one twin. These studies are based on the assumption that monozygotic (identical) and dizygotic (fraternal) twins differ only in their genetic makeup and that their environments are the same. Thus, if alcoholism is a genetic disorder, it will have a higher concordance rate for monozygotic than for dizygotic twins. In the first such twin study, conducted in Sweden, Kaij (1960) identified 174 pairs of male twins, one or both of whom had been reported to the local Temperance Board for alcohol abuse. Only 10 of these pairs were monozygotic. When compared on the number of Temperance Board convictions, duration, and complications of drinking, the monozygotic twins were more concordant for drinking problems (28%) than were the dizygotic twins (15%). After interviewing these twins, Kaij rated them again and found 54% of the monozygotic twins were assigned to the same drinking category, compared with 28% of the dizygotic twins. When he looked at only those with chronic alcoholism, the difference was greater: 71% for monozygotic to 32% for dizygotic. There have been some criticisms of this study, including the method of differentiating monozygotic and dizygotic twins; the unequal interview times; and the source of subjects, who included a high percentage of criminals.

The first twin study of drinking behavior in normal twins (e.g., those not necessarily having a diagnosis of alcoholism or problem drinking) was done by Partanen, Bruun, and Markkanen (1966) in Finland. They interviewed 902 male twins, aged 28 to 37 years, and identified three components of drinking behavior: (1) frequency; (2) amount; and (3) loss of control or dependency, as determined by the number of drunken episodes and arrests. They found that both frequency (39%) and amount (36%) had a significant heritability, but loss of control (14%) did not. The nonalcoholic population did show more concordance with regard to frequency and amount among monozygotic than among dizygotic twins, but did not indicate heredity of addictive symptoms. This finding suggests that abstinence and normal drinking have a genetic factor, while the loss of control and social consequences of drinking that are often used as criteria for the diagnosis of alcoholism may not have such a factor. When Jonsson and Nilsson (1968) questioned 750 pairs of Norwegian male twins on their drinking behaviors, however, they found no significant concordance in frequency and amount of alcohol intake. The highest indicator of heritability in their study was found when subjects were dichotomized into drinkers or abstainers, which suggests a genetic factor in abstinence.

In later research, Clifford, Fulker, and Murray (1984) also compared the drinking patterns of monozygotic and dizygotic normal twins. The correlation of the monozygotic twins was twice that of the dizygotic twins in escape and social drinking in males. These researchers concluded that genetic factors were of no importance in females, except in weekly alcohol consumption, but were of significant importance in males. In reviewing other genetic studies, however, Gurling and Murray (1984) stated, "It would be premature to conclude at this stage that there is a major genetic predisposition to the development of severe alcoholism" (p. 135).

These twin studies are flawed in a number of ways. Often, the twins are not identified by blood tests for genetic match of monozygotic twins and they may be placed in wrong groups. Furthermore, identical twins are often treated more alike than are fraternal twins simply because they look more alike and are even dressed alike in many instances. Thus, their environment, particularly their parent-child relationships, differs from that of fraternal twins. Even if identical twins are reared apart, they look alike and may be treated in a similar way by different parents because they are physically similar. In addition, generalizing from the twin to the non-twin population can cause problems. They are genetically unique in that they have higher infant mortality rates, lower birth rates, slightly lower intelligence, and higher age of mother at birth (Partanen, Bruun, & Markkanen, 1966). Although the twin studies point to some heritability of alcoholism in some pairs, the 40% to 50% discordance rates in monozygotic twins indicate a strong environmental factor.

Adoption and Half-Sibling Studies

The design of an adoption study allows researchers to separate the genetic from the environmental factors. For example, Goodwin, Schulsinger, Hermansen, Gruze, and Winokur (1973) went to Denmark to study 55 male adoptees, each of whom had at least one biological parent who had been hospitalized primarily for alcoholism. These adoptees had been removed from their homes at early ages and raised by nonrelatives who had low rates of alcohol problems. This group was matched and compared with a control group, none of whom had an alcoholic biological parent, but who had been removed from their homes. Of the 55 subjects with alcoholic parents, 10 were classified as alcoholic, a rate nearly four times that of the controls. Goodwin and colleagues concluded that there may be a genetic predisposition to severe forms of alcohol abuse, but that heavy drinking itself, even when problems resulted from the drinking, reflect predominantly non-genetic factors.

Because 85% of the alcoholic biological parents in this study were fathers, Goodwin and associates (1973) were really examining the transmission of alcoholism from father to son. Cloninger, Bohman, and Sigvardsson (1981) suggested that there may be two types of alcohol abuse heretibility: that inherited from the father and that inherited from both parents. These studies do not take into account the environmental factors that influence a baby in utero, however. Adoption studies suggest that genetic factors may play a role in alcoholism, but provide no details on the way in which a predisposition is transmitted.

In another variation of genetic research in alcoholic families, Schuckit, Goodwin, and Winokur (1972) studied 60 male and 9 female alcoholics who had half-siblings. They included subjects who had alcoholic biological parents, but were raised in foster homes with no alcoholic parents, as well as subjects who had nonalcoholic biological parents, but were raised by alcoholic parents. The results of this study indicated that 62% of the subjects who were alcoholic had at least one alcoholic biological parent, while only 19% of the subjects who were nonalcoholic had an alcoholic biological parent, suggesting a strong genetic relationship. The rates of alcoholic and nonalcoholic half-siblings who lived with alcoholic parents were the same, indicating a stronger relationship with heredity than with environmental factors. Schuckit and Haglund (1977) concluded,

> One can summarize the separation studies in alcoholism by stating that genetics appear to be of great importance in the development of alcoholism in the offspring of alcoholics. It is never possible to arrive at 100% sound conclusions in human studies because there are so many variables that cannot be controlled, but these studies seem to come close to establishing the influence of genetic factors in the development of alcoholism. In considering the conclusions, one should not under-

estimate the probable importance of social and psychological factors in the development of alcoholism. (p. 23)

Although these separation studies provide evidence of a genetic factor in the familial occurrence of alcoholism, they do not solve the nature vs. nurture debate. After reviewing the family studies of alcoholism, Goodwin (1981) concluded that these studies are plagued with difficulties. The information is retrospective and unsystematically obtained. Information is sometimes omitted or not requested. Two people from the same family may tell conflicting stories, and it is difficult to decide which story is the correct one. The definition of alcoholism also varies from study to study; it ranges from "admission to alcoholism treatment" to "drinking in excess of community standards". The uneven distribution of alcoholism in the population often leads to sample bias. For example, there are different ratios of men to women alcoholics, even between alcohol treatment centers. This makes it impossible to generalize findings. Observer bias also occurs; the "halo" effect (i.e., finding the expected) is applicable in alcohol studies. Another problem involves the ages of the subjects studied. Someone who does not have alcohol problems at age 25 may develop them at age 40, but a one-time measure obviously cannot reveal alcoholism that develops at a later date. In studies that try to predict alcoholism from a previous psychiatric morbidity the chicken and egg problem occurs. It is difficult to determine whether the subject was depressed and sociopathic and became alcoholic or was alcoholic and became depressed and sociopathic.

Other Genetic Factors Research

Genetic markers are important because they help to identify those who are at risk for alcoholism before they develop the problem. One inherited characteristic that some researchers have thought to be associated with alcoholism is color blindness. Cruz-Coke and Varela (1966) found alcoholism and cirrhosis to be associated with color blindness and suggested that an X-linked recessive gene may transmit alcoholism. Other researchers discovered that the color blindness was a consequence of the alcoholism, however. Research in this area has been contradictory, and results have been too varied to draw conclusions. Schuckit and Haglund (1977) stated, "Finding a positive and significant relationship between a known genetic marker and alcoholism is in many ways like looking for a needle in a haystack" (p. 23).

Because alcohol has marked effects on the nervous system and behavior, which varies greatly among individuals, researchers have looked for signs of a genetic susceptibility to alcoholism in alterations in certain neurobehavioral functions. Neville and Schmidt (1983) used an event-related potential (ERP) technique to compare electrical phenomena in the brains of two groups of nonalcoholic young men; one group had a family history of alcoholism, while the other did not. Recordings of brain activity both before and after the ingestion of either alcohol or a placebo revealed significant differences in brain electrical activity, especially in the feature called the P_3 wave, between the two groups. Although this may appear to point to a biological predisposition to alcoholism in the children of alcoholics, the same change in the P_3 brain wave occurred whether alcohol or a placebo was administered. It is possible that, as a result of their home environment, the children of alcoholics have developed this response to the thought of drinking alcohol. The emotional response that many children of alcoholics have to alcohol could create changes in brain wave patterns. These areas of investigation could be very useful in prevention efforts if a neurobehavioral indicator of who is at risk for alcoholism could be identified.

Schuckit has compared the subjective responses to alcohol in young nonalcoholic male drinkers who had family histories of alcoholism with the responses of a matched group who had no such family histories. In the first study, Schuckit (1984) found that the group with family histories of alcoholism reported less intense subjective feelings of intoxication after drinking, especially during the 2 hours after the maximum blood alcohol level. In the second study, Schuckit (1985a) found that a group with the family histories of alcoholism exhibited less body sway at the 0.75 mL/kg level of alcohol than did those with no family histories of alcoholism. Both these studies indicated a decreased intensity of reaction to ethanol in young men with family histories of alcoholism. Furthermore, no subjective differences were reported after the administration of a placebo, which indicated that the differences resulted from the physiological effects of alcohol and not from the expectations of drinking the alcohol. This lack of awareness of intoxication and lack of related body movement may deprive the sons of alcoholics of warning mechanisms that they have had enough to drink; thus, they are more likely to drink to excess. Schuckit believed that this indicates a biological basis for the transmission of alcoholism.

In reviewing biological studies in alcoholism transmission, Schuckit (1985b) stated, "Once the presence or absence of a biological alcoholic parent is controlled for, rearing experiences and parental loss do not increase the risk for alcoholism" (p. 31). Goodwin (1985) also reviewed the genetic studies and concluded, "Whatever biological vulnerability may be present, the development of drinking problems is obviously influenced by sociocultural factors" (p. 174). He also pointed out that not all alcoholism is familial. Approximately half of those hospitalized for alcoholism do not have a family history of alcoholism. Schuckit (1983) challenged this figure, however, in his study of hospitalized primary alcoholics; he discovered that when other sources were questioned and second-degree relatives were included, only 30% of those hospitalized did not have a family history of alcoholism.

As much as these biological studies may indicate a possible genetic cause of alcoholism, none has clearly pointed to a factor that will predict alcoholism from a biological standpoint. The research has added more evidence that children from alcoholic families are at high risk for becoming alcoholic, but the nature versus nurture controversy goes on.

PSYCHOSOCIAL INFLUENCES ON FAMILIAL ALCOHOLISM

There are 28 million people in the United States with at least one alcoholic parent (National Association for Children of Alcoholics, 1983), and it is becoming widely recognized that these children can develop a full range of problems as a result of living with an alcoholic parent—problems that continue into their adult life. These children are at high risk for developing social and emotional problems, and they are twice as likely to develop alcohol-related problems as are the children of nonalcoholics (Bosma, 1975; Goodwin et al., 1973).

Even if the alcoholic parent stops drinking, the children do not recover spontaneously. In a study of alcoholic families in Pennsylvania, Booz-Allen & Hamilton (1974) found that "the treatment and recovery of the alcoholic parent does not appear to reduce the problems experienced by the children" (p. 63).These family systems were often out of balance and unable to adjust to the newly sober parent, and the children did not give up their coping roles. In a study of 115 children aged 10 to 16 years who lived in alcoholic homes, Cork (1969) found that the children did not consider family life significantly better when their parent's drinking stopped.

Studies That Focus on Family Relationships

Both longitudinal studies (McCord, McCord, & Gudeman, 1960; Miller & Jang, 1978; Vaillant & Milofsky, 1982) and current or retrospective studies (Booz-Allen & Hamilton, 1974; Chafetz, Blane, & Hill, 1971; Haberman, 1966; McKenna & Pickens, 1981; Wilson & Orford, 1978) have revealed various problems in children who live with alcoholics. Sloboda (1974) found that alcoholic parents often do not live by society's rules; discipline is inconsistent, and the children become confused and unable to predict parental behavior. In examining the effects of the alcoholic mother, Richards (1979) discovered the prepubertal defense of splitting and pseudomaturity. The children were coping by splitting the mother into good/bad and sober/drunk. Richards (1979) stated "The inebriated mother may deliver sudden and harsh punishment followed by overindulgence" (p. 23). The mother's unpredictability creates further problems for the children.

Chafetz, Blane, and Hill (1971) compared 100 alcoholic families with 100 nonalcoholic families seen at a child guidance center and found marital instability, poor marital relationships, prolonged separations, and divorce considerably more prevalent in the alcoholic families (41% vs. 11%). In addition, these researchers discovered more serious illnesses and accidents, as well as more school problems, in alcoholic families than in nonalcoholic families. Children from alcoholic homes externalized conflict and were more often involved with the police or the courts. According to Chafetz, Blane, and Hill (1971), "This suggests that children of alcoholics have a difficult time becoming socially mature and responsible adults" (p. 696).

When Booz-Allen and Hamilton (1974) did a needs assessment of children from alcoholic families for the National Institute on Alcoholism and Alcohol Abuse, they defined alcoholism broadly to include a continuum from problem drinking to public inebriates. They interviewed children who were living with alcoholic parents and adults who had grown up with alcoholic parents. The most frequent disturbances that they found (60%) were emotional neglect of the children and family conflict, defined as violence, aggression, fighting, arguments within the home, and spouse abuse. Emotional neglect was the result of the alcoholic parent's withdrawal from the child and subsequent failure to provide the child with communication, affection, or parenting. These families also experienced the full range of other family problems, including nonfulfillment of parental responsibilities, instability, divorce, separation, death, physical abuse, and incest. The children in this study expressed strong feelings about living with an alcoholic parent. Most frequently, they resented their situation, particularly the parental duties that they had to perform and the lack of "normal" parents. Often, they expressed embarrassment about their parents' inadequacies and unresponsiveness.

School problems, delinquency, and fighting were common among the young children. A high percentage of the children had difficulties in developing relationships with peers. Less common problems included alcohol and drug abuse, depression and suicidal tendencies, repressed emotions, and lack of self-confidence and direction. Children were at higher risk of developing such problems when they (1) belonged to a lower socioeconomic group, (2) witnessed or experienced physical abuse, (3) were 6 years old or younger at the onset of the parental alcohol abuse, (4) were an only or oldest child, and (5) lived in a nonsupportive family situation. It was concluded that "having an alcoholic parent is an emotionally disturbing experience for children. If children do not resolve the problems created by parental alcoholism, they will carry them the rest of their lives" (Booz-Allen & Hamilton, 1974, p. 73).

There were some weaknesses in this study. For example, because all the children were referred by mental health professionals, any children who were not in contact with the helping services were excluded. Furthermore, it was not a generalizable study and did not determine what causes some children from alcoholic families to become alcoholic themselves, while others do not. It did indicate that the presence of a supportive parent or other relative reduced the chances of damage to the child.

Hecht (1973) noted that communication in the alcoholic family was often incongruent, unclear, and led to the isolation of family members. Watching as their parents said one thing and did another, the children received two messages and did not know which message to follow. If these messages became "double binds," the children could not win with either choice. Spouses of alcoholics often "protected" the child with half-truths about the alcoholic; unfortunately, however, the children came to believe that parents could not be trusted. To survive in this environment, the children learned to ignore verbal messages and watch for actions and deeds. Similarly, the children imitated the parental communication style of fighting and hostile sarcasm, often acting out their impulses. Children living in these systems felt alone and had difficulty trusting others.

Hecht (1973) observed that the children had a great need to love their parents, but became angry when their parents were abusing alcohol or neglecting them. This anger was not directed at their parents, but turned inward. The children also were afraid that matters would worsen and their home would disappear. They expressed their anger and resentment through rebellious behavior. Ironically, this rebellious behavior may have been the very reason for a child's removal from the home and parents. The child often became the "bad" person, while other family members hid and protected the alcoholic.

MacMurray (1979) noted that the disruption of stable patterns of family organization, combined with the abuse of alcohol, may increase the probability of neglect. No matter how damaging to the children involved, however, these cases of neglect are often not prosecuted or investigated by child protective agencies because of the lack of evidence and the difficulty of getting court convictions.

According to Clinebell (1968), four factors damage the lives of the children of alcoholics. First, children may undertake parental duties because the parent is unable or unwilling to fulfill such responsibilities. Also, the alcoholic may be treated as a child and, in turn, act helpless. Second, an inconsistent and unpredictable relationship with the alcoholic is emotionally depriving to the child. Third, the nonalcoholic parent is struggling with major problems and, because his or her own needs are unmet, is unable to attend to the needs of the children. Fourth, the family may use social isolation as a protection from further pain and suffering. Owing to embarrassment, the family builds a wall of defenses that leaves no room for social relationships or adequate peer relationships for the children. Although these conditions do not occur in all alcoholic families, they are damaging when they do exist.

Cork (1969) found that children became so absorbed in family problems that some of the children were unable to develop a sense of responsibility or an ability to solve problems. The main concerns of the children were parental fighting and quarreling, and both parents' lack of interest in them. The majority of the children had decided not to drink because they were afraid of being like their alcoholic parents. Approximately two thirds said they would never drink for various reasons, and one third said they would drink in moderation. Five children were already drinking. Ironically, if previous research is correct, 30% to 50% of the children who have decided not to drink or to drink only moderately will become alcoholic.

In considering the grandparents of the children in her study, Cork (1969) found that two thirds of the fathers of alcoholic parents were alcoholic and one tenth of their mothers were alcoholic. Fifty percent of the fathers and 7% of the mothers of the nonalcoholic parents were alcoholic. This seems to substantiate theories of an intergenerational process and makes these third-generation children truly at high risk, even though they have cognitively decided not to drink like their alcoholic parents. Although these facts may suggest a genetically inherited problem, Cork deduced from her work that "the key to alcoholism lies in the interpersonal relationships within the family" (p. 79). She felt that the major environmental stresses of the parents and grandparents in this study were difficulties in marriage and family life.

Other Studies That Focus on Children of Alcoholics

Miller and Jang (1978) conducted a 20-year longitudinal study of children of alcoholics from lower class multiproblem urban families, comparing them with other lower class multiproblem families. They gathered data in 2-hour autobiographical interviews with 259 children, 147 who had an alcoholic parent and 112 who did not. The emphasis in these interviews was on the children's patterns of coping with stress throughout their developmental years and on their relationships with their parents. The fact that this was a certain socioeconomic group does limit the study, but the results, although not generalizable to the population at large, point to specific problems of children caused by their parents' alcoholism. Miller and Jang found that the children of alcoholic parents had greater socialization difficulties than did the children of nonalcoholic parents. The degree of parental alcoholism consistently correlated with the degree of negative impact on the children, both during the children's developmental years and in their adult adaptation. If both parents were alcoholic, the adult subjects were having even greater difficulties. The children of alcoholics perceived more serious family problems (three times as many) and in retrospect had more severe marital difficulties in their own adult family lives; and were more likely to fail in marriage, employment, and ability to support themselves and their families. "Thus, among children of multiproblem families, those whose parents were alcoholics are more likely to constitute the basis for development of a new generation of multiproblem families" (Miller & Jang, 1978, p. 28).

The transmission of alcoholism was greater for the children of alcoholics. Of those who had an alcoholic parent, 36% drank heavily, whereas only 16% of those who did not have an alcoholic parent drank heavily. Not all children of alcoholics become alcoholic or have social problems, however. "A good socialization experience for the child can mitigate a history of parental alcoholism, and, similarly, a bad socialization experience can vitiate a good history of no alcoholism on the parents' part" (Miller & Jang, 1978, p. 25). They summarized, "Children reared in alcoholic multiproblem families have many more problems than do children reared in nonalcoholic multiproblem families" (Miller & Jang, 1978, p. 29). They also stated that a true predictive course of intergenerational transmission of alcoholism cannot be traced.

In another longitudinal study, McCord, and McCord, and Gudeman (1960) found that children who were raised by affectionate mothers were less likely to become alcoholic. Those who became alcoholic had often been exposed to maternal ambivalence and less clear behavior expectations. Additionally, in the families of the children who became alcoholic in later life, they found more incest, illegitimacy, maternal promiscuity, paternal deviance, maternal employment, and mutual parental role dissatisfaction. Thus, a dysfunctional family life appears to increase the risk of alcoholism for the children raised in this environment.

Symptoms in the Children of Alcoholics

Several studies have shown that children of alcoholics have an assortment of symptoms that are more severe or more numerous than are those of other children. In a study conducted by Haberman (1966), for example, interviews with their mothers indicated that the children of alcoholics have more frequent temper tantrums, fight with other children more often, and have more frequent trouble in school because of bad conduct or truancy. The children of alcoholics also suffer more often from developmental disorders and somatization of tensions (Keane & Roche, 1974). Hindman (1976) found that children from alcoholic families are isolated from the community and suffer from a lack of parenting. Using the Personality Inventory for Children (PIC), Anderson and Wentworth (1983) noted significant differences in adjustment, family relationships, and anxiety in 50 children of alcoholics whose parents were undergoing treatment for alcoholism. Males were higher in delinquency and hyperactivity, and children aged 6 to 12 years appeared to be more affected in the areas of family relationships and anxiety.

In studying children with emotional and behavioral problems who had recovering alcoholic parents, Jesse (1977) found children with faulty self-identification who were either isolated from or in opposition to their parents. They displayed gender role confusion; emotional immaturity; and feelings of shame, personal inadequacy, and alienation. Sexias (1977) reported similar findings. In describing the alcoholic family, she noted a constant atmosphere of anger, frustration, and destructive tensions that affected all family relationships. "Conflict between the parents often results in confusion, self-blame, and feelings of rejection in the child" (Sexias, 1977, p. 154). The problems that she observed in the children and their parents were role confusion, double-bind parental expectations, role reversal, and parental inconsistency.

Noll and Zucker (1983) compared the preschool sons of male alcoholics with matched controls and found significant differences on developmental assessment. The boys in the control group had better language, personal/social, fine motor, and adaptive skills. On tasks designed to measure knowledge of alcoholic beverages, however, the sons of alcoholics had earlier and more sophisticated cognitive structures. In their study sampler, Roberts and Brent (1982) found that "family members of alcoholics made more visits to physicians, and had more distinct diagnoses of trauma and stress related diseases than did members of nonalcoholic families" (p. 119). Children of alcoholics appear to be at risk not only for physical problems, but also for psychiatric problems. Bourgeois, Levigneron, and Delage (1975) discovered that, of 136 children hospitalized in a child psychiatry ward, almost 50% came from alcoholic homes. These children were four times more likely to be from families in which the parents were divorced. There were high percentages of parental abandonment and incompetence among these same parents, and 1 of 3 children of alcoholics lived outside the family environment. Similarly, Lund and Landesman-Dwyer (1979) found that 29.1% of adolescents in residential psychiatric treatment in the state of Washington had lived with an alcoholic parent. "Parental death, drug abuse, imprisonment, and physical abuse, neglect and inadequate supervision of children were reported for alcoholic families at twice or nearly twice the rate of nonalcoholic families" (Lund & Landesman-Dwyer, 1979, p. 341).

In another study of the connection between parenting and psychiatric illness, Rosenberg (1969) compared three adult groups of 50: alcoholics, drug addicts, and psychoneurotics. Less than 50% of the alcoholics and addicts reached the age of 15 with both parents living together. They viewed their fathers as punishing, uninterested, or rejecting and their mothers as unwilling or unable to provide adequate discipline. The psychoneurotic group reported high levels of parent disharmony and psychiatric illness, including excessive alcohol intake, but no overt social disruption. Therefore, Rosenberg concluded that the social disruption and tension seemed to produce alcoholics and addicts.

Moos and Billings (1982) introduced a new variable into the study of children of alcoholics: recovery versus relapse. They studied 51 families 18 months after treatment of a family member for alcoholism. Children of the 23 relapsed alcoholics evidenced more depression and anxiety and were more likely to have serious physical and emotional problems than did children in the control group. Children of the 28 recovering alcoholics were comparable to the controls, but Moos and Billings drew no conclusions about emotional disturbances in these children over time. Furthermore, this finding does not necessarily suggest that children of alcoholics will recover when their alcoholic parents do. Those who did not relapse may have had better home environments prior to treatment. The investigators did find the family environments of the relapsed alcoholics to be less cohesive and expressive, as well as less likely to promote independence, achievement, intellectual-cultural and recreational activities, and religious development.

In a longitudinal study of 698 multiracial children, Werner (1986) investigated the reasons for resilience in the offspring of alcoholics. Some of the children of alcoholics in this study population had serious learning and behavior problems, but 59% of the 49 children had not developed these problems by age 18. Males and children of alcoholic mothers had higher rates of psychosocial problems in childhood and adolescence than did females and children of alcoholic fathers. Children of alcoholics who had not developed serious coping problems by the age of 18 years differed from the others in temperament, communication skills, self-esteem, and locus of control. An important finding was the low number of stressful life events that had disrupted the resilient children's family units in their first 2 years of life.

Role Behavior Theories

In all families, members take on role behaviors. In alcoholic families, however, normal role behavior becomes rigid as family members cope with the alcoholism (Black, 1979; Booz-Allen & Hamilton, 1974; Nardi, 1981; Wegscheider, 1981b). Virginia Satir, a pioneer in family therapy, identified role behaviors that family members play when they are under stress (Bandler, Grender, & Satir, 1976). Wegscheider (1981a, 1981b), a student of Satir's, identified role behaviors specific to an alcoholic family: the dependent or alcoholic; the enabler or spouse; the family hero, who is usually the oldest or most responsible and a high achiever; the scapegoat or problem child; the lost child, who is a loner and lives in a fantasy world; and the mascot or clown, who pretends to be carefree. Family members work hard at these roles to save the family system at the expense of their own emotional and physical health. The roles hide the true feelings of these people and interfere with clear, congruent communication. When these role behaviors fail and the stress continues, family members change roles in a desperate attempt to cope.

Although these roles have obvious negative aspects, such as self-denial, repression of feelings, and denial of needs, several investigators (e.g., Nardi, 1981;

Thornton & Nardi, 1975; Wilson & Orford, 1978) have asserted that these roles may help children of alcoholics develop important life skills, such as responsibility, initiative, independence, and insight into peoples' problems.

Black (1979, 1981a, 1981b) described two roles that children of alcoholics may play: (1) the misbehaving, obviously troubled child and (2) the mature, stable, overachieving, behaving child. According to Black, most children of alcoholics are in the latter group and divides them into adjusters, placaters, and responsible ones. Black (1979) stated that the roles adopted by children of alcoholics may appear to be functional, but they really cover up problems that may emerge later, when these roles are no longer sufficient for coping. She stated that, as adults, these children of alcoholics "often find themselves depressed, and they do not understand why; life seems to lack meaning. They feel loneliness, though many are not alone. Many find great difficulty in maintaining intimate relationships. And many become alcoholic and/or marry alcoholics" (Black, 1979, p. 25).

Role behaviors are often tied to birth order. Birth order studies revealed that, in 20 of 27 separate samples of alcoholic men, more last born than firstborn in families of two or more children became alcoholic (Barry & Blane, 1977; Blane & Barry, 1973). The same was true for 6 samples of women. Moreover, the last born experienced deaths, divorces, and advanced alcoholism at a younger age, perhaps because the last born was an unwanted or rejected child, was overprotected in a prolonged dependency, or was born at a time when the alcohol problems in the family were more severe and the resources reduced.

Children of Alcoholics Research Critique

Several problems mar the psychosocial studies on children of alcoholics. Much of the material is anecdotal, based on case findings rather than on research instruments and measures; there is no standard definition of alcoholism; and controls are often taken from dysfunctional groups such as the emotionally ill. Methodological weaknesses include failure to control independent variables, such as the child's sex, age, and length of exposure to parental drinking, and failure to determine the extent of problem behaviors associated with this drinking. In addition, researchers have often failed to note which parent was alcoholic, whether one or both parents were alcoholic, and what the marital status of the parents was. Investigators who have critically reviewed studies of the children of alcoholics (el-Guebaly & Offord, 1977; Jacob, Favorini, Meisel, & Anderson, 1978) have called for more controlled studies that not only account for the variables of age, sex, education, socioeconomic class, and extent of family disorganization, but also use "blind" data collection.

Early Drinking Behavior in Children of Alcoholics

In an examination of 8 cases of alcoholism, in children aged 8 to 12 years, Mitchell, Hong, and Corman (1979) described the families of these children as unstable, disruptive, and inconsistent with discipline and supervision. All but one set of biological parents were divorced, and the parents accepted their children's drinking.

MacKay (1961) studied adolescent problem drinkers and found that each of the fathers of the boys being studied was an alcoholic and that alcoholism was common among the relatives of the girls. McKenna and Pickens (1981) reported that the children of alcoholics were likely to be younger at their first intoxication than were the children of nonalcoholics. The incidence increased when the children had two parents who were alcoholic. Children of alcoholics also had more pretreatment behavior problems and went from their first intoxication to alcoholism treatment faster than did those without alcoholic parents. Similarly, Penick, Read, Crowley, and Powell (1978) concluded that alcoholic men with family histories of alcoholism (parents or grandparents) tended to drink at earlier ages and to have more social and personal problems than did those without this history. An interesting finding of this study was the information about the families of those with no family history of alcoholism. These parents strongly disapproved of drinking of any kind, and had serious parental conflicts twice as often as the alcoholic parents. Hidden alcoholism in the grandparent generation may have produced this strict disapproval, or the risk of alcoholism may be increased in children from teetotaling families (Rekers & Hipple, 1986) or conflict-ridden families.

Children of Alcoholics as Adults

Even if children of alcoholics survive their childhood and early adulthood without becoming alcoholic, they often develop other personal and relationship problems as a result of their family environments and their role behaviors in response to these environments. Woititz (1983) noted problems with intimacy and identity. In a study of adult children of alcoholics, Black, Bucky, and Wilder-Padilla (1986) found that adult children of alcoholics do not use interpersonal resources, are more isolated, have experienced more physical and sexual abuse, and have more behavior problems, but they do not see themselves as causing problems. They reported high degrees of family disruption, high divorce rates, premature parental deaths, and sibling deaths. They witnessed excessive verbal arguing as children. As adults, they reported problems with intimacy and dependency. Sampling was a problem in this study, however. The subjects responded to advertisements in a magazine written for children of alcoholics. Therefore, they had defined themselves as children of alcoholics and had read at least some of the literature about the problems of adult children of alcoholics prior to the study.

As pioneers in group work with adult children of alcoholics, Cermak and Brown (1982) identified five major problems that these adult children commonly encounter: (1) concern with interpersonal and intrapsychic issues of control, (2) inability to trust others, (3) inattention to personal needs, (4) an exaggerated sense of responsibility for the feelings and actions of others, and (5) a fear of expressing feelings. Cermak (1984) described the problems of adult children as "a pattern of immature adaptive mechanisms that exists in alcoholics, many spouses of alcoholics and many children of alcoholics" (p. 42). In mid-life, these adult children of alcoholics often find themselves victims of their own chemical dependency or other compulsive disorders, spouses of alcoholics, survivors of many unsuccessful relationships, or parents of adolescent alcoholics or drug addicts.

Disruptive Family Environmental Factors that Lead to Alcoholism

Vaillant and Milofsky (1982) found that, although the adults in their study who were alcohol-dependent appeared to have personality disorders and to be socially inadequate, their childhoods had been no more underprivileged than those of their peers who were to drink socially as adults. They were also no less intelligent and had no more evidence of childhood emotional vulnerability. This study did reveal the influence of cultural prescriptions about alcohol consumption, however. The Irish were seven times more likely to manifest alcohol dependence than were the men of Italian, Syrian, Jewish, Greek, or Portuguese extraction. Their data suggested that the presence or absence of South European ethnicity and the number of alcoholic relatives accounted for most of the variance in adult alcoholism explained by childhood variables. Cultures that forbid drinking in children, but condone drunkenness in adults produce more alcoholics than do cultures that teach children how to drink responsibly, but forbid adult drunkenness. These prescriptions regarding behaviors and attitudes directly and indirectly related to drinking patterns may contribute a significant cultural dimension to proposed models of the alcoholic family system (Ablon, 1980).

Zucker and Gomberg (1986) believed that Vaillant and Milofsky (1982) underestimated the importance of childhood factors, personality factors, and antisocial behavior in the etiology of alcoholism. Specifically, Zucker and Gomberg pointed to indicators of early environmental difficulties that were more common among the alcoholic subjects studied by Vaillant and Milofsky (1982), especially difficulties in adolescence. The early environmental factors that Zucker and Gomberg found to be important for predicting alcoholism were father's alcoholism, marital conflict, lax maternal supervision, many moves, no attachment to father, and no family cohesiveness. In adulthood, the subsequently alcohol-dependent group had poorer mental health and more antisocial activity than did those who did not become alcoholic.

Zucker and Gomberg (1986) went on to review other longitudinal etiological studies that followed the respondents from childhood and adolescence into adulthood to establish a diagnosis of alcoholism or problem drinking. They drew several conclusions.

- Childhood antisocial behavior is consistently related to later alcoholic outcome.
- More childhood difficulty in achievement-related activity and school problems were found in later-to-be alcoholics.
- A greater activity level or hyperactivity was identified as a possible etiological factor.
- Males were more loosely tied to others interpersonally.
- There was heightened marital conflict in prealcoholic homes.
- There was inadequate parenting and lack of parent-child contact in prealcoholic homes.
- Parents were inadequate role models; they were more likely to be antisocial, alcoholic, or sexually deviant.

Zucker and Gomberg (1986) were not advocating a purely environmental explanation for the transmission of alcoholism, but rather suggesting that the etiology of alcoholism is best understood in a longitudinal-developmental framework that includes physiological, behavioral, and sociocultural factors. Lawson, Peterson, and Lawson (1983) also advocated a physiological, psychological, and sociological approach to the etiology and treatment of alcoholism.

THE ALCOHOLIC FAMILY SYSTEM

Bowen System Theory

Bowen (1974) believed the transmission process in alcoholic families involves levels of differentiation of self in the family. This is a function of the relationship that the child has with his or her parents and the way that the child handles unresolved emotional attachment to his or her parents in young adulthood. In this model of family theory and therapy, which emerged during the birth of the family movement, symptoms in one member are viewed as a function of the multigenerational family system. This intergenerational process is the basis for Bowen's theory of intergenerational family therapy that has become known as systems theory.

According to this systems theory (Bowen, 1974), the family is a system in which a change in one family member automatically produces a change in another. Bowen further believed that a person's current behavior results from a transference process in which past history and behaviors are inappropriately applied to present situations. Bowen observed families that exhibited feelings of oneness, or whose members lacked individual identities. In families whose members seemed overly dependent on one another, Bowen labeled this oneness "stuck togetherness." This stuck togetherness was the family's defense against crises or tensions; under threat, the family members pulled together to restore a delicate balance. If self-destructive behaviors, such as substance abuse, helped maintain the balance, the family would tolerate them.

In this system, the smallest unit is a triangle. Two people who feel stress bring in a third person to stabilize the unit. In alcoholic families, the third member of the triangle can be the alcohol itself. During states of calm, there are two comfortable sides of the triangle and one in conflict. These roles become fixed over a period of time. When conflict occurs between the two comfortable members, they project it onto the third, who develops symptoms in a family projection process. For example, conflict in the marriage may increase tension in the mother; she projects it onto the child, who accepts it to maintain the family oneness. The father may be the adaptive spouse who gives up his identity for the sake of the marriage and supports the mother's need, as well as her projection to the child. The father may also withdraw from the conflict by working long hours or drinking with his friends in the local tavern. Several other patterns of response to stress or conflict may occur among the three members.

The child selected for this projection is often the one closest to the mother. He or she may be the oldest child, an only child, or a child born during a crisis or with a defect. When this child leaves the family, another will take his or her place. After all the children have left, the marital problems may come to the fore, or someone outside the family may assume the role.

Families with high degrees of stuck togetherness produce children who distance themselves from the family in an attempt to gain self-identity. They may (1) become rebellious adolescents or withdraw destructively; (2) establish a physical distance by moving away from home; or (3) distance themselves not only physically, but also emotionally. These children never differentiate themselves from their parents and are consequently unable to become problem solvers in crisis situations. In addition, the adolescent who leaves this family creates a pseudoindependence that is based on anxiety and is transmitted to that person's marital relationship in a multigenerational transmission process. Therefore, the patterns of the family of origin are repeated in the nuclear family.

Bowen (1974) devised a scale for determining self-differentiation in family members. Those on the lower part of the scale are dominated by their emotions. Essentially, they lack a self; their only feeling of self-worth comes from others. The two rules of behavior for these people are (1) Does it make me feel good? and (2) Will others approve of me? Those higher on the scale of differentiation begin to use intellectual processes in decision making and develop personal opinions. Those on the upper half of the scale are goal orientated, respond with rational principles, and have less need to be defensive. They have achieved a self with a high degree of differentiation from their families. These people are able to achieve intimate relationships and are problem solvers. According to Bowen (1974), self-differentiation

> is the degree to which the person has a "solid self" or solidly held principles by which he lives his life. This is in contrast to a "pseudoself" made up of inconsistent life principles that can be corrupted by coercion for the gain of the moment. The "differentiation of self" is roughly equivalent to the concept of emotional maturity. (p. 116)

This rating is based on the amount of a person's differentiation from his or her parents, the type of relationship that exists with the parents, and the quality of emotional separation from the parents in young adulthood.

Bowen stated that people with similar scores on the scale of differentiation tend to be attracted to one another, and they pass on similar degrees of differentiation to their children. The child with the lowest degree of differentiation is at highest risk in the family projection process and for the later development of problems. When two such individuals (i.e., two pseudoselves) flee their families, blaming their parents for their problems and seeking happiness in their own marriage, it is common for one spouse to become dominant and the other to adapt to the dominant spouse because of the marital fusion. The adaptive one becomes a "no-self." "If this pattern is continued long enough, the adaptive one is vulnerable to some kind of chronic dysfunction, which can be physical illness, emotional illnesses, or a social dysfunction such as drinking, the use of drugs, or irresponsible behavior" (Bowen, 1974, p. 116). The new family can use marital conflict or projection of their immaturity onto the children as ways to adapt. This selection of adaptive patterns is not a conscious process. These patterns were programmed into the spouses by their families of origin.

Bowen believed that a continuum of behaviors lead to alcoholism. On one end is denial of the emotional attachment to the family of origin and the maintenance of a superindependent posture, despite an actual level of emotional attachment that is intense. On the other end of the continuum is an attachment so strong that the child is never able to manage a productive life. Bowen stated that most people with drinking problems fall somewhere between these two extremes. "A high percentage of adult alcoholism is in people who are married, and who have the same kind of emotional attachment in marriage that they had in their parental families" (Bowen, 1974, p. 117). Describing a similar process of symptom development, Framo (1972) stated, "Symptoms are concomitants of the universal conflict between individuation, autonomous strivings, and loyalty to the family relationship system" (p. 122). In alcoholic families, it is difficult to belong and nearly impossible to individuate in a healthy way. The effects of living in a disruptive alcoholic family system may transmit alcoholism into a second or third generation.

Family Environment

Other theorists have touched on the intergenerational process in looking at the etiology of alcoholism and a new epistemology. In a study of teen-agers with alcoholic parents, McLachlan and associates (1973) found that a sense of secure family cohesiveness clearly differentiated the controls from the teen-agers in alcoholic families. Pringle (1976) reported that the alcoholic families of origin in her study were controlling, closed systems that provided little room for self-expression and strongly encouraged competition and achievement, whereas the nonalcoholic families of origin were more cohesive, provided more support, and had less open expression and autonomy.

Kaufman (1980, 1984, 1986) described four types of family reactivity patterns: (1) the functional family system in which family members have the ability to wall off and isolate alcoholic behavior; (2) the neurotic enmeshed family system in which drinking behavior interrupts normal family tasks, causes conflict, shifts roles, and demands new adaptation; (3) the disintegrated family system in which the alcoholic is separated from the family, but family members are still available for family therapy; and (4) the absent family system that is marked by total loss of family of origin. He further stated, "There is now substantial evidence to conclude that family systems play a significant role in the genesis of alcoholism, as for example in the transmission of marital and family roles of alcoholism from one generation to the next" (Kaufman, 1984, p. 7). Kaufman (1980) also pointed out that families of drug abusers are very similar to families of alcohol abusers; however, the drug abuser may be a child, while the alcohol abuser may be the adult. In more than half of the families in which there is an identified patient with a drug problem, there is also a parent who is alcoholic. Kaufman felt that the family plays an important part in the genesis and perpetuation of substance abuse, yet it may not be the cause of all substance abuse. He concluded that there is a need for more research in the area of the substance-abusing family environments and implications for directions in family therapy.

Adaptive Consequences of Alcoholism

Steinglass, Davis, and Berenson (1977) discovered that there are adaptive consequences of alcoholism in the family system. When comparing videotapes of family sessions conducted when the alcoholic was sober with sessions conducted when the alcoholic was drinking, they observed a more relaxed and communicative system when the alcoholic was intoxicated. The family was not necessarily the cause of alcoholism, but the drinking appeared to play a part in the cohesion of the family.

Bateson (1971) hypothesized that, if the alcoholic's "style of sobriety drives him to drink, then that style must contain error or pathology; and intoxication must provide some—at least subjective—correction of this error" (p. 2). Therefore, if sobriety is somehow wrong, intoxication is in a way right. If the alcoholic's environment, or perception of the environment, is pathological, he or she can escape through intoxication. Applied to the theory that dysfunctional family systems may increase the risk of alcoholism for the offspring, this approach provides a view of alcoholism as a solution to feeling trapped in an intergenerational dysfunctional system.

Steinglass, Davis, and Berenson (1977) further developed a model to demonstrate the way in which drinking behavior is maintained. They based their model on three concepts: "interactional behavior cycling between the sober state and the intoxicated state; patterning of behavior that has reached steady state; and the hypothesis that alcohol use in the alcoholic family has become incorporated into family problem solving behavior" (Steinglass, 1979, p. 167). In addition, Steinglass (1980) pointed out that chronic alcoholism distorts the normative family life cycle. Davis, Berenson, Steinglass, and Davis (1974) postulated that the adaptive consequences of alcohol abuse "are reinforcing enough to maintain the drinking behavior, regardless of its causative factors. These adaptive consequences may operate on different levels, including intrapsychic, intracouple, or to maintain family homeostasis" (Davis et al., 1974, p. 210).

Killorin and Olson (1984) believed that, as a result of these adaptive consequences, the symptoms of alcoholism and the family style vary. Even though the families may have a common symptom, the way in which the system interacts can take many forms. Using Olson's circumplex model for evaluating family environment, these researchers found that alcoholic families fell into all types of family systems (Olson & Killorin, 1987). They found disengaged as well as enmeshed systems, and chaotic as well as rigid systems. On the scale of cohesion, approximately one third of the chemically dependent families perceived their families as disengaged, compared to 7% of the nondependent. In terms of family adaptability, more than 40% of the chemically dependent families saw themselves as chaotic, while only 8% of the nondependent families rated themselves as chaotic. Of the chemically dependent adolescents, 44% saw their families as disengaged, compared to 8% of the nondependent adolescents. The chemically dependent adolescents rated their families as connected 19% of the time, compared to 43% for the non-chemically dependent. When rating family adaptability, 52% of the chemically dependent adolescents rated their families as chaotic, compared to 20% of the nondependent adolescents. In summary, 30% of the chemically dependent adolescents rated their families in the extreme ranges on the circumplex model, while only 10% of the nondependent adolescents saw their families in these extreme ranges. The lack of cohesion reported by these families is contradictory to reports of family therapists who have reported similar families as enmeshed. What Bowen (1974) described as emotional fusion may have been mistaken for enmeshment. Families with drug-abusing adolescents may be fused, not allowing the adolescent to differentiate and, thus, producing a false reading of closeness.

Friedman and Utada (in press) found similar results. Of 143 adolescent drug abusers and their mothers, 60% of the mothers and 41% of the adolescents perceived their families as rigid-disengaged (very low adaptability and very low cohesion) compared to 8% and 7% respectively in the normative sample of FACES II.

Filstead, McElfresh, and Anderson (1981) compared the overall family environment of the alcoholic family to that of the nonalcoholic family. They collected data on 42 white families, 59% of which were families that had alcoholic male members. Each family member completed the Moos Family Environment Scale (Moos, 1986), which covers 10 dimensions of family life conceptually organized around relationships, personal growth, and system maintenance dimensions. These scores were compared to the scores of normative families and to a "normal non-clinic" population previously used by Moos (1986).

> The alcoholic families perceived their family environments to be less cohesive ($p<.001$) and less expressive ($p<.001$), perceived less emphasis on independence ($p<.001$), intellectual-cultural activities ($p<.001$), active-recreational concerns ($p<.001$) and organizational tasks ($p<.05$) than the "normal" families. The alcoholic families perceived a higher level of conflict ($p<.001$) than the "normal" families" (Filstead et al., 1981, p. 25).

Similar results were obtained in a comparison of the experimental group and the "normal non-clinic" group. In this case, the subscale for organization showed no difference, however, and the alcoholic families reported more rigidity on the subscale of control. Frost (1982), who compared families in a prevention/treatment program for children from alcoholic families with Moos normative families, supported these findings. Alcoholic families were lower in cohesion, independence, and active-recreation orientation.

In one study, adolescent drug abusers rated their families as less cohesive and less expressive ($p<.001$), having more conflict ($p<.05$), less independence ($p<.001$), fewer intellectual-cultural activities ($p<.001$), fewer active-recreational activities ($p<.001$), and more control ($p<.001$) (Friedman & Utada, in press).

Family Rituals

In an attempt to determine how the family environment may be a transmitter of alcoholism, several researchers have investigated the importance of family rituals. Wolin, Bennett, and Noonan (1979) studied a group of 25 families of middle- and upper-class background and European origin. All families included at least one parent who met their criteria for the identification of an alcoholic or problem drinker. Structured individual interviews that covered the personal history of the interviewee and the continuity of family heritage from the grandparents' generation into the current nuclear family provided information into seven areas of family rituals: (1) dinner time, (2) holidays, (3) evenings, (4) weekends, (5) vacations, (6) visitors in the home, and (7) discipline. These investigators defined family rituals as patterns of behavior that have meaning beyond their practical outcome or function. "Patterned behavior is behavior that is repetitive, stable with respect to roles, and continues over time" (Wolin, Bennett, & Noonan 1979, p. 590). They believed that these rituals were important because they "stabilize ongoing family life by clarifying expectable roles, delineating boundaries within and without the family, and defining rules so that all family members know that 'this is the way our family is'" (Wolin et al., 1979, p. 590). Steinglass, Bennett, Wolin, and Reiss (1987) stated that, "family rituals are, in effect, condensed, prepackaged training modules intended to convey to all family members the important facts about family identity" (p. 309).

Classifying families according to the impact of drinking on family rituals, Wolin and associates (1979) identified three types of families: distinctive families in which rituals did not change during drinking episodes, intermediate subsumptive families that rejected intoxicated behavior when it was present, and subsumptive families in which drinking changed the "fabric of the family" and highly disrupted the family life. They found that families whose rituals were disrupted or changed during the period of heaviest drinking by the alcoholic parent were more likely to transmit alcoholism to the younger generation than were families whose rituals remained intact. The more that alcoholism became a central organizing force and a disruption to the family rituals, the more the children were at risk for developing alcoholism. The nontransmitter families had one outstanding quality in common: "a rejection of the intoxication of the alcoholic parent through such means as confronting the alcoholic parent openly or privately or talking about his or her behavior disapprovingly" (Wolin et al., 1979, p. 591). As Steinglass and associates (1987) pointed out, however, this study had a small sample size, took a retrospective approach to the reconstruction of ritual behavior during periods of heaviest drinking, and used a nonexperimental study design. Thus, the results should be interpreted cautiously.

To follow up this study, Bennett, Wolin, Reiss, and Teitelbaum (1987) interviewed 68 married children of alcoholic parents and their spouses regarding dinner time and holiday rituals in their families of origin and in the couples' current generations. The children of alcoholics who remained nonalcoholic had limited attachments to their families of origin or selective disengagements, and the families of origin had been able to separate the rituals from the alcoholism. In summation of these ritual studies, Steinglass and associates (1987) said,

> We believe that the transmission of alcoholism from one generation to the next involves the whole family system over time. The context for transmission is the sum total of interactions, attitudes, and beliefs that define the family. The process is ongoing and dynamic, and has no particular beginning, end, or pivotal event. And it often goes on outside the awareness of the participants involved, the "senders" as well as the "receivers." (p. 304)

CONCLUSION

The family system studies have added another dimension to the nature versus nurture controversy in the etiology of alcoholism. It is quite possible that there is not one etiological prescription for all of alcoholism. Genetics may play a major role in the father-son transmission of alcoholism, while family environment may have more of an impact on women's alcoholism. The importance of finding family environment patterns that predispose children for alcoholism is that it may be possible to prevent alcoholism in these children by changing the patterns through family therapy and parent training. Kaufman (1984) called for further research on the issues of "what family patterns are more likely to generate alcoholic members; what family patterns are more likely to maintain alcoholic behavior; and how does the family life cycle interact with the developmental phases of alcoholism" (p. 8).

In an attempt to define family patterns that promote alcoholism in the offspring, Lawson (1988) investigated the relationship between the past and present perceived family environments of adults who were raised in alcoholic families and the effect of this relationship in the etiology of alcoholism. The study involved 188 subjects between the ages of 24 and 65 who were parents of children 5 years of age or older. All subjects were given the Michigan Alcoholism Screening Test (MAST) (Ward, 1980), the Children of Alcoholics Screening Test (CAST) (Jones, 1982), a Family Demographic Questionnaire, and two versions of the Moos Family Environment Scale (FES)—one to rate their families of origin and the other to rate their nuclear families. Subjects were divided into four groups: (1) alcoholic adult children of alcoholics, (2) nonalcoholic adult children of alcoholics, (3) alcoholics with no family history of alcoholism, and (4) nonalcoholic comparisons with no history of addictions. There were significant correlations between family of origin and nuclear family scores on the FES for all four groups, indicating transmission of family dynamics across generations. The three alcoholic groups reported more dysfunction in their families of origin than did the controls. The alcoholic adult children of alcoholics had significantly less cohesion and intellectual-cultural orientation than did the other two alcoholic groups, indicating that lack of these two dimensions in families may predispose children of alcoholics to alcoholism. Two types of families appeared to produce alcoholic offspring: disengaged, rigid families who are conflict-oriented and repress the expression of feelings; and rigid, moralistic families who also repress feelings. Both types stress achievement, yet provide little intellectual-cultural stimulation. Although both groups of adult children of alcoholics reported highly dysfunctional families of origin, a slight increase in cohesion and intellectual-cultural orientation in the families of origin of the nonalcoholic adult children of alcoholics may have made them more resilient and resistive to the intergenerational transmission of alcoholism. These findings support the environmental side of the nature versus nurture debate of the etiology of alcoholism. The similarities between the families of origin of the alcoholic and nonalcoholic adult children of alcoholics suggest a biological factor that predicts which adult children of alcoholics will become alcoholic, however.

Reviewing these studies of the intergenerations transmission of alcoholism in families through physiology and environment will increase the understanding of the complex nature of the etiology of alcoholism and other addictions. The more that is understood about how and why adolescents become chemically dependent, the better the treatment and prevention programs will become.

REFERENCES

Ablon, J. (1980). The significance of cultural patterning for the alcoholic family. *Family Process, 19*, 127–144.

Anderson, E.E., & Wentworth, Q. (1983). Young children in alcoholic families: A mental health needs-assessment and an intervention/prevention strategy. *Journal of Primary Prevention, 3*(3), 174–187.

Bandler, R., Grender, J., & Satir, V. (1976). *Changing with families.* Palo Alto, CA: Science and Behavior Books.

Barry, H., & Blane, H.T. (1977). Birth positions of alcoholics. *Journal of Individual Psychology, 33*, 62–69.

Bateson, G. (1971). The cybernetics of 'self': A theory of alcoholism. *Psychiatry, 34*, 1–18.

Bennett, L., Wolin, S., Reiss, D., & Teitelbaum, M. (1987). Couples at risk for transmission of alcoholism: Protective influences. *Family Process, 26,* 111–129.

Black, C. (1979, Fall). Children of alcoholics. *Alcohol Health and Research World,* pp. 23–27.

Black, C. (1981a). Innocent bystanders at risk: The children of alcoholics. *Alcoholism,* pp. 22–25.

Black, C. (1981b). *It will never happen to me.* Denver: M.A.C. Publishers.

Black, C., Bucky, S.F., & Wilder-Padilla, S. (1986). The interpersonal and emotional consequences of being an adult child of an alcoholic. *International Journal of the Addictions, 21*(2), 213–231.

Blane, H.T., & Barry, H. (1973). Birth order and alcoholism: A review. *Quarterly Journal of Studies on Alcohol, 34,* 837–852.

Booz-Allen & Hamilton, Inc. (1974). *An assessment of the needs of and resources for children of alcoholic parents.* Rockville, MD: National Institute on Alcohol Abuse and Alcoholism.

Bosma, W. (1975). Alcoholism and teenagers. *Maryland State Medical Journal, 24,* 62–68.

Bourgeois, M., Levigneron, M., & Delage, H. (1975). Les enfants d'alcooliques. Un enquete sur 66 enfants d'alcooliques d'un service pedopsychiatrique. *Annals Medico-Psychologigues, 2*(3), 592–609.

Bowen, M. (1974). Alcoholism as viewed through family systems theory and family psychotherapy. *Annals of the New York Academy of Science, 233,* 115–122.

Cermak, T.L. (1984, Summer). Children of alcoholics and the case for a new diagnostic category of codependency. *Alcohol Health and Research World,* pp. 38–42.

Cermak, T.L., & Brown, S. (1982). Interactional group therapy with adult children of alcoholics. *International Journal of Group Psychotherapy, 32,* 375–389.

Chafetz, M., Blane, H., & Hill, M. (1971). Children of alcoholics: Observations in a child guidance clinic. *Quarterly Journal of Studies on Alcohol, 32,* 687–698.

Clifford, C.A., Fulker, D.W., & Murray, R. (1984). Genetic and environmental influences on drinking patterns in normal twins. In N. Krasner, J.S. Madden, & R. Walker (Eds.), *Alcohol related problems* (pp. 136–148). Chichester, England: John Wiley & Sons.

Clinebell, H.J. (1968). Pastoral counseling of the alcoholic and his family. In R. Catanzaro (Ed.), *Alcoholism: The total treatment approach* (pp. 189–207). Springfield, IL: Charles C. Thomas.

Cloninger, R., Bohman, M., & Sigvardsson, S. (1981). Inheritance of alcohol abuse: Cross-fostering analysis of adopted men. *Archives of General Psychiatry, 38,* 861–867.

Cork, M. (1969). *The forgotten children.* Toronto: Alcoholism and Drug Addiction Research Foundation.

Cotton, N.S. (1979). The familial incidence of alcoholism: A review. *Journal of Studies on Alcohol, 46,* 89–115.

Cruz-Coke, R, & Varela, A. (1966). Inheritance of alcoholism. *Lancet, 2,* 1282.

Davis, D.J., Berenson, D., Steinglass, P., & Davis, S. (1974). The adaptive consequences of drinking. *Psychiatry, 37,* 209–215.

el-Guebaly, N., & Offord, D.R. (1977). The offspring of alcoholics: A critical review. *American Journal of Psychiatry, 134,* 357–365.

Filstead, W.J., McElfresh, O., & Anderson, C. (1981). Comparing the family environments of alcoholics and 'normal' families. *Journal of Alcohol and Drug Education, 26,* 24–31.

Framo, J.L. (1972). Symptoms from a family transactional viewpoint. In C. Sager & H.S. Kaplan (Eds.), *Progress in group and family therapy* (pp. 271–308). New York: Brunner/Mazel.

Friedman, A. & Utada, A. (in press). The family environment of adolescent drug abusers. *Family Dynamics of Addition Quarterly.*

Frost, M. (1982). *Evaluation of the children from alcoholic families program.* Unpublished research report, University of Nebraska, Omaha.

Goodwin, D.W. (1971). Is alcoholism hereditary? A review and critique. *Archives of General Psychiatry, 25,* 545–549.

Goodwin, D.W. (1981). Family studies of alcoholism. *Journal of Studies on Alcohol, 42*(1), 156–162.

Goodwin, D.W. (1985). Alcoholism and genetics. *Archives of General Psychiatry, 42,* 171–174.

Goodwin, D.W., Schulsinger, F., Hermansen, L., Gruze, S.B., & Winokur, G. (1973). Alcoholism problems in adoptees reared apart from alcoholic biological parents. *Archives of General Psychiatry, 281,* 238–243.

Gurling, H., & Murray, R. (1984). Alcoholism and genetics: Old and new evidence. In N. Krasner, J.S. Madden, & R. Walker (Eds.), *Alcohol related problems* (pp. 122–135). Chichester, England: John Wiley & Sons.

Haberman, P.W. (1966). Childhood symptoms in children of alcoholics and comparison group parents. *Journal of Marriage and the Family, 28*(2), 152–154.

Hecht, M. (1973). Children of alcoholics. *American Journal of Nursing, 10,* 1764–1767.

Hindman, M. (1976, Winter). Children of alcoholic parents. *Alcohol Health and Research World,* pp. 2–6.

Jacob, T., Favorini, A., Meisel, S.S., & Anderson, C.M. (1978). The alcoholic's spouse, children and family interactions. *Journal of Studies on Alcohol, 391*(7), 1231–1246.

Jesse, R.C. (1977). *Children of alcoholics: A clinical investigation of familial role relationships.* Unpublished doctoral dissertation, California School of Professional Psychology, San Diego.

Jones, J. (1982) *Preliminary test manual: The Children of Alcoholics Screening Test.* Chicago: Family Recovery Press.

Jonsson, E., & Nilsson, T. (1968). Alkoholkonsumtion hos monozygota och dizygota tvillingar (Alcoholism in monozygotic and dizygotic twins). *Nordisk Hygienisk Tidskrift, 49,* 21–25.

Kaij, L. (1960). *Studies on the etiology and sequels of abuse of alcohol.* Lund, Sweden: Department of Psychiatry, University of Lund.

Kaufman, E. (1980). Myths and realities in the family patterns and treatment of substance abuse. *American Journal of Drug and Alcohol Abuse, 7*(3 & 4), 257–279.

Kaufman, E. (1984). Family system variables in alcoholism. *Alcoholism: Clinical and Experimental Research, 8*(1), 4–8.

Kaufman, E. (1986). The family of the alcoholic patient. *Psychosomatics, 27*(5), 347–358.

Keane, A. & Roche, D. (1974). Developmental disorders in the children of male alcoholics. *Proceedings of the 20th International Institute on Prevention and Treatment of Alcoholism* (pp. 82–89). Lausanne: Manchester ICAA.

Killorin, E., & Olson, D. (1984). The chaotic flippers in treatment. In E. Kaufman (Ed.), *Power to change: Alcoholism* (pp. 99–129). New York: Gardner Press.

Lawson, A. (1988) *The relationship of past and present family environments of adult children of alcoholics.* Unpublished doctoral dissertation, United States International University, San Diego.

Lawson, G.W., Peterson, J.S., & Lawson, A.W. (1983). *Alcoholism and the family: A guide to treatment and prevention.* Gaithersburg, MD: Aspen Publishers.

Lund, C., & Landesman-Dwyer, S. (1979). Pre-delinquent and disturbed adolescents: The role of parental alcoholism. In M. Galanter (Ed.), *Currents in alcoholism: Vol. V. Biomedical issues and clinical effects of alcoholism* (pp. 330–342). New York: Grune & Stratton.

MacKay, J.R. (1961). Clinical observations on adolescent problem drinkers. *Quarterly Journal of Studies on Alcohol, 22,* 124–134.

MacMurray, V.D. (1979). The effect and nature of alcohol abuse in cases of child neglect. *Victimology: An International Journal, 4*(1), 29–45.

McCord, W., McCord, J., & Gudeman, J. (1960). *Origins of alcoholism.* Palo Alto, CA: Stanford University Press.

McKenna, T., & Pickens, R. (1981). Alcoholic children of alcoholics. *Journal of Studies on Alcohol, 42,* 1021–1029.

McLachlan (1973). *A study of teenagers with alcoholic parents* (Donwood Institute Research Monograph N3). Toronto: The Donwood Institute.

Midanik, L. (1983). Familial alcoholism and problem drinking in a national drinking practices survey. *Addictive Behaviors, 8,* 133–141.

Miller, D., & Jang, M. (1978). Children of alcoholics: A 20 year longitudinal study. *Social Work Research and Abstracts, 13,* 23–29.

Mitchell, J.E., Hong, M., & Corman, C. (1979). Childhood onset of alcohol abuse. *American Journal of Orthopsychiatry, 49*(3), 511–513.

Moos, R. (1986). *Family environment scale manual* (2nd rev. ed.). Palo Alto, CA: Consulting Psychology Press.

Moos, R.H., & Billings, A.G. (1982). Children of alcoholics during the recovery process: Alcoholic and matched control families. *Addictive Behaviors, 7,* 155–163.

Nardi, P. (1981). Children of alcoholics: A role-theoretical perspective. *Journal of Social Psychology, 115,* 237–245.

National Association for Children of Alcoholics Charter Statement. (1983, June). *Alcoholism*, p. 18.

Neville, H.J., & Schmidt, A.L. (1983, October). *Event-related potentials in subjects at risk for alcoholism*. NIAAA workshop on Early Identification of Alcohol Abuse, San Diego, CA.

Noll, R.B., & Zucker, R.A. (1983, August). *Findings from an alcoholic vulnerability study: The preschool years.* Paper presented at the Annual Meeting of the American Psychological Association, Anaheim, CA.

Olson, D.H., & Killorin, E.A. (1987). *Chemically dependent families and the circumplex model.* Unpublished research report, University of Minnesota, St. Paul.

Partanen, J., Bruun, K., & Markkanen, T. (1966). *Inheritance of drinking behavior: A study of intelligence, personality, and use of alcohol in adult twins* (Publication No. 14). Helsinki: The Finnish Foundation for Alcohol Studies.

Penick, E.C., Read, M.R., Crowley, P.A., & Powell, B.S. (1978). Differentiation of alcoholics by family history. *Journal of Studies on Alcohol, 39*(11), 1944–1948.

Pringle, W.J. (1976). *The alcoholic family environment: The influence of the alcoholic and nonalcoholic family of origin on present coping styles.* Unpublished doctoral dissertation, California School of Professional Psychology, Fresno.

Rekers, G., & Hipple, J. (1986, July/August). Co-dependency without alcoholism. *Focus on Family*, pp. 18–29.

Richards, T.M. (1979). Working with children of alcoholic mothers. *Alcohol Health and Research World, 3*(3), 22–25.

Roberts, K.S., & Brent, E.E. (1982). Physicians utilization and illness patterns in families of alcoholics. *Journal of Studies on Alcohol, 43*(1), 119–127.

Rosenberg, C.M. (1969). Determination of psychiatric illness in young people. *British Journal of Psychiatry, 115,* 907–915.

Schuckit, M.A. (1983). Alcoholic men with no alcoholic first-degree relatives. *American Journal of Psychiatry, 140*(4), 439–443.

Schuckit, M.A. (1984). Subjective responses to alcohol in sons of alcoholic and control subjects. *Archives of General Psychiatry, 41,* 879–884.

Schuckit, M.A. (1985a). Alcohol-induced changes in body sway in men at high alcoholism risk. *Archives of General Psychiatry, 42,* 375–379.

Schuckit, M.A. (1985b). Studies of population at high risk for alcoholism. *Psychiatric Developments, 3,* 31–63.

Schuckit, M.A., Goodwin, D.W., & Winokur, G. (1972). *Life history research in psychopathology.* Minneapolis: University of Minnesota Press.

Schuckit, M.A., & Haglund, R.M. (1977). An overview of the etiological theories on alcoholism. In N. Estes & M.E. Heineman (Eds.), *Alcoholism: Development, consequences and interventions* (pp. 15–27). St. Louis: C.V. Mosby.

Sexias, J. (1977). Children from alcoholic families. In N. Estes & M.E. Heinemann (Eds.), *Alcoholism: Development, consequences and interventions* (pp. 153–161). St. Louis: C.V. Mosby.

Sloboda, S. (1974). The children of alcoholics: A neglected problem. *Hospital and Community Psychiatry, 25,* 605–606.

Steinglass, P. (1979). Family therapy with alcoholics: A review. In E. Kaufman & P. Kaufman (Eds.), *Family therapy of drug and alcohol abuse* (pp. 147–186). New York: Gardner Press.

Steinglass, P. (1980). Life history model of the alcoholic family. *Family Process, 19*(3), 211–226.

Steinglass, P., Davis, D., & Berenson, D. (1977). Observations of conjointly hospitalized "alcohol couples" during sobriety and intoxication for theory and therapy. *Family Process, 16,* 1–16.

Steinglass, P., Bennett, L., Wolin, D., & Reiss, D. (1987). *The alcoholic family.* New York: Basic Books.

Thornton, R., & Nardi, P.M. (1975). The dynamics of role acquisition. *American Journal of Sociology, 80*(4), 870–885.

Vaillant, G.S., & Milofsky, E.S. (1982). The etiology of alcoholism: A prospective viewpoint. *American Psychologist, 37*(5), 494–503.

Ward, D. (1980). *Alcoholism: Introduction to theory and treatment.* Dubuque, IA: Kendall/Hunt.

Wegscheider, S. (1981a). *Another chance: Hope and help for the alcoholic family.* Palo Alto, CA: Science and Behavior Books.

Wegscheider, S. (1981b, January/February). From the family trap to family freedom. *Alcoholism*, pp. 36–39.

Werner, E.E. (1986). Resilient offspring of alcoholics: A longitudinal study. *Journal of Studies on Alcohol, 47,* 34–40.

Wilson, C., & Orford, J. (1978). Children of alcoholics. *Journal of Studies on Alcohol, 39,* 121–142.

Winokur, G., & Clayton, P.J. (1968). Family history studies in comparison to male and female alcoholics. *Quarterly Journal of Studies on Alcohol, 29,* 885–891.

Woititz, J.G. (1983). *Adult children of alcoholics.* Hollywood, FL: Health Communications.

Wolin, S.J., Bennett, L.A., & Noonan, D.L. (1979). Family rituals and recurrence of alcoholism over generations. *American Journal of Psychiatry, 136,* 589–593.

Zucker, R. A., & Gomberg, E.S.L. (1986). Etiology of alcoholism reconsidered: The case for a biopsychosocial process. *American Psychologist, 41*(7), 783–793.

5

An Eriksonian Developmental Matrix of Adolescents and Their Parents: The Case of Alcohol Abuse

Jim Foreman

The ideas of Erik Erikson have influenced helping professionals for years. Whether researchers and practitioners have praised and explored Erikson's developmental views (Carter & McGoldrick, 1988; Hoffman, 1988), have analyzed and extended his perspective of growth (Feinstein, 1980; Homans, 1978; Jacobson-Widding, 1983; Musto, 1980; Roazen, 1976; Rudolph & Rudolph, 1980), or have criticized and corrected his focus on the psychosocial stages of life (Franz & White, 1985; McGoldrick, 1988), each has been guided by the same assumption: The human individual is the source of psychological theory and the substance of clinical practice.

A review of Erikson's major works (1962, 1963a, 1963b, 1969, 1974, 1980a, 1982) shows that his assumption is the same. Except for one of Erikson's writings (1980b), his elaborations of his views (1978, 1981, 1987b; Erikson, Erikson, & Kivnick, 1986) have not altered his emphasis on the individual as the key to understanding what it means to be human. It is important, however, to linger on that one piece of writing, for it contains a thought-provoking comment.

> I must trace through [the Freud-Jung letters] matters of maturational conflict which characterize adulthood both as a stage within the life cycle and as a stage within the cycle of generations. (Erikson, 1980b, p. 46)

The phrases "within the life cycle" and "within the cycle of generations" suggest an extension of Erikson's individualistic view of stages to allow for the simultaneous analysis of two individuals, both with respect to each one's individual development and with respect to their intergenerational relationship. The application of this dyadic view of development and interaction to the population of adolescent substance abusers and their parents can shed new light on the etiology of substance abuse by providing a social context for that which researchers and clinicians usually perceive as a psychological problem. More specifically, the adolescent is frequently conceptualized as an isolated individual who has failed to negotiate the psychological conflicts endemic to that stage of development, and that failure supposedly exposes the adolescent to the risk of substance abuse. When an adolescent's development is seen within the context of the adolescent's interaction with his or her mother, for example, and the mother's attempts to work through her own developmental issues, a dyadic matrix emerges. Thus, the etiology of substance abuse is embedded in, to use Erikson's language, the mutuality, actuality, and activation of the adolescent and his or her mother.

Therein lie the purposes of this chapter: (1) to expand Erikson's notion of individual psychosocial stages to include a dyadic view of human development, and (2) to show how this dyadic view can be used to frame adolescent substance abuse as a problem of developmental interaction between adolescents and their parents.

THE DYAD

Mutuality

Erikson (1964) defined mutuality, a theme that runs through nearly all of his work, as "a relationship in which partners depend on each other for the development of their respective strengths" (p. 231). He called mutuality the "secret of love" (1968, p. 219), which, when pursued, "leads outward from self-centeredness to . . . communality" (1975, p. 39). Indeed, Erikson (1964) argued that, without mutuality of response between the infant and the maternal person, the appeasing of primal anxiety would be an insurmountable task. In addition, the absence of mutuality would thwart the sharing of sexual responses between adults (1963a), hinder the family's chance to unfold "potentialities for changing patterns of mutual regulation" (1963a, p. 69), and block the opportunity for building world democracy and world community (1964). In short, Erikson (1964) argued that "nothing in human life is secured in its origin unless it is verified in the intimate meeting of partners in favorable social settings" (p. 116).

Actuality

Erikson and associates (1986) linked mutuality to actuality, maintaining that they are the two chief characteristics of vital involvement. They stated that mutuality and actuality are "a sense of reality that is an active and, in fact, an interactive involvement within a communal 'actuality,' and a shared sense of 'we' within a communal mutuality" (p. 53). Erikson (1969) also called actuality "the potential for unifying action at a given moment" (p. 413). In addition, according to Erikson (1964), "actuality is the world of participation, shared with other participants with a minimum of defensive maneuvering" (pp. 164–165) and a fresh "way of relating to each other . . . of invigorating each other in the service of common goals" (1974, p. 33).

Activation

In order for an experience to be real, something factual must be connected to something actual, "that is, a consensually validated world of facts [must be combined] with a mutual activation of like-minded people. Only these two together provide a sense of reality" (Erikson, 1975, p. 103). Erikson added greater force to his view when he insisted that "mutual activation is the crux of the matter; for human ego strength . . . depends from stage to stage upon a network of mutual influences within which the person actuates others even as he is actuated" (1964, p. 165). This actuation (i.e., activation) between persons "actualizes an ethical fellowship with strong work commitments" (Erikson, 1982, p. 91). Carrying the ethical implications of activation further, Erikson recast the Golden Rule, claiming that its new form should read: "Do to another what will advance the other's growth even as it advances your own" (1982, p. 93). It is important to make certain, he added, that the doer and the other are "activated in whatever strength is appropriate to [their] age, stage, and condition" (1964, p. 233).

DYADIC MATRIX: ADOLESCENT AND PARENT

Erikson has analyzed many developmental conflicts in the psychosocial stages of an individual's life by means of a matrix (Figure 5-1). Anyone using this matrix to understand an adolescent would focus on the conflict (identity vs. confusion) at this stage of development and the adolescent's negotiation of this conflict in order to realize the virtue (fidelity) at this stage. As soon as this kind of analysis begins, however, the individuals with whom the adolescent interacts turn into developmental anonymities; they become mere means by which to show how the adolescent is moving through his or her present stage of development. As a result, the psychosocial stages of life with which these anonymities are struggling and their influence on the adolescent's development are not brought to light.

It is important, for example, to know the age of a 14-year-old's mother. If the mother is 28, she was an adolescent herself when she gave birth—two stages "too soon," according to Erikson's theory. The mother would thus be in the middle of the young adulthood stage when the child is in the beginning of adolescence. The

Old Age							Integrity vs. Despair. WISDOM
Adulthood						Generativity vs. Self-absorption. CARE	
Young Adulthood					Intimacy vs. Isolation. LOVE		
Adolescence				Identity vs. Confusion. FIDELITY			
School Age			Industry vs. Inferiority. COMPETENCE				
Play Age		Initiative vs. Guilt. PURPOSE					
Early Childhood	Autonomy vs. Shame, Doubt. WILL						
Infancy	Basic Trust vs. Basic Mistrust. HOPE						

Figure 5-1 Psychosocial Stages of Life. *Source:* Reproduced from *Vital Involvement in Old Age* by by Erik H. Erikson, Joan M. Erikson, and Helen Q. Kivnick, by permission of W.W. Norton & Company, Inc. Copyright © 1986 by Joan M. Erikson, Erik H. Erikson, and Helen Kivnick.

mother's psychosocial stage, with its intimacy versus isolation conflict and its accompanying press toward the virtue of love, would produce different mutualities, actualities, and activations with the child than would adulthood, with its generativity versus stagnation conflict and the need to realize the virtue of care.

A recasting of Erikson's matrix results in a dyadic matrix of stages (Figure 5-2). The use of this matrix in understanding developmental interaction is seen in the following example. Mother, aged 49, and Connie, aged 14, went to see the movie *Agnes of God*, and it proved to be the source of much discussion when they went to eat at a restaurant afterward. They wondered whether it is possible, as portrayed in the movie, for a modern woman, in this case a nun, to have an immaculate conception. They were intrigued by the psychotherapist in the movie and the erosion of her skepticism at the nun's faith during the course of the interviews that the court had asked the psychotherapist to carry out with the nun in order to see if the nun might have murdered the child (it was found dead) or if she was psychotic.

This interaction between Mother and Connie grounds them in the actuality of the dyad, in that "shared sense of 'we' within a communal mutuality" (Erikson et al., 1986, p. 53). Even though they draw the content of their discussion from a movie, that content is connected to the fact of actual psychotherapists and actual nuns, both of whom hold legitimate occupational roles and status in the larger community.

With their validated communal sense of actuality, Mother and Connie can experience mutuality and, therefore, the chance to unfold "potentialities for changing patterns of mutual regulation" (Erikson, 1963a, p. 69). Thus, they can move outward from their own centers—Mother through her generating actions,

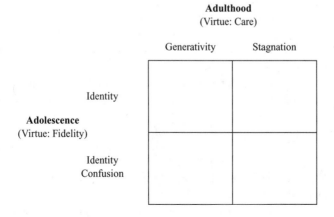

Figure 5-2 Dyadic Matrix of Stages

Connie through her identifying behaviors—to share and to explore their mutual places in their actual world. For example, Mother needs to care for Connie by nurturing the confidence that Connie has in her own inner sameness and continuity (her identity). Mother helped to prepare Connie's identity in the past and it will remain a source of meaning for Mother in the future. At the same time, Mother needs to generate in Connie a search for an identity rooted in significant other persons. So, Connie's identification with the psychotherapist and with the nun in the movie allow her to "take in and try out" their roles and to get a sense of what it would be like to be a woman other than Mother, particularly a woman in the world of work.

In this "taking in and trying out," Connie begins to experience the fidelity that Erikson details in his work, for she is seeing the contradictions in value systems that arise when the psychotherapist, who represents science, and the nun, who represents religion, ask someone to believe in them. For Erikson, this ability to sustain freely pledged loyalties in the midst of these value contradictions constitutes the definition of fidelity. So, Mother's generativity maintains Connie's trust in herself and in Mother, at the same time encouraging Connie to trust someone else or, in Erikson's terms, to give fidelity to a significant someone other than Mother. Although Connie will give this fidelity to members of her peer group in many ways, Mother lays the groundwork for Connie's movement toward fidelity by "fleshing out"—in word, deed, art, and experience—role models from the larger society that provide a context for possible ways of being for Connie. In this movement toward fidelity, Connie is beginning to discover who she is and with whom she wants to share herself.

Connie's identification with the characters in the movie and her exploration of them with Mother activate in Mother the need for generativity. For example, when Connie sees herself as a psychotherapist, Mother experiences herself as the embodiment of care and all that goes with realizing that virtue. She is the representative of the communal "we" that links tradition (a parent's passing on of work models) to the future (a child's selection of an occupation in society) and nurtures it through the present (the discussion of models of work). Also, through Connie's identifications with work models, Mother experiences her own pull toward productivity in the world of work, a pull to actualize herself as a creative person and as a contributing member of the larger society. So, Connie's need to actualize identity and fidelity activates Mother's need to actualize generativity and care. In order for Mother's actualization to be part of the communal "we," however, it must become mutual. Therefore, Mother's need to actualize generativity and care must activate Connie's need to actualize identity and fidelity. When both stage-specific needs are mutually activated, then Mother and Connie have begun, in fact, to be actualized.

The context of this interaction between Mother and Connie, a restaurant, is a movement away from the home being the only place where it is safe to be nourished and renewed with food and drink. That the food is prepared by strangers, served by strangers, and eaten in the presence of strangers is important, for these strangers are all members of the larger society who are participating in the confirmation of both Mother's generativity and care, and Connie's identity and fidelity. In their providing food and drink for Connie, these strangers are saying to Mother and Connie that they can be trusted to take temporary responsibility for Mother's need to provide food for Connie (so that Mother's generativity is freed to move into the area of other role models of work). Furthermore, because Connie need not, for a while, identify with Mother as the sole provider of the food that sustains her life, Connie can expand her identification to include Mother as the vehicle for introducing her to new models in the world of work.

These strangers, then, are representatives of the communal "we" who make it possible and legitimate for Mother and Connie to "feed" one another with their thoughts about being a psychotherapist or a nun. At the same time, Mother and Connie allow these representatives to nourish them with the literal food that sustains and renews their "food for thought." In short, these strangers are the unacknowledged representatives of the larger society who not only help to activate Mother's generativity and care, and Connie's identity and fidelity, but also ensure the communal "we" that the food for thought will act to maintain the reality of the larger society as it acts to sustain them.

This ideal-typical form of the dyadic matrix of stages shows how a functional mother and daughter might move, in part, through their respective stages.

DYADIC MATRIX: A CASE OF ALCOHOL ABUSE[*]

Mother, aged 33, and Wilma, aged 15, came to therapy because Wilma was becoming intoxicated and missing school more and more often. Mother did not know what to do to stop Wilma's drinking and truancy. The most recent incident involved the police, who arrested Wilma after they saw her staggering down the sidewalk of an inner city street, miles from home and school.

Dyadic Stage Regression: Activation, Actuality, and Mutuality

Erikson (1963a) stated that, when an individual fails to resolve the generativity versus stagnation conflict at the adulthood stage, frequently "a regression to an

---

[*]Note: the case presented here is a composite of several cases. Even though in some of these cases the substance abuser lived with a family that included the mother and other members, the focus will be on the interaction between the mother and her daughter.

obsessive need for pseudo-intimacy takes place, often with a pervading sense of stagnation and personal impoverishment" (p. 267). He expanded on this point.

> In fact, some young parents suffer . . . from the retardation of the ability to develop this stage. The meanings are often to be found in early childhood impressions; in excessive self-love based on a too strenuously self-made personality; and finally (and here we return to the beginnings) in the lack of some faith, some 'belief in the species,' which would make a child appear to be a welcome trust of the community. (p. 267)

This "lack of some faith, some 'belief in the species,' which would make a child appear to be a welcome trust of the community" is activated in Wilma during therapy sessions. So, she regresses from Stage 5 (adolescence) to Stage 1 (infancy), with its call to resolve the conflict between basic trust versus mistrust and to become a person whose basic virtue is hope. Mother regresses to Stage 4, with its accompanying tension between industry and inferiority and the need to become a person who knows herself to be the possessor of the virtue competence. Both Mother and Wilma, then, are participants in regressive activation.

> *Mother*: I don't know what else to do with you.
> *Wilma*: Give me another chance, . . . please.
> *Mother*: [*Sighing*] I've tried everything.
> *Wilma*: I'll be good, . . . I promise.
> *Mother*: That's what you said last time.
> [*Silence*]
> *Therapist*: What did she promise?
> *Mother*: Not to drink again . . . to take a babysitting job . . . you know . . . part- time.
> *Wilma*: [*Angrily*] I took that stupid job—
> *Mother*: [*Cutting her off*] Yeah! And how long did you keep it? Huh?
> *Wilma*: [*Crying*] Well, . . . I don't see . . . why must I work? None of my friends—
> *Mother*: [*Cutting her off*] Your friends! Bad kids . . . always in trouble . . . nobody can do anything with them. Now, when I was your age, I had to work. You've got to learn . . . you must be responsible. [*Turning to the therapist*] She never helps at home or cleans her room. I tell her to listen to me . . . punished her when she didn't . . . nothing worked . . . thought a part-time job would help things.

Therapist: Mom, what could Wilma do to show you that she has changed?
Mother: I've done everything I can do. It's not my fault that she won't change.

At this point, Mother is hearing questions regarding Wilma's potential for change as criticisms of Mother's own competence. Furthermore, Wilma's behavior activates in Mother a sense of inferiority and incompetence (the opposite of competence as a virtue), while Mother's behavior activates in Wilma a sense of her own mistrust and hopelessness (the opposite of hope as a virtue) as she tries to convince Mother to give her another chance to keep one of her promises. It is not uncommon for this regressive cycle of dysfunction to repeat itself in therapy sessions. For Erikson (1982), any sustained regression would be dysfunctional and unethical.

So, Mother and Wilma experience a regressive actuality, in which each one of them believes the other is "unethical," or doing wrong to the other. They have created a world in which mutuality has become reciprocal isolation. Mother, mired in stagnation, and Wilma, stuck in a confused identity, drive one another deeper into each one's own isolated realm instead of becoming more deeply connected through sharing a mutually activating and affirming common world. In her isolation, Mother inhabits a world in which she is an inferior (bad) parent who cannot raise an obedient child; in her isolation, Wilma lives in a world in which she is a mistrusting (bad) child who will not believe that a parent is a competent authority.

Mother's insistence that Wilma get a job is another sign of regressive dysfunction, for Mother uses only herself as a work model for Wilma ("Now, when I was your age, I had to work."). Moreover, she broaches the subject of work either in the therapy room or in her house, not in any place that would suggest their mutual involvement in the communal "we." Mother wants compliance from Wilma in order to allay Mother's own sense of inferiority, not to help Wilma identify with other models of work. Wilma's compliance would confirm Mother's need to be competent, but it would not expand for Wilma the range of possible occupations that the larger society promises to offer her in the future.

The regressive dyadic interaction of Mother and Wilma activates an actuality that is unethical for both their stage-specific needs, is reciprocally isolating, and results in dysfunction for both of them. Without this dyadic focus, a therapist who was treating Wilma for alcoholism would ignore the developmental stage of her mother, and there would be no way to know how Mother's failure to meet her stage-specific needs affects Wilma's desire to drink. Moreover, the regressive aspects of Wilma's development would not be adequately understood, because her regressivity is driven by Mother's regressivity.

Regression and Adolescent Alcoholism: Conjectures

Mother and Wilma are locked in their dysfunctional interaction; they experience no functional sense of mutuality, actuality, and activation. The key to unlocking this prison of their reciprocal isolation is to be found in a reworking of Erikson's notion of trust.

The First Trust: The Milk of Hope

Erikson, Erikson, and Kivnick (1986) argued that

> the tension between basic trust and mistrust reaches back to the very beginnings of life, when, through ever-growing trust in the reliable supportiveness and responsiveness of the environment, the healthy infant develops the origins of hope. (p. 218)

Therefore, hope is rooted in the first stage of life with its promise of "mutuality of recognition . . . all through life" (Erikson, 1987a, p. 579). Erikson (1968) called the ontological source of this hope "a sense of basic trust: it is the first basic wholeness, for it seems to imply that the inside [of a person] and outside [of a person] can be experienced as an interrelated goodness" (p. 82).

The need for interrelatedness and its continuity through life, then, is crucial for human development. For Erikson (1964), "to be a person, identical with oneself, presupposes a basic trust in one's own origins—and the courage to emerge from them" (p. 95). It is necessary not only to emerge from one's origins, but also to bring them along and to recognize them in each successful stage of growth as differentiated parts of an integrated life.

Erikson believed that the child in the infancy stage incorporates the outside world first through the oral zone. Thus, the child is dependent on (i.e., must trust) the delivery of objects to the mouth. Erikson (1963a) continues, "As [the] child is willing . . . to suck on appropriate objects [for example, a breast] and to swallow whatever . . . fluid [for example, milk] they emit, [s]he is soon . . . willing to 'take in' with [her] eyes what enters [her] visual field" (p. 72). To trust the world, then, is to depend on it, to take it in, to swallow it, and to make it a part of oneself. The constant repetition of this process provides a sense of the predictability of the outside world and a feeling of continuity between the outside and the inside.The child is not simply nursed by her mother: she is sucking on the world, incorporating it into her very being. No wonder Erikson (1964) said that "hope is the ontogenetic basis of faith, and is nourished by the adult faith which pervades patterns of care" (p. 118).

The Second Trust: The Meat of Fidelity

The care of an adult can transform the fidelity of adolescence into a new expression of faith. Conversely, an adult who has not successfully resolved the conflicts of adolescence cannot integrate fidelity into his or her life. Adolescence is a transitional stage, one in which an individual moves from childhood to adulthood. This movement requires "the second trust," because only an immense effort of faith will enable the adolescent to let go of parents as the source of outer predictability and inner certainty.

This "second trust" is at the core of fidelity, as the adolescent relies on it when caught in the tension between contradictory value systems and competing loyalties. The adolescent explores new identities, swallows what they have to offer, takes in their meanings, and trusts that something "meatier" than milk will provide nourishment. The adolescent finds fidelity in the world of ideas and beliefs (what Erikson calls ideological world views). Anyone who is unsuccessful in negotiating this stage does not possess the second trust. Furthermore, if a woman who does not possess the second trust gives birth to a baby, she cannot move that child past the stage at which she herself is stuck. Indeed, it is likely that she cannot fully assist the child in developing the first trust, since she was not able to trust herself to resolve the conflicts at the stage of the second trust.

Alcohol: The Poisonous Trust

It appears that Wilma's mother, who gave birth to Wilma when she was a teenager, had not successfully negotiated the conflicts of adolescence (axiomatic from an Eriksonian perspective). Therefore, because Mother was not in possession of the second trust, she could not instill in Wilma the first trust. As a result, when Wilma reached adolescence, Mother could not move her through that stage; indeed, Wilma's lack of trust and her hopelessness at not being able to grow as a person took the form of alcohol consumption. Mother's lack of trust activated in Wilma a corresponding lack of trust, with Mother regressing to the last stage she had negotiated successfully—school age, with its focus on competence.

This lack of trust frequently shows itself in dyadic interaction as suspiciousness.

> *Wilma*: You're always checking up on me.
> *Mother*: I just want to make sure you're all right.
> *Wilma*: You're only pretending to care. You're spying on me, going into my room when I'm not there.
> *Mother*: To see if your homework was done.
> *Wilma*: No! To see if I'm hiding any stuff.
> *Mother*: I only want to do what's right for you . . . to help you . . . to get close—
> *Wilma*: [*Cutting her off*]: To get close so you can smell my breath.

As can be seen in this exchange, suspiciousness is the search for betrayal and mistrust. When this search is chronic, mistrust will always be verified. Many times, both Mother and Wilma maintained their regressive states through suspiciousness. Mother refused to trust Wilma because Wilma suspected Mother of being untrustworthy. Wilma refused to trust Mother because Mother suspected Wilma of being incorrigible. This aggressive suspiciousness, then, animated each one of them to search for the facts that could prove, finally and absolutely, that her suspicions of the other were founded on the truth.

It is no wonder that, for Erikson, the two core pathologies of Stage 1 (the infancy stage) are psychosis and addictiveness. Although he does not elaborate on this, it is not difficult to guess his rationale. With even the threatened loss of basic trust, it seems to the child that the cosmic order is disintegrating into madness. When the world is not trustable, the adolescent may fill the emptiness with alcohol or other drugs, trying to poison the mistrust. It is easier to live with the predictability of the effects of the poison, which can be trusted to kill the pain of abandonment and isolation, than it is to swallow the agonizing anxiety of hopelessness.

REFERENCES

Carter, B., & McGoldrick, M. (1988). Overview: The changing family life cycle—A framework for family therapy. In B. Carter & M. McGoldrick (Eds.), *The changing family life cycle* (2nd ed., pp. 3–28). New York: Gardner Press.

Erikson, E.H. (1962). *Young man Luther.* New York: W.W. Norton.

Erikson, E.H. (1963a). *Childhood and society* (2nd ed.). New York: W.W. Norton.

Erikson, E.H. (1963b). Youth: Fidelity and diversity. In E.H. Erikson (Ed.), *The challenge of youth* (pp. 1–28). New York: Doubleday.

Erikson, E.H. (1964). *Insight and responsibility.* New York: W.W. Norton.

Erikson, E.H. (1968). *Identity: Youth and crisis.* New York: W.W. Norton.

Erikson, E.H. (1969). *Gandhi's truth.* New York: W.W. Norton.

Erikson, E.H. (1974). *Dimensions of a new identity.* New York: W.W. Norton.

Erikson, E.H. (1975). *Life history and the historical moment.* New York: W.W. Norton.

Erikson, E.H. (1978). Reflections on Dr. Borg's life cycle. In E.H. Erikson (Ed.), *Adulthood* (pp. 1–31). New York: W. W. Norton.

Erikson, E.H. (1980a). *Identity and the life cycle.* New York: W.W. Norton.

Erikson, E.H. (1980b). Themes of adulthood in the Freud-Jung correspondence. In N.J. Smelser & E.H. Erikson (Eds.), *Themes of work and love in adulthood* (pp. 43–74). Cambridge, MA: Harvard University Press.

Erikson, E.H. (1981, April). The galilean sayings and the sense of 'I.' *Yale Review,* pp. 321–362.

Erikson, E.H. (1982). *The life cycle completed.* New York: W.W. Norton.

Erikson, E.H. (1987a). The ontogeny of ritualization in man. In S. Schlein (Ed.), *A way of looking at things: Selected papers of Erik H. Erikson from 1930 to 1980* (pp. 575–594). New York: W.W. Norton.

Erikson, E.H. (1987b). Reflections on activity, recovery, and growth. In S. Schlein (Ed.), *A way of looking at things: Selected papers of Erik H. Erikson from 1930 to 1980* (pp. 531–544). New York: W.W. Norton.

Erikson, E.H., Erikson, J.M., & Kivnick, H.Q. (1986). *Vital involvement in old age.* New York: W. W. Norton.

Feinstein, H. (1980). Words and work: A dialectical analysis of value transmission between three generations of the family of William James. In M. Albin (Ed.), *New directions in psychohistory: The Adelphi papers in honor of Erik H. Erikson* (pp. 131–142). Lexington, MA: Lexington Books.

Franz, C.E., & White, K.M. (1985). Individuation and attachment in personality development: Extending Erikson's theory. *Journal of Personality, 53,* 224–256.

Hoffman, L. (1988). The family life cycle and discontinuous change. In B. Carter & M. McGoldrick (Eds.), *The changing family life cycle* (2nd ed., pp. 91–105). New York: Gardner Press.

Homans, P. (Ed.). (1978). *Childhood and selfhood: Essays on tradition, religion, and modernity in the psychology of Erik H. Erikson.* Lewisburg, PA: Bucknell University Press.

Jacobson-Widding, A. (Ed.). (1983). *Identity: Personal and socio-cultural.* Uppsala, Sweden: Almqvist & Wiksell.

McGoldrick, M. (1988). Women and the family life cycle. In B. Carter & M. McGoldrick (Eds.), *The changing family life cycle* (2nd ed., pp. 29–68). New York: Gardner Press.

Musto, D. (1980). Continuity across generations: The Adams family myth. In M. Albin (Ed.), *New directions in psychohistory: The Adelphi papers in honor of Erik H. Erikson* (pp. 117–129). Lexington, MA: Lexington Books.

Roazen, P. (1976). *Erik H. Erikson: The power and limits of a vision.* New York: Free Press.

Rudolph, S.H., & Rudolph, L.I. (1980). Authority and the transmission of values in the Rajput joint family. In M. Albin (Ed.), *New directions in psychohistory: The Adelphi papers in honor of Erik H. Erikson* (pp. 143–160). Lexington, MA: Lexington Books.

Part II

Treatment

Traditionally, treatment models for alcoholism and drug abuse have been based on the research theory of white, middle-class, male alcoholism and drug abuse. As the average age of patients admitted to substance abuse treatment programs fell, the field began to notice that adolescents could have drug and alcohol abuse problems that were serious enough to need professional treatment. Adolescents who were admitted to programs designed for adults were often unsuccessful, however. The unique issues of their developmental stage, identity formation, peer pressure, dating, school achievement, physical changes, individuation from family, negotiating more freedom from parents and parents' rules, and making life decisions, were not addressed. Consequently, these traditional treatment programs were often unsuccessful.

This section presents models of treatment that were designed especially for adolescents at various levels of severity of substance abuse. Chapter 6 points out the newness of this attempt to provide appropriate assessment and treatment for adolescent substance abusers. Adult screening and assessment instruments are not useful with this population. New instruments are being developed to get a broader picture of adolescent substance abuse and the related problems that preceded or perpetuated it. A model assessment instrument that has been used in school and clinical settings is provided.

The remaining chapters present models of treatment from peer counseling programs used in school settings to an inpatient treatment model. We have included three chapters about family therapy with adolescent substance abusers and their families because we believe that this is the most successful treatment modality. This has been demonstrated with research in the last three to four years. (For suggested readings regarding this research, see Appendix A.)

We are not discounting the effectiveness of other models of treatment with adolescents. Often the family is not available or other forms of treatment are used in conjunction with family therapy. Group therapy can be effective in dealing with peer issues and self-help groups can provide a drug-free social context. The key to successful treatment of adolescent substance abuse is to do a thorough assessment, set appropriate goals for treatment, and use all of the resources and treatment modalities available that meet those goals.

6

Assessment of Adolescent Substance Abuse

Janice Hoshino

The problem of adolescent substance abuse has been gaining increasing atten-tion in recent years. Even though it appears that there has been some leveling of the frequency of drug use by seniors in high school, survey data indicate that ado-lescents are still using drugs and alcohol at a distressingly high rate (Johnston, Bachman, & O'Malley, 1987).

The criteria used in the assessment of adolescent substance abuse differ from those used in the assessment of adult substance abuse. Owen and Nyberg (1983) cited specific problematic areas, such as

1. differentiating problematic alcohol/drug use from normal adolescent experimentation;
2. differentiating abuse of alcohol/drugs from dependency;
3. differentiating alcohol/drug problems from general behavior prob-lems, juvenile delinquency, or concomitant mental disorders; and
4. expanding standardized assessment tools to measure drug use other than alcohol, as adolescents are more likely to present with drug problems than are adults. (pp. 249–250)

The assessment process for adolescents may pose further difficulties in that the lack of research in this area has hindered the creation of a significant base for empirically significant assessment tools (Winters, 1990). The research that has been done with adolescents has tended to mirror that done with adults, which focuses on substance use in terms of opposite ends of the spectrum (i.e., normal or pathological) with little consideration given to the vast area in between (Kilty, 1990). Therefore, an abundance of materials are available for adults, while few brief screening tools are available for adolescents (Winters & Henley, 1987). Fur-thermore, validated adult alcohol assessment scales (e.g., the McAndrew Alco-holism Scale) have proved inadequate when applied to the female adolescent population (Moore, 1988).

Winters (1990) noted that 10 new adolescent assessment tools have been developed since 1985 (Table 6-1). Of these 10 assessment tools, however, 3 are unpublished. Moreover, because many of these tools are in the developmental stage, their overall comprehensiveness is unknown. According to Winters (1990), an assessment process is effective if it takes into account the following questions:

- Can adolescents be meaningfully differentiated in terms of problem severity?
- What other problems accompany adolescent chemical involvement?
- Can the identification of distinct diagnostic subgroups lead to client treatment "matches"?

Situational factors and gender differences may be important as well (Van de Goor, Knibbe, & Drop, 1990). In order to achieve maximum benefit in the adolescent assessment process, the assessment should include a lengthy examination of the family history and the family system, as well as the completion of a thorough genogram. The inclusion of the family in the therapeutic milieu may greatly affect the success of treatment. Specifically, it may broaden the scope of the problem; instead of being the problem in the family, the adolescent may simply be the symptomatic bearer of a problem within the family system. Therapeutically, this shift does not allow for the blame of any one individual. Viewing the family system not only from the present generation, but also from previous generations, and perhaps gaining insight into what Bowen termed the "multigenerational transmission process" may benefit the entire family (Papero, 1990). Additionally, treatment of an individual is probably less effective if the individual returns to the same family system and the family has not received treatment.

The assessment of the family system also provides valuable information about the family's perspective on normal versus abnormal substance use. Particular consideration should be given to the adolescent's ethnic background and the strength of the family's identification with that ethnicity. What constitutes a "family," what behaviors are problematic, what solutions to the problem are viable, and what the attitudes are toward treatment may be attributed to ethnic background (McGoldrick, 1982). As Roffman and George (1988) noted, "the therapist conducting an assessment must be particularly sensitive to potential intrafamilial value conflicts" (p. 329). Indeed, an abundance of information is necessary to complete an adolescent assessment thoroughly.

ASSESSMENT INSTRUMENTS

Covert (1988) developed several instruments to assess adolescent alcohol and substance abuse. Designed to provide a comprehensive history of substance abuse; the circumstances involved; family history; physical and emotional fea-

Table 6-1 Adolescent Assessment Tools

Instrument Name	Source	Publication Status	Administration Format	Features
Adolescent Assessment & Referral Source	NIDA [National Institute on Drug Abuse]	Unpublished	Paper & pencil	Battery of screening measures, diagnostic instrumentation guide & treatment referral guide
Adolescent Chemical Health Inventory	Renovex	Renovex, 1988	Computer self-administered	Clinically oriented scales
Adolescent Drinking Index	Harrell & Wirtz	Psychological Assessment Resources, 1989	Paper & pencil	Screening tool intended to measure drinking problem
Adolescent Drug Involvement Scale	Moberg	Unpublished	Paper & pencil	Drug abuse screening instrument adapted from Adolescent Involvement Scale (Mayer & Filstead, 1979)
Client Substance Index	Moore	Olympic Counseling Services, 1983	Paper & pencil	Organized around Jellinek's symptoms of chemical dependency
Drug Abuse Screening Test–Adolescent Version	Skinner	Unpublished	Paper & pencil	Screening instrument adapted from adult version of test
Guided Rational Substance Abuse Profile	Addiction Recovery Corp.	Addiction Recovery Corp., 1986	Semi-structured interview	Primarily organized around DSM-III criteria for substance use disorders
Minnesota Chemical Dependency Adolescent Assessment Profile	Winters & Henley	Western Psychological Services, 1988; in press, Adolescent Project, 1988	Paper & pencil, computer self-administered & structured interview	Three separate instrument battery: problem severity screening tool, multidimensional clinical inventory & DSM-III-R diagnostic interview
Perceived Benefit of Drinking & Drug Use Scales	Petchers & Singer	Petchers & Singer	Paper & pencil	Screening tool consisting of parallel alcohol and drug perceived-benefit items
Substance Involvement Instrument	Alader	Cascade Oaks, 1987	Paper & pencil	Organized around a rational theory concerning the progression of adolescent chemical involvement

Source: From "The Need for Improved Assessment of Adolescent Substance Involvement" by K.C. Winter, 1990, *Journal of Drug Issues, 20*, pp. 487-202. Journal of Drug Issues, Inc.

tures; social, vocational, and educational history features; and symptomatic formulation, the assessment process has two parts. Instruments used in the first part are completed within the therapeutic setting through a verbal interview (Exhibits 6-1 and 6-2). Those in the second part are completed by the client outside the therapy setting (Exhibits 6-3 through 6-7). The therapist can then cross-reference and examine the consistencies or inconsistencies of the client's answers. This will provide information regarding factors such as motivation, denial, or willingness to self-disclose.

The genogram should include a three-generation history of the family, with careful attention to addictive behaviors in all family members. Addictive behaviors include not only substance abuse, but also excessive behaviors such as workaholism, gambling, and eating. The genogram should also provide information on ethnicity, as well as educational, vocational, and social norms. In addition, it is important to note relationships between all family members (e.g., cut-offs, stressors, very close or distant family patterns). The family patterns that may emerge often provide insight for the client (McGoldrick & Gerson, 1985).

CONCLUSION

Even though attention to adolescent substance abuse has been increasing in recent years, an effective, standardized assessment remains in the developmental stages. The assessment process should be specialized to fit the specific needs of the adolescent population. Meeting those special assessment needs is a difficult task, however, because of the minimal historical information available. The short time that an adolescent may have been abusing substances makes it necessary to differentiate what may be acting out experimentation with alcohol and/or drugs from a more long-term addictive pattern. Furthermore, the accuracy of the information may be questionable because of lower differentiation and possibly less insight. Certainly, attention should be given to the existing assessments and longitudinal data that should be available in time.

The significance of accurately assessing and treating the substance abuse problems of adolescents is tremendously important. It is fortunate that several assessment tools are being evaluated, but assessments that rely only on clinical impressions could be detrimental for an adolescent who has many important years in front of him or her.

Exhibit 6-1 Intake Form

Evaluating Counselor: _____

1. CLIENT IDENTIFICATION:
   Name: _____ Age:_____ Client#:_____
   Year in School: _____
   Evaluation Date: _____ Marital Status:_____
   Occupation:_____
   Appearance:_____

2. SOURCE REFERRAL: _____

3. PRESENTING PROBLEM:
   A. What led to your coming here?
   B. Why are you here?

4. CHEMICAL USE HISTORY:
   A. How old were you when you had your first drink/drug? What were the circumstances?
   B. When was the first time you got intoxicated/high/etc.? What were the circumstances?
   C. What is your usual intent when you go out to drink or use drugs?
   D. What are the factors involved in your present usage? Present chemical of choice? How often do you use? Recent loss of control? Has drinking/other drugs affected your school life? If yes, how?
   E. Do you think that your drinking or other drug use is different from that of a social user? If so, in what way?
   F. When did you first notice you were drinking or using drugs differently than you would like to?
   G. Does your behavior generally change when you drink/use other drugs? In reference to your family, friends, or co-workers, in what way?
   H. Have you had any period of abstinence from drinking or other drug use? If so:
      1) For what period of time and when was it?
      2) For what reasons were you abstinent?
      3) What factors contributed to resuming alcohol/other drug use?
   I. When was your last usage?
      1) What was it? (Alcohol/other drug)
      2) How much did you use/drink?
      3) What were the circumstances and intent when you used?

5. PRIOR TREATMENT AND/OR HOSPITALIZATION:

6. PHYSICAL ASSESSMENT:
   Date of last physical exam:
   History of:

Blood pressure_____	Liver problems _____
Blood sugar levels_____	Hallucinations_____
Heart trouble _____	D.T.'s _____
Gastro-intestinal problems _____	Flashbacks_____
Sleep disturbances_____	Hangovers _____
Shakiness_____	Excessive sweating _____
Blackouts_____	Other physical symptoms _____
Seizures _____	Motor impairment_____

   Presently prescribed medications: _____

Exhibit 6-1 continued

7. EMOTIONAL STATUS:
   Depression: _____ How long? _____
   Precipitating factors: _____
   How handled? _____
   Suicidal ideation? _____ Previous attempts: _____
   Specifically ruled out due to: _____
   Fear (identify):_____
   Loneliness: _____ Paranoia: _____

8. FAMILY OF ORIGIN HISTORY:
   Year born: _____
   A. Home environment: _____
      1. What was your family environment like while you were growing up?
      2. What, if any, were the issues or concerns for you or your parents while you were growing up?
   B. Chemical dependency in family:
   C. Genogram:
   D. What family concerns (if any) are or were centered around your drinking/other drug use?
   E. How has drinking and/or other drug use affected your family life?

9. PERSONAL INFORMATION:

List family member by name	Age	Sex	Occupation	Education	Any emotional problems

10. DATING HISTORY:
    A. When did you first begin dating?
    B. Dating history (year by year): Age, how often, activities
    C. How have alcohol and/or other drugs influenced your dating history?

11. INTIMATE RELATIONSHIPS (quality of relationships):
    A. What do you consider a quality relationship?
    B. Have you had any quality relationships? (If so, when? How long? Are you in a relationship now?)

12. SOCIAL ASSESSMENT:
    A. Current living situation:
       1. With whom do you live?
       2. How is the environment?
       3. How does the environment relate to your drinking/other drug use?
    B. Peer group affiliations, social interests: _____
       1. What do you consider a friendship?
       2. What do you do with your friends?
       3. How have alcohol/other drugs affected your friendships?

Exhibit 6-1 continued

    C. Activities assessment (skills, hobbies, special interests, leisure time): _____

        1. Date of most recent activity: _____
        2. Did you participate with someone else (who?) or alone?

13. FINANCIAL STATUS: _____

14. EDUCATIONAL HISTORY: _____
    A. High School:
        1. Grade average: _____
        2. What activities did you participate in?
        3. Did alcohol or other drugs interfere with high school classes?
        4. SAT scores: _____
    B. College:
        1. Present GPA
        2. Have you ever been on academic probation?
        3. Has alcohol or other drug use interfered with academics? If so, how?

15. VOCATIONAL HISTORY:
    A. When did you first begin working?
    B. What kinds of jobs have you held? How long did you stay at each, and why did you leave?
    C. Are you presently working? If yes, what is your job, and how many hours do you work?
    D. Has alcohol and/or other drugs interfered with your work performance?

16. LEGAL HISTORY (Including DUI):

17. NUTRITION:
    A. What are your eating habits (kinds of food, meals per day, "binges," etc.)?
    B. Have you ever seen a doctor or a counselor for eating-related problems?
    C. Has there been a significant weight loss or gain in the last year?
    D. Do your eating habits change when you are nervous or upset?
    E. Do your eating habits change when you drink or use other drugs? How?

18. CLINICAL FORMULATION:
    A. Identified symptoms (Circle those specifically identified):
        1. Temporary loss of memory (blackouts)
        2. Preoccupation with drinking
        3. Hurried ingestion
        4. Binge drinker
        5. Use as a medicine
        6. Drink alone
        7. Loss of control (drinking or other drug gets out of hand)
        8. Protecting supply
        9. Increased or large tolerance
      10. Excuses or alibis
      11. Other drug use
      12. Physical symptomatology
      13. Emotional symptomatology
      14. Mental symptomatology

Exhibit 6-1 continued

    15. Guilt associated with consumption
    16. Do you ever tell yourself you are going to have only 1 or 2 drinks, but continue drinking past that amount?
    17. Did you ever tell yourself you are not going to drink at all, then drink anyway?
    18. Have you ever missed classes or exams because of drinking or other drug use?
  B. Can you identify any current problems you are having?
  C. What do you see as your primary problem?
19. If you could change anything about the way you drink/drank or used other drugs, what would that be?

20. SIGNIFICANT OTHER VERIFICATION:

Relationship to Client: _____

Congruency of information to that given by client: _____

I have read this evaluation and agree that what is stated is the information that I gave the interviewer, _____

Signature of Client: _____ Date: _____

Witness: _____ Date: _____

21. TREATMENT RECOMMENDATIONS:
  A. Inpatient treatment
  B. Intensive outpatient
  C. Misuse
  D. Psychological assessment
  E. USIU Drug Prevention Program
  F. Other referral

Client does _____ does not _____ appear to have an excluding mental disorder.

Source: From the Drug Prevention Program, United States International University. Reprinted by permission.

Exhibit 6-2 Mental Status Inventory

CCID# _____
DATE: _____

MENTAL STATUS
(Check as many items as are appropriate)

APPEARANCE

_____ clean   _____ neat   _____ appropriate
_____ soiled   _____ disheveled   _____ atypical

COMMENTS:

MANNER

_____ cooperative   _____ suspicious   _____ impulsive
_____ obsequious   _____ evasive   _____ belligerent
_____ passive   _____ manipulative   _____ hostile
_____ withdrawn   _____ negativistic   _____ bizarre

COMMENTS:

BEHAVIOR

Posture	Speech	Movement	Expressions
_____ relaxed	_____ loud	_____ retarded	_____ smiling
_____ slumped	_____ soft	_____ normal	_____ frowning
_____ rigid	_____ pressured	_____ accelerated	_____ grimacing
_____ bizarre	_____ underproductive	_____ impulsive	_____ blank
	_____ overproductive	_____ disorganized	_____ laughing
Eyes	_____ mute	_____ fidgeting	_____ crying
_____ normal contact	_____ clear	_____ pacing	_____ screaming
_____ little contact	_____ slurred	_____ trembling	_____ menacing
_____ staring	_____ articulate	_____ ritualistic	_____ gesticulating
_____ downcast	_____ incoherent	_____ catatonic	_____ other _____

COMMENTS:

EMOTION
Inferred by Evaluator: *Reported by Client:*

Emotion	Intensity	Mobility	
_____ sadness	_____ mild	____ normal	_____ sadness
_____ anger	_____ moderate	____ constructed	_____ anger
_____ fear	_____ marked	____ blunted	_____ fear
_____ anxiety	_____ extreme	____ flat	_____ euphoria
_____ guilt		____ labile	_____ guilt
_____ ambivalence	Appropriate to content		_____ ambivalence
	of verbalizations/behavior?		_____ can't/won't say
	Yes_____ No_____		_____ (Other) _____

Exhibit 6-2 continued

COMMENTS:

COGNITION

Thought Process

_____ normal   _____ loose associ-
_____ impoverished   ations
_____ blocking   _____ perseveration
_____ circumstantial _____ illogical
_____ tangential   _____ changing

Thought Content

Suicidal	Homicidal
_____ ideas	_____ ideas
_____ intent	_____ intent
_____ plan	_____ plan
_____ no suicidal thoughts	_____ no homicidal thoughts

Delusions	Preoccupations
_____ persecutory	_____ obsessional
_____ grandiose	_____ phobic
_____ religious	_____ somatic
_____ somatic	_____ self-depre-cating
_____ nihilistic	_____ sexual

COMMENTS:

PERCEPTION

_____ auditory hallucinations   _____ olfactory hallucinations   _____ gustatory hallucinations
_____ visual hallucinations   _____ tactile hallucinations   _____ illusions

---

COMMENTS: (describe disorder, i.e., is hallucination a command, an ongoing conversation, or a single voice, etc.?)

SENSORIUM

Orientation
_____ person
_____ place
_____ date

Attention/Concentration
_____ normal
_____ below average
_____ significantly impaired

Consciousness
_____ alert
_____ attentive
_____ clouded
_____ depersonalized
_____ drowsy
_____ intoxicated

Reasoning
_____ abstract
_____ concrete
_____ autistic, bizarre

Memory
_____ Impaired immediate recall
_____ Impaired short-term memory
_____ Impaired long-term memory

COMMENTS:

Exhibit 6-2 continued

JUDGMENT/INSIGHT

Judgment	Insight
(ability to act in goal-directed manner)	
_____ good	_____ true emotional insight
_____ fair	_____ intellectual insight only
_____ poor	_____ aware something wrong, but unsure of personal contribution
	_____ denies problem

COMMENTS:

_____

Source: From the Drug Prevention Program, United States International University. Reprinted by permission.

Exhibit 6-3 Substance Use Questionnaire

I WOULD SAY THAT I USE ALCOHOL OR OTHER DRUGS TO:

	YES	NO
Help me forget that I am not the kind of person I really want to be	_____	_____
Help me to get along better with other people	_____	_____
Help me to feel more satisfied with myself	_____	_____
Give me confidence in myself	_____	_____
Help me forget my problems.	_____	_____
Make me less concerned with what other people think of me	_____	_____
Help me overcome my shyness.	_____	_____
Make me less self-conscious.	_____	_____
Help me relax	_____	_____
Help me feel better	_____	_____

Source: From the Drug Prevention Program, United States International University. Reprinted by permission.

Exhibit 6-4 Personal Information Sheet

Name: _____ Client #:_____

Date: _____ Birthdate: _____ Birthplace:_____

City   State

I have attended: (no. of years) _____ Grade School

_____ High School

_____ College

List Family Member by Name	Age	Sex	Occupation	Education	Any Emotional Problems

What are your main concerns?
Check any of the following which apply to you.

_____Difficulty with mother/father   _____Not liked by others

_____Difficulty with brother/sister   _____Lack companionship

_____Away from home   _____Dating problems

_____Excessive crying   _____Religious problems

_____Poor communication   _____School

_____Sex problem   _____Lonesome

_____Fear of crowds   _____Other

Source: From the Drug Prevention Program, United States International University. Reprinted by permission.

Exhibit 6-5 Client Questionnaire

Answer all questions relating to your drinking in the past two years. Please answer all questions as honestly as you can.

YES NO

( ) ( ) 1. When you have trouble or feel under pressure, do you usually drink or use other drugs? (more heavily than usual?)

( ) ( ) 2. Have you noticed that you are able to handle more alcohol or other drugs than you did when you were first drinking?

( ) ( ) 3. Have you awakened the morning after drinking or using other drugs and found you could not remember a part of the evening even though your friends tell you that you did not pass out?

( ) ( ) 4. During drinking or other drug use with other people, do you try to have a few extra when others will not know it?

( ) ( ) 5. Do you often find that you wish to continue drinking or drugging after your friends have had enough?

( ) ( ) 6. Have you tried switching brands or following different plans for controlling your drinking or other drug use?

( ) ( ) 7. Do close relatives or friends worry or complain about your drinking or other drug use?

( ) ( ) 8. Are you having any increasing number of school, financial, or work problems?

( ) ( ) 9. Do you sometimes have the shakes and find that it helps to have a little drink or need another dose of another drug?

( ) ( ) 10. Have you ever attended a meeting of Alcoholics Anonymous (N.A., A.C.A.)?

( ) ( ) 11. Has alcohol or other drugs created problems between you and a member of your family and friends?

( ) ( ) 12. Have you often failed to keep the promises you have made to yourself about controlling or cutting down on your drinking or other drug usage?

( ) ( ) 13. Has your friend(s) or a family member ever gone to anyone for help about your drinking or drug usage?

( ) ( ) 14. Have you gotten into trouble at work/school because of your drinking or other drug usage?

( ) ( ) 15. Have you recently noticed that you cannot drink as much as you once did?

( ) ( ) 16. Have you ever gone to anyone for help with your drinking or other drug use?

( ) ( ) 17. Have you ever been told by your doctor to stop or cut down on your drinking or other drug use?

( ) ( ) 18. Do you often get into physical fights when you have been drinking or using other drugs?

( ) ( ) 19. Have you ever tried to control your drinking or other drug use by making a change in job/school or moving to a new location?

( ) ( ) 20. Do you try to avoid family or close friends when you are drinking or using?

( ) ( ) 21. Have you ever lost friendships because of your drinking or other drug use?

( ) ( ) 22. Have you ever been told you have liver problems?

( ) ( ) 23. A. Have you ever been a patient in a psychiatric hospital?
      B. Was drinking or other drug use a part of the problem that resulted in your hospitalization?

( ) ( ) 24. Have you ever had any alcohol or drug related arrests? How many?

Have any of the following relatives ever had problems with alcohol or other drugs?

A. Parents

B. Brothers and sisters

C. Husband or wife

D. Children

Source: From the Drug Prevention Program, United States International University. Reprinted by permission.

Exhibit 6-6 Confidential Client Questionnaire

CONFIDENTIAL

The following is a list of symptoms that occur frequently in the lives of some of our clients. Please indicate and comment wherever applicable to your life.

1. ( )　Blackouts (a memory lapse without loss of consciousness). If so, then how often?
   _____

2. ( )　Sneaking drinks/other drugs or hiding bottles? Beginning when? Describe.
   _____

3. ( )　Inability to consistently predict, once I start drinking/taking other drugs, when I will stop drinking/taking drugs without becoming intoxicated or having the drugs negatively affect me.

4. ( )　Rationalizing or alibis for drinking/other drug use. Please describe your most frequently used alibis.
   _____

5. ( )　Aggressive and/or abusive behavior. In what way?
   _____

6. ( )　Stopping drinking/using other drugs for a time. How often, when?
   _____

7. ( )　Did you use mood-altering medication (tranquilizers, barbiturates, sleeping pills, etc.) when drinking, or when abstinent, did you substitute medications for alcohol or other drugs?
   _____

8. ( )　Changing pattern of drinking/and other drug use (e.g., morning drinking, or drinking alone, trying another drug, etc.). Please describe.
   _____

9. ( )　Unreasonable resentments of other people and/or things or events in your life? Please describe.
   _____

10. ( )　Has the drinking/using drugs, etc., resulted in change of family/school activities? Describe.
    _____

11. ( )　Changes in sexual drive. Describe.
    _____

12. ( )　Binges or benders? Describe.
    _____

13. ( )　Tremors (shaking or trembling of the hands, etc.)? Describe.
    _____

14. ( )　Narrowing range or lack of interests (family, hobbies, etc.)?
    _____

15. ( )　Loss of friends or changing attitudes toward friends? Describe.
    _____

Exhibit 6-6 continued

16. ( ) Has your spouse/friend/lover ever left or threatened to leave you if you did not do something about your drinking or other drug use? Describe.

17. ( ) Has a physician ever told you that drinking or drug use was injuring your health? Describe.

18. ( ) Have you ever failed to do some of the things you should have done—like keeping appointments, getting things done around home or attending your job—because of drinking or other drug use? Describe.

19. ( ) Have you ever been threatened with termination from school or a job due to drinking or other drug use? Or have you ever quit a job or dropped a class to avoid termination?

20. ( ) Has any member of your family/friend ever complained that you spend too much money for alcoholic beverages or other drugs? Describe.

21. ( ) Have you ever missed or been late to classes/exams because of a hangover or other circumstances related to the use of alcohol or other drugs? Describe.

22. ( ) Have you ever been put on report for use of alcohol or other drugs? Describe.

Source: From the Drug Prevention Program, United States International University. Reprinted by permission.

Exhibit 6-7 Patient's Choice of Treatment Goals

DO YOU WANT US TO HELP YOU WITH:	YES	NO	This is not a problem for me
1. Withdrawing from alcohol?			
2. Withdrawing from drugs?			
3. Improving your physical health?			
4. Improving your eating habits?			
5. Dealing with seizures?			
6. Being able to speak clearly?			
7. Your ability to sleep?			
8. Learning how to relax?			
9. Overcoming your dependence on alcohol?			
10. Overcoming your dependence on drugs?			
11. Dealing with alcohol or drug abusing friends?			
12. Learning how to say "no" when a drink is offered?			
13. Avoiding a relapse?			
14. Talking to non-alcoholics about your drinking?			
15. Learning how to use Alcoholics Anonymous?			
16. Finding an Alcoholics Anonymous sponsor?			
17. Problem solving with your parents?			
18. Problem solving with your lover?			
19. Problem solving with your spouse?			
20. Expressing your feelings with your spouse/lover/ friends?			
21. Feeling comfortable in social settings?			
22. Making friends?			
23. Expressing your feelings to others?			
24. Handling negative emotions?			
25. Being less dependent on others?			
26. Being more self-sufficient?			
27. Handling your temper?			
28. Dealing with your sexual expectations?			
29. Dealing with depression?			
30. Handling feelings of guilt?			
31. Dealing with thoughts of suicide?			
32. Dealing with employment problems?			
33. Dealing with vocational training?			
34. Educational advancement?			
35. Spiritual beliefs?			
36. Finding a pastor?			
37. Dealing with self-doubts?			

Source: From the Drug Prevention Program, United States International University. Reprinted by permission.

REFERENCES

Covert, J. (1988). *Drug prevention program*. Unpublished manuscript, United States International University Counseling Center, San Diego.

Johnston, L.D., Bachman, J.G., & O'Malley, P.M. (1987). *Monitoring the future: Questionnaire responses from the nation's high school seniors, 1986*. Ann Arbor, MI: Survey Research Center, Institute for Social Research.

Kilty, K.M. (1990). Drinking styles of adolescents and young adults. *Journal of Studies on Alcohol, 51*(6), 556–564.

Mayer, J., & Filstead, W.J. (1979). The Adolescent Alcohol Involvement Scale: An instrument for measuring adolescent use and misuse of alcohol. *Journal of Studies on Alcohol, 40,* 291–300.

McGoldrick, M. (1982). Ethnicity and family therapy: An overview. In M. McGoldrick, J.K. Pearce, & J. Giordano (Eds.), *Ethnicity and family therapy* (pp. 3–30). New York: Guilford Press.

McGoldrick, M., & Gerson, R. (1985). *Genograms in family assessment*. New York: W.W. Norton.

Moore, R.H. (1988). The concurrent validity of the McAndrew Alcoholism Scale among at-risk adolescent females. *Journal of Clinical Psychology, 44*(6), 1005–1008.

Owen, P.L., & Nyberg, L.R. (1983). Assessing alcohol and drug problems among adolescents: Current practices. *Journal of Drug Education, 13*(3), 249–254.

Papero, D.V. (1990). *Bowen family systems theory*. Boston: Allyn & Bacon.

Roffman, R.A., & George, W.H. (1988) Cannabis abuse. In D.M. Donovan & G.A. Marlett (Eds.), *Assessment of addictive behaviors* (pp. 325–363). New York: Guilford Press.

Van de Goor, L.A.M., Knibbe, R.A., & Drop, M.J. (1990). Adolescent drinking behavior: An observational study of the influence of situational factors on adolescent drinking rates. *Journal of Studies on Alcohol, 51*(6), 548–555.

Winters, K.C. (1990). The need for improved assessment of adolescent substance involvement. *Journal of Drug Issues, 20*(3), 487–502.

Winters, K.C., & Henley, G.A. (1987). Advances in the assessment of adolescent chemical dependency: Development of a chemical use problem severity scale. *Psychology of Addictive Behaviors, 1*(3), 146–153.

7

A Model Adolescent Hospital-Based Program

Thomas F. Brock

In recent years, as psychologists, family therapists, licensed clinical social workers, and other mental health care professionals have become more active in the hospitalization of adolescents with diagnosed mental disorders and/or substance abuse, several shortcomings of such programs have been addressed. Hospital programs, whether in private free-standing psychiatric hospitals or in mental health centers that are part of larger acute care medical-surgical facilities, have become increasingly multidisciplinary in approach. In meeting the standards of the Joint Commission on Accreditation of Healthcare Organizations, hospital-based programs are now more often reflecting an educational model with stated behavioral objectives and intervention strategies, rather than the pure medical model of old.

This changing hospital environment, which is now opening doors for the licensed mental health care professionals whose training and background differ from those of the medically trained internists and psychiatrists, may soon make it possible to meet the demands of consumers and clinicians for quality hospital programs at a reasonable cost, with a reasonable length of stay, and with a return of the patient to the family and community as soon as possible. The catalyst for change may come in part from changing attitudes regarding mental health care providers. A wider variety of clinicians can now provide inpatient psychological care, once the exclusive province of the psychiatrist. In most hospital settings, however, while the nonphysician provider may, in fact, be the primary therapeutic agent, he or she serves at the discretion of the psychiatrist and as part of the physician's treatment plan. On the other hand, some inpatient health care facilities have ignored the traditional superiority of the medical license in nonmedical cases and have recently given admitting privileges and (nonmedical) order-writing privileges to licensed practitioners who are not physicians. In fact, the California Supreme Court ruled this year in *CAPP v. Rank* that hospitals who have licensed psychologists on staff must give equal privileges to those practitioners in cases that do not require medication or medical management.

The largest incentive to move away from the current behavior modification and/or psychotropic medication approach to inpatient psychological treatment for adolescents will come from the insurance companies who have grown tired of supporting lengthy stays with minimum transfer of learning to the home and community.

In a recent communication from Preferred Health Care, PsychCare delineated several of the major concerns shared by third-party payors of mental health and chemical dependency benefits.

- Psychiatric costs continue to rise while care is frequently of inferior quality and is cost-ineffective.
- Employers must arbitrarily restrict or cap benefits to avoid paying increasing and uncontrolled amounts of money, which has a negative impact on employee productivity and can result in greater utilization of medical-surgical services.
- Psychiatric diagnosis and treatment are often characterized by vagueness, inconsistency among providers, a lack of definitive effectiveness, and by multiple treatment options and levels of treatment.
- Psychiatric care is frequently highly fragmented with little or no linkage between alternative levels of care.
- The readmission rate for patients hospitalized for psychiatric treatment is very high. According to national statistics, there is a 55% likelihood that a second psychiatric admission will occur within 12 months of a first.
- There are problems in the availability and accountability of adequate after-care programs for the patient discharged from the hospital.
- Psychiatric care has been constrained by the stigma associated with mental illness.
- Inpatient admissions for children under 18 increased approximately 450% between 1980 and 1984.
- Psychiatric inpatient treatment results in an average length of stay for beneficiaries of major employers in the range of 25 to more than 40 days, compared to approximately 6 days for medical-surgical illness.

The following concerns have been raised regarding adolescent inpatient chemical dependency centers specifically:

- There is frequently a dearth of positive peer models on units devoted exclusively to adolescent chemical dependency.
- Age-appropriate school functioning, with an emphasis on necessary remediation and adaptive school skills, is frequently underemphasized.

- In homogeneously grouped chemical dependency programs, teen-agers may have the opportunity to expand their substance abuse repertoire through exposure to addictive behavior that may seem glamorous in those settings.

- By the very nature of a unit devoted exclusively to chemical dependency, there may be a minimal amount of networking with the home school and other supportive elements in the child's community.

- Units devoted exclusively to chemical dependency may not provide sufficient emphasis on individual responsibility, on age-appropriate adaptive functioning, and on the resolution of predisposing mental and familial dysfunctions.

Thus, a model treatment program for adolescents must maximize the use of dollar resources; maximize the transfer of learning, the networking possibilities for each patient, and the maintenance of home and school supportive relationships; and minimize the length of acute care stay by providing at least a three-step transitional program.

In response to these kinds of concerns, an adolescent inpatient program for the treatment of mental disorders, including a dual diagnosis program for the treatment of chemical dependency, was designed and implemented at a large medical center in Los Angeles County. The program was designed (1) to serve the unmet community needs for local acute psychiatric care for the 12- to 18-year-old population, (2) to provide quality inpatient facilities and opportunities for community practitioners, and (3) to establish a cost-effective multitiered transitional program.

The program maximizes the use of community resources, both formal and informal. For example, it involves public schools, churches, scouts, Little League, and other community agencies, as well as family and friends of family, in treatment. It provides continuity of care through a transitional program of outpatient/inpatient aftercare with at least three levels of intensity. The overall purpose of the program and structure is to increase the adolescent's adaptive level of functioning. The program as described admitted its first patient on June 1, 1988.

FACILITIES AND STAFF

The hospital is a 358-bed regional health care center that serves a wide community in southeastern Los Angeles County and portions of the San Gabriel Valley and Orange County. Founded in 1959, it is a not-for-profit organization guided by a board of directors. Its staff includes more than 350 physicians and surgeons, who represent all the major medical specialties. The hospital is accredited by the Joint Commission and is a member of several hospital associations.

The Family Practice Center is affiliated with the University of Southern California School of Medicine and provides residency training for physicians who plan to be family practitioners.

For the last 17 years, the hospital has operated a quality service mental health center. Although the center has always provided services for teen-agers, as well as for adults, a formalized adolescent program was not instituted until June of 1988. These adolescent services have come to be known as the Teen Life Connection. Teen-agers now use 17 beds in the Mental Health Center. When needed, additional beds are immediately available in an adjacent area of the hospital. The physical facilities include a large day room, an airy dining area, an enclosed outdoor patio with volleyball and basketball facilities, a fully equipped kitchen for patient use, patient laundry facilities, a fully equipped classroom, a complete occupational therapy workshop, a safety room for seclusion and restraint when necessary, a voluntary timeout room, a group therapy facility, a nursing station, and offices and consultation rooms for private practitioners.

The facilities of the Mental Health Center are open and spacious, thus preventing the feeling of cramped institutionalization that is frequently the case in adolescent treatment centers. Furthermore, the other facilities and functions of the hospital are available to the adolescent patients. These include the cafeteria, the physical therapy swimming pool, social services, and hospital transportation.

An important aspect of the program philosophy is the team approach for program services. Every practitioner and every program member is an important part of the treatment team. Minimum staff include a supervising registered nurse (RN), whose job description transcends shift changes; a charge nurse on day and night shifts; other RNs; licensed physical therapists and unlicensed counseling staff; and adequate secretarial staff, including ward clerks. In addition to these full-time staff positions, there must be adjunctive therapeutic services, including occupational therapy, recreational therapy, movement therapy, and art therapy to provide a program that is completely integrated with all other aspects of the educational and therapeutic milieu.

LEVELS OF CARE

Acute care must not be the only option available to the practitioner who is treating adolescent substance abuse. There must be a continuum of treatment levels of varying intensity to ensure that each teen-ager receives an appropriate level of care. Ideally, a treatment facility operates a number of transitional programs, each one accommodating the private clinician who will follow the patient from outpatient contact through the minimal treatment approaches necessary to meet treatment goals and return the youngster to the family and home school. Each transitional program should use the same staff, the same facilities, and the same logical consequences framework while individualizing treatment and providing the least restrictive, least costly intervention for each patient. Because the same staff and facilities are used for these programs, a patient can move up or down the continuum of treatment intensity as need and progress dictate. Transitional treatment frequently involves close communication and cooperation between the therapists and the case manager assigned by the third-party payor.

For teen-agers, the least intensive treatment beyond the support of friends, religious leaders, school counselors, and others involves weekly or biweekly therapy sessions with a licensed mental health clinician. This level of treatment is certainly appropriate for individuals who are exhibiting symptoms common to distressed teen-agers, such as school and home behavior problems, possible substance abuse, mild to moderate depression, or other less common psychological symptomatology.

Therapists who work with adolescents ought to have at least three other levels of treatment available to them: (1) intensive outpatient treatment, which requires at least half-day treatment; (2) partial hospitalization, which involves full-day treatment; and (3) inpatient treatment, which may include an intensive care unit.

Intensive Outpatient Treatment

Youngsters who do not need acute care hospitalization, whose behavior is manageable at home, and who are not suffering suicidal ideation or other mental health issues that make outpatient treatment inadvisable receive intensive outpatient treatment. These teen-agers have, at a minimum, daily contact with a licensed mental health care worker, educational therapy, and group therapy. The program provides those services that are not available at home and school, while the patient, the parents, and others in the community provide external support to the program. For instance, parents not only provide transportation, snacks, and recreational outlets, but also participate in the behavioral management aspect of the program. Outpatient day treatment is an intermediate step between the intensive, nearly constant interventions of acute and semiacute care and the once or twice a week monitoring and treatment sessions typical of outpatient psychotherapy.

Partial Hospitalization

In the partial hospitalization or full-day treatment program, a treatment modality that is appropriate for those youngsters who have successfully completed a course of acute care hospitalization and are ready to begin an incremental transition to outpatient treatment, patients receive care 5 days per week. Some patients may need to stabilize the therapeutic gains made in the acute care setting by continuing in the hospital program while sleeping at home and spending weekends with the family. The patient must not be a suicide risk or demonstrate behaviors that make out-of-hospital care inappropriate. Patients in full-day treatment see a licensed mental health care worker daily and their individual therapist two or more times each week. Treatment must include family therapy, educational therapy, a structured environment, and other aspects of full inpatient care that are provided during the day.

Inpatient Treatment

Teen-agers need inpatient treatment if they have a mental disorder and

- have failed industrious attempts at outpatient therapy, and/or
- are a clear danger to themselves or others, and/or
- are unmanageable outside of acute care, and/or
- require brief acute care for evaluation or medication management

The patient who has demonstrated unmanageability in an outpatient setting, such as the patient who is frequently suspended or has been expelled from public schools, is a runaway, and refuses or does not participate in outpatient therapy, may have to be hospitalized.

Inpatient programs provide treatment 7 days per week, 24 hours per day. The setting may be locked, unlocked, or a combination of both. A modification of an inpatient program is a residential care setting that may not provide the intensity of a hospital program, but does provide 24-hour control of a youngster and treatment outside the home setting. Again, the ideal environment is one that can be changed to meet the needs of the individual and the current inpatient population.

Even when acute care is clearly indicated and requested by the teen-age patient, rapport-building activities, goal setting, and orientation to the hospital routine are all accomplished while the youngster is an outpatient in private therapy. Support and cooperation of school personnel and other networking possibilities are sought before admission. The goal is to accomplish these tasks during the less costly outpatient hours and reserve the intense acute care resources for accelerated, maximum patient growth.

Financial Considerations

There are financial considerations as well as clinical considerations for each level of psychiatric care. Therapists and parents should ask about the daily rate of a hospital; the difference in charges for patients who are paying cash, who come with full insurance, or who enter under a rate contracted with a specific employer or insurance policy; and the items that are excluded from the daily rate. For instance, it is quite common for a hospital to charge private individuals two or three times the daily rate that insurance companies have contracted to pay. It is also common for hospitals to add charges for occupational therapy, recreational therapy, educational therapy, and group therapy to the daily rate. The hospital bill of most programs does not include the services of an independent practitioner such as the psychiatrist or primary therapist.

The type of facility is important to most insurance companies. Some will pay for psychiatric care provided in a medical-surgical hospital, but not for that provided in a free-standing psychiatric hospital. Others will pay for the treatment of a mental disorder in either setting, but consider chemical dependency a medical disease and reimburse providers only for treatment given in a medical-surgical setting.

In the Teen Life Connection program, partial hospitalization is provided for approximately half the inpatient fee. Insurance companies are increasingly apt to reimburse at the inpatient rate, usually 80% to 100% of hospital and provider charges. The savings to insurance companies and, therefore, the protection of the patient's resources are clear. Intensive outpatient treatment is usually reimbursed at the outpatient rate—generally 50% of charges—although case management personnel are beginning to see the advantages of funding intensive outpatient treatment more completely to avoid the expense of full hospitalization. Therapists want to help keep the costs down and help parents understand the costs, not only because they are advocates for the patients and the parents, and not only because they have an interest in keeping health premiums reasonable, but also because part of the therapeutic plan is to match the needs of the patients with their resources.

ELEMENTS OF TREATMENT

In the psychiatric treatment of adolescents, the emphasis of each of the therapeutic modalities is on teaching the life skills that are necessary for patients to be successful in their homes, communities, and schools. Unfortunately, many programs require a patient to adapt to an unusual set of circumstances in the hospital and thereby fail to teach those skills necessary for success outside the hospital. The rules and behavior expectancies of the hospital must be consistent with those of a reasonable home and most public schools in order to effect a transfer of learning from the intense training of the hospital to the outside world.

In order to establish a therapeutic milieu for the individualized treatment provided by the primary therapist and attending physician, the Teen Life Connection program includes a wide variety of treatment modalities for all patients. The content and emphasis of these modalities are modified for each patient in accordance with the multidisciplinary treatment plan directed by the attending therapist and psychiatrist. These treatment modalities include educational therapy, group therapy, occupational therapy, a variety of nursing interventions, and other therapeutic activities. Experience and research have indicated that the two most important elements for continued therapeutic progress for an adolescent treatment program are (1) identification with a positive model peer group and (2) commitment to continuing helpful physical activity. Both these elements have been incorporated in this program. The purpose of each intervention is to help the teen-ager accept individual responsibility for his or her own adaptive functioning.

Most teen-agers who enter an adolescent program do so because of depression, substance abuse, or behavior problems. It is the goal of this program to prepare the young person to reenter home and school as rapidly as possible. To this end, every attempt is made to identify and involve all the resources the patient has: family, public school personnel, and any other support systems that are available.

Education Component

The primary task of most 12- to 18-year-olds is to make appropriate progress toward high school graduation. Therefore, the Teen Life Connection program includes an education component designed to meet the individual academic needs of each patient so that he or she does not lose academic standing while being treated in the hospital, can progress academically as quickly as possible in the hospital setting, can have any academic deficiencies remediated as much as possible while in the hospital, and can return to the community-based school as early as possible. Effective transition may include qualifying a patient for special education and making arrangements for an individualized education program (IEP) and adequate follow-up placement. In order to accomplish these goals, the hospital classroom is completely equipped and staffed with highly trained, certified personnel who can meet the needs of the patients and provide effective positive relations. The school is accredited to allow for transfer of credits to the local school, as well as to qualify for special education funding when appropriate.

The educational program is the single most time-consuming program of the patient's day. Patients attend school in the Teen Life Connection program from 8:00 in the morning until 2:00 in the afternoon. As soon as a student is admitted, the education staff (1) contacts the home school to learn the youngster's immediate academic needs, (2) assesses the youngster individually to provide academic tasks at his or her level of achievement, and (3) begins to prepare for effective transition back to the home school. Arrangements are made for patients to receive homework assignments before discharge so that when they return to school they are turning in the same assignments as their classmates. Before discharge, the school is given a copy of hospital grades and transcripts so that work done in the hospital can be integrated into the student's record.

Logical Consequences Behavior Framework

The Teen Life Connection program does not use a behavior modification or token economy approach to teaching age-appropriate behavior. Rather, it promotes individual responsibility through a life skills-based logical consequences behavioral framework. The purpose of this structure is to promote age-appropriate adaptive behavior that has a high transfer of learning to the outside environment. Patients are given freedom and responsibility commensurate with the degree of functional independence that they demonstrate. For instance, patients who wake themselves on time and get to the classroom without assistance are given a later bed time than those who require staff reminders. (This is in contrast to many inpatient programs that do not allow clock radios in the room and require staff to wake patients. As far as safety allows, patient rooms are similar to school dormitory rooms.) Patients are encouraged not only to take care of themselves, but also to contribute to the therapeutic community and be helpful to peers and adults. Patients who are able to make these contributions receive even greater freedom and responsibility.

The logical consequences program is designed to allow patients the greatest opportunity for independent functioning and the greatest transfer of learning to the home and school setting. The program is nonpunitive, giving patients the opportunity to learn from mistakes and develop solid patterns of age-appropriate behavior. The program structure encourages independence and leadership. The life skills logical consequences program teaches self-regulation through increasing patients' self-esteem and providing real life incentives for increasingly independent behavior. This program is designed to teach patients new skills when dealing with stress through program groups and activities. Patients progress from dependent behaviors (orientation level) to age-appropriate (self-care level) to contributory behaviors (leadership level.)

Just as adults in a new setting are dependent on others until they become familiar with their surroundings, adolescent patients enter the program dependent on staff and peers for information regarding, for example, behavioral expectancies and location of activities. Every effort is made to minimize the time that patients spend at this orientation level and allow them to function in an age-appropriate manner as rapidly as possible. During this brief dependent period, however, patients may not leave the Mental Health Center, may not participate in outings, have a 9:45 P.M. bedtime, and have certain other restrictions (e.g., no school field trips). As soon as patients demonstrate that they can take care of themselves, they advance to the self-care level.

Self-care patients have a 10:30 P.M. bedtime and have certain other privileges (e.g., outings and field trips). In all aspects of the program, patients are encouraged to be responsible for themselves and to remain at least at the self-care level. Dependent behaviors (e.g., failure to get up on time, need for reminders to behave appropriately in school) return a youngster to a lower level. Again, just as rapidly as he or she can demonstrate self-care (for at least three shifts or 24 hours), the patient returns to the self-care level.

When patients demonstrate self-care for three shifts in a row *and* show that they significantly helped others during that period, they advance to the leadership level. These patients have an 11:00 P.M. bedtime and certain other privileges, many of which are determined by the patients and staff during community meetings. A patient can be on leadership status as early as 24 hours after admission. Many patients spend most of their stay on this level.

Every program activity has specific behavior expectancies for each level. Appropriate behaviors are published for the patients so they know what is expected at all times. The teen-agers are responsible for monitoring their own behaviors and keep handbooks in their rooms to see their own progress. Each staff member is able to help the patient toward self-care and leadership, and the patients are encouraged to seek help in becoming more independent.

The logical consequences approach to behavior management provides for maximum transfer of learning to the external environment. There should be no rules or expectations in the hospital that do not also make good sense at home and school. It is the goal of the program to help the patients learn self-regulation, self-care, and maximum age-appropriate functioning without the need for continuing close adult supervision or encouragement.

Family Emphasis

In addition to the teen-ager, parents and siblings are also involved in the intensive treatment program. Parents participate in an ongoing parent education class that teaches good parenting techniques and helps with current problem solving as well as future pacing. The purpose of this group is to teach the four basic skills necessary for successfully guiding a child through adolescence: (1) identifying who "owns" a problem and who needs help with an issue, (2) using listening skills and building confidence when it is the adolescent who needs help, (3) using assertion skills and limit-setting skills when it is the parent who needs help, and (4) using conflict resolution skills and negotiation skills when it is the relationship that needs help. Parents continue in this class even after the teen-ager is discharged. Each week, families receive individual family therapy, as well as multifamily therapy with other parents and patients. Families are encouraged to join their children on the weekends for special activities.

Multidisciplinary Approach

Every patient has an individualized treatment plan that includes interventions from a variety of sources. While in treatment in the hospital, the young person participates in individual family therapy from the primary therapist and attending psychiatrist, as well as in group therapy from the nursing staff, occupational therapist, and licensed clinical social workers. The education director is an integral part of the treatment team. Some of the regular interventions used in the program are

- agenda group. Patients have help in setting appropriate goals for themselves. Adolescents learn to focus on their individual issues.
- art therapy. Patients learn expressive skills and develop new awareness through insight-oriented activities.
- assertion training. Assertion groups help the patient distinguish between self-care and aggression, helping the teen-ager get what he or she needs in an age-appropriate, effective way.
- biofeedback. This modality can sometimes be a useful tool in helping the youngster gain control of his or her emotions, stress, and various symptomatology.
- chemical dependency programs. Within the adolescent program are several options for the patient with chemical dependency problems. In addition to step work, these options include groups on and off the hospital grounds, sponsorship, and other interventions.
- community meetings. Adolescents need an opportunity to meet as a group to discuss and to solve problems on the unit.
- cooking activities. Patients are given a chance to use the kitchen on the unit to learn to cook and to work both independently and in cooperation with others. These activities are designed to be fun and to increase youngsters' confidence in their own ability to take care of themselves and provide for others.
- drug awareness. As part of the overall educational program, patients are given specific factual information regarding the effects of commonly abused drugs, as well as guided discussion for the purpose of clarifying each youngster's own stance.
- field trips. Used as culminating activities, field trips emphasize and reinforce specific educational objectives of the classroom.
- goals assessment. Patients must have clearly defined treatment goals at the outset of the hospital stay. Goals assessment groups provide patients with insight and feedback regarding progress toward those goals and help the

youngsters focus on the issues leading to treatment and, more important, on the solutions to those issues.

- health and sex education. Awareness of health-promoting activities and attitudes is important. Patients are helped to avoid problems in the area of developing sexuality through didactic educational experiences, as well as through values clarification discussion groups.

- individual physical development. Patients are encouraged to assess and improve their physical conditioning, with the help of the staff, and to implement an individual plan for their physical development. Program staff work in conjunction with physical therapy staff to provide for these activities.

- leisure skills. Physical activities, as well as indoor recreational activities, provide the patient with new, productive ways of managing leisure time.

- movement therapy. Approximately once each week, patients have the opportunity to deal with their therapeutic issues nonverbally.

- personal achievement. Skill-based groups may include crafts, such as ceramics and leather working. Patients increase self-help skills such as prolonging their attention span, asking for assistance, receiving feedback, building teamwork, and persevering.

- process groups. Periodically, every patient participates in several psychotherapy groups led by a licensed professional therapist.

- relaxation groups. Patients are taught specific relaxation techniques in an effort to help them handle stress, become more aware of their physiological needs, and develop control of their bodies, as well as their cognitive and affective activities.

- time management groups. Teen-agers frequently lack the skills to manage their increasingly less discretionary time effectively. They learn to balance work, school, chores, physical activities, friends, and recreation in a way that is satisfying to them.

SUBSTANCE ABUSE PATIENTS WITHIN THE DUAL DIAGNOSIS MODEL

Patients who enter the Teen Life Connection program with chemical dependency or with substance abuse as a secondary diagnosis are given an individualized evaluation and treatment plan for their substance abuse. This three-dimensional plan is prepared separate from, but complementary to, the patient's psychiatric multidisciplinary treatment outline and can be followed in any of the three levels of treatment intensity.

The substance abuse treatment within the adolescent psychiatric treatment program takes into account recent research in which (1) commitment to physical activity, (2) participation in a peer group with a strong commitment to sobriety, and (3) continued structured meetings and activities were found to be essential to the sobriety. In addition to its use of drug abuse education; introduction of refusal and assertion skills; didactic presentations; 12-step work; Alcoholics Anonymous, NA, CA, and other peer group work, Teen Life Connection follows the Lawson model of school and family intervention in maintaining sobriety. Patients are helped to identify and connect with a sponsor and with support groups on and off campus, in and out of the hospital setting. Like other discharged patients, former substance-abusing youngsters continue to participate in family education groups, aftercare groups, and education follow-up activities.

INITIAL PROGRAM RESULTS

In its first 2 years of operation, the Teen Life Connection's logical consequences, three-step transitional program has produced the following benefits:

- Flexibility in moving up and down the ladder of treatment intensity may be difficult for the hospital administrator and billing office, but is clinically sound and cost-effective.
- Flexibility in applying benefits allows for a realistic limit to spending without sacrificing quality of care.
- This program allows for provider consistency of philosophy, approach, and implementation.
- The providers integrate prehospital and posthospital treatment and are responsible for ongoing monitoring and supervision of the patient.
- The readmission rate has been extremely low. Readmissions that have occurred have been for extremely brief periods (mean = 4.5 days).
- By involving peers, school, and other networking possibilities, the stigma of psychiatric care has been almost completely eliminated. Extended families and the school community become part of the adolescent's support group, both during hospitalization and after discharge.
- The program therapists, not just inpatient physicians, are committed to avoiding hospitalization when possible. The program provides alternatives to inpatient treatment when individual therapy is not sufficient to ameliorate the problem.
- Even before full development of the step-down transitional programs, inpatients had an an average length of stay of less than 22 days.

- The dual diagnosis program provides a heterogeneously grouped environment in which patients of varying presenting symptoms can identify positive peer models.

- While focusing on the substance abuse and other issues that brought patients to the hospital, this program focuses on adaptive functioning and provides minimal opportunity to learn additional abusing behaviors and no opportunity to glamorize the abuse of various substances.

- Even those patients who have been admitted by their parents against their own wishes have rapidly become committed to their treatment goals. Discharges against medical advice and elopements (i.e., absences from the unit without permission) are less than 5%. Readmissions are fewer than 10% per year and average fewer than 7 days length of stay.

SUGGESTED READING

Armstrong, H., Morris, R.M., Amerongen, M., & Kernaghan, P. (1983). Group therapy for parents of delinquent children. *International Journal of Group Psychotherapy, 33*(1), 85–97.

Birmingham, M.S. (1986). An outpatient treatment programme for adolescent substance abusers. *Journal of Adolescence, 9,* 123–133.

Bloor, M.J. (1986). Problems of therapeutic community practice in two halfway houses for disturbed adolescents: A comparative sociological study. *Journal of Adolescence, 9,* 29–48.

Brown, B. (1985). An application of social learning methods in a residential programme for young offenders. *Journal of Adolescence, 8,* 321–331.

Danziger, Y., Carcl, C.A., Varsano, I., Tyano, S., & Mimouni, M. (1988). Parental involvement in treatment of patients with anorexia nervosa in a pediatric day-care unit. *Pediatrics, 81*(1), 159–162.

Davids, A., Ryan, R., & Salvatore, P.D. (1968). Effectiveness of residential treatment for psychotic and other disturbed children. *American Journal of Orthopsychiatry, 68,* 470–475.

DeSantis, L., & Thomas, J.T. (1987). Parental attitudes toward adolescent sexuality: Transcultural perspectives. *Nurse Practitioner, 12*(8), 43–48.

Dittmar, H., & Bates, B. (1987). Humanistic approaches to the understanding and treatment of anorexia nervosa. *Journal of Adolescence, 13,* 57–69.

Fleischman, M.J. (1981). A replication of Patterson's "Intervention for Boys With Conduct Problems." *Journal of Consulting and Clinical Psychology, 49*(3), 342–351.

Graafsma, T., & Anbeek, M. (1984). Resistance in psychotherapy with adolescents. *Journal of Adolescence, 7,* 1–16.

Green, D. (1987). Adolescent exhibitionists: Theory and therapy. *Journal of Adolescence, 10,* 45–56.

Greenman, D.A., Gunderson, J.G., & Canning, D. (1989). Parents' attitudes and patients' behavior: A prospective study. *American Journal of Psychiatry, 146*(2), 226–230.

Gutstein, S. (1987). Family reconciliation as a response to adolescent crises. *Family Process, 26,* 475–491.

Haines, A.A., & Haines, A.H. (1987). The effects of a cognitive strategy intervention on the problem solving abilities of delinquent youths. *Journal of Adolescence, 10,* 399–413.

Holmes, P. (1984). Boundaries or chaos: An outpatient psychodrama group for adolescents. *Journal of Adolescence, 7,* 387–400.

Hunka, C.D., O'Toole, A.W., & O'Toole, R. (1987). Self-help therapy in parents. *Journal of Psychosocial Nursing, 23*(7), 25–32.

Kappelman, M.M. (1987). The impact of divorce on adolescents. *American Family Physician, 35*(6), 200–206.

Kerslake, A.S. (1983). Leadership in low intensity intermediate treatment groups. *Journal of Adolescence, 6,* 27–41.

LaBarbera, J.D., Martin, J.E., & Dozier, J.E. (1982). Residential treatment of males: The influential role of parental attitudes. *Journal of the American Academy of Child Psychiatry, 82/2103,* 286–290.

McAdam, E.K. (1986). Cognitive behavior therapy and its application with adolescents. *Journal of Adolescence, 9,* 1–15.

Perinpanayagam, K.S. (1987). Organization and management of an inpatient treatment unit for adolescents. *Journal of Adolescence, 10,* 133–148.

Prerost, F.J. (1984). Evaluating the systematic use of humor in psychotherapy with adolescents. *Journal of Adolescence, 7,* 267–276.

Pyne, N., Morrison, R., & Ainsworth, P. (1986). A consumer survey of an adolescent unit. *Journal of Adolescence, 9,* 63–72.

Rae-Grant, N.I. (1978). Arresting the vicious cycle: Care and treatment of adolescents displaying the Ovinnik syndrome. *Canadian Psychiatric Association Journal, 23,* SS22–SS40.

Rose, M. (1986). The design of atmosphere: Ego-nurture and psychic change in residential treatment. *Journal of Adolescence, 9,* 49–62.

Rose, M. (1987). The function of food in residential treatment. *Journal of Adolescence, 10,* 149–162.

Shamsie, S.J. (1981). Antisocial adolescents: Our treatments do not work—Where do we go from here? *Canadian Journal of Psychiatry, 26,* 357–363.

Singh, N. (1987). A perspective on therapeutic work with inpatient adolescents. *Journal of Adolescence, 10,* 119–131.

Tonge, B.J. (1986). Mental health, or I'm OK and so are my parents. *Australian Family Physician, 15*(9), 1181–1184.

Treffert, D.A. (1969). Child-adolescent unit in a psychiatric hospital. *Archives of General Psychiatry, 21,* 745–752.

Webster-Stratton, W. (1985). The effects of father involvement in parent training for conduct problem children. *Journal of Child Psychology and Psychiatry, 26*(5), 801–810.

Yeaton, W.H., & Sechrest, L. (1981). Critical dimensions in the choice and maintenance of successful treatments: Strength, integrity, and effectiveness. *Journal of Consulting and Clinical Psychology, 49*(2), 156–167.

8

Group Psychotherapy with Adolescents

Shari Shaw

Any discussion of adolescence elicits varied feelings and responses in both social and professional contexts. The mention of the word *adolescent* in any social situation may be met with a frown, a shaking of the head, raised eyebrows, or a knowing smile. Among professionals, statements as diverse as "I just love their energy" and "I refuse to work with them; they're too difficult" may be heard.

Theorists and researchers have a variety of opinions about this developmental period as well, although most see adolescence as primarily a Western, rather than a culturally universal, phenomenon (Ralston & Thomas, 1972; Sieg, 1971). Papanek (1987), believing that society has not deliberately planned this period, called adolescence "a cultural accident" (p. 219). Ralston and Thomas (1972) commented that, in the United States, youth has been extended into an "artificial state of adolescence" because of extended schooling in our society (p. 138). In contrast, Alissi (1972) postulated that adolescence is vanishing in our culture because of society's tendency to dampen "questioning, conflict, rebellion and all that is stressful during adolescence" (p. 500).

In spite of the opposing views of adolescence itself, many agree that the essential task of this period is character synthesis role transition. Common themes of adolescence that emerge in the literature include the struggle for increasing autonomy, identity conflict, and rebellion against authority (Malmquist, 1985). The developmental transition of adolescence so commonly involves struggle and conflict that many theorists have described it as a period of "storm and stress" (Alissi, 1972; Coleman, 1978; Stanton, 1974). This turmoil during adolescence is generally viewed as important and normal, both psychologically and behaviorally. Josselyn (1987), for example, said that adolescent behavior "is determined by an urgency to learn who the self is, to establish memories for this self" (p. 74). Similarly, Alissi (1972) stated, "Upset behavior is seen to be an external indication of internal adjustments taking place" (p. 496).

The drug and alcohol use that is prevalent during this period of life may be part of the "upset behavior," an element of the developmental conflict or identity crisis common to adolescence. Substance use among adolescents often begins by age 12 (Kornblum & Julian, 1989) and is so widespread that "virtually all (95%) of our young people experiment with mood-altering drugs by the time they are seniors in high school" (Trapold, 1990, p. 251). Group therapy is often useful to address adolescents' struggle for individuation, to facilitate role transition, and to work through the needs that frequently underlie substance abuse.

INDIVIDUATION

Definitions of adolescence reflect the search for identity and the conflict inherent in role transition. For example, Sieg (1971) defined adolescence as a pursuit of society's sanction. She described adolescence as

> the period of development in human beings that begins when the individual feels that adult privileges are due him which are not being accorded him, and that ends when the full power and social status of the adult are accorded to the individual by his society. (p. 338)

Similarly, Malmquist (1985) stressed societal acknowledgment in his description of the struggle of adolescence; "It is not a mere recognition for achievement that is sought, but a wish to be regarded, in terms of function and status, as having grown" (p. 376). In a different but complementary view, Dacey (1982) focused on the individual's self-acceptance during this period.

> The adolescent is any person, usually between the ages of 11 and 19, who has clearly started the search for a personal identity. In this process, the person examines many of the philosophical, psychological, social, and physical options which are available. The adolescent tries out numerous self-images and behaviors and accepts or rejects them. However, not until there is at least a sense of self-acceptance can adolescence end. (p. 28)

Role transition in adolescence seems to involve a search for approval, as well as a search for self-esteem and a sense of competence (Malmquist, 1985). In other terms, the search for identity is the integration of the views of others with the view of self, or "the relationship between what a person appears to be in the eyes of others with what he feels he is" (Alissi, 1972, p. 496).

Erikson (1963, 1968), who has influenced many theorists and clinicians, described adolescence as the period in which identity processes either crystallize or remain clouded. From this viewpoint, the opposite of ego identity is identity diffusion, which refers to a person's inability to establish an occupational or ideological position (Stark & Traxler, 1974).

Blos (1967, 1968) considered the adolescent identity struggle the second phase of separation-individuation, analogous to that which occurs in the first few years of life (Mahler, Pine, & Bergman, 1975). Individuation involves increasing autonomy with concomitant "diminishing emotional dependence on others" (Malmquist, 1985, p. 61). Similarly, in terms of object relations, the task of individuation is "freedom from the degree of control that internalized objects have exerted" (Malmquist, 1985, p. 62).

The adolescent who is struggling to obtain a sense of identity separates and pushes away from authority, challenging existing adult values and social norms (Ball & Meck, 1979). What begins as the adolescent's effort to be under his or her own control rather than under parental control may erupt into a rebellion (Pittman, 1987). Alissi (1972) said, "It is through the process of rebelling that the adolescent asserts his own identity and adds meaning to his life" (p. 504).

Malmquist (1985) noted that acting out, extreme negativism, violent protest, and self-destructive activities are common before the adolescent has achieved individuation. Acting out may actually be adjustive behavior (Papanek, 1987), and it can serve the adolescent as a means of mastery (Josselyn, 1987). Ellis (1979) also considered some adolescent antisocial behavior as adaptive, stating that "seemingly uncontrolled behavior may be controlled temporarily by a peer group value system that is contradictory to the accepted cultural values" (p. 107).

SUBSTANCE ABUSE

Alcohol and drug use may be one form of adolescent rebellion against authority. Rasor (1987) considered addiction a form of acting out against authority by a person who feels unloved and unwanted, "not at peace with the self or the environment" (p. 113). In addition, drug use may be a destructive and hostile impulse against the self (Rasor, 1987). Levin (1987) called it a form of "self-destruction by self-poisoning, of suicide on the installment plan" (p. 3). Pittman (1987) claimed that the self-destructive aspect may be accidental for adolescents who have little experience and may simply not know how much of a particular substance to use. Young people may be naive about an appropriate quantity of alcohol, for example, resulting in "inadvertent drunkenness" before they find a "safe" way to drink (Pittman, 1987, p. 264).

From a self-psychology perspective, addiction and its destructive effects make up a disorder of the self. Levin (1987) adopted the view of addiction as "a futile attempt to repair developmental deficits in the self" (p. 13). Therefore, according to Levin, addiction indicates a deficit in the psychic structure, an attempt to "supply externally what is missing internally" (p. 194). Similarly, a low self-concept or decreased self-esteem may contribute to substance abuse (Svobodny, 1982). Youngs (1986) commented ,"Anything that accentuates the self-doubt that kids harbor about themselves or their abilities may lead to a alcohol or drug use" (p. 195).

Anxiety is a key element in substance abuse, as it is in the adolescent struggle for identity and in rebellion. Pittman (1987) stated, "It would rarely be misleading to assume that all adolescent rebellion is fueled by anxiety" (p. 187). Kerr and Bowen (1988) also associated addiction with anxiety, stating that substance abuse is a "major binder of anxiety for the individual and within the family" (p. 119). Bowen (1978) specifically tied anxiety to substance abuse in the presence of a chronic pattern of family anxiety. He noted that "the symptom of excessive drinking occurs when family anxiety is high. The appearance of the symptom stirs even higher anxiety in those dependent on the one who drinks" (p. 259).

In addition to identity conflict and anxiety, other factors may play a role in chemical dependence for some individuals. Genetic factors, for example, often contribute to chemical dependence (Svobodny, 1982). Some adolescents seem biologically alcoholic, becoming addicted quickly because they receive "some sort of euphoriant effect" that others do not receive (Pittman, 1987, p. 179). Alcoholism in the family or parental abuse of illegal or prescription drugs may also influence the development of adolescent chemical dependence (Pittman, 1987; Svobodny, 1982; Youngs, 1986). Stressors such as sustained family conflict (particularly between parent and child), divorce or remarriage of the parents, or the death of a family member or friend often contribute to adolescent substance abuse as well (Pittman, 1987; Youngs, 1986).

Whether rebellion, self-destruction, anxiety, or other factors are central, drug and alcohol use is an intriguing temptation for an adolescent who is experiencing identity confusion. For a short time, the use of mood-altering substances may reduce physical and emotional pain (Trapold, 1990). As Levin (1987) noted, drugs are ideal for increasing self-tolerance because they give the illusion of control, power, and comfort through their seemingly magical qualities.

> They change moods, narcotize feelings, change self-perception, import either oblivion or the illusion of vitality, and give hope the the hopeless, self-esteem to the self-hating, and relief from psychic pain to the emotionally wounded. They give users a sense of power. The drug gives the illusion of magically controlling reality; it allows users to feel or be whatever they wish to feel or be. (p. 195)

Freud (1930-1961) also commented on the soothing effects of drugs when he wrote that "life, as we find it, is too hard for us; it brings us too many pains, disappointments and impossible tasks" (p. 22). He added that intoxicating substances can make us insensitive to our miseries.

GROUP PSYCHOTHERAPY

Adolescents who abuse drugs and alcohol usually lack positive reference groups or relationships with significant others; "instead most of their relationships are mediated through an inanimate object, the drug" (Ben-Yehuda, 1984, p. 275). The dependency-conflict theory of alcoholism supports this idea, as it is based on a perception of alcoholics as "people who have not succeeded in establishing, or at least in maintaining, healthy patterns of interdependence" (Levin, 1987, p. 83). For these and other reasons, outpatient group psychotherapy is generally the treatment of choice for adolescents with a substance abuse problem (Henderson & Anderson, 1989; Scheidlinger, 1985).

The goals of group therapy for adolescent drug and alcohol abusers include teaching these adolescents to value the self and others, as well as to relate to others in a positive and responsible manner. As Levin (1987) stated, "Psychological treatment aims to replace addiction with relationship and to use this emotional bond to promote integration and growth" (p. 1). Through group therapy, adolescent substance abusers may experience successes that will lead to a sense of self-confidence and self-respect. In this way, "the spirit is enhanced and energy directed in more positive ways to allow the adolescent rebellion to be more constructive and acceptable, both to himself and to society at large" (Birmingham, 1986, p. 124).

Advantages of Group Therapy

Groups, as opposed to individual therapy, are particularly effective with adolescents because young people who are in the company of peers are likely to be less threatened by authority figures (Toseland & Siporin, 1986). Ball and Meck (1979) stated, "Largely because of a shared concern with the issues of identity and independence, there is a natural cohesion among adolescents" (p. 530). The group functions partly by "mirroring" the self, to use Kohut's term, or by empathically reflecting the individual's feelings (Levin, 1987).

Group therapy offers not only peer support, but also peer confrontation. In individual treatment, patients who are impulsive or have unsatisfying relationships tend to see confrontation as personal criticism. For these patients, group therapy dilutes potentially counterproductive transference in adolescent treatment (Abt, 1987; Anderson, 1982; Levin, 1987). Groups also provide more effective confrontation, facilitating the learning of new relationship patterns. Anderson

(1982) stated, "Denial systems and feelings of depression, as well as conflicts around dependency, responsibility, and the expression of anger can be gently recognized and confronted by a supportive group" (p. 32).

Confrontation about drug use and the delusional system that often accompanies it requires the strength of a group to penetrate the denial. No one-to-one relationship can be successful with a chemically dependent person's rigid defenses; "rather, this task requires a group of people who work together over many hours to confront the omissions, the distortions of fact, and the inconsistencies in the delusional story" (Trapold, 1990, p. 266).

Group therapy facilitates the development of autonomy by exposing the group members to diverse social experiences. According to Malmquist (1985), "In a way, the peer group setting provides the adolescent with an opportunity to test his own internalized views of the world versus alternatives" (p. 6). Moreover, the therapist has an opportunity to compare actual with reported client behavior (Anderson, 1982).

In addition, group therapy facilitates the process of individuation by serving as a transitional object or as "a bridge between what is comfortably familiar and what is disturbingly unfamiliar" to the adolescent (Zabusky & Kymissis, 1983, p. 108). The group becomes a substitute family and offers a protected environment to the young person before he or she goes into the world (Scheidlinger, 1985).

Curative Factors of Group Therapy

The important functions of group therapy for adolescent substance abusers include curative factors described by Yalom (1985). For example, Butler and Fuhriman (1983) found that self-understanding, catharsis, and interpersonal learning are the most highly valued factors in outpatient therapy groups. Similarly, in a study of curative factors for adolescent group members, teens identified the following characteristics as most helpful to them in their group experience:

1. catharsis ("Being able to say what was bothering me instead of holding it in"; "Learning how to express my feelings");
2. interpersonal learning ("Other members honestly telling me what they think of me"); and
3. existential factors ("Learning that I must take ultimate responsibility for the way I live my life, no matter how much guidance and support I get from others"). (Corder, Whiteside, & Haizlip, 1981)

Selection of Group Members

Certainly, not all adolescents can benefit from group therapy. Scheidlinger (1985) suggested that "individuals with uniquely fragile egos, those in crises, sociopaths, overt sexual perverts, acute psychotics, and all paranoids" (p. 109) should be excluded from a group experience. Lawson, Ellis, and Rivers (1984) proposed the following criteria for group membership: (1) a sense of reality, (2) ability for interpersonal relations, (3) sufficient flexibility for group interactions, (4) ability to serve as a catalyst for the group, and (5) motivation.

Phillips (1989) recommended that outpatient therapy be tried first for adolescents, provided that the severity of their illness does not warrant inpatient care. Other patients who may benefit from outpatient group therapy are patients whose substance use occurs only in binges (e.g., on weekends), those with a good support system, and those recently in rehabilitation who have had a brief relapse of less than 1 week (Phillips, 1989). Lawson, Ellis, and Rivers (1984) suggested that groups for chemically dependent clients should be homogeneous in order to speed recovery; improve attendance; reduce cliques and destructive interactions; and promote identification, reeducation, and insight about psychodynamics and other issues.

In order to facilitate the process of group member selection, the group leader should meet individually with each adolescent (Corey & Corey, 1987; Henderson & Anderson, 1989). In addition to screening potential group members, the leader can begin to establish a working alliance, explain the rationale for group therapy, and discuss individual treatment goals (Henderson & Anderson, 1989). These sessions also aide in lowering resistance and determining the reservations and possible negative attitudes of any adolescent who is being sent to group by parents (Corey & Corey, 1987).

When an adolescent has reservations about participating in a group, Corey and Corey (1987) suggested that the therapist offer a trial period of three sessions during which the adolescent may decide whether to make a commitment. Such an offer may be appropriate in an open group, but a closed group with a specific time limit may be particularly appealing to many adolescents. According to Fine and associates (1989), adolescents are often relieved if a time commitment of not more than 12 sessions is requested. At the end of this time period, many individuals commit for additional sessions.

Group Therapy Techniques

Useful techniques for group therapy include providing structure and consistency for adolescent substance abusers through guidelines or "rules." Birmingham (1986), for example, suggested requiring the adolescent to sign a contract that use of substances renders him or her ineligible to continue in the group. This addresses the issue of rejection by placing responsibility on the patient rather than on the group leader.

Corey and Corey (1987) established structure for adolescents by stating expectations, such as regular attendance and confidentiality, personal responsibility for specific goals, and no smoking during group sessions. In addition, they structured sessions with adolescents by offering themes of discussion rather than asking, "What would you like to talk about today?" Possible themes include the struggle for autonomy, conflict with parents, conflict related to school, sex roles, relationship issues, and feelings (e.g., guilt, anxiety, anger, rejection, hostility, and loneliness).

Because adolescents need an active group environment, Corey and Corey (1987) recommended pointing out story-telling and excessive questioning and directing clients to focus on feelings. To keep groups dynamic, they suggested asking for a one-sentence summary of a story, requesting statements that focus on personal rather than external factors, utilizing role playing, and being flexible enough to make use of whatever happens during sessions. This may involve "going with" resistances in order to avoid defensive reactions.

Group leadership with adolescents requires special characteristics and skills. As DeBlassie and Sallee (1982) noted, "To catch and hold a young adolescent's attention so that beneficial work can be done requires talented, involved therapists" (p. 29). Phillips (1989) stressed that specific expertise in the area of adolescence, as well as chemical dependency, is necessary because of the complexity of adolescent issues; "an adolescent patient usually has many more problems than those related to a chemical problem" (p. 282).

Corey and Corey (1987) described effective group leaders as those who have resolved their own adolescent conflicts; are willing to share themselves and their struggles; and are caring, enthusiastic, and genuine. They also suggested that, while preparing for work with adolescents, leaders do some reflecting on and reliving of their own adolescent experiences.

Adjuncts to group therapy for adolescents may include self-help groups (Lawson, Ellis, & Rivers, 1984), family therapy (Henderson & Anderson, 1989), parent consultations, and/or parent and adolescent groups (Corey & Corey, 1987).

REFERENCES

Abt, L.E. (1987). Acting out in group psychotherapy: A transactional approach. In L.E. Abt & S.L. Weissman (Eds.), *Acting out: Theoretical and clinical aspects* (2nd ed., pp. 173–182). Northvale, NJ: Aronson.

Alissi, A.S. (1972). Concepts of adolescence. *Adolescence, 7*(28), 491–510.

Anderson, S.C. (1982). Group therapy with alcoholic clients: A review. *Advances in Alcohol and Substance Abuse, 2*(2), 23–40.

Ball, J.D., & Meck, D.S. (1979). Implications of developmental theories for counseling adolescents in groups. *Adolescence, 14*(55), 529–534.

Ben-Yehuda, N. (1984). A clinical sociology approach to treatment of deviants: The case of drug addicts. *Drug and Alcohol Dependence, 13,* 267–282.

Birmingham, M. (1986). An out-patient treatment programme for adolescent substance abusers. *Journal of Adolescence, 9,* 123–133.

Blos, P. (1967). The second individuation process of adolescence. *Psychoanalytic Study of the Child, 22,* 162–186.

Blos, P. (1968). Character formation in adolescence. *Psychoanalytic Study of the Child, 23,* 245–263.

Bowen, M. (1978). *Family therapy in clinical practice.* Northvale, NJ: Aronson.

Butler, T., & Fuhriman, A. (1983). Curative factors in group therapy: A review of the recent literature. *Small Group Behavior, 14*(2), 131–142.

Coleman, J.C. (1978). Current contradictions in adolescent theory. *Journal of Youth and Adolescence, 7*(1), 1–11.

Corder, B.F., Whiteside, L., & Haizlip, T.M. (1981). A study of curative factors in group psychotherapy with adolescents. *International Journal of Group Psychotherapy, 31*(3), 345–354.

Corey, M.S., & Corey, G. (1987). *Groups: Process and practice* (3rd ed.). Pacific Grove, CA: Brooks/Cole.

Dacey, J.S. (1982). *Adolescents today* (2nd ed.). Glenview, IL: Scott, Foresman.

DeBlassie, R.R., & Sallee, N. (1982). Counseling with the young adolescent. *Journal of Early Adolescence, 2*(1), 25–30.

Ellis, E.H. (1979). Some problems in the study of adolescent development. *Adolescence, 14*(53), 101–109.

Erikson, E.H. (1963). *Children and society* (2nd ed). New York: W.W. Norton.

Erikson, E.H. (1968). *Identity: Youth and crisis.* New York: W.W. Norton.

Fine, S., Gilbert, M., Schmidt, L., Haley, G., Maxwell, A., & Forth, A. (1989). Short-term group therapy with depressed adolescent outpatients. *Canadian Journal of Psychiatry, 34,* 97–102.

Freud, S. (1961). *Civilization and its discontents* (J. Strachey, Trans.). New York: W.W. Norton. (Original work published 1930)

Henderson, D.C., & Anderson, S.C. (1989). Adolescents and chemical dependency. *Social Work in Health Care, 14*(1), 87–105.

Josselyn, I. (1987). The acting out adolescent. In L.E. Abt & S.L. Weissman (Eds.), *Acting out: Theoretical and clinical aspects* (2nd ed., pp. 68–75). Northvale, NJ: Aronson.

Kerr, M.E., & Bowen, M. (1988). *Family evaluation: An approach based on Bowen theory.* New York: W.W. Norton.

Kornblum, W., & Julian, J. (1989). *Social problems* (6th ed.). Englewood Cliffs, NJ: Prentice-Hall.

Lawson, G.W., Ellis, D.C., & Rivers, P.C. (1984). *Essentials of chemical dependency counseling.* Gaithersburg, MD: Aspen Publishers.

Levin, J.D. (1987). *Treatment of alcoholism and other addictions: A self-psychology approach.* Northvale, NJ: Aronson.

Mahler, M.S., Pine, F., & Bergman, A. (1975). *The psychological birth of the human infant.* New York: Basic Books.

Malmquist, C.P. (1985). *Handbook of adolescence.* New York: Aronson.

Papanek, E. (1987). Management of acting out adolescents. In L.E. Abt & S.L. Weissman (Eds.), *Acting out: Theoretical and clinical aspects* (2nd ed., pp. 208–232). Northvale, NJ: Aronson.

Phillips, K.L. (1989). Chemical dependence treatment review guidelines. *General Hospital Psychiatry, 11,* 282–287.

Pittman, F.S., III. (1987). *Turning points: Treating families in crisis.* New York: W.W. Norton.

Ralston, N.C., & Thomas, G.P. (1972). America's artificial adolescents. *Adolescence, 6,* 137–142.

Rasor, R.W. (1987). Drug addiction: An acting out problem. In L.E. Abt & S.L. Weissman (Eds.), *Acting out: Theoretical and clinical aspects* (2nd ed., pp. 110–118). Northvale, NJ: Aronson.

Scheidlinger, S. (1985). Group treatment of adolescents: An overview. *American Journal of Orthopsychiatry, 55*(1), 102–111.

Sieg, A. (1971). Why adolescence occurs. *Adolescence, 6*(23), 338–347.

Stanton, M. (1974). The concept of conflict at adolescence. *Adolescence, 9*(36), 537–545.

Stark, P.A., & Traxler, A.J. (1974). Empirical validation of Erikson's theory of identity crises in late adolescence. *Journal of Psychology, 86,* 25–33.

Svobodny, L.A. (1982). Biographical, self-concept and educational factors among chemically dependent adolescents. *Adolescence, 17*(68), 847–853.

Toseland, R.W., & Siporin, M. (1986). When to recommend group treatment: A review of the clinical and the research literature. *International Journal of Group Psychotherapy, 36*(2), 171–201.

Trapold, M. (1990). Adolescent chemical dependency. In S.W. Henggeler & C.M. Borduin (Eds.), *Family therapy and beyond: A multisystemic approach to treating the behavior problems of children and adolescents* (pp. 246–277). Pacific Grove, CA: Brooks/Cole.

Yalom, I.D. (1985). *The theory and practice of group psychotherapy* (3rd ed.). New York: Basic Books.

Youngs, B.B. (1986). *Helping your teenager deal with stress.* Los Angeles: Tarcher.

Zabusky, G.S., & Kymissis, P. (1983). Identity group therapy: A transitional group for hospitalized adolescents. *International Journal of Group Psychotherapy, 33*(1), 99–109.

9

Peer Counseling: Positive Peer Pressure

Joy Covert and Derek Wangberg

In the 1990s, adolescents will face a world of even greater complexity and change than in the past. This will impose even more stress on an already stressed population of youth. One of the most prevalent ways to cope with the escalating stress is the use and, for some, the abuse of alcohol and drugs.

Adolescents now begin to drink 1 year younger than did their same age peers of the 1940s and 1950s (Gorden & McCalister, 1982). The number of children under 10 years of age who drink has doubled within the last 6 years (Adams, 1985). One survey of students in grades 7 through 12 in New York state found 11% addicted to alcohol (New York State Division of Alcoholism and Alcohol Abuse, 1984). Nearly two-thirds of high school seniors had used alcohol in the previous month, and 5% drank daily. A 1985 survey indicated that 37% of high school students had drunk five or more drinks on at least one occasion during the 2 weeks prior to the survey (Johnston, O'Malley, & Bachman, 1985).

Except for nicotine and caffeine, marijuana and cocaine are the two most abused drugs. Kezel and Adams (1986) found that marijuana use was declining in the 1980s, but cocaine use has risen at a steady rate among high school seniors. Furthermore, although marijuana use peaked in 1978, it still remains enormously popular.

Because many members of society continue to condone alcohol and drug use, the behavior cannot always be considered deviant. For many adolescents, the use of drugs facilitates individuation and eventual separation from the family, thus making it possible for them to complete the rite of passage into adulthood (Mitchell, 1975). It has been suggested that a society with so few more constructive ways to transcend adolescence is open to criticism, but several studies have shown that these behaviors in moderation are not always problematic (Norem-Hebeisen & Hedin, 1981).

Many approaches have been implemented to prevent problematic substance use. For example, Alcoholics Anonymous advocates complete sobriety; Beer

Drinkers of America encourages controlled and responsible drinking. Educational methods and scare tactics have also been used. On the national level, there have been several large-scale campaigns to prevent alcohol and drug abuse. Despite such programs as *Just Say No!*, however, people are continuing to use alcohol and drugs at alarming rates.

For those who abuse alcohol and drugs, rehabilitation centers have proliferated across the United States; multidisciplinary teams, including psychiatrists, psychologists, and other mental health care professionals, usually provide a 30-day course of treatment in these centers. Medical interventions may include the administration of disulfiram (Antabuse), which makes drinkers vomit if they ingest alcohol. Behavioral programs may use aversive conditioning, which involves pairing an undesirable stimulus (e.g., a moderate shock) with the abused substance. Finally, psychotherapy and counseling have been tried to mitigate the effects of problematic substance use.

None of these interventions is a panacea. All have had only limited success, although some have been more successful than others. Most authorities agree that some form of counseling should accompany any treatment method, however. Among the many different counseling modalities is one that has shown great promise for adolescents—peer counseling.

ADVANTAGES OF PEER COUNSELING

The concept of peer counseling is not a new one (Resnik, 1979), but its application to chemical dependency is relatively recent (Norem-Hebeisen & Hedin, 1981; Oster, 1983). Peer counseling can be effective with substance-abusing adolescents for many different reasons. For example, it promotes psychological growth and maturity. Adolescents can learn to understand their own feelings, as well as the feelings of their peers, and become effective counselors. Peer counseling can be more cost-effective and can reduce the stigma associated with seeing a counselor. It can also make counseling more readily available to the adolescent population.

Peer models are almost always a part of the experience of adolescents involved in alcohol and drug use. Utech and Hoving (1969) like Curtis (1979), found that the importance of parents as a reference source tends to decrease as children grow older and that there is an increasing conformity to peers, especially regarding style of dress, appearance, choice of leisure activities, language, and use of alcohol and drugs. Furthermore, as Schwieshiemer and Walberg (1976) noted, peers may have more empathy for one another, and trained peer counselors can model behaviors more conducive to personal growth. Schaps and associates (1980) concluded that peer counseling can be an effective adjunct to other treatment modalities.

TRAINING OF PEER COUNSELORS

The selection of adolescents to become peer counselors is of paramount importance (Duncan, 1976). Students, teachers, or professional counselors may make the actual selection (McCann, 1975; Rockwell & Dustir, 1979; Varenhorst & Hamburg, 1972), and they seek individuals with a high level of maturity and motivation.

In general, a typical curriculum for peer counselors training includes an initial assessment of the adolescent's problem-solving skills, empathy, genuineness, immediacy, and unconditional positive regard. Closely supervised by a professional counselor, the adolescents selected as peer counselors learn basic counseling skills through didactic techniques, role playing, and modeling by the trainer (Cocker & Churchia, 1976). For example, a 9-week training program developed by Oster (1983) emphasized problem-solving skills, such as identifying the problem, exploring alternative solutions, selecting and implementing a solution, and evaluating the result.

PEER COUNSELING EVALUATIONS

The effectiveness of peer counseling has been evaluated in several ways. Dowell (1971) used a 5-point Likert scale to rate peer counselors on degree of empathy, genuineness, and immediacy. Varenhorst and Hamburg (1972) obtained subjective reports from counselors and counselees, and Oster (1983) used multiple choice pre-test and post-test questionnaires as part of his evaluation procedure. Unfortunately, however, there have been few peer counseling studies with solid research designs. Most studies rely on subjective measures taken over short periods of time, and many have even lacked a control group.

The results of the peer counseling studies that have been done are equivocal. Schwieshiemer and Walberg (1976) found that counselees had improved significantly over the controls in attendance at school and decisiveness, but their results did not show the ameliorative effects of peer counseling conclusively. Self-reports have indicated that peer counseling was successful in academic, personal, and social areas (Varenhorst & Hamburg, 1972). In an evaluation of the effects of peer counseling on the counselees, Vriend (1969) found that those in the experimental group had improved significantly in academics.

Cocker and Churchia (1976) indicated that the communication skills of trained high school students are significantly better than are those of untrained students. Oster (1983) noted that, although neither peer counselors nor members of a control group reported a significant change in their own alcohol usage as a consequence of peer counseling training, there was a "spread of effect" that positively affected the counselor, the counselee, and ultimately, the counselee's family.

In a review of 127 treatment strategies for alcohol and drug abuse, Schaps and associates (1980) found the common denominator of the most successful programs to be that they were multifaceted and often included peer counseling. More longitudinal studies with adequate control groups are necessary, however, to determine if peer counseling should be an integral part of primary prevention strategies. In addition, more comprehensive evaluations should be built into the peer counseling programs.

MODEL PEER COUNSELING PROGRAM

There are a number of areas to be addressed when designing and implementing an adolescent peer counseling program. The first step is to conduct a needs assessment of the student body to identify the student groups that the program should target and to determine the best way to use the peer counselors so that they will have the maximum effect on the target groups. This will also assist in integrating the newly identified needs with any existing programs and services.

The selection of students to be peer counselors is critical. The peer counseling group is much more effective if it is diverse in backgrounds, nationalities, interests, and personalities—consistent with the student population. There should be minimum requirements, such as a two-semester commitment, required courses, and a minimum grade point average, for peer counselors. Because it is important to learn as much as possible about the students selected, teachers, a guidance counselor, or a vice principal may help in the selection. To attract enthusiastic, committed students, it is useful to market the program as an opportunity to help others, as a learning experience for themselves, as a way to impress colleges and potential employers, and as a great deal of fun. Most students will participate in a peer counseling program for vocational development, academic credit, and personal reasons. Students also want something in return for their service and hard work, however.

Appropriate training and supervision are essential for a successful program. Training should cover at least self-awareness; prevention models and methods; addiction models; communication and listening skills; counseling and intervention skills; presentation and facilitation skills; peer counselor responsibilities, requirements, and limitations; confidentiality; campus and community resource and referral lists; and campus policies and procedures. Program coordinators should meet regularly with peer counselors, both as a group and individually, for ongoing training and supervision. Discussions of student interaction and role playing, successes and difficulties, plans for educational presentations, continued self-awareness, retraining as needed, resources, weekly business, contact sheets, and other paperwork are all part of the supervisory process.

Once the program has been designed and the peer counselors trained, the program should be marketed to the other students and faculty. Displays, posters, fliers, advertisements in the school newspaper, letters to faculty, and presentations to classes and clubs make the program highly visible. It is most important to ensure that students know where the peer counselors are and how to contact them.

Evaluation not only contributes to the success of a peer counseling program, but also helps to obtain funding and keep the administration committed to the project. Evaluation can be done through pre- and post-tests; statistics from the contact sheets and peer counselor time cards; and feedback from peer counselors, from students served, and from the administration.

Background

A peer counseling program was developed and implemented at Monte Vista High School in Spring Valley, California, because many students were going to the school counselors with problems and these counselors lacked the time to attend to the problems. It took 4 years to develop and implement a comprehensive, diverse program.

The first steps taken were to identify a teacher with a counseling background and the willingness to take on such a project and then to find funding. It just so happened that San Diego County Drug Services was offering a grant for a consultant to train peer counselors 1 day each week in several of the county high schools. Drug Services also provided a training manual that covered information on addictions, alcohol, and other drugs; basic problem-solving skills; basic decision-making skills; and basic listening skills. Guest speakers were invited to talk on a variety of subjects, such as issues of counseling adolescents as a profession, alcoholism in the family, and adult children of alcoholics.

Some students signed up for the class, called Peer Counseling I. Others were recommended by teachers and the school counselors. The students were interviewed and their guidance counselor consulted. The peer counseling teacher made the final decisions about who could be in the class. The class met every day, and the students received credit.

In the second semester, while another group of students were in Peer Counseling I, the previously trained peer counselors were placed in classes of high-risk students, mostly first-year students and transfers, who had been identified as unsuccessful in academics. These high-risk students had a study skills class once each day to improve their skills and to facilitate their transfer to the mainstream of classes. There were two peer counselors for each study skills class, and the teacher assigned them tasks. A consultant was hired to spend one full day at school each week and to meet with the peer counselors assigned to the high-risk classes each period for supervision and ongoing training. This format proved to be very disconnecting, however. The peer counselors never met as a full group, the consultant had to teach the same lesson six times to very small groups, and the peer counselors were complaining that the teachers in the high-risk classes were using them as teacher's aides, not as peer counselors. At the end of the semester, a new peer counselor training format was adopted.

New Program

In the new program, the Peer Counseling I class stood as it was, but a Peer Counseling II class was created. Like the first class, the second class met every day, and students received regular credit. Students were required to take Peer Counseling I before they could apply for Peer Counseling II. The teachers screened the applicants and decided on the class participants. In Peer Counseling II, students expanded their information base, honed all their listening skills, learned basic counseling skills and techniques, wrote papers, took midterm and final examinations, were on committees (e.g., publicity, training, presentations), kept client records, made classroom presentations on various topics, did a community project that required at least 10 hours of volunteer time in a community social service agency, participated in the state peer counseling conference, and saw clients before school, during lunch, and after school.

One drawback of the previous program had been that, if a student could not fit Peer Counseling II in his or her schedule, the skills that had been learned in the first class were unused, and contact was lost. To rectify this, a peer counseling club was formed. Its members were previously trained peer counselors, peer counselors presently in classes, and students who were interested in becoming peer counselors. The club planned special events and networked with the peer counseling class.

In the new program, a peer counselor showed each student around the school. This established a time for the peer counselors to talk about their services and to make contact with those who might need help in adjusting to the school. Two follow-up contacts were made throughout the year. In addition, during the first 2 weeks of a semester, the peer counselors were assigned to the guidance counselors on a rotating basis to help the new students. During the rest of the semester, guidance counselors could request assistance, and a peer counselor would be assigned.

Each peer counselor was assigned one or two of the high-risk students and met with them three times a week to increase their skills, to motivate them about school, and to try to increase their attendance. The meetings usually took place before school or at lunch. The peer counselor and the student created an individual contract that highlighted goals and objectives to be reached daily and weekly.

Training Curriculum for Peer Counselors

Among the topics that were covered in the peer counselor training program were

- sociological issues
- psychological issues
- physiological issues
- effects of alcohol and other drugs, with some information on psychopharmacology
- legal and ethical issues
- treatment methods and modalities
- special problems
- communication skills
- facilitation skills
- decision-making skills
- crisis intervention skills
- attending and active listening skills
- values clarification
- feedback skills
- working with grief
- working with appropriate self-disclosure
- confrontation skills
- components for change (e.g., identifying options and projecting consequences, realistic expectations, utilization of support systems)

Since the peer counseling program was a daily class, it was initially divided into segments. Each day had a primary purpose, although the schedule was sometimes changed if there was a special event or if a topic needed more work. One day or two were for role playing, because this activity honed all the skills that were taught in the peer counseling classes. Another day was for teaching training skills, and one day was to integrate the two classes through team teaching by the two peer counseling teachers.

One day was specifically for the self-growth of the peer counselors (although almost anything that was done in class or with clients motivated self-growth). To aid in the self-growth process, some of the following questions were addressed in the training program:

- What is unique about peer counseling and peer counselors?
- Who is responsible for change, the counselor or the client?

- What happens in a counseling relationship to cause change?
- If change is to be made, who decides what those changes are?
- Can a peer counselor cause the client to change in a negative way?
- How is rapport established with a client?
- How does a peer counselor prevent the client from becoming dependent or him or her?
- How does a peer counselor know what modality to use when counseling?
- What are the differences between counseling a self-referred client and a client who is sent to counseling?
- Can a peer counselor teach a client to see all options or to solve problems? How?
- Can effective decision making be taught to clients?
- How does a peer counselor separate his or her own issues from those of the clients?
- What are the goals of counseling, and who decides what those goals are?
- What kind of special training does a peer counselor need?
- How does a peer counselor know when a client needs to be referred to someone else or to another agency?
- How are those referrals initiated and followed?
- What important paraprofessional issues (e.g., burnout, paraprofessional enabling, ethics, law) should be considered?

Occasionally, guest speakers discussed special topics, such as eating disorders, sexual abuse, and ethical issues. Care was always taken to follow school regulations regarding material presented to students. For example, when a guest speaker was asked to talk on sexual abuse, a letter was sent to the parents of all the students to get permission for the students to attend the session. If a parent refused permission, the student was assigned to another class for that period of time.

All in all, creating or developing, implementing, and evaluating a peer counseling program is a challenge. It is a rewarding challenge, but it is also a good deal of work. In the process, there is an enormous amount of self-growth, both for the peer counselors and for the teachers.

REFERENCES

Adams, R. (1985). *Drug usage prevalence questionnaire*. Atlanta: Pride—Parents Resource Institute for Drug Education.

Cocker, P.G., & Churchia, P.G. (1976). Effects of communication skills training on high school students' ability to function as peer group facilitators. *Journal of Counseling Psychology, 23*(5), 464–467.

Curtis, R.C. (1979). Parents and peers: Serendipity in a study of shifting reference sources. *Social Forces, 52*(3), 368–375.

Dowell, R.C. (1971). *Adolescents as peer counselors: A program of psychological growth.* Unpublished manuscript, Harvard University, School of Education, Cambridge, MA.

Duncan, J.A. (1976). Ethical consideration in peer group work. *Elementary School Guidance and Counseling, 11,* 59–61.

Gorden, N.P., & McCalister, G. (1982). Adolescent drinking: Issues and research. In T.J. Coates (Ed.), *Promoting adolescent health* (pp. 201, 203, 210). New York: Academic Press.

Johnston, L.D., O'Malley, P.M., & Bachman, J.G. (1985). *Use of licit and illicit drugs by America's high school students, 1975–1985* (DHHS Publication No. ADM 85-L394). Washington, DC: U.S. Government Printing Office.

Kezel, N.J., & Adams, E.H. (1986, November 21). *Science,* pp. 970–974.

McCann, B.G. (1975). Peer counseling: An approach to psychological education. *Elementary School Guidance and Counseling, 9*(3), 180–187.

Mitchell, J.J. (1975). *The adolescent predicament.* Toronto: Holt, Rhinehart, Winston of Canada.

New York State Division of Alcoholism and Alcohol Abuse. (1984). *Alcohol abuse among secondary students in New York State.* Buffalo: New York Research Institute on Alcoholism.

Norem-Hebeisen, A., & Hedin, D.P. (1981). Influences on adolescent problem behavior: Causes, connections, contexts (DHHS Publication No. 6 ADM). Washington, DC: U.S. Government Printing Office.

Oster, R.A. (1983). Peer counseling: Drug and alcohol abuse prevention. *Journal of Primary Prevention, 3*(3).

Resnik, H.S. (1979). It starts with people: Experiences in drug abuse prevention (DHEW Publication No. 79-590). Rockville, MD:

Rockwell, L.K., & Dustir, R. (1979). Building a model for training peer counselors. *School Counselor, 26*(5), 311–316.

Schaps, E. (1980). *A review of 127 drug abuse prevention program evaluations.* Lafayette, CA: Pacific Institute for Research Evaluation.

Schwieshiemer, W., & Walberg, H.J. (1976). A peer counseling experiment: High school students as small group leaders. *Journal of Counseling Psychology, 23*(4), 398-401.

Varenhorst, B., & Hamburg, B. (1972). Peer counseling in the secondary schools: A community mental health project for youth. *American Journal of Orthopsychiatry, 42,* 566–581.

Vriend, T.J. (1969). High performing inner city adolescents assist low performing peers in counseling groups. *Personnel and Guidance Journal, 47*(9), 897–904.

10

Hanging On for Dear Life: Family Treatment of Adolescent Substance Abuse

David C. Treadway

The mother in my office was distraught. Her 13-year-old son had run away three nights earlier, after she had confronted him about the marijuana that she had found in his room. In therapy I had been encouraging her to take a tougher stance with the boy. When she had grounded him for the upcoming weekend, he had just turned on his heels and walked out of the house. She had called all of his friends' mothers, but no one had seen him. She had driven around town for hours looking for him, but to no avail. Each morning she checked at the school to see if he had come in. They had not seen him. She called the police; they had not been able to find him either. She even called her ex-husband who lived out of state. He responded by blaming her for ruining his son. She felt helpless, scared, and alone. She kept coming back to the question of where the boy had found a place to sleep. At one point she said to me, "You know, sometimes when I have to wake him up in the morning, I just stand there and watch him sleep. His face looks so soft and young. I look at him and he's still my little boy."

Before I had children, I was pretty good in these situations. I would encourage the mother to hang in there, reassure her that the boy was probably all right, and tell her that it would be good for him to find out how tough it might be out on the streets. The answers came easily to me back then.

My son turns 11 this year. Sometimes, when he is angry, his face takes on a cold, hard look. He looks like a stranger to me. Sometimes he tells me that he can't stand our home and that he wants to be free and to live on his own. A cold fear stirs inside me. I can imagine driving the streets late at night, looking. I can imagine the round of phone calls and the sitting around. I can imagine the waiting. Sometimes I find myself watching my son while he is sleeping.

Source: "Hanging on for Dear Life: Family Treatment of Adolescent Substance Abuse" is reprinted from *Before It's Too Late: Working with Substance Abuse in the Family* by David C. Treadway, Ph.D., by permission of the author and W.W. Norton & Company, Inc. Copyright 1989 by David C. Treadway.

The answers don't come so easily anymore.

*   *   *   *   *

Working with adolescent substance abusers scares me. By the time these children are in serious trouble with chemicals, the family, the school, and the community have often lost a significant degree of control over them. Their own self-destructive impulses have taken over. It was right for the mother to confront her child about the pot, but the risk was real. The streets are not safe for a 13-year-old.

For me the hardest part of working with adolescents is that, when it comes to a confrontation over control, many kids are willing to die in order to win. Adolescents are able to intimidate adults because they will go to such extremes in order to resist being controlled. Kids always have the power to hurt themselves. When a four-year-old angrily declares that he hates his mother and is going to live at his friend's house, his mother will shake her head and make the child get dressed anyway. When a 16-year-old says that if he can't go out on Saturday night he's going to run away from home and live on the streets, his mother and his father are quite likely to be immobilized by fear. Parents frequently need to be more assertive with their children, but it is profoundly hard to do when their adolescent has shown a reckless disregard for his or her own safety.

Parents do not really have much power, and neither do therapists. Work with out-of-control adolescents can feel like driving a huge tractor trailer that has lost its brakes and is careening down the mountainside. You can't stop the truck. Somehow you have to either run into a snowbank or steer it all the way down to safety. It's really a matter of hanging on for dear life.

There are several key elements that make working with adolescent substance abuse especially difficult:

1. Since abusing chemicals is a rite of passage for most adolescents in our culture, it is sometimes difficult to distinguish between the adolescents who are going through the normal developmental stage of learning how to handle chemicals through experimentation and the adolescents who are in serious trouble. Yet, it is clear that many adolescents have real problems with handling chemicals right from the start. This is particularly true for children who are growing up in dysfunctional families. For many of these teenagers, who have a considerable amount of chronic anxiety, low self-esteem, and residual anger, the discovery of drugs and alcohol may be overwhelmingly powerful. The chemical magically brings them relief from anxiety, an enhanced feeling of self-worth, and often much greater ease in their relationships with their peers. For these children, normal experimentation can lead quite quickly to a pattern of abuse and then addiction. Yet, it is hard to distinguish between the kids whose abuse of drugs and alcohol is

simply a part of adolescent acting-out behavior and those who really are drug-dependent almost immediately.

2. Adolescents are quite resistant to treatment and are rarely candid about their use of chemicals with either their families or therapist. Thus, serious substance abuse can go unrecognized while the family and the therapist attempt to deal with poor grades, a surly attitude, and breaking curfew. When the therapist does attempt to confront the possibility of substance abuse in the adolescent, it may lead to the adolescent's escalating his/her defiance into a real crisis, which may include running away from home, threats of suicide, or a refusal to obey any rules.

3. Once teenagers do acknowledge their dependency and seek to change, there is often little support or understanding within their peer groups. This is particularly true for kids who are trying to be completely abstinent. Adolescents who may desperately need a support group in order to stay sober feel like outcasts when they reenter their school and home environment after treatment. Having built their social life around their use of chemicals, they have difficulty relating to their peers straight. For adults, AA and Al-Anon groups are so widespread that almost everyone can find a group that feels comfortable. Unfortunately, there are simply fewer self-help groups for kids.

FAMILY PATTERNS

By the time parents and adolescents arrive in my office, the parents have usually lost control of the child. The parents may have been too permissive and allowed the child too much freedom, or they may have been excessively rigid and controlling. Most frequently, the parents are split between permissive and rigid positions and thus provide an inconsistent and incoherent point of view to the child. Whatever particular positions the parents have taken, they are usually helplessly flailing at their surly, unresponsive adolescent and blaming each other for the problem.

When adolescents have too much freedom, they feel internally unsafe and abandoned. Thus, the escalation of acting-out behavior can be seen as an attempt by the adolescent to engage the parents and to force them to exercise some control and authority. It is developmentally normal for adolescents to learn how to define their own identity through the process of struggle with their parents and other authority figures. When the responses of the adult world are excessively rigid, permissive, or inconsistent, adolescents tend to become more out of control, as they anxiously seek both their sense of independence and the feeling of protection that comes from external limits set by caring adults.

During this invariably difficult time for developing adolescents, the family itself is undergoing significant stress and transition as it enters the leaving-home stage of the family life cycle. The parents have to allow their children progressively more autonomy. In addition, the parents have to renegotiate their lives with each other as they make the transition from being primarily a parenting team to being a couple. They may experience considerable unacknowledged anxiety about the prospects of facing their relationship after the children leave home. On an individual level, the mother may be putting more effort into her career, while the father is simultaneously arriving at his own mid-life crisis and coming to terms with the limits of his career and questions about his own future. Finally, adolescents themselves have to resolve their struggle between needs to be separate and unresolved dependency. A crisis with an adolescent has the effect of distracting the family from all these normal developmental processes and in that respect may protect family members from the stress of facing these transitions.

I remember a very striking case in which three family members (a father, stepmother, and son) came for treatment. The presenting problem was the son's heroin addiction. The family was in a rigid pattern of conflict, with the father caught between the son and the stepmother. The most salient aspect of the case was that the father was 80, the stepmother was 75, and the son was 49. The family had simply never been able to go through the normal developmental process of having the child successfully leave home. The family was in a tableau like the couple on Keats' Grecian urn, always chasing and never changing. The symptom allowed the family to maintain the old status quo while going through time. Not surprisingly, treatment, which had also become part of the family's pattern, was unsuccessful. In a five-year follow-up study, we learned that the father had died and the son had given up heroin. The urn had finally broken.

There is invariably tension between the adults attempting to manage an out-of-control teenager. Some adults will be sponsoring more support, understanding, and freedom for the child; others will be arguing that the child needs firmness, limits, and confrontation. The adults often actively undermine each other and this further empowers the child in the struggle. These splits between the adults appear in many different patterns. The husband and wife may be detouring their marital issues by focusing on the child. In a single-parent family the mother and child may be reenacting the unresolved struggle between the divorced parents. In other families, the child may be a scapegoat who unites the family. Sometimes the split is between the family on one side and the school or courts on the other.

The common thread in each of these patterns is that there is significant disagreement among the adults about how to manage the adolescent. They split on the age-old debate between firmness/discipline and nurturance/understanding. Clearly, both elements are essential to growth. What frequently happens is that the adults involved become polarized, with each side pushing its position harder in an attempt to counterbalance the other. Thus, firmness becomes punitive and nurturance becomes enabling.

SIX-STAGE TREATMENT MODEL

Stage 1: Engage the Whole System

The first step is to engage the family in the therapy. I emphasize to parents that they are the ones who can most directly help their child in trouble and that my role is to facilitate their working with their adolescent more effectively. Almost always I have to counter the parents' response: "We've tried everything. You're the doctor. We want you to make him better." People often feel the need to remind me that I am "the expert." I usually accept that designation and use it to reinforce my efforts to get the family involved right from the beginning of treatment.

Engaging the whole system means doing considerable leg work to make contact and build working alliances with other professionals working with the family. Since a very high proportion of adolescent substance abuse cases involves active splitting among the adults as to how to respond to the teenager, it is essential that I enter the case not on one side or the other but as someone who can help the various sides resolve their disagreements. For example, when a school refers an adolescent and the family does not feel that there is a problem, I establish my role with the school and the family as a potential negotiator. I don't represent the school's position to the family because that will usually stiffen the family's resistance to treatment. By the same token, I don't simply join the family by scapegoating the school. In order to establish my role as "honest broker," I show equal respect for both sides.

Careful networking to engage the other professionals can also be beneficial in providing leverage. Often the other professionals (school and counselor, probation officer, department of social services worker, etc.) have the clout to put external pressure on either the adolescent or the parents, if that becomes necessary. When other professionals are treated with respect as colleagues, they are often willing to collaborate on these cases and to play the role of the "heavy." This variation on the "good cop/bad cop" games allows me to be tough with the family without risking my alliance with them. In one case, the most critical interview in the whole course of treatment took place when the probation officer came to a therapy meeting and described in vivid detail what it would be like for the boy to be in a youth detention center. The family's level of cooperation rose dramatically after that session.

Stage 2: Assessment

The key question in assessing and treating adolescents' substance abuse is: When do you treat the acting-out behavior as the main issue and when do you treat the chemical dependency as the central problem? This is particularly difficult when there is little clear-cut evidence of the degree of dependency. Here I use the same basic approach that I use in treating adults, which is to remain very vigilant to the possibility of chemical dependency while initially treating the presenting problems. The treatment itself becomes a diagnostic process. Adolescents who are using substances as part of the whole gamut of rebellious behavior will tend to be responsive to effective family therapy, but teenagers who are really "hooked" on drugs will generally be unable to respond to the family treatment. This failure to respond leads to the exposure of the drug problem in much the same way as the disengagement stage in couples treatment often leads to a confrontation of the hidden alcoholism. Using the treatment process itself as a diagnostic tool enables one to avoid the typical "cops and robbers" game, in which the parents make accusations about their kids' drug use that they cannot prove and thus set up endless rounds of recriminations and denial.

Rarely do families initially seek treatment because of an adolescent's problems with chemicals. More frequently the presenting problem is related to the child's performance at school or rebellious behavior at home. The parents are usually locked in a hopeless power struggle with the child, in which every position they take is quickly countered by escalating defiance. We first need to consider whether there is a substance abuse problem at all. Since kids generally do not volunteer this information in sessions, I am constantly on the alert for signs of a potential problem. The following are some habits and behaviors that strongly indicate potential substance abuse:

1. significant deterioration of school performance
2. change of peer group and unwillingness to have friends meet parents
3. significant swings in mood
4. unwillingness to accept authority and limits, e.g., curfews and other responsibilities
5. major disturbances in sleep patterns and eating patterns
6. loss of interest and involvement in previously valued activities, such as athletics, hobbies, and church groups
7. an excess amount of unaccounted for money or possessions
8. an excessive need for money
9. withdrawal from participation in family life

Whenever I hear parents report a cluster of these behaviors, I consider substance abuse as a potential underlying catalyst for many of the adolescent's difficulties. Chemical dependency should also be kept in mind when assessing teenagers' resistance to therapy and difficulty changing their behavior. Adolescents are even less likely than adults to be able to manage their need for chemicals. The therapist should consider a teenager's inability to respond to therapy as an indicator that he/she is already too dependent on chemicals.

As in the case of hidden adult substance abuse, the adolescent's abuse is usually not out in the open. I begin by joining the family around immediate concerns. The primary task of the first session is to address the presenting problems. However, as part of the early joining I do ask circular questions about family members' feelings, philosophies, and behavior around substance use issues:

- Which member of the family worries about drugs the most?
- Which child is most likely to be drawn to chemicals and why?
- Which of your parents is most likely to understand why kids lie about their use of drugs?
- Which of your children would have the hardest time confiding in you if he or she were in trouble with chemicals?
- What are the most effective ways that parents deal with kids who abuse drugs? What are the least effective ways?
- What are the ways that kids learn how to manage their own experimentation with drugs and booze?
- (To the kids) What is the best way to help a friend who is in serious trouble with drugs and booze?
- (To the parents) How did your parents manage this issue? What was helpful and what was not helpful?

These questions are not simply thrown at the family; rather, they are worked into the general questions about how the family works asked at the beginning of the first couple interviews. The questions usually allow the subject of adolescent substance abuse to be brought up and discussed without threatening or accusing anyone. When the parents do begin to accuse the identified patient, I steer the conversation in another direction. How family members respond to these questions usually provides me with a strong sense of how much covert substance abuse is going on in the system, even through they have not been asked directly about their own patterns of use. The clue may be a giggle between siblings, a slight shake of the head, a description of a friend's problem, or an evasive answer. What is most important for me is not the exact amount of substance abuse but rather the fact of possible covert abuse and the family's repertoire of ideas about how to address it.

In addition to opening up the topic of drug and alcohol use in a general way, I normalize adolescents' experimentation with chemicals and their dishonesty with parents and therapists about such experimentation. Rather than getting caught in a game of "Miami Vice," in which the parents try to get the "goods" on the teenager, I encourage them to focus on observable behavior and whether or not the child is making any progress on that front. I review with the parents and the adolescents the behavioral indicators of substance abuse outlined earlier. Just as with a controlled drinking contract, I set up the therapy as a potential test of whether the adolescent is out of control with chemicals. I explain to the parents that genuine progress in the therapy may indicate that the child is managing his/her covert experimentation with chemicals responsibly and that a lack of progress or cooperation in the therapy may signify that there is a much bigger problem with substance abuse than anyone in the family suspects.

This benign double bind, which naturally infuriates adolescents, sends a strong message that, if they do not cooperate with their parents, their use of chemicals will come under much greater scrutiny. It also sets up in advance the possible shift from treating the child as simply an acting-out adolescent who needs limits to thinking of him as a drug-dependent child who is out of control and needs to be treated as "sick" rather than "bad." Frequently, when the limit-setting confrontational approach does not work, it is because the adolescent cannot control his need for chemicals and thus is unable to respond to the treatment.

Stage 3: Empower the Parents

Since parents usually enter therapy only when they have already lost effective control of their adolescent, our task is to empower them so that they can respond more effectively to their teenager. The initial strategies involve having the parents stop flailing at the adolescent in a way that perpetuates their sense of helplessness and inadequacy. Empowering parents means helping them take charge of their own responses and become less reactive to the adolescent.

This process begins with the conduct of the interview and the therapist's way of responding to the struggle between the parents and the adolescent in the room. I invariably make an alliance with the parents around the difficulties of managing their children rather than maintaining a neutral and evenhanded position. Although I truly enjoy kids, including thoroughly obnoxious, mouthy adolescents, I do not undercut the parents by making an alliance with the children, particularly at the parents' expense. Invariably, this means that parents feel supported by me and kids feel that therapy is some form of punishment initially.

In one first interview with a mother and her adolescent son, the boy reviled the woman in extremely vulgar language. She sat motionless, like a frightened child being berated by an abusive parent. Being a very astute clinician, I sensed a possible problem in the hierarchy. When I encouraged the mother to confront the boy, he simply became louder and more abusive and turned some of his abuse toward me. I was in a dilemma. If I confronted him successfully, then I would have saved the mother, but I also would have disempowered her even further. If I didn't confront the boy, then I would essentially be taking the same helpless position that she was taking. Finally, I said to her, "It is really helpful to me that you are letting your son demonstrate how angry and rude he is. If you had insisted on his behaving better in our meeting today I never would have had such a clear sense of how difficult he must be to manage at home. Would you like to continue to let him berate you for the rest of the hour, or would you like to simply excuse him from the room if he can't keep from swearing at you?"

Reframing her behavior in this way did not create a dramatic shift in the hierarchy. It was only the beginning of her learning that she had a choice. She told her son to leave the room.

There are many ways for therapists to empower the parents in the room. It is useful to talk to parents first and encourage them not to allow interruptions by obstreperous children. The parents should decide whether it is better for them to talk with unresponsive teenagers or ignore them when they will not participate. I point out that it is not their responsibility to make the child talk in the session. I also prepare parents for the possibility that the teenager might bolt from the room if the session gets to difficult. I encourage them not to be overly concerned if this happens; it simply means that the adolescent was unable to communicate in any other way that he was feeling too much pressure. Since I began giving this message to parents, fewer adolescents have found it necessary to precipitously leave the room.

Despite this focus on allying with the parents, it is important to make therapy a safe place for the kids also. I make sure that they have opportunities to present their points of view about how the family works and to voice their complaints about their parents. It often helps to put kids at ease by telling them that it is normal and appropriate for them to maintain a sense of privacy about themselves and that it is okay if they do not want to be totally open with their parents, siblings, and me. When an adolescent won't talk at all in the session, I tell parents that they should not attempt to force him to talk; rather, they should just accept that, although he may not be ready to express himself, he can't help listening.

The primary difficulty in empowering the parents is resolving the split between them about how to manage the children in the first place. Since the struggle over the adolescent is often a metaphor for other unresolved issues between the spouses, it may be difficult for them to formulate a united plan of action. Patiently helping the couple negotiate and struggle over how best to respond to the child is essential. It is important to keep the identified patient in the negotiating process, since the experience of watching the parents learn how to work together allows him/her to begin to give up the role of protective lightning rod.

I also keep the siblings involved because building some bridges among the siblings in the system allows me to broaden the problems from simply the difficulties of this "bad" child to less toxic general parenting issues with all the children. In one part of the room parents may be involved in negotiating a new set of rules, while in another part the siblings are working on what they as a group would like to see changed in the family. The parents may take some time to work out a particular position vis-à-vis the child in trouble; then one of them will be selected to negotiate the new parental position with the child. When the parent gets into a snag with the kid, I encourage both parents to go back to their discussion and work on their response to the teenager's objection. Whether the parents are able to struggle through to a consensus or end up agreeing to disagree is less important than the process of their confronting each other directly and learning how to negotiate. I normalize disagreements and encourage the parents to accept the value of their having different perceptions and solutions. I help the parents practice taking turns being in charge, presenting a united front, and even working independently.

At this stage, however, I am careful to keep the focus of the negotiation on parenting rather than allowing them to open up marital conflicts. If the parents begin to expose their marital fights, the adolescent is likely to act out again in a distracting and protective manner. I almost always keep the kids in the room and engaged in the process, because then it is much easier to keep the parents focused on parenting.

When there is only one parent involved, I help the parent lay out her agenda for the session and then direct her to engage the child. When the parent gets caught in a struggle, I help her sort out the range of possible responses. I work only minimally with the kids. If I engage the kids too much, then I inevitably slip into the role of the missing parent; that often disempowers the single parent even further. I also engage the other parent in the treatment by contacting him and, whenever possible, having him come to sessions with the adolescents. This brings into focus the unresolved issues with the distant parent.

In terms of confronting the teenager's behavior, I direct the parents to work at setting limits only on the behaviors over which they have the possibility of exercising some control. For example, a rule that a child cannot smoke pot is impossible to enforce. However, a rule that says a child who gets caught smoking pot will not be allowed to use the family car is within the parent's power to enact. This is a particular problem when the child's attitude is a source of contention. It is virtually impossible to legislate a positive attitude, and yet parents will be drawn to confrontation over their teenager's surliness like moths to a flame. I tell parents that a negative attitude is worn by many kids like a fig leaf. It protects them from feeling too exposed. It protects their pride. The message to the parents is, "Focus on the behavior and don't get hooked on the attitude. There's no crime in your son's not feeling like doing what he has to do as long as he is doing it."

The key to effective empowerment is to have the parents set reasonable limits with practical consequences and avoid empty threats. The rules and consequences need to be adjusted to the age of the adolescent; also, at different ages the parents will have different forms of leverage. There are several elements that help parents develop effective limits and consequences:

1. Involve adolescents in creating rules and consequences through the use of family meetings and contracts. Adolescents should be encouraged to make specific suggestions about how the parents might also work on their own behavior, so that the contracts are mutual rather than unilateral. Contracts that adolescents feel are fair are much easier to enforce than parental orders.

2. Negotiate limits and consequences that are in line with the community standards for adolescents. It is very difficult for teenagers, who are so oriented toward peer relationships, to handle rules and punishments that are either significantly more permissive or significantly more restrictive than the community norms. Whenever possible, work with other parents in the community to develop standards of behavior.

3. Although it is useful for the parents to be flexible in creating the contract, once it is agreed upon they should be rigid in enforcing it. Contracts should be kept to the letter for an agreed length of time; then they can be renegotiated. Adolescents usually want to change the contract the minute they get caught breaking one of its provisions.

4. Choose consequences that can be applied without expressing a lot of critical or angry feelings. Parents frequently betray their sense of helplessness by resorting to angry outbursts. These tend to be harshly judgmental and much more punitive than a consequence administered without rancor.

5. Apply limits consistently and do not be manipulated into modifying the terms of punishment. A relatively short-term punishment carried out to the letter is much more effective than a long-term punishment from which the parents ultimately retreat because they feel guilty about the harshness.

6. Regularly adjust the contract and parental expectations to reflect adolescents' constant state of change and increased autonomy.

7. With adolescents 17 and older, parents need to stop trying to control and direct the adolescent and to learn how to negotiate with the child as an adult. At this age, parents cannot legislate behavior; however, they can decide what they will and will not support. They cannot order a child to go to school, come in at a certain time, or abstain from drugs, but they can withhold financial support, forbid him from living at home, or insist that he pay room and board. The message to the child is that with adult freedom comes adult responsibility.

8. Parents need to be reminded that it is normal and appropriate for kids to struggle with their parents. Adolescents develop their own identity and

sense of autonomy through their conflicts with the adult world. Parents' willingness to struggle is itself more important than winning or losing.

9. Finally, parents need to be reminded that adolescence is not a terminal disease and that most kids grow up in spite of themselves. Parents also need to be reminded that they are human, make mistakes, routinely forget all the good advice listed above, and are simply "holding on for dear life."

Frequently, parents are too disempowered to effectively set any limits, I encourage them simply to stop fighting so many losing battles with their kids. The parents need to gain control over their helpless reactivity to the child's rebellious behavior. I want them to take charge of their not being in charge. I often ask them to write a letter that basically acknowledges their powerlessness. The following is a letter written to one 16-year-old boy by his parents.

Dear Daniel,

It must be obvious to you that we have been completely unable to get you to accept our rules and authority as your parents. At this point, we feel that we simply cannot control you or protect you from continuing on a very self-destructive course.

We strongly believe that you are using drugs frequently. You have been skipping school and coming and going as you please. When we tell you that you have to be home at a certain time, you just ignore us, and when we attempt to ground you, you just walk out and go to a friend's house to stay for a couple of days.

Daniel, we are scared for you. We feel that you are doing things that are dangerous and we cannot stop you right now. We love you. We wish we could protect you. We're going to work hard to learn how to reach you and help you get some control over yourself. But for now we're going to stop fighting with you all the time. It is not good for you or for us for there to be constant fighting about your behavior.

At this point you are basically a man. You have the power to wreck your life if you choose, but we will not give up trying to find a way to help you.

Love,

Mom and Dad

A letter such as this is not the answer, but at least it is a step toward helping "the tail stop wagging the dog."

Whenever possible in this stage of empowering parents, I encourage them to seek out support groups like Tough Love or Al-Anon in order to feel less isolated and overwhelmed by their problems with their adolescents. Too frequently these families live in complete isolation, and the parents feel too ashamed of their failings with their children to reach out to friends or relatives for support. Joining a group of other parents who are struggling with the same issues often brings a strong sense of relief to clients who suffer from the fear that they are all alone. I also tend to be quite open about my own concerns and frustrations about parenting, as another way of helping parents with their isolation and their shame.

The two key elements for empowering parents are for the therapist (1) to communicate to the parents that they represent the core of the solution rather than the cause of the problem and (2) to help them learn how to pick their battles carefully. Parents cannot truly control adolescents, but they can learn how not to be controlled by them.

Stage 4: The Crisis of Change

When the parents become a more effective and empowered team, a significant family crisis invariably results. Adolescents are similar to toddlers in their need to test limits strenuously before they accept them. This is particularly true when parents have changed their behavior as a result of therapy. The adolescent needs to challenge the change in order to find out if the parents are really committed to it and willing to follow though. It will not be enough for parents to set limits with strong consequences. Invariably, adolescents will break the limit and attempt to avoid the consequence. Parents must be carefully prepared for this eventuality and have a series of alternatives in anticipation of the teenager's resistance. I find myself posing questions such as, "If he decides to test you by breaking curfew and when you ground him for a weekend he doesn't show up after school on Friday, then what are you going to do?"

Adolescents will test their parents' resolve either flagrantly disobeying the rule and seeing if the parents have the will to impose the maximum consequence or by skillfully finding a little loophole in the rule and exploiting it. In the latter case the parents are left with the dilemma of choosing between imposing the consequence "unfairly" or backing off and acknowledging that the child was successful in finding a legitimate loophole. Some teenagers are able to see that contracts can be used to reduce parental control and scrutiny if the adolescent simply insists that the terms of the contract be taken literally.

It is at this point of crisis that the adolescent's level of dependency on chemicals becomes more clearly defined. As the parents and the other adults in the system become united and effective, kids who are only superficially involved with chemicals will tend to resist mightily and protest loudly, but their behavior will begin to improve and they will generally be able to accept limits. Teenagers who are in serious trouble with drugs and alcohol will not be able to change easily because they are not really in control. Thus, the crisis will escalate as the adolescent's inability to respond to parental limits becomes more apparent.

When this happens I begin to focus the family treatment on the likelihood that the teenager cannot respond to limits due to his being involved in hidden chemical dependency. I explain that it is not that the adolescent is unwilling to change; rather, he/she is no longer able to change. By introducing the disease model of addiction at this point, I am softening the scapegoating process that has become intensified by the parents' becoming assertive. If the parents are setting limits and imposing consequences and the situation is simply becoming more out of control, then the disease model becomes a way of reframing the adolescent's behavior. This defuses the power struggle and provides the adolescent with a face-saving way of accepting parental control.

Introducing the idea that the adolescent is powerless over his behavior because he cannot handle his drug use often has a paradoxical effect. Many teenagers resist mightily the notion that they cannot control themselves and so set out to prove that they have no chemical dependency problem. The way to prove that they are not chemically dependent is to conform to the contacts that have been agreed upon; therefore, some adolescents begin to accept the contracts almost in spite of themselves.

However, most teenagers in serious trouble with chemicals cannot respond to this paradox. A direct confrontation of the substance abuse is usually in order. If there is clear-cut evidence of substance abuse, as well as friends and other concerned adults who know about the problem and are willing to help, an intervention is extremely effective.

There are two elements to doing a successful intervention with adolescents. First, other teenagers whom the adolescent cares about and respects need to be involved. The impact of the adolescent's peers confronting the substance abuse is enormous, because so much of the substance abuse is intertwined with anxieties around peer relationships. When your friends tell you that they are worried about you and think that you have a problem, you're likely to take their warnings much more seriously than your parents' constant nagging. Secondly, it is very important to involve adults other than parents. The voices of one or two caring adults who have no particular involvement in the power struggle between the parents and the adolescents will be heard over the parents' complaints during an intervention.

During this crisis period, whether an intervention is done or not, inpatient treatment becomes a possibility. I think a residential program that uses a solid therapeutic community model, is sophisticated about chemical dependency, and offers a strong family program for all family members is ideal for teenagers with serious chemical dependency, since there are so few resources and supports for abstinent adolescents in the community. Often the month of inpatient treatment, during which there is intensive peer support and encouragement to stay sober, is necessary to start adolescents on the road to recovery.

Family members need to learn how to handle the newly sober adolescent, who will seem like a stranger to them when he comes home. It is not unusual for kids to come out of a residential programs with a fanatical commitment to their own sobriety and the values that they have learned in the program. They are often intolerant of their parents and siblings who have not "dealt with their issues." The whole family needs to be educated about the recovery process and teenagers' appropriate need for rigidity about their sobriety. Family members need to develop new ways of relating rather than retreating toward the old pattern; otherwise they might end up scapegoating the adolescent who is now in recovery.

Residential treatment programs are effective when the adolescent is chemically dependent and when the parents themselves have so thoroughly lost control over the adolescent that they cannot protect the child from himself. However, if a program has already been tried and it has not been successful, then that usually indicates that there may be an underlying function to having the adolescent in the scapegoat role that is actively being reinforced by inpatient treatment.

Parents who have viewed their adolescent as "bad" are often relieved by shifting their perception to seeing their child as "sick." That reframe may break the impasse. Unfortunately, many families too readily identify their child as "sick" and are quite comfortable about turning the child over to the doctors and the inpatient program to be cured. These families tend to use the "sick" label to avoid putting pressure on the adolescent to be responsible for himself and to get caught in helpless enabling behavior. In these situations repeat hospitalizations protect the family from actually letting go of the child. The old family pattern is perpetuated, with the hospital becoming an unwitting partner in maintaining a dysfunctional homeostasis.

With some inpatient programs that work specifically with chemically dependent teenagers a new difficulty sometimes arises. The treatment staff may be too ideologically committed to the family disease model of addiction. This can lead them to confront parents on their own "disease" in a way that alienates rather than joins. If parents are challenged too early in the treatment process, they will sabotage the treatment and the child's recovery.

When the adolescent is older, i.e., in the late teens or twenties, or when residential programs have already been tried, the crisis-of-change stage may involve supporting the parents through difficult tasks. They must resist rescuing the abuser by simply putting him/her into inpatient treatment. Further, they must become powerful enough and detached enough to simply set limits, with the ultimate consequence being that the child can no longer live at home or be supported by the parents. The parents must state to the adolescent that they will be supportive if the abuser seeks treatment on his own but that initiating and following through with treatment are his responsibilities.

At this critical juncture, when the parents are faced with having to tell their out-of-control adolescent that he can no longer live at home or be supported by them, the situation becomes very scary. Almost always, when the parents are able to take such a strong position, the kid will escalate the level of defiance to the point of threatening to harm himself or members of the family.

Mr. and Mrs. Harris finally decided to stand up to their 25-year-old heroin-addicted son, Alan. It had taken them a long time to genuinely believe that kicking him out of the house was necessary and that letting him continue to stay dependent on them was like putting junk in his veins. They had already forced Alan into three hospitalizations, so they basically knew that there was no other choice. They were just scared.

The first weekend after they told him to leave home, Alan found an exquisite way of trying to undermine their will to hold firm. Many times during the weekend he went to various subway stations, chose a phone close to the tracks, and called his folks. When they answered the phone he wouldn't say anything. He would simply hold the phone out towards the tracks, so that the parents could hear the rumble of the trains going by. Then he would say into the phone in a harsh whisper, "I'm going to throw myself in front of the next train that comes in because that's what you want. You want to get rid of me. Thanks." Then he would hang up before the parents could say anything.

It was a long, long weekend. The parents were scared and so was I. We knew he was capable of doing what he was threatening. There was nothing to be done. On Monday he signed himself into detox and for the first time took responsibility for his own recovery.

That case worked out. Some don't. Parents are not simply pathological, resistant, or stupid when they cannot confront their children. They're scared and they know that it is a matter of life and death. I don't want to be the one who aggressively pushes the parents in this crisis-of-change stage, because they ultimately have to be prepared to hold the line and take the consequences of what might happen. I spend a considerable amount of time helping parents prepare for this confrontation and appreciating their fears. The parents are ready for the crisis when they truly believe that continuing on the current path will lead to permanent disablement and possible death and that confronting the child may be the only way to help him.

Stage 5: Restraint from Change

After the family has successfully gone through the crisis stage and the adolescent is functioning much better in terms of both chemical use and behavior, we enter a somewhat awkward stage. The family continues to come into treatment and yet no one knows what to talk about. The sessions begin with family members' description of how much better the identified patient is; then there is a period of mutual congratulations. Yet before long the conversation becomes strained and the tension level in the room begins to rise. At first everyone seems to feel the warm, soothing glow that one might have while drinking a cup of hot soup after being out on a cold winter's day. Then you can almost hear the "dum, dum, dum" of the theme music from the movie *Jaws*. You can almost see the black fin circling around ominously in the cup of nice, hot soup.

The shark in the soup represents all the unresolved issues, conflicts, and secrets that have not been addressed in the therapy because the family members have been devoting their attention to the scapegoat. Just as in the early stages of recovery for one of the parents, they do not know how to interact now that the crisis has passed and the adolescent is better. This stage is particularly awkward because the tension around the underlying question: Should the therapy move on to address other family or marital problems? There is also considerable confusion about how best to relate to the recovering adolescent.

Usually in these sessions following the adolescent's improvement, when no one is quite sure what the topic of the therapy should be, one of the parents inadvertently broaches a new issue. Often this has to do with a significant marital or individual problem. Almost before he or she realizes it, the unwary therapist is working on topics that have never been agreed upon as part of the therapy and that some members of the family may actively resist discussing.

Suddenly Mrs. Jones wants to tell about how Mr. Jones only pays attention to her when there is a crisis in the family. Now that Bobby is better Mr. Jones is ignoring her again. Mr. Jones responds defensively. Then there is abruptly a marital argument in the room. Mrs. Jones turns to the therapist for help and requests some sessions for the couple to work on their relationship. Clearly Mr. Jones does not like the idea and the kids look uncomfortable. Perhaps by the next session Bobby will have created a crisis again and this talk of marital therapy will be swept away.

During this strained transitional stage I strongly encourage the family to resist the temptation to move on to other issues. It is important to stay focused in the every day mechanics of recovery without expecting that long-standing family disputes will be opened up and resolved. While appreciating the wish of some family members to address other problems, I keep the work focused on the adolescent and his recovery until the family has sustained a solid period of stability without relapses. I make explicit the possibility that, if we move too quickly to other issues in the system, the adolescent may take it upon himself to rescue the family by getting into trouble again.

While restraining the family from moving on to other issues, I go through many of the same steps that I do when working with the alcoholic couple system. I work with each member of the family in the presence of the others around adjustment difficulties. I teach family members how to negotiate and manage conflict. We address the family's grief over the time lost to the struggle with the adolescent.

Adolescents go through this stage of recovery in two quite different ways. Some, particularly those who are coming out of intensive residential treatment centers, return to the family with a reformer's zeal. They feel that their recovery is dependent on the other family members' acknowledgment that they, too, are "sick" and need to be in recovery. Naturally, other family members may resist this idea. I actively support the adolescent's zeal in terms of his/her own recovery. Then, without overtly criticizing his efforts to reform the family, I encourage him to let the family members come along at their own pace and not to risk his own recovery by becoming too involved in theirs. I usually communicate this perspective through the language and teachings of AA and Al-Anon ("one step at a time"; "easy does it"; "don't take other people's inventory"). The wish to change the whole family is also in part an expression of the adolescent's unresolved grief as he begins to face the possibility that the family will not ever be the way he or she would like it to be and that it is time to leave the family behind.

The second typical pattern is one of occasional relapses. It is important that neither the parents nor I get overly excited by relapses. I normalize them as part of the adolescent's continuing effort to become more autonomous and learn by making mistakes. I encourage the parents to practice what they learned earlier in the therapy around setting limits and enacting consequences. I hypothesize in their presence that the adolescent is not feeling sufficiently grown up to be completely successful and needs the slips to keep the parents involved. I also hypothesize that perhaps the adolescent does not feel that the family is ready to have him be completely retired from the scapegoat position. What issues will they have to deal with if the adolescent is no longer center stage? The key to managing relapses is to block the event from completely dominating the family and to keep the parents from returning to their previous crisis mentality in their responses.

Regardless of whether the adolescent is overly zealous or caught in a relapse pattern, continuing involvement in support groups such as AA or Al-Anon is essential. I also encourage the families to practice having meetings on their own to address ongoing family problems, rather than relying on the therapy as the only place to talk. I begin to space out the meetings, so that the family members come to rely more on themselves and support systems in their community. To ensure success, they need to develop confidence that they can handle crises on their own without the therapist.

Stage 6: Individuation

When the family members are feeling more independent and competent, it is time for a shift in the focus of the therapy. Even though the adolescent is doing well, he may still have some developmental issues that he would like to work on without his parents' involvement. Kids who have been preoccupied with being symptomatic and the center of family turmoil often have not had the opportunity to address normal adolescent confusion and anxiety about self-image, sexuality, future planning, and peer relationships.

The goal of the last stage of therapy is to enable family members to individuate and facilitate the adolescent's autonomy and independence. The adolescent is encouraged to work individually on his own personal issues. In order to maintain my alliance with the whole family and ensure the adolescent's privacy, I usually refer the teenager to an individual therapist at this stage. If the adolescent chooses to handle developmental issues the way that most adolescents do (that is, the trial and error method) I encourage the parents to back off and try not to be control- ling. This is particularly important if the adolescent is living at home, but old enough to be considered an adult—17 or older. The parents and the adolescent have to negotiate the difference between the parents' asserting their rights as the providers of food and shelter and their attempting to impose their values and standards. It needs to be made clear that the adolescent has the right to reject the parents' rules or values as long as he/she is willing to be self-supporting and find his/her own place to live. Thus, the issue is defined as the negotiation of "board- inghouse rules" rather than a parent-child struggle over values and lifestyles.

Not only is the adolescent focusing on his individual issues and separating himself from the family, but the parents are also having to address the underlying issues of letting the child go, accepting him for who he is rather than who they wanted him to be, and beginning to face their own relationship as a couple. Mak- ing this transition to the marital issues is often a very delicate process. As I encourage the adolescent to deal with developmental issues independently of the family, I gently open up the marital relationship by encouraging the parents to reward themselves for having worked so hard at this difficult process. Perhaps, I say, they might try an activity that would not involve the children. This rather benign suggestion often reveals the lack of connection and intimacy between the parents that has been covered over by their struggle around the adolescent's behavior.

I want to make it safe for the couple to address marital issues in the therapy, but I do not want to push too hard. It is not my place to decide whether spouses should or should not use therapy as the way to readjust their marriage as the chil- dren begin to leave home. All couples go through considerable stress at this point and most of them weather the storm without therapy. Rather than push marital therapy, I normalize the transitional difficulties and make explicit the possibility that the adolescent may have a relapse in order to protect them from focusing too intensely on their couple relationship.

If spouses decide they would like to work on their marriage with me, I point out that there are several steps to go through to ensure that the family is really ready to handle the change in focus. First, I want the family members to have a successful recess from therapy, in order to enhance their self-confidence in their abilities to manage problems. Secondly, I want to be sure that both spouses want to pursue marital therapy. Frequently one really wants the therapy and the other is going along with the idea to placate the spouse. Finally, I want the parents to explain to the kids that, even though there may be increased tension between them as they do the therapy, they would really like the kids to stay out of trouble and not to rescue them by creating diversionary crises. These preliminaries both prepare the parents for the normal tensions of marital therapy and block the return of the symptom. During the individuation stage the therapist becomes less central. In such an active and directive therapy it is a complicated task for the therapist to effectively disengage. Crises that happen during this late stage of therapy are usually related to the family's anxiety about losing the therapist. Individuation is hard for everybody in the treatment system, including me. It is hard not to be needed anymore.

NECESSITY IS THE MOTHER OF INVENTION

How does one translate generic treatment models into actual clinical situations? Models are never more than the frameworks for thinking about a family system and a preliminary way of organizing treatment. Each family is unique; ultimately every therapy is different. Treating adolescent substance abuse often means confronting life-threatening situations. Sometimes such desperate circumstances demand desperate responses.

As in the following case, sometimes I need to let go of my neat formulas and pat strategies and simply trust my intuition that doing something is safer than doing nothing.

It was the first session. The parents, Mr. and Mrs. Moss, were sitting close together on the sofa, wringing their hands and looking at me anxiously. The "child," Patrick, was a rude, foul-mouthed, 19-year-old adolescent who responded to most of my questions by swearing under his breath while refusing to answer directly. When I encouraged the parents to confront Patrick they looked at me with abject terror, as if I had asked them to jump out of an airplane without a parachute.

It turned out that Patrick had been a drug addict for several years. He had been in inpatient treatment twice with no apparent success. As I tried to find out what the situation was at home, it quickly became apparent that the boy was running the show. About once every six weeks he would steal the family TV set and hock it for drug money. Then he would badger the parents into buying a new one. When the parents searched his room and found drugs they would flush the drugs down the toilet. He would simply replace the drugs in the exact same hiding places. Mr. and Mrs. Moss ran a small travel agency together. Naturally Patrick worked for them and just as naturally he stole money out of petty cash on a daily basis.

By the end of the interview I was feeling quite overwhelmed by these helpless parents and their difficult child. As the parents and I were discussing the possibility of another interview, the boy turned to them and said, "This shit is a waste of my fuckin' time. I don't care how much money you pay me, I'm not coming back to one of these stupid things." At this point I found out that the boy had been paid twice as much as I was being paid for the session. That information helped me understand why I felt so powerless throughout the interview. It is always a good idea to get paid more than the identified patient!

I decided that my first major intervention would be to tell the parents that they should either pay me twice as much as Patrick for our sessions or not pay him at all. The boy resolved the dilemma by stomping out of the room.

The therapy was launched in this rather shaky manner, and the following sessions were not a great improvement. Patrick didn't return and the parents took turns undermining my suggestions on my part that involved challenging their "poor sick" son. They had decided that he was ill and therefore they couldn't confront him. After all, he was not responsible for his behavior. They also carefully explained to me that they could not set limits on Patrick because obviously he was too big to be punished; further, they could not throw him out of the house because then he would get arrested and sent to jail, where he might get in "serious trouble." I was beginning to feel a little exasperated.

In session seven a significant shift in the therapy took place. This was precipitated by the boy's once again lifting the family TV set. The parents were desperately upset and turned to me to save their son. I was beginning to see that I had been pushing them too hard. They needed to find a response to this boy that genuinely empowered them and yet did not scare them so much that they couldn't do it. Clearly they were not ready to confront the boy directly, but they were desperate and said they would do anything I told them to do. I gave them the following four homework assignments:

1. Mrs. Moss was instructed to get up one morning at 3 and cook Patrick an elaborate breakfast in bed. Then she was to carry the tray into his room, turn on the lights, wake him up, and put the tray gently on his chest. She was to greet him with a big smile and announce that she loved him so much that she just couldn't resist the urge to make him breakfast in bed.

2. Mr. and Mrs. Moss were encouraged to go all over the house finding the boy's hiding places for drugs. Instead of removing the drug, they were to leave in each place a note that said, "Surprise! Old dogs can learn new tricks."

3. The father was encouraged to pick up a bunch of crisp new $10 bills from the bank. Each day he was to leave one of the bills around the office; attached to it would be a note saying, "Don't spend it all in one place."

4. The mother was told to fill up the refrigerator with jars of baby food. When her son asked her what the jars were doing in the refrigerator, she was to say, "Well, you never know when we might have a new little someone around here." (This last intervention, an apparent flight of fancy, was related to my knowing that the boy was the youngest of two adopted children and my being struck with how comfortable he was being the permanent baby of the family.)

The parents were somewhat perplexed by these ideas, but they were quick to acknowledge that conventional strategies had always failed and they did not have a lot to lose. They were also clearly intrigued with the possibility that for once Patrick would not be calling all the shots.

The change in the parents at the next interview was quite dramatic. They had done all the assignments and thoroughly enjoyed their son's bewilderment and discomfort. Their son had become quite upset and accused the parents of being crazy. He also told them that their "shrink" was crazy and should be fired. Feeling united and empowered, the parents decided that it was time Patrick either went into treatment on his own or lived somewhere else. I was very pleased and, I might add, very impressed with my "moves."

I should have known better. A week later the parents called me at 11 o'clock at night. They were hysterical. The mother said, "We did what you told us, Dr. Treadway. We kicked him out of the house and told him he could not come back in the house for nine months."

(I always get nervous when people call me at 11 o'clock at night to tell me that they did what *I* told them to do.)

Mrs. Moss went on to explain that Patrick's response was to go out in the middle of this cold December night in his shirtsleeves, with the intent of freezing himself to death in front of their living room picture window. The parents didn't know what to do. They didn't want to back down on their position. They did not want to call the police and have him dragged off the lawn. They thought he might just be stubborn enough and stoned enough to freeze himself to death.

I didn't know what to do. None of my treatment models prepared me for front lawn suicides. After some hesitation I told the parents to cajole their son into spending the night in the family car. I encouraged them to take turns sitting in the car with the boy, but not to allow him to talk them into letting him come back into the house. I encouraged the mother to make some coffee and take some blankets out to the car. It took some work, but eventually the parents were able to get their son into the car, where they took turns staying with him.

At 7 o'clock in the morning I arrived at their house to do an emergency session. You might wonder why I didn't insist that the family come to my office. The truth is that I was quite rattled by this turn of events. Naturally, we met in the car. I had Mom and Dad in the front seat, in the proper hierarchical position; Patrick and I were in the back seat. By this time he was cold sober and convinced that his parents and I were out of our minds. When it sank in that the parents were serious about not letting him live in the house, he opted to put himself in the hospital.

After two weeks in the hospital, he called his parents and announced that he was cured and willing to come home as long as they fired me. Without consulting me, the parents told him that, although they wanted to see him and were encouraged about his treatment, they would neither support him nor allow him back into their home for eight months and two weeks.

The son ended up going through an extended rehabilitation program. When he completed it, he found a job and a place to live in a neighboring state. I continued to see the parents for a while for check-up sessions. They went on their first vacation together in 12 years.

At the eight-month mark the son called the parents and told them he had a girlfriend and would like to bring her home to meet the folks. The parents told him that they thought this was great news, but suggested that they either meet in a restaurant or postpone the visit for another month.

Sometimes old dogs can learn new tricks. Even therapists.

11

The Adolescent Module in Multidimensional Family Therapy

Howard A. Liddle, Gayle Dakof, Guy Diamond,
Michelle Holt, Jacqueline Aroyo, and Michael Watson

Basic clinical research has clarified the family's role in the formation, mainte-nance, and treatment of adolescent drug abuse (e.g., Baumrind, 1989; Baumrind & Moselle, 1985; Bernal & Flores-Ortiz, 1991; Brook, Whiteman, Nomura, Gor-don, & Cohen, 1988; Coombs & Landsverk, 1988; Dishion, Patterson, & Reid, 1988; Dishion, Reid, & Patterson, 1988; Pandina & Schuele, 1983). Although a review of family intervention programs indicates that family treatment is a prom-ising approach for adolescent drug abuse (Bry, 1988; Davidge & Forman, 1988; Liddle & Schmidt, 1991; Todd & Selekman, 1991), only carefully constructed, empirically based clinical models will fulfill the promise of family systems inter-ventions (Liddle, 1991b).

In the mid-1980s, the National Institute on Drug Abuse (NIDA) launched an initiative to address the possibilities of constructing family therapy models to treat adolescent drug abuse. Because several clinical research teams had empiri-cally established successful family therapy approaches for drug abuse (e.g., Stan-ton & Todd, 1982; Szapocznik, Kurtines, Foote, Perez-Vidal, & Hervis, 1983), the NIDA was interested in determining whether effective family therapy treat-ment models could be developed with adolescents (Joanning, Lewis, & Liddle, 1990; National Institutes of Health, 1983; Todd & Selekman, 1991). The NIDA's

The clinical work and research described in this chapter were supported by grants to the senior author from the National Institute on Drug Abuse (R01 DA 03714 and P50 DA 07697-01), and the United States Department of Education.

Source: Adapted from "Adolescent Substance Abusers in Family Therapy: The Critical Initial Phase of Treatment" by H.A. Liddle and G. Diamond, 1991, *Family Dynamics of Addiction Quar-terly, 1*, pp. 55–68. Copyright 1991 by Aspen Publishers, Inc.

interest in this area has continued with its funding of the first treatment evaluation research center to study family therapy approaches for adolescent drug abuse—the Center for Research on Adolescent Drug Abuse. The first approach developed in a NIDA-funded study, the Adolescents and Families Project, continues to be tested and refined in the Center. The Adolescents and Families Project began in 1985 at the University of California, San Francisco and moved to Temple University in April of 1990.

MULTIDIMENSIONAL FAMILY THERAPY

A multisystemic treatment approach for adolescent substance abuse and its correlated behavior problems (Liddle, 1991a, 1991c), multidimensional family therapy has its roots in the integrative structural-strategic family therapy tradition (Fraser, 1986; Stanton, 1981; Todd, 1986). It incorporates additional notions about the targets, mechanisms, and methods of change, however. The multidimensional family therapy approach developed for the Adolescents and Families Project, for instance, (1) does not use paradoxical interventions, (2) does not employ a function of the symptom concept, (3) does not draw primarily from other schools of family therapy for its tenets and methods, (4) is not ahistorical in its focus, (5) uses adolescent development research to guide its assessments and interventions, (6) requires working with individuals in the course of treatment more than the structural-strategic models, and (7) employs knowledge and methods from the skills-based intervention approaches with adolescents.

The clinical research program's mandate to construct a specialized treatment model for adolescent substance abuse led to the model's refinement. This activity, tailoring an existing integrative approach, was also influenced by two contemporary trends in drug abuse treatment (Liddle & Schmidt, 1991; National Institutes of Health, 1983) and psychotherapy (Miller & Prinz, 1991)—treatment development (i.e., greater particularization of treatment models, population-specific treatment manuals, theory-specific outcome, therapy process specification) and model enhancement (i.e., the reconstruction of treatment packages for specific purposes).

Conceptually, multidimensional family therapy reflects the growing, perhaps standard, trend to conceive of adolescent problems such as drug use and delinquency as correlated behaviors (Elliott, Huizinga, & Ageton, 1985; Kazdin, 1987). Dishion, Reid, and Patterson (1988) argued that drug abuse and delinquency are "somewhat different aspects of a unified behavioral process" (p. 189). This perspective typifies the contemporary work in this area, which is beginning to clarify the strong relationship of adolescent substance abuse to conduct disorder (Bukstein, Brent, & Kaminer, 1989). Investigators and clinicians alike have reached a consensus on the importance of understanding adolescent problems in a multivariate, multisystemic, nonreductionistic fashion (Dishion & Loeber, 1985; Fishman, 1986; Henggeler et al., 1986; Jessor & Jessor, 1977; Pandina & Schuele, 1983). Newcomb and Bentler (1989) summarized the treatment implications of this empirically derived perspective:

> Substance use and abuse during adolescence are strongly associated with other problem behaviors such as delinquency, precocious sexual behavior, deviant attitudes, or school dropout. Any focus on drug use or abuse to the exclusion of such correlates, whether antecedent, contemporaneous, or consequent, distorts the phenomenon by focusing on only one aspect or component of a general pattern or syndrome. (p. 243)

Multidimensional Family Therapy in the Context of Other Family Therapy Approaches

The multidimensional family therapy approach has several features that distinguish it from contemporary family therapy models. First, it is a research-based approach. Although there are several well articulated, empirically based family treatment models for adolescent problems of drug abuse and conduct disorder (e.g., Alexander, Klein, & Parsons, 1977; Alexander & Parsons, 1973; Barton, Alexander, Waldron, Turner, & Warburton, 1985; Henggeler et al., 1986; Lewis, Piercy, Sprenkle, & Trepper, 1990a; Robin & Foster, 1989; Szapocznik et al., 1988), others fall outside the context of systematic evaluation and research (Fishman, 1986; Jurich, 1990). Family therapy, however, is now in a era that is less tolerant of approaches that lag behind in evaluation, regardless of their logical or intuitive appeal (Erickson, 1988; Liddle, 1990b).

Second, developed in a specific context for particular purposes, multidimensional family therapy is a specialized model designed to treat the problem behavior syndrome (Jessor & Jessor, 1977) or cluster (Kazdin, 1987) of adolescent problems of substance abuse and conduct problems. Philosophically, it is consistent with calls for specialization in therapy model construction (Achenbach, 1986; Goldfried & Wolfe, 1988; Gurman, 1988; Liddle, 1990a; Pinsof, 1989).

Third, this approach takes into account the problems associated with the tendency of some family therapy models to endorse family reductionism—the crediting or blaming of health and pathology on the family. Accordingly, multidimensional family therapy emphasizes individuals as systems and subsystems more than do many other contemporary family therapy approaches.

Its multidimensional focus is a fourth distinguishing feature of this model. For example, integrating assessment dimensions such as cognitive attributions, affective states, and recollections of the past with communication and social skills training is not the usual fare for family therapy models. Another aspect of multidimensionality is the import of extrafamilial factors in maintaining and treating adolescent problems. Peer, educational, and juvenile justice systems, in addition to individual and family domains, are principal areas of assessment and intervention in any multisystemic, multidimensional model.

A fifth factor concerns the integrative nature of the model. Although still lagging behind that in the psychotherapy field, the integrative tradition in family therapy is beginning to take hold (Lebow, 1987). Still, most family therapy integrative models, particularly those designed for the treatment of adolescent drug abuse, have relied on other models of family therapy for their sources of integration. For instance, approaches for adolescent substance abusers, such as those outlined by Ellis (1986), Lewis, Piercy, Sprenkle, and Trepper (1990b), and Todd and Selekman (1991), rely primarily on structural, strategic, brief therapy, behavioral, and systemic schools of family therapy, while the approach developed by Joanning (1991) represents the radical constructivist wing of family therapy. Existing within a family psychology framework (Kaslow, 1987; Liddle, 1987a, 1987b), multidimensional family therapy is more comprehensive than are most contemporary family therapy models and makes it possible to avoid the problems of some integrative family therapy models that underutilize basic knowledge of psychological principles and content (Liddle, Schmidt, & Ettinger, in press).

A sixth distinguishing characteristic of multidimensional family therapy concerns its emphasis on the adolescent in the context of family therapy for adolescent problems. The adolescent is a prominent figure in the successful conduct of this therapy, and treatment is seen as disadvantaged if he or she does not participate fully. Therefore, engagement is a primary emphasis of the clinician's early work. The adolescent should feel that therapy can be a context in which his or her individual concerns can be met.

Finally, the incorporation of empirical findings of developmental and adolescent psychology into the clinical model is a core characteristic of multidimensional family therapy (Liddle, Schmidt, & Ettinger, in press). Too few have appreciated the need for this activity in family therapy. Many family therapists (1) make incorrect assumptions about adolescent development (e.g., Pittman, 1987); (2) urge mobilization a priori to counter anticipated adolescent resistance (Jurich, 1990); and (3) ignore or minimize individual adolescent development issues (Berg & Gallagher, 1991; Durrant & Coles, 1991; Fisch, 1989; Heath & Ayers, 1991), while overfocusing on parental power and authority (Fox, 1991; Haley, 1981) and correction of "incongruous hierarchies" (Madanes, 1981, 1985). Multidimensional family therapy, in contrast, uses existing knowledge of the ways in which families serve as buffering or protective mechanisms against the influence of deviant peer and societal influences (e.g., Burke & Weir, 1978, 1979; Greenberg, Siegel, & Leitch, 1983; Larson, 1983; Steinberg & Silverberg, 1986; Wills, 1990), as well as empirical work on the ways in which positive family relations in the adolescent years foster competence, such as self-confidence (Ryan & Lynch, 1989), self-regulation and exploratory behavior (Hartrup, 1979; Hill, 1980; Hill & Holmbeck, 1986), autonomy (Steinberg, 1987, 1990), and ego development of both the teen-ager (Hauser et al., 1984) and the parent (Hauser, Borman, Jacobson, Powers, & Noam, 1991).

Clinical Use of Adolescent Development Research

The history of adolescent psychology has been dominated by the theoretically derived belief that separation/individuation constitutes the central task of adolescence. Modern day developmental research challenges this position. Empirical evidence demonstrates, for example, that positive parent-child relationships foster and predict healthy adolescent development (Hauser et al., 1985; Hill, 1980; Montemayor, 1983, 1986) and that families serve as a primary context of adolescent development (Grotevant & Cooper, 1983; Hauser et al., 1984). Research in this area also indicates that emotional support from the family has a protective or buffering effect against substance abuse (Burke & Weir, 1978; Greenberg, Siegel, & Leitch, 1983; Larson, 1983). Wills and Vaughn (1989) found that, when there is a high level of substance abuse in the peer network, family, but not peer, support had protective effects. Wills (1990) concluded:

Many parents believe that they are powerless in the face of peer pressures toward adolescent deviance. To the contrary, my findings indicate that parents, through the support they provide to teens, can have considerable favorable influence . . . parents protect their teens by being interested in and available to talk about problems. (p. 91)

Research findings such as these have helped to depose separation/individuation as the goal of adolescence. Parent-child interdependence has come to be seen as the optimal developmental condition. As Steinberg (1990) noted,

Transformations in family relations at adolescence reflect the adolescent's growing understanding of his or her *interdependence* within the family and the parents' willingness to engage in a process through which close ties are maintained but the young person's individuality is not threatened. (p. 265)

Youniss and Smollar (1985) stated,

Both parent and adolescent actively participate in the mutual and reciprocal process of redefining the relationship. Transformation of the rela-

> tionship from one of unilateral authority to one of cooperative negotiation is necessary for the adolescent's social and psychological development to proceed on course; a severing of the parent-child bond jeopardizes this process. (p. 265)

When the parent-child relationship falters or remains poor over time, an adolescent's psychosocial growth deviates from normative parameters (Baumrind & Moselle, 1985; Kellam, Brown, Rubin, & Ensminger, 1983; Newcomb & Bentler, 1988a, 1988b; Shedler & Block, 1990).

The two primary dimensions of family relations, organization and cohesion, have important clinical implications. Given the degree of disengagement and lack of cohesion in the families of adolescent drug abusers, interventions that rely primarily on parental hierarchy and power (organization) can further alienate an already estranged teen-ager. Therefore, increasing cohesion (i.e., developmentally appropriate attachment) among the family members becomes an essential goal. Rather than unilateral closeness, cohesion between adolescents and parents involves, as indicated, the negotiation of new modes of interdependence (Silverberg & Steinberg, 1987; Steinberg, in press)—a relationship definition that coincides with the developmental needs of teen-agers.

Reformulated to fit the developmental period of the second decade of life, attachment has been an important concept in multidimensional family therapy (Greenberg et al., 1983). Youniss and Smollar (1985) reached a conclusion that is representative of those reached by a wide array of adolescent development researchers.

> In healthy families, adolescents remain responsive to parental authority and continue to seek parents' advice, but they do so in a context of greater freedom. The parents, at the same time, retain their authority through giving more freedom to adolescents by recognizing their personal needs and capabilities. . . . It is clear that parental relationships have not been discarded nor have they lost their binding power. In fact, the adolescents said that the transformation helped to bring them and their parents closer. (pp. 162–163)

Conceptual Framework

Multidimensional family therapy draws from contemporary work that emphasizes the continuous interplay and reciprocally determining relationship between cognition, affect, behavior, and environmental input and feedback (e.g., Bandura,

1978; Greenberg & Safran, 1987; Mahoney, 1984; Wachtel, 1977). In the words of Bandura (1986),

> Conceptions of human behavior in terms of unidirectional personal determinism are just as unsatisfying as those espousing unidirectional environmental determinism. (pp. 22–23)
>
> Rather, human functioning is explained in terms of a model of triadic reciprocity in which behavior, cognitive and other personal factors, and environmental events all operate as interacting determinants of each other. (p. 18)

Fundamental to the treatment model as well are the ecological (Bronfenbrenner, 1983), dynamic-interactional (Lerner, 1978), and interactional (Magnusson, 1988) perspectives on human development. This holistic conception of development underscores "the organization and integration of capacities in various developmental domains" (Reider & Cicchetti, 1990, p. 382). Also influential has been developmental psychopathology with its roots in a thorough understanding of problems in their developmental context (Achenbach, 1990; Cicchetti, 1984; Kazdin, 1989; Rutter & Sroufe, 1984).

The key assumptions of multidimensional family therapy, which have been drawn in large part from the theories that have been briefly mentioned, include the following:

- complexity of human functioning. The premise that people function simultaneously in numerous domains of human existence (e.g., affective, cognitive, behavioral, temporal, moral/ethical, spiritual, interpersonal) is hardly a new revelation. For more than 20 years, for example, the social cognition area has contributed substantially to the understanding of the links between cognition, emotion, and behavior (Shantz, 1983).
- interconnectedness across domains. Although the domains of human existence are interconnected, the mechanisms that govern these relationships are not always apparent.
- practical implications of this perspective. In therapy, problems can be accessed through these related domains of human functioning. By implication, solutions to these problems can be generated within any one (or more) of these domains. Work in the domain of emotion, for example, is related to the belief systems and behavioral repertoires. The therapist must maintain access to these interrelated areas and must understand the accessing and potentiating aspects of one domain upon another.
- potential pitfalls of a univariate or narrow perspective. Therapists are handicapped if they work only in one domain or consider one domain more impor-

tant than another. Multidimensional family therapy avoids a univariate focus at both assessment and intervention levels.

- clinical advantages. At a practical, clinical, decision-making level, a clinician who uses multidimensional family therapy has available multiple targets for change.

WHITHER INTERVENTIONS: THE CASE FOR MODULES

Because the term *intervention* infers a single technique or method, the term *modules* better organizes and defines the content domains of the multidimensional family therapy model. Modules indicate the "territories" in which the therapist needs to operate. Cognitive psychologists may refer to the module notion as a therapist's schemata. Just as "chunking" allows chess masters to think of several moves and countermoves at once, in a series of interconnected "chunks," modules allow therapists to think in larger units.

A vignette from live supervision may help to illustrate the usefulness of this thinking device. Live supervision is a training method in which a supervisor observes a session as it occurs. It allows the supervisor to offer suggestions to the therapist-trainee through a telephone connection between the observation and therapy room. As Haley (1976) said in describing this method, live supervision provides help to a therapist when he or she needs it most—during the conduct of an actual session. At its worst, live supervision can be disorienting and therapeutically harmful (Liddle & Schwartz, 1983; Montalvo, 1973), particularly when there is poor case planning, difficulty in formulating overall working themes, and/or a therapist with a low skill. If, for example, a therapist repeats a phrase phoned in by a supervisor, but does not have a broader theme in which the phrase or single intervention fits, the therapist has no broader direction to follow after the single intervention has run its course. Left without a theme to play, the therapist sits in the session waiting for the supervisor to call with the next (decontextualized) "intervention."

Rather than relying on single interventions per se, therapists who follow the multidimensional family therapy model operate according to essential modules or units of treatment. These modules include territories to be covered, agenda items to be developed, and generic themes to be explored. They are inextricably connected to the treatment model within which they were developed.

There are different levels of modules as well. At one level, modules are broadly defined as themes or foci. These basic building blocks of the content of therapy become actualized in a majority of cases. Such modules include engaging the adolescent, working with the parental subsystem, establishing and working with themes with parental and adolescent subsystems together, and including extrafamilial influences in treatment.

Modules at a more narrow level are "subroutines" or conceptual content units that help operationalize therapeutic strategy and research-based knowledge. At this more prescriptive level, modules are suggested "lines" or minispeeches that the therapist is prepared to deliver when the occasion arises. Modules also assist in establishing certain content domains over others. They give therapists a practical way of creating certain content themes within the session. In this therapy, not all content is created equal, and some conversations are judged more important than are others.

Modules are advantageous for other reasons as well. They prepare the therapist for several common situations. They also provide a shorthand or code that allows the therapist and supervisor to communicate expeditiously about volumes of content with a single phrase. Most important, however, modules are meant to be "worked," interactionally, in conversation with the family members. They are vehicles by which to establish content themes in sessions. Finally, in addition to establishing a content territory in a session, modules develop the therapist's position about that content territory.

CLINICAL APPLICATIONS

The overall goal of multidimensional family therapy is the improvement of family relationships so that the family can act as a buffering mechanism against the deviant and destructive behavior of its youth (e.g., Wills, 1990). Care is taken to avoid the excesses of approaches with teen-agers that overemphasize parental control functions, because such approaches can exacerbate the alienation and disengagement of the teen-ager. Therapy not only helps to renegotiate the parent-adolescent transition, but also addresses and heals prior relationship hurts.

A new developmentally appropriate relationship evolves between parent and adolescent. This relationship allows a parent to begin anew, offering guidance and influence within new, developmentally guided parameters. The parent is available to the teen-ager for support, yet is not afraid to make demands. Parents learn to balance the two principal aspects of their parenting practices—guidance and support. Therapy helps them to rekindle their commitment, hopes, and dreams for their adolescent, despite the problems that he or she has caused.

At the same time, the teen-ager in this relationship is not in a reactive or avoidant stance vis-à-vis the parents. Adolescents in a developmentally appropriate relationship with their parents are able to discuss certain aspects, although certainly not all of their life with their parent(s), and they remain connected to a healthy, vital peer network and sphere of activities. The therapist connects and at times translates the parent's and adolescent's experience of the other. Seeing the adolescent and parents separately throughout therapy accentuates this intermediary function. When a crisis has occurred or the affect regulation ability of parents and teen-ager is low, separate sessions buy time until each can adopt a less extreme stance and can constructively address and communicate the strong emotions aroused by the other.

The instigation of these processes is challenging, given the degree of (often longstanding) emotional distance, disenchantment, and hostility evident in these families (Burke & Weir, 1978, 1979; Mann, Borduin, Henggeler, & Blaske, 1990). Participation in environments such as these extracts a severe psychological price (Rook, 1984). A critical step in reconnecting the parent and adolescent occurs at therapy's outset. Without success in this area, therapeutic efforts to repair the relationship often remain incomplete.

Defining Therapy with the Adolescent

Adolescents who abuse drugs commonly feel disrespected, abused, and believe themselves to be hardly worth listening to—mostly, they are told to listen and be quiet. Many people (e.g., family members, school personnel, and probation officers) have agreed the teen-ager's behavior and/or personality is undesirable. The therapist should aim to create a new experience for the adolescent, one that is in keeping with some the most basic elements of any counseling relationship. Alliance building is not simply a strategy to obtain the adolescent's cooperation; it represents a genuine interest in and commitment to the adolescent's well-being. Presenting the possibility of a relationship in which the adolescent will be cared about, respected, and listened to is a basic first step of engagement.

> *Therapist:* So what do you think of this?
> *Larry:* It's cool.
> *Therapist:* You've never been in therapy like this have you?
> *Larry:* No, not like this.
> *Therapist:* Do you feel nervous, do you feel . . .
> *Larry:* No. It's just another counseling?
> *Therapist:* I don't think it's going to be another counseling. That's not the way I work. I think we could do a lot here. But, I guess one thing I want to know is whether you're going to work with me. You know what I mean by that?
> [Larry nods.]
> *Therapist:* You see, I'm really interested in who you are, and I really want to know more about you. I want to know who you are in this family, and who you want to be, as your own person, Larry.

The therapist tries to make this therapy different from other attempts at therapy by clearly inviting the teen-ager's full participation. Great care is taken to help the adolescent feel that he or she will be an inherent part of the treatment. New expectations are offered. The therapist tries to enable and challenge the teen-ager to assume a proactive stance toward therapy—to use each therapy session as a place to clarify thoughts, feelings, and future dreams. Anchored in the therapeutic alliance, this activity creates a laboratory in which to address some of the normal developmental challenges of adolescence, as well as to solve some of the current areas of stress for the adolescent.

Developing a Collaborative Set

The adolescent's conception of therapy must be discussed. This discussion is an opportunity for the therapist to define the work as different from that which may have taken place in the past. The therapist works quickly to define some concrete areas that can be the focus of therapy. These areas, of course, must have salience for the teen-ager.

> *Therapist:* But, I'm going to need your help. Do you think you can help me with it?
> *Larry:* I can try.
> *Therapist:* Yeah? You think it's going to be hard?
> *Larry:* Yeah.
> *Therapist:* What do you think it'll mean?
> *Larry:* I don't know, man. I don't think counseling does any good. If you want to get in trouble, you get in trouble no matter who tells you not to. If you don't wanna get in trouble you won't get in trouble no matter who tells you to get in trouble. So I don't really think counseling does anything.
> *Therapist:* Hm. Well, . . .
> *Larry:* But I could be wrong.
> *Therapist:* Well, you told me last week when the big fight happened with your father, that you don't like dealing with your anger that way.
> *Larry:* I don't, man, but that doesn't mean any of you are gonna make me change. . . . Maybe I'm wrong, I'm not saying I'm not.
> *Therapist:* Would you be interested in learning how to deal with things better?
> *Larry:* Yeah. I would.
> *Therapist:* That's something we could do here.

In this case, the adolescent initially resists the therapist's requests. His disbelief in counseling indicates a pessimistic attitude and an inability to imagine a meaningful future. Themes of meaninglessness have been common in the identities of adolescents involved with drugs (Bentler, Harlow, & Newcomb 1986; Newcomb & Harlow, 1986). Furthermore, drug-using adolescents are at high risk for what has been called identity diffusion—a failure to develop the skills necessary to take hold of their own lives and, as a result, consolidation of their identities around a negative self-image (Baumrind, 1985). The therapist resuscitates or creates the adolescent's natural desires for growth and health. The individual sessions with the teen-ager often focus on the development of an expanded repertoire of interpersonal skills, which have frequently been found to be in need of work with troubled adolescents (Dodge, 1980; Dodge, Murphy, & Buchsbaum, 1984; Hansen, Watson-Perczel, & Christopher, 1989).

Understanding the Adolescent's Affect

Teen-agers frequently present themselves with an aura of impermeability (e.g., "I'm tough," "I'm hip," "I don't care"). Professional and public perceptions of adolescents further these stereotypes (Offer, Ostrov, & Howard, 1981). Therapists must not be taken in by these false and misleading characterizations. Multidimensional family therapy facilitates therapist-adolescent engagement by accessing different aspects of the teen-ager's emotional world that, too often, go unexplored. Feelings of vulnerability, sadness, and tenderness, for example, are frequently assumed to be therapeutically inaccessible with teen-agers. Yet, with skill and an appreciation of these sensitive themes, the therapist can facilitate engagement and develop substantive content by working with these underappreciated and sometimes avoided domains of a teen-ager's existence.

The adolescent's ability to process and constructively express emotions is often weak. In fact, emotion regulation and the management of aggressive impulses have been found to be significant deficit areas in clinical populations (Aber, Allen, Carlson, & Cicchetti, in press). Many teen-agers become overwhelmed and cognitively disorganized when dealing with their emotions in the early stage of treatment. This domain of work has benefits for engagement and substantively for the therapy as well, however. For example, the therapist may use an event that he or she witnessed (e.g., the fight between Larry and his dad) to connect with the affective domain of the teen-ager and offer alternatives that therapy can address.

> *Therapist:* You know, you didn't look so happy when you were hitting your dad. You told me you hate when you get mad at him. I didn't think you looked too happy. Tonight you didn't look happy. Maybe you didn't like what they were saying, or you feel they don't understand you. Maybe you feel like you get caught between them when they argue. You know, it's a hard situation, your parents being separated. They're still working out their own problems. It's going to affect you. I know that's

rough. So, I want to help you work through some of this in a way that would make things better for you.

Larry: [Indifferently]: Yeah.

Therapist: Would you like to see things change?

Larry: Sure.

The therapist has specified some salient emotional themes (e.g., anger, marital conflict, parents' separation) that are rarely acknowledged in this teen-ager's life. By communicating therapy's possibilities for addressing the significant issues of this teen-ager's life, the therapist makes the sessions an arena for a teen-ager's developmental growth. Adolescents learn to manage difficult emotions; take another's perspective; cope with life's disappointments; and make mature claims for attention, respect, and love.

Meeting Developmental Challenges

For adolescents who abuse drugs, cognitive sophistication often lags behind developmental expectations. Teen-agers should be acquiring the skills in formal operational thinking, self-reflection, and the ability to make choices based on abstract ideas rather than on concrete experience. Amotivational syndrome, which is characterized by apathy, mental laziness, and withdrawal from demanding social stimuli (Baumrind & Moselle, 1985) and is thought to be exacerbated by drug use, particularly extensive marijuana use, may contribute to inhibitions in this area.

At its best, therapy stimulates the growth of these skills. The therapist asks the adolescents to reflect on their behavior; to confront avoided interpersonal problem situations (with new attributions and skills); and to wrestle with ideas about what they want from therapy, from the family, and from life.

Therapist: It sounds like Dad would like to be closer to you. Is that something you share also?

Larry: I don't know.

Therapist: You don't know? Hm . . . Well, . . . it's perfect that you say that, because that's exactly the kind of thing I'm going to ask you *not* to do. I'm going to ask you to struggle with things in here, and say "Yeah, this is what I hate" or "This isn't what I want." Even when it's difficult. Because I know you've got a voice in there that wants things. But, sometimes they're hard to say. You're afraid you're going to hurt somebody, or get angry with them, or you might not get what you want. But I want to help you discover that things can be different. That you can be different.

Throughout treatment, the therapist requests mature, active, responsible behavior from the adolescent, who usually welcomes this challenge. Furthermore, these requests convey the message that the therapist believes the teen-ager is capable of mature behavior. This is a radical departure from the environment of criticism and neglect that the adolescent often experiences in the family and social environment.

Making the Strange Familiar

Therapy is a strange and foreign environment for many teen-agers. The therapist must succinctly, yet deftly, sketch in this landscape, always stressing core themes of collaboration, compassion, experimentation, communication, and responsibility.

> *Therapist:* There are times I will ask you to talk to your folks, and be straight with them. There are times I will ask you to do things in here or at home and try out new things. There will be times when we meet alone, and I'll want you to be straight with me and say what's on your mind so that you can get some of your own needs met. Because I feel like you're not getting what you want right now. [Pausing] What does that all sound like? Do you want to give it a try?

In the early stages of therapy, the therapist often uses such "speeches" in an attempt to establish an agenda and a direction for the treatment. They define expectations and set forth propositions to be considered by the teen-ager and the family.

Calibrating Expectations

Although the therapist must avoid becoming overorganized and pessimistic because of a therapy-disinclined teen-ager, it is essential to respect to the adolescent's caution and distrust. He or she must be given the opportunity to work out a way to participate in the treatment. Therefore, the therapist must be careful to pace the presentation of the treatment program and requests for participation and commitment.

WALKING THE TIGHTROPE: A GUIDING METAPHOR

When working with adolescents and their families, clinicians must learn to "walk the tightrope." They must establish and maintain alliances with both the adolescent and the parents. Thus, at one time, they must be the voice of the adolescent; at other times, the voice of the parent(s). To support and speak for both teen-agers and parents, while also taking into account extrafamilial systems (e.g., juvenile justice and school), is a daunting task. Yet, maintaining multiple alliances is not only possible, but also essential, for successful therapy with drug-abusing adolescents and their families.

The initial challenge is to engage the adolescents in therapy. The majority of substance-abusing adolescents come to therapy only because their parents or the juvenile justice system has ordered them to do so. As the teen-ager's active participation in the therapeutic process increases chances for success, it is vital to help the adolescent formulate a personal therapeutic agenda. Without this viable agenda, engagement is compromised.

Establishing the adolescent's agenda is one of the primary therapeutic challenges. The adolescent must be persuaded that therapy can be personally worthwhile. To accomplish this goal, the therapist must prove to the teen-ager, through both words and actions, that therapy will be more than just helping the parents become more powerful and controlling. Engagement and alliance-building strategies must continue throughout the therapy.

In multidimensional family therapy, the clinician tries to facilitate both in-session and out-of-session change. Fostering in-session change through enactment is a core component of this approach. The therapist must be very careful to prepare the adolescent, the parent(s), and other family members adequately for these conversations to maximize the possibilities for success. Preparation consists of meeting with each family member alone to explore, highlight, question, and acknowledge personal beliefs, attitudes, opinions, and feelings about themselves, other family members, and the family as a whole. Family members often need help in ascertaining how they feel and what they think about the important themes that the therapist or other family members have brought to the therapy.

By working individually with each family member before the enactment, the therapist is able to (1) solidify alliances so that the therapist will be free to challenge in the upcoming enactment sequence, (2) help family members formulate the content and style of what they want to say to other members, and (3) elicit from the family members their most helpful statements. The definition of helpful statements, of course, varies from family to family, person to person, and issue to issue. For example, a parent's statement of willingness to listen to the adolescent's perspective, despite many previous disappointments and hurts, is a helpful statement.

Many substance-abusing adolescents have little control of their emotions, thoughts, behaviors, and daily life. Although they may not be able to articulate precisely how they experience the world, many adolescents have an unmistakable sense that something in their life is desperately wrong. Several interventions are used in this situation. First, the therapist should have high expectations for the adolescent and should attempt to increase the adolescent's self-expectations by providing alternatives—holding up certain desirable behaviors and, in essence, saying, "This is what you can do, this is what you can be, this is how you can get along in the world, and this is how you can interact with your parents." For each family, the therapist may use different materials to sketch this portrait of higher expectations (e.g., attributions, emotions, the past), but the message is always the same: "You can do better, and I'm going to help you do better."

The therapist also presents to the adolescent high expectations of the parents and explains to the teen-ager the therapeutic goal of helping the parents be better parents—to be more fair, to listen and acknowledge the adolescent, and to be more responsive. By talking to the adolescent about the parents' parenting, the therapist counters the teen-ager's fear that the responsibility for change will lie solely with him or her. It is important not only to help parents understand that they will need to do some things differently for the adolescent to change, but also to help the teen-ager understand that he or she has a role (insofar as family atmosphere and relationships are concerned) in making things better as well. This serves to counter the adolescent's pessimism as well. It can be a difficult balance for the therapist to maintain, but the adolescent should feel *some degree* of responsibility to help alter the parents' behavior. The therapist creates a partnership with the teen-ager that, among other things, helps the adolescent deal with the parents and the way that they treat the adolescent. Teen-agers appreciate having and often need a spokesperson, even one who is not always completely on their side. They are accustomed to a world that does not respect them, expects them to be unreasonable, and in general perceives adolescence, incorrectly so, as a time of inevitable storm and stress (Offer et al., 1981).

In addition to increasing expectations, the therapist helps the adolescent, literally and figuratively, find a different language and, thus, a different way of being in the world. One teen-ager may need to learn to communicate unhappiness and frustration through words rather than through violence and self-destructive actions. Another may need to learn how to talk directly to the parent about past hurts and betrayals rather than continuing to punish the parent indirectly by repeated drug use and suicide attempts. The language that we aimed for is one in which the adolescents can, to the best of their ability, explain their subjective experiences, world views, hopes and dreams, complaints, and disappointments.

In conclusion, multidimensional family therapy accepts and uses the complexity of human existence and experience. It helps adolescents and their families work together in various realms to achieve multidimensional changes. Because families of teen-agers who are abusing drugs often have longstanding problems, comprehensive, developmentally rooted models are needed to address their problems. For therapeutic models to improve, the systems models of tomorrow must be empirically based and sufficiently intensive in design and execution. The families who come for help need and deserve no less than this.

REFERENCES

Aber, J.L., Allen, J., Carlson, V., & Cicchetti, D. (in press). The effects of maltreatment on development during early childhood: Recent studies and their theoretical, clinical, and policy implications. In D. Cicchetti & V. Carlson (Eds.), *Child maltreatment: Theory and research on the causes and consequences of child abuse and neglect.* New York: Cambridge University Press.

Achenbach, T.M. (1986). The developmental study of psychopathology: Implications for psychotherapy and behavior change. In S.L. Garfield & A.E. Bergin (Eds.), *Handbook of psychotherapy and behavior change* (pp. 117–154). New York: John Wiley & Sons.

Achenbach, T.M. (1990). What is "developmental" about developmental psychopathology? In J. Rolf, A.S. Masten, D. Cicchetti, K.H. Nuechterlein, & S. Weintraub (Eds.), *Risk and protective factors in the development of psychopathology.* New York: Cambridge University Press.

Alexander, J.F., Klein, N.C., & Parsons, B.V. (1977). Impact of family systems intervention on recidivism and sibling delinquency: A model of primary prevention and program evaluation. *Journal of Consulting and Clinical Psychology, 45*(3), 469–474.

Alexander, J.F., & Parsons, B.V. (1973). Short-term behavioral intervention with delinquent families: Impact on family process and recidivism. *Journal of Abnormal Psychology, 81*(3), 219–225.

Bandura, A. (1978). The self system in reciprocal determinism. *American Psychologist, 33,* 334–358.

Bandura, A. (1986). *Social foundations of thought and action: A social cognitive theory.* Englewood Cliffs, NJ: Prentice-Hall.

Barton, C., Alexander, J.F., Waldron, H., Turner, C.W., & Warburton, J. (1985). Generalizing treatment effects of functional family therapy: Three replications. *American Journal of Family Therapy, 13*(3), 16–26.

Baumrind, D. (1985). Familial antecendents of adolescent drug use: A developmental perspective. In C.L. Jones & R.J. Battjes (Eds.), *Etiology of drug abuse: Implications for prevention* (pp. 13–44). NIDA Research Monograph No. 56, DHHS Publication No. (ADM 85–1335). Rockville, MD: NIDA.

Baumrind, D. (1989). *Influence of parenting style on adolescent development.* Paper presented at the 97th annual convention of the American Psychological Association, New Orleans, LA.

Baumrind, D., & Moselle, K.A. (1985). A developmental perspective on adolescent drug abuse. *Advances in Alcohol and Substance Abuse, 4,* 41–67.

Bentler, P.M., Harlow, L.L., & Newcomb, M.D. (1986). Depression, self-derogation, substance use, and suicide ideation: Lack of purpose in life as a mediational factor. *Journal of Clinical Psychology, 42*(1), 5–21.

Berg, I.K., & Gallagher, D. (1991). Solution-focused brief treatment with adolescent substance abusers. In T. Todd & M. Selekman (Eds.), *Family therapy with adolescent substance abusers* (pp. 93–111). Needham Heights, MA: Allyn & Bacon.

Bernal, G., & Flores-Ortiz, Y. (1991). Contextual family therapy with adolescent drug abusers. In T. Todd & M. Selekman (Eds.), *Family therapy with adolescent substance abusers* (pp. 70–92). Needam Heights, MA: Allyn & Bacon.

Bronfenbrenner, U. (1983). The context of development and the development of context. In R.M. Lerner (Ed.), *Developmental psychology: Historical and philosophical perspectives* (pp. 147–184). Hillsdale, NJ: Lawrence Erlbaum Associates.

Brook, J.S., Whiteman, M., Nomura, C., Gordon, A.S., & Cohen, P. (1988). Personality, family and ecological influences on adolescent drug use: A developmental analysis. In R.H. Coombs (Ed.), *The family context of adolescent drug use* (pp. 123–162). New York: Haworth Press.

Bry, B.H. (1988). Family based approaches to reducing adolescent substance use: Theories, techniques and findings. In E.R. Rahdert & J. Grabowski (Eds.), *Adolescent drug abuse: Analysis of treatment research* (pp. 39–68). NIDA Monograph 77. Rockville, MD: DHHS.

Bukstein, O.G., Brent, D.A., & Kaminer, Y. (1989). Comorbidity of substance abuse and other psychiatric disorders in adolescents. *American Journal of Psychiatry, 146*(9), 1131–1141.

Burke, R.J., & Weir, T. (1978). Benefits to adolescents of informal helping relationships with their parents and peers. *Psychological Reports, 42,* 1175–1184.

Burke, R.J., & Weir, T. (1979). Helping responses of parents and peers and adolescent well-being. *Journal of Psychology, 102,* 49–62.

Cicchetti, D. (1984). The emergence of developmental psychopathology. *Child Development, 55,* 1–7.

Coombs, R.H., & Landsverk, J. (1988). Parenting styles and substance use during childhood and adolescence. *Journal of Marriage and the Family, 50,* 473–482.

Davidge, A.M., & Forman, S.G. (1988). Psychological treatment of adolescent substance abusers: A review. *Children and Youth Services Review, 10,* 45–55.

Dishion, T.J., & Loeber, R. (1985). Male adolescent marijuana and alcohol abuse: The role of parents and peers revisited. *Journal of Alcohol and Substance Abuse, 11*(12), 11–25.

Dishion, T.J., Patterson, G.R., & Reid, J.B. (1988). Parent and peer factors associated with drug sampling in early adolescence: Implication for treatment. In E.R. Rahdert & J. Grabowski (Eds.), *Adolescent drug abuse: Analyses of treatment research* (pp. 69–93). NIDA Research Monograph 77. Rockville, MD: DHHS.

Dishion, T.J., Reid, J.R., & Patterson, G.R. (1988). Empirical guidelines for a family intervention for adolescent drug use. In R.H. Coombs (Ed.), *The family context of adolescent drug use* (pp. 189–224). New York: Haworth Press.

Dodge, K.A. (1980). Social cognition and children's aggressive behavior. *Child Development, 51,* 162–170.

Dodge, K.A., Murphy, R.R., & Buchsbaum, K. (1984). The assessment of intention-cue detection skills in children: Implications for developmental psychopathology. *Child Development, 55,* 163–173.

Durrant, M., & Coles, D. (1991). Michael White's cybernetic approach. In T. Todd & M. Selekman (Eds.), *Family therapy with adolescent substance abusers.* Needham Heights, MA: Allyn & Bacon.

Elliott, D.S., Huizinga, D., & Ageton, S.S. (1985). *Explaining delinquency and drug use.* Beverly Hills, CA: Sage Publications.

Ellis, D.C. (1986). *Growing up stoned: Coming to terms with teenage drug abuse in modern America.* Pompano Beach, FL: Health Communications.

Erickson, G.D. (1988). Against the grain: Decentering family therapy. *Journal of Marital and Family Therapy, 14,* 225–236.

Fisch, R. (1989). Training in the brief therapy model. In H.A. Liddle, D.C. Breunlin, & R.C. Schwartz (Eds.), *Handbook of family therapy training and supervision* (pp. 78–92). New York: Guilford Press.

Fishman, H.C. (1986). *Treating troubled adolescents: A family therapy approach.* New York: Basic Books.

Fox, M.R. (1991). Strategic inpatient family therapy with adolescent substance abusers: The Fox system. In T. Todd & M. Selekman (Eds.), *Family therapy with adolescent substance abusers* (pp. 190–208). Needham Heights, MA: Allyn & Bacon.

Fraser, J.S. (1986). Integrating systems-based models: Similarities, differences, and some critical questions. In D.E. Efron (Ed.), *Journeys: Expansion of the strategic-systemic therapies*. New York: Brunner/Mazel.

Goldfried, M.R., & Wolfe, B.E. (1988). Research on psychotherapy integration: Recommendations and conclusions from an NIMH Workshop. *Journal of Consulting and Clinical Psychology, 56,* 448–451.

Greenberg, L.S., & Safran, J.D. (1987). *Emotion in psychotherapy: Affect, cognition, and the process of change*. New York: Guilford Press.

Greenberg, M.T., Siegel, J.M., & Leitch, C.J. (1983). The nature and importance of attachment relationships to parents and peers during adolescence. *Journal of Youth and Adolescence, 12*(5), 373–386.

Grotevant, H.D., & Cooper, C.R. (Eds.). (1983). *Adolescent development in the family*. San Francisco: Jossey-Bass.

Gurman, A.S. (1988). Issues in the specification of family therapy interventions. In L.C. Wynne (Ed.), *The state of the art in family therapy research: Controversies and recommendations*. New York: Family Process Press.

Haley, J. (1976). *Problem solving therapy*. San Francisco: Jossey-Bass.

Haley, J. (1981). *Leaving home*. New York: McGraw-Hill.

Hansen, D.J., Watson-Perczel, M., & Christopher, J.S. (1989). Clinical issues in social-skills training with adolescents. *Clinical Psychology Review, 9,* 365–391.

Hartrup, W. (1979). Two social worlds of childhood. *American Psychologist, 39,* 955–960.

Hauser, S.T., Borman, E.H., Jacobson, A.M., Powers, S.I., & Noam, G.G. (1991). Understanding family contexts of adolescent coping: A study of parental ego development and adolescent coping strategies. *Journal of Early Adolescence, 11*(1), 96–124.

Hauser, S.T., Liebman, W., Houlihan, J., Powers, S.I., Jacobson, A.M., Noam G.G., Weiss, B., & Follansbee, D. (1985). Family contexts of pubertal timing. *Journal of Youth and Adolescence, 14*(4), 317–337.

Hauser, S.T., Powers, S., Noam, G.G., Jacobson, A.M., Weiss, B., & Follansbee, D.J. (1984). Family context of adolescent ego development. *Child Development, 55,* 195–213.

Heath, A.W., & Ayers, T.C. (1991). MRI brief therapy with adolescent substance abusers. In T. Todd & M. Selekman (Eds.), *Family therapy with adolescent substance abusers* (pp. 49–69). Needham Heights, MA: Allyn & Bacon.

Henggeler, S.W., Rodick, J.D., Bourduin, C.M., Hanson, C.L., Watson, S.M., & Urey, J.R. (1986). Multisystemic treatment of juvenile offenders: Effects on adolescent behavior and family interaction. *Developmental Psychology, 22,* 132–141.

Hill, J.P. (1980). The family. In M. Johnson & K.J. Rehage (Eds.), *Toward adolescence: The middle school years. Part I* (pp. 32–55). Chicago: University of Chicago Press.

Hill, J.P., & Holmbeck, G.N. (1986). Attachment and autonomy during adolescence. *Annals of Child Development, 3,* 145–189.

Jessor, R., & Jessor, S.L. (1977). The social-psychological framework. In R. Jessor & S.L. Jessor (Eds.), *Problem behavior and psychosocial development: A longitudinal study of youth* (pp. 17–42). New York: Academic Press.

Joanning, H., Lewis, R., & Liddle, H. (1990, May 1). Using family therapy to treat adolescent drug abuse. *Congressional Record* (U.S. Senate), 55506–55507.

Joanning, H., Thomas, F., Newfield, N., & Lamur, B. (1991). Organizing a coordinated family treatment model for the inpatient and outpatient treatment of adolescent drug abuse. *Journal of Family Psychotherapy, 1*(4), 29–47.

Jurich, A. (1990). The jujitsu approach: Confronting the belligerent adolescent. *Family Therapy Networker*, (64), 43–45, 47, 64.

Kaslow, F.W. (1987). Trends in family psychology. *Journal of Family Psychology, 1,* 77–90.

Kazdin, A.E. (1987). Treatment of antisocial behavior in children: Current status and future directions. *Psychological Bulletin, 102,* 187–203.

Kazdin, A.E. (1989). Developmental psychopathology: Current research, issues and directions. *American Psychologist, 44*(2), 180–187.

Kellam, S., Brown, C.H., Rubin, B.R., & Ensminger, M.E. (1983). Paths leading to teenage psychiatric symptoms and substance abuse: Developmental epidemiological studies in Woodlawn. In S.B. Guze, F.J. Earls, & J.E. Barrett (Eds.), *Childhood psychopathology and development.* New York: Raven Press.

Larson, R.W. (1983). Adolescents' daily experiences with family and friends: Contrasting opportunity systems. *Journal of Marriage and the Family, 45,* 739–750.

Lebow, J.L. (1987). Developing a personal integration in family therapy: Principles for model construction and practice. *Journal of Marital and Family Therapy, 13*(1), 1–14.

Lerner, R.M. (1978). Nature, nurture, dynamic interaction. *Human Development, 21,* 1–20.

Lewis, R.A., Piercy, F.P., Sprenkle, D.H., & Trepper, T.S. (1990a). Family-based interventions for helping drug-abusing adolescents. *Journal of Adolescent Research, 50*(1), 82–95.

Lewis, R.A., Piercy, F.P., Sprenkle, D.H., & Trepper, T.S. (1990b). The Purdue brief family therapy model for adolescent substance abusers. In T. Todd & M. Selekman (Eds.), *Family therapy with adolescent substance abusers.* Needham Heights, MA: Allyn & Bacon.

Liddle, H.A. (1987a). Family psychology: The journal, the field. *Journal of Family Psychology, 1*(1), 5–22.

Liddle, H.A. (1987b). Family psychology: Task of an emerging (and emerged) discipline. *Journal of Family Psychology, 1*(2), 149–167.

Liddle, H.A. (1990a). *Clinical practice and research in family therapy: Why the gap persists.* Paper presented at the 1990 annual meeting of the American Association for Marriage and Family Therapy, Washington, DC.

Liddle, H.A. (1990b). *What's wrong with family therapy?* Paper presented at the 1990 annual meeting of the American Association for Marriage and Family Therapy, Washington, DC.

Liddle, H.A. (1991a). *The Adolescents and Families Project: Multidimensional family therapy in action* (ADAMHA monograph from the first national conference on the treatment of adolescent drug, alcohol and mental health problems, Public Health Service). Washington, DC: U.S. Government Printing Office.

Liddle, H.A. (1991b). Empirical values and the culture of family therapy. *Journal of Marital and Family Therapy, 17,* 327–348.

Liddle, H.A. (1991c). Engaging the adolescent in family systems therapy. In T. Nelson (Ed.), *Interventions in family therapy.* New York: Haworth Press.

Liddle, H.A., & Schmidt, S. (1991). *Family therapy with drug abusing adolescents: The state of the art.* Invited technical report prepared for the NIDA meeting on the 5-year plan for the Treatment Research Branch, Bethesda, MD, February 7–8.

Liddle, H.A., Schmidt, S., & Ettinger (in press). Adolescent developmental research: Guidelines for clinicians. *Journal of Marital and Family Therapy.*

Liddle, H.A., & Schwartz, R.C. (1983). Live supervision/consultation: Conceptual and pragmatic guidelines for family therapy training. *Family Process, 22,* 477–490.

Madanes, C. (1981). *Strategic family therapy.* San Francisco: Jossey-Bass.

Madanes, C. (1985). *Behind the one way mirror.* San Francisco: Jossey-Bass.

Magnusson, D. (1988). *Individual development from an interactional perspective: A longitudinal study.* Hillsdale, NJ: Lawrence Erlbaum Associates.

Mahoney, M.J. (1984). Integrating cognition, affect, and action: A comment. *Cognitive Therapy and Research, 8,* 585–589.

Mann, B.J., Borduin, C.M., Henggeler, S.W., & Blaske, D.M. (1990). An investigation of systemic conceptualizations of parent-child coalitions and symptom change. *Journal of Consulting and Clinical Psychology, 58,* 336–344.

Miller, G.E., & Prinz, R.J. (1991). Enhancement of social learning family interventions for childhood conduct disorder. *Psychological Bulletin, 108*(2), 291–307.

Montalvo, B. (1973). Aspects of live supervision. *Family Process, 12,* 343–359.

Montemayor, R. (1983). Parents and adolescents in conflict: All families some of the time and some families most of the time. *Journal of Early Adolescence, 3*(1–2), 83–103.

Montemayor, R. (1986). Family variation in parent-adolescent storm and stress. *Journal of Adolescent Research, 1*(1), 15–31.

National Institutes of Health. (1983). *NIH Guide for Grants and Contracts, 12*(8).

Newcomb, M.D., & Bentler, P.M. (1988a). Impact of adolescent drug use and social support on problems of young adults: A longitudinal study. *Journal of Abnormal Psychology, 97*(1), 64–75.

Newcomb, M.D., & Bentler, P.M. (1988b). The impact of family context, deviant attitudes, and emotional distress on adolescent drug use: Longitudinal latent-variable analyses of mothers and their children. *Journal of Research in Personality, 22,* 154–176.

Newcomb, M.D., & Bentler, P.M. (1989). Substance use and abuse among children and teenagers. *American Psychologist, 44,* 242–248.

Newcomb, M.D., & Harlow, L.L. (1986). Life events and substance use among adolescents: Mediating effects of perceived loss of control and meaninglessness in life. *Journal of Personality and Social Psychology, 51,* 564–577.

Offer, D., Ostrov, E., & Howard, K.I. (1981). The mental health professional's concept of the normal adolescent. *Archives of General Psychiatry, 38,* 149–152.

Pandina, R.J., & Schuele, J.A. (1983). Psychosocial correlates of alcohol and drug use of adolescent students and adolescents in treatment. *Journal of Studies on Alcohol, 44*(6), 950–973.

Pinsof, W.M. (1989). A conceptual framework and methodological criteria for family therapy research. *Journal of Consulting and Clinical Psychology, 57,* 53–59.

Pittman, F.S. (1987). *Turning points.* New York: W.W. Norton.

Reider, C., & Cicchetti, D. (1990). Organizational perspective on cognitive control functioning and cognitive-affective balance in maltreated children. *Developmental Psychology, 25,* 382–393.

Robin, A.L., & Foster, S.L. (1989). *Negotiating parent adolescent conflict: A behavioral-family systems approach.* New York: Guilford Press.

Rook, K.S. (1984). The negative side of social interaction: Impact on psychological well-being. *Journal of Personality and Social Psychology, 46,* 1097–1108.

Rutter, M., & Sroufe, L.A. (1984). The domain of developmental psychopathology. *Child Development, 55,* 17–29.

Ryan, R.M., & Lynch, J.H. (1989). Emotional autonomy versus detachment: Revisiting the vicissitudes of adolescence and young adulthood. *Child Development, 60,* 340–356.

Shantz, C.U. (1983). Social cognition. In J.H. Flavell & E.M. Markman (Eds.), *Handbook of child psychology* (Vol. 3, pp. 495–555). New York: John Wiley & Sons.

Shedler, J., & Block, J. (1990). Adolescent drug use and psychological health: A longitudinal inquiry. *American Psychologist, 45*(5), 612–630.

Silverberg, S.B., & Steinberg, L. (1987). Adolescent autonomy, parent-adolescent conflict, and parental well-being. *Journal of Youth and Adolescence, 16*(3), 293–311.

Stanton, M.D. (1981). An integrated structural/strategic approach to family therapy. *Journal of Marital and Family Therapy, 7,* 427–439.

Stanton, M.D., Todd, T.C., & Associates (1982). *The family therapy of drug abuse and addiction.* New York: Guilford Press.

Steinberg, L. (1987). Family factors in delinquency: A developmental perspective. *Journal of Adolescent Research, 2*(3), 255–268.

Steinberg, L. (1990). Autonomy, conflict, and harmony in the family. In S.S. Feldman & G.R. Elliott (Eds.), *At the threshold: The developing adolescent.* Cambridge, MA: Harvard University Press.

Steinberg, L. (in press). *Interdependency in the family: Autonomy, conflict and harmony in the parent-adolescent relationship.* New York: Carnegie Council on Adolescent Development.

Steinberg, L., & Silverberg, S. (1986). The vicissitudes of autonomy in early adolescence. *Child Development, 57,* 841–851.

Szapocznik, J., Kurtines, W., Foote, F., Perez-Vidal, A., & Hervis, O. (1983). Conjoint versus one-person family therapy: Some evidence for the effectiveness of conducting family therapy through one person. *Journal of Consulting and Clinical Psychology, 51,* 889–899.

Szapocznik, J., Perez-Vidal, A., Brickman, A.L., Foote, F.H., Santiseban, D., Hervis, O., & Kurtines, W.M. (1988). Engaging adolescent drug abusers and their families in treatment: A strategic structural systems approach. *Journal of Consulting and Clinical Psychology, 56*(4), 552–557.

Todd, T.C. (1986). Structural-strategic marital therapy. In N.S. Jacobson & A.S. Gurman (Eds.), *Clinical handbook of marital therapy* (pp. 71–105). New York: Guilford Press.

Todd, T.C., & Selekman, M.D. (Eds.). (1991). *Family therapy with adolescent substance abusers.* Needham Heights, MA: Allyn & Bacon.

Wachtel, P.L. (1977). *Psychoanalysis and behavior therapy: Toward an integration.* New York: Basic Books.

Wills, T.A. (1990). Social support and the family. In E.A. Blechman (Ed.), *Emotions and the family: For better or worse.* Hillsdale, NJ: Lawrence Erlbaum Associates.

Wills, T.A., & Vaughn, R. (1989). Social support and smoking in early adolescence. *Journal of Behavioral Medicine, 12,* 321–339.

Youniss, J., & Smollar, J. (1985). *Adolescent relations with mothers, fathers and friends.* Chicago: University of Chicago Press.

12

Taming the Chemical Monsters: Cybernetic-Systemic Therapy with Adolescent Substance Abusers

The cybernetic-systemic approach of Michael White has provided the family therapy field with an innovative and creative therapeutic method for working with a wide range of presenting problems (White, 1984, 1985, 1986, & 1987). White's cybernetic approach is based on the theoretical principles of Gregory Bateson (1972 & 1980), the philosophical ideas of Michael Foucault (White, 1987), and the work of Second Cybernetics theoreticians. What is most unique about the cybernetic-systemic therapy approach is the therapist's commitment to maintaining a non-blame stance with families. For the cybernetic family therapist, problems develop in families as a result of the activation of vicious cycles of family interaction following the mishandling of a problematic situation, random events, or family stressors (Durrant, 1985 & 1987). Over time, the family members become stuck or restrained in how they interact with the problem and with one another. This leads to the perpetuation of vicious guilt/blame cycles of interaction and scapegoating in the family. According to Durrant, "the notion of restrained participation around the problem removes the need for the popular family therapy idea of 'the function of the symptom'" (Durrant, 1987). The cybernetic family therapist views the family restraints as the problem, not the symptomatic person or some structural abnormality in the family system. The family as a whole is oppressed by the problem, including the symptomatic person.

CYBERNETIC-SYSTEMIC QUESTIONING

Among the most important and innovative aspects of White's therapy approach is his careful use of client language to externalize the problem out of the symp-

Source: From "Taming the Chemical Monsters: Cybernetic-Systemic Therapy with Adolescent Substance Abusers" by M. Selekman, 1989, *Journal of Strategic and Systemic Therapies, 8,* pp. 5–9. Copyright 1989 by Journal of Strategic and Systemic Therapies. Reprinted by permission.

tomatic person. Through the use of the family's description of the problem, the cybernetic family therapist co-constructs with the family a new objectified and metaphorical description of the problem—i.e., cocaine addiction becomes Coke. Some examples of *externalizing questions* are as follows: "How long has Coke been pushing Johnny around?" "What kinds of things does Coke make Johnny do?" "So when you ask Johnny to clean up his bedroom, Coke makes him cuss you out?" Problems can be externalized into oppressive lifestyles, careers, or patterns—i.e., "how long has The Pattern been pushing all of you around?" These kinds of questions begin to challenge the outmoded family beliefs that the locus of the problem is inside the symptomatic person.

Another category of questions which help pave the way to solution are *relative influence* questions. These questions elicit from family members information regarding periods of time when the problem is not pushing them around. Families that are stuck or are operating from a restrained belief system have a difficult time accessing successful past solutions or recognizing times when they have control over the problem. DeShazer (1985) contends that nothing happens all of the time, that there are always exceptions to the rule. Exception sequences of behavior can be used to construct a solution. Relative influence questions capitalize on these exceptions and help facilitate for the family the discovery of "newsworthy" information that may make a difference. A few examples of relative influence questions are as follows: "I'm curious, are there times when Coke is not pushing you around?" "Have there been any times lately, Johnny, when you have achieved victories over Coke?" and "Johnny, can you think of times when your parents have achieved victories over Coke?"

Raising dilemma questions are useful for creating intensity and emotionality within the family. These questions present to the family a double description of their current state-of-affairs—you may remain the same or you may decide to change. The therapist argues strongly for both positions, presenting the advantages and disadvantages of both, and leaves the dilemma resting in the hands of the family. All dilemmas presented to the family must be framed interactionally (Durrant, 1987). Some examples of raising dilemma questions are as follows: "Johnny, are you going to continue to allow Coke to make you get into trouble at school, or do you prefer to be known around school as being a popular guy?" "Are you (parents) going to continue to allow Coke to push your son around or are you planning to assist Johnny in putting a stop to Coke's reign over him?"

The last major category of cybernetic questions are known as *complimentary questions*. These questions are excellent for interactionalizing the problem description. Similar to raising dilemma questions, complimentary questions can create emotionality in the family. Two examples of this line of questioning are: "Do you (the adolescent) see how Coke puts your parents in charge of your future?" and "Do you (parents) see how Coke is taking away your son's future?"

ADOLESCENT SUBSTANCE ABUSE IN CONTEXT

Family therapists who work fairly regularly with adolescent substance abusers are quite familiar with the repetitive guilt/blame patterns of interaction that operate in these families. These patterns of interaction are maintained by ineffectual attempted solutions—i.e., lectures about the dangers of using drugs or power struggles; and dormitive explanations of why the substance abuse problem exists —i.e., the adolescent has a progressive disease or low self-esteem. Often times, the alcohol or drug problem develops a life of its own in families. This author has worked with several families where alcohol problems had been oppressing them for three or four generations. Typically, the adolescent substance abuser is blamed for the family problems and may end up being hospitalized. The major problem with this popular attempted solution is the fact that the old family patterns and beliefs about the substance abuser are left untouched while the latter is in the hospital. Shortly after being discharged, the substance abuser most likely will relapse, which in turn, will further exacerbate the vicious guilt/blame cycles of interaction in the family. It is also important to examine the role the substance abuser's peer group and larger systems (the school and juvenile justice systems) play in the maintenance of the problem life support system (Tomm & White, 1987).

According to White, relapses can be framed to the family as being an opportunity for come back practice (White, 1987). The author has found it most useful to normalize drug and alcohol relapses as being an opportunity for growth and springboards toward further changes (Selekman, 1987). The family should be told that relapses are inevitable, particularly with adolescent substance abusers. Once drug or alcohol abstinence occurs, the author routinely predicts potential relapses in between sessions as a way of keeping the family "on their toes" and reinforcing changes. "Go Slow!" messages and restraint from immediate change are useful interventions in the context of substance abuse problems. This author frequently uses the strategic intervention of asking the substance abuser to pay close attention to what he does to avoid the temptation to get "high" between sessions (DeShazer, 1985).

Besides introducing "newsworthy" information to the family through the use of cybernetic questioning, experiments or rituals will be prescribed between sessions to help consolidate gains and facilitate the family learning process. An example of a ritual this author frequently employs with adolescent substance abusers is as follows; the parents may be asked to expose the adolescent to potentially frustrating situations, which in the past, would have led to drug use; the family would be asked to keep track of both the adolescent's and The Chemical Monster's victories over one another; special privileges can be given to the adolescent for being victorious over The Chemical Monster. Another variation of this ritual is to have the adolescent keep track of the various things that he does to avoid giving in to peer pressure to get "high." The parents and adolescent can develop a point/level system based on the various ways the youngster positively handles peer pressure and remains "straight."

Therapy tends to be brief, three to six sessions, with long intervals between each session. Palazzoli (1980) believes that longer intervals between sessions provide the family with time to provide an answer to therapeutic inputs, which in turn, may lead to "news of a difference" and observable changes. A small change or difference when noted in the first session by the family, may be adequate enough to set in motion a positive feedback loop process which will lead to the development of a virtuous cycle of family interaction (Durrant, 1987). The second and subsequent sessions consist of highlighting differences and having the family do experiments. Therapy concludes with a celebration party.

Finally, all major changes are to be responded to with amazement and celebration (Tomm & White, 1987). Family members are asked to make distinctions between the past and present family patterns of interaction to help highlight "the news of a difference, that made a difference." Trophies, plaques, or certificates can be given to the adolescent for successfully Taming the Chemical Monster (Menses & Durrant, 1986). The creative concept of end of therapy celebration activities was developed by the New Zealand family therapist David Epston (Tomm & White, 1987).

The author has also found the cybernetic-systemic approach to be quite useful in other treatment contexts for adolescent substance abusers. The author has developed a relapse prevention group in a day treatment setting for chronic adolescent alcohol and drug abusers based on the cybernetic-systemic approach. Relapses are first normalized, which proves to be "newsworthy" information for these troubled youths. Through the use of cybernetic questioning, relapses are externalized from the students into external "just keeping you honest friends," or "beasts" and "monsters." The students keep track of which type of relapse they interact with on a daily basis. Students are to write in their daily journal entries exceptions where they remain "straight," as well as keep track of times when the Relapse Monster is pushing them around. Systemic role plays are performed with each student to help demonstrate the various ways that they invite the Relapse Monster to interact with them, their family, and larger systems—i.e., the probation officer. The school staff keep track of both the students' and the Relapse Monsters' victories over one another. Cybernetic language and questions are employed in daily interactions with students to help highlight differences. At the end of each school semester, students receive medals, plaques, trophies, and a special luncheon to celebrate their victories over the Relapse Monsters.

CASE EXAMPLE

What was most unusual about the Brown case, was the fact that Robert, a seventeen-year-old heavy alcohol abuser, made the initial call for help. Typically, the mother or a school counselor involved with the adolescent substance abuser is the complainant. Robert had decided to call the author's agency due to his "loss of control with alcohol." Robert allegedly had been drinking beer four to five times per week. At one sitting, Robert claimed he could consume a quart of beer. Robert also mentioned over the telephone that lately when he drinks he becomes "physically out of control" as well—i.e., punching holes in his bedroom wall and threatening to strike his mother. An appointment was scheduled for Robert and his mother the next day with the author.

First Interview

The therapist spent the first fifteen minutes of the initial session joining with Robert and his mother. Mrs. Brown (Carol) reported to him that she had worked as an executive secretary for a small company for twelve years. Mr. Brown (George) had worked for the same company until his death from "alcoholism" two years ago. Carol disclosed to the therapist that "alcoholism had claimed the lives" of George's brother, an uncle, and the paternal grandfather. Carol further added: "I think Robert may be an alcoholic." Robert responded with: "No way man!" In response to this brief exchange of words between Robert and his mother, the therapist decided to shift gears and begin establishing rapport with Robert. He began by complimenting Robert on his courage to ask for help. Robert was also complimented on how he had "one hell of a grip" when it comes to handshakes. Robert proudly proclaimed to the therapist that he was a former "State Wrestling Champion" two years ago. The therapist explored with Robert how he had accomplished such an incredible feat. Robert shared with him that he used to run daily close to five miles and lift free weights four times per week. The therapist disclosed to the family that he used to wrestle in junior high school, but decided to hang up his wrestling career for good after being pinned in less than two minutes in the finals of a tournament. Robert and his mother laughed. The therapist joined in on the laughter. Carol began to brag about what an "outstanding wrestler" Robert used to be. She further added: "I used to love going to his wrestling matches." At this point in the session the therapist decided to shift gears—i.e., explore with each family member his or her view of the problem. It soon became quite clear to the therapist that Robert and his mother were in disagreement over whether or not Robert was "an alcoholic." Robert, however, did feel that he had "lost control" over his alcohol consumption and "anger."

After discovering how important wrestling was for this family, the therapist decided to utilize wrestling language in the majority of his questions and future interventions. The first major task with the Browns was to begin to challenge the family beliefs that Robert was an "alcoholic" and that "all the men in the Brown family die from alcoholism." This genetic/biological disease-based explanation is a hopeless view. In the Brown family, this belief system had been perpetuated for four generations. Alcoholism problems had not only been maintained by this outmoded belief system, but were also supported by vicious guilt/blame cycles that had been transferred down through the generations. In the present family drama, Carol blamed herself for not saving her husband from the "death grip of alcoholism." While talking about George, Carol began to cry and share her concerns about the alcoholism "claiming the life" of her only child Robert. Robert remained fairly cool while his mother expressed her concerns. Carol began to yell at Robert in the session about having a "nonchalant attitude." Robert responded to his mother's angry voice with "Don't worry so much . . . I can take care of myself."

In an effort to help disrupt restrained patterns of interaction around the problem, the therapist began to reconstruct the family view of the problem through the use of externalizing questions. He asked the following questions: "So, the Alcohol Monster has been pushing you two and the Brown men around for some time, hasn't it?"; (To Carol) "How long has the Alcohol Monster been ruling over Robert's life?" and (Carol) "When the Alcohol Monster is trying to pin Robert, what sort of things does it make the two of you do?" Both Robert and his mother were in agreement that they had been oppressed by the Alcohol Monster for several years. In fact, Carol had disclosed for the first time that her "father" and paternal "grandfather" were also "pushed around" by the "Alcohol Monster." Robert reacted strongly to the second and third questions by saying: "Ruling over me?" "Trying to pin me?" "I'm not going to allow alcohol to put me in a grave, no way!" Carol reported to the therapist that Robert gets physically out of control when he is drunk. Apparently, Robert has punched several holes through his bedroom walls. On one occasion, Robert had "threatened to punch" his mother. Carol admitted that she was scared of Robert.

At this point in the session, the therapist decided to explore with the family how things are different in their relationship when the Alcohol Monster is not pushing them around. Robert was asked: "Have there been any times lately when you have tricked the Alcohol Monster and not allowed it to take you down on the wrestling mat?" Carol was asked: "Can you think of any times lately where you have blocked the Alcohol Monster from taking advantage of Robert?" Robert responded to the first question by sharing that the days he "lifts weights" he usually remains "straight." The therapist made a mental note of this important exception as being a potential building block for solution. Carol mentioned to him that she had "poured down" the kitchen sink drain "many bottles of booze" that belonged to Robert. Robert was able to point out another important exception where he had control over his drinking. When Robert stood clear of a particular group of school peers, he would avoid the temptation to use alcohol.

In order to create more emotional intensity in the session, the therapist began to raise dilemmas with the family regarding the various ways that they invite the Alcohol Monster to reign over them. He asked the following questions of Robert: "Will you continue to follow the family tradition of allowing the Alcohol Monster to make you a passenger in life, or do you prefer to establish a new tradition of succeeding in life?" and "Do you want to continue to allow the Alcohol Monster to broadcast to the world that you are an 'alcoholic,' 'burnout,' or 'loser,' or do you want to develop a new reputation of being a winner?" Robert responded to these challenging questions with: "I know I'm a winner!"; "I'm not going to allow the Alcohol Monster to claim my life!" These questions did a nice job of eliciting Robert's competitive spirit.

Since the session time was coming to a close, the therapist decided to take a brief break to design an appropriate intervention. Utilizing the Browns' love for wrestling and Robert's competitive spirit, he developed a wrestling ritual which would capitalize on their strengths. Each day Robert was to keep track of all of the various things that he did to avoid the temptation to be pushed around or pinned by the Alcohol Monster. At the end of each day, Robert was to go to his mother to receive a score for his performance. The wrestling scoring system was employed (3 points = near pin, 2 points = reversal, and 1 point = an escape). The criterion for each point category was determined by Robert and his mother. A *near pin* situation would consist of Robert's "drinking a soda," rather than beer with his alcohol-using friends. *Reversal* points could be earned if Robert would go to a party, "think about drinking," but "avoid" the temptation to drink instead. An *escape* would consist of Robert's "walking away" from peer pressure to "get drunk." Robert would receive a special privilege for pinning the Alcohol Monster—i.e., "taking mother's Cadillac car out for a spin." Carol was put in charge of documenting on a chart both Robert's and the Alcohol Monster's victories over one another. The therapist encouraged Robert to train hard for this tough wrestling match. In fact, he suggested that Robert should utilize his former "champion training" methods. Before ending the session, the therapist predicted that most likely Robert would get pinned at least twice prior to our next appointment. After receiving the intervention, both Robert and his mother appeared fired up for this big challenge in their lives. The next appointment was scheduled for two weeks later.

Second Interview

Two weeks later, Robert and his mother came in smiling and proud of their accomplishment. Not only did Robert achieve daily pins over the Alcohol Monster, but the mother was now convinced that her son was "not an alcoholic." The fact that Robert did not have "shakes," "cravings," or "relapses," sold the mother on the idea that her son was "not physically addicted" to alcohol. Robert proudly shared with the mother and the therapist his plans to be the "first man in the Brown family to defeat the Alcohol Monster!" The therapist explored with Robert how he avoided the temptation to drink. Robert reported that he had been working out almost daily over the two-week period between sessions. Robert also was associating with some of his "old jock friends." The therapist cautioned Robert and his mother about Alcohol Monsters being sneaky characters and not giving up easily. Again, he predicted that Robert would be pushed around and pinned by the Alcohol Monster a few times over the next four weeks. As a vote of confidence for the family, the third session was scheduled for four weeks down the road. The family was asked to continue the wrestling ritual.

Third Interview

Prior to the third session, the therapist purchased a small trophy and an achievement certificate which he had planned to use as last session awards to celebrate the family changes. The Browns entered his office smiling and quite pleased with how well things were going. There were a number of changes that had occurred over the break period. Robert had no relapses, he secured a part-time job at a gas station, and he had announced his plans to go out for the wrestling team. Carol pointed out to the therapist that Robert "got to drive" her "Cadillac" practically on a daily basis "as a reward" for his "straightening out." Carol also reported that she was "getting out of the house more." While highlighting differences for the family, it was clear to the therapist that the Browns could make distinctions between their old and new family dance steps. He asked the Browns what they would need to do to "go backwards." Again, it was clear that news of a difference that made a difference was quite evident with the Browns. Towards the end of the session, Carol shared with the therapist that she had thought of "cancelling the appointment" because things were "going so well." The therapist and family mutually agreed to terminate therapy. Before allowing Robert and his mother to leave the room, the therapist presented the twosome with individual awards for their great achievement—defeating the Alcohol Monster. Robert was given a trophy for being a *Champion, Alcohol Monster Wrestler.* Carol was given a certificate for being a *Champion Wrestling Coach.* Robert and the mother were quite pleased with their awards. The final session concluded with hugs and handshakes.

Follow-up

Follow-up phone calls were made at three, six, and twelve months. Although Robert was not available for any of the therapist's calls, the mother reported that

Robert had remained abstinent from alcohol. The best news was hearing that Robert had achieved a "16-4 record" on his high school "wrestling team."

CONCLUSION

As the reader can clearly see, the cybernetic-systemic approach can be quite effective with chronic adolescent substance abuse problems. In the Brown case, the therapist carefully utilized client language and family strengths in externalizing the problem and with the wrestling ritual to break up the problem life support system in this family. The cybernetic questions alone are quite effective at challenging outmoded family beliefs and restrained patterns of interaction. The author has found the cybernetic approach to be most useful in the context of relapse prevention as well.

The interventions presented in this chapter are not meant to imply that their use in any way is a panacea for successful treatment with adolescent substance abusers and their families. Some heavy adolescent substance abusers may require periodic hospital-based detoxification or short-term hospitalization for physical withdrawal complications. With families where there are multiple substance abusers, the author has found it useful to structure sessions by intervening through individual family members or subsystems. With highly chaotic and disorganized families, the author has found a structural-strategic therapy approach to be the treatment of choice. Further clinical experimentation and research is needed with the cybernetic-systemic model in order to determine which type of adolescent substance abuse case situations may best benefit from this family therapy approach.

REFERENCES

Bateson, G. (1972). *Steps to an ecology of mind.* New York: Ballantine Books.

Bateson, G. (1980). *Mind and nature: A necessary unity.* New York: Bantam Books.

DeShazer, S. (1985). *Keys to solution in brief therapy.* New York: W. W. Norton.

Durrant, M. (1985). *Temper taming.* Unpublished manuscript.

Durrant, M. (1987). *Foundations of systemic/cybernetic family therapy.* Unpublished manuscript.

Menses, G., & Durrant, M. (1986). Contextual residential care: The applications of the principles of cybernetic therapy to the residential treatment of irresponsible adolescents and their families. *Dulwich Centre Review,* 3–13.

Palazzoli, M.S. (1980). Why a longer interval between sessions? The therapeutic control of the family-therapist suprasystem. In M. Andolfi & I. Zwerling (Eds.), *Dimensions of family therapy* (pp. 161–171). New York: Guilford Press.

Selekman, M. (1987). Conquering a chemical monster: A case of adolescent substance abuse. *Family Therapy Case Studies,* 51–57.

Tomm, K., & White, M. (1987, October). *Externalizing problems and internalizing directional choices.* Training Institute presented at the Annual Conference of the American Association for Marriage and Family Therapy, Chicago, IL.

White, M. (1984). Pseudoencopresis: From avalanche to victory, from vicious to virtuous cycles. *Family Systems Medicine, 2*(2), 150–160.

White, M. (1985). Fear busting and monster taming: An approach to the fears of young children. *Dulwich Centre Review,* 29–33.

White, M. (1986). Negative explanation, restraint and double description. *Family Process, 25*(2), 169–184.

White, M. (1987). Family therapy & schizophrenia: Addressing the in-the-corner lifestyle. *Dulwich Centre Newsletter,* 14–21.

13

Neurolinguistic Programming and Hypnosis during Intervention with Substance-Abusing Adolescents

Kirt J. Baab

Substance abuse, or substance dependence, involves the ingestion of a substance with the intent to alter mood, affect, thinking, and behavior patterns. "Getting high" creates a change in consciousness.

Rossi (1986) described in detail how human physiology is changed by stress and how "states" may be conceptualized in terms of both body and mind. In outlining the interaction between mind and body, Rossi made it clear that what occurs in one state and what occurs in another ("altered") state may or may not be consciously retrievable in the "natural" state. The possibility that altering the physiology alters the state experienced by the individual is known to both the substance abuser and the psychotherapist.

THERAPEUTIC COMMUNICATION

A procedure for communicating with a person who moves in and out of one (or more) states into another (or others) has been one of the hallmarks of the work of Erickson (1981). How does this relate to communicating with a substance-abusing adolescent? How do hypnosis, body-mind healing, communication, and substance dependence relate to one another? An adolescent who gets high is making the statements, "I don't like things the way they are, so I'll alter them by whatever means are at my disposal" and "I'll do this independent of you." Hypnosis in the appropriate context can also alter experience from one way of being and doing to another way of being and doing. Hypnosis may be autosuggestive or suggested by a therapist. It is beneficial for adolescents to learn methods of altering their way of being and doing other than through the use of substances.

Body-mind healing is a process in which states are identified, their functions understood, and the person assisted in changing his or her way of being and doing by using these states and developing others (Rossi, 1986). Metacommunication is analogous to body-mind healing in hypnosis (Bandler & Grinder, 1975). Adolescents who have used drugs and/or alcohol have injured both body and mind. They develop different states through the use of substances, which may inhibit the body's normal production of mood-altering substances. This is counterproductive. In the long run, the use of substances to get high robs the body of its natural ability to get high. A method that uses these states is a parsimonious method for healing body-mind injuries. Hypnotherapy and metacommunication are two different methods of using these states. They do so through the dialogue between the counselor and the adolescent.

Planning the Use of Therapeutic Communication

The counselor's relationship with the substance-abusing adolescent provides a context in which both the body-mind injuries and the information necessary to heal those injuries are revealed. In the relationship, the counselor confronts one of the primary indicators of a substance abuse problem. The teen-ager denies use, denies dependence, denies its consequences, denies his or her previous communication, and/or denies his or her attributes (which may be the very resources necessary to break the cycle of addiction). Denial, which often appears as resistance to treatment, is a primary symptom of addiction (Meagher, 1987). Resistance to treatment is generally believed to be under conscious control and to have a malicious intent to violate the values of the counselor, social worker, or therapist (Bandler & Grinder, 1979). In fact, the power struggles between adolescents and adults that abound in the treatment of adolescents often revolve around the disagreement between client and counselor about the "intention" of the client when he or she "denies" that a problem exists.

An alternative to seeing denial as resistance or a deliberate intent to deceive is to see the "substance-abusing part" of the personality as subconsciously (or preconsciously) motivated. According to this view, the substance-abusing part is state-dependent, or linked to the physiological arousal level of the drug-intoxicated state. Furthermore, the substance-abusing part may indeed be oppositional to the counselor *and* to the healthy part of the adolescent's personality that wants to comply with treatment demands. The procedure for using the resistance is a paradoxical one (Erickson, 1981; Rossi, 1986; Watzlawick, Weakland, & Fisch, 1974).

This paradoxical procedure is relatively simple for the counselor. First, the counselor must be able to distinguish between the "parts" of the adolescent. Second, the counselor must know the goals and objectives of counseling this specific adolescent. Third, the counselor must identify the sequence of intermediary steps that he or she is willing to take in the dialogue with the client to build and retain rapport with the healthy part(s) of the adolescent. Fourth, the counselor must have a means of gaining access to the individual state-dependent parts with the adolescent. Fifth, the counselor must be able to direct the adolescent toward the goals and objectives of treatment, while carefully taking the time to complete fully each task.

Dynamics within the Personality

The healthy part(s) of the personality exist at one level of conscious awareness (i.e., one state of physiological arousal); the unhealthy part(s) of the personality, at another level of arousal. In some cases, the suppressed or repressed material may resurface periodically for the client. This is the "unfinished business" or family-of-origin material that may be the adolescent's explanation for the use of substances.

The conscious, healthy part of the personality can be compared to a driver in the front seat of a car. In the back seat are two 3-year-old children who clamor so loudly from time to time that they distract the driver. If one of those children screams in pain, the distraction may be so great that the driver may slam on the brakes, swerve uncontrollably, or turn around while still driving and, thus, stop watching the road. The back seat occupants, the unhealthy part of the personality are indulged, are but unwittingly jeopardize both themselves and the driver.

Similarly, the unhealthy part(s) of a 15-year-old boy are unlikely to understand the importance of coming home from the beach earlier than his peers instead of staying out late with his friends who drink, even though the police arrest students for drinking at the beach. An explanation usually leads to one of three responses. The boy may say, "Yeah, Mom. I know! I know!" and come home late anyway. He may say, "You *always* tell me I hafta come home early. *Nobody* else does!" and slam the door as he leaves; or he may say, "Fine! . . . I won't go then!" and sulk in his room, closing the door, sitting in the dark, and turning up the stereo.

Two messages are actually conveyed in each situation. One occurs at the verbal level: "I'm answering, so you can't say I don't listen." The other is nonverbal and is conveyed through the behavior accompanying the verbal response, effectively eliciting another response from the adults. An angry verbal response with an oppositional behavioral response elicits anger or fear in the parents. An angry, attacking response elicits anger, guilt, or fear in the parents. An angry verbal response with a "complaining" behavioral response elicits guilt, worry, or anger in the parents. The 3-year-old children are reigning supreme.

IMPLEMENTATION OF THE TREATMENT PROGRAM

The counselor's first step in the treatment of a substance-abusing adolescent is to distinguish between the self-destructive part of the adolescent and the constructive, self-nurturing part. In some treatment programs, the destructive part is called the large addictive self, and the self-nurturing part is called the small whole self. The large addictive self is the using self, or the self that plans how to acquire, where to use, how to use, whom to select as using friends, what to do in order to hide the use, and how to maintain the use of the substance. Sometimes, the large addictive self minimizes the importance of the small whole self by discounting the feelings of the small whole self.

The addictive self reveals itself in a style of thinking, feeling, and behaving that promotes poor self-image and low self-esteem. The roles that may be taken by the addictive self include, but are not limited to, "scapegoat," "mascot," "addict" or "identified patient," and "enabler." The small whole self aspires to be creative, constructive, learned, compassionate, productive, and socially involved in activities that promote physical, intellectual, and spiritual well-being. The roles used by the small whole self are often those of "natural child," "inquisitive student," "brother," "sister," and "friend." Finer distinctions may be made through the use of minimal cues, such as posturing; facial expressions; tonal variations; skin color changes; muscle tone changes; and—in the case of the addictive self—language styles evident while describing use, activities related to use, and thoughts or feelings associated with preparing to use, using, or hiding the consequences of use. These minimal cues and the larger complexes of thinking, feeling, and behaving associated with them may be used as reference points to distinguish between the large addictive self and the small whole self, as well as to determine when the adolescent is in an unhealthy state. This distinction between the large and small selves is also useful in helping the client track the developmental progress as he or she eliminates addictive behavior and replaces it with constructive, self-nurturing care.

To explain to clients the process of changing from addictive behavior to healthy behavior, once it has begun, many counselors use the acronym HOW: Honesty about self in relation to substance use, its consequences, and others; Openness in communicating with others by sharing personal thoughts, feelings, and behaviors; and Willingness to listen to others, to try new behaviors, and to choose new feeling responses. These are the hallmarks of HOW recovery from addiction takes place; they are the hallmarks of a healthy "whole self."

In order to improve the effectiveness of intervention, an important question for counselors to ask themselves during assessment is, If the substance-abusing adolescent is behaving according to the minimum expectations (e.g., attending school, coming home on time, eating dinner with his or her family, earning passing grades in school), what is destructive about his or her use? The answer to this question helps to clarify what the large addictive self is doing. For example, the use of substances when and where the behavior has negative consequences indicates the time and place that the addictive self is operating.

A counselor who wants to follow this method must use communication and information to identify the specific goals, the specific objectives, and the specific means that will empower the client to reach the goals and meet the objectives. These goals fall into four categories: (1) skills, (2) behavior, (3) abstinence, and (4) esteem. The objectives are to meet medical, familial, social, educational, and psychological needs. The art of counseling is the eliciting of the state(s) conducive to meeting these goals and objectives. The identification of the roles, thoughts, feelings, behaviors, and the minimal cues of the whole self allows the counselor to "metacommunicate" with the client (Bandler & Grinder, 1975), bringing the client to greater focus in pursuit of the goals of sobriety.

The counselor who uses this model must be flexible in his or her thinking. The overall response to intervention and treatment will vary from client to client. The circumstances will vary from family to family. The amount of emotional and financial support will vary from household to household. The pragmatics of participation will vary from one type of treatment to another. So, whether clients require inpatient care, long-term residential care, outpatient care, or simply participation in self-help groups, the overall strategy of distinguishing between an addictive self and a whole self is valuable in the intervention process. This distinction facilitates the development of rapport with the client and communicates the hopeful, positive outlook of the counselor to the client. The distinction also further clarifies throughout the intervention, treatment, and aftercare process the client's ability to determine the difference between self-destructive behavior and self-nurturing behavior, to use the whole self instead of the addictive self as an identity, and to solve problems by using the information being acquired in recovery.

Motivation

Different clients have different motivations for abusing substances. Some adolescents abuse substances to punish their parents for real or imagined wrongs. Others attempt to self-medicate other psychiatric disorders. Still others abuse substances to belong to a group. Even others do so because it is a repetition of a family behavior. Sometimes, adolescents abuse substances because they believe that no other goal or objective is available to them.

Many professionals believe that adolescents do not stop using drugs because they are not motivated to stop. According to this model, those who use drugs are caught in a conflict between an addictive self, which is motivated by self-destructive impulses, and a whole self, which is motivated by constructive impulses. The yielding to the self-destructive impulses of the addictive self is evidence of that self's development to the detriment of the whole self. The misunderstanding of the intention to think, feel, and use substances, coupled with the effects of the substances and the body's susceptibility to the influence of the substances, promotes the development of the addictive self. When a counselor explains the effects of substance use as a self-defeating attempt to satisfy an impulse in a way that makes the impulse stronger, the energy expended in satisfying the impulse may be freed to be used in satisfying the whole self.

Observing the distinctions between the whole self and the addictive self, the counselor can provide the adolescent with accurate and effective feedback about his or her state. In this way, the counselor can help the adolescent learn how to direct his or her intention so that it comes in line with sobriety. Many times, this is difficult, and the use of other metacommunication techniques, such as anchoring and reframing, enhances the process of change in the adolescent (Bandler & Grinder, 1975, 1979; Bandler, DeLozier, & Grinder, 1977).

For some adolescents, the fear of death, jails, or institutions is enough of a reason to quit. For others, repairing family relationships, learning a trade, or receiving appropriate medical treatment strengthens their motivation to stay sober. For still others, learning that someone will help them protect themselves from their families will end their tendency to yield to the self-destruction of the addictive self. The counselor who wants to communicate with a substance-abusing adolescent must be able to convey the desire to know both the motivation to use and the motivation to stop using. In addition, it is important to communicate to the adolescent that the counselor knows how to solve problems, empathizes with the adolescent, and will help the adolescent to reach the goals and objectives of sobriety. This entails more than saying, "I will help you." The counselor must foster the feeling of "I trust you" in the adolescent, which very often means clearly demonstrating the counselor's recognition of the adolescent as a unique individual.

Role of the Counselor

The counselor who wishes to apply this model of communication must decide how far to go in assisting the adolescent substance abuser. The counselor must know the answers to several questions in order to anticipate the emotional needs of the adolescent.

- Will the counselor see the adolescent one, two, or three times?
- Will the counselor see the adolescent weekly until a specific goal is met?
- Will the counselor referee between the adolescent and the parents?
- Will the counselor visit the adolescent in the hospital?
- Will the counselor take emergency calls 24 hours a day?

- What will the counselor report to Child Protective Services? the police? the parents?
- What will the counselor do if the adolescent threatens to commit suicide?

Answering these questions in a way that frames the actions involved as beneficial to the adolescent gives the counselor an opportunity to talk with the adolescent about several emotionally charged issues. This discussion quickly clarifies the adolescent's ability to make good judgments, the extent to which the addictive self is operating in the adolescent, and the emotional needs of the whole self in relation to these issues.

In addition, the counselor must decide how to respond to the anger, fear, guilt, and discouragement of the substance-abusing adolescent in order to help the adolescent solve problems in his or her relationships with others and to cope with the consequences of his or her substance abuse. When these decisions have been made, the counselor can focus on the adolescent; identify the roles, thoughts, feelings, behavior, and minimal cues that are associated with either the addictive self or the whole self; and concentrate on the goals and objectives of the intervention or treatment.

The counselor must be able to gain access to the parts within the adolescent. In this process, the roles, thoughts, feelings, and behaviors are anchored to a stimulus deliberately paired with them (Bandler & Grinder, 1975). The counselor-originated stimuli are usually associated with the indicators of the adolescent's state(s) or part(s) beyond the conscious awareness of the client (Bandler et al., 1977). The counselor may use a particular voice tone, posture, or label for a given part, in addition to a touch to make such an association. In fact, Bandler and Grinder (1975), Watzlawick and colleagues (1974), and others (Erickson, 1981; Rossi, 1986) noted that these associations occur in communication. Since the processes of reinforcement and conditioning occur naturally, it is wise to use them.

For example, when an adolescent whines, "My friends *always* get to stay out late" and "My parents *never* let me" stay out late, the counselor may note the whining tone and the accompanying facial expression as minimal cues, the whining as a behavior, and the exaggerations of always and never as descriptions of his or her experience—all associated with the role of victim. Of course, the adolescent had to learn the role, but does not need to perpetuate it in the belief that it is the only viable option and is a sufficient reason for using drugs.

On the other hand, an adolescent who sits down with a counselor, looks at the desk top, pauses for a moment, then looks at the counselor with moist eyes wide open and says, "Will you help me?" while maintaining eye contact is demonstrating healthy behavior. The pause, the widened eyes, and the voice tone in the question are minimal cues. Furthermore, the assertive nature of the request indicates a more level-headed adult role. The counselor may respond with a warm, empathetic voice tone and "anchor" or "pair" the empathy with the assertive behavior of the adolescent. In all subsequent discourse, either empathic warmth or the label of "victim" (if the therapist had articulated the term concurrently with the adolescent's request) may be used as cues to elicit the emotional "state" in the adolescent that was present when the adolescent requested the help.

Finally, the counselor must explain to the adolescent what is and is not confidential; what may be expected of the counselor; what the purposes, goals, and objectives of counseling are; and what methods will be used to reach those goals and objectives. As the adolescent reacts to the discussion, the counselor may track the unhealthy state (or healthy state) by watching the minimal cues; they will reveal the emotional state associated with the topic areas in the adolescent's mind and will guide the therapist in a way that surpasses the "self-knowledge" reflected in the self-disclosure of the adolescent. Thus, the counselor may monitor the adolescent's progress without the awareness of the adolescent.

This may be beneficial. After anchoring the healthy state to a particular stimulus, the counselor may reframe the solving of problems associated with the telltale minimal cues into the goals and objectives of chemical dependency treatment. This approach increases motivation of the adolescent, as the goals and objectives of chemical dependency treatment then more closely reflect the adolescent's goals and objectives.

The counselor may anchor, accept, recognize, and reflect the adolescent's unhealthy state and cues with empathy without condoning them. When the adolescent demands solutions or expectations from the counselor, his or her defenses will drop. When they do, the resulting healthier state may be anchored with an anchor different from that used with the unhealthy state. Over time, as the adolescent feels the effects of rapport in both the healthy and unhealthy states, he or she will come to trust the counselor more. Self-disclosure will increase spontaneously. As this occurs, the counselor may more frequently elicit the healthy state (the whole self) and, thus, extinguish the unhealthy state. The counselor and the adolescent may discuss the steps that the adolescent needs to take, is taking, or has taken to reach the goals of sobriety. This will promote the maintenance of sobriety.

Variations in the use of these basic nonverbal communication methods, verbal communication, and metacommunication techniques include paradoxical interventions, therapeutic double binds, 5-step reframing, 6-step reframing, and future pacing, to name a few (Bandler & Grinder, 1975, 1979; Bandler et al., 1977; Watzlawick et al., 1974). A myriad of combinations is possible. Denial, resistance, and power struggles are not necessarily indicators of failure in the counseling relationship with adolescents. Instead, they may be critical junctures, or choice points, for the adolescent. They are indicators of emotional conflict, illustrating the ambivalence of adolescents and the developmental task of identity formation.

In this model, these "problems" indicate that the stage has been set for a choice between intimacy and isolation. The script has been written, but the adolescent is discovering that it is not too late for last minute rewriting before opening night. The counselor may help by recognizing that the resources for recovery are found within the adolescent. The motivation for change is found in releasing the energy bound up in the conflicts within the adolescent.

REFERENCES

Bandler, R., & Grinder, J. (1975). *Patterns of hypnotic techniques of Milton H. Erickson, M.D.* (Vol. 1). CA: Meta Publications.

Bandler, R., & Grinder, J. (1979). *Frogs into princes.* Provo, UT: Real People Press.

Bandler, R., De Lozier, J., & Grinder, J. (1977). *Patterns of hypnotic techniques of Milton H. Erickson, M.D.* (Vol. 2). CA: Meta Publications.

Erickson, M.H. (1981). *Experiencing hypnosis.* New York: Irvington.

Meagher, M.D. (1987). *Beginning of a miracle.* Miami, FL: Health Publications.

Rossi, E.L. (1986). *The psychobiology of mind-body healing.* New York: W.W. Norton.

Watzlawick, P., Weakland, C.E., & Fisch, R. (1974). *Change.* New York: W.W. Norton.

14

Urine Drug Screens in Adolescent Programs

Thomas F. Brock

Substance abuse among adolescents is an issue of increasing concern to school officials, to therapists, and to other health care providers. There has been a corresponding increase in public funding for educational programs to teach the dangers of use and abuse, to teach refusal skills, to increase self-esteem, and to arm the school population in other ways against the potential of abuse. Public school programs are being developed to identify potential abusers, to prevent abuse, and to provide treatment options for youngsters in trouble. There are more and more adolescents in both inpatient and outpatient treatment programs. In both the educational and clinical settings, there is an increasing interest in testing young people for involvement with drugs of abuse. As Kwong, Chamberlain, Frederick, Kapur, and Sunshine (1988) stated, "There is increasing pressure to use urine drug screens to determine the prevalence of substance abuse, to deter illicit drug use, and to identify substance abusers for rehabilitation."

The well-considered use of urine drug screens holds the promise of both identifying youngsters in need of treatment and preventing experimentation among adolescents who do not currently abuse substances. When best used, laboratory tests can identify an individual who has recently used one of several drugs of abuse. Urine drug screens commonly test for five recreational drugs: marijuana, cocaine, opiates, amphetamines, and phencyclidine (PCP). A test for alcohol is sometimes included in a urine test, and some screens test for other frequently abused psychoactive substances.

Data are not sufficient to report conclusively on the effectiveness of UADS in adolescent program settings. After learning that 48% of sailors aged 18 to 24 were using illicit drugs, however, the Navy instituted a drug plan that included 10 million drug tests each year. Two years after beginning the drug testing program, the Navy reported that the percentage of use was less than 10%; in 1989, the percentage of sailors using illicit drugs was less than 5%. An independent study revealed that 83% of the sailors in that age group cited random testing as the chief deterrent to drug abuse. Of additional significance, 26% reported that they would resume usage if the testing program were dropped. The experience of this branch of the armed services could conceivably be replicated in educational settings and in adolescent mental health care settings.

TYPES OF PROGRAMS

There are two major types of adolescent programs in which drug screens may be used—educational and clinical. In addition, some juvenile justice programs that affect both the educational and the therapeutic populations may conduct drug tests.

Educational Settings

If drug screens were perfectly accurate, their use in the educational setting would be likely to benefit several groups of teen-agers. For example, those who are currently using drugs and who are

- experiencing difficulty in their lives with no identifiable etiology may be directed to appropriate treatment modalities
- experiencing few or no problematic areas in their lives could avert potential problems by early identification and intervention
- trying to cease and/or control their use may find the additional incentive—discovery—that will give them the impetus to achieve sobriety or control
- acting on the assumption that they are merely living within the established behavioral norms of the school may be confronted with a new public set of norms
- thinking that their age mates value getting high may find that their peers no longer accept or elevate the user to a lofty position, that their use ceases to have its secretive allure, and that peer models have a demonstrated positive value for sobriety

Drug screens would also benefit teen-agers who are not using drugs and

- deserve to be part of the mainstream and to feel part of the mainstream, rather than believing that they are on the fringe of adolescent behavioral norms
- want to stay away from drugs and may need the extra incentive
- want to be educated in a drug-free environment

With a firm knowledge of who is using and who is not using drugs, educational administrators can create the kind of environment and make the kind of statement regarding drug use that is appropriate to their educational setting. Embry-Riddle Aeronautical University, an institution designed to train pilots, has an additional incentive for using drug screens: "To make sure its students are drug free when they enter that work force" (Laboda, 1990, p. 93). Embry-Riddle wants to ensure a drug-free campus as well as to set an example for other schools.

Involuntary vs. Voluntary Drug Testing

When considering a drug testing program, the school district must first consider whether the program will be involuntary or voluntary. In the public schools, involuntary drug testing has several inherent difficulties. Because school attendance is compulsory, public schools come under a great deal of judicial scrutiny regarding any involuntary participation.

Urine drug screens in the public schools are subject to Fourth Amendment protections. Thus, students have a constitutional right to be protected against unreasonable searches and seizures. Urine drug tests have been determined to be searches, and mandatory testing will be found constitutional only if school officials have probable cause to believe that an individual has violated the school's lawful drug policy (Hogan & Hartson, 1986). Even then, the search must be reasonable and must be related to the lawful functions of the school. Appeals courts have ruled that the observation of voiding to obtain a urine specimen is an excessive intrusion on a student's legitimate expectation of privacy and that the excessive intrusiveness is not justified by the need.

A drug test cannot demonstrate impairment, nor can it show with precision the recency of use. Therefore, a school that has a policy of mandatory drug testing, even if probable cause is shown, will be subject to criticism for attempting to regulate off-campus behavior. A positive test result does not prove a youngster has violated legitimate campus rules, and the school will not be justified in taking any adverse action against the student based upon the result of the drug test.

School districts must consider the implications of the Education of the Handicapped Act, which could place a district at financial risk if a school identified an impaired youngster and took action against the student. The courts may rule that the youngster is handicapped by virtue of the drug addiction.

Finally, involuntary drug testing in the school, by its very nature, may be detrimental to the educational atmosphere. The learning environment is likely to suffer demonstrably if youngsters are forced to provide urine specimens as part of their school activities. Even if the involuntary testing were part of a nonpunitive, humane educational program, the mandatory element is antithetical to the goals of the democratic school environment. According to Hogan and Hartson (1986), the Carlstadt–East Rutherford Regional School District had a rehabilitative track for students whose mandatory comprehensive medical examination, which required the submission of a urine specimen, showed drug or alcohol use. The purpose of the program was to help the students recognize the dangers of drug abuse and to remedy any existing problem. While the goals may have been laudable, the New Jersey court found such blanket testing to be unconstitutional.

There are several good reasons for public school districts to participate in a program of voluntary drug testing. Such a program may well serve as a preventive measure. Some teen-agers who may otherwise be tempted to use drugs may decline if their use is likely to be discovered by parents or by school authorities. The possibility of a drug test may strengthen the moral courage of certain youngsters who prefer to decline use. Perhaps more important, testing allows the school, the parents, and the students to make a public statement against drug use and abuse. Voluntary drug testing may also help identify youngsters who are in need of counseling or more intensive substance abuse intervention.

The American Academy of Pediatrics (1989) has suggested that true voluntary screening is an ambiguous concept in a school population of minor children, however, and that screening can be truly voluntary only with older adolescents. Furthermore, peer pressure in so-called voluntary programs in athletic departments, for instance, can stigmatize a nonvolunteering youngster to such a degree that the student may volunteer for testing. In general, voluntary screening programs are those that have the cooperation and consent both of the children's parents and the children themselves.

Guidelines for School Districts

Any school district that is contemplating a drug testing program for junior and senior high school students should consider several guidelines and caveats. Public education about drugs and about drug testing should precede the establishment of a drug testing program. Parents and students should be aware of the prevalence of substance abuse in their community and nationwide, as well as the financial, educational, personal, physiological, and psychological consequences of that abuse. Urine drug screening may be an important part of the district's drug program, but it should not be the entire program.

Several professional positions must be coordinated in a drug testing program.

Clinical Laboratory. The professional laboratory must be evaluated, its procedures understood, its cutoffs and sensitivities known, and its chain of specimen custody documented. The laboratory personnel must work closely with the clinician.

Licensed Clinician. Clinical interpretations of the test results ought to be done by a licensed therapist who is not a member of the school staff. Theoretically, this person can be a licensed psychologist, a licensed physician, a licensed family therapist, or another mental health care professional who agrees to keep the results of the drug testing confidential and the communication about the student with the school district minimal. The type of license that the mental health care professional holds is much less important than is the degree of training and experience that the clinician has in adolescent therapy. The treatment of adolescent substance abuse is much different from the treatment of adult addiction, and the clinician must have experience in working with teen-agers who do not abuse substances, as well as with those who do.

The clinician should discuss the results of the drug test with the parents of the student, whether the test result is positive or negative. That discussion may be brief, but it should allow time to question the student and parents about other indicators of possible abuse. Behavioral indicators may be as meaningful, if not more so, as the results of the drug testing.

School Staff. Whether a nurse, athletic coach, counselor, or teacher, the school staff must be composed of the kinds of people who have a rapport with students and will give the drug program a positive image.

Procedure

A student should understand the nature of the voluntary drug testing program, the drug tests themselves, and the confidentiality of those tests. The sample should be collected in the clinician's office or in the laboratory so that the collection can be supervised, the chain-of-custody procedures followed, and the school protected from involvement in what may seem an invasive process.

Because of the short half-life of many chemicals, the drug test must be given randomly. Student names must be drawn at random, and the test must be given on a random day and time. The clinician who is interpreting the test results should, within 48 to 72 hours of the collection of the sample, report the results to the parents of the student. The school district and the clinician should agree on the options for treatment, if the results are positive, prior to implementation of the program. Options should range from low intensity outpatient to high intensity inpatient programs. Both privately and publicly funded programs should be included so that the clinician, together with the parents, can match treatment resources with the individual needs of the student.

At the end of a certain period of time, in a manner that protects the identity of all students involved, the clinicians should be required to report to the school district about the drug testing program. The report should include a tabulation of the recommendations made to parents. This reporting makes it possible to evaluate the efficacy of the program.

It should be clear that the students or their parents can revoke a voluntary consent to participate in the drug testing program at any time. There should be a written agreement that the school will not be informed of the results of any test and that the test results can neither be used for school disciplinary proceedings nor be communicated to another person without the parents' and students' permission. As an additional safeguard, a volunteer committee may supervise the program rather than school staff members, who may be involved in disciplinary or punitive activities. Edison High School in Huntington Beach, California, reported that 90% of students in their target populations (i.e., athletes, coaches, and school administrators) participate in the voluntary testing (Committee for Voluntary Drug Testing, 1988).

Clinical Settings

Treatment programs, whether inpatient or outpatient, generally institute drug testing for two reasons: (1) to diagnose a patient's problem accurately and (2) to monitor the progress of treatment. A clinician needs to know if a patient's disturb-ance of conduct or depression is related to the effects of mood- or behavior-altering substances. Once substance abuse has been identified as part of a teen-ager's problem, frequent testing is used to help monitor the patient's sobriety.

In inpatient settings, a urine drug screen is done on every patient at admission for the purpose of ruling out substance abuse. It is also useful for the clinician doing the initial assessment to say to the youngster, "You will be given a urine drug screen. What do you believe will come up positive?" That statement alone makes it easier for the teen-ager to talk about his or her substance use. Knowing or believing that the use will be discovered anyway, the patient will generally want to be open about the drug use; this certainly can facilitate the healing process. For those patients who are suspected of using or abusing recreational drugs, a UADS is given on their return from a visit outside the facility. In either instance, the use of the drug screen can be helpful in correctly identifying the patient's difficulties, as well as in opening positive lines of communication.

In outpatient treatment, the thorough practitioner uses a urine drug screen as an adjunct to a functional assessment when substance abuse is suspected. In this way, the UADS becomes a diagnostic tool as well as a monitoring device. The urine drug screen can increase communication; make it possible for the therapist and the client to work together to reduce or eliminate use; and, rather than putting the therapist in the position of an authoritarian monitor, place the therapist in the position of a colleague helping the youngster toward the stated goal of sobriety or higher functioning.

LIMITATIONS OF URINE TESTING

While attending to the possible benefits of drug testing and before developing any policy for testing in either the educational or clinical setting, those who are considering such a program must develop an awareness of the inherent limitations of laboratory testing for drug abuse.

General Limitations

It is quite possible for a laboratory to issue a positive report from a urine sample when the true result is negative. Although they are relatively rare, false positive reports can result from either clinical or clerical error. In heroin testing programs, it was found that the ingestion of products containing poppy seeds (e.g., in rolls or bagels) produces urine that tests positive for morphine/codeine in routine urine drug screens. Mule and Casella (1988) reported a sensitive rapid quantitative test to detect a metabolite that is not found in poppy seeds.

False positive reports can be eliminated for all practical purposes by the use of a confirmatory test. Lundberg and Hawks (1985) stated that "false positive urines are, however, rare, particularly when suitable confirmation methods have been used" (p. 791).

From 1972 through 1981, the National Institute on Drug Abuse, in conjunction with the Centers for Disease Control, studied a number of laboratories that performed drug screening. They found that some laboratories often failed to detect drugs at concentrations called for in their contracts. "False negatives tended to occur much more frequently than false positives" (Hansen, Caudill, & Boone, 1985). Because underreporting of drugs may threaten the treatment process, mental health care practitioners should have a clear idea of the level of confidence that they can place in a negative report.

According to Lundberg and Hawks (1985), "Drug use may be the primary cause of academic underachievement; family disintegration secondary to adolescent rebellion; acting out behavior such as theft, vandalism, physical violence, or cruelty to people or animals; unpredictable dysphoric mood changes and irascible behavior; apathy or chronic fatigue" (p. 789). However, urine drug screens cannot tell the practitioner to what degree, if any, drug use has contributed to the adolescent's symptomatology. These behaviors may be independent of drug use, even when laboratory analysis confirms drug use.

Current drug screening methods do not clearly indicate when the drug was used, how much of the drug was used, or for how long the drug had been used. A true positive result on a test for marijuana, for instance, does not mean that the client was under the influence of THC when the test was collected, it means merely that the person whose urine was tested used marijuana in the preceding hours, days, or weeks. Repeated testing over time may give a more refined picture of use, but such a picture should emerge from programmatic or therapeutic contacts.

> Drug concentrations in urine vary with dose, route of administration, time elapsed since administration, and the individual's physiological status. . . . Therefore a urine test result only indicates the presence or absence of drugs (as defined by the chosen thresholds). It cannot support any interpretation as to the amount of drug taken, the time it was taken or the absence or presence of impairment. (Kwong et al., 1988, p. 610)

Adolescent folklore and several popular periodicals describe methods of falsifying a urine drug screen by (1) adulterating the sample, (2) replacing the subject's urine with a clean sample, and (3) preparing the subject to void a misleading sample. Adolescents commonly add water to their own urine when giving a sample, thereby reducing the concentration of the drug to a level below the threshold; add vinegar, salt, or other adulterate to the urine; bring a clean sample in a condom or balloon stored under the arm (to maintain approximate body temperature); and drink large volumes of water and exercise actively prior to a scheduled drug test. Some youth-oriented magazines frequently carry advertisements for instructions on producing substance-free test results. For $3, teenagers can purchase an instruction sheet that details the common ways to ensure clean observed or unobserved specimens. The risk that some teen-agers will use these techniques can be minimized if the test is random and if the sample is voided under the direct supervision of a concerned adult (Lundberg & Hawks, 1985). Kwong and associates (1988) noted that "urine specimens can easily be tampered with by substitution, dilution or adulteration. Only by direct observation of its collection can the integrity of the specimen be assured" (p. 610), even though it may be a disagreeable task for the observer. If it is not possible to have a witnessed collection, the temperature of the sample should be recorded at the time of the collection; the specific gravity of the sample, as well as the pH, should be tested in the laboratory. Some authors have suggested using a bluing agent in the toilet when voiding is not observed; however, such a procedure does not prevent a client from using tap water if a sink is available. A client who has consumed a great deal of water will have clear urine. Such a dilute specimen should not be sent to the laboratory; another more concentrated specimen should be collected on the following morning.

Specific Limitations

Drugs frequently included in a test program are amphetamines, barbiturates, benzodiazepines, cannabinoids, cocaine, ethanol, methadone, methaqualone, opiates, and PCP (Kwong et al., 1988). The medium used for testing these drugs is usually the subject's urine. Breath is easily collected, but its use is restricted to the testing of volatiles, such as alcohol. Saliva and hair are readily available, but their drug concentrations are low; furthermore, laboratories often lack experience in testing them. Drugs are usually present in high concentrations in the blood, and their presence in the blood may indicate recent use. Except for that on alcohol, however, there is a paucity of research correlating blood concentrations and concomitant behavioral impairment. In addition, it is more expensive and invasive to collect blood. Therefore, because urine is readily available, contains relatively high concentrations of drugs or metabolites, and can be collected noninvasively, urine is the specimen of choice.

Two types of tests are usually given: a screening test and a confirmation test. The screening procedure, or preliminary test, is usually less expensive and can efficiently identify samples that contain target drugs below an established threshold in a large number of specimens. The confirmatory test should be given to any sample that fails to pass the initial screening. It should have a threshold that is as low or lower than that of the initial test, be based on a different chemical or physical principle (Kwong et al., 1988), and be administered by different personnel. When informed of a positive test result, a clinician should be told the technique used to confirm the result, as well as the threshold used for both the preliminary and the confirmation tests.

A threshold that is useful to an emergency department physician may not be useful to a therapist in an adolescent chemical dependency program. If, for example, a teen-ager who recently smoked a large amount of marijuana and had a true urine cannabinoid quantity of 90 ng/mL went to a hospital emergency room complaining of depression, the emergency room physician who orders a complete drug screen will be satisfied with a 100 ng/mL cutoff for cannabis. A negative test result indicates that the patient is not currently high on marijuana, which is probably the case. The mental health care clinician, however, is not so interested in current physiological impairment as in patterns of use. The youngster could well be depressed as a result of daily pot use. The patient could be emotionally and physiologically impaired, even though the result of the drug test was negative. The therapist wants a lower threshold, as a cannabinoid threshold of even 20 ng/mL indicates use.

There are two primary methods of urine drug testing—immunoassay and chromatographic techniques. The immunoassay techniques, which require only a small specimen, are generally used for the preliminary or initial screen. Types of immunoassay techniques include radioimmunoassay (RIA), enzyme immunoassay (EIA), and fluorescence polarization immunoassay (FPIA). According to Kwong and associates (1988), many immunoassays are not specific for single drugs, and the antibodies often cross-react with related drugs and metabolites. This property makes many immunoassays specific for families of drugs, but not for individual drugs. "Therefore, a positive immunoassay result requires confirmation and definitive identification by chromatographic assay" (Kwong et al., 1988, p. 611).

Chromatography relies on the expertise of the laboratory technicians to a greater degree than do immunoassays. Thin layer chromatography can be used as an initial test, if confirmed by one of the other chromatographic techniques. In the drug programs, thin layer chromatography can be used to confirm an assay technique. Gas chromatography (GC) can be used to confirm a test, although it is labor-intensive. High performance liquid chromatography is also used as a confirmatory test.

The best confirmatory test is the combination of gas chromatography with mass spectrometry (GC-MS). According to Kwong and associates (1988), "This combines the resolving capabilities of GC with the high sensitivity and specificity of a mass spectrometer. GC-MS is currently considered to be the technique of choice for identification of drugs or metabolites in urine" (p. 612). The laboratory should provide the practitioner with test sensitivity, threshold, and durations of detectability (Table 14-1).

Despite their limitations, urine drug screens can be effective in improving the quality of treatment, as well as in helping prevent substance use or abuse. Awareness of the limitations encourages clinicians to interpret both negative and posi-

---

Table 14-1 Average Times That Drugs Can Be Detected in Urine

Drug	Time
Marijuana	
Occasional users (once a week)	3–5 days
Frequent users (1 joint a day)	7–10 days
Chronic users (4 joints a day)	Several weeks
Cocaine	2–4 days
Phencyclidine (PCP)	10–14 days
Amphetamines and methamphetamines	2–4 days
Opiates (heroin and prescription narcotics)	1.5–3 days
Barbiturates	
Short acting	1 day
Long acting	14 days

tive findings. The clinician cannot rely on drug screens alone, however, but must take into account the clinical interview, age-appropriate adaptive functioning, and the reports of other adults (e.g., parents, school officials) in diagnosing substance abuse. The clinician's best tool is the therapeutic relationship established with the youngster and members of the adolescent's network.

REFERENCES

American Academy of Pediatrics, Committee on Adolescence, Committee on Bioethics, & Provisional Committee on Substance Abuse. (1989). Screening for drugs of abuse in children and adolescents. *Pediatrics, 84*(2), 396–398.

Committee for Voluntary Drug Testing. (1988). *The voluntary drug-testing program for Edison High School students.* Huntington Beach, CA: Edison High School.

Hansen, H.J., Caudill, S.P., & Boone, D.J. (1985). Crisis in drug testing: Results of CDC blind study. *Journal of the American Medical Association, 253,* 2382–2387.

Kwong, T.C., Chamberlain, R.T., Frederick, D.L., Kapur, B., & Sunshine, I. (1988). Critical issues in urinalysis of abused substances: Report of the Substance-Abuse Testing Committee. *Clinical Chemistry, 34*(3), 605–632.

Laboda, A. (1990, August). Drug testing at Embry-Riddle. *Flying.*

Lundberg, R.H., & Hawks, R.L. (1985). Laboratory detection of marijuana use. *Journal of the American Medical Association, 254,* 788–792.

Mule, S.J., & Casella, G.A. (1988). Rendering the "poppy-seed defense" defenseless: Identification of 6-monoacetylmorphine in urine by gas chromatography/mass spectroscopy. *Clinical Chemistry, 34*(7), 1427–1430.

SUGGESTED READINGS

Chamberlain, R.T. (1985). Optimization of a toxicology program. *Clinical Biochemistry, 19,* 122–126.

Colbert, D.L., & Childerstone, M. (1987). Multiple drugs of abuse in urine detected with a single reagent and fluorescence polarization. *Clinical Chemistry, 33*(10), 1921–1923.

Dobbins, T., & Lipman, G. (1988, April 5). T*he evolution of a successful district-wide drug prevention plan.* Paper presented at the meeting of the Board of Simi Valley United School District.

Holmes, S.D., Lipshultz, L.I., & Smith, R.G. (1983). Effect of cannabinoids on human Sertoli cell function in vitro. *Archives of Andrology, 11,* 245–251.

Jones, R.T. (1987). Drug of abuse profile: Cannabis. *Clinical Chemistry, 33*(11B), 72B–81B.

Manno, B.R., Manno, J.E., & Dempsey, C.A. (1986). A thin layer chromatographic method for high volume screening of urine for methylphenidate abuse. *Journal of Analytical Toxicology, 10,* 116–119.

McBay, A.J. (1986). Problems in testing for abused drugs [Letter to the editor]. *Journal of the American Medical Association, 255,* 39.

McBay, A.J. (1987). Drug-analysis technology—Pitfalls and problems of drug testing. *Clinical Chemistry, 33*(11B), 33B–38B.

McBay, A.J., Dubowski, K.M., & Finkle, B.S. (1983). Urine testing for marijuana use [Letter to the editor]. *Journal of the American Medical Association, 249,* 881.

Medelson, J.H., Mello, N.K., & Ellingboe, J. (1985). Acute effects of marijuana smoking on prolactin levels in human females. *Journal of Pharmacology and Experimental Therapeutics, 2321,* 220–222.

Peat, M.A. (1988). Analytical and technical aspects of testing for drug abuse: Confirmatory procedures. *Clinical Chemistry, 34*(3), 471–473.

Podkowik, B.I., Smith, M.L., & Pick, R.O. (1987). Experience with a sulfonamide diuretic in a large urine drug testing program. *Journal of Analytical Toxicology, 11,* 215–218.

Poklis, A. (1987). Evaluation of TDX cocaine metabolite assay. *Journal of Analytical Toxicology, 11,* 228–230.

Powell, D.J., & Fuller, R.W. (1983). Marijuana and sex: Strange bedpartners. *Journal of Psychoactive Drugs, 15*(4), 269–280.

Svensson, J.O. (1986). Determination of benzoylecgonine in urine from drug abusers using ion pair high performance liquid chromatography. *Journal of Analytical Toxicology, 10,* 122–124.

Tatel, D.S., & Heffernan, E.B. (1986, November). *Drug testing and public schools: An analysis of issues and summary of case law.* Paper presented at the meeting of the American Association of School Administrators, Arlington, VA.

Tilak, S.K., & Zimmerman, A.M. (1984). Effects of cannabinoids on macromolecular synthesis in isolated spermatogenic cells. *Pharmacology, 29,* 343–350.

15

Twelve-Step Programs and the Treatment of Adolescent Substance Abuse

Gary W. Lawson

Given the large number of programs for the treatment of adolescent substance abuse and the current rate of which they are opening, closing, and changing across the United States, it would be almost impossible to determine the specific number of programs that use a 12-step model. It would be even more difficult to determine the extent to which such programs use a 12-step model similar to that developed by Alcoholics Anonymous (AA) in their overall treatment programs. There are indications, however, that a majority (perhaps as much as 75% or more) of both inpatient and outpatient adolescent substance abuse treatment programs across the United States base some treatment on a 12-step philosophy or model ("Youth Treatment," 1983).

Of 11 adolescent substance abuse treatment programs profiled in different states across the United States, for example, 9 were found to have adopted the 12-step model to some degree or another ("Youth Treatment," 1983). Sample comments from program staff included, "We are very supportive of the AA philosophy"; "We feel that AA and occasionally NA (Narcotics Anonymous) are ideal"; "Our program is based on AA philosophy and encourages the residents to explore the community and find different AA meetings to attend weekly." In one case, the 12 steps had been condensed to 7 steps, but the program philosophy remained basically the same as that for a 12-step model.

Although there is a general lack of research to support the effectiveness of a 12-step or any other approach to adolescent substance abuse treatment (Institute of Medicine, 1989), a 12-step approach appears to be pervasive. Part of the reason for this is the fact that many of these adolescent treatment programs were founded and are run by recovering alcoholics or drug addicts who themselves gained sobriety as the result of a 12-step program (Selekman & Todd, 1991). From a research standpoint, however, a staff that fully believes in the effectiveness of a 12-step program usually feels no need for actual outcome or comparison studies of different treatment approaches. The idea that "what worked for me will work for you" does not necessarily encourage scientific inquiry into important questions such as when it works, why it works, whom it works for, and why it does not always work. A favorite cliché in the AA community is, "Utilize; don't analyze." That may be useful advice for a new member of AA, but not for treatment personnel who are trying to provide the best treatment regimen for an individual adolescent. It is scientific and useful to analyze.

Most of the research that is available on the effectiveness of 12-step programs has been conducted with AA or NA members. The few studies that have been done have had many methodological problems, however. There has been a lack of agreement on the meaning of affiliation with such groups, as well as a lack of valid measures to assess the characteristics under investigation (McCrady & Irvine, 1989).

Perhaps the primary reasons for the wide acceptance of these programs are that they are readily available, they are free, they are simple to use, and they are flexible enough to be used in a manner that seems appropriate to the individual in need of them. These programs are supposed to be programs of attraction; attendance is usually voluntary. In some cases, judges or probation officers require individuals to attend meetings, but what these individuals take from the meetings and how they utilize it is up to each one—which makes the program seem more voluntary. The basic reason that people who attend 12-step programs are able to change their behavior is that they learn to believe that they can change. Before there is a behavior change, however, there must be motivation to change, which is usually precipitated by some negative consequence of the drinking or using behavior. These consequences usually come from family members, employers, health problems, or law enforcement agencies rather than 12-step programs. Motivation may be the most important factor in the treatment of adolescent substance abusers, because adolescents usually believe that they can do anything they choose to do, including giving up drugs or alcohol.

THE 12-STEP PHILOSOPHY

In the mid-1930s, the founders of AA devised a set of principles known as the Twelve Steps to help alcoholics achieve sobriety (Alcoholics Anonymous, 1976). The 12 steps of AA are the basis for nearly all the other 12-step programs.

1. We admitted that we were powerless over alcohol and that our lives had become unmanageable.
2. We came to believe that a Power greater than ourselves could restore us to sanity.

3. We made a decision to turn our will and our lives over to the care of God as we understood Him.
4. We made a searching and fearless moral inventory of ourselves.
5. We admitted to God, to ourselves, and to another human being the exact nature of our wrongs.
6. We were entirely ready to have God remove all these defects of character.
7. We humbly asked Him to remove our shortcomings.
8. We made a list of all persons we had harmed, and became willing to make amends to them all.
9. We made direct amends to such people wherever possible, except when to do so would injure them or others.
10. We continued to take personal inventory and when we were wrong, promptly admitted it.
11. We sought through prayer and meditation to improve our conscious contact with God as we understood Him, praying only for knowledge of His will for us and the power to carry that out.
12. Having had a spiritual awakening as the result of these steps, we tried to carry this message to alcoholics and to practice these principles in all our affairs.

In the beginning, AA's basic tenets were that only an alcoholic could help another alcoholic and that psychiatric or other treatment was usually unsuccessful (Cain, 1964). Alcoholics, by banding together in a spirit of mutual help and understanding, and by turning their lives over to God as they understood Him, could manage to lead relatively normal lives. Above all, alcoholics were expected to face the fact that they must never again take even one drink of alcohol; it was an explicit AA belief that, once an alcoholic, always an alcoholic (Cain, 1964). For the first 5 years, AA had no more than a few hundred members, almost all of whom were middle-aged, middle-class white men. In 1941, after the famous reporter Jack Alexander wrote an article about AA for the *Saturday Evening Post*, membership leaped to more than 8,000 (Cain, 1964). Today, the number of AA members has been reported to be close to 2 million (Kurtz, 1990). One person may participate in several of these groups and could be counted several times, so the estimates of numbers of members could be exaggerated. Regardless, 12-step programs have had a major impact on our society. The movement, which Kurtz (1990) referred to as "a twentieth century revelation of the Holy Spirit to counteract the emotional problems which our present pace of living is producing in plague-like proportions" (p. 93), has apparently filled some need that more traditional institutions (e.g., church and family) had not been meeting.

Although AA has been credited with beginning the disease concept of alcoholism, AA's founders attempted to avoid the controversy by using the word *malady* when referring to alcoholism. Most members of AA do believe that alcoholism is a disease, however. The most popular and most often repeated definition of alcoholism is that it is "a physical allergy, coupled with a mental compulsion" (Cain, 1964, p. 69). Most members of AA believe that alcoholism is not a "mental disorder"; they prefer to believe that "there is nothing wrong with alcoholics except alcohol."

There seems to be some disagreement about compulsive drug use and disease. Members of NA seldom see themselves as alcoholics and have been known to claim that they can use alcohol without abusing it. Although most alcoholics abuse some other substance as well, they see drug addicts as somehow different. Most treatment professionals see addiction to one substance the same as addiction to another, however.

Therapeutic Aspects of a 12-Step Model

Some of the therapeutic value of a 12-step program is obvious; some of it is not quite so evident. Much of the therapeutic value of a 12-step model comes from the steps themselves. For example, the first step of admitting powerlessness is the same as recognizing and admitting the problem. Most emotional, psychological, or behavioral problems improve when the person with these problems acknowledges them. This is simple on the surface, but the therapeutic dynamics of the first step are very complex and go far beyond just admitting to the problem. The real therapeutic value has to do with the etiological issues of addiction, particularly the issue of control. Alcoholics drink to demonstrate their control of drinking, even when they know that they have lost control. Paradoxically, it is only by giving up control, admitting powerlessness, and turning the problem over to a "Higher Power" that the addicted person is able to regain control of his or her life. This is one of many paradoxes in a 12-step program to promote therapeutic change.

Steps 1, 2, and 3 are designed to help the individual admit the problem, ask for help, and turn the problems over to a "Higher Power." This is not bad advice for any such problem. Steps 4 through 10 are designed to deal with the guilt that alcoholics or addicts often feel for the problems they have caused others. In some cases, alcoholics drink to relieve guilt feelings, only they feel more guilty after they sober up, and drink again because of the guilt—the circle never ends. There is always an excuse to drink or to use drugs. These steps also help the alcoholic or addict deal with anger by acknowledging his or her part in it and asking for forgiveness from the other party.

Step 11 encourages the person to stay with the program and to continue the self-evaluation, while step 12 asks the individual to carry the message to other alcoholics and to practice the 12 steps in all activities. Step 12 is one of the most therapeutic of all the steps; not only does it provide another chance to reduce guilt for past behavior, but also there is no better way to build self-esteem than to help another person.

Another major therapeutic aspect of a 12-step program is the group interaction. The things that make any group helpful to an individual—empathy, support, encouragement—happen very often in 12-step groups. Groups may be harmful, as well as helpful, however. With more than 36,000 different AA groups in the United States alone, there are bound to be some groups that are not always helpful for all who attend (Lawson, Ellis, & Rivers, 1984). Groups are like families: some are good for all, some are good for a few, and some are bad for everyone.

A new participant in a 12-step program usually selects a sponsor from the group, someone who has a solid sobriety and can act as an individual guide. The sponsor helps the new member on an individual basis as needed. The idea is that the new member will benefit from the experience of the member who has been sober longer. Members can keep their sponsors as long as they wish; some keep them for life. Again, although the sponsor can be a source of strength, some caution is necessary. Not everyone has the ability to be therapeutic for another human being. In fact, there are individuals with the best of intentions who often give harmful advice to others or just lack emotional availability in a time of need.

One final therapeutic benefit of AA and most other 12-step programs is their availability. If there is a telephone close at hand, there is someone to call 24 hours a day. If an alcoholic feels like drinking or an addict like using, there is usually a meeting being held nearby. This ready availability is the reason that so many treatment programs recommend AA or other 12-step programs as a major part of their aftercare plans.

Criticisms of 12-Step Programs

Kurtz (1990) noted four major criticisms of AA and the other 12-step programs: (1) attachment to AA or another 12-step group is an acting out of intrapsychic pathology, in other words, people change one addiction for another; (2) these groups are antiscience and antiprofessional; (3) these groups have never been proved effective; and (4) AA, specifically, is culturally inappropriate for other than middle-class white men. There are perhaps different degrees of truth in all these criticisms. Alcoholics Anonymous, in particular, has been taken to task in the literature many times over the years (Kalb & Propper, 1976; Tournier, 1979); it was even compared to a cult as long as 25 years ago (Cain, 1964). The problem with criticizing this type of organization is that many people owe their very lives to the organization, and they perceive any critical remarks against the program as a personal attack or as a threat to their sobriety.

One of the major critics of AA is a newer group, called Rational Recovery (RR), which offers an alternative approach to alcoholism based on the principles of rational emotive therapy as developed by Dr. Albert Ellis (1979). One of the major complaints that the members of RR have about AA is its perceived status as the "only" alternative for the treatment of alcoholism. They see AA as a religious sect that has unlawfully become the "only" referral source for many city, state, and federal law enforcement and mental health care agencies. There may be many court cases before the matter is resolved. In the meantime, RR seems to be growing steadily. (Information about RR is available through RR Systems, Box 800, Lotus, CA 95651.)

TWELVE-STEP PROGRAMS FOR ADOLESCENT SUBSTANCE ABUSERS

Although 12-step programs for adolescents vary greatly, in general, they are based on the following set of beliefs and values:

1. Physical or psychological addiction to drugs/alcohol is one disease with a common set of symptoms.
2. This disease is progressive and has physical, social, and spiritual aspects; left untreated, it can only lead to death or insanity.
3. The alcoholic or addict must admit that he or she is powerless over the substance.
4. In order to live a sober life, the addict must never use the mind-altering substance again.
5. Once an addict, always an addict.
6. Turning one's life over to a "Higher Power" is an important aspect of maintaining sobriety.
7. In most cases, those not actively attending meetings and working their program are doomed to a return to addictive behavior.
8. Sobriety is more important than any interpersonal relationship.
9. Life must be lived "one day at a time."
10. It is important to rely on those who have had a similar experience of addiction for advice and help in maintaining sobriety.

Some of these statements have never been endorsed or even suggested by AA or any other 12-step programs. They are part of the treatment philosophy by those who practice the 12 steps, however.

Adolescent substance abusers who go to treatment programs vary from first-time drug experimenters to long-time, hard-core addicts who must be admitted for drug abuse treatment. Many of these adolescents exhibit a psychiatric condition, such as depression or anxiety, along with the effects of their substance use. In many cases, family problems (e.g., divorce, incest, or parental alcoholism or drug abuse) have precipitated the drug use in the adolescent. Programs based on 12 steps tend to focus on the substance abuse, sometimes to the exclusion of these other problems. At times, 12-step residential and hospital-based programs are too quick to diagnose adolescents as addicts or alcoholics; they are too ready to use the standard treatment package for everyone. To prevent adolescents from being wrongfully diagnosed, it is advisable to address adolescent substance abusers by means of a systematic approach, ranking the relative severity of problems in different domains. Such an approach has been suggested by Tarter (1990) and colleagues at the University of Pittsburgh School of Medicine.

It is relatively easy to diagnose substance abuse in adults who show physical symptoms and have long histories of substance use. Adolescents, on the other hand, are often short-term substance users in whom little physical damage is evident. They are sometimes labeled chemically dependent simply because they have used an illegal substance. Many adults who would not be considered alcoholics or addicts today have, during their adolescence, had periods of drug or alcohol use that could have been perceived as chemical dependence. These individuals actually may be more healthy as adults than are nonusers (Shedler & Block, 1990). If they had they been labeled chemically dependent and placed in a 12-step treatment program during their adolescence, however, peers and staff would have encouraged them to admit that they were addicted to chemicals and would have accused them of being in a state of denial if they did not. Most 12-step programs spend whatever time is necessary to cajole new patients into admitting that they are alcoholics or addicts. The fact is that, during any 10- to 20-year period, approximately one third of alcoholics "mature out" into various forms of moderate drinking or abstinence. The rate of maturing out is even higher among heavy drinkers who are not diagnosed as alcoholics (Fillmore, 1988).

It is impossible to predict what effect an inaccurate diagnosis would have on its victim, but the effect is likely to be negative or neutral at best. In some cases, a diagnosis of drug addiction or alcoholism could reduce an individual's potential and even cost him or her a job, for example, a career in the military or law enforcement. Such labels also tend to raise an individual's life, health, and auto insurance premiums forever. Ultimately, there is a possibility that the individual will accept the label and will begin to take drugs or drink because that is what an addict or alcoholic does. All these things should be considered before an adolescent is sent to a 12-step–based substance abuse treatment program that is more likely than not to use the addict or alcoholic label.

Doing Well in 12-Step Programs for Adolescents?

Research has shown that older individuals (above 30) generally do better in substance abuse treatment programs and that younger participants, particularly adolescents, are often noncompliant with treatment recommendations (Anderson, 1992). Given that negative information, there are several specific questions that a therapist should consider before placing an adolescent in a 12-step program.

- Is the adolescent really chemically dependent, and are there other problems that should be addressed before diagnosis is made?
- Does the adolescent have family support in the 12-step work?
- Is the group that the adolescent attends appropriate for the adolescent's age and values?
- Is the adolescent likely to respond to a group experience?
- Will the adolescent feel comfortable in a spiritual program?
- Is the adolescent mature enough to understand and relate to the concepts of a 12-step program?
- Does the adolescent believe in the disease concept of addiction?

The typical inpatient treatment regimen for adolescent clients consists of attending daily AA or NA meetings, individual and group therapy, and educational lectures on problem areas or on one of the 12 steps. When they enter a program, adolescents are given a chance to "take the first step," which usually involves admitting to themselves, their parents, the treatment staff, and other patients that they have become powerless over their drug or alcohol use. Adolescent clients who refuse to acknowledge that they have a problem with substance abuse are perceived as in a state of denial (Selekman & Todd, 1991).

A sponsor can play a critical role in 12-step treatment and must be selected carefully. Adolescents are particularly vulnerable to bad advice from trusted adults and may lump their sponsor with "all those other adults who don't understand me." Because of their need for immediate gratification, adolescents may need a sponsor who is immediately available at all times. Furthermore, when adolescents choose immature adolescents as sponsors, the potential for negative results may be even greater. Although adolescents can sometimes be appropriate sponsors, they often lack the life experience to guide another person on a lifelong journey.

Each group is different; each has a personality of its own. Although all AA groups are supposed to be open to any AA member, many are close-knit and have been for years. New members are tolerated, but are not really made to feel welcome. Other groups are very large, and an adolescent who is new to the program may feel out of place or overwhelmed. A therapist should attend open meetings of several different groups before referring an adolescent to a specific group.

Twelve-Step Programs and Other Therapies

The success of any effort to integrate 12-step programs with other therapeutic approaches depends a great deal on the therapist involved. The therapist's philosophy regarding substance abuse or addiction is critical. Even such diverse approaches as those of AA and behavioral therapy can be integrated, however. Given the substantial disagreements between the two approaches, particularly around the issue of controlled drinking versus total abstinence, they have many aspects in common, such as the role of skills acquisition, affective change, cognitive changes, and the use of social supports. Both approaches emphasize avoiding drinking environments, developing interests and activities incompatible with drinking, developing skills to use when alcohol is present, and having clearly defined behaviors to draw on when experiencing a desire to drink (McCrady & Irvine, 1989).

If the therapist understands 12-step programs and can support the adolescent's use of such a program, individual therapy is usually compatible with a 12-step program. It is important that the therapist and the adolescent agree on the goals for therapy and on the usefulness of a 12-step program. It is not therapeutic to have the therapist say one thing and the 12-step sponsor or other group members say something else. Most 12-step members have accepted the value of therapy from a professional therapist.

Group therapy and 12-step meetings are usually offered in the same treatment program, but the rules of conduct and the goals are different for each modality. Group therapy should not become a 12-step meeting, nor should 12-step meetings become therapy groups. The latter is particularly true, because there is no trained therapist available to intervene if the group situation should become therapeutically harmful. The therapist should be the controlling agent in group therapy; experienced members, general rules, and the principles of the organization tend to control 12-step meetings.

Family therapists should have an understanding of other 12-step groups available for family members, such as Al-Anon and Co-Dependents Anonymous. Recently, there has been a growth and development of family therapy as a major treatment approach for addictions. Davis (1980) pointed out the similarities between AA and family therapy and suggested ways in which they might be mutually reinforcing. He stated that cessation of drinking should be the first goal in family treatment and, in general, family therapists have agreed (Bepko, 1985).

ALTERNATIVE MODELS

With the acceptance of 12-step programs by treatment professionals and the popular press, it is easy to believe that they work for just about everyone. Despite their growing popularity, however, the numbers are still not good. For example, if AA has 2 million members and there are more than 20 million people with alcohol problems in the United States, then AA helps less than 1 in 10 people with an alcohol problem. There are many reasons for this. Some people with alcohol problems are not ready for the kind of help that AA has to offer. They may not believe that they have a disease or that their problem is bad enough to require outside help. The concept of a "Higher Power" dissuades some from attending AA. Adolescents in the first phases of substance abuse may find it hard to relate to the older alcoholic or addict who has years of abuse. In these cases, alternatives to the 12-step approach should be used.

Alternatives to 12-step models include those devised by groups such as RR or groups for special segments of the population such as Women for Sobriety. The 12 steps have also been modified to appeal to others; for example, behavioral psychologist B.F. Skinner (1987) wrote the Humanist Alternative Steps.

1. We accept the fact that all our efforts to stop drinking have failed.
2. We believe that we must turn elsewhere for help.
3. We turn to our fellow men and women, particularly those who have struggled with the same problem.
4. We have made a list of the situations in which we are most likely to drink.
5. We ask our friends to help us avoid those situations.
6. We are ready to accept the help they give us.
7. We earnestly hope that they will help.
8. We have made a list of the persons we have harmed and to whom we hope to make amends.
9. We shall do all we can to make amends, in any way that will not cause further harm.
10. We will continue to make such lists and revise them as needed.
11. We appreciate what our friends have done and are doing to help us.
12. We, in turn, are ready to help others who may come to us in the same way.

These steps avoid any mention of a "Higher Power," which may make them more acceptable to some people than are the 12 steps in AA. Many alternatives should be considered, perhaps even before the traditional 12-step model. In some cases, the alternatives do not require that an adolescent accept the label of alcoholic or addict so quickly. If less restrictive alternatives are ineffective, the 12-step approach will always be there.

REFERENCES

Alcoholics Anonymous. (1976). *Alcoholics Anonymous: The story of how many thousands of men and women have recovered from alcoholism* (3rd ed.). New York: Alcoholics Anonymous World Service.

Anderson, L.P. (1992). Differential treatment effects. In L. L'Abate, J. Farrar, & D.A. Serritella (Eds.), *Handbook of differential treatments for addictions* (pp. 23–40). Boston: Allyn & Bacon.

Bepko, C. (1985). *The responsibility trap.* New York: Free Press.

Cain, A. (1964). *The cured alcoholic.* New York: John Day.

Davis, D.I. (1980). Alcoholics Anonymous and family therapy. *Journal of Marital and Family Therapy, 6*(1), 65–74.

Ellis, A. (1979). Rational emotive therapy. In R.J. Corsini (Ed.), *Current psychotherapies* (pp. 97–108). Itasca, IL: Peacock Press.

Fillmore, K.M. (1988). *Evaluating Recovery Outcomes.* San Diego: University of California.

Institute of Medicine. (1989). Mutual help groups. In *Report of a study prevention and treatment of alcohol problems research opportunities.* Washington, DC: National Academy Press.

Kalb, M., & Propper, M. (1976). The future of alcohology: Craft or science? *American Journal of Psychiatry, 133,* 641–645.

Kurtz, L.F. (1990). Twelve step programs. In T.J. Powell (Ed.), *Working with self-help* (pp. 93–118). Silver Spring, MD: NASW Press.

Lawson, G., Ellis, D, & Rivers, C. (1984). *Essentials of chemical dependency counseling.* Gaithersburg, MD: Aspen Publishers.

McCrady, B.S., & Irvine, S. (1989). Self-help groups. In R.K. Hester & W.R. Miller (Eds.), *Handbook of alcoholism treatment approaches: Effective alternatives* (pp. 154–169). New York: Pergamon Press.

Selekman, M., & Todd, T.C. (1991). Crucial issues in the treatment of adolescent substance abusers and their families. In T.C. Todd & M. Selekman (Eds.), *Family therapy approaches with adolescent substance abusers* (pp. 3–19). Boston: Allyn & Bacon.

Shedler, J., & Block, J. (1990). Adolescent drug use and psychological health: A longitudinal inquiry. *American Psychologist, 45,* 612–630.

Skinner, B.F. (1987, July/August). A humanist alternative to A.A.'s twelve steps. *Humanists,* pp. 5–6.

Tarter, R. (1990). Decision-tree for adolescent assessment and treatment planning. *American Journal of Drug and Alcohol Abuse, 16,* 1–46.

Tournier, R.E. (1979). Alcoholics Anonymous as treatment and as ideology. *Journal of Studies on Alcohol, 40,* 230–239.

Youth treatment program profiles. (1983, Summer). In *Alcohol and Research World* (pp. 19–40). Rockville, MD: National Institute on Alcohol Abuse and Alcoholism.

Part III

Related Problems

Previous sections of this book have defined adolescent substance abuse as multicausal and multidimensional. It is a complex disorder that is made more complex by the problems that are often associated with or co-exist with adolescent substance abuse. These related problems are as dangerous and as destructive as the abuse itself.

Although suicide and incest are long-standing problems for adolescents, they are sometimes overlooked in their relationship to substance abuse. Chapters 16 and 17 have been included not only to address these problems directly, but to point to the strong relationship between these problems and substance abuse.

Gangs are an ever-growing problem in the United States, and where there are gangs there are usually drugs. The gangs are often substitute families for adolescents and their loyalty to the gangs may put them in life-threatening situations. Chapter 18 provides special insight into the world of the substance abusing gang member.

Satanic cults have some of the same attractions as gangs. Adolescents' interest in the occult is often a passing fascination with Ouija™ boards and tarot cards. Some may listen to heavy or black metal music and even read about witchcraft. This is often done for excitement or to alarm parents. However, those adolescents who gain a substitute family from a cult or begin using drugs may become more deeply involved. Chapter 19 describes various levels of occult involvement, assessment issues with adolescents involved with the occult, and treatment suggestions.

Perhaps the most frightening consequence of drug abuse is AIDS. Adolescents are the fastest growing population of the newly infected and often the most difficult to reach with prevention messages. Part of being an adolescent is feeling invincible. Warnings of health risks for smoking, drinking, and taking drugs are often countered with, "It won't happen to me." This is a particularly deadly belief for those intravenous drug users who share needles or those who practice unsafe sex.

Chapter 21 deals with the unique subject of steriod use. Steroids are not mind-altering drugs that adolescents take to get high but they do pose a threat. Steroid use is an increasing problem and is particularly disturbing because it involves otherwise outstanding youth. It is a drug problem connected to competitive athletes concerned with their bodies and how they function. The pressure to win can lead to steroid use that may end a promising career or destroy an athlete.

Chapter 22 defines anorexia, bulimia, and overeating as life threatening problems, especially for adolescent girls. Eating problems themselves are addictive disorders involving compulsive, physically damaging behaviors. Adolescents with eating disorders are often children of alcoholics, or, they develop their own drug or alcohol problem. It also appears that eating disorders are part of an inter-generational family addictive process.

Chapter 23, about vision problems, is the most unique in this section. Therapists or school counselors may miss an opportunity to prevent or intervene in a drug problem that had its antecedents in a visual perceptual disorder. That disorder often leads to school failure, juvenile delinquency, and drug use. An astonishing number of adolescents in juvenile detention facilities have a variety of visual perceptual disorders that are treatable. Recent research in this area is showing much lower recidivism rates for those adolescents in detention facilities who receive this treatment.

This section ends on a positive note. Lewayne Gilchrist and her associates have studied drug use among pregnant adolescents. Their study indicates that adolescents often stop or reduce their drug use when they become pregnant. This certainly is good news for their children, our next generation. This concern for the well-being of their unborn children could be used to help adolescent mothers continue this trend after the children are born.

16

Suicide Solution: The Relationship of Alcohol and Drug Abuse to Adolescent Suicide

Steven G. Daily

In all their talk about waging and winning the "War on Drugs," the politicians and the media fail to emphasize the fact that the Number 1 drug problem in the United States is not cocaine, marijuana, lysergic acid diethylamide (LSD), or any other illegal substance, but a solution called alcohol. According to the National Institute on Alcohol Abuse and Alcoholism, there are approximately 3.5 million teen-age alcoholics in the United States—that is 1 in every 9 teen-agers. Drunk driving is the leading cause of death for adolescents in the United States and is responsible for the maiming of an additional 2.5 million people on U.S. highways each year (Johnston, 1987).

The second leading cause of death for teen-agers in the United States is suicide. Before 1960, teen-age suicide comprised a relatively negligible percentage of the total number of suicides committed each year and was a distant fifth cause of adolescent fatalities. In the last three decades, however, teen-age suicide has increased by nearly 300% (Johnston, 1987). Often, these two leading causes of death cannot be separated. Many drivers who apparently intended to commit suicide by ramming their cars into trains, trucks, and other vehicles or by driving off steep embankments have significantly high amounts of alcohol in their blood. Other drivers who are totally inebriated kill themselves and others in accidents that appear to be unintentional, although not even the coroner knows for sure. As a rule, suicide is ruled out when there is any doubt, which helps to explain why deaths by suicide tend to be grossly underreported (Grollman, 1988). It is fair to say, however, that adolescent alcohol and drug abuse are important contributors to the rising teen-age suicide rate. Alcohol, particularly, is a suicide solution.

THE GROWING PROBLEM

Textbooks on sociology or social problems that were published before the year 1960 generally contain no mention of teen-age suicide or adolescent drug abuse.

Such problems were so rare that U.S. society seemed to be unconcerned about them. In the year 1960, the U.S. Bureau of Narcotics reported that 1 in every 4,000 U.S. citizens was addicted to some form of narcotic (Horton & Leslie, 1965), drug addiction was not even linked to adolescent suicide, and only 22% of arrests in U.S. cities involved persons under the age of 21. The percentage of individuals in this age group arrested for drunkenness, driving while intoxicated, and violation of drug laws was significantly lower (Raab & Selznick, 1964).

The numbers shown in Table 16-1 are hard to believe when compared with the annual figures reported by the U.S. Department of Justice in the 1980s. In 1983, for example, there were 661,400 arrests for drug law violations and 1,921,100 arrests for driving under the influence in the United States (Neubeck, 1986). These figures represent an increase of much more than 1,000% in each of these two categories. In addition, more than 40% of arrests each year after 1978 have involved offenses committed by people under the age of 21 (Birren, Kinney, Schaie, & Woodruff, 1981).

The dramatic increase in adolescent drug abuse has had a direct impact on teen-age suicide. Prior to 1960, the use of firearms, hanging, and exhaust gases were by far the most frequent means of suicide in the United States, but drug suicides triples during the 1960s (Berger, 1967). By 1971, not only did drugs account for 31% of all suicides (McGuire, Birch, & Gottschalk, 1976), but also teen-age suicide had increased so rapidly that, in a decade, it had moved from a distant fifth to the third leading cause of adolescent fatalities (Hosier, 1978).

As mentioned earlier, the line that separates substance abuse from suicidal behavior is often blurred. It may be impossible to distinguish between "suicidal gestures" and "serious suicide attempts." Research has indicated that approximately one third of drug overdose cases cannot be classified in either category (Ianzito, 1970). This element of uncertainty should be kept in mind when the following figures from studies on teen-age suicide and adolescent alcohol and drug abuse are considered:

- The highest percentage of drinkers among males is found in the 18 to 20 age group; among females, in the 21 to 34 age group (Zimburg, 1979).

Table 16-1 Total Arrests in U.S. Cities (over 2,500 population) in 1960

Offense	Total	% under age 21
Drunkenness	1,326,407	3.8
Driving while intoxicated	146,381	4.7
Violation of drug laws	23,430	16.9

Source: From *Major Social Problems* (p. 42) by E. Raab and G.J. Selznick, 1964, New York, Harper & Row.

- Among seventh graders, approximately two thirds of all boys and half of all girls have used alcohol. These percentages increase by the twelfth grade to 93% for boys and 87% for girls (Neubeck, 1986).
- Drivers between the ages of 16 and 21 make up only 12% of all licensed drivers, but are responsible for 26% of drinking driver fatalities (U.S. Department of Commerce, 1985).
- Seventy-four percent of drug-related deaths and 75% of drug emergencies involve legally prescribed drugs (U.S. Drug Enforcement Administration, 1981).
- Drug abuse in the United States has generally leveled off since 1983. Abuse of cocaine and the synthetic drugs has increased, however, contributing to the rise in drug-related deaths (Lamar, 1986; Shafer, 1985).
- Twelve percent of teen-agers are on both alcohol and drugs (polabuse), the most dangerous form of drug abuse (Seligman, Martin, & Peterson, 1984).
- The suicide rate for 15- to 24-year-olds has tripled in the past two decades and is rising most rapidly for white males in this age group (Stengel, 1984).
- At least 500,000 and possibly as many as 2 million teen-agers attempt suicide every year in the United States (Ross, 1984).
- Girls attempt suicide 3 times more frequently than do boys, and boys succeed 4 times more frequently.
- Thirty-four percent of U.S. teen-agers have "seriously considered" committing suicide.
- Thirty-two percent of U.S. teen-agers have made plans to commit suicide, and 14% have actually attempted suicide.
- Ninety percent of teen-aged attempters have known another attempter, a phenomenon referred to as the "cluster effect" (Stengel, 1984).

SELF-DESTRUCTIVE BEHAVIOR

Empirical evidence relating to both chemical abuse and drug-related suicide indicates that these behaviors are essentially gambles with death (Adams, Giffen, & Garfield, 1973; Lester & Lester, 1971), a phenomenon that has been referred to as "psychopharmacological roulette" (Mayo, 1974). Teen-agers who abuse drugs or alcohol often develop self-destructive behavior patterns that lead to a form of "slow suicide," even when there is no indication of intentional suicidal behavior or ideation. These patterns of slow suicide generally include (1) strong feelings of self-derogation or self-rejection, (2) extreme risk-taking behaviors, (3) physical degeneration and health problems, and (4) an inclination toward accident-prone behavior.

Research indicates that there is a significant correlation between high scores (i.e., indicating low self-esteem) on a self-derogation scale and various forms of deviant behavior, including substance abuse. In a 3-year study involving 7,618 teen-agers, for example, Kaplan (1976) found that students (particularly white middle- and upper-class males) whose responses to a seven-item self-derogation scale most often revealed low self-esteem were most inclined to abuse drugs and engage in various forms of antisocial behavior (Table 16-2).

A number of other studies have also found strong relationships among chemical abuse, risk-taking behaviors, and chronic and acute suicidal behaviors. In a study of 114 persons who requested drug abuse services from the Orange County Department of Mental Health (Saxon et al., 1978 as cited in Buetow, 1988, p. 31), for example, it was found that 57% had been involved in auto accidents in which they had been driving, 52% had taken drug overdoses that were nonsuicidal, 46% had thought seriously about committing suicide, and 19.2% had actually attempted suicide. All these figures are significantly above national norms.

Table 16-2 Correlation between Low Self-Esteem and Antisocial Behavior

1. I wish I could have more respect for myself (true).
2. On the whole, I am satisfied with myself (false).
3. I feel I do not have much to be proud of (true).
4. I am inclined to feel I'm a failure (true).
5. I take a positive attitude toward myself (false).
6. At times I think I am no good at all (true).
7. I certainly feel useless at times (true).

Behaviors	Level of Significance
Took narcotic drugs	$p < .001$
Used alcohol more than 2 times	$p < .01$
Thought about or threatened suicide	$p < .001$
Attempted suicide	$p < .001$
Carried dangerous weapons	$p < .001$
Cheated on exams	$p < .001$
Failed in school	$p < .001$
Engaged in public vandalism	$p < .001$
Stole other people's property	$p < .001$

Source: From "Self-Attitudes and Deviant Responses" by H.B. Kaplan, 1976, *Social Forces, 54*, pp. 788–801. University of North Carolina Press.

Other studies show an even higher rate of suicide ideation and behavior for alcohol and drug abusers. In a study of 62 alcoholics, Kendall and Stanton (1966, as cited in Buetow, 1988) found that the alcoholics' mortality rate was 5 times higher than general population norms and their suicide rate was 58 times greater than the national average. In another study, 30% of the alcoholics had made suicide attempts, and 92% had some history of expressing suicidal thoughts (Murphy et al., 1979, as cited in Buetow, 1988, p. 28). Goodwin (1982, as cited in Buetow, 1988) found that alcohol is a major factor in at least 25% of all suicides, and Wheeler (1987) reported that alcohol is a significant factor in 90% of all child abuse cases, which MacFarlane and Waterman (1986) have shown to correlate with self-destructive behavior and suicide.

The link between drug addiction and suicide is particularly strong. James (1967, as cited in Buetow, 1988) found that the suicide rate for male drug addicts was 50 times greater than the national average; Frederick and associates (1973, as cited in Harris, Linn, & Hunter, 1979) discovered that 43% of drug addicts expected to die by suicide. Even among drug users who are not addicts, the rate of suicide is approximately 15 times higher than it is in the general population (Harris, Linn, & Hunter, 1979). Other studies linking the problems of adolescent drug abuse and suicide have produced the following findings:

- The average mean age of drug addicts who commit suicide is 21.1 years, more than 10 years under the national mean (Roy & Linnoilas, 1986, as cited in Buetow, 1988).
- The white male between 14 and 20 years of age is the most likely candidate to commit suicide (Hawton, 1982, as cited in Buetow, 1988).
- Males are at least 4 times as likely to commit suicide as are females (Mercy et al., 1984, as cited in Buetow, 1988, p. 31).
- Male drug abuse and suicide has been strongly linked to (1) an unwillingness to seek help, (2) a lack of purpose in life, and (3) self-degradation based on feelings of meaninglessness (Harlow, 1986; Saxon et al., 1980, as cited in Buetow, 1988, p. 31).
- The factors most related to suicidal thoughts for both high school and college students are family problems, parental conflicts, and drinking or drug abuse problems (Wright, 1985b).

Therapists have approached the problems of drug abuse and suicide in a variety of ways. Psychoanalysts have generally viewed addiction as an inability to cope with adult responsibilities, resulting in regression to a childlike narcissistic state of dependence on a drug that becomes addictive and self-destructive. Suicide is the ultimate fulfillment of the death instinct, what Freud referred to as Thanatos (Lettieri, 1978), the deepest human drive toward aggression and destructiveness.

It is seen as the consequence of internalized rage; the desire to kill another is redirected upon the self.

According to behavioral and cognitive learning theorists, drug addiction occurs because the substance provides social or psychological reinforcement that makes it attractive. Drug use can be treated by pairing positive stimuli with slow withdrawal or through aversive therapy used in various detoxification programs. Suicide occurs because social or psychological pressures have built up to the point at which the individual sees death by suicide as a positive reinforcer rather than as a self-destructive act; death appears more attractive than life.

Existential theorists argue that addicts use drugs or alcohol as a primary source of pleasure because they lack the ability to play or to find pleasurable meaning in life through other activities. Recreational users, in contrast, see the use of drugs or alcohol as just one of the many pleasures that they enjoy. Suicide occurs because life is seen as ultimately absurd or meaningless. According to Camus, the question of suicide is the only serious philosophical problem (as cited in Lettieri, 1978). Humanistic theorists understand both drug abuse and suicide as byproducts of low self-esteem or feelings of worthlessness. They are two different forms of self-destructive behavior that grow out of the same root cause—deep feelings of inadequacy and self-rejection.

Developmental theorists see both drug dependence and suicide as a consequence of the failure to mature through one or more developmental stages. The individual who fails to develop basic attributes such as trust, autonomy, self-esteem, and initiative becomes dependent on sources other than the self to meet these needs. Whereas the non–drug-using suicidal individual often becomes overly dependent on other human beings, the addict chooses drugs as a substitute and, when the drugs fail, may turn to suicide. Family systems theorists suggest that both drug addiction and suicidal behavior grow out of unhealthy or dysfunctional relationships in a family, to which all family members contribute. The addict or suicidal person cannot be treated as an isolated client who needs therapy, because he or she is part of a system that must be treated as a whole; the family itself must be viewed as the client (Lettieri, 1978; Lawson, Peterson, & Lawson, 1983).

ALCOHOL AND DRUGS IN PREADOLESCENTS AND YOUNG ADOLESCENTS

According to the National Council on Alcoholism, 30% of the 9-year-olds in the United States today feel pressure to drink (Ordovensky & DuBois, 1986). Although alcohol is clearly the substance with which preadolescents and young adolescents are most likely to have problems, there is also plenty of evidence to indicate that students who abuse hard drugs in high school generally have their first exposure to these drugs in their preadolescent years.

The most recent national study on preadolescent and early adolescent chemical abuse was conducted by the Search Institute, which is based in Minneapolis, Minnesota (Benson, Williams, & Johnson, 1987). Its sample of 8,165 young people taken from fifth through ninth graders across the United States slightly over-represents the north central states, families with college-educated parents, and Protestants while it slightly underrepresents black and Hispanic youth, youth from single-parent families, and youth with no religious background; nevertheless, the study contains some important findings.

- Boys report considerably more use of alcohol, marijuana, and other drugs than do girls.
- Experimentation with alcohol is more common among current fifth graders than it was among older youth when they were in the fifth grade.
- The percentage of youth who drank alcohol 10 or more times "in the last 12 months" doubles between the eighth and ninth grades.
- During the 12 months prior to the survey,
    1. more than one in five (22%) fifth graders reported alcohol use
    2. more than half (53%) of all ninth graders had used alcohol
    3. 47% of ninth graders attended a drinking party with peers
    4. 13% of all youth in the study report that they used marijuana

A recurring theme throughout the entire study is that today's young adolescents are facing more difficult decisions, tougher temptations, and more pronounced pressures than young people their age have ever faced before. The sophistication and complexity of modern society is forcing many young people to grow up before they are ready emotionally. Of the fifth graders surveyed in this study, 16% said that they worried very much or quite a bit about the possibility that "I might kill myself." The use of drugs and alcohol has become one unfortunate way of coping with the fears and pressures of preadolescence. Twenty-seven percent of fifth graders said that they were 10-years-old or younger when they first started using alcohol, for example, a figure 12% higher than the figure that the ninth graders reported at the same age. Furthermore, the percentage of fifth graders involved with harder drugs was equal to or greater than the percentages of their counterparts in grades 6 through 9 in almost every category (Tables 16-3 and 16-4).

The findings of Benson and associates (1987) are encouraging because they show that the great majority of young adolescents in the United States are still not using or abusing hard drugs—although it must be kept in mind that this sample does not fully represent the poorest socioeconomic classes. This research is also

Table 16-3 Early Adolescent Use of "Hard" Drugs

In the last 12 months, have you used a drug like cocaine, angel dust, or LSD?

Number of Times	Percentage of Young Adolescents				
	5th	6th	7th	8th	9th
None	88	90	92	92	90
1 or 2 times	3	3	2	3	3
3–9 times	6	5	4	4	3
10–19 times	1	1	1	1	1
20 times or more	1	2	1	1	2
Once or more	12	10	8	8	10

Source: From *The Quicksilver Years: The Hopes and Fears of Early Adolescence* by P. Benson, D. Williams and A. Johnson, pp. 143–156, 1987, New York, Harper & Row.

Table 16-4 Early Adolescent Use of Pills

In the last 12 months, have you taken pills to get more energy (such as uppers, speed, or bennies) or pills to relax (such as downers or goofballs)? (Don't count pills ordered by doctors.)

Number of Times	Percentage of Young Adolescents				
	5th	6th	7th	8th	9th
None	86	91	91	90	85
1 or 2 times	4	3	3	3	5
3–9 times	7	4	5	4	5
10–19 times	1	1	1	1	1
20 times or more	2	1	1	2	4
Once or more	14	9	9	10	15

Source: From *The Quicksilver Years: The Hopes and Fears of Early Adolescence* by P. Benson, D. Williams and A. Johnson, pp. 143–156, 1987, New York, Harper & Row.

disturbing, however, because it shows that young people are getting involved with both alcohol and other drugs at earlier ages. Finally, this research demonstrates a strong correlation between the rapid increase in early alcohol and drug abuse and the significant increase in suicidal fears experienced by the youngest participants in this study.

CAUSES OF SUICIDAL SUBSTANCE ABUSE

The causes of adolescent substance use and abuse are generally complex. The developmental issues alone include separation from parental control in order to establish a distinct and individual identity, self-acceptance and peer pressure, the development of sexual relationships, and the pressures of the vocational choices and career decisions that all bombard the adolescent when he or she is trying to make the difficult transition from childhood to adulthood. "Drug use results from a complex interaction of genetic endowment, behavior patterns, motives, and social and psychological determinants. Reasons for use may be extremely complex or as simple as availability" (Archambault, 1989, p. 225). The causes of substance use appear to be significantly broader than the causes of the most self-destructive forms of substance abuse, however.

Many adolescents use or experiment with drugs for reasons that "appear to be divorced from any particular pattern of deviant behavior or severe emotional distress" (Segal, 1983, p. 430), such as curiosity, recreation or relaxation, relief of boredom, expanded awareness or insight, excitement, the drug effect (to "get high" or "mellow out"), and social interaction (Beschner & Friedman, 1979; Buetow, 1988; Zuckerman, 1979). Others turn to alcohol and drugs in an attempt to cope with serious personal or interpersonal problems and emotions, such as loneliness, anger, depression, feelings of low self-esteem, pressure, and frustration (Beschner & Friedman, 1985; Segal, 1983). Members of this second group, who tend to become compulsive users or substance abusers, make up approximately 5% of the teen-aged population in the United States between the ages of 14 and 18 (Beschner & Friedman, 1985). These adolescents are most likely to engage in deviant or self-destructive behaviors, experience extreme depression, and become suicidal.

In an attempt to substantiate the validity of this 5% figure among Southern California public high school students, a representative sample of 156 students from a typical high school in Riverside County were asked to fill out a drug use inventory (Buetow, 1988) and the Back Depression Inventory (Beck, Rush, Shaw, & Emery, 1979). The following is a brief summary of the findings:

- Seventy-seven percent of the students surveyed were using, or had used, either alcohol or other drugs.
- Of the 156 respondents, 45 (28.8%) were experiencing significant depression, ranging from borderline clinical depression to extreme depression.
- Thirty-nine (25%) of the students were using alcohol or drugs on a weekly basis, and 26 (17%) of these students were among those who reported significant depression.

- Forty-six (29.4%) of the students had contemplated or desired suicide; 38 (24%) of these had used alcohol or drugs, and 26 (17%) were weekly substance users/abusers.
- Twenty-four (15.3%) of the students said that they wanted to kill themselves or that they would kill themselves if they had the chance, and two thirds of these teen-agers were habitual alcohol or drug users/abusers.

Rather than the 5% figure of Beschner and Friedman (1985), this study showed that approximately 14% of high school students are teen-agers who simultaneously experience substance abuse, significant depression, severe emotional problems, and strong suicidal desires. In addition, 82% of this problem group indicated on the drug use inventory that they had major parental and family problems. This finding seems to support the conclusions reached in research conducted by Wright (1985a).

In a group of 207 high school students and 901 college students who had strong suicidal inclinations, Wright (1985a) found four distinct factors to be the most significant contributors to their suicidal thoughts and behaviors. First, these young people viewed their parents as two people with interpersonal conflicts. From a family systems perspective, this finding is not all surprising. Generally, therapists who work with the families of teen-aged drug addicts find that these families are engaged in a number of dysfunctional practices and patterns that reinforce the addictive behaviors of their "problem teen." Labeled the identified patient or client by other family members, this adolescent becomes the family scapegoat.

Second, according to Wright (1985b), these teen-agers viewed their relationship with their father as very poor. There seem to be two probable explanations for singling out their relationships with their fathers. First, male adolescents are twice as likely as are female adolescents to become heavily involved in substance abuse. Males are also more inclined to have conflictual relationships with their fathers than with their mothers. Second, cultural biases still dictate that a higher percentage of fathers will fill authoritarian roles in their families than do mothers, a factor that naturally leads them to more conflicts with their children of either sex who engage in rebellious or disorderly behavior.

Third, the teen-agers in this study viewed at least one parent as angry or depressed. Children introject or internalize negative parental emotions that have been modeled, and they become more likely to engage in self-destructive behavior. The fact that each of these first three factors are tied directly to the adolescent's family system underlines the importance of family therapy in the treatment of substance abuse. Finally, these adolescents viewed their drinking or drug use as a problem. Substance abuse is a major contributor to teen-age suicidal behavior, but it is not as powerful a force as the family. Adolescent drug abuse and teen-age suicide seem to have their roots firmly planted in dysfunctional family systems.

In addition to low self-esteem, loneliness, and family problems, teen-age suicide has been linked to peer rejection and social isolation, obsession with heavy metal rock music, sexual relationships gone awry, involvement with Satanic cults, and obsession with games such as Dungeons and Dragons (Johnston, 1987). Most of these items have a high correlation with teen-age substance abuse, but there are still many suicidal adolescents who abstain completely from all forms of alcohol and drugs or use such substances only rarely and moderately.

Various factors have been linked to both teen-age substance abuse and suicide. A lack of purpose or meaning in life and a lack of internalized moral values, for example, are adolescent problems that have become increasingly common in recent years and are highly correlated with self-destructive behaviors, such as substance abuse and suicide (Harlow, 1986; Wynne & Hess, 1986). Adolescents who drop out of school are much more likely to be substance abusers and potential suicide victims than are teen-agers who remain in school (Sherraden, 1986). Black male adolescents are particularly vulnerable to substance abuse, depression, and self-destructive behavior, largely because cultural expectations for males seem out of their reach and because their involvement in gang-related activities is often high (Spaights & Simpson, 1986). Premarital sex, out-of-wedlock births, youth homicide, and delinquency have been correlated with teen-age substance abuse and suicide (Wynne & Hess, 1986). Running away from home is also a behavior that is strongly associated with adolescent substance abuse and suicide (Sommer, 1984).

ASSESSMENT AND TREATMENT

Adolescents are a distinctive population that demands special attention from those involved in chemical dependency or suicide counseling. Too often, the methods of treatment designed for adult populations are applied with unfortunate consequences to adolescents who need treatment (Ehrlich, 1987). For example, adolescents who are herded into Alcoholics Anonymous programs and told that they have an incurable disease called alcoholism—when their problem is actually traceable to a dysfunctional family system—may become even more rebellious or antisocial in their behavior. It is essential to treat adolescent substance abuse and suicide-related problems in a context that permits consideration of the developmental, family systems, and other special issues relating to the adolescent experience.

The first step in treating the teen-ager who struggles with either substance abuse or suicide-related problems is an accurate assessment. To accomplish this, the counselor must explore the physiological, sociological, and psychological factors that may be contributing to the adolescent's condition (Lawson, Peterson,

& Lawson, 1983). Physiological considerations include a family history that suggests hereditary or genetic predispositions toward alcoholism, drug addiction, or severe depression. The use of a genogram can be quite valuable in revealing such a history (McGoldrick & Gerson, 1985). The teen-ager's own physical and medical history, particularly in regard to the physical changes that occur during adolescence (e.g., acne, change of voice, menstruation), may also be causing significant emotional or psychological stress.

Sociological considerations include the impact of family, school, and peer environments on the adolescent's substance abuse or depression. What behaviors are the parents modeling in the home? Are there strong religious or moral views in the home that either contribute to the problem or provide potential avenues for positive change? Are there ethnic or cultural issues involved? How is the adolescent performing in school, and what other factors at school may be contributing to the condition. Finally, what are the adolescent's friendship patterns? Have they undergone a recent change? Is there a pattern of increasing isolation from friends? Is there any discussion or behavior relating to substance abuse or suicide with peers? To what degree does the adolescent have a group-dependent personality?

Psychological considerations focus on the development of the teen-ager's personality and that way in which parents, siblings, and significant life events have affected it. The counselor must determine the teen-ager's level of self-esteem or ego strength. Is the adolescent involved with activities and hobbies (e.g., music, sports, school offices) that help him or her to feel productive and worthwhile? Have parents demonstrated conditional or unconditional love? Have parental attitudes generally been caring or uncaring? Overdemanding or respectful? Understanding or condemning? Overprotective or liberating? Is sibling birth order a significant factor? What pressures does the adolescent feel as a result of parental comparisons with siblings and peers? What are the adolescent's fears and hopes, and what persons or events have been most influential in shaping them?

Other issues that have particular relevance for the treatment of adolescents include the following:

- Most treatment programs and facilities are not equipped or designed primarily for adolescents. Approximately 20.6% of all drug abusers in treatment are 19 years of age or younger, but only 5.1% of available treatment programs have adolescents as their primary clientele (Beschner & Friedman, 1985).

- In some cases, nonintervention is actually more effective than is intervention with teens who are working through a developmental stage and need some space to sort out their own feelings of depression or attitudes toward substance use/abuse. The counselor should be careful not to disenfranchise the adolescent or to rob the adolescent of self-esteem by labeling him or her

(Archambault, 1989). Empowerment is an important goal in the treatment of teen-agers.

- Compared to adult substance abusers in treatment, teen-aged abusers are more often required to seek treatment by legal authorities, more likely to be pressured into treatment by family members, tend to be less educated, and tend to come from more chaotic family systems (Beschner & Friedman, 1985; DeLeon & Deitch, 1984).
- Research with depressed and suicidal drug abusers suggests that cognitive therapy is particularly effective as a means of treatment for high school or college students with average or above average intelligence (Chabon & Robins, 1986). Cognitive restructuring, problem solving, and nondirective approaches have all proved to be generally helpful in treating substance abuse and suicide behaviors (Patsiokas & Clum, 1985).

Inaccuracies in the initial diagnosis and the general unreliability of the assessment methods that are commonly used with adolescent borderline patients involved with substance abuse and suicidal behavior demonstrate the need for better prognostic procedures for adolescents (Simon, 1986). According to Beschner and Friedman (1985), the treatment of adolescents involved with substance abuse is most likely to be successful if the counselors

- are at ease and comfortable with adolescents
- can project a positive model of treatment
- have several years of counseling experience
- have an understanding, empathic attitude
- can confront self-destructive behaviors
- provide a great deal of support
- provide practical assistance in solving the client's real life problems

Rossman (1986) suggested that the following five steps are applicable to the treatment of both adolescent substance abuse and teen-age depression:

1. Help them to recognize that drugs are not working.
2. Help them substitute interpersonal relationships for drugs.
3. Help them to recognize the root reasons for their abuse.
4. Help them see the value of finding new power over their lives.
5. Help them see that recovery and social rehabilitation are bigger issues than the question of abstinence.

ISSUES IN PREVENTION

> In the preindustrial Western world, the body of suicide was frequently spat upon, hung on public gallows, left unburied for vultures or dragged through the streets to be buried at the crossroads with a stake through the heart and a stone on the face. Such condemnation, along with the small matter of roasting in hell, was what passed for suicide prevention. (Breskin, 1984, p. 27)

Early approaches to the prevention of alcohol and drug abusers were often equally horrifying. Even in the last half of the 20th century, however, there has not been nearly enough emphasis on positive prevention. Because substance abuse and suicide are the two leading killers of adolescents in the United States today, treatment is not enough. Efforts to create and implement education and prevention-oriented programs must increase. Despite the fact that the United States currently has the highest rates of adolescent drug abuse and suicide, surveys of high school and college students show a sad lack of knowledge in these areas (American Association of School Administrators, 1985; Vinal, 1986). Some of the most recent attempts at creative prevention of adolescent substance abuse and suicide include various media approaches (Sokploff, 1987), the QUEST program of social and skills development (Little, 1985), prevention novels written for adolescents (Hipple, 1984), and approaches that involve the entire family (Lawson et al., 1983; Robson, 1984).

Primary prevention attempts to eliminate problems before they occur, while secondary prevention is concerned with arresting the progress of a disorder early in its development. In either case, the family unit is in the best position to play the key preventive role in adolescent substance abuse and suicide. Family members must learn to recognize the warning signs, such as the following warning signals of adolescent suicide (Madison, 1978):

- mental depression, especially during the time when recovery seems imminent
- changes in behavior or personality, especially the discontinuation of habitual activities
- making final arrangements, such as giving away prized possessions
- suicidal talk, especially direct threats (which require immediate help)
- a previous attempt

The ability to recognize drug and suicide problems is crucial to effective prevention, but it is also important to understand the ways in which families can function to make the emergence of substance abuse or suicidal behaviors most unlikely. Families with the following characteristics have been found to be most immune to problems such as adolescent substance abuse and suicide (Blum, 1972; Strong & DeVault, 1986):

- The families stressed love and the physical expression of affection. Family members showed mutual concern and interest.
- They showed a tolerance of differences and forgiveness of failings.
- Self-confidence and respect among family members allowed for a variety of self-expression.
- Parents assumed leadership and were strong, but not autocratic. They were not afraid to make mistakes or to show emotion.
- They expressed a basic conviction of the goodness of the world and its people.
- Their interaction was characterized by humor and good-natured teasing.
- They communicated clearly and valued honesty and outspokenness.
- The family was a source of joy and happiness to its members.

The Search Institute found that adolescents were much less likely to use alcohol or drugs and, thus, to engage in suicidal behavior when their families provided nurturance, a sense of closeness, affection, a commitment of the young person to the church, and centrality of religion in the home. The opposite was true in families that emphasized coercive discipline and authoritarian control (Benson et al., 1987). These findings indicate the importance of family therapy and the need for more family life education in schools, churches, and communities if the war against adolescent substance abuse and suicide is to be won the only way it can ultimately be won—through prevention.

REFERENCES

Adams, R.L., Giffen, M.B., & Garfield, F. (1973). Risk taking among suicide attempters. *Journal of Abnormal Psychology, 82,* 262–267.

American Association of School Administrators. (1985). *Successful approaches to preventing youthful drug and alcohol use.* Arlington, VA: Author.

Archambault, D. (1989). Adolescence: A physiological cultural, and psychological no man's land. In G. Lawson & A. Lawson (Eds.), *Alcoholism and substance abuse in special populations* (pp. 223–246). Gaithersburg, MD: Aspen Publishers.

Beck, A.T., Rush, A.J., Shaw, B.F., & Emery, G. (1979). *Cognitive therapy of depression.* New York: Guilford Press.

Benson, P., Williams, D., & Johnson, A. (1987). *The quicksilver years: The hopes and fears of early adolescence.* New York: Harper & Row.

Berger, F.M. (1967). Drugs and suicide in the United States. *Clinical Pharmacology and Therapeutics, 8*(2), 219–223.

Beschner, G.M., & Friedman, A.S. (1979). *Youth drug abuse: Problems, issues and treatment.* Lexington, MA: D.C. Heath.

Beschner, G.M., & Friedman, A.S. (1985). Treatment of adolescent drug abusers. *International Journal of the Addictions, 20,* 977–993.

Birren, J.E., Kinney, D.K., Schaie, K.W., & Woodruff, D.S. (1981). *Developmental psychology: A lifespan approach.* Boston: Houghton Mifflin.

Blum, R.H. (1972). *Horatio Alger's children.* San Francisco: Jossey-Bass.

Breskin, D. (1984, November 8). Dear mom and dad. *Rolling Stone,* pp. 26–35.

Buetow, C.A. (1988). *An investigation of the suicide risk factors associated with substance use among adolescents.* Unpublished doctoral dissertation, United States International University.

Chabon, B., & Robins, C.J. (1986). Cognitive distortions among depressed and suicidal drug abusers. *International Journal of the Addictions, 21*(12), 1313–1329.

DeLeon, G., & Deitch, D. (1984). Treatment of the adolescent abuser in the therapeutic community. *Treatment services for adolescent drug abusers.* Rockville, MD: National Institute on Drug Abuse.

Ehrlich, P. (1987). 12-step principles and adolescent chemical dependence treatment. *Journal of Psychoactive Drugs, 19*(3), 311–317.

Grollman, E.A. (1988). *Suicide: Prevention, intervention, postvention.* Boston: Beacon Press.

Harlow, L.L. (1986). Depression, self-derogation, substance use, and suicide ideation: Lack of purpose in life as a mediational factor. *Journal of Clinical Psychology, 42*(1), 5–21.

Harris, R., Linn, M.W., & Hunter, K. (1979). Suicide attempts among drug users. *Suicide and Life-Threatening Behavior, 9,* 25–32.

Hipple, T.W. (1984). Twenty adolescent novels. *School Counselor, 32*(2), 142–148.

Horton, P.B., & Leslie, G.R. (1965). *The sociology of social problems.* New York: Appleton, Century, Crofts.

Hosier, H. (1978). *Suicide: A cry for help.* Irvine, CA: Harvest House.

Ianzito, B.M. (1970). Attempted suicide by drug ingestion. *Diseases of the Nervous System, 31*(7), 453–458.

Johnston, J. (1987). *Why suicide?* New York: Thomas Nelson.

Kaplan, H.B. (1976). Self-attitudes and deviant responses. *Social Forces, 54*(4), 788–801.

Lamar, J.V. (1986, June 2). Crack: A cheap and deadly cocaine is a spreading menace. *Time,* pp. 16–18.

Lawson, G., Peterson, J.S., & Lawson, A. (1983). *Alcoholism and the family.* Gaithersburg, MD: Aspen Publishers.

Lester, G., & Lester, D. (1971). *Suicide: The gamble with death.* Englewood Cliffs, NJ: Prentice-Hall.

Lettieri, D.J. (Ed.). (1978). *Drugs and suicide.* London: Sage Publications.

Little, R. (1985). The excellence movement: What's the connection to student needs? *NASSP Bulletin, 69*(484), 64–69.

MacFarlane, K., & Waterman, J. (1986). *Sexual abuse of young children.* New York: Guilford Press.

Madison, A. (1978). *Suicide and young people.* New York: Clarion Books.

Mayo, J.A. (1974). Psychopharmacological roulette: A follow up study of patients hospitalized for drug overdose. *American Journal of Public Health, 64,* 616–617.

McGoldrick, M., & Gerson, R. (1985). *Genograms in family assessment.* New York: W.W. Norton.

McGuire, F.L., Birch, H., & Gottschalk, L.A. (1976). A comparison of suicide and non-suicide deaths involving psychotropic drugs in four major U.S. cities. *American Journal of Public Health, 66*(11), 1058–1061.

Neubeck, K.J. (1986). *Social problems: A critical approach.* New York: Random House.

Ordovensky, P., & DuBois, J. (1986, June 25). Students: Alcohol is enemy no. 1. *USA Today*, pp. 1–2D.

Patsiokas, A.T., & Clum, G.A. (1985). Effects of psychotherapeutic strategies in the treatment of suicide attempters. *Psychotherapy, 22*(2), 281–290.

Raab, E., & Selznick, G.J. (1964). *Major social problems.* New York: Harper & Row.

Robson, J. (1984). Alcohol abuse in adolescence. *Alcohol and Alcoholism, 19*(2), 177–179.

Ross, C. (1984). *Youth suicide and what you can do about it.* (Available from the National Committee for Youth Suicide Prevention, 1811 Trousdale Dr., Burlingame, CA 94010)

Rossman, P. (1986). *Drug abuse in adolescence.*[Video Lecture]. San Diego: United States International University Video Library.

Segal, B. (1983). Drugs and youth: A review of the problem. *International Journal of the Addictions, 18*(3), 429–433.

Seligman, J., Martin, E.P., & Peterson, C. (1984, June 4). Getting straight. *Newsweek*, pp. 62–69.

Shafer, J. (1985). Designer drugs. In *Drugs, society and behavior 88/89* (pp. 83–89). Guilford, CT: Dushkin.

Sherraden, M.W. (1986). School dropouts in perspective. *Educational Forum, 51,* 15–31.

Simon, J.I. (1986). Day hospital treatment for borderline adolescents. *Adolescence, 21*(83), 561–572.

Sokploff, M. (1987). Adolescent social issues: Using media to address crucial concerns. *Media and Methods, 24*(2), 8–16.

Sommer, B. (1984). The troubled teen: Suicide, drug use, and running away. *Women and Health, 9,* 117–141.

Spaights, E., & Simpson, G. (1986). Some unique causes of black suicide. *Psychology: A Quarterly Journal of Human Behavior, 23*(1), 1–5.

Stengel, E. (1984). The suicide attempt. In F. Shneidman (Ed.), *Death: Current perspectives.* Palo Alto, CA: Mayfield Press.

Strong, B., & DeVault, C. (1986). *The marriage and family experience.* New York: West Publishing.

U.S. Department of Commerce. Bureau of the Census. (1985). *Statistical abstract of the United States.* Washington, DC: U.S. Government Printing Office.

U.S. Drug Enforcement Administration. (1981). *Drug abuse warning network: 1980 annual report.* Washington, DC: U.S. Government Printing Office.

Vinal, D. (1986). A determination of the health protective behaviors of female adolescents: A pilot study. *Adolescence, 21,* 87–105.

Wheeler, C. (1987, February 23). Healing scars of parental drinking. *Insight*, p. 64.

Wright, L.S. (1985a) High school polydrug users and abusers. *Adolescence, 20,* 853–861.

Wright, L.S. (1985b). Suicidal thoughts and their relationship to family stress and personal problems among high school seniors and college undergraduates. *Adolescence, 20,* 575–580.

Wynne, E.A., & Hess, M. (1986). Long term trends in youth conduct and the revival of traditional value patterns. *Educational Evaluation and Policy Analysis, 8*(3), 294–308.

Zimburg, S. (1979). Alcohol and the elderly. In C. Petersen (Ed.), *Drugs and the elderly* (pp. 28–40). Springfield, IL: Charles C. Thomas.

Zuckerman, M. (1979). *Sensation seeking.* Hillsdale, NJ: Lawrence Earlbaum Associates.

17

Alcohol, Incest, and Adolescence

Steven G. Daily

Half a century ago, incest was reported in the Western world so rarely that it was considered to be virtually nonexistent. For every 1 million people in the U.S. population census of 1930, there were 1.1 cases of reported incest (MacDonald, 1979). In 1937, there were approximately 4 cases per 1 million population reported in Scotland, 5 cases per 1 million in Canada, and 7 cases per million (the highest rate in the Western world) in New Zealand (Mendlicott, 1967). These figures reveal very little about the actual occurrence of incest during this period, but they do indicate that incest was not generally perceived to be a problem. The cultural denial concerning this practice ensured that there would be no adequate social provisions to deal with any cases that were detected. The cultural prohibitions and fears surrounding incest also made it difficult to study such behavior and its relationship to other factors, such as substance abuse, until the last few decades.

Today, in contrast, there is such a variety of research available in the fields of substance abuse and child abuse that the findings often appear contradictory and require some kind of interpretation. For example, several researchers have criticized the widely discrepant results of studies that claim to demonstrate a strong correlation between alcoholism and child molestation (Scavnicky-Mylant, 1984). They argue that these studies are so varied in their operational definitions and methodologies that it is impossible to compare and evaluate their results. On the low end of the spectrum, studies have indicated that approximately 12% of identified child abusers are also alcoholics; on the high end of the scale, studies have shown that fully 65% of incest perpetrators have a history of alcoholism (Scavnicky-Mylant, 1984). Other surveys of the literature on alcoholism and incest provide an even higher range of scores in measuring the percentage of incest perpetrators who are alcoholics. For example, after examining 15 major studies, Barnard (1983) found reports that 15% to 80% of incest offenders were also alcoholics. Whatever the correct figure, the relationship between incest and alcoholism is clearly more than coincidental.

For years incest and alcoholism were treated as individual disorders that resulted primarily from psychological dysfunction or a specific personality weakness. Today, however, both these problems are considered to be best understood within the context of severe family dysfunction. Research findings over the last decade provide a helpful framework for counseling or understanding adolescents in such a family system.

- There are approximately 3 to 4 million children in the United States living in homes that are both alcoholic and incestuous (Liles & Childs, 1986).

- Twenty-six percent of children raised in alcoholic homes are also the victims of incest (Black, 1982). Furthermore, 41.5% of female adolescents who are substance abusers report that they were victims of intrafamilial or extrafamilial sexual abuse (Flanigan, 1988; Harrison, 1989).

- Forty-five percent of incest offenders consume alcohol just before molesting their victims, and at least 38% of these offenders are judged to be alcoholics (Liles, 1984).

- Thirty-eight percent of women and 8% of men report that they were the victims of sexual abuse at least once before the age of 18 (Pellauer, Chester, & Boyajian, 1987).

- Eighty-five percent of child molesters were sexually abused themselves as minors, usually at the same age as their victims. The great majority of these offenders also became substance abusers in their teens (MacFarlane & Waterman, 1986).

- Seventy-eight percent of all incest victims are assaulted in their own homes by relatives or people they know well. Eighty-six percent of such incest cases involve fathers or stepfathers as offenders (Groth & Burgess, 1977; Liles & Childs, 1986).

- Incest victims are much more likely to become substance abusers in their teens than are teen-agers in the general population. Other long-term effects of incest include delinquency, antisocial behavior, promiscuity, prostitution, heterosexual disorders, depression, and homosexuality (MacDonald, 1979; MacFarlane & Waterman, 1986).

- The average age of the daughter-victim when incest begins is 9.05 years. The incestuous behavior typically lasts for 36.3 months and is the major cause of runaway cases involving teen-aged girls (Graham, 1984; Liles & Childs, 1986).

- In a major study of incestuous families, Muldoon found a 65% rate of alcohol abuse by the offender, a 47% rate of physical abuse of the children, and a 39% rate of physical abuse of the wife (as cited in Taylor, 1984).

An examination of these studies from the perspective of dysfunctional family systems reveals some basic general patterns. First, most incest cases involve father figure offenders who generally demonstrate a high incidence of alcohol abuse. Second, an unusually high percentage of women who are treated for chemical dependency were the victims of incest when they were adolescents or children (Harrison, 1989; Yeary, 1982). Mother-son, mother-daughter, and father-son incest are believed to be significantly more rare than is either father-daughter incest or sibling (peer) incest. Because it does not involve the use of power or coercion, peer incest is believed to be much less harmful (Yeary, 1982).

DYNAMICS OF THE INCESTUOUS FAMILY

In the incestuous family, the mother generally relinquishes her role to the older daughter. In some cases, there is actual role reversal, but the mother-daughter relationship more often resembles that of competitive siblings. This explains why the incidence of incest is much higher with older daughters than it is with younger daughters and why the inadequate relationship between the oldest daughter and the mother often becomes a pattern that recurs generation after generation (Spencer, 1978). The parentification of one child while the others are ignored, spoiled, or scapegoated is also a common pattern in alcoholic families. Another similarity is that the spouse of the incest offender, like the spouse of the alcoholic, may be the chief enabler who consciously or unconsciously contributes to and perpetuates the family addiction and dysfunction (Wegscheider, 1981).

Justice and Justice (1979) focused specifically on the family dynamics of father-daughter incest, emphasizing the role that alcohol and alcoholism play in such family systems. They noted that the cycle of incest includes the following predisposing conditions and factors:

- The father, under severe job or family stress, increases his drinking.
- The father seeks his fantasy of an "all loving" mother in his daughter.
- Sex ceases between the father and the mother (husband and wife).
- The mother leaves her husband and daughter alone (e.g., works nights).
- The daughter is hungry for attention and affection.
- The family's sexual climate is either very lax or very repressive.

Justice and Justice concluded that 80% to 85% of incestuous fathers have "symbiotic personalities" that crave intimacy, but cannot appropriately achieve it. These men are either tyrants or introverts, who are expert rationalizers and generally alcoholics. The daughter in such a relationship usually has many of the following characteristics: (1) a poor relationship with her mother, (2) low self-esteem, (3) strong needs for attention and affection, (4) development of a seductive manner, (5) excessive attachment to her father, and (6) a willingness and desire to become her father's "rescuer" or to overcompensate for his alcoholism and neediness.

In both incestuous and alcoholic families, the addictive behavior of the identified patient is generally a symptom that develops in the family's attempt to deal with pervasive fears of abandonment and chaotic family disintegration. The dysfunctional family desperately assimilates the symptoms of incest and/or alcoholism for the sake of its own self-preservation (Lustig, 1966; Satir, Bandler, & Grinder, 1976; Wegscheider, 1981). Two of the most common family problems that contribute to the development of both incest and alcoholism are (1) marital sexual incompatibility and (2) overly rigid or chaotic family authority structures.

Sexual Patterns of Incest Offenders

Incestuous behavior may result from pedophilia, an abnormal and intense sexual craving for young children, or it may be part of a larger pattern of indiscriminate promiscuity. Most commonly, however, incest involves the selection of a specific child, usually the oldest daughter, as a substitute sexual partner when the incest offender is incapable of sharing or cultivating satisfying intimate relations with the spouse and is unwilling or afraid to seek a partner outside the nuclear family (Meiselman, 1978). The spouses in incestuous marriages have often been raised themselves in homes with family intimacy dysfunctions. The same is also true of substance abusers, particularly those who have grown up in alcoholic homes.

Coleman (1982) noted that "a significantly high proportion of chemical abusers have histories of family-intimacy dysfunctions" (p. 155) and that these dynamics play an important causal role in subsequent substance abuse patterns. Bowen (1966) further stated, "In many cases, chemical abuse becomes the coping mechanism for family-intimacy dysfunction. This abuse pattern leads to further intimacy dysfunction in adolescence and adulthood and is transmitted from generation to generation" (p. 266). Bowen (1966) demonstrated that couples who marry tend to function at the same basic levels of self-differentiation (emotional separateness from their family of origin or individuality), which helps to explain why two people with similar developmental deficits are attracted to each other. The marriage of such a couple produces a generational cycle in which individuals who have been raised in environments with family intimacy dysfunction choose each other as mates, experience their own marital sexual problems, and lay the foundation for incest and/or substance abuse in the family system.

Research on the less common problem of father-son incest has revealed that this kind of incest is found in three basic types of family situations: (1) homosexual families, (2) promiscuous families, and (3) physically abusive families. Furthermore, alcohol abuse is strongly linked to incest in each of these family systems (Pierce, 1987). The weight of evidence suggests that both "incest and alcoholism are family problems in which there is a primary illness interacting with a dysfunctional family system" (Kellerman, 1984, p. 84), and these problems are often interrelated and much more closely associated than has been recognized in previous decades.

Authority Structure in the Incestuous/Addictive Family

The authority structure of the family system is a precursor of potential incestuous and/or alcoholic patterns. For example, Hoorwitz (1983) found that, in most cases of incest, not only is the marital relationship sexually and emotionally unsatisfying, but also the father is likely to be devout, moralistic, and fundamentalist in his religious beliefs. Brucki (1986) found that the most common characteristics in incestuous families are authoritarianism, social isolation, and poor impulse control among fathers, with dependency and emotional absence among mothers. Both the short-term and long-term effects of incest in these families included serious problems with substance abuse.

Finally, in an overview of past research on incestuous families, Luther and Price (1980) found that the authority structures in these families tend toward the extremes of passive, introverted (secretive), and disconnected types or strong, authoritarian, and dominating styles. Thus, the major parental models found most commonly in alcoholic families are also most prominent in incestuous families. Not only do studies show that up to 80% of incest offenders have a history of substance abuse (Barnard, 1983), but also they indicate that as many as 84% of drug or alcohol addicts have a history of child abuse/neglect or come from homes with family intimacy dysfunctions (Cohen, 1982). When compared with marijuana use and other forms of substance abuse, alcoholism has been shown to be most connected to the influence of the family of origin (Sommer, 1984).

TREATMENT ISSUES IN ALCOHOLIC AND INCESTUOUS FAMILIES

The similarities in the family dynamics of alcoholic and incestuous families are striking, but families that struggle with both problems need treatment for both. "The inherent problem in treating one of these problems, but not the other, is that potential for prevention of recidivism is diminished" (Barnard, 1983, p. 139). The following characteristics are shared by alcoholic and/or incestuous families and should be recognized in the diagnosis and treatment of both conditions:

- Both problems may be partially caused by maladaptive responses to family stress, unmet needs for emotional closeness, low self-esteem, and a hunger for control and/or power (Giaretto, 1976).

- Both problems are characterized by a dysfunctional marital relationship and, generally, a deteriorating or dysfunctional sexual relationship between husband and wife (Barnard, 1983).

- Both problems commonly exist in families in which generational boundaries are blurred and family roles are pathologically and rigidly assigned (Barnard, 1983).

- Incestuous fathers resemble alcoholic fathers in their heavy use of denial, minimization, and rationalization (Liles & Childs, 1986).

- Secrecy is the hallmark of both alcoholic and/or incestuous families. Though highly destructive, these secrets preserve and "maintain the delicately fragile equilibrium of the family" (Barnard, 1983, p. 137; Wegscheider, 1981).

- In both cases, family affect is muffled and distorted, creating an environment that short-circuits or mutes normal inhibitory anxieties (Barnard, 1983).

- In both alcoholic and incestuous families, sibling relationships become pathologically disturbed as children become

   1. pseudoadults or parental caregivers

   2. scapegoats who act out their anger, fear, or confusion as a cry for help

   3. lost or withdrawn children, isolated in the family system

   4. guilt-stricken individuals who wrongly assume fault for the problem

   5. nontrusting individuals in their relationships with family and others (Black, 1982; Deutsch, 1982)

- Both problems are often perpetuated by colluding spouses who become chief enablers or co-dependents who deny their role in such family problems (Liles & Childs, 1986).

- In both family systems, there tends to be either extreme enmeshment (excessive belongingness) or extreme detachment (disconnectiveness) in family relationships (Minuchin, 1974).

- Both alcoholic and incestuous families have dependency problems (i.e., a lack of ability to function interdependently) and family intimacy problems (Bowen, 1974).

- Both types of families are known for their social isolation or "negative anonymity, and their extreme deficits in basic communication skills (Ackerman, 1983; Sgroi, 1982).

- Both problems represent attempts to maintain a homeostasis that will keep the family system together (Liles & Childs, 1986).

Patterns in incestuous and/or alcoholic families can continue without significant disruption for generations, as such families rarely fragment or view divorce as an option unless an external intervention uncovers the dysfunctional nature of the family system. Framo (1965) pointed out that individuals often "unconsciously seek parents instead of spouses" when they marry (p. 98). They choose mates with whom "they can prove or correct something about themselves" or "can duplicate or master an old conflictual relationship" from their family of origin (p. 98). Because such individuals are generally trying to make up for a deficit in their past, they have much higher and more unrealistic expectations of the marital relationship than do those who enter marriage with a healthy sense of self-identity and a solid self-esteem. Individuals from alcoholic and/or incestuous families are most likely to enter into marital relationships that, according to Framo (1965), are characterized by "threats of divorce," although "the possibility of separation or divorce almost does not exist" because "separation means psychic death."

ADOLESCENTS IN ALCOHOLIC AND/OR INCESTUOUS FAMILIES

Adolescence is a developmental period in life that is generally associated with great stress, uncertainty, and frustration even in a relatively healthy family system. When dysfunctional factors in the family such as alcoholism and/or incest compound these problems, the demands of adolescence become overwhelming. In many cases, adolescents in such environments are forced to create elaborate defense systems simply to survive, much less to complete the major developmental tasks required for their transition to adulthood:

- achieve a gender-appropriate social role
- accept one's body image
- achieve independence from parents
- find a responsible sexuality
- complete requisite academic goals
- prepare for an occupation
- develop a set of values necessary for filling later roles as spouse and parent
- evolve a set of values and a philosophy of life that will be compatible with a successful evolution into adulthood (Garmezy, 1981)

The typical stages that the child/adolescent passes through in an alcoholic or incestuous home can clearly complicate these developmental changes. The act of incest is generally more invasive and threatening to a child or adolescent than are the behaviors of an alcoholic parent, which are commonly viewed as either dominant and abusive or neglectful and uncaring. The dynamics in both kinds of families are often so similar that patterns of adolescent response bear a great deal of resemblance, however. Therefore, the five stages of what Summit (1983) called "the accommodation syndrome" in incestuous families is applicable to the dynamics of adolescent development in both the incestuous and alcoholic family.

Accommodation

Stage 1: Denial, Secrecy, and Fear

Because of the social stigma connected with alcoholism and incest, the adolescent in such a family system naturally participates in the "conspiracy of silence" that is characteristic of such cases. Often, the adolescent either blindly refuses to acknowledge that his or her family is abnormal or internalizes a sense of guilt or shame that leads to extreme secrecy about the family problem. There is a constant fear of exposure. Adolescents do not invite their friends and peers to the house because they dread the embarrassment that potential parental interactions or behavior may produce. In many cases, their parents are very highly respected individuals in the community, which makes the hypocrisy of their family behavior all the more difficult to tolerate and all the more necessary to hide.

Stage 2: Helplessness and Victimization

Even in their teens, children generally feel helpless to change the complex dysfunctional dynamics in the alcoholic and/or incestuous family. Many adolescent girls who are molested in their own beds while other family members are sleeping in the house fail to cry out or to express their outrage because they are paralyzed with fear about the potential consequences of such behavior. "Violation of a person's most secure retreat overwhelms ordinary defenses and leads to disillusionment, severe insecurity, and a process of victimization" (Summit, 1983, p. 6). To a lesser degree, the same is often true of adolescents whose physically or emotionally abusive alcoholic parent violates the privacy of their room. Teen-agers need some boundaries that are sacred; they desperately need to have some privacy that will be respected. When such limits are not provided, particularly in an abusive environment, adolescents either internalize their anger into self-hatred or attempt to overcompensate for their helplessness through extreme rebellion or perfectionism.

Stage 3: Accommodation and Acceptance of Blame

The extremes of neglect or abuse that confront adolescents in alcoholic and/or incestuous family systems drive teen-agers to one of two conclusions about who is responsible for their suffering. They come to believe either that they themselves are "bad, deserving of punishment and not worth caring for" or that their parent(s) is(are) "bad, unfairly punishing and not capable of caring" (Summit, 1983, p. 67). When victimized teen-agers come to the second conclusion, they often become runaways. Adolescents much more commonly blame themselves, however, because they have been raised in a family system that has neither prepared them nor given them permission to believe that either of their parents is bad. Self-scapegoating becomes the almost universal alternative for such young people.

In alcoholic and/or incestuous families, there is "an inevitable splitting of conventional moral values: maintaining a lie to keep the secret is the ultimate virtue, while telling the truth would be the greatest sin" (Summit, 1983, p. 8). The teen-ager is constantly forced to restructure reality in a manner that will protect the family. In such an environment, the male adolescent is more likely than is the female adolescent to channel frustration and anger into antisocial and aggressive forms of behavior, but substance abuse is common among both sexes. Parents have often modeled this kind of behavior, particularly in the alcoholic home, and it becomes a natural course of escape. Even when there is no parental alcoholism or drug abuse, the adolescent in such an environment is very likely to choose substance abuse to escape from the hellish realities of an abusive environment.

Stage 4: Delayed and Conflictual Disclosure

The normal conflicts between parents and children who are passing through adolescence are significantly compounded and accentuated in alcoholic and/or incestuous families. Accommodation mechanisms such as substance abuse, truancy, promiscuity, delinquency, attempted suicide, rebellion, or attempts to run away from home are common symptomatic teen-age reactions to abusive or neglectful family environments and may become the focus of tension between parents and their frustrated adolescents. As these problems develop into full-blown conflicts, adolescents often find themselves in trouble at school, with the law, or in a counselor's office as the identified patient. Under these circumstances, the teen-ager who feels enough pressure often subtly discloses or angrily exposes the family secret of alcoholism and/or incest.

Tragically, the adolescent is most likely to opt for disclosure and "seek understanding and intervention" during the rebellious teen-age years when he or she is least likely to find adult support (Summit, 1983). The very adults who have been entrusted with this information for the first time often discredit or minimize such an attempt at disclosure. As the story unfolds, it is easy for adult counselors or officials to identify with the distraught parents who are trying to raise a "rebellious" or "depressed" teen-ager and to question the adolescent's credibility. If alcohol abuse or incest has occurred for years, why is the adolescent just exposing the problem now? Is it not likely that the adolescent has invented this story to retaliate against one or both parents for their attempts to provide reasonable discipline or control? How much credibility can a delinquent, drug-abusing, or "problem" adolescent have? The adult may believe that the adolescent must take responsibility for his or her own problem and focus on solving it, rather than placing blame on others. Such deductions betray the trust and vulnerability that the adolescent displays through this kind of difficult disclosure.

Rebellion is not always part of the disclosure process. Some adolescents who are model offspring, honor students, and classic overachievers occasionally attempt to disclose a major family secret such as alcohol abuse or incest only to be greeted with incredulous statements (e.g., "It obviously hasn't hurt your success or affected your accomplishments!"). More often than not, however, these kinds of deep family secrets are never disclosed by family members even during adolescence. It is usually outside intervention that brings such a family to counseling.

Stage 5: Retraction of Complaint

In the chaotic aftermath of their disclosures about incest or alcohol-related abuse, many adolescents begin to back away from their accusations or complaints. The same kinds of considerations that generally cause adolescents to feel uncomfortable about disclosing such problems in the first place are usually responsible for such retractions. They may fear criminal prosecution, they may experience guilt for the angry accusations that have been made, or they may feel ashamed and responsible for fragmenting or destroying the family. Their concerns about occupational loss and the financial security of the family are also significant. Ultimately, it takes a tremendous amount of therapeutic support to sustain the adolescent who chooses the courageous course of disclosure in the face of strong family pressures to preserve a system built on secrets and silence.

Incest-Related Sexual Problems

Several studies have revealed the intergenerational cycle that occurs when marital sexual incompatibility and family intimacy dysfunctions lead to incest and/or substance abuse, which in turn contribute to sexual maladjustment and dysfunction in the next generation. In many cases, the sexual dysfunctions that occur in this pattern involve fears of intimacy and healthy sexual relationships, as a person who is coerced into sexual activity naturally develops distrust and fear about such an activity. In other cases, however, incest and alcoholism in the family can create an environment in which adolescents are more inclined to become involved in promiscuity, prostitution, and various forms of sexual addiction.

Although many incest offenders consume alcohol immediately before committing their crimes, incest is seldom a physically violent crime conducted in a drunken rage. Rather, it often begins as the gentle seduction of a sexually naive child or adolescent for the genital pleasure of the offender. This act frequently introduces the inexperienced victim to new found genital pleasures, however, and may lead to an unhealthy longing for sexual pleasure that is disconnected from any relational context. The body becomes objectified and is viewed as a "sexual pleasure machine" that can be manipulated, used, or exploited. The body becomes a thing or an object that is seen as isolated, rather than as an inseparable part of a person. Such a mentality destroys healthy self-esteem and lays the foundation for every form of sexual addiction (Joy, 1986). The healthy, mutual sexual exploration that is commonly practiced by pre-adolescent children who "play doctor" has been positively correlated with "warm interpersonal relations" in adulthood (Joy, 1986), but any kind of one-up–one-down relationship, whether it be abusive or just exploitative, will leave scars that generally affect the victim throughout adolescence and adulthood.

Promiscuity and Premarital Sex

In the last two decades, there has been a radical shift in the attitudes of U.S. families toward premarital sexual behavior. In 1985, for the first time in the history of the Gallup Report, the majority of U.S. citizens (52%) expressed the opinion that premarital sex is not wrong; only 39% stated that it was wrong. As recently as 1969, however, 68% of U.S. citizens had said that premarital sex was wrong, and only 21% had said that it was not wrong (Gallup, 1986). A radical change in behavior has accompanied this radical change in attitude. Between 1970 and 1985, for example, the rate of teen-age pregnancy skyrocketed in the United States. While births in general have not increased at all, births to unmarried women have increased 213.6% (a figure that would be even higher were it not for the dramatic increase in abortions). In addition, the practice of premarital cohabitation has increased by 380%, and births to unmarried couples have increased 313.3% (Strong & DeVault, 1986).

The fact that reported cases of incest (Pellauer et al., 1987) and adolescent arrests for drunk driving (Neubeck, 1986; Raab & Selznick, 1964) have both more than doubled during this same period is not just coincidental. Most of the major cultural changes that have affected families in the United States during the last three decades are to some degree interrelated. For example, the incidence of incest among adolescent females who are indiscriminately promiscuous or who engage in prostitution is extremely high (Brennan, 1978; Volpe, 1983). There is also a correlation between adolescent practice of premarital sex, promiscuity, or rape and teen-age use or abuse of alcohol (MacDonald, 1979; Spees, 1987). In other words, the adolescent who is raised in an alcoholic and/or incestuous family is much more likely to experience major sexual problems or to act out promiscuous or sexually addictive behaviors than is the average teen-ager.

The Problem of Rape

Because 50% to 90% of all rape and incest cases are probably never reported or prosecuted, research findings about such behavior vary widely and generally require cautious interpretation. It is still fair to say that alcohol plays a significant role in all types of rape, however. Alcohol is by far the most significant factor in date, acquaintance, and gang rapes, which involve teen-agers far more than does any other kind of rape. This is known to be true in spite of strong evidence that fewer than 1 in 100 of these rapes are actually reported to law enforcement authorities (Parrot, 1988). Male victims of rape are even less likely to report it, although surveys indicate that approximately 10% of all rapes involve male victims.

According to Adams and Abarbanel (1988), the incidence of all forms of acquaintance rape has increased rapidly in recent years, making it the most reported kind of rape in the United States—even though studies indicate that 99% of these crimes go unreported. Anonymous survey responses in a number of national studies indicate that 15% to 17% of college women admit to having been raped, while 7% to 8% of college men admit to having committed rape. In addition, according to a major study, 77.6% of college women and 57.3% of college men at Texas A&M University said that they had been involved in male-against-female sexual aggression in dating situations (Muehlenhard, 1987).

Acquaintance rape is the most traumatic and devastating form of rape because it can destroy the victim's ability to exercise trust in established relationships or to initiate relationships with new acquaintances. Here again, an alcoholic and/or incestuous family heritage is positively correlated with rape victimization and perpetration. Men who were victims of incest as children are much more likely to become rape or incest offenders as adults than are those who have not been raised in such a family system (MacFarlane & Waterman, 1986; Tufts New England Medical Center, 1984). Women who were victims of incest as children are much more likely to develop the very characteristics that make them extremely vulnerable to acquaintance rape and generally incapable of reporting such crimes, namely, low self-esteem, submissive or nonassertive behaviors, promiscuous or seductive mannerisms, and, in many cases, masochistic inclinations (Parrot, 1988). Although such characteristics do not make a woman in any way responsible for or deserving of rape, they do make her much more vulnerable to rape.

The great majority of teen-age rapes involve the use and abuse of alcohol. In fact, the most important circumstantial factor in marital rape (Barnard, 1990) and acquaintance rape is substance abuse (Parrot, 1988). There is a direct correlation between the occurrence of acquaintance rape and the degree of intoxication of both the offender and the victim. Offenders who drink or get drunk generally lose their inhibitions; become overly aggressive; insist that their victim "wanted it," "provoked it," or "owed it to him"; and often excuse, justify, or blame their behavior on having had "too much to drink." This rationalization allows the offenders to keep on believing that they are not rapists. Victims who drink too much also lose their inhibitions, their judgment or ability to set preventive limits, and their ability to deal with such a crime once it has occurred.

Development of Sexual Disorders or Homosexuality

Although no direct cause-and-effect relationship has been established between either incestuous victimization or alcoholism and adolescent sexual disorders or homosexuality, important correlational studies have demonstrated that these factors are inseparably linked. For example, research suggests that feminine behavior is negatively correlated with alcohol consumption for both men and women, and that masculine behavior is positively correlated with alcohol consumption for men (Chomak & Collins, 1987). Not only drinking, but also the sex roles that are modeled by drinking parents affect an adolescent's perception of sex roles. The family intimacy dysfunctions in an alcoholic and/or incestuous family also contribute to a number of sexual disorders in adolescence or adulthood.

Research has also linked the practice of homosexuality to both incest and alcoholism. For example, Groth (1982) found that males who were molested when they were young are much more likely to molest young boys as adults than are men in the general population. Sexual identity and role confusion can also be an adolescent symptom of an extended incestuous relationship (MacDonald, 1979). Finally, homophobia is common in male adolescents or adults who have been the victims of incest (MacFarlane & Waterman, 1986). Alcoholism is 2 to 3 times as prevalent in the homosexual community as it is in the general population (Zehner, 1984). This correlation may mean only that the social pressures felt by homosexuals drive them to drink more; it may mean, however, that the family dynamics in the alcoholic and/or incestuous home create an environment in which sexual role confusion is more likely to occur, leading to bisexual or homosexual experimentation in adolescence.

CONCLUSION

Because marital sexual maladjustment and incompatibility are so common in the alcoholic and/or incestuous family system, it is often almost impossible for adolescents to observe proper or healthy parental modeling at any stage in their sexual development. Therefore, it is not surprising that such teen-agers feel incapable of developing warm, trusting, and appropriately affectionate relationships with peers. Family intimacy dysfunction is often the only norm that they have known. The unique developmental challenges facing adolescents in alcoholic/ incestuous family systems make the treatment of these individuals significantly more complex than the treatment of family members in less demanding developmental stages.

REFERENCES

Ackerman, R. (1983). *Children of alcoholics.* Holmes Beach, FL: Learning Publications.

Adams, A., & Abarbanel, G. (1988). *Sexual assault on campus: What colleges can do.* (Available through Santa Monica Rape Treatment Center, Santa Monica, CA)

Barnard, C.P. (1983). Alcoholism and incest: Improving diagnostic comprehensiveness. *International Journal of Family Therapy, 5*(2), 136–143.

Barnard, C.P. (1990). *Aggression, family violence and chemical dependency.* New York: Haworth Press.

Black, C. (1982). *It will never happen to me.* Denver: M.A.C. Publishers.

Bowen, M. (1966). The use of family theory in clinical practice. In R. Green & J. Framo (Eds.), *Family therapy: Major contributions* (pp. 265–311). New York: International Universities Press.

Bowen, M. (1974). Toward the differentiation of self in one's family of origin. In F. Andres & J. Lorio (Eds.), *Georgetown family symposia: A collection of papers* (Vol. 1, 1971–1972). Washington, DC: Georgetown University Medical Center, Department of Psychiatry.

Brennan, T. (1978). *The social psychology of runaways.* Lexington, MA: Lexington Books.

Brucki, H. (1986). An overview of incest with suggestions for occupational therapy treatment. *Occupational Therapy in Mental Health, 5*(4), 63–76.

Chomak, S., & Collins, L. (1987). Relationship between sex-role behaviors and alcohol consumption in undergraduate men and women. *Journal of Studies on Alcohol, 48*(3), 194–200.

Cohen, F. (1982). A study of the relationship between child abuse and drug addiction in 178 patients. *Child Abuse and Neglect, 6*(4), 383–387.

Coleman, E. (1982). Family intimacy and chemical abuse: The connection. *Journal of Psychoactive Drugs, 14,* 153–158.

Deutsch, D. (1982). *Broken bottles, broken dreams.* New York: Teacher's College Press.

Flanigan, B. (1988). Alcohol and marijuana use among female adolescent incest victims. *Alcoholism Treatment Quarterly, 5,* 231–248.

Framo, J. (1965). *Emerging trends: Religion in America.* Princeton, NJ: Princeton Religious Research Center.

Gallup, G. (1986). *Emerging trends: Religion in America.* Princeton, NJ: Princeton Religion Research Center.

Garmezy, N. (1981). *Adolescence and stress.* Washington, DC: U.S. Government Printing Office.

Giaretto, H. (1976). Humanistic treatment of father-daughter incest. In Hefner & Kempe (Eds.), *Child abuse and neglect* (pp. 143–158). Cambridge, MA: Bollinger.

Graham, M. (1984, May 20). Breaking the silence. *West Magazine, San Jose Mercur,* 17.

Groth, A.N. (1982). Undetected recidivism among rapists and child molesters. *Crime and Delinquency, 28,* 450–458.

Groth, A.N., & Burgess, A.W. (1977). Motivational intent in the sexual assault of children. *Criminal Justice and Behavior, 4*(3), 253–264.

Harrison, P. (1989). Differential drug use patterns among sexually abused adolescent girls in treatment for chemical dependency. *International Journal of the Addictions, 24*(6), 499–514.

Hoorwitz, A. (1983). Guidelines for treating father-daughter incest. *Social Casework, 64*(9), 515–524.

Joy, D. (1986). *Re-bonding: Preventing and restoring damaged relationships.* Waco, TX: Word Books.

Justice, B., & Justice, R. (1979). *The broken taboo: Incest.* New York: Human Sciences Press.

Kellerman, J. (1984). *The family and alcoholism.* Center City, MN: Hazelden Foundation.

Liles, R. (1984). *Therapist ascription to theoretical statements taken from the literature on father-daughter incest.* Ann Arbor, MI: University Microfilms International.

Liles, R., & Childs, D. (1986). Similarities in family dynamics of incest and alcohol abuse. *Alcohol Health and Research World,* 66–69.

Lustig, N. (1966). Incest: A family group survival pattern. *Archives of General Psychiatry, 14,* 31–40.

Luther, S., & Price, J. (1980). Child sexual abuse: A review. *Journal of School Health, 50*(3), 161–165.

MacDonald, J.M. (1979). *Rape: Offenders and their victims.* Springfield, IL: Charles C. Thomas.

MacFarlane, K., & Waterman, J. (1986). *Sexual abuse of young children.* New York: Guilford Press.

Meiselman, K.C. (1978). *Incest: A psychological study of causes and effects with treatment recommendations.* San Francisco: Jossey-Bass.

Mendlicott, R.W. (1967). Parent-child incest. *Australian and New Zealand Journal of Psychiatry, 1,* 180.

Minuchin, S. (1974). *Families and family therapy.* Cambridge, MA: Harvard University Press.

Muehlenhard, C. (1987). Date rape and sexual aggression in dating situations. *Journal of Counseling Psychology, 34*(2), 186–196.

Neubeck, K. (1986). *Social problems: A critical approach.* New York: Random House.

Parrot, A. (1988). *Date rape and acquaintance rape.* New York: Rosen Publishing Group.

Pellauer, M., Chester, B., & Boyajian, J. (Eds.). (1987). *Sexual assault and abuse: A handbook for clergy and religious professionals.* New York: Harper & Row.

Pierce, L. (1987). Father-son incest. *Social Casework, 68*(2), 67–74.

Raab, E., & Selznick, G. (1964). *Major social problems.* New York: Harper & Row.

Satir, V., Bandler, R., & Grinder, J. (1976). *Changing with families.* Palo Alto, CA: Science and Behavior Books.

Scavnicky-Mylant, M. (1984). Children of alcoholics: Children in need. *Family and Community Health.*

Sgroi, S. (1982). *Handbook of clinical intervention in child sexual abuse.* Lexington, MA: Lexington Books.

Sommer, B. (1984). The troubled teen: Suicide, drug use and running away. *Women and Health, 9,* 117–141.

Spees, E. (1987). College students' sexual attitudes and behaviors. *Journal of College Student Personnel, 28*(2), 135–140.

Spencer, J. (1978). Father-daughter incest: A clinical view from the corrections field. *Child Welfare, 57*(9), 581–590.

Strong, B., & DeVault, C. (1986). Self-esteem and primary demographic characteristics of alcoholics in a rural state. *Journal of Alcohol and Drug Education, 30*(2), 51–59.

Summit, R. (1983, February). *The accommodation syndrome*. Paper presented at the Family Life Workshop at Loma Linda University, Loma Linda, CA.

Taylor, R. (1984). Marital therapy in the treatment of incest. *Social Casework: The Journal of Contemporary Social Work*, 195–202.

Tufts New England Medical Center. (1984). *Sexually exploited children*. Washington, DC: U.S. Department of Justice.

Volpe, J. (1983, January 17). Send all drunk drivers to jail? *U.S. News*, p. 71.

Wegscheider, S. (1981). *Another chance: Hope and health for the alcoholic family*. Palo Alto, CA: Science and Behavior Books.

Yeary, J. (1982). Incest and chemical dependency. *Journal of Psychoactive Drugs, 14*, 133–135.

Zehner, M. (1984). Homosexuality and alcoholism. *Journal of Social Work and Human Sexuality, 2*, 75–89.

18

Gangs and Drugs

Tully S. Lale

The existence of gangs is not a new phenomenon. Groups of people have banded together in "gangs" for physical, psychological, and sociological support and protection since time immemorial. In recent history, however, the term *gang* has generally had a negative connotation (e.g., chain gang, street gang). Hollywood immortalized gangs of "juvenile delinquents" in such film classics of the 1950s as *West Side Story* and the *Blackboard Jungle*. Today, gang activities can be witnessed almost daily on live television news in just about every U.S. city. The "zip guns" and "rumbles" of the 1950s seem benign when compared to the assault weapons and drive-by shootings of the 1980s and 1990s. It is the introduction of drug entrepreneurship that has escalated gang activity to these unprecedented levels of violence and death. Unlike the victims of intragang or intergang warfare of the past, many of the victims of today's drug profit-driven turf battles are innocent bystanders.

> We are comprised of a group of mothers who have gotten fed up with the gang violence, the terror, and the drugs in our area and the slayings of our innocent children and innocent adults. We came forth as citizens, concerned citizens, and parents to address the issues of gang violence because we feel that the police, anybody that's in office cannot conquer this problem alone, because it starts in the home.
>
> — Patricia Patrick, Director, Mothers Against Gangs in the Community (MAGIC) (as cited in California Council on Criminal Justice State Task Force on Gangs and Drugs, 1989)

ETIOLOGY OF GANGS

The involvement of young people in gangs and drugs generally results from a combination of life skills deficiencies and subsequent lack of personal responsibility and accountability for self. This at-risk profile originates in numerous social, cultural, psychological, and environmental influences: parental neglect; lack of positive role modeling; peer pressure; low self-esteem; the attraction of gang support, structure, and drug profits; and the need for acceptance and identity. Not only do gangs have their own hierarchy (Table 18-1), but also they have their own language (Table 18-2), signs, and dress codes to identify their members as "family." Although gang membership occurs across all racial, ethnic, and socioeconomic levels, gangs generally attract those youth who are economically deprived and discriminated against because of their racial and ethnic origin.

Family Contribution to Gangs and Drugs

Parental and adult role models play a vital role in a youngster's attitude toward gangs and drugs. Almost all gang members become involved in gang activities in

Table 18-1 Hierarchy of Gang Structure

Affiliation	Description
Hard-core	Usually the leaders, hard-core members, comprise approximately 5% to 10% of the gang. They have been in the gang the longest and are knowledgeable in legal matters, having been in and out of jail. Often unemployed, they are usually involved with drug distribution and/or use. Average age is early to mid-20s. They are very influential in establishing the character and setting the priorities for the gang.
Regular members	Already initiated into the gang, regular members tend to back up the "hard-core" gang members. If they stay with the gang, they become the next generation of "hard-core" leaders. Average age is generally 14 to 17 years.
"Wanna-be's"	Although not officially members of the gang, wanna-be's act like they are. They may hang around the gang and try to achieve status and recognition by acts of daring, such as writing the graffiti of the gang. Average age is 11 to 13 years.
Fringe/claimers	Some individuals who are not members may "claim" to be in order to feel protected in their neighborhoods. They tend to be in and out based on the gang's activity (e.g., in for partying, but out for committing serious crime). Age can fluctuate between 11 and 18. These youngsters put themselves in jeopardy by sometimes "being in the wrong place at the wrong time."
"Could-be's" (potentials)	Youngsters who are elementary school age, live in or close to an area where there is gang activity, and may have a family member already involved in gangs are could-be's. The potentials do not necessarily have to join a gang. If alternatives are available, there is an excellent opportunity for intervention that would preclude gang affiliation.

Table 18-2 Gang Slang Terminology

Term	Meaning
Ace kool	Best friend/backup
Blood	Piru/family/non-Crip
Book	Run, leave, get away
Breakdown	Shotgun
Bullet	One year in custody
Busted, popped a cap	Shot at someone
Busting	Fighting with fists or weapons
Choias	The police
Courting in/ checking in	Initiation into a gang
Courting out/ checking out	Expulsion from a gang
Crip	A gang faction associated with the color blue, enemies of the Piru
Cuzz/crab	A member of the Crips
Drop a dime	Snitch on someone
Durag	Bandana worn on the head
Esseys	Mexicans/Chicanos
Firme/homegirl	Girl friend/comrade of a gang member
From nowhere	An individual not a gang member
Gang banger	Gang member
Gang banging	Involved in gang activity
Gavachos	Anglos/whites
Graffiti	Coded slang used by gangs to claim turf, brag, challenge rival gangs and honor fallen comrades
Jammed	Be jumped or accosted
Homeboy	A fellow gang member or comrade
La Hura	The police
Low rider	An individual sometimes involved in gang activity
Mad-dogging	Staring down someone in a challenge that often escalates into violence
Payback	Vendetta or retaliation
Piru	A gang faction associated with the color red, enemies of the Crips
Placa	Graffiti that identifies a particular gang or individual
Pulling you on	Making a fool of you
Ride	A car or vehicle
Rifa	Term used in a Placa to mean "we rule," reign, or control this area
Ruca	Female companion/wife or girl friend
Signs	Hand gestures that identify a particular gang set
Surfer	A white individual sometimes involved in gang activity
Tacked out	Covered with tattoos; also called wearing "sleeves"
Throwing Signs	Using hand gestures in challenging gang rivals to confrontation

their youth, usually through the influences of other gang members. In some cases, family members who are already gang members themselves may actually encourage gang membership. In other cases, parents, guardians, or family members may not recognize a youngster's affiliation with gangs, or the youngster may be adept at concealing the gang membership. Other parents or guardians may not see the gang involvement as a threat to their children's future. In all cases, however, the youth involved in gang activities is, potentially, involved in drug use or sales.

> I'm not proud to say that I'm a mother of gang members, some of my boys became involved in gangs and drugs. I lost two boys in connection with drugs. Programs should be established where the parents can have time to face the truth of their children's involvement in gangs and drugs, for parents to seek out appropriate counseling.
>
> — Virginia Lopez, Concerned Parents Group, East Los Angeles (California Council on Criminal Justice, 1989)

Although a stable family and home environment does not ensure that a child will avoid gangs and drugs, gang counselors concur that guidance from a parent or guardian is important in deterring young people from gang and drug involvement. Many gang youths come from broken or single-parent homes and do not have the support and guidance of a parent or similar role model to keep them from succumbing to the temptations of gang activities. Male role models are particularly important in parenting, yet some fathers fail to accept their responsibilities as co-parents and decline to provide support.

> We know that in 50 percent of Black homes—and the rate among non-Blacks is climbing also—there is no significant role model or father figure. . . . So we provide role models . . . young Black men who have come up through the ghetto, who know the language of the streets, but who know that somehow with the help of God you can transcend what you have been.
>
> — Dr. Cecil Murray, Counselor, Youth Look-In Program, Los Angeles (California Council on Criminal Justice, 1989)

Even though parents or guardians may be aware of their children's gang involvement, they may not have the skills and knowledge to intercede with a potential gang- or drug-related problem. To complicate matters further, some parents or guardians may not wish help from outside authorities for fear of shaming their families.

Additional problems arise when parents fail to take responsibility for their children and do not provide a nurturing, positive structuring for the children's self-esteem. Parents who are themselves involved in gangs or drugs provide little positive role modeling for their children; in fact, they provide damaging negative role models. Other families may actually be economically dependent on the illicit profits that their children obtain from gangs' drug sales and other criminal behavior.

> I find parents who are denying the fact that their children are drug users or gang-bangers; who are fearful of their own children; who are supportive of the fact that their children are bringing in money that helps them buy a better car, helps them improve their house.
>
> — Sister Elisa Martinez, Coordinator, Concerned Parent Program, East Los Angeles (California Council on Criminal Justice, 1989)

The Peer Component

When the various influences on adolescents are studied systematically, it appears that the greatest influence on the troubled adolescent is wielded by the peer group (Henggeler, 1989), the group that gives the adolescent a sense of belonging. Everyone must feel he or she has a place and a purpose in this world in order to make life worth living. The family is the beginning base to that sense of belonging for a child. As children grow older and begin to enter adolescence, however, they need to disassociate and individuate from the family in order to find their own identity. At this point, they may find gang involvement attractive because they may feel that it provides

- fellowship/brotherhood
- identity/recognition
- sense of belonging
- surrogate family
- protection/security
- excitement/attention
- family tradition
- financial benefit

When adolescents select peer groups, they are molding their future. If teenagers join a group that strives to better their lives, become educated, and plan positively for their future, they will benefit from learning about team work, helping, sharing, and, thus, accepting personal and social responsibility. This is the essence of positive self-esteem. On the other hand, if they join a group that is not focused on schoolwork or education; is involved with the use/abuse and sale of drugs; and promotes violence, criminal activity, or other antisocial behavior, these teen-agers are likely to become wards of the state as future welfare recipients or penal institution residents.

> Gang members come from broken, unloved families. The kids say "Nobody cared. The gang offered me love." Without prevention, there are only three ways out of gangs: death, drugs, or prison.
>
> — Ida Sydnor, Executive Director, Black Sacramento Christian Club Organizers (California Council on Criminal Justice, 1989)

A unique and innovative forum was provided by the 1989 San Diego Urban Youth Revitalization Conference (Ellis, 1990) in which 10 current and former gang members acted as a panel in responding to three major questions regarding gangs and drugs. First, when asked how and why kids get involved in gangs, the panel gave the following answers:

- Adolescents join gangs because of the whole peer/friendship group experience. They grow up together in the same neighborhood and want to follow in the footsteps of their older siblings and friends, who may have joined gangs. In a way, it is a natural thing for friends to band with friends. The situation gets serious because of rivalries that develop and people's desire to protect their own.
- Often, there is not much else to do. Limited recreational or after-school activities leave a great deal of time to fill.
- Gangs are like families. Its members feel welcomed and loved . . . a part of something important.
- Teen-agers want to have the kinds of cars, money, and respect that gang leaders seem to have. Such leaders and/or local drug barons become role models for many aspiring youths.
- Youth gangs provide protection for their members; teen-agers often "claim" a gang as security against harassment.

Second, the gang panel was asked whether gangs and drugs are separate problems in their community, are generally connected, or are the same. The panel responded as follows:

- Gangs were active long before the drug issue emerged. Drugs are found everywhere, not just in communities where there are gangs.

- Most adolescents who are active in gangs have some knowledge of drugs. Some try it just as an experiment; others become involved for money purposes, particularly the hard-core gang members.
- Latino gangs tend not to be involved in profiteering from drug trafficking, but rather to use and abuse drugs such as phencyclidine (PCP). African-American gangs, on the other hand, tend to focus on making money through illicit drug enterprise, notably involving "crack" and other forms of cocaine.

When asked whether the *War on Drugs* or *Just Say No!* campaigns were effective deterrents to drugs in their communities, most youths on the panel responded that they had no effect at all.

As the third and last question, the panel was asked what is needed to turn adolescents away from gangs and/or drugs.

- Most panelists said that jobs are critical to reversing current gang trends. Older gang members, particularly, need jobs that will enable them to make more than minimum wages and help them to support their families.
- For younger adolescents, the panelists recommended recreation and after-school programs that would remove them from the streets and reduce their interests in gang membership. Also the provision of part-time jobs was considered potentially helpful.

When asked, "If you were offered minimum wage pay, would it deter you from present gang involvement?", those who were currently gang-involved replied yes—especially if the jobs would lead to training and better pay in the future. The risks of physical injury or incarceration associated with their current life style seemed to make any steady employment attractive. Two youths indicated that they would not be available for minimum wage pay, however.

GANG INVOLVEMENT PREVENTION AND INTERVENTION STRATEGIES

The key to successfully interceding with youth who are "at risk" of joining gangs or becoming involved in drugs is to identify the risk early in their lives and provide constructive, viable alternatives to the gang/drug life style. In this effort, it is important to provide them with the ethical and personal skills needed to handle the stresses placed on them in today's society.

The problem of gangs and drugs is multivariate in its etiology, and effective prevention/intervention strategies require a multimodal approach. Programs that involve the cooperation of the family, schools, businesses, religious organizations, law enforcement groups, and government agencies are essential to combat gang and drug activities, as well as to prevent the intimidation of the community from gang and drug violence. Furthermore, intervention strategies are necessary for adolescents at each level of gang involvement. No single approach can address all the needs of a community in fighting this problem.

> Money doesn't solve problems; people solve problems. We have given these gangs the right to exist, the people are responsible for it, and the people have to turn it around.
>
> — Edward Vincent, Mayor, City of Inglewood, California (California Council on Criminal Justice, 1989)

Family-Based Strategies

For an adolescent from a dysfunctional family, a gang may become a surrogate family. However legally and socially ostracized the gang may be, its members are meeting each other's needs for affiliation, nurturing, and validation.

> Gangs offer three things: prestige, excitement, and camaraderie. Each of these should be achievable outside of gangs. Schools and community services should consider such alternatives.
>
> — Brian Van Camp, Chair and Founder, Citizens for a Better Sacramento (California Council on Criminal Justice, 1989)

Comprehensive parental awareness and training programs should be established to teach parents how to address the problems that are precursors to youth gang and drug involvement. When there is no positive parental role model, the community may intercede with support groups, role model pairing, and counseling. Role model programs, such as the San Francisco–based mentoring program, not only provide guidance, emotional support, and camaraderie, but also help youth to achieve their full potential through employment opportunities. Youth role models or peer counseling has proved effective in guiding youth away from gang and drug activity. Some reformed gang members, when carefully screened, monitored, and trained, have been able to impress on young people the adverse and detrimental effects of gang and drug involvement.

> If we give them other alternatives, if we give them other options, we will eradicate the disease, we'll prevent the problems. The funding which we hope will be forthcoming will be for the prevention. It's an

old saying, everyone's heard it, "an ounce of prevention is worth a pound of care."

— David Rosenberg, Gang Intervention Program, San Diego (California Council on Criminal Justice, 1989)

Family prevention and intervention strategies should encourage parental responsibility, establish parental support programs, and provide 24-hour hotlines and counseling. Parental awareness is the key to prevention and is critical to effective early intervention. Through community-based programs, at risk youngsters can be identified, their parents or guardians notified, and family counseling provided to address and resolve the causes of the gang- and/or drug-related problem. Parents and guardians may be encouraged to take responsibility for their children, to teach them social values, and to instill self-esteem. Community-based agencies should develop parental support programs that provide 24-hour hotlines and counseling for parents of gang members and parents of victims of gang- and drug-related crimes. Self-help groups, where parents or guardians can meet to share their problems and work together to identify solutions (Exhibit 18-1), are also desirable components of a comprehensive parental support program.

We need a comprehensive innovative program capable of bringing families back together, restoring respect for adults, parents, teachers, and property.

— Robert Henning, Council, City of Lynwood, California (California Council on Criminal Justice, 1989)

School-Based Strategies

As the drug trade becomes increasingly lucrative, the reach of drugs and gangs is extending into even smaller communities throughout the United States. In order to fend off this impending threat, concerted efforts in school-based prevention education are essential.

When we began, 31 percent of all fifth graders indicated attitudes in favor of gangs and drugs. At the end of the program, only 7 percent indicated at risk attitudes.

— Ernie Paculba, Coordinator, Gang Alternatives Project, Los Angeles Unified School District (California Council on Criminal Justice, 1989)

Exhibit 18-1 Prevention Agenda for Parents

1. Be a positive role model. What is your relationship with gangs, alcohol, nicotine, and illegal substances?
2. Know your children's friends and acquaintances; birds of a feather do flock together!
3. What influence do their friends have on your children?
4. What do your children do with their free time?
5. What can you do to fill that free time with constructive alternatives?
6. What activities can you participate in with your children?
7. Keep communication channels open with your children.
8. Give your children responsibilities for which they are accountable.
9. Educate yourself on the use of alcohol and drugs, as well as gang dress, colors, language, and paraphernalia.
10. Develop and foster an antidrug, antigang attitude in your home.
11. Do not allow your children to dress in gang colors, use gang slang, or have gang or drug paraphernalia in your home.
12. Keep alcohol and weapons locked up and away from children.
13. Do not allow your children out after curfew or late at night.
14. Know where your children are going and with whom.
15. Participate in your children's education; provide a suitable place in your home for homework, and monitor completion.
16. Get to know your neighbors, and participate in community and school programs; promote a sense of community togetherness.
17. Do not be afraid to discipline your children and hold them accountable for their behavior.
18. Support community alternatives to drugs and gangs, such as sports/recreational programs and church-sponsored activities.

Teacher, administrator, and student awareness alone will not resolve the growing problem of youth involvement with gangs and drugs. In cooperation with community organizations and law enforcement agencies, schools must develop and provide a parental skills curriculum. Once parents or guardians have been notified that their child is involved with gangs and drugs, they need a remediative resource to instruct them on methods for guiding and controlling the child's behavior and actions. Parental skills training is a critical component in the prevention equation.

> I think we must teach standards, we must get away from the 1960s idea that there are no values. We must begin to focus on the values that we hold dearly in America, the values that got us to where we are, and we must be willing to enforce those standards with quick justice, especially for the very young.
>
> — Dr. B. David Brooks, President, Thomas Jefferson Research Center (California Council on Criminal Justice, 1989)

Schools should be safe harbors, not a realm of intimidation where gang members use and sell drugs with little fear of exposure. To recapture their grounds and prevent further gang and drug influence on campus, schools must establish and enforce codes that prohibit the display of gang colors and the use of pagers or car telephones on school grounds. The wearing of gang colors publicizes gang presence and control; the use of pagers, car telephones, and other such devices on or near the school grounds to arrange drug deals increases a gang's visibility and ability to intimidate other students. In cooperation with local media, schools may sponsor short public service announcements: "Kids, do you know someone using or selling drugs on your school campus? You have a right to a healthy and safe environment. . . . Call ROPE-A-DOPE at XXX-DOPE." A strategy such as this would certainly turn the intimidation factor back on the users and pushers.

> When I was going to elementary school . . . they know [teachers] there's kids out there now that are starting from eight to nine years old . . . going out there selling drugs . . . taking care of business . . . they're supposed to be educating people, but they don't tell people about real life, reality, what's really happening out there. . . . I guess they're scared to tell anyone.
>
> — Secret Witness, California State Task Force on Gangs and Drugs (California Council on Criminal Justice, 1989)

In cooperation with local government and state agencies, schools should expand after-school, weekend, and summer youth programs to appeal to broader based groups, especially in the age range of 10 to 18 years. Youth need a safe alternative to gangs. All agencies at all levels are encouraged to work with the schools in implementing youth alternative programs.

The key to the success of school-based programs to prevent gang and drug involvement is to start such programs as early as kindergarten. Several school districts have developed programs that include the teaching of social values, gang awareness, and methods for effectively averting gang involvement and drug use. For example, the Paramount Program, the Los Angeles Police Department Drug Abuse Resistance Education (DARE) program, and the Los Angeles Sheriff's Department Substance Abuse Narcotics Education (SANE) are on the cutting edge of prevention curricula. The Paramount Program is designed for antigang education; DARE and SANE focus primarily on drug use/abuse prevention, but include components to prevent gang involvement. Programs to counsel and intervene with at risk youth are also valuable in providing critical life skills, such as communication skills, values clarification, stress management strategies, and self-esteem. Optimum school-based education programs to prevent gang involvement and drug use should

- teach social values and self-esteem to children, commencing with kindergarten.
- teach personal responsibility and, most important, family values and parenting skills.
- teach students in all grades peer refusal skills to avoid gang and drug involvement.
- train teachers and administrators to implement the prevention curriculum and to detect and intervene with gang- and/or drug-related at risk behavior.
- emphasize to all teachers and administrators the importance of modeling appropriate behavior in regard to substance use and/or abuse (e.g., smoking and drinking behaviors). Hypocrisy will undermine the best of preventive education programs.
- require all teachers and administrators to complete the gang involvement/ drug use prevention training program as a requirement for certificate renewal.
- enlist support from the teachers' unions and the community, (e.g., PTA) in implementing and evaluating these programs.

Business- and Industry-Based Strategies

Employment opportunities are attractive alternatives to involvement with gangs and drugs. While they are attracted to the possibility of large drug profits, very few gang members actually earn large amounts of money selling drugs. More inner-city youth become the victims of the drugs, so the need for viable career opportunities remains.

> The often stated sentence that "somebody that's making $400 a day dealing drugs is simply not going to take a job at a fast food place" is wrong. Not everybody's making $400 a day dealing drugs.
>
> — Bill Dawson, Executive Director, Community Resources and Self-Help (CRASH) (California Council on Criminal Justice, 1989)

Many gang- and drug-affected communities are plagued with high unemployment rates. Local businesses that hire gang members and at risk youth have proved successful in extricating these adolescents from the gang environment.

Employment provides camaraderie and guidance to the employee; in return, it requires responsibility and accountability. Employment often acts as a "positive gang" in that it provides a forum for acceptance, teamwork, and recognition for achievement. In addition, employment offers a fair wage for a day's work. Many current and former gang members have testified that they prefer to make their living in legitimate employment.

Many gang members and at risk youth do not possess the skills either to seek a job or to perform a job well once they have obtained it. Businesses and industrial communities should participate in job training, development, and placement programs to provide career-oriented job opportunities to these individuals. Such programs provide valuable skills to the labor force, promote economic security within the community, and encourage overall economic growth for business and industry.

> I say the business community has to be there with the kind of compact or business partnership program that we've been working on really in the later years. I think it has to get to that level in the schools, and this is going to be done by tutors or mentoring programs or adopt-a-school, where the business people come into the schoolroom. They show that, yes, it is possible to make some money if you stay in this program, and there is excitement and camaraderie and prestige.
>
> — Brian Van Camp, Chair and Founder, Citizens for a Better Sacramento (California Council on Criminal Justice, 1989)

The business community can offer valuable assistance to economically depressed and gang-affected areas. Through an "adopt-a-school" program, for example, businesses provide schools with additional needed equipment, financial resources, and expertise in the classrooms. Business sponsorship of sports activities provides positive alternatives to gang involvement for juveniles. Local businesses may encourage their employees to participate in mentor programs, in which they are paired with teen-agers who need guidance in selecting positive alternatives to gang and drug involvement.

> At the age of 12, I ran away from home and joined a gang. At the age of 14, I joined a program that was called Neighborhood Youth Corps. This individual spoke to me, sat me down, counseled me, and I really got touched by the idea that this individual was trying to help me.
>
> — Alfredo Rosa, President, Los Angeles BACA (California Council on Criminal Justice, 1989)

Community-Based Strategies

Communities should implement programs to encourage teen-agers to serve as role models and to participate in peer counseling and community development programs. The National Crime Prevention Council's model programs; the City of Pasadena Youth Advisor programs; and youth-oriented organizations such as the Girl Scouts, Boy Scouts, Girls' Clubs, Boys' Clubs, and YWCA/YMCA have been effective in providing positive alternatives to youth, teaching social values and self-esteem, and encouraging participation in the community.

Religious organizations play an important role within the inner city and within gang- and drug-affected communities. They are often focal points for community activities and family gatherings, providing spiritual support to the neighborhood. Several programs operated by religious organizations have been successful at removing youth from their associations with gangs and drugs. The success of these programs lies in the individual interaction between youth and positive adult role models who take an active and ongoing interest in the youth, guiding them in their growth and counseling them to avoid the influences of gangs and drugs.

Sports and church-sponsored activities often provide the same rewards that adolescents claim to receive for joining gangs (e.g., camaraderie, identification, united purpose, excitement, ventilation of stress). The standards and values of "good sportsmanship" and teamwork are important concepts derived from athletics. The moral and ethical principles provided in spiritual guidance, particularly those espoused in the Golden Rule, are incompatible with gang values. These principles could be said to be antidotal to the gang ethic.

Explicit media coverage of the gang and drug situation throughout the United States has been beneficial in raising community awareness of the severity of the gang and drug problem. It is important that the media inform the public of the gang- and drug-related incidents in their communities. Reporting techniques must be responsible and careful, however, so that the coverage does not perpetuate the gang phenomenon. Sensational reporting styles should be avoided because they glamorize the gang life style and add to the gang mystique.

It would seem prudent to make initial investments in activities and facilities that will pay off as long-term social dividends in diminishing the power and attraction of drugs and gangs. Only through a concerted and coordinated multimodal effort that includes parents and guardians, schools and educators, business and industry representatives, law enforcement officials, religious and community leaders, and the media will it be possible to make at risk youth less susceptible to the gang and drug culture.

REFERENCES

California Council on Criminal Justice State Task Force on Gangs and Drugs. (1989). *Final Report.*
Ellis, A. (Ed.). (1990). *San Diego Urban Youth Revitalization Conference, Final Report.*
Henggeler, S.W. (1989). *Delinquency in adolescence.* Newbury Park, CA: Sage Publications.

19

The Occult and Our Youth

Sophia M. Hyzin and Ann W. Lawson

Today's adolescents are growing up in a world saturated with satanic and occult symbols and suggestions through black/heavy metal music, fantasy role-playing games (e.g., Dungeons and Dragons), horror movies, and diabolical paraphernalia. To young Satanists, the devil is a friend who offers money, drugs, sex, excitement, and whatever else they may desire. When parents and society say no, the devil says yes. Under this creed of rebellion and self-centeredness, and the "me first" philosophy of Satanism, such acts as lying, cheating, all imaginable sexual perversions, murder, and use of illicit drugs are condoned if they bring satisfaction to the individual.

The ultimate design of Satanists is to become deities with all of Lucifer's passions and goals. By participating in sacrificial ceremonies, the Satanists experience the raw essence of evil that seems to induce altered states of consciousness. In nontraditional Satanic cults, drugs play an important part in the ceremonies. In teen-age satanic cults, drugs and alcohol are integral.

HISTORY OF THE OCCULT

The study of magic and/or black arts is a purposefully complex and convoluted undertaking. Those who study magic intentionally surround their activities in mystique because, through an understanding of magic and its use, they can obtain power over others, nature, and the universe—ultimately becoming a god (Cavendish, 1967).

Black arts magicians differ from devil worshippers and/or Satanists in that they are seeking a balance in the universe in their quest to become gods. The Satanist, on the other hand, worships and serves the devil's will. Paganism, the earliest religion that involved magic, originated during the Ice Age, when, supposedly, humans were making the transition from hunting and gathering to farm-ing. This transition required technology, and the teachings of this technology, or "magic," appear to have fallen to a small group of people called the "shamans" or "magickians." Spelled with a *k,* the term *magick* means the art of producing a desired effect through the use of spells, incantations, and other arcane techniques (Kahaner, 1988).

Sacrifice, human or animal, has been a part of many magical rituals. The prim-itive ritual of human sacrifice has a long history. The Old Testament records the sacrifice of infants to the pagan male deity Molech (1 Kings 11:5, 2 Kings 23:10, Jeremiah 32:35). The image of Molech was made of brass and was hollow. A fire kindled within the idol; when the extended hands became hot, Molech's priest took the baby from the father's hands and placed it in Molech's hands to the accompaniment of drums so that the father could not hear the screams of his dying offspring (Harris, Archer, & Waltke, 1980). Other ancient peoples also offered human victims in propitiatory rites—at times to atone for the wrongs of an entire group and at other times to appease the gods after a natural disaster (Larson, 1989).

The organized worship of an entirely evil entity known as Satan or the devil did not take place until after Christianity was established (Kahaner, 1988). In Hebrew, the word *satan* in a verb form literally means "be an adversary, resist." In a noun form, it means "adversary, one who withstands." In the Biblical view, Satan is the preeminent opponent of mankind. Although created as an angel with perfect wisdom and beauty, and anointed for a position of great authority in Heaven (Ezekiel 28:12–15), he fell into condemnation through pride that induced him to rival God (i.e., he wanted to be God).

SATANISM TODAY

Those who adhere to Satanism today include public religious Satanists, hard-core satanic cults, self-styled satanic groups, teen-aged dabblers, and genera-tional Satanists.

Public Religious Satanists

The religious Satanists are highly structured and organized. The best known orthodox groups include the Church of Satan, the Temple of Set, and the Process Church of Final Judgment (Lyons, 1988). The most famous of these is the Church of Satan, which diametrically opposes everything that the Christian Church supports.

Hard-Core Satanic Cults

Members of the extremely well organized hard-core satanic cults are known to abduct, brainwash, and kill their victims. Such cults are found throughout the world. It has been estimated that between 40,000 and 60,000 human beings are killed through ritual homicides in the United States each year (Johnston, 1989).

Self-Styled Satanic Groups

Typically, teen-aged self-styled Satanists are loners, have above average IQs, and are under- or overachievers who strive for control or power, take drugs, and appear to be preoccupied with death. They are often secretive, may be involved with pornographic material, and have a sociopathic background (Kahaner, 1988; Pulling, 1989). The Son of Sam, Charles Manson, and other serial killers belong to the self-styled satanic groups. Followers are held in the group by the use of drugs, mind control, intimidation, and the cult confession. The leader of the cult may demand that members perform criminal acts.

Aleister Crowley, an occultist, is considered to be the father of modern black magick and modern Satanism. The basic philosophy of a self-styled satanic group (or coven) follows his laws (Crowley, 1971, 1974a), such as "do what thou wilt"; "good is evil, and evil is good"; "man has the right to kill those who would thwart these rights." Self-styled Satanists also take basic creeds and rituals from the writings of La Vey (1969).

Each self-styled satanic group shapes its teachings and ceremonies to its common interest. If the main interest of a coven is sexual experience, for example, their belief system and rituals will relate to sex. Whatever the interest (e.g., using and dealing drugs, producing pornography, selling illegal weapons, kidnapping, sacrificing and mutilating animals, sacrificing and dismembering human beings, having sex with animals), a satanic group is an ideal setting for doing "what thou wilt" and getting away with it. The belief that evil spirits monitor a member's every move and thought guarantees loyalty to the group, even when other members of the group are not present (Johnston, 1989).

Teen-aged Dabblers

A person who experiments with occult practices is a dabbler. Most teen-aged dabblers acquire pieces of information from various sources and mix them together to arrive at their own unique philosophy. A dabbler may try to cast spells and perform certain rituals based on instructions that he or she has found in books and magazines or may imitate the actions of characters in occult movies and television shows (Pulling, 1989). Teen-aged dabblers get involved with fantasy role-playing games, suggestive black/heavy metal music, drugs, seances, and a quest for power. They practice chants and incantations, and they faithfully read *The Satanic Bible* (La Vey, 1969). Occasionally, these young people form small covens.

Teen-aged dabblers have been known to cause emotional and physical harm to others. "The greatest amount of documentation now on file and the greatest number of criminal [satanic] cases that have gone to court and have been adjudicated have involved teenage occult dabblers in Devil worship" (Pulling, 1989, p. 34).

Generational Satanists

Some teen-agers are involved in Satanism simply because they are born into it.

Generational cult membership is an inherited way of life, passed from one generation to another. It is the elitist group of members consisting of intermarriages to form a high level of blood purity. The cult carefully selects a child's parents, who will produce an offspring with a high IQ and spiritual and racial superiority. A child's parents may be married to each other, or both may be married to separate spouses. Multigenerational intermarrying produces a clan-like network, which assures safety and continuance of the cult. (Johnston, 1989, p. 96)

These families are known to "practice wild satanic orgies at least eight times a year and sacrifice animals, and babies" (Johnston, 1989, p. 33).

SATANISM AND DRUGS

For centuries, Satanism and drugs have been uniquely joined. In the last several decades, there has been a resurgence of the occult sciences and/or fascination with the "Eastern mind" wherein experience takes precedence over logic and reason. Through Satanism, individuals believe that they are invoking supernatural sources of power and that, by the use of hallucinogenic drugs and alcohol, they can also release inhibitions. Drugs are considered a shortcut to various occult planes, frequently called the "astral plane." Huxley (1954) made similar observations; in his experiment with mescaline, he noted that the drug allowed him to bypass what he called the "reducing valve" of his senses and central nervous system and to escape almost immediately to the astral plane. Crowley (1974b), a heavy drug user, made many of the same observations.

The Greek word meaning 'sorcery' and 'magic arts.' is the root of *farmakeia*, the word *pharmacy* and/or drugs (Arndt & Gingrich, 1957). Archeologists have noted that pre-Colombian cultures forged a link between sadism, terrorism, and human sacrifice by using drugs. The Meso-American folk religions of the Mayas and Aztecs required human sacrifices and used drugs to induce apathy in the victims. Castaneda (1969), who has been influential in today's drug use and Satanism, idealized black magic practices of human-animal communication and spell casting. He suggested that such occult practices are possible under the influence of hallucinogenic drugs, such as psilocybin and peyote. Many teen-agers today imitate Castaneda's fusion of the occult and narcotics (Larson, 1989).

Drug use is prevalent in ritual abuse. Child victims of ritual abuse describe being drugged or hypnotized and, on awakening, being told that they have had "magic surgery." The blood that has been smeared on their bodies constitutes compelling evidence that such surgery has taken place. In some cases, children are told that a bomb has been placed inside them and that, if they disclose the abuse, the bomb will explode and kill them, as well as anyone to whom they disclose the abuse. Most typically, child victims of magic surgery are told that a monster, a demon, or "the devil's heart" has been placed inside them and that it will attack them if they disclose the abuse. They are also told that the monster, demon, or the devil is now in charge of their thoughts and behavior, and will cause them to "be bad." Child victims are made to believe that this entity will cause them pain if they fail to comply with its wishes. "Ritually abused children often report somatic complaints such as abdominal pain in connection with this phenomenon" (Los Angeles County Commission for Women, 1989, pp. 9–10). It is important to keep these facts in mind when working with teen-agers who have been ritually abused as children (Gould, 1988).

The lure of drugs is an enticement that adults may use to attract teen-agers to Satanism. Once involved in the cult, the use of drugs, along with hypnotic suggestion, becomes a form of brainwashing (Larson, 1989). When used to indoctrinate and control the youths, drugs may be administered in suppositories, hidden in food or drink, swallowed under duress, or injected. The hypnotic and paralytic effects of the drugs cause victims to experience mental and emotional states that range from confusion and drowsiness to passivity and helplessness. Memory distortions occur as well; victims tend to recall very real and painful experiences only with difficulty. Cult leaders capitalize on drug-induced reality distortions to create the illusion that they have absolute power to which the victim must submit (Los Angeles County Commission for Women, 1989). Consequently, drugs serve as a form of continued entrapment. Teen-agers often use drugs as a means of coping in cults. Those who sincerely want to become a member of a satanic group will do anything to join.

Drinking blood is distasteful, yet that's what is required to join some Satanic cults. Drugs make it possible to do the unthinkable. Also, many new members have to cut or torture themselves to prove their devotion to the devil. Drugs help them withstand the pain. Once they become an active member of the cult, drugs become even more necessary to heighten the mystique of some ceremonies. (Larson, 1989, p. 89)

Drugs may also be used to numb the person who will serve as a sacrifice. In the investigations of scenes involving sacrifices, either human or animal, "it never appears that those victims died willingly" (Wedge, 1989, p. 83).

Some teen-agers who join satanic cults becomes involved in drug trafficking. New members may serve as "mules," carriers who transport the drugs across borders and state lines. The illicit distribution of drugs generates an underground cash economy and enables cult members to spend their time pursuing satanic activities (Larson, 1989).

Religion, mysticism, and magic all spring from the same basic "feeling" about the universe: a sudden feeling of "meaning" (Wilson, 1971). Teen-agers today are searching for meaning, security, and love. If unable to find them, the disillusioned youth often seek control over their neglected and helpless circumstances. Some believe that drugs, Satanism, and other forms of the occult are the answer.

ASSESSMENT OF ADOLESCENT INVOLVEMENT

Two categories of youngsters are involved in satanic worship. One category includes children who have been ritually abused by a satanic cult. These children have a pattern of symptoms that differs from the patterns observed in other children who have been physically or sexually abused. The second category includes adolescents who are in varying stages of involvement with the occult. Children who have been ritually abused and are also involved in the occult by virtue of growing up in families who are involved in the satanic practices (generational) may comprise a third group.

Although there is little research about the prevalence of this problem, a survey conducted in Provo, Utah, found that 62 of 92 psychotherapists (67%) have treated adolescents involved in satanism (Wheeler & Wood, 1987). An adolescent's involvement in satanic activities may be symptomatic of several disorders, such as substance abuse, depression, borderline personality disorders, disruptive behavior, or antisocial personality (Wheeler, Wood, & Hatch, 1988). On the other hand, the rituals of satanism may intrigue adolescents because they appear to provide power and may be a rebellion against their parents. The level of involvement varies dramatically from adolescents who are innocently intrigued with Dungeons and Dragons, ouija boards, or tarot cards, or who listen to black/heavy metal music to adolescents who have joined a cult and attended or participated in their rituals. Most of the adolescents involved are experimenters or dabblers, but a few become more deeply involved.

These adolescents have some common personality characteristics. They feel disconnected from their peer group and family and may have disdain for conventional peer group activities. They feel a lack of love in their lives and are often scapegoated by their families. They are unhappy with their families, and they believe that their families are unhappy with them (Wheeler et al., 1988). They may be drawn to the occult because of thoughts of suicide and death. If they are bored, the occult offers excitement. Feelings of powerlessness due to poverty, racism, or rigid family values are common among these followers of the occult. Their knowledge of mysterious or taboo things that upset others gives them a sense of power.

Thus, a typical adolescent involved in satanic practices is an intelligent young male who is creative, often artistic, and curious; he is frequently an underachiever in school. He may come from a middle- or upper middle-class family; he may have low self-esteem, difficulty with peers, and be isolated from others; he may be bored, restless, and easily influenced by peers; and he may abuse alcohol and other drugs. Such young men are often alienated from their families because of physical abuse, sexual abuse, or chemical dependencies in the family (Grady & Spohn, 1988). The signs of active involvement with satanic practices include

- obsession with fantasy role-playing games
- obsession with black/heavy metal rock music
- unusual number of books on magic, witchcraft, Paganism, rituals, Satanism, or the occult
- objects used for spells, such as red and black candles, incense, knives, pentagrams, bones, inverted crosses, chalice-like cups, and written chants
- symbolic jewelry (especially silver jewelry), including pentagrams, skulls, goat heads, the number 666, demons, dragons, and swastikas
- drug use and drug paraphernalia
- unexplained fear of the world or people beyond the youth's bedroom
- doodles, diagrams, or graffiti drawings that depict violence, inverted crosses, demons, werewolves, pentagrams, or obvious references to the devil, Satan, or Lucifer
- body tattoos that have been burned or carved, especially on the left side of the body or between the thumb and index finger, with reference to the occult
- changes in eating and sleeping patterns
- heavy alcohol and other drug use
- unusual behavior, such as vandalism, graffiti, and cruelty to animals
- diaries or recordings of rituals or cult meetings (Grady & Spohn, 1988)

Many of these behaviors are merely experiments with the occult; they may be done to provoke a reaction from parents and other adults. These adolescents often spontaneously turn away from these behaviors. Problems develop with deeper levels of involvement.

A comprehensive assessment for satanic involvement must include a consideration of self-esteem, family, unmet needs, social relationships, school performance, and health in order to establish a baseline for intervention (Wheeler et al., 1988). Although most adolescents involved in satanic practices are not committed worshippers, some have serious problems. The vast continuum of possible involvement calls for a thorough assessment of the degree of involvement and other coexisting psychopathologies. For example, adolescents who were ritually abused as children may suffer from dissociative disorders or multiple personality disorders.

Wheeler et al. (1988) listed the following behaviors of adolescents involved in Satanism:

- using ouija boards and tarot cards to obtain answers to questions and to predict future events
- meeting in covens on a regular basis to worship Satan
- conducting seances to form covenants with Satan, to cast spells, to request Satan's presence, and to place hexes on enemies
- chanting to unify Satan worshippers in a common activity
- raising of objects into the air, presumably through supernatural powers
- conducting "black weddings" symbolically to wed female followers to Satan
- sacrificing animals and drinking animal blood
- conducting ceremonies involving sexual activity and the use of drugs and alcohol
- conducting ceremonies in cemeteries and focusing on death
- reading books on Satanism such as *The Satanic Bible* and *The Satanic Rituals* (La Vey, 1969, 1972) to provide followers with information about philosophy, activities, and symbolism
- listening to heavy metal rock music because of its strong emphasis on death, destruction, sex, and Satanism
- selling one's soul to Satan in return for power, money, fame, and success

Adolescents who belong to a satanic cult may celebrate sabbats or attend rituals on special dates of the satanic calendar. A host of crimes, including animal or human sacrifices, sexual orgies, and kidnappings, may be committed before, during, and after the ceremonies.

For the adolescent having difficulties, joining a cult may ease the pain of isolation or may be an escape from the pain of his or her life. Therapists should assess the extent of the adolescent's involvement with the occult, personality factors, relationships with peers, and the dynamics of the family system.

INTERVENTION FOR INVOLVEMENT WITH SATANISM

The goals of intervention for adolescents who are involved in Satanism should be individualized, but there are some common themes. Wheeler et al. (1988) recommended an approach in which the first step is to strip the adolescent's environment of all symbols and paraphernalia associated with the occult. This may be accomplished either by removing the adolescent from the environment (i.e., through inpatient treatment) or by removing the symbols from the home. Separation from the peers who are also involved in the occult is necessary. In an inpatient or residential setting, the adolescent should be prohibited from telling stories about the occult to other patients or staff, writing journals about rituals, or drawing symbols.

Therapists should help the adolescent understand his or her motivation to be involved with the occult. This may help the adolescent verbalize life conflicts without having to act them out. The therapeutic relationship should provide the adolescent with a safe place to deal with the fears, anger, pain, frustration, and alienation that drew him or her to the occult. Because power is so often the motivation for involvement, the therapist should avoid power struggles. The therapist is often seen as another authority figure who is ignorant or frightened of the occult. To counter this, the therapist should listen intently—both verbally and nonverbally—to the adolescent's belief and knowledge of Satanism and should avoid being judgmental. Also, the therapist should help the adolescent build identity, increase self-esteem, and find personal power through mastery, self-control, and assertiveness. Alternative activities that provide some of the same features that attracted the adolescent to the occult should be explored and new peer groups encouraged. Substance abuse should be evaluated and an appropriate treatment plan developed. The powerless approach of Alcoholics Anonymous may not appeal to these adolescents who are, clearly, looking for power. A paradoxical approach of gaining power through admitting powerlessness may be more successful.

Family therapy is very important with these adolescents. The goals of the family therapy should include (1) reducing the scapegoating of the adolescent, (2) building cohesion and closeness, and (3) creating appropriate expectations and parenting strategies for adolescents. The adolescents in these families need to feel that they are connected to their families. They need to develop the personal skills that will allow them to be involved in important personal relationships outside the satanic cult. Parents may benefit from networking with other parents who are struggling with the same problems.

Families with severe dysfunctions may need more intense work. Any ongoing physical and/or sexual abuse must be reported to the proper agencies. The adolescent may need to be placed into a residential program or foster family for safety while continuing in family therapy with the goal of family reunification.

REFERENCES

Arndt, W.F., & Gingrich, F.W. (1957). *A Greek-English lexicon of the New Testament and other Christian literature*. Chicago: University of Chicago Press.

Castaneda, C. (1969). *The teachings of Don Juan: A yogi way of knowledge*. New York: Ballantine Books.

Cavendish, R. (1967). *The black arts*. New York: G.P. Putnam & Sons.

Crowley, A. (1971). *Confessions of Aleister Crowley*. New York: Bantam Books.

Crowley, A. (1974a). *Magick in theory and practice*. New York: Dover Publications.

Crowley, A. (1974b). *The book of law*. New York: Samuel Weiser.

Gould, C. (1988). *Signs and symptoms of ritualistic child abuse*.

Grady, & Spohn (1988). *Cult involvement and satanic practices*. Handout from workshop at Parkside Hospital, Oceanside, California, 1989.

Harris, R.L., Archer, G.L., & Waltke, B.K. (1980). *Theological wordbook of the Old Testament*. Chicago: Moody Press.

Huxley, A. (1954). *The doors of perception*. New York: Harper & Row.

Johnston, J. (1989). *The edge of evil*. Dallas: Word Publishing.

Kahaner, L. (1988). *Cults that kill*. New York: Warner Books.

Larson, B. (1989). *Satanism: The seduction of America's youth*. Nashville, TN: Thomas Nelson Publishers.

La Vey, A.S. (1969). *The satanic bible*. New York: Avon Books.

La Vey, A. (1972). *The satanic rituals*. New York: Avon Books.

Los Angeles County Commission for Women. (1989). *Ritual abuse*. Los Angeles: LA County Commission for Women.

Lyons, A. (1988). *Satan wants you*. New York: The Mysterious Press.

Pulling, P. (1989). *The Devil's web*. Lafayette, LA: Huntington House.

Wedge, T.W. (1989). *The Satan hunter*. Canton, OH: Daring Books.

Wheeler, B., & Wood, S. (1987). *Adolescents involved in satanism: Assessment and interventions*. Unpublished manuscript, Brigham Young University, Provo, UT.

Wheeler, B., Wood, S., & Hatch, R.J. (1988, November/December). Assessment and intervention with adolescents involved in satanism. *Social Work*, 547–550.

Wilson, C. (1971). *The occult*. New York: Random House.

20

The Fastest Growing AIDS Population—Adolescents

Evelyn Palmquist

The complexity of problems confronting people with acquired immunodeficiency syndrome (AIDS) and the terror that this disease engenders set it apart from other contemporary public health problems. AIDS is currently a low-incidence, highly lethal disease found primarily in specific, identifiable groups. As a public health issue, however, the AIDS epidemic is having a broad impact on the education of children, the psychological lives of high-risk and low-risk youth, and the relationship between parents and children (Belfer, Krenner, & Miller, 1988). Given the fact that the human immunodeficiency virus (HIV) that causes AIDS is transmitted by intravenous (IV) use of contaminated blood or blood products, in perinatal contact of mother and infant, during breast-feeding, or through unprotected sexual activity with an HIV-positive partner, no segment of the population will be left unaffected by AIDS.

AIDS has become a major cause of morbidity and mortality in the United States, and it is the leading cause of death among people with hemophilia and IV drug users (Agle, Gluck, & Pierce, 1987; Des Jarlais & Friedman, 1989; Heyward & Curran, 1988; Mason, Olson, Meyers, Huszti, & Kenning, 1989). It has been estimated that 1 to 1.5 million U.S. citizens are already infected with HIV and will eventually develop AIDS. By the end of 1992, there are likely to be approximately 365,000 cases in the United States (Heyward & Curran, 1988). According to data released by the Centers for Disease Control (CDC) in 1990, there were 35,238 newly reported cases in 1989, an increase of 9% over the previous year. The most significant increases reported were a 27% increase in the number of cases among the heterosexual population and a 35% increase in metropolitan areas with a population of less than 100,000.

ADOLESCENT BEHAVIOR

Adolescents between the ages of 13 and 19 make up approximately 10% of the U.S. population, accounting for approximately 25 million people. This age group is not currently identified as a high-risk group for the acquisition or spread of HIV infection, although the definition of risk has been changing to focus on risk behavior rather than on risk groups. As of spring 1989, AIDS had been diagnosed in more than 18,000 individuals between the ages of 20 and 29, and many of these individuals had probably been infected with HIV when they were teen-agers (Department of Health and Human Services, 1990). Adolescents have now been targeted as a "bridging" group to those currently infected (Hein, 1987), largely because the typical cognitive processing of adolescents increases the like-lihood that they will ignore warnings of risk in the belief that they are personally invulnerable to negative consequences (Elkind, 1967).

Many aspects of the life-styles of adolescents, especially those in the inner cit-ies, seem to place them directly in the path of the epidemic (Hein, 1987). The youngest members of each of the groups known to be at highest risk for contract-ing and transmitting AIDS are themselves adolescent (i.e., bisexual and homo-sexual men and IV drug users). More critically however, the chain of heterosexual partners of these adolescents forms a bridge to a much larger ado-lescent population whose patterns of sexual behavior may expose them to the virus (Hein, 1987; Heyward & Curran, 1988).

Because most adolescents do not seek health services on a regular basis, their risk status for HIV infection must be inferred from data collected for other pur-poses. This information can be summarized in three categories: sexual behavior and relevant consequences, physiological considerations, and drug abuse (Flora & Thoresen, 1988; Hein, 1987; Olson, Huszti, Mason, & Seibert, 1989).

A high percentage of teen-agers in the United States have had intercourse. In a national survey conducted in 1983 (Hofferth & Hayes, 1987), 60% of white male teen-agers reported sexual intercourse by age 18 years; 60% of white female teen-agers by age 19 years. Among blacks, 60% of the male teen-agers had inter-course by age 16 and 60% of female teen-agers by age 18.

Among the 25 million adolescents in the United States, there are subgroups who either have had intercourse at an early age or whose patterns of sexual behavior may put them at increased risk. Sorenson (1973) defined two such pat-terns of sexual relationships as the "serial monogamous" pattern and the "sexual adventurer" pattern. According to Sorenson's survey of U.S. adolescents, roughly one-half of the nonvirginal females and one-quarter of the nonvirginal males could be described as serially monogamous, although some occasionally had intercourse with other partners besides the primary partner. Sorenson also found that more that half of all sexually experienced adolescent females had intercourse with male partners who were 20 years of age or older.

Sorenson (1973) defined the sexual adventurer as an adolescent who, by the age of 19, had had a total of 17 sexual partners and who, in the month preceding the interview, had had an average of 3.2 sexual partners. The sexual adventurers, then, make up another subgroup of adolescents at risk for the acquisition of AIDS or the spread of the disease to their partners. Approximately 41% of the sexually experienced adolescent males and 13% of the sexually experienced females are sexual adventurers (Sorenson, 1973). Further increasing the risk of HIV infection, approximately one-half of all teen-agers do not use contraceptives the first time that they have sexual relations (Zelnick & Shah, 1983).

The magnitude of the adolescent problem became even clearer when the CDC (1987) reported 145 cases of AIDS in teen-agers aged 13 to 19 years. When the age range was expanded to include young people from ages 11 to 24 years, more than 10 times as many cases were noted. Of the young adult cases, 79% were linked to homosexual or bisexual behavior (Remafedi, 1988). The 1987 CDC report also showed that an alarming number of youths already had AIDS and an even larger number had subclinical HIV infections (Remafedi, 1988).

Although the number of AIDS cases among adolescents is small compared to the number among adults, it is likely that many people who were infected as teenagers will not become ill until they reach adulthood and the infection will remain undetected until then. Furthermore, adolescence seems to be a peak period for most sexually transmitted diseases (Hein, 1987), and the future spread of AIDS among youths can be expected. Patterns of sexual behavior, contraceptive underuse, and drug abuse make adolescents especially vulnerable to AIDS.

ADOLESCENT AWARENESS

The lack of accurate knowledege about AIDS seems to be a major problem for adolescents. In general, adolescents define illness in terms of the absence of disease, rather than in terms of well-being or prevention (Brooks-Gunn, Boyer, & Hein, 1988). Therefore, the idea that anyone can be an asymptomatic carrier of a deadly disease may be particularly difficult for them to accept.

DiClemente, Korn, and Temoshok (1986) found that high school students in San Francisco, where the public awareness of AIDS is probably the highest, showed remarkable levels of ignorance and misinformation. They reported that only 60% of the students were aware that the use of condoms reduced the risk of AIDS. Also, the majority thought that AIDS could be transmitted through kissing; few were aware that no vaccine was available and that AIDS cannot be cured through early treatment. Girls were more likely to be concerned about getting AIDS, even though most AIDS patients were male.

Information gathered from other surveys (DiClemente, Boyer, & Morales, 1988; Struin & Hingson, 1987) similarly revealed that most adolescents knew that having sexual intercourse and sharing needles were major routes for the transmission of HIV infection; however, significantly fewer adolescents were aware that using condoms reduced the risk of disease transmission (DiClemente et al., 1988). DiClemente and colleagues (1988) found white high school students in San Francisco were more knowledgeable than were black and Hispanic adolescents about HIV transmission and prevention. Although some teen-agers reported changes in casual behavior because of the fear of AIDS, few reported changes in the behaviors that actually transmit the virus (Struin & Hingson, 1987). In New York, for example, most adolescents who were engaging in the highest risk sexual behavior perceived themselves to be at low risk and did not use precautionary measures during sexual intercourse.

Misconceptions about HIV transmission often lead to high levels of anxiety about personal susceptibility to HIV infection. Jaffe and Wortman (1988) noted that healthy, but frightened, adolescents are approaching physicians for reassurance; many are requesting HIV testing for their own peace of mind. Fear-reducing messages rather than fear-arousing messages, realistic assessments of risk, and information on ways to change behavior may be more effective than HIV testing when working with the adolescent population, however (Brooks-Gunn et al., 1988).

PREVENTION

On the ground that adolescents' health beliefs are likely to influence their response to the AIDS epidemic, 94% of all parents surveyed by Meade (1988) indicated that they wanted their teen-agers to receive instruction in the schools about HIV transmission. As of 1987, only a small percentage of teen-agers had received formal instruction in school about AIDS—despite the fact that the vast majority of teen-agers and their parents wanted schools to provide such information (DiClemente et al., 1988). Furthermore, although education has been identified as a crucial component of any attempt to stop the spread of AIDS in the adolescent population, few schools are currently offering programs that specifically address AIDS prevention. The implementation of such programs is complex. Because of the nature of the material, community concerns about the "appropriateness" of the information given to children must be considered. Differences in program content may also be necessary for particular school districts or neighborhoods.

Brooks-Gunn and associates (1988) emphasized that effective programs must take into account the developmental differences in the ability of elementary, middle, and senior high school students to understand HIV transmission. In terms of content, Brooks-Gunn and associates (1988) proposed a program that begins in elementary school with a focus on the role of blood products in transmitting disease. In junior high school, the program can be expanded to include a focus on transmission through sexual activity and IV drug use as well. In high school, more information on drug and sexual transmission can be added. Brooks-Gunn and associates (1988) further explained that such topics as HIV transmission by same-sex acts, as well as by heterosexual acts, and the effectiveness of contraceptive methods can be included if appropriate. Kirby (1984) noted that training in decision-making skills should be included at all levels, but that very few, if any, school districts include decision making about sexuality as a goal of their sex education programs.

Many problems can arise in the process of developing a prevention program for students who have gaps in knowledge about both sexuality and AIDS. Information alone does not solve a problem of such magnitude. If specific protective methods are to be taught, adolescents must feel empowered to alter the course of their own behavior and to exert control over situations in which they may find themselves at risk. Melton (1988) stated that knowledge about sex and contraception is largely unrelated to reproductive decisions, although there is a definite relationship with the use of contraceptives.

According to Melton (1988), two problems may limit the usefulness of a conventional sex education program to teach AIDS prevention. First, general information about reproductive processes may not be helpful unless education that increases skills in the use of the particular information accompanies it. Second, information about sex and AIDS may need to be substantially more graphic and detailed than is common in a high school sex education course. In addition, Melton noted that even a well-designed sex education program may be ineffective if the source is not perceived as credible. Because of the dramatic changes in sexual norms in the 1960s and 1970s, peers may be more effective than are adults in presenting AIDS-related information. Melton (1988) suggested experimenting with AIDS prevention programs in nontraditional, peer-oriented settings, such as neighborhood teen centers or peer counseling programs. Solomon and DeJong (1986) emphasized that not only should the information be presented in an acceptable, realistic, clear, positive, and nonjudgmental manner, but also in a culturally sensitive fashion.

Henderson and Peterson (1988) commented that children and adolescents are becoming increasingly knowledgeable about AIDS. Students in their survey reported obtaining information about AIDS from television and radio (57%), and from magazines or newspapers (16%). Given the volume of AIDS information that appears daily in the media, the lack of classroom educational programs may not be the only reason for adolescent misinformation or resistance to behavioral change. Remafedi (1988) pointed out that adolescent cognitive patterns, which are characterized by concrete and dichotomous thinking, may contribute to a misunderstanding of information and a resistance to change.

In an effort to develop a basis for a successful AIDS education program. Nader, Wexler, Patterson, Mckusick, and Coates (1989) conducted a comparison study of beliefs about AIDS among opportunistic samples of 1,572 urban public high school students, suburban private school students, youth incarcerated in a detention facility, and a group who were contacted through a gay youth organization. The questionnaire items formed four important theoretical constructs derived by an expert group extensively involved with AIDS education: (1) agreement with health guidelines, (2) perceived personal threat of AIDS, (3) a sense of personal efficacy to prevent infection and the spread of AIDS, and (4) perceived norms of safe sex behaviors. In all groups, females were more likely to endorse higher norms for safe sex practices than were males. Older adolescents of both sexes tended to perceive a less personal threat of AIDS and also rated lower norms for safe sex practices than did the younger adolescents.

ADOLESCENT SPECIAL NEED POPULATIONS

There is little information about how many male adolescents identify themselves as homosexual or what percentage of such youth have had same-sex experiences. Of all adolescent males, however, 10% probably have had some same-sex experiences (Remafedi, 1987). Because of a polarized view of AIDS as a "gay" disease, some adolescents attribute the illness to a homosexual identity rather than to a virus that transverses discrete social boundaries (Owen, 1985; Remafedi, 1988).

Several surveys of young adolescent males (Finger, 1947; Kinsey, Pomeroy, & Martin, 1948; Ramsey, 1943; Sorenson, 1973) indicated a 17% to 37% incidence of homosexual activity to orgasm on a least one occasion. Thus, the total population of young men who are or will become members of an AIDS high-risk group is sizable. Of special concern are young men who engage in unprotected genital-anal intercourse. The likelihood of an adolescent's exposure to the virus increases when his partners are older, multiple, or anonymous. Also, the use of alcohol or drugs can impair an individual's willingness or ability to use condoms or take other precautions during sexual activity (Remafedi, 1988).

The social stigma of sexual minority status specifically impedes a young gay person's learning about AIDS. In the process of acquiring a homosexual identity, young men often hide, deny, or dismiss their homosexual feelings (Remafedi, 1988); they may also avoid confronting the reality and the risks of their sexual experimentation, commonly avoiding or completely withdrawing from schools that have sexually transmitted disease prevention programs (Remafedi, 1987). Others escape family disapproval or rejection by turning to the streets in search of a gay-identified peer group and means of financial support (Deisher, Robinson, & Boyer, 1982). In many cases, overwhelming concerns about day-to-day survival overshadow their interest in illness prevention.

Incarcerated youth seem to be in special need. Nader and associates (1989) reported that incarcerated adolescents demonstrate significantly poorer knowledge and lower compliance with health guidelines, lower perceived personal threat of AIDS, lower personal efficacy to prevent AIDS, and lower perceived norms of safe sex practices, as compared to other adolescents. They proposed that programs for this potential high-risk population be developed in a way that not only would alter peer norms and support, but also would give specific information on high-risk sexual behaviors and effective strategies to avoid HIV infection and transmission.

Weber, Elfenbein, Richards, Davis, and Thomas (1989) used responses to a health history questionnaire to study the sexual experiences of 1,255 adolescents admitted to a juvenile detention facility. More than 80% reported some sexual experience. The age of first intercourse acknowledged by females was early (mean 13 years), but rarely prepubertal, and was similar for blacks and non-blacks. Males commonly reported beginning their sexual experience before age 10 years (40% in blacks and 20% in non-blacks). Sexual activity continued in most, with 73% of the sexually experienced teen-agers reporting intercourse in the month prior to admission. Reports of recent sexual activity increased with age in all groups. This information suggests that sex education and AIDS prevention programs should be directed to high-risk groups at an earlier age.

Presently in the United States, 25% of all AIDS patients and 58% of all pediatric AIDS patients are black; 15% and 22% of all adult and pediatric AIDS patients are Hispanic (Schinke, Holden, & Moncher, 1989). To put these figures in perspective, blacks and Hispanics make up approximately 12% and 6% of the U.S. population, respectively. The CDC (1986) reported that the incidence of AIDS among black children is 15.1 times higher than that among white children; the incidence among Hispanic children is 9.1 times higher. Of AIDS patients who were infected heterosexually, 50% are black and 25% are Hispanic. Black and Hispanic women currently account for 51% and 21%, respectively, of all female AIDS cases in the United States (CDC, 1986).

The CDC (1986) reported that AIDS patients who were IV drug abusers were predominantly black (51%) or Hispanic (30%). Children who had AIDS and whose parents were IV drug abusers were also predominantly black (51%) or Hispanic (30%). The CDC noted that education and prevention programs may be less effective in reaching minority populations unless such programs are specifically designed for those groups (CDC, 1986). Schinke and associates (1989) suggested that theory-based, culturally sound, and empirically tested interventions are necessary to prevent HIV infection among black and Hispanic adolescents in the United States. They believed that intervention strategies for these adolescents should reflect concepts of cultural orientation, social learning, and support networks.

CONCLUSION

The epidemic of AIDS has compelled society to face numerous complex and sometimes painful realities regarding youthful sexuality and its expressions, drug use, discrimination, and individual rights and public responsibilities. The ability to find ethical and rational approaches to these and other issues will determine the ultimate success or failure of the battle against AIDS among the adolescent population in the United States.

REFERENCES

Agle, D., Gluck, H., & Pierce, G.F. (1987). The risk of AIDS: Psychological impact on the hemophilic population. *General Hospital Psychiatry, 9,* 11–17.

Belfer, M.L., Krenner, P.K., & Miller, F.B. (1988). AIDS in children and adolescents. *Journal of the American Academy of Child and Adolescent Psychiatry, 27*(2), 147–151.

Brooks-Gunn, J., Boyer, C.B., & Hein, K. (1988). Preventing HIV infection and AIDS in children and adolescents. *American Psychologist, 42*(11), 958–964.

Centers for Disease Control. (1986). AIDS among blacks and Hispanics in the United States. *Morbidity and Mortality Weekly Report, 35*(42), 655–666.

Centers for Disease Control. (1987). Acquired immunodeficiency syndrome (AIDS). *CDC Weekly Surveillance Report.*

Centers for Disease Control. (1990). AIDS data for 1989. *CDC Weekly Surveillance Report.*

Deisher, R., Robinson, G., & Boyer, D. (1982). The adolescent female and male prostitute. *Pediatric Annual, 11,* 819–825.

Department of Health and Human Services, Public Health Service, Centers for Disease Control. (1990). *AIDS prevention guide: For parents and other adults concerned about youth.* Atlanta: Centers for Disease Control.

Des Jarlais, D.C., & Friedman, S.R. (1989). AIDS and IV drug use. *Science, 245*(8), 578–579.

DiClemente, R.J., Boyer, C., & Morales, E.D. (1988). Minorities and AIDS: Knowledge, attitudes, and misconceptions among black and Latino adolescents. *American Journal of Public Health, 78,* 55–57.

DiClemente, R.J., Korn, J., & Temoshok, L. (1986). Adolescents and AIDS: A survey of knowledge, attitudes and beliefs about AIDS in San Francisco. *American Journal of Public Health, 76,* 1145–1148.

Elkind, D. (1967). Egocentricism in adolescents. *Child Development, 38,* 1025–1026.

Finger, F.W. (1947). Sex beliefs and practices among male college students. *Journal of Abnormal Social Psychology, 42,* 57–67.

Flora, J.A., & Thoresen, C.E. (1988). Reducing the risk of AIDS in adolescents. *American Psychologist, 43*(11), 965–970.

Hein, K. (1987). AIDS in adolescents: A rationale for concern. *New York State Journal of Medicine, 5,* 290–295.

Henderson, S.D., & Peterson, L.R. (1988). AIDS and secondary school students: Their knowledge is limited and they want to learn more. *Pediatrics, 81,* 350–355.

Heyward, W.L., & Curran, J.W. (1988). The epidemiology of AIDS in the U.S. *Scientific American, 259*(4), 72–81.

Hofferth, S.L., & Hayes, C.D. (Eds.). (1987). *Risking the future: Adolescent sexuality, pregnancy, and childbearing. Working papers and statistical appendices* (Vol. 2). Washington, DC: National Academy of Sciences.

Jaffe, L.R., & Wortman, R.N. (1988). The fear of AIDS: Guidelines to the counseling and HIV-III antibody screening of adolescents. *Journal of Adolescent Health Care, 9*(1), 84–86.

Kinsey, A.C., Pomeroy, W.B., & Martin, C.E. (1948). *Sexual behavior in the human male.* Philadelphia: W.B. Saunders.

Kirby, D. (1984). *Sexuality education: An evaluation of programs and their effects.* Santa Cruz, CA: Network Publications.

Mason, P.J., Olson, R.A., Meyers, J.G., Huszti, A.C., & Kenning, M. (1989). AIDS and hemophilia: Implications for interventions with families. *Journal of Pediatric Psychology, 14*(3), 341–355.

Meade, J. (1988). What parents should know when AIDS comes to school. *Children, 4,* 59–65.

Melton, G.B. (1988). Adolescents and prevention of AIDS. *Professional Psychology: Research and Pratice, 19*(4), 403–408.

Nader, P.R., Wexler, D.B., Patterson, T.L., Mckusick, L., & Coates, T. (1989). Comparison of beliefs about AIDS among urban, suburban, incarcerated, and gay adolescents. *Journal of Adolescent Health Care, 10,* 413–418.

Olson, R.A., Huszti, A.C., Mason, P.J., & Seibert, J.M. (1989). Pediatric AIDS/HIV infection: An emerging challenge to pediatric psychology. *Journal of Pediatric Psychology, 14,* 1–21.

Owen, W.F. (1985). Medical problems of the homosexual adolescent. *Journal of Adolescent Health Care, 6,* 278–285.

Ramsey, G.V. (1943). The sexual development of boys. *American Journal of Psychology, 56,* 217–222.

Remafedi, G.J. (1987). Adolescent homosexuality: Psychosocial and medical implications. *Pediatrics, 79,* 331–337.

Remafedi, G.J. (1988). Preventing the sexual transmission of AIDS during adolescence. *Journal of Adolescent Health Care, 9,* 139–143.

Schinke, S.P., Holden, G.W., & Moncher, M.S. (1989). *Adolescent sexuality: New challenges for social work.* New York: Haworth Press.

Solomon, M.Z., & DeJong, W. (1986). Recent sexually transmitted disease prevention efforts and their implications for AIDS health education. *Health Education Quarterly, 13,* 301–316.

Sorenson, R.C. (1973). *Adolescent sexuality in contemporary America.* New York: World Publishing.

Struin, L., & Hingson, R. (1987). Acquired immunodeficiency syndrome and adolescents: Knowledge, beliefs and attitudes and behaviors. *Pediatrics, 79,* 825–828.

Weber, F.T., Elfenbein, D.S., Richards, N.L., Davis, A.B., & Thomas, J. (1989). Early sexual activity of delinquent adolescents. *Journal of Adolescent Health Care, 10,* 398–403.

Zelnick, M., & Shah, F.K. (1983). First intercourse among young Americans. *Family Planning Perspectives, 15*(2), 64–70.

21

Steroids

Robert E. Banks

> Drug screening, banning athletes, loss of medals, rescinding records, and threats of permanent disqualification have not stopped the use of steroids. . . . One of the saddest spin-offs from the use of steroids (and other drugs) is that the athlete learns to believe that success lies in external powers (drugs) rather than in the fact that he or she is a good athlete—the internal power. (Grandjean, 1985).

The demands of society have quickly outgrown the abilities of the human to respond. The expectation of perfection in all facets of life has created a paranoia that seems to make drug use the cure-all to any facet of stress. Athletes are really no different from the majority of people in society, but they learn quickly that they must perform well in order to enter and remain in the society of athletes.

Contests of physical skill were once occasions of sacred honor. Today, there seems to be widespread acceptance of subtle and even outright cheating at all levels of sports. Furthermore, the pressure to win has driven many athletes to take drugs. The extent to which drugs aid in athletic performance has long been known, but the extent of drug detection and the subsequent elimination of athletes are new.

Athletes, indeed all of society, must learn that taking drugs is cheating. In addition, it compromises the ethics of individuals who are often perceived as role models.

Unfortunately, athletes who take drugs seem to lack any sense of wrongdoing. Coaches, athletic department administrators, and other administrative personnel either actively or passively condone substance abuse. Publicly, these individuals decry the abuse of drugs such as anabolic steroids. However, they feel that their jobs are on the line if they don't have winning records. A tremendous amount of pressure is put on these people to win. Like the student-athlete, they have the attitude that winning is everything and that the end justifies the means. Attempts to beat the competition through chemistry have been going on for decades, and many young athletes are wrongfully convinced that the only way to become a champion is to use drugs in an abusive manner.

DRUG ABUSE IN SPORTS

According to the the American Osteopathic Academy of Sports Medicine ([AOASM] 1989), the earliest reports of drug abuse by athletes were in 1865 when swimmers in Amsterdam's canal races were charged with taking drugs. Greek wrestlers of ancient times were thought to have eaten 10 pounds of lamb a day to increase their strength, however, and the distance runners of that time period believed sesame seeds increased their endurance. Ancient Norse warriors fought under the influence of psychoactive mushrooms (AOASM, 1989).

The International Olympic Committee defined the term *doping* as the administration to or use by a competing athlete of any substance foreign to the body or any physiological substance taken in abnormal quantity, or taken by an abnormal route, or taken into the body with the sole intention of increasing in an artificial and unfair manner the athlete's performance in competition (United States Olympic Committee [USOC], 1989a). The USOC doping control program has listed six doping classes that include banned substances (USOC, 1989a): (1) stimulants, (2) narcotics, (3) anabolic steroids, (4) beta-blockers, (5) diuretics, and (6) peptide hormones and analogues.

There are two classes of sports drugs. Restorative drugs are taken for some kind of injury or stress in order to return the athlete to his or her normal state. Such drugs include aspirin, painkillers, muscle relaxants, tranquilizers, sedatives, anti-inflammatories, enzymes, and topical anesthetic sprays or ointments. Ergogenic drugs, on the other hand, are taken to increase an althlete's performance beyond the level that he or she would normally achieve. Ergogenic substances can be pharmacological, physiological, or nutritional.The most controversial and dangerous drugs are included in this group, for example, anabolic steroids, amphetamines, cocaine, and caffeine. Athletes' abuse of ergogenic substances is of great concern to coaches and administrators (AOASM, 1989; Goldman, Bush, & Klatz, 1984).

Kennedy (1987), one of the foremost authorities in body building, gave the following account of the effect of steroids:

> Steroids give you size that you would never get from normal training. They add strength, chase fat away, and give you a vastly improved recuperative ability. They add vascularity and even allow you to train longer with less fatigue . . . yes, steroids work for the bodybuilder. Don't let anyone tell you it's just a placebo effect. They could legitimately be

described as miracle drugs—if they didn't have the reputation for side effects.

Ali Malla, a successful professional body builder, had the following to say about steroids:

> When I used drugs, I would average 315 (pounds) on the bench press for at least 10 reps; without drugs I could manage only 205 . . . when you take steroids, you get a very rapid pump in the muscles while training and you feel bigger all of the time. This "big feeling" promotes a self-confident manner sometimes called a "feeling of well-being." (Brainum, 1988).

Lyle Alzado, former National Football League defensive end, had these comments about steroids among the professionals:

> On some teams, between 75 and 90 percent of all athletes use steroids. Steroids create more raw power, speed and endurance. Some of the old-time players have gotten by without using them, but a player cannot compete today at a topnotch level of football without an aid of some sort. (Johnson, 1985).

Even though the use of steroids is very dangerous, these drugs have become popular among athletes. According to DeMarco (1986), athletes and sports medicine experts estimate that users now include almost all competitive power lifters, 80% to 95% of competitive body builders, 30% to 50% of professional football players, and smaller percentages of most other professional and college athletes.

Borgen (1986) reported that more and more very young athletes are using anabolic steroids. Virtually all high school athletes can use steroids without fear of being penalized or even caught in competitions. Harry Edwards, a professor of sociology at the University of California at Berkeley and an expert on amateur sports, stated in an article by Flax (1988) that "kids are using steroids because we as a society believe that winning is more important than integrity, honesty, and health itself."

Because of the increased use of steroids, a vast and lucrative black market has developed to distribute these drugs. Nightingale (1986) estimated that the steroid users are served by a black market that was estimated at $100 million annually (excluding veterinary grades and imported steroids). Studies of steroid-using athletes have reported that from 85% to 100% obtained their steroids on the black market (Burkett & Falduto, 1986; Taylor, 1985; Woolley & Barnett, 1986). A major distribution point for steroids has been health clubs. Health clubs often obtain their supply of steroids and other drugs from illegal distributors who stockpile steroids diverted from pharmaceutical companies and veterinary drug houses in the United States and abroad (Taylor, 1985).

MECHANISMS OF STEROID ACTION

The androgens are the most significant of the anabolic steroids. They are synthetic derivatives of testosterone, the male hormone that functions androgenically to stimulate male characteristics and anabolically to increase muscle mass, body weight, general growth, bone maturation, and virility (Mannie, 1989). Steroid hormones easily pass through the bloodstream and into the plasma membrane of the target cell. Once in the cell, the hormone binds to a protein receptor site in the cytoplasm, and the hormone-receptor complex is translocated into the nucleus of the cell. The complex interacts with specific genes of the nuclear DNA and activates them to form the enzymes necessary to alter cell function (Tortora & Anagnostakos, 1984).

Steroids generally have two messages that activate the genes to create an anabolic effect. One message is to direct the cell's ribosomes to manufacture greater amounts of protein (Hatfield, 1982), mostly structural and contractile proteins. The second message is to stimulate the synthesis of creatine phosphate, an organic molecule that restores contractile energy during anaerobic work (Wolf, 1984).

SIDE EFFECTS OF STEROIDS

Hatfield (1982), a steroid researcher and power lifter, said that drug use occurs "when the intended or sought-after effect(s) of a drug are obtained with a minimum of hazard." He added that abuse occurs "when a drug is taken such that the hazard is greatly increased, or such that an individual is no longer capable of functioning normally or coping with his/her environment adequately." In accordance with the goal of the medical profession "to restore and protect health" and the guiding principle *primum non nocere* 'first do no harm,' drugs should be used only in disease deficiency or injury states. The evidence is clear that the abuse of androgenic-anabolic steroids, for example, can disturb a natural homeostatic function of the body and greatly increase the risks associated with these drugs.

Steroids have many side effects, some even life-threatening, in both males and females. Some generalized side effects for both sexes include acne, liver tumors, premature strokes, allergic reactions, weakness and rupture of ligaments and tendons, increase in recovery time between exercise periods, premature heart disease, chronic fatigue, high blood pressure, acquired immunodeficiency syndrome

(AIDS), and even death (AOASM, 1989; Chambers & Kozubowski, 1988; DeMarco, 1986; Epstein, 1988; Goldman et al., 1984; Groves, 1987; Lamb, 1984, 1989; Larsen & Wright, 1989; McIntyre, 1990; Mirkin & Shangold, 1985; Petersen, 1989; Ribadeneira, 1988; Schiller, 1988; Thompson, 1988; USOC, 1989b). Side effects in men include sterility, decreased sperm count, enlarged prostate gland, decreased sex drive, breast enlargement, and impotence. Side effects for women include menstrual irregularities, sterility, enlargement of the clitoris, decrease in breast size, decreased sex drive, lower voice, male pattern baldness, heavier bones, and excessive body hair (Larsen & Wright, 1989).

In women's bodybuilding, it has been estimated that between 15% and 30% of the national-international level competitors have used steroids (Dayton, 1984). Anabolic steroids may aid the performance of the female athlete by building lean body (muscle) mass and increasing strength. This is accomplished by elevating the level of the male hormone testosterone in the body, increasing nitrogen and potassium retention, enhancing protein synthesis, blocking the uptake of cortisol in the muscles, reducing fatigue, and slowing protein breakdown (Nevole & Prentice, 1987). Because most scientific research on anabolic steroids has been done with male subjects, the full effect of anabolics on women is not yet known. It is known, however, that the androgenic side effects in woman are generally not reversible—even with prompt discontinued steroid use (Johnson, 1990; Nevole & Prentice, 1987).

Anabolic steroids act on all tissues of the body. In women, therefore, they affect the hormone-sensitive receptors on the ovaries, in the pituitary gland, and in the hypothalamus. The effects that steroids have on a woman's reproductive system or her ability to have children have not yet been determined conclusively, but female rhesus monkeys that had been given male hormones early in their pregnancies gave birth to abnormal female offspring. The young monkeys exhibited more aggression, their clitorises were extremely enlarged, and their labia majora were partially fused, seemingly to form a scrotal sac (Dayton, 1984).

Borgen (1986), a female body builder, decided that the only way to uncover the truth about steroids was to conduct a personal experiment. She intended to take methandronstenolone (Dianabol) and keep a meticulous record to determine the positive and negative effects of steroid use. After 1 week, she noted the following changes:

1. vaginal bleeding, resulting from the steroid's interference with the blood's clotting mechanism, and marked discomfort near the ovaries
2. bronchial tightness, stiffness in the joints, and cranial pressure 1 hour after taking a dose each day
3. random muscle spasms at rest and in the gym
4. increase in bench press maximum to 20 pounds (which Borgen attributed in part to the intense mental commitment)

Borgen stopped her experiment after a short time. She stated that the physiological gains did not outweigh the physiological complications. She implied that her psychological complications were much harder to overcome, however, in that she noted an increase in her workout intensity at the end (Borgen, 1986).

THE ADOLESCENT AND STEROIDS

In interviews with 400 high school athletes in Connecticut, Anderson and Garber (1988) found that one third had tried marijuana, 4 in 10 drank at least once a month, and 8 of 10 knew of athletes in their school who had abused drugs or alcohol. Nearly one third of the athletes interviewed said that they had observed teammates under the influence of drugs or alcohol in practices or games. Studies show that male athletes abuse substances marginally more than do female athletes.

In a steroid-specific study, Buckley (as cited in Larsen & Wright, 1989) surveyed 150 high schools across the United States with some astounding results. The overall rate of steroid use in high schools was 6.64%. The users were more likely to be athletes, especially football players and wrestlers. The percentage of first use at age 15 or younger was 38.3%. Approximately 18.2% used a single cycle, 40% used five or more cycles, and 12% used cycles of 13 weeks or longer. Most of the steroids (60.5%) were obtained on the black market, but 20% were obtained from health care professionals. Buckley concluded that students underreported steroid use. Charles Yesalis (as cited in Flax, 1988), a professor of health and human services at Pennsylvania State University, stated that from 250,000 to 500,000 teen-agers may be using steroids.

The National Federation of State High School Associations is launching a program against the use of steroids and other drugs. In an interview with Mares (1989), Dr. Herbert Kleber, deputy director for demand reduction in the U.S. Office of National Drug Control Policy and assistant to the former federal drug czar William Bennett, suggested that schools nationwide must take a more stringent approach to the steroid problem by developing clear policies and drug education programs. Roger Svendsen (as cited in Mares, 1989) outlined several factors that high school officials and athletes need to be aware of to prevent steroid use. First, a school must provide the proper information about steroids to the students. Second, the school must be able to recognize coaches who may persuade an athlete to use steroids—a win-at-all-costs coach. Third, coaches not only must be assertive with athletes, but also must be effective communicators. Fourth, there must be an environment of positive reinforcement and support for the student athletes. Finally, coaches must present their athletes with alternatives to steroid use.

CONCLUSION

Connie Carpenter-Phinney, a 1984 gold medal–winning cyclist who is a member of the USOC Advisory Committee on Substance Abuse, Research and Education, said that "the one really good thing that's coming out of the Olympics regarding positive drug tests is that it will serve as a deterrent in the future" (as cited in Brown & Brady, 1988, p. 1E). Drug testing is not infallible, however. Some athletes know when to stop taking drugs before an event to avoid testing positive (Brown & Brady, 1988) or how to mask steroid abuse by taking other drugs (Moore, 1988).

Baasher (1985) suggested that it is necessary to identify the underlying motivation for using a drug and then to overcome the motivation. Policies, goals, priorities, and lines of action for prevention must be in harmony with local conditions and relevant to the social setting. In one program to help student leaders of athletic teams acquire the knowledge, skills, and confidence to be assertive role models for healthy and chemical-free living (Griffin & Newman, 1988), students identified by peers or their coaches as leaders attended a 3-day residential workshop designed to help them improve their decision-making skills, as well as to develop an awareness of and personal commitment to good health.

REFERENCES

American Osteopathic Academy of Sports Medicine. (1989, May). *Anabolic androgenic steroids and substance abuse in sport* (American Osteopathic Academy of Sports Medicine Position Paper).

Anderson, W., & Garber, G. (1988, June). Athletes caught in the web. *Hartford Courant*, pp. A1–A3.

Baasher, T. (1985, August/September). Preventing drug problems. *World Health*, pp. 6–9.

Bergman, R., & Leach, R.E. (1985). The use and abuse of anabolic steroids in Olympic caliber athletes. *Clinical Orthopaedics and Related Research*, 169–172.

Borgen, J. (1986, February). Steroid confessions. *Flex*, pp. 80–84, 87.

Brainum, J. (1988, June). Unchained from drugs. *Muscle and Fitness*, p. 92.

Brown, B., & Brady, E. (1988, September). Positive test could have positive result. *USA Today*, p. 1E.

Burkett, L.N., & Falduto, M.T. (1986). Steroid use by athletes in a metropolitan area. *Phys Sportmed*, *12*, 69–74.

Chambers, R.L., & Kozubowski, J.M. (1988, September). What to say to your athletes about steroids. *Athletic Business*, pp. 54–57.

Dayton, L. (1984, July). Women on steroids. *Strength Training for Beauty*, pp. 72–77.

DeMarco, T. (1986, July). Steroids: Frightening growth industry. *Miami Herald*, pp. 1D–3D.

Epstein, W. (1988, July). The rising cost of beef. *Tampa Tribune*, pp. 1H–3H.

Flax, E. (1988). Steroids: Few demanding that high school athletes "Just Say No." *Education Week*, *8*(6), 1–2.

Goldman, B., Bush, P., & Klatz, R. (1984). *Death in the locker room*. Tucson: The Body Press.

Grandjean, A. (1985). Anabolic steroids—Where we stand today. *National Strength and Conditioning Journal*, *7*, 58–64.

Griffin, T., & Newman, M. (1988). *Athletics and chemical use. The role of student athletes as peer leaders.* Paper presented at the 35th International Congress on Alcoholism and Drug Dependence, Oslo, Norway.

Groves, D. (1987, September). The Rambo drug. *American Health*, pp. 43–46.

Hatfield, F. (1982). *Anabolic steroids—What kind, how many?* Madison, WI: Fitness Systems.

Johnson, L. (1990). History and development of anabolic steroids. In R. Banks, Jr. (Ed.), *Substance abuse in sports: The Realities* (pp. 13–23). Dubuque, IA: Kendall/Hunt.

Johnson, W.O. (1985). Steroids: A problem of huge dimensions. *Sports Illustrated, 62*(19), 38.

Kennedy, R. (1987). *Rock hard.* New York: Warner Books.

Lamb, D.R. (1984). Anabolic steroids in athletics: How well do they work and how dangerous are they? *American Journal of Sports Medicine, 12*(1), 31–38.

Lamb, D.R. (1989, February). *The consequences of anabolic policy* (Missouri Baptist College Athletic Policy).

Larsen, R.E., & Wright, S.K.B. (1989). *Anabolic steroids and athletes.* Minnesota Extension Service.

Mannie, K. (1989, September). What coaches and athletes should know about steroids. *Scholastic Coach,* p. 51.

Mares, F. (1989). Kleber urges help of athletic officials in fight against anabolic steroids. *National Federation News, 7*(4), 1–2.

McIntyre, D.E. (1990). Steroids: The double lie. *MSHSAA Journal, 54*(5), 2.

Mirkin, G., & Shangold, M. (1985, February). The steroid scourge. *Sports Fitness,* pp. 17–20.

Moore, W.V. (1988). Anabolic steroid use in adolescence [Editorial]. *Journal of the American Medical Association, 260,* 3484–3486.

Nevole, G., & Prentice, W. (1987, Winter). The effects of anabolic steroids on female athletes. *Athletic Training,* pp. 297–299.

Nightingale, S.L. (1986). Illegal marketing of anabolic steroids to enhance performance charged [Letter to the editor]. *Journal of the American Medical Association, 256,* 1851.

Petersen, R.C. (1989). *The use of steroids in sports can be dangerous.* National Clearinghouse for Alcohol and Drug Information.

Ribadeneira, D. (1988, November). Steroid revolution youngsters increasingly using the drug just to look good. *Houston Chronicle,* pp. 1B–2B.

Schiller, B. (1988, July). Beating the drug rap: Athletes say steroid use is rampant. *Toronto Star,* pp. A1–A2.

Taylor, W.N. (1985). *Hormonal manipulation: A new era of monstrous athletes.* Jefferson, NC: McFarland and Company.

Thompson, L. (1988). Chemistry of competition drugs and the Olympic athletes. *Washington Post,* pp. 12–15.

Tortora, G., & Anagnostakos, N. (1984), *Principles of anatomy and physiology* (4th ed.). New York: Harper & Row.

United States Olympic Committee. (1989a). *Doping control program policies and procedures for in competition testing—1989–92.* Colorado Springs, CO: author.

United States Olympic Committee. (1989b). *Drug free: USOC drug education handbook, 1989–1992.* Colorado Springs, CO: author.

United States Olympic Committee. (1989c). *Guide to banned medications.* Colorado Springs, CO: author.

Wolf, M. (1984). *The complete book of nautilus training.* Chicago: Contemporary Books.

Woolley, B.H., & Barnett, D.W. (1986). The use and misuse of drugs by athletes. *Houston Medical Journal, 2,* 29–35.

22

Eating Disorders in Adolescents

Divya Kakaiya

Anorexia nervosa, bulimia nervosa, and compulsive eating are increasingly common, complex disorders that are baffling clinicians. These disorders are difficult to treat, especially during adolescence when a person's preoccupation with their bodies is at its peak. Eating disorders include various symptom complexes for which there is no single, simple explanation. They are neither purely physiological nor totally physiochemical. Neither are they due to psychological or social factors alone; instead, they develop as an expression of disturbances in the interaction of these various forces (Bruch, 1973).

ANOREXIA NERVOSA: DEFINITION, DIAGNOSIS, AND INCIDENCE

Diet programs make up the fastest growing industry in the United States. It is estimated that more than 20 million U.S. citizens are dieting seriously at any given moment, spending more than $10 billion a year in the process (Neuman & Halvorson, 1983). In a nation infatuated with slimness and the good life, being thin is equated with happiness.

Anorexia nervosa has been recognized in the medical literature for more than 100 years. Extreme, potentially life-threatening weight loss is the primary clinical feature of anorexia. The weight loss results from restrictive eating and, in most cases, excessive exercising and/or purging (e.g., self-induced vomiting or laxative abuse).

Anorexics are driven by a strong fear of becoming fat, or the pursuit of thinness. They tend to see themselves as fat even when they are emaciated. They notice the slightest changes in the tightness of their clothing. Their obsession with thinness may lead them to weigh themselves as many as 20 times a day, frequently before and after a bowel movement, after the consumption of a glass of water or a carrot stick, and certainly before and after exercising.

The current revision of the *Diagnostic and Statistical Manual of Mental Disorders (DSM III-R*; American Psychiatric Association, 1987) defines anorexia as follows:

1. refusal to maintain body weight above 15% below that which is expected
2. extreme fear of weight gain, despite being significantly underweight
3. disturbance in body image, for example, feeling fat even when underweight
4. in females, amenorrhea for at least three consecutive menstrual cycles

The diagnostic criteria suggest that fear of obesity and body image distortion play a major role in the etiology and maintenance of anorexia nervosa.

Anorexia nervosa may first appear in early to late adolescence, with the highest risks at ages 14 and 18. It occurs mostly in the upper socioeconomic classes, although in recent years the distribution among classes has been more equal (Eckert, 1985). Approximately 1% of women have anorexia nervosa (Crisp, Palmer, & Kalucy, 1976). Anorexia Nervosa and Related Eating Disorders, Inc. (ANRED) estimates that roughly 10% of anorexics are male. One particularly striking fact is that this disorder develops strictly in industrialized nations where food is abundant and plentiful.

BULIMIA NERVOSA: DEFINITION, DIAGNOSIS, AND INCIDENCE

Because their victims share many of the same behaviors and concerns—particularly the intense fear of becoming fat—bulimia nervosa and anorexia nervosa have often been called sister ailments (Neuman & Halvorson, 1983). Individuals with either disorder assess their worth by the "numbers" on the scale or the protrusion of their stomachs. The drive for thinness is the surface symptom that reveals a person for whom success and perfectionism are major motivational factors. Schwartz (1988) argued that slimming is the modern expression of an industrial society confused by its own desires and, therefore, never satisfied.

Bulimia is a complex, emotional disease characterized primarily by an obsession and preoccupation with food and weight. Often, bulimics alternate fasting with binge eating. They starve themselves and then may resort to binges, followed by vomiting or the use of laxatives, diuretics, and/or vigorous exercising to remove food from the body and prevent weight gain. Unlike anorexics, bulimics usually maintain a normal or near normal body weight; they may even be somewhat overweight, when the primary symptom is gorging rather than starvation (Neuman & Halvorson, 1983).

Even during periods of remission, eating is seldom normal for the individual afflicted with bulimia. Typically, only the binge eating and the purging are in remission, not the dieting behavior. The obsessive thoughts and fears regarding weight gain are ever present in the bulimic person's mind. Perfectionism, negativity, dichotomous thinking, personalization, fear of alienating others, and superstitious thinking are some cognitive patterns that have been evidenced among individuals who suffer from bulimia (Johnson & Pure, 1986).

Until the 1970s, bulimia was usually considered symptomatic of anorexia nervosa rather than a separate entity. In 1980, however, bulimia was recognized as a separate eating disorder. The *DSM III-R* (American Psychiatric Association, 1987) established the following criteria for a differential diagnosis of bulimia nervosa:

1. recurrent episodes of binge eating (i.e., rapid consumption of a large amount of food in a discrete period of time)
2. a feeling of lack of control over eating behavior during the eating binges
3. regular use of self-induced vomiting, laxatives or diuretics, strict dieting or fasting, or vigorous exercise in order to prevent weight gain
4. A minimum average of two binge eating episodes a week for at least 3 months
5. persistent overconcern with body shape and weight

Since a distinction has been made between bulimia and anorexia nervosa only recently, the relationship between these two entities remains controversial. Three major subgroups of patients have been identified to date.

1. individuals with anorexia nervosa who continuously restrict their food intake and never indulge in binge eating
2. individuals with anorexia nervosa who intermittently engage in binge eating and use vomiting, exercise, dieting, or diuretics to prevent weight gain (this symptom being called bulimia)
3. individuals with bulimia (the syndrome) who are not underweight and are, therefore, not anorexic (Neuman & Halvorson, 1983)

Movement from one condition to the other is possible and quite common. Some anorexics have had a primary episode of anorexia nervosa and then moved to binge eating and purging. Occasionally, the reverse may occur; an individual afflicted with bulimia may lose substantial weight and then be identified as anorexic.

The National Association of Anorexia Nervosa and Associated Disorders (ANAD) has estimated that 20% to 30% of college women engage in bulimic behavior, but the actual incidence of bulimia has not been clearly established. The guilt and shame associated with the secretive binge eating behavior precludes many requests for professional help. Among the 410 female students who responded to a survey conducted at the University of Virginia, however, 12%

admitted to having the disorder (Pennbaker, Barrios, & Hoover, 1983). A study conducted at Ohio State University indicated that up to 30% of female college students engage in some bingeing and purging (Svensdsen & Cusin, 1980).

Although bulimia predominantly affects females, the disorder is not unique to women. The *DSM III-R* (American Psychiatric Association, 1987) noted a recent study of college freshmen indicating that 4.5% of the females and 0.4% of the males had a history of bulimia. According to ANAD statistics, 5% to 10% of people afflicted with bulimia are male. Many of these men are involved in sports and professions in which weight plays an important role (e.g., wrestling, gymnastics, and weight lifting).

Physicians tend to overlook many of the symptoms of bulimia because their presence is benign. Bulimics may allude to having trouble eating, but because of their normal to low body weight, most physicians do not probe this further. Hence, the true incidence of bulimia is difficult to assess (Neuman & Halvorson, 1983).

COMPULSIVE OVEREATING: DEFINITION, DIAGNOSIS, AND INCIDENCE

Recent research has suggested that 20% to 40% of obese patients have significant problems with binge eating. This particular subgroup of patients often does not receive appropriate care, since the outward signs of the illness may not be severe. It is the compulsive overeater who supports the multibillion dollar diet industry in the United States. Most commercial diet programs thrive on the patient who chronically gains weight. This person's yo-yo syndrome may be a manifestation of unresolved psychological issues.

Williamson (1990) proposed the following diagnostic criteria for compulsive overeating:

1. recurrent episodes of binge eating at least twice per week for 3 months
2. at least three of the following:
   a. consumption of high caloric, easily ingested food during a binge
   b. inconspicuous eating during a binge
   c. repeated attempts at dieting to lose weight
   d. negative affect often associated with binge eating
   e. frequent weight fluctuations greater than 10 pounds due to alternating bingeing and fasting
3. no use of extreme methods, such as vomiting, laxative abuse, severe dieting, or extreme exercise, to lose or control weight
4. no evidence of body image disturbances other than dissatisfaction with body size

5. bulimic episodes not attributable to anorexia nervosa, bulimia nervosa, or any other known physical disorder

In the diagnostic evaluation of compulsive overeating, a history of repeated interventions, such as medical supervision for periods of 6 months or longer, stapling of the stomach, or wiring of jaws, needs to be assessed. This particular group of eating disorders has secondary problems similar to those of bulimia. For example, many of these patients are depressed, and dependent, passive aggressive, and avoidant personality styles are common. Substance abuse is also common among these patients, and many have experienced incest and/or other forms of sexual abuse.

According to most studies, binge eating is a frequent behavior. Hawkins and Clement (1980) and Pyle and associates (1983) reported binge eating in 57% to 79% of U.S. women. Additionally, 15% of female high school students consider themselves binge eaters (Halmi, Falk, & Schwartz, 1981).

Recent estimates have indicated that 5-10% of present preschool children, 10% of schoolage children, 15% of adolescents, and 30% of American adults are obese (Maloney & Klykylo, 1983). Considering that most obese and overweight children become obese adults, early intervention is a necessity.

ETIOLOGICAL ANALYSIS

No single perspective has been shown to describe the illness of bulimia nervosa comprehensively (Garner & Garfinkle, 1985). Various factors interact to produce a person who is vulnerable to the symptoms of compulsive overeating, or undereating, and/or purging. As Pope and Hudson (1988) argued, the etiology is heterogenous (i.e., due to the interaction of an individual with multiple biological, psychological, and environmental factors) rather than homogenous (i.e., due to the presence of some specific abnormality). An eclectic, multidimensional perspective does increase the understanding of this illness.

Sociocultural Perspective

Bulimia appears to be a woman's disease, with more than 90% of those afflicted being women (Sights & Richards, 1984). Women of high socioeconomic status are most likely to emulate closely the trendsetters of beauty and fashion (Banner, 1983); not surprisingly, therefore, they exhibit greater weight preoccupation. Obesity, traditionally, has been the least punished in lower socioeconomic classes.

Women in certain environments also appear to be at a particularly high risk. College campuses seem to be breeding grounds for eating disorders such as bulimia, for example. One study found a dramatically higher weight gain among women during their first year of college than in women of similar socioeconomic backgrounds who did not go to college (Hovell, Mewborn, Randle, & Fowler-Johnson, 1985). Several factors may contribute to this observation. As was discussed earlier, those in middle and upper class environments—such as college campuses—are at higher risk since there is a strong emphasis on success at any cost, and success and thinness are often linked together for women. A woman's struggles with autonomy often are manifested through struggles with weight. In addition, the competitive school environment may foster not only competition in terms of academic achievement, but also competition in terms of the achievement of a beautiful (i.e., thin) body. Appearance is of much greater importance in dating for women than for men, and there is preliminary evidence that, in schools where there is a heavy emphasis on dating, there is a higher prevalence of bulimia than in schools where there is less emphasis on dating (Rodin, Striegel-Moore, & Silberstein, 1985).

Other kinds of subcultures also amplify sociocultural pressures and, hence, place their members at a greater risk for eating disorders. Among professionals whose weight is a primary job factor, such as dancers, models, actresses, and athletes, Vincent (1980) found clinical evidence that suggested a high prevalence of bulimia, although no percentages are cited. The eating pathology seems to be linked more to the requirement of form and shape, rather than to the stressful nature of these professions. Furthermore, it seems to be precipitated after the person enters the subculture, as is the case with women who develop bulimia in their freshmen year of college.

Developmental Processes

In assessing which particular women are at risk for eating disorders, a developmental perspective clarifies many issues.

Vulnerability Factors

Girls learn from an early age that appearance is a very important aspect of their femininity (Valette, 1988). Young girls learn that being attractive and pleasing to others secures love and attention. In school environments, little boys receive praise for their intellectual pursuits, while little girls often receive praise for neatness and care of their appearance (Ambert, 1976). A time of particular vulnerability appears to be adolescence, when young girls and boys are challenging their notions of self-identity and attempting to find their place in the world

(Root, Fallon, & Friedrich, 1986). Coupled with the physical changes of puberty, these challenges make the world a very confusing place for the young adult.

Prior to puberty, girls have 10% to 15% more body fat than do boys; after puberty, however, girls have twice as much fat as boys do (Marino & King, 1980). Girls gain weight at puberty primarily in the form of fat tissue, while boys gain muscle and lean tissue. Biologically, the female body is preparing for the start of her reproductive cycle. Although girls typically want to be thinner, boys express dissatisfaction and want to gain more weight.

In addition to the physical changes that adolescents undergo, there are three primary developmental tasks that adolescents must master: (1) achieving a new sense of self; (2) establishing peer relationships, particularly heterosexual ones; and (3) developing independence (Havinghurst, 1972). Like several authors, Chodorow (1978) has suggested that women define themselves primarily in relation and connection to others, whereas men rely on individuation and a sense of accomplishment in forming the sense of self.

In regard to the first task, achieving a new sense of self, Chodorow's (1978) theory applies in that girls appear to be more interpersonally oriented than are boys. Girls also seem to be more self-conscious and try harder to avoid negative reactions from others. In response to feeling insecure and in an effort to avoid negative evaluation by others, the adolescent girl becomes more and more sensitive to and compliant with the demands of society. In the process, she becomes increasingly vulnerable to an "other" orientation, negating her own internal perceptions of who she is.

In assessing the second task of adolescence, forming peer relationships, particularly heterosexual ones, Rosenberg and Simmons (1975) reported conclusive findings. They found, for example, that girls were more likely than boys to rank popularity as more important than independence and competence. The authors also discovered that those who emphasized popularity had a less stable self-image and a greater susceptibility to others' evaluations. Given that attractive (i.e., thin) females are rewarded in the interpersonal and especially the heterosexual domain, the wish to be popular and the pursuit of thinness may become synonymous in the mind of the teen-aged girl.

The third task, establishing independence, also seems to pose a different challenge for girls than for boys. According to Gilligan (1982), a girl's relationship orientation becomes an issue during adolescence, when the tasks of separation and individuation emerge. Gilligan reported that adolescent girls conceptualize dependence as a positive attribute, with isolation as its polar opposite. When the world views dependence as problematic, these girls often begin to feel insecure, confused, and inadequate; they become stuck in a world of bewildering and ambiguous sex roles. Hence, adolescent girls' increasing preoccupation with weight and dieting is tied to the issue of independence. When other aspects of life seem out of control, these girls may perceive weight as one of the few areas that they can control (Hood, Moore, & Gardner, 1982).

Because society views efforts to lose weight as a sign of maturity, dieting may reflect a girl's desire to show others, as well as herself, that she is growing up (Steele, 1980). In this case, dieting may be a metaphor for movement toward independence. On the other hand, losing weight may also represent an effort to delay and defy the body changes that signal maturity and adulthood. A successful diet would indeed preserve the prepubertal look, perhaps reflecting a desire to remain in childhood (Bruch, 1973; Crisp, 1980; Valette, 1988).

High-Risk Women

The timing of development and personality variables may make some women particularly vulnerable to eating disorders. Life span theory suggests that being "out of phase" with cohorts is a special stressor for the adolescent and increases the likelihood of a developmental crisis (Neugarten, 1972). Male early developers have been found to be more relaxed, less dependent, and more self-confident than female early developers; they also enjoy a more positive self-image than do late-developing girls (Clausen, 1975). For girls, the outcomes of early maturation are less clear. Although early-maturing girls are generally more popular among males, they tend to be less popular among same-age, same-sex peers. Issues of jealousy, rivalry, and competition seem to outweigh the benefits of an attractive, mature body. Early-developing girls also tend to be fatter than their peers and less satisfied with their body image. Thus, maturing faster than her peers may place a girl at a greater risk for eating disorders (Simmons, Bluth, & McKinney, 1983).

The dissatisfaction of young women with their bodies has been documented repeatedly. Dwyer, Feldman, Seltzer, and Mayer (1969) reported that 80% of the high school senior girls and approximately 20% of the high school senior boys wanted to lose weight. Consistent with their statements, 30% of these girls were dieting, only 6% of the boys were dieting. In a separate study, Nylander (1971) found that the majority of female Swedish adolescents "felt fat," while their male peers seldom expressed such feelings. In addition, the girls' body dissatisfaction increased with age, with 50% of the 14-year-olds and 70% of the 18-year-olds indicating that they felt fat.

The specific personality variables that seem to place certain women at risk for eating disorders have to do with women's tendency to be "other" oriented. Qualities such as warmth, emotional availability toward others, and sensitivity to others' needs are considered strong feminine traits. Peggy, a 28-year-old bulimic anorexic, described one aspect of the "other" orientation as follows:

> I'm not sure where my family really stands on this, but what is important is that I perceived an implied pressure never to show any of my

feelings. You know big girls don't cry; they don't get angry, much less swear; they love their families, their teachers, the whole town and they are always happy. To please everybody else, I took care of their feelings and left mine to the last. Anorexia and bulimia were my means of coping with this. All these buried feelings and all the pressure I felt to have a good body, got saved for a binge. (Cauwels, 1983).

Studies conducted on women with eating disorders have noted that they have a high need for approval and difficulty in asserting their needs (Boskind-Lodahl, 1976). Although research indicates that there is no single personality profile of individuals with an eating disorder, certain consistent patterns emerge. For example, women who have an eating disorder seem to have significant difficulties in identifying and articulating internal states, which makes coping with impulsive and anxiety-ridden stimuli a much more difficult task. Therefore, as Johnson and Pure (1986) suggested, it is important in interviewing women with eating disorders to observe how quickly and accurately they report their feelings.

Johnson and Pure (1986) also highlighted certain cognitive distortions. Perfectionism, a characteristic often observed in depressed patients, is a hallmark for many eating disorder patients. They set rigid standards for themselves, which they would not ascribe to others, and usually feel that they could have done better. They also work out of a negative filter, failing to see the positives, and to see their world in terms of polar opposites. Thus, they consider a diet successful only if they adhere to it completely; they see any slip as a total failure that makes it permissible to have a binge.

Personalization is another cognitive distortion found in individuals who have eating disorders. They feel that they are the center of attention. Extremely sensitive to criticism, they tend to feel that they are constantly being judged with scorn and derision. They also have an intense fear of alienating others and must have love and approval from all their loved ones (Johnson & Pure, 1986).

Women who have eating disorders also engage in superstitious thinking. They may connect two seemingly unrelated events and predict an outcome, even though the two are not associated. For example, they may believe that a certain "forbidden" food will increase their weight by 10 pounds, even though they consumed only a few calories.

The cognitive style of patients with an eating disorder is often diffuse and chaotic. They may experience feelings as "out-of-control" phenomena. Binge eating, in contrast, is a behavior that is predictable, reliable, and under their control. Also, because of the highly ritualized and repetitive nature of the binge, it can be used to organize thoughts and behavior (Johnson & Pure, 1986). Those who have stronger compulsive personalities may use the binge as a way of being impulsive.

Depression is common among women who have an eating disorder. There is evidence that depressive symptoms increase during or after binge eating and purging episodes (Johnson & Larson, 1982). For some of these women, the binge-purge cycle serves a self-punishing purpose. For others, however, eating may serve as an antidote to depression in terms of self-nurturance and self-medication, as well as an attempt to fill the emptiness.

Psychological Variables

Anorexia, bulimia, and compulsive eating are complex disorders that involve the interplay of a broad range of psychological factors. For example, anorexic patients are eager to please others, especially authority figures, and have generally tended to be "model" children. They are very compliant and follow directions with meticulous perfectionism. They tend to be A students and to excel in extracurricular activities. There is a rigidity in their thinking process, however. Additionally, the need to please others often results in a paranoid style of functioning. Therefore, this strange, noncompliant behavior of stubbornly refusing to eat puzzles the anorexic's parents.

An important aspect of the bulimic personality is a vague, diffuse sense of identity (Cauwels, 1983). Bulimics depend heavily on others to approve of them and are fearful of taking risks and being honest, lest they lose the comfort and the security of a status quo. They passively comply with the expectations of others at the expense of developing an identity of their own. As Cauwels aptly put it, "At any particular time, a bulimic's personality is likely to be a collage of what she has picked from other people, yet somehow the pieces don't fit into a promising whole."

In some individuals, bulimia appears to take on a life of its own, operating not only in response to stress, but also as an independent habit (Neuman & Halvorson, 1983). Many clinicians have noted the similarity between bulimia and chemical dependency. Mitchell, Pyle, Hatsukami, and Eckert (1985), in their study on the characteristics of bulimia, reported that 8 of their sample of 34 women had previously completed chemical dependency treatment and one additional patient was believed to be alcoholic. Herzog (1982) reported that 10 of the 30 bulimic patients in his series reported alcoholism in at least one first-degree family member, suggesting a familial relationship between bulimia and alcoholism. Steele (1980) described an addiction as a "habit gone out of control." According to Steele, bulimia functions like other addictions in that it "manages to ward off anxiety, pain and an awareness of the immediate problem" (pp. 823–824). Bulimics' belief in magical solutions facilitates their adoption of a "quick fix" ideology.

The binge-purge cycle has a ritualized aspect that creates structure and stability for the affected individual. This cycle consumes an inordinate amount of time and, hence, affects outside involvements. Bulimics are unable to maintain intimacy in relationships, because the binge eating and purging take priority over close relationships, jobs, school, health, and budgetary considerations. The central focus of the person's life becomes acquiring food and establishing secret times to carry out the cycle. All this affects the person's self-esteem and fills him or her with self-hatred (Neuman & Halvorson, 1983).

Bulimic individuals commonly have a pervasive feeling of powerlessness within themselves and over their environment. Weiss and Ebert (1983) found that, in comparison to women with no eating disorder, bulimics exhibited a lower internal locus of control. An external locus of control tends to decrease the individual's sense of self-efficacy and control over the environment. Furthermore, many bulimics have been victims of physical or sexual abuse, rape, or battering (Kakaiya, 1991; Root & Fallon, 1985). Of 172 women in one sample, 66% had been victimized. As adults, they may still be in relationships that entail physical, sexual, and verbal abuse. Constant criticism, manipulativeness, and emotional nonavailability of significant people in their lives have led them to feel powerless and resigned to lack of personal control.

Thus, the bulimia may start out as an individual's attempt to gain self-control and internal mastery through the ritualization of eating. A vicious cycle is established whereby the more out of control the bulimics get with the food, the more depressed they feel, the more they eat, the more powerless they feel (Root & Fallon, 1985).

Biological Theories

From a biological perspective, eating disorders can be regarded as affective disorders, metabolic disturbances, and/or a genetic vulnerability (Weiss & Ebert, 1983). It has not yet been determined, however, whether anorexia is an affective disorder. Anorexics are not as overtly depressed as are patients with affective disorders (Pyle, Mitchell, & Eckert, 1981). Their depression may be associated with complex changes in weight and appetite.

Clinical evidence has shown that many bulimic patients are depressed. Using the experience sampling method, Johnson and Larson (1982) investigated the daily moods and behavior of 15 bulimic individuals. Participants wore electronic pagers and, when they were beeped, filled out self-reports on their current mood and behavior. The bulimic participants in the study showed a wider fluctuation of mood and more dysphoria than did the control group. Following a purge, the bulimic sample reported decreased anger and increased feelings of control, adequacy, and alertness; overall, however, they reported being sadder, lonelier, weaker, more irritable, more passive, and more constrained than did the control group. These findings suggested to Johnson and Larson that bulimics experience an agitated depressive state and that food and overeating may be used as self-medication.

Pyle and associates (1983) found that individuals with more severe forms of bulimia were more likely to have sought treatment for depression previously than were those with less severe forms of the disorder. They hypothesized that there may be a link between affective disorders and the more severe forms of bulimia, although no causal link between bulimia and depression has been established. A genetic disposition toward an affective disorder may be linked to a biochemical disturbance of appetite; for example, depression is sometimes associated with a loss of appetite and is sometimes associated with an increased appetite. The authors also suggested that the loss of control experienced by the individuals may enhance their tendency toward depression.

In their study of 10 bulimic women, Hudson, Laffer, and Pope (1982) found that 15% of the women's 46 first-degree relatives had probable or possible major depression; 4% had alcohol dependence; and 2% displayed cyclosthymic disorder, agoraphobia, or possible bulimia. In another study, in which the subjects were 14 women with anorexia nervosa and 45 with bulimia, Hudson and associates (1983) reported that 16% of the first-degree relatives had a major affective disorder. The authors suggested that "genetics offer the most likely explanation"

Some eating disorders may be associated with a metabolic imbalance. The fact that many bulimics and compulsive overeaters binge on carbohydrates suggests not only that they like carbohydrates, but also that a carbohydrate craving relates to some of their other symptoms. Eating carbohydrates speeds up the synthesis of serotonin, a neurotransmitter, in the brain; therefore, a carbohydrate craving may reflect the body's need for increased serotonin. When researchers treated a study group of students with fenfluramine hydrochloride, an appetite suppressant that is thought to release serotonin, and with tryptophan, an amino acid that is thought to contribute to serotonin synthesis, they found that the two substances significantly reduced the subjects' carbohydrate consumption without significantly affecting other aspects of their appetites.

Women who are genetically programmed to be heavier may have a genetic vulnerability to eating disorders. It has been shown that adopted children resemble their biological parents in weight far more than they resemble their adoptive parents (Stunkcard, 1985). The set point theory states that the proper weight for each person is metabolically coded in each person's genetic makeup. When individuals allow their weight to drop below the set point, their body responds by sending off binge triggers (Cauwels, 1983). Most theorists state that by no means are any, or all, of these theories complete in themselves and that specific vulnerability factors must be taken into account.

Familial Variables

With a growing research data base, family variables that seem to predispose certain individuals to anorexia, bulimia, and compulsive overeating are emerging. Only in the past 5 to 7 years has the family system of the bulimic been scrutinized, however. Until that time, generalities were developed from classic studies done on anorexia nervosa by Minuchin (1974). These studies emphasized the psychosomatic nature of illness in families, with the main issues being lack of conflict resolution, overprotectiveness, enmeshment, rigidity, and involvement of the patient in parental conflict. This systems approach takes into account the family's need for homeostasis and the function of the anorexic symptom in stabilizing the family. In applying this theory to bulimic family systems, Schwartz, Barrat, and Saba (1985) stressed three additional factors: (1) heightened consciousness of appearance, (2) special meaning attached to food and eating, and (3) isolation.

Root and associates (1986) have highlighted the multigenerational factors of bulimia. Addressing these aspects helps to reduce treatment resistance because responsibility can be diffused. Also, it becomes possible to explore and work through family secrets. Through generations, bulimic families appear to have elaborate rituals around food. The bulimic learns to approach food ambivalently, and mealtime may be an arena where messages are conflicting. In most families with eating disorders, food takes on a special language of its own—for sustenance as well as expression of love and anger.

In the families of compulsive overeaters, an adolescent's initial struggle with food may have been about establishing autonomy from overintrusive parents. Further assessment of the family reveals the enmeshment in the family system. Usually, there is a role reversal, with the compulsive eater becoming the primary caregiver. If one parent is alcoholic, the other parent may be preoccupied with "fixing" the alcoholic parent; as a result, one of the children fills the role of the caregiver. Triangulation is commonly present, with the "symptom" fulfilling a special role of homeostasis in the family system.

Kakaiya (1991) used the responses of 121 women between the ages of 18 and 37 on the Moos Family Environment Scale (FES) to compare the perceptions of family environments and the severity of bulimia in adult children of alcoholic women and nonadult children of alcoholic women. Subjects were divided into four groups.

1. adult children of alcoholic women who were bulimic
2. nonadult children of alcoholic, bulimic women
3. adult children of alcoholic women who were not bulimic
4. women who were neither bulimic nor adult children of alcoholics

Women who had alcoholic parents rated their families of origin higher on the scale of conflict, lower in cohesion, lower in expressiveness, and lower in intellectual cultural orientation than did the others.

Figure 22-1, which is a graph of the FES T-score means for the four groups, shows the predictable peaks and valleys, with the bulimic adult children of alcoholics group scoring lowest on cohesion, expressiveness, and independence, while scoring highest on conflict. Women in these families are not allowed to be assertive, outgoing, and gregarious. The bulimic adult children of alcoholics group scored the highest on achievement, which is probably an indicator of the push to look good in these families. On the scale of conflict, alcoholism created a specific tension, as is seen in both groups of adult children of alcoholics (Kakaiya, 1991).

When the subjects who reported alcoholism for themselves were studied in terms of their FES means (Figure 22-2), it was found that the alcoholic women who were "plain" binge eaters scored the lowest on cohesion, expressiveness, and independence; they scored the highest on achievement. It seems that they used alcohol to deal with the repression in the family. Comparing their peaks to those of the bulimic adult children of alcoholics group suggests that the presence of alcoholism gave them some freedom of expression, slightly more cohesion and independence, and less emphasis on achievement (Kakaiya, 1991).

Figure 22-3 shows the means for the specific parents' alcoholism for both the bulimic and nonbulimic groups; 54% of the first group and 55% of the second group had alcoholic fathers. Women who grow up with an impaired alcoholic father have a poor role model of a man. Alcoholic fathers are very controlling, and many bulimic women who have alcoholic fathers talk about the anger and passivity they feel toward the controlling men in their lives. The bulimic adult children of alcoholics were more likely to have an alcoholic mother than were their nonbulimic counterparts.

Therapists must be aware that the families of adolescents with various eating disorders are likely to be quite different. For example, anorexics and their families are traditionally the most resistant to treatment. They have excellent coping strategies because of their need to look good, and the "pseudoresolution" of their issues may cloud the clinical picture. They are very compliant and do all the homework that the therapist may assign. The amount of rigidity and control in the family will become apparent to the clinician. Disengagement from the anorexic's symptoms must be a primary task.

Bulimic families exhibit a little more chaos and drama, and they may have more affect. This is a family in which there may be multiple addictions, especially parental alcoholism. Therefore, the issues of family violence, abuse, neglect, and sexual trauma must be explored. Most bulimics report a history of victimization, and their need to keep some control at any or all costs becomes an arena in which the therapist must tread gently in order to maintain the therapeutic alliance and trust.

In working with families of compulsive eaters, the therapist should determine whether there is a history of parental alcoholism. It is likely that the compulsive eater has experienced some form of sexual abuse, and the resultant repression of feelings through food is a core issue. The regulation of affect is an important variable. By the time compulsive eaters reach adolescence, they have been teased and

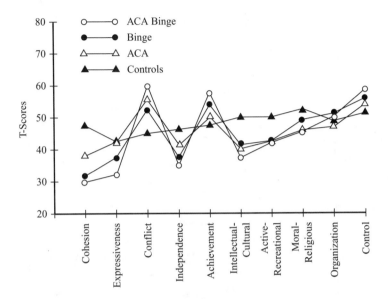

Figure 22-1 FES T-Score Means for Four Groups. ACA, Adult children of alcoholics.

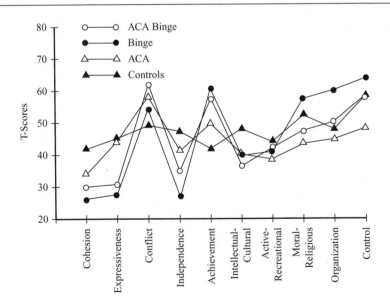

Figure 22-2 FES T-Score Means for Four Groups Using Subjects Reporting Self-Alcoholism. ACA, Adult children of alcoholics.

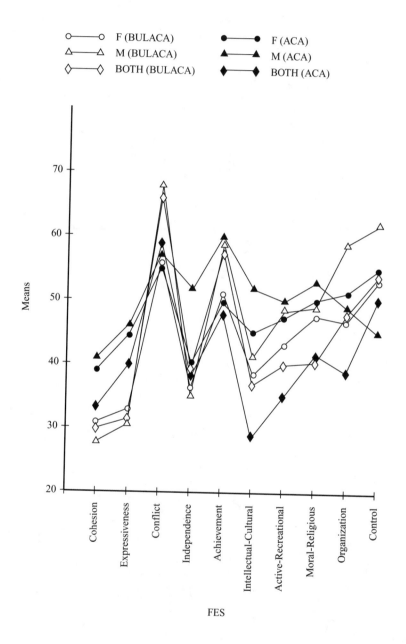

Figure 22-3 Graph of Means for Specific Parents' Alcoholism for BULACA Group (*N* = 39) and ACA Group (*N* = 22). BULACA, Bulimic adult children of alcoholics; ACA, Adult children of alcoholics; F, Father; M, Mother.

ridiculed mercilessly by their peers, and a core depressive element may have established itself. Also, since the parents have been impaired in some way (e.g., through alcoholism), compulsive eaters have learned self-nurturing through food. Identification of feelings and assertiveness are key goals in early therapy. In the later stages of therapy, the safe expression of anger and the development of a clearer, more autonomous identity are relevant issues.

TREATMENT MODALITIES

The treatment of anorexia, bulimia, and compulsive eating is in its infancy, and a great deal of further research is necessary. The modalities that have been used successfully in the past include inpatient management, individual psychotherapy, family therapy, group therapy, and self-help groups. The approach that appears to be most effective for the client and reduces burnout for the therapist is a multidimensional approach that involves a treatment team (Garner & Garfinkle, 1985).

The process of recovery from bulimia is slow. Primary among the many difficulties that must to be overcome, as identified by Neuman and Halvorson (1983), is the addictive quality of the binge eating and vomiting that makes it more resistant to treatment than is pure anorexia. The bulimic behavior is a powerful reinforcer, because it reduces anxiety. For many bulimic clients, being "good" means maintaining a diet, and they may skip or avoid sessions if they have had a relapse (Root et al., 1986). Since perfectionism is a major part of the clinical picture, it becomes a primary task to keep the client engaged in therapy, particularly at vulnerable times, when the bingeing and vomiting may be at its worst. Most bulimics have had their primary relationship with food, and their interactive social skills may be minimal to nonexistent. Thus, any form of treatment is a slow process.

Types of Therapy

Patients who do not recover with outpatient psychotherapy or drug therapy for eating disorders are candidates for inpatient management. The existence of a major depressive disorder and suicide intent is a clear indication for a more structured form of treatment. The medical complications of anorexia and bulimia may also indicate inpatient treatment: cardiac arrhythmias, acute gastric dilation, electrolyte imbalances, irritation of the gastrointestinal tract, hypertrophy of the salivary glands, dental problems, and endocrine problems. Severe disability in terms of job, school, or finances because of the preoccupation with binge eating and elimination is another indicator for inpatient management. Bulimics who abuse laxatives often will not stray too far from a bathroom and sometimes even refuse to leave the home (Kaye & Gwirtsman, 1985).

Most inpatient treatment modalities are structured in three phases. In the initial phase, the goal is to interrupt the binge-purge cycle and regularize meals. In the second phase, which takes place once the symptom has been resolved, individual, family, and group therapy can begin to address the underlying issues. The third phase consists of a transition to an outpatient form of treatment and the continued intensification of psychotherapeutic management. Ongoing education is crucial (Garner & Garfinkle, 1985), body image issues and continued exploration of feelings are primary tasks of therapy (Root, Fallon, & Friedrich, 1986).

Individual therapy is usually oriented toward a combination of insight and cognitive behavioral approaches (Neuman & Halvorson, 1983). It addresses issues commonly seen with late adolescent and young adult women: relations with and individuation from family of origin; friendships and intimacies; loneliness; femininity; physical appearance and its importance; personal goals and values; role confusion; frustrating tensions and releases; trust in one's own judgment; and need for personal control (Kaye & Gwirtsman, 1985). Therapy is directive with an emphasis on understanding the payoffs of the symptoms and learning more appropriate channels to work through anxiety. The cognitive component of the therapy teaches the patient to identify distorted cognitive beliefs, to adopt accurate new beliefs, and to deal with situations that require assertiveness. Food diaries are a helpful tool to enhance the individual's awareness of the precipitating factors and emerging patterns of behavior. Individual therapy, according to Cauwels (1983), offers the advantage of helping the bulimic obtain her badly needed special attention, special caring, and sense that she is important for herself. She can feel secure, relaxed, and reinforced without having to binge and purge.

Family therapy has usually been provided in conjunction with individual or inpatient management. The primary model developed by Schwartz and associates (1985) takes into consideration that bulimia and anorexia nervosa function very efficiently for women and their families. Their model has three stages: (1) creating a context for change, (2) challenging patterns and expanding alternatives, and (3) consolidating changes. Interventions at each stage are designed to restructure the individual's dysfunctional interactions with food, self, and others in order to eliminate the bulimic behavior. Additional goals are to assist the individual in feeling more differentiated, more grown-up, and more in control of relationships with family and others, as well as to inoculate the family against relapse (Schwartz, Barrat, & Saba, 1985).

Cauwels (1983) asserted that group therapy is one of the more effective ways of treating bulimia. The curative powers of sharing the "secret" are paramount. The demystification of the illness removes a great deal of power and pleasure from the binge. The establishment of a strong networking alliance within the groups decreases the isolation characteristic of bulimics. The group members offer support by setting good examples for each other. The confrontation provided by the group assists the bulimic in being more honest with herself. Specific elements of group therapy include discussions of the personal isolation and shame resulting from the behavior; an examination of relationship problems and the use of specific behavioral strategies, such as daily journals to record feelings and factors that precede binges; short-term goal contracting; role playing of feared situations; and assertiveness training (Mitchell et al., 1985). A combination of group therapy and individual therapy with dietary counseling is the most effective treatment, according to Mitchell and associates (1985).

A more recent development in the treatment of bulimia is the emergence of self-help groups. These community-based, outpatient programs come from various schools of therapeutic thought and engage various approaches. Some are successful; others are not. They are appropriate adjunctive support to individual counseling, in that they provide a forum in which people can exchange ideas and hopes (Cauwels, 1983).

Overeaters Anonymous is a self-help, nonprofit organization patterned after Alcoholics Anonymous. Founded in 1960, it has become an adjunctive support and resource used by many eating disorders units. More recently, an organization called Anorexics/Bulimics Anonymous has been gaining popularity among anorexics and bulimics. Enright, Butterfield, and Berkowitz (1985) suggested that, since support groups are nonauthoritarian in nature, women who have struggled with authority have an easier time letting go of their defensive structures and accepting the comfort provided by people who have "been there." Overeaters Anonymous is a very popular program among compulsive eaters.

Pharmacological Treatment

Many clinicians attempt to combine pharmacological treatment with therapy. Very little follow-up research has been conducted to gauge the efficacy of these treatment guidelines, however, and there is much controversy surrounding this approach.

Monoamine oxidase inhibitors have been controversial in the treatment of the affective component of bulimia nervosa. When Walsh, Stewart, Roose, Gladis, and Glassman (1984) conducted a double-blind, placebo-controlled trial of the inhibitor phenelzine sulfate in women with bulimia nervosa, they found that those who took the drug rather than the placebo improved; however there was a time effect in favor of improvement during the second phase of the study. Of the 11 patients who started the first phase of the study, 7 failed to complete the second phase. Additionally, even though there was an improvement in the depression, the bulimic symptoms did not improve. The dropout group had a high prevalence of borderline personality disorders, which suggests that personality disturbances may be important in predicting poor compliance. Firm conclusion about the efficacy of monoamine oxidase inhibitors in treating bulimia must await clear confirmation (Garner & Garfinkle, 1987).

Since 1982, treatment with tricyclic antidepressants for the bulimia syndrome has been researched aggressively. In one of the first reports, Pope and Hudson (1982) noted that 75% of their 8 patients had at least a 50% decrease in their bulimic behavior within 3 weeks of beginning the treatment with medication. Amitriptyline, clomipramine, imipramine, desipramine, and mianserin have all been researched and responses have been favorable (Garner & Garfinkle, 1987). The studies have been criticized for the small numbers of subjects in the double-blind placebo-controlled studies, however. Additionally, it is necessary to assess the efficacy of the tricyclic antidepressants over a longer period.

Anxiety plays a major role in the genesis and maintenance of bulimia and anorexia. An important goal of treatment is to reverse the association between anxiety relief and food restriction so that eating is paired with relaxation. Antianxiety agents such as lorazepam or oxazepam are more frequently used with anorexia than with bulimia. There is a potential for abuse of the addictive antianxiety agents in bulimics because of their tendency toward multiple addictions (Garner & Garfinkle, 1987).

FAMILY THERAPY PHILOSOPHY

In addressing eating disorders, therapists must understand family influences in order to understand the complexity of the disorders.

Communication Model

The core belief of the communication model of family therapy is that communication between family members is the most important factor of family life (Lawson, Petersen, & Lawson, 1983). According to this theory, symptoms emerge because blocked communication has produced family tension and the family has scapegoated one or more of its members (Lawson et al., 1983). All people are motivated by the need to maintain or restore their optimum level of interpersonal stimulation; insufficient or excessive stimulation automatically causes tension and sets in motion the behavior required to achieve equilibrium (Jackson, 1968). Thus, when their needs are not being met, family members seek alternative ways of need gratification in order to maintain family homeostasis.

Jackson (1960) developed the double bind theory, which is a popular concept in the field of family therapy. The child is given a conflicting message in which the verbal and nonverbal parts of the message contradict each other. One message carries a negative connotation, and the other is more abstract and contradictory. With these double messages, children may assume that communication is worthless, and they may withdraw from the relationship and turn to a substance.

Through the years, women have used food to bolster their self-esteem and personal power. In an alcoholic family system, for example, the mother may "treat" the daughter to goodies as a way to make up for the turmoil caused by the drinking father. If the father values thinness in women, the daughter begins to lose weight to gain her father's approval (McFarland & Baker-Baumann, 1988). If, however, the mother sees her daughter's weight loss as a threat to her own control of her daughter, she may send a message of hurt, disappointment, or disapproval. The daughter picks up on this conflicted message and abandons her efforts to be thin, thus entering the yo-yo syndrome of gaining and losing weight to satisfy both her parents.

Clearly, the communication that people receive from significant others in their lives determines their view of self. Satir (1967), a strong proponent of the communication theory, stated that a child who is 5 years old has received 5 million pieces of communication and the child's self-esteem has already been set. She also believed that dysfunction results from people's inaccurate perception of interactions and their unwillingness to accept other's differences. Most treatment programs for eating disorders have a strong emphasis on communication patterns and relearning healthier ways of communication and conflict resolution.

Systems Model

Bowen (1978) defined a family as a system and hypothesized that a person's current behavior results from a process that he called a "family projection process." Through this process, past history and behaviors are inappropriately applied to the present. Unresolved issues from the past, including those from the family of origin, are reenacted. In a family system, the child with the least degree of differentiation runs the highest risk in the family projection process and will develop problems later in life.

Bowen (1978) defined self-differentiation as the degree to which a person has a solid self or solidly held principles by which he or she lives life. This differentiation of self is similar to the concept of emotional maturity. Some characteristics of a differentiated self are (1) defined opinions, (2) goal orientation, (3) ability to achieve intimate relationships, and (4) differentiation from family. In the initial mate selection process, people are attracted to those with similar scales of differentiation, and they pass on their level of differentiation to their children. Thus, the child with the least degree of differentiation has a tendency to become involved in the marital dyad.

An advantage of the systemic viewpoint is the circular understanding of symptoms. The person with an eating disorder is not considered symptomatic because of a neurotransmitter imbalance or a "bad mother" (Root et al., 1986). Instead, family members and others adopted into the system have acted and reacted upon each other in unpredictable ways and continually change the nature of the field (Hoffman, 1981). This becomes especially clear when multigenerational issues are addressed. As the symptom diffuses, the system balances and harmonizes itself, and new rules and roles begin to emerge.

Structural Model

Minuchin (1974) emphasized that children learn function or dysfunction through family structure. Transactions that are unique to the family, such as levels of authority, power structures, and mutual expectations, make up the family structure (Lawson et al., 1983). This structure, created so that the spouses can meet each other's needs, becomes the core of the nuclear family. When children enter this family system, the functions need to be renegotiated. Dysfunction occurs if boundaries are not created between parent and child functions.

Parent-child relationships can be enmeshed, clear, or disengaged. In addictive families, enmeshment is clearly present; family members can read each other's minds, finish each other's sentences, and are reactive to each other. The boundaries in enmeshed families are diffuse and fluid. Such ambiguous boundaries that do not clearly define areas of authority and responsibility lead to confusion and a random method of problem solving. Boundary violations are a common occurrence in bulimic families. An extreme case of violation is sexual molestation; milder forms, such as the use of each other's belongings without asking for permission, also occur.

Social Learning Model

The work of Patterson (1971) led to the development of the social learning model, which is based on behaviorism and behavior modification. Patterson stated that children learn their style of interacting through the reactions that they received from their families in the past. Patterson's main theory is that reinforcement will increase the probability of the desired behavior and repeated nonreinforcement will decrease the probability of the desired behavior. Problems arise when negative behaviors are unknowingly reinforced.

There are four types of reinforcers (Patterson, 1971). The first type is a positive reinforcer, which is a reward for appropriate behavior and can be external or internal; the goal is to move toward internal reinforcers, such as self-worth and positive feelings. The second type is a negative reinforcer, which occurs when an unwanted experience is removed. The third type is punishment, which therapists do not use because of the carryover to positive behaviors. Finally, the fourth type is nonreinforcement; in this case, either the person is removed from the reinforcing environment, or the positive reinforcer (e.g., praise or attention) is removed. According to Patterson's theory of social learning, dysfunctional behavior, having been learned through parents and families, can be easily unlearned through operant conditioning and reinforcement techniques.

Family Transactions Model

Developments in sociopsychological theory, psychoanalytical/dynamic/ego psychology, general systems theory, communication theory, child development, group dynamics and sociology of family, and family therapy are blended together in the family transactions model (Framo, 1981). Symptoms are viewed as "disordered relationship events," and intrapsychic and transactional levels are considered necessary to understand the complete picture. Certain symptoms are designed to "help" family members remain in the family system. Consequently, there are a range of symptoms that help family members escape. In the example given by Framo, the child was so out of control that he had to be institutionalized; as a result, he did not have to deal with the guilt of having abandoned his family or feelings of disloyalty. In some couples, symptoms are necessary for the maintenance and survival of the relationship; in some families, symptoms are passed from one family member to another, usually an indicator that there is some imbalance in the family system.

REFERENCES

Ambert, A.M. (1976). *Sex structure*. Don Mills, Canada: Longman.

American Psychiatric Association. (1987). *Diagnostic and statistical manual of mental disorders* (3rd ed., rev. ed.). Washington, DC: Author.

Banner, L.W. (1983) *American beauty*. New York: Alfred A. Knopf.

Boskind-Lodahl, M. (1976). Cinderella's step-sisters: A feminist perspective on anorexia nervosa and bulimia. *Signs: Journal of Women in Culture and Society, 2,* 342–356.

Bowen, M. (1978). *Family therapy in clinical practice*. New York: James Aronson.

Bruch, H. (1973). *Eating disorders: Obesity, anorexia and the person within*. New York: Basic Books.

Cauwels, J. (1983). *Bulimia—The binge purge compulsion*. New York: Doubleday.

Chodorow, N. (1978). *The reproduction of mothering: Psychoanalysis and sociology of gender*. Berkeley: University of California Press.

Clausen, J. (1975). The social meaning of differential physical and sexual maturation. In S. Dragastin & J. Elder (Eds.), *Adolescence in the life cycle: Psychological change and social context* (pp. 77–89). Washington, DC: Hemisphere.

Crisp, A. (1980). *Anorexia nervosa: Let me be*. London: Academic Press.

Crisp, A.H., Palmer, R.L., & Kalucy, R.S. (1976). How common is anorexia nervosa: A prevalence study. *British Journal of Psychiatry, 218*, 549–554.

Dwyer, J., Feldman, J., Seltzer, C., & Mayer, J. (1969). Body image in adolescents: Attitudes towards weight and perception of appearance. *American Journal of Clinical Nutrition, 20*, 1045–1056.

Eckert, E.D. (1985). Characteristics of anorexia nervosa. In J.E. Mitchell (Ed.), *Anorexia nervosa & bulimia: Diagnosis & treatment* (pp. 3–28). Minneapolis: University of Minnesota Press.

Enright, A.B., Butterfield, P., & Berkowitz, B. (1985). Self help and support groups in the management of eating disorders. In D. Garner & P. Garfinkle (Eds.), *Handbook of psychotherapy of anorexia nervosa & bulimia*. New York: Guilford Press.

Framo, J. (1981). *Explorations in marital and family therapy: Selected papers of James L. Framo*. New York: Springer.

Garner, D., & Garfinkle, P. (Eds.). (1985). *Handbook for psychotherapy for anorexia nervosa and bulimia*. New York: Guilford Press.

Garner, D., & Garfinkle, P. (Eds.). (1987). *The role of drug treatments for eating disorders*. New York: Brunner/Mazel.

Gilligan, C. (1982). *In a different voice: Psychological theory and women's development*. Cambridge, MA: Harvard University Press.

Halmi, K.A., Falk, J.R., & Schwartz, E. (1981). Binge eating & vomiting: A survey of a college population. *Psychological Medicine, 11*, 697–706.

Havinghurst, R. (1972). *Developmental tasks and education*. New York: McCay.

Hawkins, R., & Clement, P. (1980). Development and construct-validation of a self report measure of binge eating tendencies. *Addictive Behaviors, 5*, 219–226.

Herzog, D. (1982). Bulimia: The secretive syndrome. *Psychosomatics, 23*, 481–483.

Hoffman, L. (1981). *Foundations of family therapy*. New York: Basic Books.

Hood, J., Moore, T., & Gardner, D. (1982). Locus of controls as a measure of ineffectiveness in anorexia nervosa. *Journal of Clinical and Consulting Psychology, 50*, 3–13.

Hovell, M., Mewborn, C., Randle, Y., & Fowler-Johnson, S. (1985). Risk of excess weight gain in university women: A three year community controlled analysis. *Addictive Behaviors, 10*, 15–28.

Hudson, J., Laffer, P., & Pope, H. (1982). Bulimia related to affective disorder by family history and response to dexamethosone suppression test. *American Journal of Psychiatry, 139*, 685–687.

Hudson, J., Pope, H., Jonas, J., Laffer, P., Hudson, M., & Melby, J. (1983). Hypothalamic-pituitary-adrenal axis hyperactivity in bulimia. *Psychiatry Research, 8*, 111–117.

Jackson, D. (Ed.). (1960). *The etiology of schizophrenia*. New York: Basic Books.

Jackson, D. (1968). *Communication, family and marriage*. Palo Alto, CA: Science and Behavior Books.

Johnson, C., & Larson, R. (1982). Bulimia: An analysis of moods and behavior. *Psychosomatic Medicine, 44*, 341–353.

Johnson, C., & Pure, D. (1986). Assessment of bulimia: A multidimensional model. In K. Brownell & J. Fozeyt (Eds.), *Handbook of eating disorders: Physiology, psychology and treatment of obesity, anorexia nervosa, and bulimia* (pp. 125–132). New York: Basic Books.

Kakaiya, D. (1991). *A comparison of perceptions of family environments and severity of bulimia in adult children of alcoholics and non-adult children of women*. Unpublished doctoral dissertation, United States International University, San Diego, CA.

Kaye, W., & Gwirtsman, H. (Eds.). (1985). *A comprehensive approach to the treatment of normal weight bulimia*. Washington, DC: American Psychiatric Press.

Lawson, G., Petersen, J., & Lawson, A. (1983). *Alcoholism and the family: A guide to treatment and prevention*. Gaithersburg, MD: Aspen Publishers.

Maloney, M.J., & Klykylo, W. (1983). An overview of anorexia nervosa, bulimia and obesity in children and adolescents. *Journal of American Academy of Child Psychiatry, 22,* 99.

Marino, D., & King, J. (1980). Nutritional concerns during adolescence. *Pediatric Clinics of North America, 27,* 125–139.

McFarland, B., & Baker-Baumann, T. (1988). *Feeding the empty heart: Adult children and compulsive eating*. Center City, MN: Hazelden.

Minuchin, S. (1974). *Families and family therapy*. Cambridge, MA: Harvard University Press.

Minuchin, S., Rosman, B., & Baker, L. (1978). *Psychosomatic families*. Cambridge, MA: Harvard University Press.

Mitchell, J., Pyle, R., Hatsukami, D., & Eckert, E. (1985). Characteristics of 275 patients with bulimia. *American Journal of Psychiatry, 142,* 482–485.

Neugarten, B. (1972). Personality and aging process. *Gerontologist, 12,* 9.

Neuman, P., & Halvorson, P. (1983). *Anorexia nervosa and bulimia: A handbook for counselors and therapists*. New York: Van Nostrand Reinhold.

Nylander, J. (1971). The feeling of being fat and dieting in a school population: Epidemiologic interview investigation. *Acta Sociomedica Scandinavica, 3,* 17–26.

Patterson, G. (1971). *Families*. Champaign, IL: Illinois Research Press.

Pennbaker, J., Barrios, B., & Hoover, C. (1983). *Psychological factors influencing the incidence of bulimia nervosa*. Unpublished manuscript available from J. Pennbaker, Department of Psychology, University of Virginia, Charlottesville, Virginia 22903.

Pope, H.A., & Hudson, J.I. (1982). Treatment of bulimia with antidepressants. *Psychopharmacology, 78,* 176–179.

Pope, H., & Hudson, J. (1988). Is bulimia nervosa a heterogenous disorder: Lessons in history and medicine. *International Journal of Eating Disorders, 2,* 155–166.

Pyle, R.L., Mitchell, J.E., & Eckert, E.D. (1981). Bulimia: A report of 34 cases. *Journal of Clinical Psychiatry, 42*(2), 60–64.

Pyle, R., Mitchell, J., Eckert, E., Halvorson, P., Neumann, P., & Goff, G. (1983). The incidence of bulimia in college freshmen students. *International Journal of Eating Disorders, 2*(3), 75–85.

Rodin, J., Striegel-Moore, R., & Silberstein, L. (1985). Women and weight: A normative discontent. In T.B. Sonderegger (Ed.), *Nebraska symposium on motivation: Vol. 32. Psychology and gender* (pp. 267–307). Lincoln, NE: University of Nebraska Press.

Root, M., & Fallon, P. (1985). *Victimization experiences as contributing factors in the development of bulimia in women*. Manuscript submitted for publication.

Root, M., Fallon, P., & Friedrich, W. (1986). *Bulimia: A systems approach to treatment*. New York: W.W. Norton.

Satir, V. (1967). *Conjoint family therapy*. Palo Alto, CA: Science and Behavior Books.

Schwartz, R. (1982). Bulimia and family therapy: A case study. *International Journal of Eating Disorders, 2,* 75–82.

Schwartz, R. (1988). *Bulimia: Psychoanalytic treatment and theory*. Madison, WI: International Universities Press.

Schwartz, R.C., Barrat, M.J., & Saba, G. (1985). Family therapy for bulimia. In M. Garner & P.E. Garfinkle (Eds.), *Handbook of psychotherapy for anorexia nervosa & bulimia* (pp. 280–310). New York: Guilford Press.

Sights, J., & Richards, H. (1984). Parents of bulimic women. *International Journal of Eating Disorders, 3,* 3–13.

Simmons, R., Bluth, D., & McKinney, K. (1983). The social and psychological effects of puberty on white females. In J. Brooks-Gunn & A. Petersen (Eds.), *Girls at puberty* (pp. 168–175). New York: Plenum Press.

Steele, C. (1980). Weight loss among teenage girls: An adolescent crisis. *Adolescence, 15,* 823–829.

Stunkcard, A. (1985). *A twin study of human obesity.* Unpublished manuscript, University of Pennsylvania, Philadelphia.

Svensden, D., & Cusin, J. (1980). *Eating disorders in the college student: Anorexia and bulimia.* Paper presented at the American College Health Association Annual Meeting, San Diego, CA.

Valette, B. (1988). *Eating disorders.* Deresden, TN: Avon.

Vincent, L.M. (1980). *Competing with the sylph: Dancers and the pursuit of the ideal body form.* New York: Andrews and McMeel.

Walsh, B.T., Stewart, J.W., Roose, S.P., Gladis, M., & Glassman, A.H. (1984). Treatment of bulimia with phenelzine: A double-blind placebo controlled study. *Archives of General Psychiatry, 41,* 1105–1109.

Weiss, S., & Ebert, M. (1983). Psychological and behavioral characteristics of normal-weight bulimics and normal-weight controls. *Psychosomatic Medicine, 45,* 293–303.

Williamson, D. (1990). *Assessment of eating disorders: Obesity. anorexia, and bulimia nervosa.* New York: Pergamon Press.

23

Vision Problems, Juvenile Delinquency, and Drug Abuse

Ann W. Lawson and Robert Sanet

The link between vision disorders and adolescent drug abuse lies in understanding the commonalities shared by the fields of optometry and psychology—the study of perception. "Perception is the process by which we organize and interpret the patterns of stimuli in our environment" (Hilgard, Atkinson, & Atkinson, 1979, p. 129). Perception of things and events takes place within space and time. Vision and hearing supply these perceptions, but vision is the dominant sense in that it gives a perception of succession, movement, and change. Eighty percent of our information about the world comes through the eyes.

Just as there is a difference between hearing and listening, there is a difference between sight and vision. Sight is a function of the eyes alone, while vision involves the interplay of the eyes and the brain. The eyes do not send images directly to the brain. They are carried by nonvisual electrical impulses through the optic nerves. The brain then interprets the eye's images and gives meaning to the eye's messages (Seiderman & Marcus, 1989). People are born with sight; vision is learned. Perspective is a learned concept of the eye and brain. To the eye, something appears small in the distance, or the road appears to narrow; experience has taught the brain that appearances can be misleading, however. Interpretation is also a factor in perception, as is clearly evident in the variance of multiple eye witness reports to crimes. All the witnesses saw the same thing, yet they may all give slightly different interpretations of what they saw.

Psychologists study visual perceptions such as figure-ground relationships, shape and size constancy, brightness and color constancy, optical illusions, movement and depth perception, learning in perception, attention, and even extrasensory perception. They are concerned with the functional processes of the brain. Optometrists are concerned with eye disorders and vision, the "individual's ability to react to and interact with his environment on the basis of information received through the eyes" (Peiser, 1972, p. 152). Optometric evaluations are concerned with eye problems, physiological vision problems, and visual-perceptual difficulties (Seiderman, 1976). Eye problems include the following:

- ocular pathology
- visual acuity
- refractive errors, such as myopia (i.e., nearsightedness), hyperopia (i.e., far-sightedness), and astigmatism
- strabismus, the condition in which the eyes are not both directed toward the fixation point or the turning in or out of the eye (also called cross-eye or wall-eye)
- amblyopia, a reduction in visual acuity that cannot be improved with corrective lenses or is not a result of a disease (also called lazy eye)
- nystagmus, an involuntary to-and-fro movement of the eye; a disturbance of the mechanisms that hold images steady

Physiological vision problems include defects in the functioning of the visual system, such as binocular fusion or the inability to use both eyes simultaneously, accommodation or the ability to focus, fixation, and eye movements. The third area of evaluation, visual-perceptual skills, is of particular interest to the developmental optometrist concerned with learning-disabled children. These skills include visual-verbal match, figure-ground perception, directionality in space, visual form perception, visual-motor coordination, and visual imagery. Seiderman (1976) stated that, because "perception is the end-product of the total process of vision, the eye practitioner must or should be concerned with perception" (p. 336). It is this last area that links the optometrist and the psychologist, as both need to understand the role that visual problems play in juvenile delinquency and adolescent drug abuse.

VISION DEVELOPMENT

More than 98% of infants are born with healthy eyes. Having normal, healthy eyes does not guarantee good vision, however. Vision takes at least 10 years to develop in humans (Seiderman & Marcus, 1989). Gesell, a pioneer in the study of children's vision, explained that a child is "born with a pair of eyes, but not with a visual world. He must build that world himself, and it is his private creation. . . . The space world thus becomes part of him. To no small degree, he is it" (Gesell, as cited in Seiderman & Marcus, 1989, p. 28). Visual development occurs in stages much like physical, emotional, and social development does. Yet, it is much more subtle and hard to recognize (Gessell, 1949).

Vision development is measured in inches and feet. The vision of a newborn is focused at approximately 8 inches, just enough to see the mother's face. It is not yet the dominant sense. As motor development occurs, so does vision development. Binocular vision begins to develop, which in turn helps the child understand space. This space extends to approximately 3 feet with mid-range vision to 10 feet when the child is 8 to 12 months old. This is also when visual memory and recognition of familiar faces and objects begins. By the time the child is 2 years old, vision must be coordinated with walking and talking. Language and vision work together to create words for the objects seen. The 2-year-old has binocular vision of 2 to 3 feet and can recognize a face at 5 to 8 feet. This is also the stage at which cause-and-effect thinking begins and object constancy develops.

At 3 years of age, the child understands the concepts of near and far, up and down; his or her personal space has expanded to 7 to 10 feet. Full binocular vision is present. The child is able to scan and coordinate hand and eye movements. Half-way through this third year, however, the child regresses and becomes less coordinated in his or her visual and motor systems. He or she is exploring space in a new way. For this reason, his or her eye-hand movements and binocular vision may seem to work less well than they did previously. By the fourth year, however, the child's visual space has expanded to 10 to 16 feet, and visual-motor coordination is advanced enough for complicated movements such as throwing a ball (Seiderman & Marcus, 1989).

Hendrickson (1969) reported on the vision development process and reviewed A.M. Skeffington's model of four overlapping, intertwining circles of vision performance.

1. Antigravity. A child must struggle against gravity to lift the head, to roll over, to sit, and then to stand. This process gives the child information about his or her space in the world and a zero point from which to move. This stage focuses on the question, Where am I in space?

2. Centering. The child learns to shift attention from one sense or one object to another. This is also a process of whereness, of knowing where things are. Binocular vision is important at this stage. Eye teaming, the use of two eyes together, is learned through movement. Out of this movement comes directionality, the knowing of where sides are. This allows the child to distinguish a *b* from a *d* or to determine which side of the *n* is correct for the *o* (*on* or *no*). This is the stage of the question, Where is it?

3. Identification. The child uses all of his or her senses to identify texture, temperature, size, shape, color, loudness, odors, tastes, distances, etc. This is the stage of the question, What is it?

4. Speech-auditory. The child matches patterns of sound and speech to form language throughout development. During this process, visualization and visual memory occur. The child can create a visual image of someone or something even though he or she is not currently looking at the person or object.

Dzik (1966) renamed these four stages of preschool perceptual skills, calling them Locomotion, Location, Labeling, and Language: the Four Ls. These are the skills that children use to understand the printed word. They are learned through a combination of visual and motor skills and make up visual perception—"seeing for meaning–getting meaning from what you see" (Dzik, 1966, p. 466).

Visual problems are multicausal, having physiological, social, and psychological variables. Vision must be stimulated. Children who are confined inside a building or spend too much time watching television are limiting their visual experience. Unfortunately, video games have replaced good motor development games, such as hopscotch, jump rope, and jacks. A delay in motor development can retard the learning of visual skills. Children who wear orthopedic braces or are restricted in sitting up, crawling, creeping, or walking are at an increased risk for visual problems. Fine motor coordination problems, such as difficulty in buttoning buttons or tying shoes, may also signal vision problems. Furthermore, nutrition is important for good vision development. The eyes and brain use up one fourth of the body's nutrition (Seiderman & Marcus, 1989). Poor nutrition can weaken the structure of the eyes and may cause myopia.

Even personality may be a factor in the development of myopia. Researchers have been able to predict which subjects have myopia simply from the subjects' responses on psychological and vocational interest tests (Young, Singer, & Foster, 1975). There is also some evidence that poor vision development is correlated with poor intellectual development in infancy and preschool years (Gottfried & Gilman, 1985). Some learning disabilities are believed to result from vision problems, and vision therapy has been effective in remedial work with learning-disabled children (Seiderman, 1980). Vision problems and learning disabilities are believed to be predecessors of substance abuse and juvenile delinquency (Dunivant, 1982).

VISION TRAINING

Often referred to as vision training, "vision therapy trains the brain to give the correct instructions to the muscles of the eye" (Seiderman & Marcus, 1989, p. 21). The goal of vision training is a balance between central and peripheral awareness. This training or therapy is helpful in remediating learning disabilities that have their basis in visual-perceptual problems.

The use of the Snellen Eye Chart to screen school-aged children does not detect visual-perceptual problems. This procedure reveals only the student's ability to read the chart (or blackboard) with each eye from 20 feet away, thus explaining the term 20/20 vision. In spite of this "perfect vision," however, many children cannot learn to read or achieve academically to their intellectual potential. A comprehensive vision screening is necessary to detect any visual blocks to learning that are detrimental. This screening should include tests of

1. visual acuity for far vision for seeing the blackboard and near vision for seeing books and close work clearly
2. eye movement control for keeping place when reading, copying from one place to another, and aligning math problems
3. focusing ability for copying from the blackboard to the desk and for sustaining focus when reading and writing
4. eye teaming or convergence for enduring desk work
   a. fusion, near for reading accuracy, speed, and comprehension
   b. fusion, far for ability to see the chalkboard without stress
   c. stereopsis for all tasks involving depth perception
   d. phoria, near for accuracy in sustained desk work
   e. phoria, far for attentional skills
   f. phoria, vertical for proper posture and head alignment
5. eye structure for seeing clearly and comfortably at all distances
6. visual-motor integration for discriminating letters, words, and handwriting, as well as for copying from one place to another

Children with vision problems may do well in school from kindergarten through the third grade, but find the increased demands of reading and written work in the fourth grade more than they can handle with their perceptual problems. Thus, teachers and school nurses are often able to identify children who would benefit from vision training. Exhibit 23-1 is a checklist that educators can use to screen students in the classroom for vision problems. This screening process has pass, fail, or borderline criteria. It does not quantify or specify the exact problem or needs of the child.

A more exact diagnostic process requires an optometrist with training in developmental optometry and vision training. The College of Optometrists in Vision Development certifies optometrists in this speciality (Seiderman & Marcus, 1989), but the theory and procedures of diagnosis and management of vision disorders are taught in all schools of optometry (Cohen, 1988). A complete diagnostic evaluation includes exact measurement of the following areas:

1. eye health
2. visual acuity
3. visual tracking
4. focusing
5. eye coordination (e.g., muscle balance)
6. refractive error (e.g., need for glasses)
7. visual-perceptual skills

Exhibit 23-1 Educator's Checklist: Observable Clues to Classroom Vision Problems

Student's
Name_____ Date_____

1. **APPEARANCE OF EYES:**

   One eye turns in or out at any time _____
   Reddened eyes or lids _____
   Eyes tear excessively _____
   Encrusted eyelids _____
   Frequent styes on lids _____

2. **COMPLAINTS WHEN USING EYES AT DESK:**

   Headaches in forehead or temples _____
   Burning or itching after reading or desk work _____
   Nausea or dizziness _____
   Print blurs after reading a short time _____

3. **BEHAVIORAL SIGNS OF VISUAL PROBLEMS:**

   A. *Eye Movement Abilities (Ocular Motility)*
      Head turns as reads across page _____
      Loses place often during reading _____
      Needs finger or marker to keep place _____
      Displays short attention span in reading or copying _____
      Too frequently omits words _____
      Repeatedly omits "small" words _____
      Writes up or down hill on paper _____
      Rereads or skips lines unknowingly _____
      Orients drawings poorly on page _____

   B. *Eye Teaming Abilities (Binocularity)*
      Complains of seeing double (diplopia) _____
      Repeats letters within words _____
      Omits letters, numbers, or phrases _____
      Misaligns digits in number columns _____
      Squints, closes, or covers one eye _____
      Tilts head extremely while working at desk _____
      Consistently shows gross postural deviations at all desk activities _____

   C. *Eye-Hand Coordination Abilities*
      Must feel of things to assist in any interpretation required _____
      Eyes not used to "steer" hand movements (extreme lack of orientation,
         placement or words or drawings on page)
      Writes crookedly, poorly spaced: cannot stay on ruled lines _____
      Misaligns both horizontal and vertical series of numbers _____
      Uses hand or fingers to keep place on the page _____
      Uses other hand as "spacer" to control spacing and alignment on page _____
      Repeatedly confuses left-right directions _____

Exhibit 23-1 continued

D. *Visual Form Perception (Visual Comparison, Visual Imagery, Visualization)*
Mistakes words with same or similar beginnings   ____
Fails to recognize same word in next sentence   ____
Reverses letters and/or words in writing and copying   ____
Confuses likenesses and minor differences   ____
Confuses same word in same sentence   ____
Repeatedly confuses similar beginnings and endings of words   ____
Fails to visualize what is read either silently or orally   ____
Whispers to self for reinforcement while reading silently   ____
Returns to "drawing with fingers" to decide likes and differences   ____

E. *Refractive Status (Nearsightedness, Farsightedness, Focus Problems, etc.)*
Comprehension reduces as reading continues: loses interest too quickly   ____
Mispronounces similar words as continues reading   ____
Blinks excessively at desk tasks and/or reading; not elsewhere   ____
Holds book too closely; face too close to desk surface   ____
Avoids all possible near-centered tasks   ____
Complains of discomfort in tasks that demand visual interpretation   ____
Closes or covers one eye when reading or doing desk work   ____
Makes errors in copying from chalkboard to paper on desk   ____
Makes errors in copying from reference book to notebook   ____
Squints to see chalkboard, or requests to move nearer   ____
Rubs eyes during or after short periods of visual activity   ____
Fatigues easily; blinks to make chalkboard clear up after desk task   ____

OBSERVER'S SUGGESTIONS:

Signed (Print) _____

(Encircle) Teacher, Nurse, Remedial Teacher, Psychologist, Vision Consultant, Other

Phone _____

Address _____

_____

_____

Source: Reprinted with permission from the Optometric Extension Program Foundation, Santa Ana, CA.

If these tests reveal any visual problem, the optometrist creates a treatment plan. Training routines often isolate the functions of binocular vision and remediate those that are inadequate. Such routines commonly involve familiar tasks done under unfamiliar conditions (Siederman & Marcus, 1989). Sometimes devices are used to separate the sight in the two eyes (Polaroid glasses) or stimulate the focusing system (prisms). With practice, the brain learns to send the correct instructions to the eye. Other kinds of vision, such as peripheral vision and reaction times, can be improved with this form of therapy. For learning-disabled children, vision training can improve eye-hand coordination, visual memory, and figure-ground perception. These training activities involve a kind of visual biofeedback and gamelike exercises with materials such as strings with beads (Brock String) and parquetry blocks.

> The treatment may appear to be relatively uncomplicated, such as patching an eye as part of amblyopia therapy. Or, it may require complex infrared sensing devices and computers which monitor eye position and provide feedback to the patient to reduce the uncontrolled jumping of an eye with nystagmus. (Cohen, 1988, p. 95)

Vision therapy is provided in the optometrist's office, usually by a staff of trained specialists who work under the optometrist's supervision. Sessions are scheduled for 1 to 2 hours weekly for 3 to 9 months. Homework assignments consist of exercises that the patient does for 10 to 20 minutes per day, depending on the patient's age. Because the patient's motivation is very important in order to obtain maximum benefits from the exercises, it is essential to provide praise and other reinforcement for all efforts. This is especially true for children who have experienced nothing but failure; often their self-esteem needs repair. Vision training should begin at a level where these children can be successful and then build on that success. Once the therapy has been completed, the results are usually lasting because the habit of doing it correctly is reinforced daily.

VISION AND JUVENILE DELINQUENCY

Optometrists first began to explore the link between poor vision performance and juvenile delinquency when Dzik (1966, 1968) found that 91% of 350 children in the Hamilton County, Tennessee, juvenile facilities were low-achieving students who read below grade level. All these students had failed some sort of vision examination. In 1965, Dzik (1966) found that 94% of 125 youths at a detention home were reading below their grade level. Given a battery of vision tests, 48% of these juveniles failed near vision tests, 35% failed both near and far tests, 53% failed perception tests, and a total of 72% failed one or more of the tests of their visual skills. In a third study, in 1967, Dzik (1968) found 90% of the youths in these same facilities reading one to seven grades below their grade level. Dzik proposed that stress-relieving glasses and vision training could help these adolescents to read better and enhance their school performance. He believed that avoidance of the close (near point) work that stressed their eyes resulted in lower reading abilities, loss of self-esteem, and misbehavior.

Many of these adolescents may have shown signs of vision problems early in life; because these problems went undiagnosed, the children were labeled hyperactive, mischievous, or hard to discipline. Such a label can shape the responses that children receive from their parents. By the time they enter school, they may have a failure identity. The visual demands of school reinforce this identity. Bright, underachieving children often find destructive ways to channel their energy.

After completing these studies, Dzik (1975) compiled a list of five preconditions to juvenile delinquency.

1. lack of proper supervision by the family
2. improper discipline (i.e., too much or too little)
3. lack of family projects, preventing family members from feeling like part of the team
4. a great deal of energy and aggressiveness that is unsupervised
5. nonachievement in the classroom, resulting in a failure identity

School failure shuts off adolescents even further from sports and other activities in which they may be successful. Additionally, Dzik found that juvenile delinquents often had 20/20 for distance vision, but poor near vision.

Dzik might just as well have been describing an alcoholic family environment with their preconditions. When one or both parents are alcoholic(s) or addict(s), parenting and a sense of family belonging or cohesion are usually unavailable for the adolescent. Children of alcoholics are at an increased risk for developing addictions and other destructive behaviors. It is no wonder that many of the juvenile delinquents with vision problems reported in studies of this population had high drug use (Kaseno, 1986).

More recent studies have replicated Dzik's findings. In a study conducted in 1972, less than 10% of the juveniles in the Indiana Boys School passed a perceptual motor test battery (Dowis, 1977, 1984). Visual training was given to 158 of 391 boys for 10 weeks. At the end of the training, their reading level had increased two grade levels. Only 11 of the boys (6.5%) returned to the school, compared to a 31% average recidivism rate.

In 1973, Dowis tested 444 adjudicated delinquents at the Colorado Division of Youth Services. He found that 90.4% had multiple learning disorders and were reading an average of 2.7 years below their grade level. Vision training was given to 48 of these juveniles for $4^{1}/_{2}$ months. Recidivism was reduced in this group from 18% to 4% ($p < .005$).

Bachara and Zaba (1978) attempted to improve on the previous research designs by using a control group. They tested a total of 79 juvenile delinquents from Tidewater, Virginia, for learning disabilities and divided them into two groups. They were two grade years behind in reading as measured by the Wide Range Achievement Test, and 90% were at least 1 year behind academically according to age equivalent grade placement. The subjects fell within a normal range of intelligence (90–110) as measured by the Wechesler Intelligence Scale for Children (WISC) and the Wechesler Adult Intelligence Scale (WAIS). In each case the problem was diagnosed as learning disabilities based on psychological testing and supplemental data. Group A (n = 48) was given traditional treatment, including counseling, remediation, and drug treatment. Group B (n = 31) received help with learning disabilities, including vision training, close supervision, and group counseling. The recidivism rate over 2 years was 41.6% for Group A and 6.5% for Group B ($p < .01$). This study had several flaws, however. The subjects were not randomly assigned, and there was a significant age variable (mean age 15 years, 3 months versus 13 years, 1 month). Younger, more motivated subjects may have been assigned to the vision training group.

Harris (1989), working with the Optometric Center of Maryland, conducted one study at a juvenile detention facility in Baltimore County. They conducted a double-blind study with random group assignment. Juveniles were divided into three groups: (1) a control group that received no treatment; (2) an alternate treatment group that received 24 half-hour sessions of individualized reading instruction in the same vicinity as the vision training; and (3) an experimental group that received 24 half-hour sessions of one-to-one vision training and glasses, if needed. Nonservice providers were unaware of which treatment was being provided to which subjects during the pre- and post-testing. Only preliminary data were reported, but Harris found slightly more than 98% of the subjects had visual problems. Most of the subjects did not have the basic developmental visual abilities necessary to handle the demands of the educational environment. He surmised that they had given up in the first grade (Harris, 1989). Unfortunately, this project was abandoned; the second and third stages of the project were not conducted (Optometric Extension Program, 1992).

Kaseno (1986) attempted to determine if the conclusions that Dzik had reached in the 1960s were still true today. He discovered that 9 of 10 adolescents incarcerated in San Bernadino, California, Juvenile Hall had major visual perceptual disorders. Between July 1980 and June 1985, Kaseno provided vision training to 506 adolescents at the juvenile facility. These adolescents were given 24 half-hour sessions. Of this group, 85% had been in some kind of special education, and 80% had failed at least one grade. They were an average of 6 years behind in reading. As a result of this project, the adolescents increased their average reading level by 3.1 grade levels and improved their IQ by 5 points. This institution had a record of 60% recidivism. There was a 46% decrease in recidivism in this group; only 14% of those who were treated returned. This has become an ongoing project that treats the 400 wards of San Bernadino Juvenile Hall. They provide 5,000 annual patient contacts, including visual examinations, perceptual-visual evaluations, consultations, vision therapy, progress evaluations, audiograms, dyslexia determination tests, and miscellaneous services (Berman, 1989). To date, approximately 10,000 adolescents have been evaluated and helped at the San Bernadino project (Shapiro, 1992). Similar results of vision therapy with juvenile offenders have been reported in South Africa (Stekli, 1990) and Australia (Pitt, 1990).

DRUG ABUSE PREVENTION

Many of the juvenile delinquents in whom vision problems were diagnosed also had drug abuse problems. The San Bernadino Project has proposed a study that will examine the connection between vision problems and substance abuse of incarcerated adolescents. In considering the ways in which vision training could be useful in drug prevention, it is easy to see how early screening, testing, and intervention with vision problems could give these children the tools that they need to be successful in school, to have a better family life, to improve their self-esteem, and to become productive citizens. Figure 23-1 illustrates the spiraling problems that can result from undiagnosed and untreated vision problems.

Pitt (1990) tested 75 incarcerated juveniles in Australia between the ages of 13 and 22; the mean age being 17.37. Of the 75 subjects, 36% (27) showed problems with accommodation (focusing). Because substances such as caffeine, alcohol, prescription and nonprescription drugs have some effect on the autonomic nervous system, and therefore accommodation, Pitt was interested in the drug use of his subjects. Through voluntary admission of his subjects, he determined that many of them were using nonprescribed drugs such as cocaine, marijuana, heroin, and amphetamines in addition to alcohol and tobacco. Of the 27 subjects with reduced accommodation, 63% (17) reported drug abuse compared to 33.3% (16) with normal accommodation. Pitt concluded that the drug use may be affecting accommodation instead of being a result of accommodation problems and thus school failure. Whether the drug use precedes the vision problems or is a consequence of them, there is an unusually high percentage of incarcerated juveniles with vision problems.

The expectations of society and the school system are often overwhelming for these children. To achieve at the college level, for example, students need a visual system that enables them

1. to read comfortably and rapidly for long stretches of time,
2. to keep their attention concentrated for all that time,

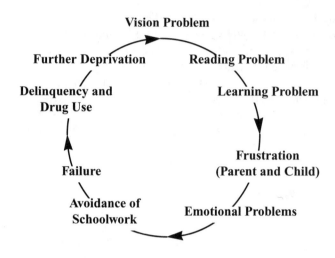

Figure 23-1 Spiraling Problem of Delinquency

Exhibit 23-2 Optometric Resources

RESOURCES FOR LOCATING AN OPTOMETRIST SPECIALIZING IN VISION TRAINING

1. College of Optometrists in Vision Development
   P.O. Box 285
   Chula Vista, CA 92012
   (619) 425-6191

2. Optometric Extension Program Foundation Inc.
   2912 South Daimler Street
   Santa Ana, CA 92705-5811
   (714) 250-8070

OPTOMETRIC PROFESSIONALS

Optometrists	Complete 4 years postcollege professional school of optometry; examine and treat eyes for disease; prescribe glasses, contact lenses, and vision therapy (varies from state to state)
Opthalmologists	Have medical specialty; treat disease and perform surgery; may or may not prescribe glasses and contact lenses
Opticians	Make glasses prescribed by others
Oculists	Once applied to both optometrists and opthalmologists but no longer used

3. to process the information contained in what they are reading quickly and accurately, and
4. to store it accurately and efficiently for quick retrieval. (Seiderman & Marcus, 1989, p. 75)

It seems logical that students who are able to do these things will succeed in school and other activities, will develop a positive self-image, and will resist using drugs. The ideal way to provide these skills and remediation for the children who need them is early screening. Wheeler (1984) advocated a prevention program with the following guidelines:

1. State legislatures must enact laws that mandate developmental vision evaluations for juvenile delinquents.
2. Court intake forms should have a vision referral component.
3. State juvenile service commissions should have optometric consultants.
4. State training schools should have optometric consultants.
5. Schools should examine children at an early age to identify those at high risk for vision problems.
6. States must require vision screening programs in primary grades that go beyond the Snellen Eye Chart.
7. Public Law 94-142 should be changed to require the identification of children with visually based learning disabilities and to mandate the provision of vision therapy through the individualized education program (IEP) process.
8. Educational programs must be developed to increase community awareness and public support.
9. Preventive family counseling should be available to educate all family members about the learning-disabled juvenile and to repair poor relationships, improve parenting, and create a sense of family cohesion.

Considering the costs of remediation of drug abuse (often $30,000) and juvenile delinquency ($28,000 per year of incarceration), it would be cost-effective for local, state, and federal government to provide these services. It seems logical that the War on Drugs should focus on saving children at an early age.

REFERENCES

American Optometric Association Board of Trustees. (1966). *Policy Manual.* Alexandria, VA.

Bachara, G., & Zaba, J. (1978). Learning disabilities and juvenile delinquency. *Journal of Learning Disabilities, 11*(4) 58–62.

Berman, M.S. (1989). Vision care in a juvenile detention facility. *Optometry and Vision Science, 66*(1), 23–25.

Cohen, A. (1988). The efficacy of optometric vision therapy. *Journal of the American Optometric Association, 59*(2), 95–105.

Dowis, R. (1977). The effect of a visual training program on juvenile delinquency. *Journal of the American Optometric Association, 48*(9), 1173–1176.

Dowis, R. (1984). The importance of vision in the prevention of learning disabilities and juvenile delinquency. *Journal of Optometric Vision Development, 15*(3), 20–22.

Dunivant, N. (1982). *The relationship between learning disabilities and juvenile delinquency.* Williamsburg, VA: National Center for State Courts.

Dzik, D. (1966). Vision and the juvenile delinquent. *Journal of the American Optometric Association, 37*(5), 461–468.

Dzik, D. (1968, January 25). Behavioral optometric vision—A practical and comprehensive plan for juvenile delinquency control. *Optometric Weekly*, pp. 23–29.

Dzik, D. (1975). Optometric intervention in the control of juvenile delinquents. *Journal of the American Optometric Association, 46*(6), 629–634.

Gesell, A. (1949). *Vision: Its development in infant and child.* New York: Paul B. Hoeber.

Gottfried, A., & Gilman, G. (1985). Visual skills and intellectual development: A relationship in young children. *Journal of the American Optometric Association, 56*(7).

Harris, P. (1989). The prevalence of visual conditions in a population of juvenile delinquents. *Curriculum II, 61*(4), 1–24.

Hendrickson, H. (1969). The vision development process. In R.M. Wold (Ed.), *Visual and perceptual aspects for the achieving and underachieving child* (pp. 45–57). Seattle: Special Child Publications.

Hilgard, E., Atkinson, A., & Atkinson, R. (1979). *Introduction to psychology* (7th ed.). New York: Harcourt Brace Jovanovich.

Kaseno, S. (1986). Screening and treatment program for vision and learning disabilities among juvenile delinquents. *Curriculum II, 58*(7), 1–8.

Optometric Extension Program. (1992). Personal communication.

Peiser, I.J. (1972). Vision and learning disabilities. *Journal of the American Optometric Association, 43*, 152–159.

Pitt, A. (1990). Accommodation deficits in a group of young offenders. *Australian Orthoptic Journal, 16*, 1–5.

Seiderman, A. (1976). An optometric approach to the diagnosis of visually based problems in learning. In G. Leisman (Ed.), *Basic visual processes and learning disability* (pp. 330–343). Springfield, IL: Charles C. Thomas.

Seiderman, A. (1980). Optometric vision therapy—Results of a demonstration project with a learning disabled population. *Journal of the American Optometric Association, 51*(5), 489–493.

Seiderman, A., & Marcus, S. (1989). *20/20 is not enough.* New York: Alfred A. Knopf.

Shapiro, S. (1992). Vision and juvenile delinquency. *Eyecare Business, 7*(3), 23–25.

Stekli, A. (1990). Visual dysfunction, learning disability, and juvenile delinquency. *South Africa Optometry, 49*(4), 189–193.

Wheeler, T. (1984). *Vision, juvenile delinquency and learning disorders* (Series 1, Number 12). Santa Ana, CA: Optometric Extension Program.

Young, F., Singer, R., & Foster, D. (1975). The psychological differentiation of male myopes and nonmyopes. *American Journal of Optometry and Physiological Optics, 52*, 679–686.

24

Drug Use Among
Pregnant Adolescents

Lewayne D. Gilchrist, Mary Rogers Gillmore, and Mary Jane Lohr

Although problem behaviors in adolescence are often discussed as part of a "syndrome" of deviance (see Donovan & Jessor, 1985; Jessor & Jessor, 1977), surprisingly little research focuses specifically on the interaction of two or more such behaviors. One reason is that the structure of federal funding in the United States has resulted in the study of separate problems without particular concern for interconnections among problem behaviors (Baumrind, 1987).

Rates for both sexual intercourse and drug use among adolescent women have risen substantially in recent decades (Hayes, 1987; Johnston, O'Malley, & Bachman, 1988). One important negative consequence of high substance use among young sexually active women is underscored in research identifying drug use during pregnancy as a major cause of fetal abnormalities and developmental anomalies in children (Chasnoff, 1988; Little, Snell, Klein, & Gilstrap, 1989; Zuckerman et al., 1989). The spread of AIDS into the heterosexual population and rising incidence of human immunodeficiency virus (HIV) infection in infants have added to concern about patterns of sexual behavior and drug use among sexually active and pregnant women. However, despite concern over the co-occurrence of substance use and unplanned pregnancy among adolescents and despite the recognized importance to infant health of preventing drug use during pregnancy, surprisingly little information is available about drug use before, during, and after pregnancy in adolescence (Irwin & Millstein, 1986; Yamaguchi & Kandel, 1987; Zuckerman, Amaro, & Beardslee, 1987).

Research on drug use among sexually active and pregnant adolescent women is important for other reasons. The bulk of studies to date that have shaped thinking about the etiology and prevention of drug use have been conducted with in-

Source: From *Drug Use Among Pregnant Adolescents* by L.D. Gilchrist, M.R. Gillmore and M.J. Lohr, 1990, *Journal of Consulting and Clinical Psychology, 58*, pp. 402–407. Copyright 1990 by the American Psychological Association, Inc. Reprinted by permission.

school populations (Johnston, O'Malley, & Bachman, 1988; Jones & Battjes, 1985). One important group of adolescents who are routinely missed by school-based programs are pregnant young women. Some sexually active young women drop out of school for many reasons prior to pregnancy (Hofferth, 1987). Some drop out because of pregnancy. Even when a young woman plans to complete high school, in very few school districts do pregnant students remain in regular classes. Later, even for well-motivated young mothers, child care and financial problems often interfere with completion of schooling (Hofferth & Hayes, 1987). Thus, agencies that serve pregnant and parenting adolescents may be important sites for etiological and survey research related to drug use and for delivery of interventions to prevent or reduce drug use.

This chapter reviews what is known about substance use among sexually active adolescent women. The authors report early data from a longitudinal study in progress on drug use before and during pregnancy in adolescence to support the contention that these young women constitute a special high-risk group.

DRUG USE AND SEXUAL ACTIVITY IN ADOLESCENT WOMEN

Drug Use and Sexual Activity

In the United States, 42% to 50% of adolescent women ages 15 to 19 are sexually active (Hayes, 1987; Moore, 1988). In one of the very few non–school-based studies of drug use and sexual activity in adolescent women, Zabin (1984) demonstrates unusually high rates of smoking in these young women compared with school-based counterparts. Zabin's study documents a strong negative relation between age of first intercourse and level of cigarette smoking. Smoking is also negatively associated with consistent contraceptive behavior and thus potentially with higher rates of unintended pregnancy.

Positive associations between drug use and sexual behavior for both male and female adolescents have been observed by a number of researchers (Elliott & Morse, 1988; Mott & Haurin, 1988; Newcomb & Bentler, 1988; Yamaguchi & Kandel, 1987; Zabin, Hardy, Smith, & Hirsch, 1986). Growing evidence supports consistent differences between Blacks and Whites in the relation between rates of substance use and rates of sexual activity. Nationally, the prevalence of substance use is relatively low among Black adolescents, whereas the incidence of sexual initiation and premarital pregnancy at early ages is high. For White adolescents, the prevalence of substance use is considerably higher, but the incidence of sexual initiation, especially at young ages, is lower than that of Blacks. Yet within each of these groups, a positive relation exists between substance use and sexual activity (Zabin et al., 1986).

In a well-designed longitudinal study, one of the few addressing the relation between sexual activity and drug use in a national sample of adolescents, Elliott and Morse (1988) found positive relations at the bivariate level between prevalence and incidence of intercourse and extent of drug use (and incidentally extent of delinquency). Although the prevalence of both sexual intercourse and substance use was greater for young men than for young women, as is typically found, positive associations for these behaviors were apparent for both genders. Elliott and Morse also examined the risk of pregnancy within 1 year of the onset of sexual intercourse for unmarried female adolescents. They found that, relative to the risk of pregnancy for the sample as a whole, for those who engaged in no drug use at the time of onset of sexual activity, the probability of a premarital pregnancy was less than or equal to that of the general adolescent population. For those who used illicit drugs at the time of onset of sexual intercourse, the probability of becoming premaritally pregnant was higher than that of the general adolescent population.

The only other study employing a national probability sample in which the relations among sexual activity and drug use have been examined is that reported recently by Mott and Haurin (1988). A limitation of this study is the retrospective data collection procedure requiring subjects to recall their drug use some 7 years earlier. Despite this limitation, these investigators have presented one of the few studies that addresses alcohol use, marijuana use, and sexual intercourse for each of three racial/ethnic groups: Whites, Hispanics, and Blacks. For girls in all racial groups and all but the youngest age groups, marijuana use appears to be more strongly associated with sexual initiation than does regular monthly (but not regular weekly) alcohol use. Despite this finding linking sexual initiation and marijuana use, the most common pattern identified by Mott and Haurin (1988) for all adolescent subgroups was sex only (i.e., no use of alcohol or marijuana just before or just after initiation of sex).

Drug Use and Pregnancy

Among sexually active women, 23.9% experience at least one pregnancy before age 18 (Hayes, 1987). Many of these unintended pregnancies in adolescence end in abortion. Hayes reports that 40% of pregnancies in women ages 15 to 19 are aborted; for women under the age of 15, the rate is 1.4 abortions for every live birth. Nonetheless, substantial numbers of young women choose to carry their pregnancies to term. Many oft-reported correlates of early pregnancy and childbearing (e.g., lower socioeconomic status [SES], low educational achievement, dropping out of school, lack of parental guidance, family conflict, and peer influence) are notably similar to correlates reported for early substance use (Hawkins, Lishner, Catalano, & Howard, 1986; Hayes, 1987; Lancaster &

Hamburg, 1986; Robins & Przybeck, 1985; Schinke, 1984). Adolescents who carry their pregnancies to term are more likely than aborters to be younger at first intercourse and at first pregnancy, to be poor, to have lower educational aspirations and achievement, and to have rapid repeat pregnancies (Hardy, 1982; Lancaster & Hamburg, 1986). Findings from Jessor and Jessor (1977), Donovan and Jessor (1985), and others (Irwin & Millstein, 1986; Murray & Perry, 1985) regarding common etiology for multiple problem behaviors strongly suggest that these young women are highly likely to be current substance users or at high risk of becoming substance users.

To date, none of the major national studies supply data on drug use among pregnant adolescents. Data from a regional sample of 232 pregnant and nonpregnant Black adolescents in Chicago show that patterns of substance use among pregnant subjects receiving prenatal care were very similar to patterns among nonpregnant control subjects, except that pregnant subjects were much more likely to smoke cigarettes (Pletsch, 1988). Data from studies of pregnant women over age 21 suggest that drug use may be affected, either increased or decreased, by health information received during pregnancy or by the pregnancy experience itself (see Boyd, 1985; Hickner, Westenberg, & Dittenbir, 1984). With regard to changes in substance use that pregnant adolescents may make, available reports conflict. Merritt, Lawrence, and Naeye (1980) found that pregnant adolescents actually increased rates of substance use. In contrast, Zuckerman et al., (1983) found that drug-using young women decreased drug use during pregnancy.

In summary, on the basis of the literature, it is very likely that pregnant adolescents have been involved in multiple problem behaviors including substance use before pregnancy occurred. Little is known about substance use rates before pregnancy or about how such rates change with pregnancy among adolescents. The following data from a study in progress address some of the gaps in current literature. These data provide drug use rates for a sample of pregnant young women seen in community agencies serving school-age pregnant and parenting adolescents. The data provide information on use rates before and during pregnancy; comparisons of these use rates with national data from nonpregnant, in-school adolescents; and description of environmental factors that may be related to maintenance of drug use in this special adolescent group.

METHOD

The data reported here represent all ($N = 241$) subjects interviewed in an ongoing longitudinal study of patterns of drug use among pregnant and parenting school-age adolescents. Unmarried, pregnant adolescents, 17 years of age or under, living in a large metropolitan area in the Northwest were recruited from prenatal clinics serving inner-city, low-income populations; from alternative educational programs for pregnant and parenting teenagers; and from social service agencies serving inner-city adolescents. Because recruitment procedures included using advertising to encourage eligible adolescents to contact study staff, a conventional overall response rate could not be calculated. In the only agency (a large county hospital prenatal clinic) where recruitment procedures allowed collection of complete approach and consent data, 75% of eligible informed adolescents consented to participate in the study.

Subjects were interviewed in a location of their choice, typically their homes. The initial interview, the basis for the data reported here, lasted approximately 2 hours. Information was obtained on a wide variety of topics including living situation; sociodemographic characteristics; school status; work status; social support; peer, family, and sexual partner relationships; sexual history and current sexual activities; contraceptive use; drug use; and antisocial behaviors. Drug use items were patterned after those used in the Monitoring the Future study (Johnston et al., 1988) and employed the same pattern of recall-use in the last year. In addition, urine samples were obtained from a randomly selected 50% subsample. To verify self-reported drug use, these samples were laboratory analyzed for the biochemical by-products of alcohol, amphetamines, barbiturates, cocaine, heroin and other opiates, and tobacco. One participant refused to provide a urine sample. Subjects were paid $15 for this interview.

RESULTS

Subject Characteristics

At the time of the initial interview, subjects were on average 28 weeks pregnant. Seventy-one percent of the sample were experiencing their first pregnancy. Subjects ranged in age from 12 to 17 ($M = 16$ years). Slightly more than half (51%) were White, 32% were Black, and the remainder were from Asia, Pacific Islander, Hispanic, and Native-American backgrounds. Overall, subjects were representative of the national profile of teenagers who carry their premarital pregnancies to term in that they came from low SES backgrounds (35% of parents received welfare in the last year) and had mothers with relatively low educational achievement and unskilled or semiskilled occupational status. One hundred fifty-four subjects (64%) were living with a parent or guardian, 19% lived with a male sexual partner, and the remainder lived with friends or other relatives. With regard to school, 38% labeled themselves official dropouts; 24% had not been attending school regularly even before this pregnancy; and 62% reported that they had been suspended or expelled at least once during the time they were in school. With regard to minor delinquent behavior, 48% said they had been in trouble with the police at least once (22% in the last year); 70% had run away from home at least once before their current pregnancy, and 14% had run away at least once after this pregnancy. When the 13 subjects who had engaged in prostitution were removed from the analyses, the mean number of lifetime sexual partners was 4.8 (mode = 2).

Data Quality

Of the 119 subjects for whom laboratory verification of self-reported drug use was available, only 3 cases (2.5%) had discrepant data. Thus, self-report is assumed to be a reasonably accurate record of current use. One limitation of this study is the retrospective nature of the prepregnancy drug use data. The period of recall, 1 year ago, is relatively short, however, and is the same as that used in national studies of adolescent drug use (Elliott & Morse, 1988; Johnston et al., 1988). Social desirability factors may lead some subjects to under- rather than overreport earlier drug use. On the other hand, some pregnant subjects may overreport their prepregnancy drug use in order to rationalize their current use (e.g., "My use during this pregnancy isn't so bad since it is considerably less than what I used to use"). Also, the rates are not representative of all pregnant adolescents. Young women in detention or who had police records for prostitution were not actively recruited. The sample is intended to reflect those young women who show up voluntarily at health and social services agencies in the general community. The primary purpose of our study was to examine relations among drug use, sexual behaviors, and repeat pregnancy rather than to establish prevalence rates.

Drug Use

Table 24-1 compares pregnant subjects' reported drug use with national data from the Monitoring the Future study of male and female high school seniors (Johnston et al., 1988). Virtually all research on adolescent drug use rates show that rates increase with age into young adulthood. Underscoring the elevated drug use rates reported by the pregnant sample is the fact that the Monitoring the Future sample is older and thus might be expected to report more lifetime use. Nonetheless, the pregnant sample reports comparable or higher lifetime use rates for all substances when compared with the high school senior sample. Particularly high rates are reported for marijuana and cocaine use. Additional analyses suggest that the earlier the age of sexual initiation, the greater the frequency of prepregnancy drug use. Such an association was present in varying degrees for all measured substances, but the association achieved significance only in the case of cocaine. (First age of intercourse: alcohol, .14; marijuana, .16; cocaine, .25; other drugs, .09.) Only 11 (4.6%) subjects reported ever using needles for drug injection.

Table 24-1 Lifetime Prevalence (Percentage Ever Used)

| | High School Seniors | | | |
| | Class of 1987 | | Class of 1988 | |
Substance	All	Female Students	All[a]	Pregnant Sample
Alcohol	92.2	92.2	92.0	93.8
Marijuana	50.2	48.0	47.2	78.0
Cocaine	15.2	13.6	12.1	30.3
Inhalants	17.0	14.2	16.7	17.8
Stimulants	21.6	22.9	19.8	29.5
Sedatives	8.7	8.0	7.8	7.1[b]
Barbiturates	7.4	6.7	6.7	—
Tranquilizers	10.9	11.0	9.4	7.5
Cigarettes	67.2	68.9	66.4	78.8
Nonprescription stimulants	25.5	42.2	—	32.4

[a]Breakdowns by sex and use of nonprescription drugs not yet available for 1988.
[b]Combines sedatives and barbiturates.
Note: The data on high school seniors are from *Illicit Drug Use, Smoking, and Drinking by America's High School Students, College Students, and Young Adults* (p. 36) by L.D. Johnston, P.M. O'Malley, and J.G. Bachman, 1988. Washington DC: U.S. Government Printing Office, and supplemental news release (p. 6) by L.D. Johnston, February 24, 1989. (All data in the public domain.) Dashes indicated data not available.

Table 24-2 summarizes data bearing on changes in drug use with the occurrence of pregnancy. This table contains comparisons of substance use rates before pregnancy with reported (and verified) use rates during pregnancy. These analyses included only those subjects who reported using the substance a year ago. As illustrated, rates for use for all measured substances dropped significantly during pregnancy. Information is not available on change in rates of cigarette smoking. Subjects were not asked to give specific frequency of cigarette use for 1 year ago. However, 71% of the 188 subjects who smoked before pregnancy reported smoking less or much less during pregnancy.

Pro-Drug Environment and Predictors of Drug Use

Subjects as a group live in environments containing relatively high rates of both licit and illicit drug use and easy access to drugs. Table 24-3 summarizes subject-reported rates of use of alcohol, cigarettes, marijuana, and cocaine for subjects' fathers, mothers, current boyfriends/sexual partners, and best friends—

Table 24-2 Mean Level of Drug Use Before and During Pregnancy for Subjects Reporting Drug Use One Year Ago

Substance	Prepregnancy		Pregnancy		Difference		n	t^b
	M^a	SD	M^a	SD	M^a	SD		
Alcohol	3.63	1.25	1.35	0.72	2.28	1.22	162	23.76
Marijuana	3.82	1.28	1.61	1.19	2.21	1.34	121	18.18
Cocaine	3.70	1.39	1.16	0.44	2.54	1.43	37	10.84
Other drugs	3.11	1.33	1.05	0.23	2.05	1.31	37	9.53

[a]Drug use measures are monthly frequencies ranging from *no use* (1) to *daily use* (6).
[b]Paired t test of difference between means.
Note: $p < .001$ for all substances

Table 24-3 Percentage of Drug Use by Others in Subjects' Environment

Relationship	Cigarettes	Alcohol	Marijuana	Cocaine
Mother's use				
%	50	33	10	6
n	237	233	237	236
Father's use				
%	57	49	11	2[a]
n	194	177	194	199
Best friend's use				
%	59	65	36	6
n	218	206	216	216
Boyfriend's use				
%	62	76	48	9
n	177	175	176	174

[a]Combines cocaine with all other illicit drugs except marijuana.

Note: All percentages indicate use in the past month. *N*s reflect number of subjects who reported knowledge of the person's drug use.

---

presumed influences on subjects' drug use. In addition 28% of the sample reported that their current sexual partner had sold drugs, and 38 (15.8%) subjects reported that they themselves had sold drugs. The influence of subjects' prepregnancy use, boyfriends' current use, and best friends' current use of cigarettes, alcohol, and marijuana on whether pregnant subjects were using these drugs was examined. The zero-order correlations presented in Table 24-4 show positive and significant relations between each of these variables and subjects' use of the substance. However, when multivariate methods—specifically multiple regression—were used to examine the influence of these variables, with the exception of cigarette and alcohol use, only prepregnancy use remained significantly associated with subjects' current use of drugs (see Table 24-5). That is, when prepregnancy drug use was taken into account, neither boyfriends' use nor best friends' use of marijuana contributed to the explained variance in subjects' use of these drugs. For cigarettes and alcohol, however, best friends' use remained significantly associated with subjects' use even after taking into account prepregnancy use and boyfriends' use.

IMPLICATIONS FOR RESEARCH

Although still confined to relatively small regional samples, early research suggests that pregnant adolescents may have rates of prepregnancy substance use

Table 24-4 Correlations Between Prepregnancy Use, Boyfriend's Use, Best Friend's Use, and Subject's Use of Drugs

Subject's Use of	Prepregnancy Use	Boyfriend's Use	Best Friend's Use
Cigarettes	.40***	.30***	.34***
Alcohol	.54***	.25***	.38***
Marijuana	.59***	.34***	.35***

*p < .05.
**p < .01.
***p < .001.
Note: Listwise deletion of missing/inapplicable data resulted in $n = 158$ for cigarette use, $n = 150$ for alcohol use, and $n = 156$ for marijuana use.

that exceed national rates even for older adolescents but that a significant drop in substance use may occur during pregnancy for at least some young women. Data suggest that pregnant adolescents planning to carry their infants to term live in environments where drugs are easily available and where interpersonal partners and social supports have greater than average drug use. However, some data suggest that during pregnancy some subjects are able to maintain no or low drug use in spite of use among key members of their social support network. One opportunity for preventive intervention seems to lie in capitalizing on and extending the voluntary drop in drug use that may occur during pregnancy. Because pregnant and parenting adolescents are frequently not in conventional classrooms, prevention programmers will need to look beyond conventional school-based programs to influence this group of drug-using adolescents.

With regard to future etiological research, unanswered questions with significant preventive implications for reducing high-risk behavior among adolescent girls include the following: What is the association and temporal ordering of substance use and unprotected sexual activity among adolescent women? How long does the observed drop in rates of drug use during pregnancy remain once the pregnancy is over? To what extent does drug use predict which adolescents experience multiple pregnancies and which do not? Do situational or interpersonal factors have more influence on female adolescents than more traditionally examined personality or family background factors? How influential are sexual partners in initiation and maintenance of substance use among adolescent women? Very little data currently relate sexual partners' drug use to drug initiation and use among adolescent women. Dating relationships often expose females to or incorporate them into their male dating partners' social networks. If, by virtue of her relationship with a sexual partner who is often older than she, an adolescent girl is incorporated into an older, more experienced social network, she may through

Table 24-5 Influence of Pre-pregnancy Drug Use, Boyfriend's Use, and Best Friend's Use on Drug Use During Pregnancy

Dependent Variable	β [a]	SE	t
Cigarette use			
Prepregnancy	.29	.08	3.84***
Boyfriend's use	.14	.01	1.86
Best friend's use	.22	.01	3.02*
Alcohol use			
Prepregnancy	.44	.02	5.69***
Boyfriend's use	.10	.02	1.37
Best friend's use	.16	.02	2.13*
Marijuana use			
Prepregnancy	.53	.02	6.82***
Boyfriend's use	.13	.01	1.76
Best friend's use	.02	.02	.22

[a]Standardized regression coefficients.
*$p < .05$.
**$p < .01$.
***$p < .001$.
Note: Listwise deletion of missing/inapplicable data resulted in $n = 158$ for cigarette use, $n = 150$ for alcohol use, and $n = 156$ for marijuana use.

modeling and social influence processes be prematurely (i.e., in advance of normal developmental processes) introduced to substance use. Little is known about this avenue of drug onset or drug use maintenance for adolescent females. Sexual partners may constitute a special kind of peer group for sexually active adolescent women. Sexual partners may have more influence on the type, amount, and progression of female adolescents' drug use than may peers and same age friends. Although early data from the study show no relation between subjects' use during pregnancy and boyfriends' use of drugs, after taking subjects' prepregnancy use into account, boyfriends may be influencing prepregnancy use and thereby indirectly influencing subjects' use of drugs during pregnancy. More research is needed regarding postpregnancy drug use and the relation of partner variables to escalating or declining rates of substance use after pregnancy resolution. Prospective research with adolescent girls not yet pregnant but at risk for pregnancy would eliminate potential bias in retrospective reporting of prepregnancy drug use. At a minimum, given our review of the extant literature and preliminary findings from this examination of drug use and pregnancy, future research regarding sexual activity and drug use should be race and sex specific.

REFERENCES

Baumrind, D. (1987). A developmental perspective on adolescent risk taking in contemporary America. In C.E. Irwin, Jr. (Ed.), *Adolescent social behavior and health* (pp. 93–125). San Francisco: Jossey-Bass.

Boyd, M.D. (1985). Patient motivation during pregnancy. *Maryland Medical Journal, 10,* 977–981.

Chasnoff, I.J. (1988). *Drug use in pregnancy: Mother and child.* Lancaster, England: MTP Press.

Donovan, J.E., & Jessor, R. (1985). Structure of problem behavior in adolescence and young adulthood. *Journal of Counseling and Clinical Psychology, 53,* 890–904.

Elliott, D.S., & Morse, B. (1988). *Delinquency and drug use as risk factors in teenage sexual activity and pregnancy.* Unpublished manuscript, Institute of Behavioral Science, University of Colorado, Boulder.

Hardy, J.B. (1982). Adolescents as parents: Possible long-range implications. In T.J. Coates, A.C. Peterson, & C. Perry (Eds.), *Promoting adolescent health: A dialog on research and practice* (pp. 255–267). New York: Academic Press.

Hawkins, J.D., Lishner, D.M., Catalano, R.F., & Howard, M.O. (1986). Childhood predictors of adolescent substance abuse: Toward an empirically grounded theory. *Journal of Children in Contemporary Society, 81*(1), 11–48.

Hayes, C.D. (1987). *Risking the future: Adolescent sexuality, pregnancy, and childbearing, Vol. 1.* Washington, DC: National Academy Press.

Hickner, J., Westenberg, C., & Dittenbir, M. (1984). Effect of pregnancy on smoking behavior: A baseline study. *Journal of Family Practice, 18,* 241–244.

Hofferth, S.L. (1987). Social and economic consequences of teenage childbearing. In S.L. Hofferth & C.D. Hayes (Eds.), *Risking the future: Adolescent sexuality, pregnancy, and childbearing, Vol. 2: Working papers and statistical appendixes* (pp. 123–144). Washington, DC: National Academy Press.

Hofferth, S.L., & Hayes, C.D. (Eds.). (1987). *Risking the future: Adolescent sexuality, pregnancy, and childbearing: Statistical appendixes.* Washington, DC: National Academy Press.

Irwin, C.E., & Millstein, S.G. (1986). Biopsychosocial correlates of risk-taking behaviors during adolescence: Can the physician intervene? *Journal of Adolescent Health Care, 7*(6, Suppl.), 82S–96S.

Jessor, R., & Jessor, S.L. (1977). *Problem behavior and psychosocial development: A longitudinal study of youth.* New York: Academic Press.

Johnston, L.D., O'Malley, P.M., & Bachman, J.G. (1988). *Illicit drug use, smoking, and drinking by America's high school students, college students, and young adults.* Washington, DC: U.S. Government Printing Office.

Jones, C.L., & Battjes, R.J. (Eds.). (1985). *Etiology of drug abuse: Implications for prevention* (NIDA Research Monograph 56). Washington, DC: U.S. Government Printing Office.

Lancaster, J.B., & Hamburg, B.A. (Eds.). (1986). *School-age pregnancy and parenthood: Biosocial dimensions.* New York: Aldine.

Little, B.B., Snell, L.M., Klein, V.R., & Gilstrap, L.C., III. (1989). Cocaine abuse during pregnancy: Maternal and fetal implications. *Obstetrics and Gynecology, 73,* 157–160.

Merritt, T.A., Lawrence, R.A., & Naeye, R.L. (1980). The infants of adolescent mothers. *Pediatric Annals, 9,* 200–220.

Moore, K. (1988, November). *Facts at a glance.* Washington, DC: Child Trends.

Mott, F.L., & Haurin, R.J. (1988). Linkages between sexual activity and alcohol and drug use among American adolescents. *Family Planning Perspectives, 20,* 128–136.

Murray, D.M., & Perry, C.L. (1985). The prevention of adolescent drug abuse: Implications of etiological, developmental, behavioral, and environmental models. In C.L. Jones & R.J. Battjes (Eds.), *Etiology of drug abuse: Implications for prevention* (NIDA Research Monograph 56, pp. 236–256). Washington, DC: U.S. Government Printing Office.

Newcomb, M.D., & Bentler, P.M. (1988). *Consequences of adolescent drug use: Impact on the lives of young adults.* Newbury Park, CA: Sage.

Pletsch, P.K. (1988). Substance use and health activities of pregnant adolescents. *Journal of Adolescent Health Care, 9,* 38–45.

Robins, L.N., & Przybeck, T.R. (1985). Age of onset of drug use as a factor in drug and other disorders. In C.L. Jones & R.J. Battjes (Eds.) *Etiology of drug abuse: Implications for prevention* (NIDA Research Monograph 56, pp. 178–192). Washington, DC: U.S. Government Printing Office.

Schinke, S.P. (1984). Preventing teenage pregnancy. In M. Hersen, R.M. Eisler, & P.M. Miller (Eds.), *Progress in behavior modification* (Vol. 16, pp. 31–64). New York: Academic Press.

Yamaguchi, K., & Kandel, D. (1987). Drug use and other determinants of premarital pregnancy and its outcomes: A dynamic analysis of competing life events. *Journal of Marriage and the Family, 49,* 257–270.

Zabin, L.S. (1984). The association between smoking and sexual behavior among teens in U.S. contraceptive clinics. *American Journal of Public Health, 74,* 261–263.

Zabin, L.S., Hardy, J.B., Smith, E., & Hirsch, M.B. (1986). Substance use and its relation to sexual activity among inner-city adolescents. *Journal of Adolescent Health Care, 7,* 320–331.

Zuckerman, B.S., Alpert, J.J., Dooling, E., Hingson, R., Kayne, H., Morelock, S., & Oppenheimer, E. (1983). Neonatal outcome: Is adolescent pregnancy a risk factor? *Pediatrics, 71,* 489–493.

Zuckerman, B.S., Amaro, H., & Beardslee, W. (1987). Mental health of adolescent mothers: The implications of depression and drug use. *Developmental and Behavioral Pediatrics, 8,* 111–116.

Zuckerman, B.S., Frank, D.A., Hingson, R., Amaro, H., Levenson, S.M., Kayne, H., Parker, S., Vinci, R., Aboagye, K., Fried, L.E., Cabral, H., Timperi, R., & Bauchner, H. (1989). Effects of maternal marijuana and cocaine use on fetal growth. *New England Journal of Medicine, 320,* 762–768.

Part IV

Special Groups

At the same time the field of substance abuse treatment recognized adolescents as a special population, they also had to acknowledge the special needs of women and minorities. They discovered that not all alcoholics and drug addicts were the same and many of these special groups did poorly in traditional treatment programs that were often designed for white, middle-class males. The current trend in the field is to define the various and differing needs of these groups and to create treatment theories and programs that will be more successful. Although adolescents themselves are a special population, treating them all in the same manner or assuming their problems are the same can lead to treatment failure.

This section divides adolescent substance abusers further by examining three special populations: female adolescents, Native American youth, and adolescents from alcoholic families. Women are affected by strong role expectations and socialization in our society. Even with the women's movement it is less acceptable for women than for men to drink alcohol or take drugs. Chapter 25, about female adolescent drug and alcohol abusers, lends insight for therapists working with this special group.

Native Americans are truly a high risk population with regard to alcohol and drug abuse. Whole tribes and cultures are in danger of being lost to this abuse. Chapter 26 explores various risk factors for Native American youth and points to differences within this population and between tribes.

Another high risk group is children of alcoholics. Clearly, alcoholism and other addictive disorders are more prevalent in some families than in others. Children of alcoholics are at risk for the intergenerational transmission of alcoholism in three domains: biological, sociological, and psychological. Yet not all children of alcoholics become alcoholic. The current research on resiliency of this population may help in developing prevention programs specifically for this high risk population.

The two remaining chapters focus on specific drugs of abuse, cocaine and methamphetamine. Although these are not the only or most widely used drugs by adolescents, they are most appealing to this group. They are both widely available and are relatively inexpensive, but are also among the most harmful of illegal drugs. These chapters examine the special groups of adolescents who use these as their drugs of choice.

This is certainly not an exhaustive list of the special groups that are found within the adolescent substance abusing population, but this is a beginning look at the diversity of the population. Therapists working with any of these groups should be aware of these issues when assessing and treating adolescents for substance abuse and related problems.

25

Alcohol and Drug Abuse Among Female Adolescents

Nancy Waite-O'Brien

Drug addiction and alcohol abuse in adolescent females are infrequently researched. Adolescents, as a whole, are an underserved population in treatment and research on substance abuse. Because females make up a minority of that population, they tend to be ignored or included in research that is more descriptive of the adolescent male population. Young females who abuse substances face some special problems, however.

NORMAL ADOLESCENCE

Adolescence is a tumultuous time of change and adjustment for young people. Around the age of 13, a girl begins to abandon her concrete childhood construction of reality and to see some of the imperfections of the adult world. She begins to question authority, particularly that of her parents, and to challenge social expectations. Her sense of morality is no longer based on social conventions, but on personal principles. She both emulates and rebels against the adults in her life.

At the same time, her peer group becomes increasingly important. The influence of her peers supplants the values that she has learned from her parents. For some parents, this time of change and rebellion is confusing and frightening, and they respond by withdrawing. When this happens, the girl is apt to become overly reliant on her peers.

Early adolescence is characterized by a heightened consciousness of self and others. The girl becomes more self-centered and, paradoxically, more able to understand the viewpoints of others. Simultaneously, self-esteem ebbs, and this newly formed self-awareness can become focused on real and imagined inadequacies. Along with these internal changes, the physical transitions surrounding puberty and, frequently, the change to a larger and more intimidating school environment confuse the young girl even more.

Because of adolescents' poor perspective on change, they tend to view these changes as cataclysmic and have trouble seeing an end to their difficulties. One of the major tasks of adolescence is to learn to tolerate change, even though this frequently means pain. It is not uncommon for the child who is unable to learn this to escape this disequilibrium into problematic behavior such as drug use, anorexia, phobias, psychosis, or suicide.

According to Baumrind (1985), normal adolescence includes puberty; lowered academic values; more value on independence; tolerance of deviation from adult norms; more social criticism and activism; less religiosity; increase in perceived friends' support instead of parents' support; more relaxation of parental standards; and more drinking, drug use, and sexual activity. Some drug and alcohol use is a normal part of adolescence. The task of parents and therapists is to differentiate between "normal" use and problematic or addictive use.

NATURE OF THE PROBLEM

Availability

Alcohol and drugs are readily available to adolescent females. At least at the beginnings of their use, most girls do not have to pay for them. As one young recovering addict said, "Just go down to the boardwalk and within five minutes a sailor will give you a beer or anything else. You're just not likely to have to buy it" (Anonymous, personal communication). In view of the difficulties that an adolescent struggles with in terms of self-image, it is easy to imagine the kinds of confusing messages that she receives about self-worth as men or boys supply her with drugs or alcohol.

Bowker (1977) suggested a process model for a young girl's introduction to drug use and sexual behavior. Beginning with two assumptions—that females are more sensitive to social pressures from intimate associates than are males and that males control access to drugs through their connection with dealers—Bowker postulated that the process begins with dating or with some other social contact. Drug use then becomes intertwined with sexual behavior, especially when the female joins the male in drug use and the drugs lower her inhibition so that she can participate in sex. The male maintains his sexual power because he has a ready supply of drugs, and the female maintains her dependence because she does not control her source of supply.

Bowker (1977) reported that, in comparing the influence of opposite-sex friends versus same-sex friends on the use of alcohol, girls were more influenced by male friends than by female friends. Males were more likely to be influenced by same-sex friends. Thus, girls are more likely to be influenced by their boyfriends than by their girlfriends in regard to alcohol use.

Patterns of Use

Most high school girls drink. The percentage of high school girls who drink increased dramatically through the 1960s, but in recent years has stayed fairly constant (Wilsnack & Beckman, 1984). A large minority get drunk repeatedly and have one or more social problems as a result, however. Girls are less likely to drink hard liquor and are more likely to drink alone. Boys drink faster and tend to drink with same-sex friends (Wilsnack & Beckman, 1984).

Hundleby (1987) compared exploratory drug use to the beginnings of sexual behavior for teen-agers. First, both activities are related to an increased need for stimulation, especially for new and different types. Second, both provide a vehicle for social acceptance or an entree into a group. Third, both give the young person greater perceived prestige, because each is an imitation of adultlike behaviors. Finally, both drug use and sexual behavior are rebellious acts that can provide a way for the adolescent to break away from family ties and mores.

Adolescent female drug users are somewhat likely to engage in other delinquent behaviors, are likely to engage in social behaviors such as "hanging around with friends" rather than staying at home, often have lower academic achievement, and are less religious than are girls who do not use drugs or alcohol.

Stages of Use

In general, adolescent drug use begins with wine, beer, and tobacco; moves to hard liquor and marijuana use; and finally reaches other illicit drug use (Murray & Perry, 1985). For girls, their first experiences may be with diet pills or other stimulants related to weight loss. Involvement at one stage is not predictive of involvement at the next stage, but involvement at later stages assumes involvement at an earlier stage in the progression. For example, a teen-ager who drinks beer is not necessarily a prospective user of cocaine or heroin. A teen-ager who is using heroin or cocaine, however, is likely to have also used alcohol, cigarettes, and marijuana in the past.

For a girl, previous involvement in minor delinquency and problematic drinking in her parents seem to predict a progression to the use of hard liquor. The movement from hard liquor to marijuana use is correlated with the use of marijuana by her peer group and with her adoption of values that are favorable to the use of drugs. The progression to the use of other drugs is associated with poor relations with the parents and with the modeling of drug use by parents or peers (Kandel, Kessler, & Margulies, 1978; Murray & Perry, 1985).

Girls tend to drift into alcohol use, but they seem to seek the use of illicit drugs in response to intrapsychic pressures (Kandel, Kessler, & Margulies, 1978). For younger girls, drug use is often a mark of social transition or acceptance. For older teens, it is more often a means to reduce stress.

PREDICTIVE INFLUENCES

Age

Not unexpectedly, girls are more likely to drink and to use drugs as they get older. They are more likely to drink more and to drink in more socially inappropriate ways. When drinking or other drug use begins early, later problems with these chemicals develop more often. (Murray & Perry, 1985; Wilsnack & Beckman, 1984).

Education and Socioeconomic Class

Drug use is negatively correlated with educational expectations; for example, girls who expect to graduate from 4-year colleges are less likely to use drugs problematically (Johnston, Bachman, & O'Malley, 1982). Drinking is generally associated with lower academic performance (Wilsnack & Beckman, 1984). In both cases, it is difficult to determine if the drug or alcohol use is a way to cope with negative feelings about school, or if the drug or alcohol use itself has caused the declining performance. It is necessary to examine changes in school performance over time. If the declining grades follow substance abuse, it is likely that the substance abuse is the cause of the problem.

There is no evidence that drug or alcohol use is more prevalent in any particular socioeconomic class. It is probable that socioeconomic class determines the specific drug used, but not the overall pattern of use.

Ethnicity and Regional Use Patterns

White teen-agers are more likely to use alcohol than are black or Hispanic adolescents. In study samples that included them, Native Americans have been found to drink more than do other ethnic groups. Teens who are of Irish descent are more likely to drink, get drunk, and have problems related to drinking than are their Italian, English, or Jewish counterparts. Jewish adolescents are more likely to use alcohol, but less likely to use it problematically (Wilsnack & Beckman, 1984).

Adolescents in the northeastern and northcentral parts of the United States tend to drink more than do those in the South or the West. In areas where there are high rates of abstinence (e.g., Utah), young people who do drink tend to have more alcohol-related problems than do drinkers from other areas. There are no reported differences between boys and girls in this aspect of research (Wilsnack & Beckman, 1984).

Parental Attitudes

Girls are more likely to drink if their relations with their parents are unsupportive, alienated, or hostile. When there is tension in the home, boys are likely to drink in ways that are rebellious or acting out. Girls in this situation, however, tend to drink to get drunk. If the parents are tolerant of their son's drinking, their daughter is likely to drink, too. Parents' emphasis on the harmfulness of drugs is not effective in influencing a child's attitudes or drug behavior (Kandel, 1985). One study showed that parents' efforts to control the drinking behavior of their children reduced their sons' drunkenness, but not their daughters' (Wilsnack & Beckman, 1984).

A girl whose relationship with her father is tense and who feels rejected by her mother is more likely to drink. In fact, as girls grow older, the lack of parental affection becomes an increasingly more significant dynamic in connection with their alcohol use. One study showed that a conflict with the parents in early adolescence increases the probability of a girl's alcohol use and problem drinking 4 years later (Thompson & Wilsnack, 1982).

The quality of the parent-child relationship has its greatest impact on the use of drugs other than marijuana. In her family, the female opiate addict often feels helpless. Characterized by avoidance and denial, the family is generally not cohesive as a family unit. The young addict is often competitive with her mother and has a difficult relationship with her father. This dynamic is different from that seen in a family with a male addict. With males, the addict is more often enmeshed with his overly protective mother. These families generally avoid separation. Even when there is a crisis, it becomes a mechanism to keep the young addict's family together—especially if the addict is female (Glynn, 1984).

In a 10-year longitudinal study of drug use in teen-agers, Block, Block, and Keyes (1988) found that early family environment played a significant role in subsequent drug use. They found that an unstructured, laissez faire home environment in which few expectations were placed on a nursery school–aged girl was predictive of drug use 10 years later. These homes, which tended to be messy, crowded, unkempt, busy, noisy, and interpersonally informal, seemed on the surface to be headed by "progressive" parents. In actuality, these parents were inept, distracted, and ineffective. This dynamic was true for girls, but not for their brothers.

The authors here suggest that the girls' home environment creates a facade of independence and progressiveness that really masks parental inadequacy. The daughters learn independence but not achievement. As a result, the girls pick up a mixed message: the need to be independent without the tools to accomplish this goal. In contrast, their brothers' environment *outside* the family is more supportive of independent action.

Within these homes, the father tended to de-emphasize competitiveness, to foster low achievement, to emphasize early autonomy, to have few strict rules, to be permissive, and to oppose sex role typing. The mother also had few expectations; in addition, she was frequently angry with her daughter, made unwilling sacrifices for her, had difficulty punishing her children, and allowed them to question her decisions.

In general, the parents of adolescent users tend to have deficient parental styles. Parents of substance-abusing teen-agers tend to be rigidly fixed to their roles; any attempt to change them is apt to precipitate a family crisis (Glynn, 1984). Communication in these families is usually problematic. It is characterized by denial of the addiction, guilt, little physical expression of affection, and an absence of joy. These families tend to be overly intellectual and to share few of their intimate feelings. Their decision-making ability is poor, and they seem, in many ways, like the families of emotionally disturbed children (Glynn, 1984).

Family Size and Structure

There is no clear evidence that family size has any influence on drug use in adolescent females. It is possible, however, that a larger family size may contribute to this problem (Glynn, 1984).

The structure of the female opiate addict's family often contains a triad made up of (1) the addict, (2) an overinvolved parent, and (3) a distancing, punitive, or absent parent. In single-parent families, another adult from outside of the family may become involved (Glynn, 1984).

The presence of only one parent in the home contributes slightly to drug abuse, but the quality of the parent-child relationship within that home is more important. If the family broke up after the child was 12 years old or if the parent was lost through death, there is a greater risk of later drug abuse (Glynn, 1984).

Peer Influences

Female adolescent drinkers tend to associate with other people who drink. When this occurs, the individual is likely to see the world through the eyes of her peer group. It is unclear whether an adolescent chooses to drink and then finds a peer group to match this preference or whether she chooses her friends and then changes her drinking patterns because of their influence. Although it appears that peer pressure can lead adolescents to experiment with alcohol, there is no evidence to show that peer pressure is responsible for continued drinking. In the long run, parental influence is likely to be a more powerful force in this regard.

Kandel (1985) found that girls were more influenced by their friends' use of alcohol than were boys. For girls, the effect of peer use was 10 times that of the effect of parental drinking. For boys, the effect of peer use was 7 times that of parental drinking. In addition, a brother or sister's perceived use of amphetamines or barbiturates tends to influence a girl's choice to use these drugs. This influence is not so great for boys (Bowker, 1977).

As a girl moves away from alcohol into illicit drugs, the influence of one single friend becomes more important. Although not necessarily a close friend, this person has a powerful influence on the girl's life. This friendship may represent a move away from long-term friendships to one that is less intimate. Bowker (1977) found that, as females increase their drug use, the perceived social distance from a same-sex drug user decreases more rapidly for females than for males. Thus, as the drug use progresses, the female is apt to become attached to one person whose drug use is similar to her own and then to establish a quasi-intimate friendship. The emphasis is on the singularity of the friendship rather than on its intimacy, however.

PERSONALITY FACTORS AS A CORRELATE OF DRUG USE

Alienation and Independence

It is thought that a sense of anomie and distrust are related to heavy drinking among adolescent girls. This sense of isolation and alienation may be related to problem drinking through one of three mechanisms: (1) the feeling of alienation leads directly to drinking; (2) the sense of detachment removes constraints on drinking, resulting in heavier alcohol use; or (3) the drinking itself drives others away, leaving the adolescent powerless and socially devalued (Wilsnack & Beckman, 1984).

Block, Block, and Keyes (1988), in their longitudinal study of the correlates of marijuana use, found that female users could be described as rebellious, unable to delay gratification, unlikely to favor conservative values, and unambitious. As nursery school–aged children, these girls were described as interpersonally importunate, impatient, and resentful if not given their own way. Additionally, these children were described as cautious, whiny, selfish, sulky, uncoordinated, and liable to spend a great deal of time daydreaming.

Ego Strength

One of the major tasks of becoming a healthy adult is developing the ego resiliency that makes it possible to weather life's difficulties. Adolescents who have little faith in their ability to control their own behavior and the consequences of that behavior are likely to use alcohol or other drugs to handle feelings of helplessness. This may become a circular process, however, because alcohol may intensify feelings of helplessness and, to cope with these feelings, the adolescents may drink more. If they can control their behavior, they may still drink, but not problematically. This is true of both boys and girls.

In a study of the irrational beliefs of drug users from a rational emotive therapy perspective, Denoff (1987) found that drug use is correlated with catastrophizing, approval seeking, and blame and punishment. Catastrophizing and approval seeking are associated with ego anxiety. People who catastrophize tend to overestimate the cost of not succeeding. Approval-seeking people are fearful and anxious in situations in which self-worth is threatened. Together, these attributes distort the individual's interpretation of a situation. As a result, the person, whether male or female, magnifies the cost of not being accepted. Alcohol and drugs work to alleviate this anxiety.

Antisocial Behaviors

Females who drink heavily tend to engage in some masculine forms of delinquency, such as theft, vandalism, or staying out all night. This behavior is associated with the drinking behavior of either or both of the parents (Widseth & Meyer, 1971). In contrast, a boy's antisocial drinking behavior tends to be more strongly associated with his father's drinking behavior (Zucker & Devoe, 1975).

Affiliative Needs

As already mentioned, females tend to have much stronger affiliative needs than do males (Hundleby & Mercer, 1987; Kandel, 1985; Wilsnack & Beckman, 1984). In fact, their drug or alcohol use may allow them to satisfy some of these needs through being a part of a drug-using community. One young woman whose drug use began in adolescence said that women feel the pain of addictive use in their relationships, however. She felt that the threatened loss of a close relationship would finally bring reality to an addicted woman. She saw that as a significant difference between men and women. She suggested that the threatened loss of job or possessions would have a greater impact on men (Anonymous, personal communication).

SOCIETAL ATTITUDES

Even in the wake of the Women's Movement, intoxication with alcohol or drugs is viewed as a threat to traditional feminine values and role performances. It tends to be associated with rebelliousness and reduced self-control. In fact, adolescent females who are hostile or indifferent to traditionally feminine values and standards do tend to be heavier drinkers (Wilsnack & Beckman, 1984). One aspect of traditional femininity—the valuing or respecting of social obligations, along with concern for others and desire to get along with others—is negatively correlated with drinking for both males and females (Wilsnack & Wilsnack, 1979; Wilsnack, Thompson, & Wilsnack, 1981).

Norms regarding drinking are gender-specific. Drinking or drug-using females suffer a greater social stigma than do men. Women are still considered the bearers of social manners and virtues, and a drunk woman suffers the loss of her virtue in the eyes of the world. No matter what her age, she will be judged more severely than a man. More ominously, a young woman who is drunk is often looked on as a helpless and irresponsible sex object, and she frequently receives unwanted sexual advances (Gomberg, 1982).

PHYSIOLOGICAL DIFFERENCES

The adopted sons of alcoholic biological parents (most frequently, alcoholic biological fathers) are at high risk for alcoholism (Wilsnack & Beckman, 1984). The risk does not appear to be as great for the adopted daughters of alcoholic biological parents. Females may be less likely to inherit the predisposition toward the disease. Other possible reasons for this gender difference are (1) the tendency toward inheriting alcoholism may be a sex-linked characteristic; (2) the conditions necessary to express this characteristic may be more likely to occur in males than in females; or (3) females are more susceptible than are males to the influences that override this predisposition.

Gender differences in alcohol abuse may also be related to differences in body weight or the amount of body fluid. Because girls tend to weigh less and have a lower percentage of body fluid, intake of the same amount of alcohol will produce a higher blood-alcohol level in a girl than in a boy (Ray, 1978; Wilsnack & Beckman, 1984). For this reason, a smaller amount of alcohol will cause drunkenness in a girl than in a boy.

It is not known if absorption or metabolism rates differ between adolescent males and females, but the wide swings in hormonal levels that occur in a female's body throughout her menstrual cycle make such a difference seem likely. Alcohol's effects are known to vary markedly during this cycle. A woman is most affected by alcohol just before her period, for example. This difference probably applies to other drugs, too. Furthermore, the greater the amount of body fat, the lower the rate at which alcohol is metabolized. Because females tend to have more body fat, it can be assumed that they will metabolize alcohol more slowly. Additionally, the use of birth control pills slows alcohol metabolism. These lower rates prolong the effects of the substance (Wilsnack & Beckman, 1984).

SPECIAL PROBLEMS

Rape

> As I look back, there were a lot of situations where I wasn't safe at all, but when you're high you have complete confidence. Not just confidence, but like if they would get you, or if anything would happen to you, who really cares? It's not like anyone can really hurt you. It's like if they happened to hurt you, I wouldn't really get hurt. (Anonymous, personal communication)

Nearly half of chemically dependent women have been battered or raped (Peluso & Peluso, 1988). With adolescents, the cycle of battering often begins with childhood incest or molestation, followed by running away from home, followed by rape and battering on the streets or in new relationships. Drugs become part of the survival system for these girls.

In their study of juvenile assaultive and sexual offenses, Vinogradov, Dishotsky, Doty, and Tinklenberg (1988) found that alcohol is the drug most likely to be associated with these offenses. Although their focus was on the offenders, they reported that both the victim and the attacker had been drinking in 39% of all rapes. They also reported another study in which 63% of the victims had been drinking. Females who have been drinking or are drunk are vulnerable to rape not only because drunk women are generally viewed as women of easy virtue, but also because alcohol affects judgment and the victim is less able to determine when a situation is dangerous or to break off an interaction when it becomes dangerous.

Depression

During adolescence, depression becomes more prevalent among females than among males (Formanck & Gurian, 1987). At this point, gender appears to be the strongest predictor for the development of depression (Lewis, 1985; Radloff & Rae, 1981), perhaps because of hormonal influences or perhaps because of women's greater vulnerability to the environmental influences that lead to depression. In adolescence, a girl is under increasing stress. She finds that sex roles are much narrower; she may no longer be rewarded for academic excellence. Because she tends to see her roles in terms of her relationships, she may be experiencing more anxiety about her attachments. The physical changes that she experiences at puberty may bring additional stresses. Menstruation may bring on new tension and irritability, as well as depression. If she acts on her sexual feelings, she may fear pregnancy.

Females tend to respond to stress with self-blame, which leads to additional feelings of shame and guilt. The Women's Movement has created new opportunities for women, but has also blurred some sex role differences. "Traditional" feminine roles conflict with the assertiveness associated with these new roles.

All these factors establish a favorable environment for the use of drugs or alcohol. If a girl has little ego resiliency, the pain and sadness associated with any one of these circumstances will make the use of these chemicals very attractive.

Parenting

With the likelihood that a drug-using girl is sexually active and with the unlikelihood that she is practicing birth control, she may well become a child-mother. Such young girls are ill-equipped for the job of parenting. There is a good chance that these girls are immature, even for their young age. As they have not yet finished their own emotional growth, they have little emotional strength to give to an infant. If the mother used drugs during the pregnancy, the infant may have special needs that will create even more strain on the parent-child relationship. These girls have a high probability of perpetuating the cycle of abuse and neglect that began in their own childhood by passing it to their own children (Peluso & Peluso, 1988).

TREATMENT

Drug abuse and alcoholism in adolescent females does not emerge from a vacuum. The influence of the family is felt in all stages of substance abuse. Therefore, it is of fundamental importance that treatment for these young women incorporates their families. It is possible that the substance abuse has been a way to divert attention from other family problems. Family treatment provides a way for the family to make changes without using the substance-abusing adolescent as a scapegoat for other family problems.

The special needs of adolescent female drug users must be incorporated into the treatment plan. For example, issues related to dependency are important. It is necessary to determine how a girl has become dependent on others, both for her source of drugs and for her self-definition. She needs to develop a belief and trust in her own feelings and to learn to assert herself appropriately. Often, feelings of dependence and low self-esteem come from a lack of self-care skills. These young women do not have the vocational skill to find satisfying and well paying employment. Therefore, an appropriate component of treatment includes vocational counseling and some minimal job training skills.

Sexual abuse, promiscuity, and rape are common occurrences for young female addicts and alcoholics. Because of the shame and embarrassment associated with such events, these issues are frequently not addressed in treatment, especially in a mixed group. For a young female addict or alcoholic, preparing a history of her sexual experiences and sharing it with other girls can be very helpful, however. She should also learn that it is normal and healthy to desire sex and that a sexual relationship can be loving as well as pleasurable. In addition, she must learn to take responsibility for preventing both pregnancy and infection with sexually transmitted diseases.

Since some young women in treatment for substance abuse will already be parents, it is important to include training in effective parenting. Teaching these young women about child development, appropriate discipline, and ways to provide support and encouragement will go a long way toward changing the patterns of abuse and neglect often associated with teen-aged mothers.

The association of depression with chemical dependency for women is nearly universal. Depression tends to be a way a girl handles her feelings of powerlessness, inadequacy, anger, and rage. Treatment facilities should provide ways for the young women to explore these feelings and to learn appropriate ways to handle them. Issues related to self-esteem should also be an integral part of treatment for female adolescents. Learning to share with and receive encouragement from other girls can begin the process of restoring a hurt and struggling inner self.

REFERENCES

Baumrind D. (1985). Familial antecedents of adolescent drug use: A developmental perspective. *National Institute on Drug Abuse Research Monograph Series, 56,* 13–44.

Block, J., Block, J.H., & Keyes, S. (1988). Longitudinally foretelling drug usage in adolescence: Early childhood and personality and environmental precursors. *Child Development, 59,* 336–355.

Bowker, L.H. (1977). *Drug use among American women, old and young: Sexual oppression and other themes.* San Francisco: R. & E. Research.

Denoff, M.S. (1987). Irrational beliefs as predictors of adolescent drug abuse and running away. *Journal of Clinical Psychology, 43,* 412–423.

Formanck, R., & Gurian, A. (1987). *Women and depression: A lifespan perspective.* New York: Springer.

Glynn, T.J. (1984). Adolescent drug use and the family environment: A review. *Journal of Drug Issues, 14,* 271–295.

Gomberg, E.L. (1982). Historical and political perspective: Women and drug use. *Journal of Social Issues, 38,* 9–23.

Hundleby, J.D. (1987). Adolescent drug use in a behavioral matrix: A confirmation and comparison of the sexes. *Addictive Behaviors, 12,* 103–112.

Hundleby, J.D., & Mercer, G.W. (1987). Family and friends as social environments and their relationship to young adolescents' use of alcohol, tobacco and marijuana. *Journal of Marriage and the Family, 49,* 151–164.

Johnston, L.D., Bachman, J.G., & O'Malley, P.M. (1982). *Student drug use in America: 1975–1987* (DHHS Publication No. ADM-82-1208). Washington, DC: U.S. Government Printing Office.

Kandel, D.B. (1985). On processes of peer influence in adolescent drug use: A developmental perspective. *Advances in Alcohol and Substance Abuse, 4,* 138–163.

Kandel, D.B., Kessler, R.C., & Margulies, R.Z. (1978). Antecedents of adolescent initiation into stages of drug use: A developmental analysis. *Journal of Youth and Adolescence, 7,* 13–40.

Lewis, H.B. (1985). Depression versus paranoia: Why are there sex differences in mental illness? *Journal of Personality, 53,* 150–178.

Murray, D.M., & Perry, C.L. (1985). The prevention of adolescent drug abuse: Implications of etiological, developmental, behavioral and environmental models. *Journal of Primary Prevention, 6*(1), 31–52.

Peluso, E., & Peluso, L.S. (1988). *Women & drugs: Getting hooked, getting clean.* Minneapolis: CompCare.

Radloff, L.S., & Rae, D.S. (1981). Components of sex differences in depression. *Research in Community and Mental Health, 2,* 111–137.

Ray, O. (1978). *Drugs, society and human behavior.* St. Louis: C.V. Mosby.

Thompson, K.M., & Wilsnack, R.W. (1982). *Parental influences on adolescent drinking: Modeling attitudes or conflict?* Paper presented at the 46th annual meeting of the Midwest Sociological Society, Des Moines, IA.

Vinogradov, S., Dishotsky, N.I., Doty, A.K., & Tinklenberg, J.R. (1988). Patterns of behavior in adolescent rape. *American Journal of Orthopsychiatry, 58,* 179–187.

Widseth, J.C., & Meyer, J. (1971). Drinking behaviors and attitudes toward alcohol in delinquent girls. *International Journal of the Addictions, 6,* 453–461.

Wilsnack, S.C., & Beckman, L.J. (1984). *Alcohol problems in women.* New York: Guilford Press.

Wilsnack, R.W., Thompson, K.M., & Wilsnack, S.C. (1981). *Effects of gender-role orientation on adolescent drinking: Patterns over time.* Paper presented at the annual meeting of the Society for the Study of Social Problems, Toronto, Canada.

Wilsnack, S.C., & Wilsnack, R.W. (1979). Sex roles and adolescent drinking. In H.T. Blane & M.E. Chafetz (Eds.), *Youth alcohol and social policy.* (pp. XX). New York: Plenum Press.

Zucker, R.A., & Devoe, C.I. (1975). Life history characteristics associated with problem drinking and antisocial behavior in adolescent girls: A comparison with male findings. In R.D. Wirt, G. Winokur, & M. Roff (Eds.), *Life history research in psychopathology* (Vol. 4, pp. XX). Minneapolis: University of Minnesota Press.

26

Substance Abuse Among Native American Youth

Thomas J. Young

According to the latest census, there are 1,418,195 Native Americans in the United States, a 71% increase over the 1970 count (U. S. Bureau of the Census, 1980). Some demographers believe that this figure is too low, however, and have estimated that a more accurate figure may be 2 million. Regardless of the exact count, it is evident that this population is growing rapidly and is quite young. The median age for this ethnic group is 18 years, compared to 29 years for the general U. S. population (May & Broudy, 1980; U. S. Bureau of the Census, 1980). Among the Navajo, the largest tribe in the United States, the median age is 16 years; only 4% of the Navajo population is 65 years of age or older, compared to 11% nationally (May & Broudy, 1980; Young, 1988).

In the 1960s and 1970s, large numbers of Native Americans moved to urban areas, especially along the West Coast. The percentage of Native Americans living in urban areas increased from 13.4% in 1950, to 17.9% in 1960, to 44.5% in 1970. It is currently estimated that approximately 50% of Native Americans reside in urban areas, primarily in unstable, lower working class areas (Fuchs & Havighurst, 1972; Sorkin, 1978). Poverty remains a harsh social reality for this ethnic group, as 27.5% have incomes below the poverty line (Shepard, 1987). The economic situation is often even worse among Native Americans on reservations. On the Rosebud Indian Reservation in South Dakota, for example, the unemployment rate is 80% (Chaze, 1985).

According to U. S. Indian Health Service statistics, Native Americans are generally healthier today than in the past. From the mid-1950s to the mid-1970s alone, the tuberculosis mortality rate decreased 75%, infant mortality declined 51%, and death due to influenza and pneumonia dropped 36% (Schaefer, 1979). Diseases such as otitis media, gastroenteritis, impetigo, gonococcal infections, pneumonia, and influenza continue to pose significant health problems, however. Even so, the greatest health problem in many Native American communities is the abuse of alcohol and other substances.

USE OF ALCOHOL

The "drunken Indian" stereotype has become an entrenched aspect of American folklore. Actually, there is considerable tribal variation in drinking patterns, ranging from chronic intoxication to abstinence (Westermeyer, 1974). For example, the Navajo generally accept drinking and episodic drunkenness, while the Hopi tend to condemn drinking and intoxication as an irresponsible threat to cosmic harmony (Kunitz, Levy, Odoroff, & Bollinger, 1971). Despite the considerable tribal variation in the use of alcohol, the U. S. Indian Health Service (1977) has cited alcohol abuse as the most urgent health problem facing Native Americans. The Services' hospital discharge rate for alcohol-related diagnoses is approximately 3 times the U. S. national rate and 2 times the rate for races other than non-Hispanic whites (U. S. Indian Health Service, 1982). The discharge rates for nondependent abuse of alcohol and for alcoholic liver disease are 3.4 times the national rates (5.8 vs. 1.7 per 100,000 and 6.4 vs. 1.9 per 100,000, respectively), while the alcohol dependency discharge rate is nearly twice the national rate (35.8 vs. 19.7 per 100,000) and the alcohol psychosis discharge rate is 4 times the national rate (11.8 vs. 2.9 per 100,000).

Without question, the single most disturbing statistic is that 75% of all Native American deaths can be directly or indirectly linked to alcohol. Indeed, 5 of the 10 leading causes of death among Native Americans are directly related to alcohol: (1) accidents, (2) cirrhosis of the liver, (3) alcohol dependency, (4) suicide, and (5) homicide (Andre, 1979). Alcohol-related accidents represent the leading cause of death among Native Americans; the mortality rate in this group is 3 times the national average (U. S. Indian Health Service, 1977). The mortality rate for cirrhosis of the liver is 4.4 times the national rate and is 85% alcohol related (May, 1982). The suicide and homicide rates are 1.6 and 2.9 times that of the general population (Abbas, 1982), and alcohol is a factor in approximately 80% of all Native American suicides and 90% of all homicides (Young, LaPlante, & Robbins, 1987).

Prevalence of Alcohol Use

According to epidemiological data, 67% of all adults in the United States who are 18 years or older consume alcohol at least once a year (National Institute on Alcohol Abuse and Alcoholism, 1981). Data on the prevalence of alcohol use among Native Americans are less precise; researchers have reported a striking range of use from one reservation to the next. For example, Levy and Kunitz (1974) found that 30% of the Navajo of the Southwest use alcohol, although the adult prevalence rate was as high as 42% in some communities. This is in comparison to 69% of the Standing Rock Sioux in South Dakota (Whittacker, 1972), 80% of the Ute of Igacio in Colorado (Jessor, Graves, Hanson, & Jessor, 1969), and 84% of the Ojibwa of the Brokenhead Reserve in Canada (Longclaws, Barnes, Grieve, & Dumoff, 1980).

Likewise, the range of reported "heavy use" is considerable. For the general U.S. population, the prevalence of heavy use has been estimated to be between 9% (National Institute on Alcohol Abuse and Alcoholism, 1981) and 18% (Cahalan & Cisin, 1968). In comparison, heavy use has been reported among 9% to 24% of the Standing Rock Sioux (Whittacker, 1972), 14% of the Navajo (Levy & Kunitz, 1974), 26% of the Ute (Jessor et al., 1969), and 42% of the Ojibwa (Longclaws et al., 1980).

With regard to youth, the National Institute on Alcohol Abuse and Alcoholism (1981) statistics indicated that 73% of the white non-Hispanic students in Grades 7 through 12 have used alcohol and that 11% use alcohol heavily. In a national sample, Oetting, Goldstein, and colleagues (1980) found that 78% of Native American youth in Grades 7 through 12 have tried alcohol, with 61% reporting use in the 2 months preceding the survey. In another study, Oetting, Edwards, Goldstein, and Garcia-Mason (1980) found that 89% of the youth in five Southwestern tribes had used alcohol and that 2% had used alcohol heavily. At the Ojibwa reservation in Canada, Longclaws and associates (1980) discovered that 56% of the youth had tried alcohol, that 39% had used alcohol in the preceding month, and that 17% used alcohol heavily. In a study of Native American youth on the Wind River Reservation in Wyoming, the prevalence of "ever use" and "heavy use" was 76% and 46%, respectively (Cockerham, 1977).

Unfortunately, these studies probably do not indicate the true extent of alcohol use among Native American adolescents, as only those attending school were represented in the data. Consequently, two risk groups, absentee students and dropouts, were generally excluded from the reports. This is a serious methodological limitation, considering that the absentee rates for Native American youth in many schools range up to 40% and that less than one third of all Native American youth complete high school (Beauvais, Oetting, & Edwards, 1985; Sorkin, 1978).

The literature suggests that alcohol use is more prevalent among Native Americans, but gathering precise information on Native American substance use and abuse is extremely difficult. First, cultural barriers to communication and understanding often frustrate data collection and interpretation. Second, obtaining samples of adequate size is a problem in most studies because researchers must opt for the investigation of either large scattered tribes or the limited population of small sedentary tribes. Finally, the lack of data that pertain to the aboriginal past may cause researchers to make inferences that reflect preconceived and unverifiable notions (Levy & Kunitz, 1973).

Patterns of Alcohol Use

There are at least four types of Native American drinking patterns: abstinence, social drinking, recreational drinking, and anxiety drinking. Abstinence is most commonly found among Native American women and adults over 30 years of age. It is socially unacceptable and, therefore, quite rare for Navajo and Pueblo women to drink once they have passed their mid-20s, and far more Native American adults stop drinking than do non–Native American adults. Among the Navajo, for instance, 37% of the adults over age 30 have stopped drinking, compared to 8% nationally. The tragedy, as May (1982) has indicated, is that too many Native American youth do not live long enough to change their drinking style.

Native American social drinking is similar to social drinking within the dominant culture in that it promotes group cohesion. Rodeos, ceremonials, and other social events provide a festive atmosphere for alcohol consumption. Drinking is viewed as a gesture of friendship, and declining an offer of a drink is a faux pas. Among the Navajo, relatives commonly drink together. The composition of Navajo drinking groups mirrors the cultural emphasis placed on the maintenance of warm and stable interpersonal relationships and the preservation of the universal harmony ethic (Heath, 1964).

Like social drinking, recreational drinking fosters social cohesion, but it differs in terms of the volume, speed, and duration of the alcohol consumption. Typically, a group consumes a large amount of alcohol quickly. Drinking is sporadic, however, and is marked by long periods of abstinence between each binge. Nevertheless, this drinking pattern increases the probability for arrest, injury, or accidental death. Yet some tribes not only tolerate recreational drinking, but also prescribe it, particularly for teen-aged males. Among the Santee, for example, this style of drinking is considered part of a normal rite of passage from "hell-raiser to family man" (Hill, 1974).

Cirrhosis of the liver and other alcohol-related degenerative diseases usually occur among anxiety drinkers. These individuals, who are physically and psychologically addicted to alcohol, tend to drink alone. They are usually marked by downward social mobility and are often socially ostracized, like the Hopi rural skid row alcoholics (Young, 1989).

USE OF OTHER SUBSTANCES

Native American youth are more likely than are non–Native American youth to use not only alcohol, but also inhalants and marijuana. The voluntary use of inhalants for mind-altering purposes among Native American youth appears to be twice as high as among the general population of youth 12 to 17 years of age. The national prevalence rate for all youth in this age group is 11% compared to 22% for a national sample of Native American youth (Young, 1987).

Inhalants are popular because they are inexpensive and easy to obtain, and because they provide the user with a rapid onset and dissipation of intoxication. It is a mistake simply to dismiss inhalant use as "childish behavior." There is always a danger of sudden or accidental death with inhalant use. In most cases of acute toxicity, death is due to cardiac arrest and a variety of cardiac arrhythmias. Of course, accidental death may also result from antisocial behavior, self-destructive acts, and excessive risk taking. The chronic use of inhalants can lead to a variety of health problems, such as bone marrow depression; leukemia; encephalopathy; and liver, kidney, chromosome, and immune system damage (Young & Lawson, 1986).

National statistics indicate that 30.9% of U.S. adolescents (12- to 17-years-old) have at least tried marijuana (Fishburne, Abelson, & Cisin, 1980). In comparison, Oetting, Goldstein, and associates (1980) surveyed a national sample of Native American youth in Grades 7 through 12 and found that 46% had tried marijuana. Considerable tribal variation has been reported, however, ranging from 62% of the students in five Southwestern tribes (Oetting, Edwards, et al., 1980) to 22% of the youth on a reservation in central Canada (Longclaws et al., 1980). Still, in overall terms, it appears that Native American youth are more likely than are non–Native American youth to experiment with marijuana.

THEORETICAL PERSPECTIVES

It is commonly heard that Native Americans are inherently vulnerable to the abuse of alcohol and other drugs. In the early 1970s, this "firewater" theory gained some scientific support when Fenna, Mix, Schaefer, and Gilbert (1971) found that whites metabolized alcohol at a significantly faster rate than did Native Americans. Lieber (1972) criticized this study on methodological grounds, however, and Bennion and Li (1976) found in a subsequent study that the mean rates of alcohol metabolism for whites and for Native Americans were virtually identical.

Another popular explanation of the high prevalence of substance abuse among Native Americans is the sociocultural theory of anomie. According to this theory, Native Americans are "mourning the loss of a historical tradition and reacting to the stresses of acculturation, including the demand to integrate and identify with mainstream society" (Lewis, 1982, p. 319). Historical events such as the forced relocation of tribes, the breakup of families, the constant harassment from settlers and soldiers, and the failure of the reservation system to provide a well-defined set of social roles, it is argued, resulted in the disintegration of Native American cultures and fostered a state of anomie. Hence, many Native Americans now attempt to assert their "Indianness" through drinking and drunkenness.

Critics of anomie theory contend that "it is a self-proving argument which explains all findings no matter how contradictory" (Levy & Kunitz, 1973, p. 234). They question the idea that aboriginal cultures were free of social pathologies and contend that Native American substance abuse can be explained by preexisting elements of aboriginal life. Several historians, for example, have argued that drinking and drunkenness were compatible with the aboriginal goals and values of many tribes and that much of the drinking behavior was learned by emulating white settlers (Dailey, 1968; MacAndrew & Edgerton, 1969; Winkler, 1969).

Oetting, Beauvais, and Edwards (1988) criticized researchers for their "tendency to search for extraordinary cultural factors to explain Indian alcohol use" (p. 87). They argued that "many of the factors that underlie alcohol use in non–Indians have the same effects on Indians" and that "Indians might be better served by applying general knowledge of alcohol abuse to the resolution of problem drinking among Indians" (p. 88). Four contributing factors have consistently emerged in the literature on adolescent drug use: sociocultural background, family interaction, peer relationships, and personal characteristics.

Most scholars believe that adolescent drug use results from the interaction of several factors rather than from one single variable. As the number of risk factors increases, the likelihood of drug use increases. Sociocultural factors and peer relationships appear to have the greatest impact on an adolescent's decision to experiment with drugs; psychological adjustment and psychosocial competency have a greater influence on the transition from experimentation to regular use (Gullotta & Adams, 1982; Lettieri, 1985).

Some researchers disagree with the contention that too much effort has been spent on a search for culturally unique factors relating to Native American substance use. These researchers do not dismiss the general importance of family turmoil, peer groups, or psychological adjustment, but they do believe that monocultural explanations tend to obscure the diversity of the population and the complexity of Native American drug use.

RATIONALES FOR DRUG USE

Adolescents' rationales or justifications for drug use determine what drugs they use, the conditions under which they use drugs, and the effect that they expect from drugs. An understanding of their rationales for drug use may provide the clinician with important information for counseling. If Native American and non–Native American youth use different rationales for drug use, multimodal treatment may be indicated.

To study this issue, Binion, Miller, Beauvais, and Oetting (1989) administered anonymous self-report substance use surveys to eighth grade Native American students from two reservations in the western United States and to non–Native American eighth grade students from three small towns in the same region. Among alcohol users, there were significant differences between Native American and non–Native American youth on 11 of the 13 rationales. Non–Native American youth attributed more importance to parties and sex, for example, while Native American youth attached more importance to independence; sensation seeking; relief of boredom, loneliness, unhappiness, and anger; and social interaction. No significant differences were found on the rationales of feeling drugged and nervousness.

Non–Native American youth also attached significantly more importance to parties and sex as rationales for marijuana use. For other drugs, they attributed more importance to the rationales of parties, sensation seeking, boredom, feeling drugged, and nervousness. Native American youth did not attach significantly more importance to any of the rationales than did non–Native American youth.

Both Native American and non–Native American youth placed a great deal of importance on the altered affect that drugs provide. This was the rationale that most of the adolescents surveyed felt was important for their drug use, regardless of the type of drug. Since other rationales interacted with and supported altered affect, however, the authors were unable to conclude that altered affect is the most important rationale for drug use. The findings suggested that Native American youth use alcohol for multiple and interrelated reasons, forming an intricate and elaborate network of rationales. Therefore, clinical interventions with Native American youth on reservations will have to go beyond educational efforts and adopt a multifaceted milieu approach to the treatment and prevention of substance abuse.

CONCLUSION

The need for further research on substance abuse among Native American youth is evident in the fact that there is controversy over the two most fundamental issues: the prevalence of Native American substance abuse and the reason why Native Americans use/abuse alcohol and other drugs. Both the biological and the cultural components of substance use and abuse among members of this ethnic group should be investigated. Unfortunately, as Heath (1975) noted, many researchers may deliberately avoid the firewater theory and its claim of genetic vulnerability because it is as emotionally charged as the black IQ controversy. If a meaningful body of literature is to evolve on this topic, however, the dogma and polemics that have prevailed so far must be transcended. This goal can be accomplished only through an interdisciplinary approach.

Intervention strategies must begin with the realization that Native Americans represent a diverse population. Treatment modalities that prove effective among one group of Native Americans may not be useful or appropriate among another group (Stone, 1962; Vogel, 1970). Even within specific groups, clinicians must remain sensitive to social, psychological, and biological variation among individuals. Thus, treatment must be multimodal, designed to meet the needs of each client. In some cases, therefore, the clinician must be prepared to transcend the so-called clinical mentality through the use of indigenous healers and Native American health care practices.

REFERENCES

Abbas, L. (1982). Alcoholism among Native Americans. In W. Mitchell & M. Galletti (Eds.), *Native American substance abuse* (pp. 44–54). Tempe, AZ: Arizona State University.

Andre, J.M. (1979). *The epidemiology of alcoholism among American Indians and Alaska Natives.* Albuquerque: U.S. Indian Health Service.

Beauvais, F., Oetting, E.R., & Edwards, R. (1985). Trends in the use of inhalants among American Indian adolescents. *White Cloud Journal, 3,* 3–11.

Bennion, L., & Li, T.K. (1976). Alcohol metabolism in American Indians and whites. *New England Journal of Medicine, 294,* 9–13.

Binion, A., Miller, C.D., Beauvais, F., & Oetting, E.R. (1989). *Rationales for the use of alcohol, marijuana, and other drugs by Indian youth.* Unpublished manuscript, Colorado State University, Psychology Department, Fort Collins, CO.

Cahalan, D., & Cisin, H. (1968). American drinking practices. *Quarterly Journal of Studies in Alcohol, 29,* 130–151.

Chaze, W.L. (1985, September). Alcohol, poverty—The killing fields of Rosebud. *U.S. News and World Report,* pp. 52–53.

Cockerham, W.C. (1977). Patterns of alcohol and multiple drug use among rural white and American Indian adolescents. *International Journal of the Addictions, 12,* 271–285.

Dailey, R.C. (1968). The role of alcohol among North American Indian tribes as reported in the Jesuit relations. *Anthropologica, 1,* 45–49.

Fenna, D., Mix, L., Schaefer, O., & Gilbert, J.A.L. (1971). Ethanol metabolism in various racial groups. *Canadian Medical Association Journal, 105,* 472–475.

Fishburne, P.M., Abelson, H.I., & Cisin, I. (1980). *National survey on drug abuse: Main findings* (DHHS Publication No. ADM-80-976). Washington, DC: U.S. Government Printing Office.

Fuchs, E., & Havighurst, R. (1972). *To live and die on this earth: American Indian education.* New York: Doubleday.

Gullotta, T.P., & Adams, G.R. (1982). Substance abuse minimization: Conceptualizing prevention in adolescent and youth programs. *Journal of Youth and Adolescence, 11,* 409–424.

Heath, D.B. (1964). Prohibition and post-repeal drinking patterns among the Navajo. *Quarterly Journal of Studies on Alcohol, 25,* 119–135.

Heath, D.B. (1975). A critical review of ethnographic studies of alcohol use. In R.J. Gibbins, Y. Israel, H. Kalant, R.E. Popham, W. Schmidt, & R.G. Smart (Eds.), *Research advances in alcohol and drug problems* (Vol. 2, pp. 1–92). New York: John Wiley & Sons.

Hill, T.W. (1974). From hell-raiser to family man. In J. Spradley & D. McCurdy (Eds.), *Conformity and conflict: Readings in cultural anthropology* (pp. 186–200). Boston: Little, Brown.

Jessor, R., Graves, T., Hanson, R., & Jessor, S. (1969). *Society, personality and deviant behavior: A study of a tri-ethnic community.* New York: Holt, Rinehart & Winston.

Kunitz, S.J., Levy, J.E., Odoroff, C.L., & Bollinger, J. (1971). The epidemiology of alcoholic cirrhosis in two Southwestern Indian tribes. *Quarterly Journal of Studies on Alcohol, 32,* 706–720.

Lettieri, D.J. (1985). Drug abuse: A review of explanations and models of explanation. *Advances in Alcohol and Substance Abuse, 4,* 9–40.

Levy, J.E., & Kunitz, S.J. (1973). Indian drinking: Problems of data collection and the interpretation. In M. Chafetz (Ed.), *Proceedings of the 1st annual alcoholism conference* (DHEW Publication No. HSM 73-9074, pp. 217–236). Washington, DC: U.S. Government Printing Office.

Levy, J.E., & Kunitz, S.J. (1974). *Indian drinking: Navajo practices and Anglo-American theories.* New York: Wiley-Interscience.

Lewis, R.G. (1982). Alcoholism and Native Americans: A review of the literature. In National Institute on Alcohol Abuse and Alcoholism (Ed.), *Alcohol and health: Special population issues* (DHHS Publication No. ADM 82-1193, pp. 315–328). Washington, DC: U.S. Government Printing Office.

Lieber, C.S. (1972). Metabolism of ethanol and alcoholism: Racial and acquired factors. *Annals of Internal Medicine, 76,* 326–327.

Longclaws, L., Barnes, G., Grieve, L., & Dumoff, R. (1980). Alcohol and drug use among the Brokenhead Ojibwa. *Journal of Studies on Alcohol, 41,* 21–36.

MacAndrew, C., & Edgerton, R.B. (1969). *Drunken comportment.* Chicago: Aldine.

May, P.A. (1982). Substance abuse and American Indians: Prevalence and susceptibility. *International Journal of the Addictions, 17,* 1185–1209.

May, P.A., & Broudy, D.W. (1980). *Health problems of the Navajo and suggested interventions.* Window Rock, AZ: Navajo Health Authority.

National Institute on Alcohol Abuse and Alcoholism. (1981). *Fourth special report to the U.S. Congress on alcohol and health* (DHHS Publication No. HSM 73-9124). Washington, DC: U.S. Government Printing Office.

Oetting, E.R., Beauvais, F., & Edwards, R. (1988). Alcohol and Indian youth: Social and psychological correlates and prevention. *Journal of Drug Issues, 18,* 87–101.

Oetting, E.R., Edwards, R., Goldstein, G.S., & Garcia-Mason, V. (1980). Drug use among adolescents of five South-western Native American tribes. *International Journal of the Addictions, 15,* 439–445.

Oetting, E.R., Goldstein, G.S., Beauvais, F., Edwards, R., Goldstein, L., & Valarde, J. (1980). *Drug abuse among Indian children.* Fort Collins, CO: Western Behavioral Studies.

Schaefer, R.T. (1979). *Racial and ethnic groups.* Boston: Little, Brown.

Shepard, J.M. (1987). *Sociology* (3rd. ed.). St. Paul, MN: West.

Sorkin, A.L. (1978). *The urban American Indian.* Lexington, MA: Lexington Books.

Stone, E. (1962). *Medicine among the American Indians.* New York: Hafner.

U.S. Bureau of the Census. (1980). *Census of the population: Subject reports, American Indians* (Publication No. PC 80-2-10). Washington, DC: U.S. Government Printing Office.

U.S. Indian Health Service. (1977). *Alcoholism: A high priority health problem* (DHEW Publication No. HSA 77-1001). Washington, DC: U.S. Government Printing Office.

U.S. Indian Health Service. (1982). *Analysis of fiscal year 1981 IHS and U. S. hospital discharge rates by age and primary diagnosis.* Washington, DC: U.S. Government Printing Office.

Vogel, V.J. (1970). *American Indian medicine.* Norman, OK: University of Oklahoma Press.

Westermeyer, J. (1974). "The drunken Indian": Myths and realities. *Psychiatric Annals, 4,* 29.

Whittacker, J.O. (1972). Alcohol and the Standing Rock Sioux tribe. *Quarterly Journal of Studies on Alcohol, 23,* 468–479.

Winkler, A.M. (1969). Drinking on the American frontier. *Quarterly Journal of Studies on Alcohol, 29,* 413–445.

Young, T.J. (1987). Inhalant use among American Indian youth. *Child Psychiatry and Human Development, 18,* 36–46.

Young, T.J. (1988). Substance use and abuse among Native Americans. *Clinical Psychology Review, 8,* 125–138.

Young, T.J. (1989). Indigent alcoholics on skid row. In G.W. Lawson & A.W. Lawson (Eds.), *Alcoholism and substance abuse in special populations* (pp. 305–313). Gaithersburg, MD: Aspen Publishers.

Young, T., LaPlante, C., & Robbins, W. (1987). Indians before the law: An assessment of contravening cultural/legal ideologies. *Quarterly Journal of Ideology, 11,* 59–70.

Young, T.J., & Lawson, G. (1986). Voluntary inhalation of volatile substances: A clinical review. *Corrective and Social Psychiatry, 32,* 49–54.

27

Methamphetamine and Adolescents

Jeanne Tarter

The Southwest and Pacific Coast are experiencing another drug plague. An army of amateur street chemists are developing a new industry of "home-brewed" dope that has a great deal in common with the old industry of "home-brewed" booze that arose in the Depression years. The laboratories are hidden, but within easy reach of the market. The substance produced can have impurities that may be harmful, if not fatal. The product that is produced is illegal, and merchants sell their wares to anyone who can pay the price, even children. The product is methamphetamine. In accordance with its renewed popularity, methamphetamine is known by a number of street names that vary from one area to another. A few of the common names are

- *chalk:* named for the gritty, chalklike appearance of some methamphetamine tablets from illicit manufacturers
- *driver:* short for "truck driver," a methamphetamine tablet used by truck drivers
- *water:* methamphetamine to be mixed with water for injection
- *crank:* usually, illicit methamphetamine
- *speed:* any amphetamine
- *fives:* 5-milligram tablets of any amphetamine
- *leaper:* any amphetamine
- *dice:* methamphetamine, probably Desoxyn
- *crystal:* methamphetamine in powder form
- *lightning:* any amphetamine
- *yellow bam:* methamphetamine, probably Desoxyn
- *meth:* methamphetamine
- *zip:* any amphetamine

HISTORICAL OVERVIEW

Methamphetamine use by young people is a growing problem in the western section of the United States (Johnston, O'Malley, & Bachman, 1988). During the year 1986–1987, the University of California Medical Center in San Diego found evidence of amphetamine, methamphetamine, or both in 297 toxicology test profiles (Bailey, 1987). The *Los Angeles Times* (Isikoff, 1989) reported that there were 87 methamphetamine-related deaths in Los Angeles, San Francisco, and San Diego in 1986. The trend of methamphetamine use is rapidly moving across the continent to the East. The fear that parents once felt about psychedelic drugs is being transferred to "speed." The phrase *speed kills* is being revived from the late 1960s.

The first epidemic of methamphetamine abuse broke out after World War II in the United States (Angrist & Gershon, 1969) and Japan (Kato, 1969). Many adolescents began to use the methamphetamine that they obtained from inhalers. They chewed and swallowed pieces of the wick of the inhaler or boiled the wick down to a fluid and injected it into the body with a hypodermic needle. Methamphetamine in pill form was also easy to obtain, either legally or illegally. In 1966, Sadusk wrote that legal amphetamine production had increased to approximately 8 billion tablets per year. Each man, woman, and child in the United States could have 35 doses of 5-milligram amphetamine tablets per year.

High-dose and/or intravenous use of methamphetamine became popular in the late 1960s and early 1970s. Smith and Fischer (1970) described methamphetamine as a "major adolescent abuse problem" (p. 117). By the late 1960s, approximately one in four adolescents in the United States had used the drug at least once. Occasional and/or one-time users of methamphetamine were usually adolescents who came from middle-class families and had tried the oral form of the drug.

The adolescent use of methamphetamine decreased from 1975 to 1981 and then leveled off until 1985. The Southwestern and Pacific Coast states are again seeing an increase of adolescent methamphetamine abuse, however (Bailey, 1987; Newmeyer, 1988). The trend is likely to spread throughout the United States and other nations. Japan is already experiencing another methamphetamine epidemic; many of those who are now using methamphetamine are the adolescents who inhaled glue and toluene in their early teen-age years (Kato, 1983).

Methamphetamine use is a serious obstacle to a young person's maturation process. The period of young adulthood is a transition period in which the young person develops individuality and an adult value system. Methamphetamine use prolongs dependence and immaturity, however, and may result in lifelong physical problems or even death. The worst effect of all may be chronic psychiatric problems that will follow a person for a lifetime.

Seymour and Smith (1987) pointed out that the route of administration of methamphetamine varies. The drug can be taken orally, by nasal insufflation, or by intravenous injection. Interviews with a number of adolescent users in southern California revealed that smoking the drug is now the preferred route of administration, however. The intravenous route is used primarily by individuals who are high-dose, long-time users (Anonymous, personal communication, March 1989).

The *Physicians' Desk Reference* (1982) noted that the normal dose for methamphetamine is 10 to 20 milligrams per day. The effects of the drug begin approximately 30 minutes after administration and last from 4 to 8 hours. Methamphetamine, like the other amphetamines, varies greatly in its half-life and in the duration of its effects. The reason for the variations is that the drug is excreted in the urine and the amount excreted depends on the acidity of the urine. The higher the acid content of the urine, the faster the excretion of the methamphetamine. King and Coleman (1987) advised treating methamphetamine toxicity by administering ammonium chloride to acidify the urine. Street abusers drink large quantities of cranberry juice when they want to reduce the effects of the drug and take sodium bicarbonate when they want to prolong the effects.

The central nervous system effects of methamphetamine are restlessness, increased wakefulness, anorexia, alertness, agitation, and increased motor and speech activity. Headaches, cardiac palpitations, dizziness, and elevated pulse and blood pressure rates are peripheral nervous system effects (King & Coleman, 1987). The contraction of the smooth muscles of the bladder neck in response to the methamphetamine may cause urinary retention. Bennett and Delrio (1980) reported an idiopathic rupture of the bladder that was associated with simultaneous methamphetamine and alcohol use; the rupture appeared to be due to the diuretic effect of the alcohol in combination with the bladder neck constriction.

Tolerance to methamphetamine develops rapidly, and the individual finds it necessary to increase the dose of the drug in order to achieve the desired effects. If the dose of methamphetamine is high (more than 50 milligrams per day), psychosis can occur. A combination of physical and psychiatric factors determines the toxicity of methamphetamine in different individuals. Smith (1969) reported that some severe reactions had occurred when a nontolerant individual was given 30 milligrams of methamphetamine by rapid intravenous push, but that some individuals were injecting themselves with 100 to 500 milligrams of street methamphetamine per day without developing an acute psychosis.

A number of cases of cerebral hemorrhage have been associated with methamphetamine abuse (D'Souza & Shraber, 1981; Goodman & Becker, 1970; Yu, Cooper, Wellenstein, & Block, 1983). Intravenous use of the drug can cause infections from contaminants, renal damage, strokes, heart attacks, and death due to circulatory collapse (Radcliffe, Rush, Sites, & Cruse, 1985).

MEDICAL USES OF METHAMPHETAMINE

Like those for the other amphetamines, prescriptions for methamphetamine cannot exceed a 30-day supply and are not refillable. Methamphetamine can be medically prescribed for only three conditions: (1) obesity, (2) narcolepsy, and (3) hyperkinesis (King & Coleman, 1987; Lasagna, 1979; Young & Lawson, 1988).

Of the three conditions, methamphetamine is most frequently prescribed for obesity. Amphetamines have a limited anorexic effect, however, because tolerance to the drug occurs in a few weeks (Young & Lawson, 1988). Furthermore, medication does not solve the psychological problems and the poor dietary habits that go along with obesity, and treatment should address these problems. As noted in the *Physicians' Desk Reference* (1982), "The limited usefulness of Desoxyn [methamphetamine] should be weighed against possible risks inherent in use of the drug" (p. 513).

Narcolepsy is a sleep disorder. Its symptoms may include sleep attacks, sleep paralysis, cataplexy, and hypnagogic hallucinations. Methamphetamine is the amphetamine of choice in the treatment of this condition, as it has the fewest sympathomimetic side effects (Soldatos, Kales, & Cadieux, 1979). Precautions should be taken in the use of methamphetamine, because treatment can be complicated by the abuse potential of the drug.

Some physicians prescribe methamphetamine for hyperkinetic syndrome or attention deficit disorder. Methamphetamine has been shown to have a stabilizing effect on children over 6 years of age who have a number of behavioral problems, but it is not the drug of choice. Most pediatricians have found that the drug methylpenidate (Ritalin) is much more effective (Bolter, 1979).

PREVALENCE OF METHAMPHETAMINE ABUSE

The National Institute on Drug Abuse sponsors two national research surveys to assess the prevalence of drug abuse in the adolescent population. The surveys are (1) National Trends in Drug Use and Related Factors Among American High School Students and Young Adults and (2) The National Household Survey of Drug Abuse (National Institute on Drug Abuse, 1987).

The National Trends Survey, which has been in existence since 1975, is conducted in approximately 130 high schools in different regions throughout the United States. More than 16,000 high school seniors are polled. The study covers 18 classes of drugs and monitors the current drug use trends, prevalence data, student attitudes about drugs, and effectiveness of drug education information.

The National Trends Survey does not include adolescents who have dropped out of school, however. The Census Bureau estimates the dropout rate to be approximately 15%. The prevalence of drug use among dropouts is extremely high; for this reason, government officials feel that the National Trends Survey grossly underestimates the adolescent drug abuse problem.

In this survey, methamphetamine is listed under stimulants (amphetamines). Students have been instructed to exclude not only the use of physician-prescribed stimulants, but also the use of over-the-counter stimulants since the 1984 survey, when new questions were included on controlled and uncontrolled stimulant use. From 1979 through 1983, the sharp rise that was reported in amphetamine use is attributed to the survey respondents' including over-the-counter stimulants on their answer sheets (Johnston, O'Malley, & Bachman, 1988).

The National Household Survey, like the National Trends Survey, is based on questionnaires and personal interviews. Because the National Household Survey covers a broader age range than does the National Trends Survey, it permits a comparison of drug use among different age groups. The results of both surveys indicate that overall drug use by U.S. high school seniors dropped in 1988 on a national level (Freedlund, Spence, & Maxwell, 1988; Johnston, O'Malley, & Bachman, 1988). Adolescents in the United States continued to surpass their counterparts in all other nations in using and experimenting with legal and illegal drugs, however.

The surveys have shown wide differences in both licit and illicit drug use in various regions of the United States. Stimulant (amphetamine and methamphetamine) use is the highest in the West and lowest in the Southeast (Johnston, O'Malley, & Bachman, 1988). Some of the other trends are as follows:

- Amphetamines are the second most popular illicit drugs among adolescents. (Marijuana is the first.)
- Amphetamines are the fourth most popular of licit and illicit drugs among adolescents. (Alcohol, cigarettes, and marijuana are used more often.)
- Amphetamines have been tried by 22% of high school seniors surveyed. Approximately 5% use them daily.
- Amphetamines are used slightly more frequently by girls (9%) than by boys (8%).
- Amphetamine use is higher in large cities than in rural areas.
- Amphetamine use is higher among high school students who do not expect to go to college.

In 1988, the Texas Commission on Alcohol and Drug Abuse conducted a survey on substance abuse in secondary schools (Freedlund, Spence, & Maxwell, 1988). The information gathered indicated that substance abuse among Texas youth had increased considerably since the previous survey, which had been taken in 1980. According to the earlier survey, substance abuse in Texas was well below the national averages. In 1988, however, substance abuse patterns in Texas were very similar to the national averages (Figure 27-1).

The Texas survey sample consisted of 7,500 public school students in Grades 7 through 12. Private school students and school dropouts were not included in this study. The eight-page questionnaire focused on usage patterns of 14 drugs and covered problems relating to substance abuse. The term *uppers* was used to indicate amphetamines. Prescription drugs (stimulants) taken to experience a "high" rather than in accordance with a doctor's order were also included in the upper category.

- Amphetamine use among Texas adolescents increased 93% from 1980 to 1988. Other trends in amphetamine use among Texas youth reported in the survey (Freedlund et al., 1988) are
- Amphetamines are the fifth most frequently used substance by adolescents in the 7th, 8th, and 9th grades. (Alcohol, cigarettes, marijuana, and inhalants are used more often.)
- Amphetamines are the fourth most frequently used substance by adolescents in the 10th, 11th, and 12th grades.
- Amphetamines have been tried by 11% of 7th graders and 25% of 12th graders.
- Current use of amphetamine by adolescents stands at 6% for all grades— twice as high as it was in 1980.

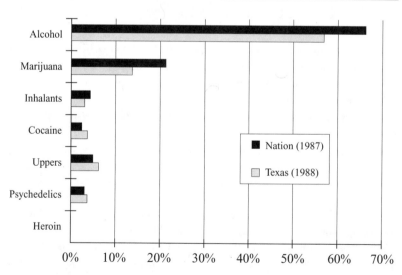

Figure 27-1 Thirty-Day Prevalence of Substance Use Among High School Seniors. *Source:* From *Substance Use Among Students in Texas Secondary Schools—1988* by F.V. Freedlund, R.T. Spence, and J.C. Maxwell, 1988, Austin, TX: Texas Commission on Alcohol and Drug Abuse.

- Amphetamines are used by more white high school seniors (33%) than by any other race or ethnic group. Black high school seniors (8%) have the lowest rate of amphetamine use.
- More girls than boys report amphetamine use.
- Students from two-parent families are less likely to use amphetamines, compared to students from other family situations.
- Amphetamines are used more frequently in large metropolitan areas.

FACTORS THAT INFLUENCE METHAMPHETAMINE USE

The popularity of one drug over another varies from one region to the next. Several factors have enhanced the popularity of methamphetamine. For example, the drug is relatively easy to manufacture from chemicals that are inexpensive and easy to obtain. In some states, the chemicals (e.g., acetic anhydride and ephedrine) can be purchased in bulk from legitimate chemical wholesalers. Isikoff (1989) estimated that $10,000 worth of chemicals and $2,000 worth of laboratory equipment yield approximately $200,000 worth of methamphetamine.

The quality of the methamphetamine depends on the skill of the "cook" and the "recipe" used. A large laboratory can produce between 5 and 25 pounds of methamphetamine a week, but this amount can be increased by the addition of other substances, such as caffeine, ephedrine, aspirin, and aminophylline (Cox & Smart, 1972). Most of the large laboratories are in isolated areas and have skilled chemists or "cooks" to process the drug. Small laboratories are usually run by novice "cooks" in high-use areas. Both types of laboratory produce methamphetamine that adolescents can easily obtain and afford to buy (Jehl, 1989).

Over time, the "in" method of methamphetamine ingestion has changed. In the late 1960s, the drug was taken orally or intravenously. Today, adolescents may (1) snort the drug as an off-white or brownish powder, (2) drink it after dissolving the power in a soft drink, or (3) smoke it in a smokeless cigarette or aluminum foil. The adolescent who is looking for the ultimate "high" uses an intravenous injection of methamphetamine powder that has been diluted in water. Once the individual begins using this method, he or she uses injections repeatedly in an effort to recapture that first high (Anonymous, personal communication, March 1989).

Because methamphetamine has not received the media coverage that cocaine has had, adolescents do not associate the two drugs with the same dangers and may believe that they can use methamphetamine frequently without ill effects. Youngsters are drawn to the chemical because it is cheaper and produces a longer lasting high than does cocaine. The diet pill effect attracts a number of adolescents, especially girls. The drug is both physically and psychologically addicting, however. Tolerance and physical dependence develop rapidly. Life-threatening infections from contaminants and unsterile needles develop from intravenous use.

Drug dealers take advantage of the lack of public awareness, pushing the medicinal aspects of the drug and playing down its dangers (Isikoff, 1989).

Methamphetamine is a party drug; users want their friends to participate in their high. Thus, adolescents usually begin to use methamphetamine with friends who supply it and use it themselves. They need to be part of the group and to feel as if they belong. Cox and Smart (1972) observed that the majority of their subjects used speed in a group so that they could have people to "rap" with.

Adolescents search for independence, but fear being independent. Methamphetamine makes it easy for adolescents to communicate with others, because it gives them a sense of self-confidence and self-esteem. Some users feel it gives a general feeling of well-being and happiness. Other users say that it gives them an ability to think faster, helps them to relax more fully, and increases their awareness of their surroundings (Cox & Smart, 1972).

The amphetamines are reported to be aphrodisiacs, and the initial use of methamphetamine does indeed enhance sexual activity. Male users, for example, insist that it enables them to have prolonged erections and prolonged intercourse. Chronic use generally results in impotence, but even the user's knowledge of this fact seldom inhibits drug use (Smith, Buxton, & Dammann, 1979).

DIAGNOSIS

The amount of methamphetamine used and the frequency of use determine the signs and symptoms that appear. Some of the signs and symptoms are nonspecific, and parents often attribute them to adolescence per se. A diagnostic pattern forms when the signs and symptoms occur together, however. In this event, the parents should examine not only the methamphetamine abuse, but also other situations in the adolescent's life (Kozicki, 1986).

Among the signs of methamphetamine use are

- concomitant use of alcohol, tobacco, and/or marijuana. Methamphetamine is usually used in combination with other drugs, most frequently alcohol and marijuana. Adolescents who use inhalants in their preteen years tend to switch to stimulants in high school (Johnston, O'Malley, & Bachman, 1988).

- peer group change. The users drift away from "straight" friends, because they no longer feel comfortable with them (Cox & Smart, 1972).

- chronic lack of money. The need for money to buy drugs can lead to borrowing money, stealing, selling valued possessions, dealing drugs, or turning to prostitution (Cox & Smart, 1972).

- mood shifts. Hyperactivity and garrulousness are usually followed by depression, anxiety, and irritability.

- possession of paraphernalia for "shooting," "snorting," or "smoking" methamphetamine. An adolescent whose parents find drug paraphernalia in his or her possession usually swears that the equipment belongs to a friend. Most parents want to believe what their child tells them but accepting this explanation without question only prolongs the adolescent's drug use (Emmelkamp, 1988).

The symptoms of methamphetamine abuse vary according to the type of use. With occasional methamphetamine use, the adolescent may have chronic upper respiratory infections, fatigue, and weight loss. With regular intermittent use, such as two or three times a week for several months, the adolescent may experience mood swings, deterioration of schoolwork, loss of interest in outside activities, sleep difficulties, and an exacerbation of the symptoms associated with occasional methamphetamine use. Frequent use of the drug creates a crawling sensation on the skin, and the adolescent may pick or dig at parts of the body in an effort to remove "bugs." Grating or grinding of the teeth (bruxism) is also a common symptom.

Malnutrition, weakening of the immune system, depression, anxiety, helplessness, thirst, suspicion, fear of being watched, insomnia, and a distortion of time sense are symptoms of high doses and daily use of methamphetamine. As the adolescent begins to ingest higher doses, an amphetamine psychosis that resembles paranoid schizophrenia may occur. Ellinwood (1969) noted that the symptoms mentioned earlier become more pronounced as the psychosis develops. Hallucinations and delusions of persecution are common and can lead to violent acts of aggression against self or others.

High-dose intravenous methamphetamine use can lead to drug "runs" that last for days or even weeks. During this time, the adolescent goes without food or sleep. Psychosis and violent behavior are common. When the "crash" occurs, the individual may be severely depressed and/or may sleep for long periods, even days (Smith & Fischer, 1970; Young & Lawson, 1988).

During the late 1960s, liquid methamphetamine was legally manufactured for intravenous use and packaged in glass ampules. Methamphetamine is no longer legally produced in ampules, but the term *overamp* is still used to describe an overdose. The adolescent who has "overamped" on methamphetamine remains conscious, but lacks the ability to move or speak. Other symptoms are elevations in temperature and blood pressure, rapid pulse, and respiratory distress (Smith & Fischer, 1970).

TREATMENT

The appropriate treatment strategy depends on the signs and symptoms that are present. Methamphetamine use or abuse is usually a symptom of other problems in the adolescent's life. Because every adolescent is an individual with individual needs and issues that should be addressed, no one treatment strategy fits every adolescent. Care should be taken to fit the treatment to the particular adolescent's needs. Archambault (1989) stated, "As professionals, the first duty is to do no harm. With this concept clearly in mind, one can then proceed to help" (p. 241). The following treatment strategy can be the basis for a more individualized approach:

1. A complete drug history should be taken from both the parents and the adolescent. The simultaneous use of several drugs is common in adolescents. Laboratory tests of a blood or urine sample may be necessary to determine what other chemicals the adolescent has used.
2. A complete medical examination should be performed to rule out any medical or psychiatric disorders.
3. Hospitalization may be necessary in cases of significant overdose, psychosis, or recurring drug hunger.
4. The general strategy should be one of support and reassurance. The adolescent should be told that the symptoms are the result of the methamphetamine and that the effects will slowly disappear in approximately 2 to 4 hours. A quiet room with a minimal amount of stimulation helps to reduce the symptoms.
5. Psychosis requires the use of the precautions that are extended to all paranoid clients. For example, it is necessary to explain procedures to obtain permission before touching the individual, and to avoid any rapid movements in the individual's presence.
6. Medication is generally not needed. If medicine does appear to be necessary, diazepam (Valium) or chlordiazepoxide hydrochloride (Librium), given one or two times, maybe helpful in reducing anxiety.
7. Long-term treatment usually involves drug abuse counseling on an outpatient basis. During therapy, an attempt should be made to address all the adolescent's life problems, not just the methamphetamine abuse.
8. The family systems approach to drug treatment should be recommended to the adolescent and his or her family, as it deals with all aspects of the family environment.

PREVENTION

Those who are working to prevent adolescent methamphetamine use should have a clear understanding of (1) the adolescent stage of the human development cycle and (2) the chemical dependence syndrome (DuPaint, 1987). Smart and Fejer (1974) suggested that one approach to prevention is to decrease the attractive way that drugs are presented to the adolescent in the media. Appropriate monitoring and control are necessary, for commercial interests have made the United States a drug-taking society.

Over the years, there has been a general erosion of social policy about intoxicants, and many children are becoming adolescents without clear and consistent guidelines on the proper use of various substances. Archambault (1989) stated, however, that "a healthy home environment can buttress an adolescent in a relatively sick society" (p. 243). Spotts and Shantz (1985) theorized that adolescent substance abuse is based on dysfunctional relationships with parental figures.

Families that have taken firm, consistent stands against drug use and have strong parental control have fewer children involved with drugs than do families that have more permissive attitudes about drug use. Adolescents whose parents are drug-free role models are less likely to use chemicals themselves. Of adolescent drug abusers, 81% have a parent or parents who also abuse drugs (Perry & Murry, 1985). Johnston, O'Malley, and Bachman (1988) indicated that children from two-parent families are less likely to use drugs than are children from one-parent families. Research studies often show that children who have low self-esteem are more likely to abuse drugs. Jessor and Jessor (1975) listed inadequate bonding to family and society, inadequate communication and assertiveness skills, inability to defer gratification, and the inability to accept the logical consequences of their actions as contributing factors in adolescent substance abuse. Building these skills should be a goal of all parents in order to help their adolescents get through the teen-age years without using chemicals as a crutch.

REFERENCES

Anonymous. (1989, March). [Interviews with nine adolescents who have used methamphetamine and wish to remain anonymous. The interviews took place in Redlands, San Diego, and Riverside, California.]

Angrist, B.M., & Gershon, S. (1969). Amphetamine abuse in New York City. *Journal of Psychedelic Drugs, 2*(2), 84–91.

Archambault, D. (1989). Adolescence: A physiological, cultural and psychological no man's land. In G. Lawson & A. Lawson (Eds.), *Alcoholism and substance abuse in special populations* (pp. 223–245). Gaithersburg, MD: Aspen Publishers.

Bailey, D.N. (1987). Amphetamine detection during toxicology screening of a university medical center patient population. *Clinical Toxicology, 25*(5), 399–409.

Bennett, A.H., & Delrio, A. (1980). Idiopathic rupture of the bladder: Association with methamphetamine and alcohol. *Journal of Urology, 124*(3), 429–430.

Bolter, A. (1979). The therapeutic use of methylphenidate (Ritalin) in the private practice of pediatrics. In D. Smith (Ed.), *Amphetamine use, misuse, and abuse* (pp. 153–159). Boston: G.H. Hall.

Cox, C., & Smart, R.G. (1972). Social and psychological aspects of speed use. *International Journal of the Addictions, 7*(2), 201–217.

D'Souza, T., & Shraber, D. (1981). Intracranial hemorrhage associated with amphetamine use [letter]. *Neurology, 31*(7), 922–923.

DuPaint, R.L. (1987). Prevention of adolescent chemical dependency. *Pediatric Clinics of North America, 34*(2), 495–505.

Ellinwood, E.H., Jr. (1969). Amphetamine psychoses I: Description of the individual and process. *Journal of Psychedelic Drugs, 2*(2), 42–51.

Emmelkamp, P.M. (1988). Drug addiction and parental rearing style: A controlled study. *International Journal of the Addictions, 23*(2), 207–216.

Freedlund, E.V., Spence, R.T., & Maxwell, J.C. (1988). *Substance use among students in Texas secondary schools—1988.* Austin, TX: Texas Commission on Alcohol and Drug Abuse.

Goodman, S.J., & Becker, D.P. (1970). Intracranial hemorrhage with amphetamine abuse. *Journal of the American Medical Association, 212,* 428.

Isikoff, M. (1989, February 12). In rural American, crank, not crack, is drug plague. *Los Angeles Times,* pp. 1, 4.

Jehl, D. (1989, March 1). Specific strategy on drug war eludes Bennett. *Los Angeles Times,* p. 14.

Jessor, R., & Jessor, S.L. (1975). Adolescent development and onset of drinking. *Journal of Alcohol Studies, 36,* 27–51.

Johnston, L., O'Malley, P., & Bachman, J.G. (1988). *National trends in drug use and related factors among American high school students and young adults* (DHHS Publication No. ADM 89-1602). Washington, DC: National Institute on Drug Abuse.

Kato, M. (1969). Drug dependence in Japan. *International Journal of the Addictions, 4,* 591.

Kato, M. (1983). A bird's eye view of the present state of drug abuse in Japan. *Drug and Alcohol Dependence, 11,* 55–56.

King, P., & Coleman, J.H. (1987). Stimulants and narcotic drugs. *Pediatric Clinics of North America, 34*(2), 349–361.

Kozicki, Z.A. (1986). Why do adolescents use substances (drug/alcohol). *Journal of Alcohol and Drug Education, 32*(1), 1–7.

Lasagna, L. (1979). Proper prescribing practices for therapeutic uses of amphetamines. In D. Smith (Ed.), *Amphetamine use, misuse, and abuse* (pp. 107–111). Boston: G.H. Hall.

National Institute on Drug Abuse. (1987). *National household survey on drug abuse* (DHHS Publication No. ADM 87-1539). Washington, DC: U.S. Government Printing Office.

Newmeyer, J.A. (1988). The prevalence of drug use in 1987. *Journal of Psychoactive Drugs, 20*(2), 185–189.

Perry, C.L., & Murry, D.M. (1985). The prevention of adolescent drug abuse: Implications from etiological, developmental, behavioral and environmental models. *Journal of Primary Prevention, 6,* 31–52.

Physicians' desk reference. (1982). Desoxyn (methamphetamine hydrochloride). Oradell, NJ: Medical Economics.

Radcliffe, A., Rush, P., Sites, C.F., & Cruse, J. (1985). Psychomotor stimulants. In A.D. Radcliffe (Ed.), *Pharmer's almanac* (pp. 89–98). Denver, CO: M.A.C. Printing.

Sadusk, J.F. (1966). Non-narcotic addiction: Size and extent of the problem. *Journal of the American Medical Association, 196,* 707–709.

Seymour, R., & Smith, D. (1987). Amphetamine. In R. Seymour & D.E. Smith (Eds.), *Guide to psychoactive drugs: An up-to-the-minute reference to mind altering substances* (pp. 63–71). New York: Harrington Park Press.

Smart, R., & Fejer, D. (1974). The effect of high and low fear messages about drugs. *Journal of Drug Education, 4,* 225–235.

Smith, D.E. (1969). An analysis of variables in high dose methamphetamine dependence. *Journal of Psychedelic Drugs, 2*(2), 60–62.

Smith, D.E., Buxton, M.E., & Dammann, G. (1979). Amphetamine abuse and sexual disfunction: Clinical and research considerations. In D.E. Smith (Ed.), *Amphetamine use, misuse, and abuse* (pp. 228–248). Boston: G.H. Hall.

Smith, D.E., & Fischer, C.M. (1970). An analysis of 310 cases of acute high-dose methamphetamine toxicity in Haight Ashbury. *Clinical Toxicology, 3*(1), 117–124.

Soldatos, C.R., Kales, A., & Cadieux, R. (1979). Narcolepsy. In D.E. Smith (Ed.), *Amphetamine use, misuse, and abuse* (pp. 128–139). Boston: G.H. Hall.

Spotts, J.V., & Shantz, F.C. (1985). Theory of substance abuse. In J. Brooks, D. Lettiere, D. Brooks, & B. Stimmel (Eds.), *Alcohol and substance abuse in adolescence* (pp. 117–138). New York: Hawthorne Press.

Young, T., & Lawson, G. (1988). Central nervous system stimulants. In G. Lawson & C. Cooperrider (Eds.), *Clinical psychopharmacology* (pp. 137–141). Gaithersburg, MD: Aspen Publishers.

Yu, Y.J., Cooper, D.R., Wellenstein, D.E., & Block, B. (1983). Cerebral angitis and intracerebral hemorrhage associated with methamphetamine abuse. *Journal of Neurosurgery, 1*(9), 411–413.

28

Cocaine and Adolescents

James T. Donoghue

Cocaine is a stimulant. It is the active ingredient of the leaf of the *Erythroxylon* plant (which has no resemblance to the cocoa bean or kola nut). The plant is native to Peru and Colombia, but has been cultivated in Bolivia, Brazil, Ceylon, Chile, Ecuador, France, India, Jamaica, Java, and the United States.

The drug is available from street sale as a paste, powder, or rock. Paste, also known as base, pasta, pistillo, and buscuso, comes from dissolving the leaves in a chemical solution; the paste contains cocaine, sulfate, other coca alkaloids, diluents, and adulterants. Powder, also known as snow or coke, comes from adding chemicals to the paste to make cocaine hydrochloride. Free base, a term often heard in the 1980s about smokable cocaine, is the free molecule that the user makes by dissolving the cocaine hydrochloride powder in water with a base of ammonia or baking soda added and then extracting the cocaine. Ordinary extraction for free base preparation fails to remove many of the adulterants or diluents that are added to the paste and powder, however. Crack or rock cocaine is a marketing version of the free base. Prepared by the dealer from the cocaine hydrochloride powder, it is sold in small, white, pebblelike rocks ready to be smoked. The crack sound that the rocks make when they burn in a pipe is the source of the name. Crack cocaine surfaced as a less expensive and more easily accessible form of free base smoking that does not require users to deal with elaborate equipment or flammable solvents.

EFFECTS OF COCAINE AND CRACK

Cocaine produces a sense of euphoria, well-being, and alertness, while increasing self-confidence, self-perceptions of mastery, interpersonal communication, and capability of doing work (Estroff, 1987; Siegel, 1987; Washton, 1989; Weiss & Mirin, 1987). It enhances emotions and sexual feelings, decreases anxiety and social inhibitions, and relieves pain. The method of ingestion, history and frequency of use, and dosage determine physical changes. The majority of users ingest the drug by sniffing powder into the nasal mucosa, causing stimulation but limited euphoria, much like high doses of caffeine do. This is the slowest route; it takes 1 to 3 minutes for the cocaine to reach the brain, compared to 30 to 120 seconds following injection and 5 to 10 seconds following smoking. Intranasal sniffing of the powdered form is typically done by placing the cocaine on a smooth flat surface (e.g., a mirror), chopping the crystallike substance into a finer powder with a razor blade, and then pushing the powder into very narrow lines 1 or 2 inches in length. The powder is ingested up the nostril by sniffing the line through a straw or rolled up dollar bill or from a small spoon. Intranasal sniffing increases the heart rate and elevates the blood pressure. Intranasal use can produce dependence with large doses, but dependence more often follows smoking and injection.

Smoking paste placed at the end of marijuana or tobacco cigarettes increases the pulse, blood pressure, respiratory rate, and body temperature. It can also dilate pupils, change muscle tension, and cause shakiness and heavy sweating. Repeated smoking of paste often causes anxiety, hostility, and severe depression; it can also lead to numbness in the mouth, a burning sensation in the eyes, pounding heartbeat, shaking limbs, headache, insomnia, dizziness, abdominal pain, heavy sweating, auditory and visual hallucinations, frightening anxiety, and paranoid ideas.

Free base smokers move readily through four stages of intoxication, depending on the level of dosage and the chronicity of use: (1) euphoria, (2) dysphoria, (3) paranoia, and (4) psychosis—sometimes all within a single episode of use that lasts only a few hours. Smoking free base in a pipe or in a tobacco or marijuana cigarette gives almost immediate euphoria and increases blood pressure, pulse, body temperature, and respiratory rate. The effect of free base smoking declines rapidly, however, with the euphoric sensation peaking in as little as 5 minutes and leading quickly to a "crash" sensation of depression, anxiety, and agitation, as well as a craving for more drug as soon as 10 minutes after the euphoria. Because of the continual craving, users may smoke in a "binge," possibly until the supply of the drug is gone. Smoking free base not only causes the same body changes as does smoking paste, but also may lead to burns from a combination of flames, volatile chemicals, and intoxicated users. Other physical effects of smoking free base include wispy voice, bleeding gums, dizziness, episodic unconsciousness, urination difficulties, complications of syncope, myoclonic jerking and seizures, bronchitis, and pneumonia. Psychological effects include attention and concentration problems, hyperexcitability, violent loss of impulse control, memory problems, and decrease in the number of dreams.

Intravenous injection of cocaine (typically 1/8 to 1/4 gram placed on a spoon with water, strained, drawn into a syringe, and injected) produces the same body changes as does smoking, but the use of the paraphernalia carries additional risks, such as skin infection, hepatitis, acquired immunodeficiency syndrome (AIDS), endocarditis, and other conditions that can come from needle sharing. One variation of intravenous injection is the "speedball" injection of a cocaine and heroin solution, which increases the risk of fatal respiratory consequences.

Cocaine and crack have a variety of other health consequences. For example, the drug may lead to more rapid brain electrical activity and elevated blood sugar levels that can be problematic for diabetics. Nasal problems are common, including congestion, cold symptoms, frequent nosebleeds, chronic cough, allergylike symptoms without the presence of the allergen, recurrent sinus infections, perforation of the nasal septum, sinus abscesses, and a diminished sense of smell. Grand mal seizures and a reduction of the seizure threshold have been reported in epileptics who use cocaine (Estroff, 1987). Lung problems, such as a decreased capacity to transport oxygen into the blood and damage from injection of adulterants (e.g., talc) in the cocaine powder, may occur. Appetite suppression can lead to weight loss, vitamin deficiency, and malnutrition. The sexual difficulties that may occur include male impotence, male inability to ejaculate, and decreased desire for both males and females. Chronic smoking can lead to spitting up of black, nonbloody material and anterior chest wall pain (Estroff, 1987; Miller, Gold, & Millman, 1989; Washton, 1989; Weiss & Mirin, 1987). An overdose can lead to rapid irregular heartbeat, cerebral hemorrhage, seizure, heat stroke, and respiratory failure. Possible psychiatric problems include depression, paranoia, and withdrawal from family and friends. Death can occur from suicide, automobile accidents, and homicide through interaction with criminals.

In teen-agers, the use of cocaine has been linked to frequent sniffing, sinus problems, diminished olfaction, nasal crusts or scabs, recurrent nosebleeds, chronic illness, abdominal pain, chest pain, and pneumomediastinum (Schwartz & Estroff, 1988; Schwartz, Estroff, Fairbanks, & Hoffmann, 1989; Shannon, Lacouture, Roa, & Woolf, 1989). Crack use has been linked to loss of consciousness (10% of those who had smoked 10 to 50 times, 30% of those who had smoked more than 50 times) and seizure (10% of those who had smoked 10 to 50 times and 90% of those who had smoked more than 50 times) (Schwartz, 1989). It has also been linked to sexually transmitted diseases in teen-agers; 41% of black teen-aged crack users reported a lifetime history of at least one sexually transmitted disease. Rapid heartbeat, paranoid thinking, cold sweat, impotence in males, and miscarriage or premature labor in females have also been reported (Fullilove & Fullilove, 1989).

Cocaine dependence involves repeated use, greater doses, and high-dose bingeing. The use of cocaine has been referred to as a kind of "cerebral masturbation" in that the user enjoys the pleasure alone and ignores the increasingly apparent negative environmental contingencies. Compulsive bingeing is linked to the availability of high doses and a rapid, high-intensity route of ingestion (i.e., smoking or injection). Binges create extreme euphoria and memories that stimulate craving. Binges are interrupted by periods of abstinence that may last several days or longer. Typically, binges occur 1 to 3 times a week and last from 8 to 24 hours.

A common post-binge pattern includes a period of 1 to 4 hours of depression, agitation, and craving. This is a period of increasing exhaustion and desire for sleep, although the user may employ marijuana, sedatives, opiates, or alcohol to allow sleep. The length of the crash sleep, which is punctuated by brief periods of wakefulness during which the user eats a great deal, depends on the duration and intensity of the binge. Following the crash sleep, there may be a period of decreased activity, low motivation, boredom, and anhedonia. The user experiencing this and recalling the euphoria of use can experience a severe craving and may resume use, resulting in continued binge cycles. Withdrawal can be even more severe for users with predisposing psychiatric problems. The anhedonia may lift in 2 to 12 weeks if the user is able to maintain abstinence through the period of extinction. Objects or events linked to cocaine use, such as specific persons, locations, events, times of year, interpersonal conflict previously managed by cocaine, paraphernalia, and mood states that produce memories of cocaine euphoria, may cue cravings even years after the last use. Abstinence requires experiencing these cravings without relapse. In time, the cravings are extinguished because the cues are no longer linked to euphoria (Gawin & Ellinwood, 1989).

ADOLESCENT USE OF COCAINE

There is no single accepted theory of the etiology of adolescent cocaine use. A stage or gateway theory is attributed to Kandel (1980) who investigated the different social and psychological factors that predict adolescent entry into drug use. Three sequential stages were suggested (hard liquor, marijuana, and illicit drugs) and predictive variables noted. Risk factor theory used in epidemiology has produced a broad range of variables leading to initial adolescent involvement in drug use and has produced much research into the risk factors and predictors correlating to drug use. A multiple pathway model of adolescent drug use has also been suggested (Newcomb, Maddahian, & Bentler, 1986) in which several different factors may result in the same outcome of use and abuse.

Some writers have suggested that teen-agers use stimulants like cocaine to increase assertion, self-esteem, and frustration tolerance (Weider & Kaplan, 1976); others have suggested that, because cocaine gives them a sense of mastery, control, invincibility, and grandeur, teen-agers use it to eliminate boredom and emptiness, and to defend against depression and feelings of unworthiness and weakness (Wurmser, 1974). Use is linked to an inflated sense of worth and a defense style that allows an active confrontation with the environment (Milkman

& Frosch, 1973), as well as to the control of fatigue and depletion associated with depression (Khantzian, 1975).

Spotts and Shontz (1985) described male adult cocaine users as proud, ambitious, highly competitive, stubborn, isolated individuals who avoid dependency of any kind. In addition, these men dominate women, displaying little interest in developing mutual relationships with them and describing their mothers as cold, stern, and stronger than their fathers (whom they describe as supportive). Brower and Anglin (1987) noted the need for longitudinal studies that track adolescent cocaine users over time and may point to possible biological factors (e.g., dopamine depletion–prone individuals, as dopamine depletion is linked to cocaine addiction), behavioral psychological factors (e.g., prior drug use, psychopathology, self-medication for attention deficit disorder, intent to use, antisocial behaviors, normal risk taking), and social factors (e.g., peers; family life; and demographics, such as age, race, sex, and religion) that may be involved.

Correlate research into characteristics and predictors of adolescent cocaine users has produced some limited findings in the 1980s. Grades in school, available spending money, and frequency of marijuana use were found to be good predictors of cocaine use (Mills & Noyes, 1984). Frequency of adolescent marijuana use for both sexes and father's educational level for females were the only significant indicators of cocaine use. The typical cocaine user (more than 10 times) is described as unmarried, having an unstable work and marital history, involved in car accidents while drunk or stoned, having a history of being arrested, and suffering psychiatric problems (Kandel, Murphy, & Karus, 1985). Increased frequency of use is linked to cutting classes, low religious involvement, gender (males more likely), and religious faith (more risk for Jewish and less risk for Protestant)—but not to race. Cocaine use has been linked to income, reported depression, and intent to use, although intent to use is less common in those adolescents who are more pleased with their appearance, less ambitious, less law-abiding, more liberal, and less committed to religious beliefs (Newcomb & Bentler, 1986).

The adolescent cocaine user has been found to engage in greater use of other drugs, show more deviant behaviors, have more difficulty in acquiring adult role responsibilities, be in poorer health, and have a greater tendency toward psychotic conditions than do non-users (Newcomb & Bentler, 1987). Male users report less happiness with their handling of feelings and with their accomplishments, while female users report less satisfaction in intimate relationships and accomplishments, as well as psychiatric treatment. In a survey of 7th, 9th, and 11th graders, Newcomb, Fahy, and Skager (1988) found that certain predictors were best for cocaine use by particular grades, but that only other drug use was significantly and uniquely correlated when other factors were controlled. These authors did find increased use in older grades, more use by continuation school students, racial correlations (e.g., higher use by blacks and American Indians), but no gender correlation. Newcomb, Chou, Bentler, and Huba (1988) confirmed that actual cocaine use correlated significantly with the reported motivations for alcohol and marijuana,

- reducing negative affect (e.g., stop boredom; get rid of anxiety or tension; feeling sad, blue, or depressed)
- enhancing positive affect and creativity (e.g., know myself better, be more creative and original, enjoy what I am doing more, understand things differently, feel better about myself)
- increasing social cohesion (e.g., feel good around people, friends pressuring me into using, everybody else uses, get along better with friends)
- coping with addiction (e.g., helps me get through the day, feel bad when I don't use, helps me with problems)

Of adolescent cocaine users in treatment who had used more than 50 times, more than half reported that their parents had no suspicions about their use, more than half reported committing vandalism while intoxicated, and 86% reported amphetamine abuse (Smith, Schwartz, & Martin, 1989).

When they compared adolescent cocaine (not crack) and crack users, Ringwalt and Palmer (1989) found that users of crack (with or without cocaine) were likely to be younger, to make poorer grades, to be depressed more often, to be more alienated from friends and family, and to have talked to a teacher or counselor about their problem. Adolescent cocaine use is linked to a history of sexual abuse, a link not found in adolescent marijuana use (Singer, Petchers, & Hussey, 1989). Finally, it appears that males who participate in religious services and score lower on deviancy measures, and females who become a parent or have a lower income, are most likely to stop using cocaine by age 25; the use of illicit drugs by friends is the primary deterrent to cessation (Kandel & Ravels, 1989).

INCIDENCE OF ADOLESCENT COCAINE USE

Surveys are the most direct measures of the scope of drug abuse. They have the advantages of possible repetition over time and in-depth questioning. Surveys can be done by questionnaire or interviews (face to face, telephone, or mail; privately or in groups). Their limitations include exclusion of certain population segments (e.g., dropouts and absentees in school surveys, homeless and street people in home interviews), expense, time, and reliability and validity—especially with sensitive issues such as drug abuse (Kozel, 1990). The possibility of underreporting and lying must be kept in mind, as indicated by a recent finding in one study that 35% of the pregnant teen-agers who tested positive for cocaine had denied use (Zuckerman, Amaro, & Cabral, 1989).

Factual knowledge of the number of adolescent drug users comes primarily from two ongoing surveys: the National Household Survey sponsored by the National Institute on Drug Abuse (NIDA) and the high school seniors study of the University of Michigan Institute of Social Research. The NIDA study has been done seven times, most recently in 1988 (National Institute on Drug Abuse, 1989). Trained interviewers used self-administered answer sheets and other procedures designed for anonymity and confidentiality to obtain data on the incidence of cocaine (including crack) use and the incidence of crack use only among 1,557 males and 1,538 females aged 12 through 17 (Table 28-1). The statistics suggest that, at the time of the interviews, some 683,000 of those aged 12 through 17 had used cocaine ever, some 591,000 had used in the previous year, some 225,000 had used in the previous month, and some 95,000 were using once a week or more. Incidence levels among Hispanics, among females, and among teen-agers in the West are notable.

Table 28-2 shows crack use findings from the same NIDA survey. At the time of the interviews, it appears that some 188,000 of those aged 12 through 17 had used crack ever, some 132,000 had used in the previous year, and some 56,000 had used in the previous month. Incidence levels among females and among Hispanic teen-agers are notable.

The University of Michigan Institute for Social Research Survey, sometimes referred to as the High School Senior Survey, has addressed issues in adolescent drug use since 1975 (Johnston, O'Malley, & Bachman, 1989). The 1990 survey sampled approximately 15,000 seniors in 135 high schools by means of questionnaires given by researchers in the students' classrooms. The questionnaires covered such issues as incidence of use, incidence of discrimination of use, values regarding harmfulness of use and disapproval of users, and perceived availability for many drugs. Table 28-3 shows the High School Senior Survey findings on cocaine use by seniors from the 1975 through 1990 graduating classes. The statistics indicate that approximately 7.8% of the 1991 seniors have used cocaine ever and 1.4% have used in the past 30 days. A marked decline in use since the 1985 survey is notable.

Table 28-4 shows cocaine findings from the High School Senior Survey of perceived harmfulness of cocaine (physically or in other ways), disapproval of users, and perceived availability of cocaine. According to these statistics, 51% of the 1990 seniors reported that cocaine is easy to get, 59.4% of the 1990 seniors reported that they perceived a great harmfulness of cocaine for users who use 1 to 2 times. There is a marked rise in perceived harmfulness, disapproval of users, and availability of cocaine since the 1986 survey. The period of 1985 to 1990 is notable for a decline in use ever (17.3% in 1985 and 7.8% in 1991, according to Table 28-3), during a rise in availability (48.9% in 1985 and 51% in 1991, according to Table 28-4).

Table 28-1 Cocaine Use in 1988 by 12- Through 17-Year-Olds (Including Crack)

	Use Ever		Use Past Year		Use Past Month		12 or More Times in Past Year		Once a Week or More in Past Year	
	Observed Estimate (%)	Population Estimate (1000s)	Observed Estimate (%)	Population Estimate (1000s)	Observed Estimate (%)	Population Estimate (1000s)	Observed Estimate (%)	Population Estimate (1000s)	Observed Estimate (%)	Population Estimate (1000s)
All aged 12–17	3.4	683	2.9	591	1.1	225	1.1	222	0.5	95
Race										
White	3.6	521	3.2	470	1.3	183	1.2	174	0.5	78
Hispanic	4.6	97	3.6	77	1.3	28	1.3	28	0.3	6
Black	2.1	65	1.4	43	*	*	1.3	20	*	*
Sex										
Male	3.3	345	3.0	308	0.9	89	0.9	88	0.6	60
Female	3.4	338	2.9	283	1.4	138	1.4	135	*	*
Region										
Northeast	3.9	144	3.3	125	0.9	33	1.5	58	*	*
North-Central	3.9	207	3.5	184	1.7	89	*	*	*	*
South	1.5	121	1.3	106	*	*	*	*	*	*
West	6.5	211	5.5	176	2.5	81	1.5	47	*	*

*Indicates low precision; no estimates reported.
Source: From *National Household Survey on Drug Abuse*, D.H.H.S. Pub. No. ADM-89-1636, 1989, Rockville, MD: National Institute on Drug Abuse.

Table 28-2 Crack Use in 1988 by 12- Through 17-Year-Olds

	Use Ever		Use Past Year		Use Past Month	
	Observed Estimate (%)	Population Estimate (1000s)	Observed Estimate (%)	Population Estimate (1000s)	Observed Estimate (%)	Population Estimate (1000s)
All aged 12–17	0.9	188	0.7	132	0.3	56
Race						
White	0.9	135	0.7	102	*	*
Hispanic	1.3	27	0.9	19	*	*
Black	0.9	26	*	*	*	*
Sex						
Male	0.9	88	0.5	56	0.3	28
Female	1.0	100	0.8	76	*	*
Region						
Northeast	*	*	*	*	*	*
North-Central	1.4	75	1.4	*	*	*
South	0.4	29	*	75	*	*
West	1.8	59	*	*	*	*

*Indicates low precision; no estimates reported.
Source: From *National Household Survey on Drug Abuse*, D.H.H.S. Pub. No. ADM-89-1636, 1989, Rockville, MD: National Institute on Drug Abuse.

Table 28-3 Cocaine Use by Seniors for Graduating Classes 1975–1991

	1975	1976	1977	1978	1979	1980	1981	1982	1983	1984	1985	1986	1987	1988	1989	1990	1991
Approximate sample size (1,000s)	9.5	15.4	17.1	17.8	15.5	15.9	17.5	17.7	16.3	15.9	16.0	15.2	16.3	16.3	16.7	15.2	16.0
Use ever (%)	9.0	9.7	10.8	12.9	15.4	15.7	16.5	16.9	16.2	16.1	17.3	16.9	15.2	12.1	10.3	9.4	7.8
Use in past year (%)	5.6	6.0	7.2	9.0	12.0	12.3	12.4	11.5	11.4	11.6	13.1	12.7	10.3	7.9	6.5	5.3	3.5
Use in past 30 days (%)	1.9	2.0	2.9	3.9	5.7	5.2	5.8	5.0	4.9	5.8	6.7	6.2	4.3	3.4	2.8	1.9	1.4
Use daily in past 30 days (%)	0.1	0.1	0.1	0.2	0.2	0.2	0.3	0.2	0.2	0.2	0.4	0.4	0.3	0.2	0.3	0.1	0.1

Source: From *Drug Use, Drinking and Smoking: National Survey Results from High School, College and Young Adult Populations* by L.D. Johnston, D.M. O'Malley and J.B. Bachman, 1990, Rockville, MD: National Institute on Drug Abuse.

Table 28-4 Perceived Harmfulness, Disapproval of Users, Perceived Availability of Cocaine by Seniors for Graduating Classes 1975–1991

	1975	1976	1977	1978	1979	1980	1981	1982	1983	1984	1985	1986	1987	1988	1989	1990	1991
Sample size	2804	2918	3052	3770	3250	3234	3604	3557	3305	3262	3250	3020	3315	3276	2796	2553	2549
Think people at great risk of harming selves by use																	
If use 1–2 times	42.6	39.1	35.6	33.2	31.5	31.3	32.1	32.8	33.0	35.7	34.0	33.5	47.9	51.2	54.9	59.4	59.4
If use occasionally	NA	NA	NA	NA	NA	NA	NA	NA	NA	NA	NA	54.2	66.8	69.2	71.8	73.9	75.5
If use regularly	73.1	72.3	68.2	68.2	69.5	69.2	7.2	73.0	74.3	78.8	79.9	82.2	88.5	89.2	90.2	91.1	90.4
Sample size	2677	2977	3085	3686	3221	3261	3610	3651	3341	3254	3265	3113	3302	3311	2799	2566	2547
Disapprove of use by those 18 or over																	
If use 1–2 times	71.3	82.4	79.1	77.0	74.7	76.3	74.6	76.6	77.0	79.7	79.3	80.2	87.3	89.1	90.5	91.5	93.6
If use regularly	99.3	93.9	92.1	91.9	90.8	91.2	90.7	91.5	93.2	94.5	93.8	94.3	96.7	96.2	96.4	96.7	97.3
Sample size	2627	2865	3065	3598	3172	3240	3578	3602	3385	3269	3774	3077	3271	3231	2806	2549	2476
Think it would be very easy or fairly easy to get	37.0	34.0	33.0	37.8	45.5	45.9	47.5	47.4	43.1	45.0	48.9	51.5	54.2	55.0	58.7	54.5	51.0

Source: From *Drug Use, Drinking and Smoking: National Survey Results from High School, College and Young Adult Populations* by L.D. Johnston, D.M. O'Malley and J.B. Bachman, 1990, Rockville, MD: National Institute on Drug Abuse.

Table 28-5 shows crack use findings from the High School Seniors Survey of use ever, use in the past year, use in the past 30 days, and use daily in the past 30 days for seniors from the 1986 to 1991 graduating classes. A decline in use ever and use in the past year since the 1986 and 1987 surveys is notable.

Other surveys have produced drug use statistics for rural U.S. teen-agers (Oetting & Beauvais, 1990), Native American teen-agers (Oetting & Beauvais, 1990), Mexican-American teen-agers (Oetting & Beauvais, 1990), Canadian teen-agers (Smart & Adlaf, 1987) and pregnant teen-agers (Gilchrist, Gillmore, & Lohr, 1990). Rural rate of drug use ever (lifetime prevalence) is found to parallel nonrural use, except for marijuana use; rural use of marijuana is somewhat less (Oetting & Beauvais, 1990). Drug use ever is found generally to be greater for pregnant teen-agers than for nonpregnant teen-agers. While cocaine use ever for pregnant teen-agers was reported to be 34% and cocaine use in the month prior declined during pregnancy from 3.95 times in a month to 1.32 times in a month (Gilchrist et al., 1990), teen-agers are noted for underreporting (Zuckerman et al., 1989).

The possible health consequences of cocaine use, the physically reinforcing properties of the drug, the powerful myths affecting teen users, and the continued availability of cocaine all suggest that the psychologist, nurse, teacher, and counselor must be highly sensitive to adolescent cocaine use.

Table 28-5 Crack Use by Seniors for Graduating Classes 1986–1991

	1986	1987	1988	1989	1990	1991
Sample size	3,400	6,520	6,520	5,566	15,200	16,000
Use ever (%)	NA	5.4	4.8	4.7	3.5	3.1
Use past year (%)	4.1	3.9	3.1	3.1	1.9	1.5
Use past 30 days (%)	NA	1.3	1.6	1.4	0.7	0.7
Use daily past 30 days (%)	NA	0.1	0.1	0.2	0.1	0.1

Source: From *Drug Use, Drinking and Smoking: National Survey Results from High School, College and Young Adult Populations* by L.D. Johnston, D.M. O'Malley and J.B. Bachman, 1990, Rockville, MD: National Institute on Drug Abuse.

REFERENCES

Brower, K., & Anglin, M.D. (1987). Adolescent cocaine use: Epidemiology, risk factors, and prevention. *Journal of Drug Education, 17*(2), 163–180.

Estroff, T.W. (1987). Medical and biological consequences of cocaine abuse. In A.M. Washton & M.S. Gold (Eds.), *Cocaine: A clinician's handbook* (pp. 23–32). New York: Guilford Press.

Fullilove, M.T., & Fullilove, R.E. (1989). Intersecting epidemics: Black teen crack use and sexually transmitted disease. *Journal of the American Medical Women's Association, 44*(5), 146–153.

Gawin, F.H., & Ellinwood, E.H. (1989). Cocaine dependence. *American Review of Medicine, 40,*149–161.

Gilchrist, L.D., Gillmore, M.R., & Lohr, M.J. (1990). Drug use among pregnant adolescents. *Journal of Consulting and Clinical Psychology, 58*(4), 402–407.

Johnston, L.D., O'Malley, D.M., & Bachman, J.B. (1989). *Drug use, drinking and smoking: National survey results from high school, college, and young adult populations 1975–1985.* Rockville, MD: National Institute on Drug Abuse.

Kandel, D. (1980). Drug and drinking behaviors among youth. *Annual Review of Sociology, 6,* 235–285.

Kandel, D.B., Murphy, D., & Karus, D. (1985). Cocaine use in young adulthood: Patterns of use and psychosocial correlates. In N.J. Kozel & E. Adams (Eds.), *Cocaine use in America: Epidemiologic and clinical perspectives* (pp. 76–110). Rockville, MD: National Institute on Drug Abuse.

Kandel, D.B., & Ravels, V.H. (1989). Cessation of illicit drug use in young adulthood. *Archives of General Psychiatry, 46*(2), 109 –116.

Khantzian, E.J. (1975). Self selection and progression in drug dependence. *Psychiatry Digest, 10,* 19–22.

Kozel, N.J. (1990). Epidemiology of drug abuse in the U.S.: A summary of methods and findings. *Bulletin of the Pan American Health Organization, 24*(1), 53–62.

Milkman, H., & Frosch, W.A. (1973). On the preferential abuse of heroin and methamphetamine. *Journal of Nervous and Mental Diseases, 156,* 242–248.

Miller, N.S., Gold, M.S., & Millman, R.L. (1989). Cocaine. *American Family Physician, 39* (2), 115–120.

Mills, C.J., & Noyes, H.L. (1984). Patterns and correlates of initial and subsequent drug use among adolescents. *Journal of Consulting and Clinical Psychology, 52*(2), 231–243.

National Institute on Drug Abuse. (1989). *National household survey on drug abuse.* (DHHS Publication No. ADM-89-1636). Washington, DC: U.S. Government Printing Office.

Newcomb, M.D., & Bentler, P.M. (1986). Cocaine use among adolescents: Longitudinal associations with social context, psychopathology, and use of other substances. *Addictive Behaviors, 11,* 263–273.

Newcomb, M.D., & Bentler, P.M. (1987). Cocaine use among young adults. In M.S. Gold, M.I. Galanter, & B. Stimmel (Eds.), *Cocaine: Pharmacology, addiction, and therapy* (pp. 73–96). New York: Haworth Press.

Newcomb, M.D., Chou, C., Bentler, P.M., & Huba, G.J. (1988). Cognitive motivations for drug use among adolescents: Longitudinal tests of gender differences and predictors of change in drug use. *Journal of Counseling Psychology, 35*(4), 426–438.

Newcomb, M.D., Fahy, B.N., & Skager, R. (1988). Correlates of cocaine use among adolescents. *Journal of Drug Issues, 18*(3), 327–354.

Newcomb, M.D., Maddahian, E., & Bentler, P.M. (1986). Risk factors for drug use among adolescents: Concurrent and longitudinal analyses. *American Journal of Public Health, 76*(5), 525–531.

Oetting, E.R., & Beauvais, F. (1990). Adolescent drug use: Findings of national and local surveys. *Journal of Consulting and Clinical Psychology, 58*(4), 385–394.

Ringwalt, C.L., & Palmer, J.H. (1989). Cocaine and crack users compared. *Adolescence, 24*(96), 851–859.

Schwartz, R.H. (1989). Seizures associated with smoking 'crack'—A survey of adolescent 'crack' smokers. *Western Journal of Medicine, 150*(2), 213.

Schwartz, R.H., & Estroff, T. (1988). Seizures and syncope in adolescent cocaine abusers. *American Journal of Medicine, 85,* 462.

Schwartz, R.H., Estroff, T., Fairbanks, D.N.F., & Hoffmann, N.G. (1989). Nasal symptoms associated with cocaine abuse during adolescence. *Archives of Otolaryngology, Head and Neck Surgery, 115,* 63–64.

Shannon, M., Lacouture, P.G., Roa, J., & Woolf, A. (1989). Cocaine exposure among children seen at a pediatric hospital. *Pediatrics, 83*(3), 337–342.

Siegel, R.K. (1987). Cocaine smoking: Nature and extent of coca paste and cocaine freebase abuse. In A.M. Washton & M.S. Gold (Eds.), *Cocaine: A clinician's handbook* (pp. 175–191). New York: Guilford Press.

Singer, M.I., Petchers, M.K., & Hussey, D. (1989). The relationship between sexual abuse and substance abuse among psychiatrically hospitalized adolescents. *Child Abuse and Neglect, 13*(3), 319–325.

Smart, R.G., & Adlaf, E.M. (1987). *Alcohol and other drug use among Ontario students in 1987 and trends since 1977.* Toronto: Addiction Research Foundation.

Smith, D.E., Schwartz, R.H., & Martin, D.M. (1989). Heavy cocaine use by adolescents. *Pediatrics, 83*(4), 539–542.

Spotts, J.V., & Shontz, F.C. (1985). A theory of adolescent substance abuse. *Advances in Alcohol and Substance Abuse, 4*(2), 117–138.

Washton, A.M. (1989). *Cocaine addiction.* New York: W.W. Norton.

Weider, H., & Kaplan, E. (1976). Drug use in adolescents. *Psychoanalytic Study of the Child, 24,* 399–431.

Weiss, R.D., & Mirin, S.M. (1987). *Cocaine.* Washington, DC: American Psychiatric Press.

Wurmser, L. (1974). *Methadone and the craving for narcotics: Observations of patients on methadone maintenance in psychotherapy.* Papers presented at the Fourth National Methadone Conference, San Francisco.

Zuckerman, B., Amaro, H., & Cabral, H. (1989). Validity of self-reporting of marijuana and cocaine use among pregnant adolescents. *Journal of Pediatrics, 115*(5, Part 1), 812–815.

29

Adolescents in Alcoholic Families

Christine M. O'Sullivan

In the best of families, adolescence is a time of turmoil. Even in well-balanced, healthy families, the storm and strife associated with a child-becoming-adult can cause stress and problems. In an alcoholic family, however, this important period of development is a period of chaos and trauma for the child who is in the process of becoming an adult. Adolescence can consist of many woundings and problems that the individual can carry for many, many years.

DEVELOPMENTAL TASKS OF ADOLESCENCE

The life cycle stage termed adolescence is the bridge between childhood and adulthood. At its best, adolescence brings about tremendous physical, emotional, mental, and social changes. The person who is in this stage of life must adjust to a changing body, learn to relate to opposite-sex peers in a sexual manner, prepare for a vocation in life, and become more attached to peers and less attached to family. Given a healthy family life, this time is a period of some stress and turmoil for an adolescent. For those adolescents living in an alcoholic home, adolescence becomes a time of severe stress and turmoil that can lead to serious consequences. Parental alcoholism can negatively affect all the developmental tasks of this era of the life cycle.

Before entering puberty, children are not generally self-conscious about their bodies. As puberty progresses, however, their bodies seem to undergo changes overnight. The proportions of their bodies begin to resemble those of mature adults rather than children. Aside from any external problems that these adolescents may be experiencing, the growth spurts alone can make them uncomfortable with their bodies. Tanner (1971) noted that growth causes self-consciousness in adolescents. The earliest structures to reach adult growth are the head, the hands, and the feet. At this point, children become *very* aware of their bodies and, because of the uneven growth, appear to be awkward and gangly. Both girls and boys are at the mercy of fluctuating hormones on the physical level, as well as changing ideas, expectations, and aspirations on the psychosocial level.

In the cognitive sphere of development, adolescents go from concrete operations, to formal operations, then to abstract operations. They begin to manipulate more than two categories of information within their head; for example, they can compare time, speed, and distance. They become future-oriented rather than present-oriented. They are able, at this point in their development, to hypothesize about future events and to anticipate the consequences of their actions.

Along with the body and cognitive changes, children are beginning to become independent of their families. Adolescents form attachments to their peers that seem stronger than are their attachments to their families. Formal and diversified, these peer groups develop their own culture and identity. Membership in these peer groups becomes a primary focus for an adolescent. The subculture and values of the peer group may conflict with parental rules, expectations, and values, and the adolescent often resolves such conflicts in favor of the peer group. Although appearing to rebel against parental and social standards, the adolescent peer group paradoxically demands conformity to its own standards of dress and behavior.

The final major task of adolescence is the development of the adult sex role identity. The adolescent begins to expand the same-sex relationships that existed before adolescence into the heterosexual sphere. Teen-agers begin to date and to practice the roles that they will eventually be required to assume. Both sexes begin to make occupational and vocational choices in selecting particular kinds of education in high school. All these tasks take place within the context of the family unit.

ALCOHOLIC FAMILIES

The family is a social unit that provides nurturance, support, and guidance for its members. According to Bowen (1974), the family is a system composed of individual members. There is a central oneness that holds its members together in a family, however. If this oneness of the family becomes unhealthy, differentiation and uniqueness may not occur, and the members of the family become overly dependent on each other. The dysfunctional family maintains the enmeshed status quo at the expense of its individual members (Walsh, 1981).

An alcoholic family is a prime example of a dysfunctional family and, as such, does not provide the nurturing and protection that a healthy family provides.

There is no single alcoholic family dysfunctional style. The degree and kind of dysfunction reflected by the family vary according to the type and progression of alcoholism in the alcoholic. Bowen (1974) theorized that alcohol formed the third side of a triangle between the parents that allowed them to regulate the closeness and distance between the marital pair.

Kaufman (1985, 1986), who maintained that alcoholism can be the central organizing principle in a family, identified four basic kinds of alcoholic family structures. One kind of alcoholic family seems to reorganize itself by ignoring the alcoholism since the alcoholic usually drinks outside the home. The members of this family appear to be quite functional and, as Kaufman noted, seem to have little psychological insight. In the second type of alcoholic family, which Kaufman termed the "neurotic enmeshed" family, the family is organized around the alcoholic's behavior. The third and fourth kinds of alcoholic families are really nonfamilies. In one case, the alcoholism has progressed so far that the alcoholic has lost the family. In the other case, the alcoholic, usually young, has left the family.

There is a complex relationship between alcoholism and the family that reinforces drinking. Steinglass (1980a, 1980b, 1981, 1987) studied a cohort of 31 families with one alcoholic parent in three different settings: their own homes, a family interaction laboratory, and a multiple family discussion group. He described three states of interactions within the families, depending on the state of the alcoholism—stable wet (alcoholic actively drinking), stable dry (alcoholic abstinent), and transitional. A couple's behavior during periods of intoxication may have adaptive consequences for the family that reinforces the drinking. Spouses of alcoholics are found to react to alcohol abuse to the extent that the alcoholism invades the family more than to the severity of the drinking. The degree of psychiatric symptoms experienced by a nonalcoholic spouse correlates closely with the alcoholic spouse's perception of the degree of social and behavioral consequences of the alcoholism—except when the alcoholism is dormant. Steinglass noted that nonalcoholic spouses experience stress because they must cope with the spouse's alcoholism. The level of psychopathology of the nonalcoholic spouse is a critical determinant of the impact of alcoholism on the family. If the psychiatric symptoms are associated with underlying personality and ego disturbances combined with alcoholism, there is the likelihood that drinking behavior will have negative consequences on work and in social and family areas.

The denial that exists in an alcoholic family serves two purposes. First, the alcoholic denies the alcoholism so that drinking can continue. Second, the spouse and children deny to avoid feelings of shame or to protect self-esteem. Because denial requires lies and actions, it is exhausting and enervating. Denial breeds fear of discovery and adds to the mistrust and isolation of the members of the alcoholic's family.

EFFECTS ON ADOLESCENCE

If the family can organize so that the alcoholic does not affect the family functioning in the manner of the functional alcoholic family described by Kaufman (1984), the family can maintain its emotional balance, and adolescence will probably proceed in its usual bumpy course. The family that is the most problematic, however, is Kaufman's neurotic enmeshed family. In this family, the developmental stage of adolescence becomes fraught with problems and, for some children of alcoholics, is a living nightmare.

Development of Pathology

Adolescents in alcoholic families are at an increased risk for alcoholism, sociopathy, depression, anxiety, eating disorders, difficulty with intimacy, and a host of other obsessive-compulsive disorders. Parentification of children leads to what Woodside (1982) called "pathological independence," as their assumption of parental tasks causes adolescents to become adult at an inappropriate age. Pathological independence cuts short the adolescent's process of socialization with peers and can make it impossible for the adolescent to explore alternative identities. The age of the child when alcoholism is recognized as such makes a difference in the issues that surface later in adulthood. The later in development that a child must deal with parental alcoholism, the more developmental resources that child is likely to have acquired.

Almost all the risk research on alcoholic families show that children of alcoholics are at a three- to fourfold risk of becoming alcoholics (Monteiro & Schuckit, 1988). Goodwin (1981) found an excess of depression, "criminality," sociopathy, and "abnormal personality" in families of alcoholics. In the main, depression was found in female relatives; sociopathy and alcoholism in males. Although most of the studies indicate a genetic link, that link occurs as a potential for the disorder. Alcoholism is far more complex in that the environmental factors greatly influence the development of the disorder.

Seixas (1977) noted that the parents in an alcoholic family are usually in continual conflict, with the arguments being repetitious and illogical. The children are robbed of attention, are inconsistently disciplined, and lack a trustworthy environment. They are usually physically and psychically pushed aside in a constant atmosphere of anger and tension. Children are often scapegoated and suffer from role confusion, double bind expectations, and the role reversals of the parentified child. Because few children of alcoholics develop strong emotional ties with their parents, they have little opportunity to experience the normal process of breaking away. Parental unreliability increases a child's isolation and leads to a lack of respect for authority.

Ackerman (1987, 1988) conducted a nationwide study of adult children of alcoholics and found that the quality of child care is lowest when both parents are alcoholic, with the probability of child abuse being the greatest under this condition. There are four basic kinds of abuse that can occur in an alcoholic family: neglect, physical, psychological, and sexual abuse (O'Sullivan, 1990). Various studies have shown correlations of .45 to .80 between alcoholism in the family and abuse.

Hecht (1973) called the problem of children of alcoholics "the fourth most important public health problem" (p. 1764). The family is the primary place where children learn how people relate to each other and form ideas of control, relationships, and responsibility, principally through identification. Hecht noted that anger at an alcoholic parent can be turned inward, causing depression and other problems in children of alcoholics. He believed that it is important to view a child in the context of the child's family system.

Wilson and Orford (1978) noted the contrasts in the drinking patterns of different alcoholics, for example, men and women. In a study of alcoholic families in London, they found that the pattern of parental drinking strongly influences the family process. Marital conflict and separation may be a critical variable in the ill effects of parental alcoholism on children. They found a variety of patterns of parent-child relationships and communications, and differences in family atmospheres due to the tension from anticipation of moods in the alcoholic. When the mother is the alcoholic parent, family stability is lowest and the probability of neglect is highest (probably because men will leave alcoholic women, but women will stay with alcoholic men). Seixas (1977) commented that the children of alcoholic mothers are more seriously curbed in terms of lack of input from the mother; therefore, they tend to have more behavioral and emotional problems than do children of alcoholic fathers. In her opinion, the alcoholic mother is incapable of fulfilling her role, so the children are emotionally ignored and isolated. The lack of stimulation hampers the children's movement from one stage of development to the next. According to Seixas, behavioral problems can be attributed to the mother's arrested ego development.

When Seixas (1977) studied 39 children of alcoholics, she found 39 behavioral disorders. She found the children of alcoholics to be exceptionally sensitive to noises, bright lights, heat or cold, and other physical stimuli. They were emotionally detached and withdrawn from social stimulation. They were usually aggressive and domineering toward other children. Adolescents from alcoholic families also indulged in unethical behavior and could be domineering, sadistic, or expansive with poor emotional control. They also evidenced schizoid withdrawal, an inability to delay gratification, and anxious self-blame.

In their studies about adolescents in trouble, El-Guebaly and Offord (1977) found that juvenile delinquents who abuse alcohol or were addicted to alcohol often came from families in which there had been parental alcoholism and family breakdown. Other studies have shown that parental alcoholism is associated with antisocial behavior, suicide attempts, institutionalization, acting out, serious psychiatric disorders, and anorexia nervosa in adolescents. These studies had several problems, however, including nonrandom samples, small samples, and poor data collection procedures. Furthermore, it is not clear whether alcoholism made a specific contribution to the etiology of antisocial behavior or whether alcoholism's main contribution is through its tendency to place the family in lower socioeconomic levels.

Blane and Barry (1973) noted that firstborn sons of alcoholics are overrepresented in samples of alcoholics with a preponderance of small families. A sample of alcoholics also has a high proportion of only children. As a result of these findings, Blane and Barry concluded that individuals in certain birth positions may be more likely to develop alcoholism in response to certain disturbing experiences. For example, the last born may be unwanted and rejected, especially in large families. Risk for alcoholism is also higher for later born men whose parents are firstborn and who have older brothers rather than older sisters.

In a study of children referred for psychiatric treatment and evaluation, Chafetz, Blane, and Hill (1971) grouped these children into 100 controls who had no alcoholic parents and 100 children who had one or two alcoholic parents. They found that there were more only children, fewer second borns, and no Jewish children in the group who had alcoholic parents. However, there were Jewish children in the control group. They also found that the alcoholic families had lower income. Although there was no difference in health status or symptoms between the two groups, the children of alcoholics had a higher incidence of school problems and involvement with the police and courts. They theorized that children of alcoholics learned socially disapproved ways of behaving from parental models. There is cognitive confusion in these children because their world is different from the real world. They experience conflict, blame, anger, and guilt. They see themselves as the cause of parental drinking. Furthermore, they cannot understand the role and behavior of the sober parent as that parent becomes caught up in the alcoholic's behavior. These adolescents may be more preoccupied with inner thoughts. Girls usually somaticize their problems, while boys tend to become hyperactive and have difficulties concentrating. There is usually continual tension and anger at home, along with neglect by the sober parent.

Resilience in the Children of Alcoholics

Although the majority of the research on alcoholism and the family has focused on the pathology evidenced in the nonalcoholic family members, children who become symptomatic because of parental alcoholism are in the minority. Most of the children of alcoholics manifest a quality called resilience and are able to transcend the problems of growing up in an alcoholic family. As Pickens (1984) noted, "Not every child of an alcoholic will develop these disorders. Fewer than 50 percent develop any problems" (p. 14). According to Miller and Jang (1977), "A good socialization experience for the child can mitigate a history of parental alcoholism, and, similarly, a bad socialization experience can vitiate a good history of no alcoholism on the parents' part" (p. 25). They also look to the school for the opportunity for the child to develop other definitions of self.

Berlin and Davis (1989) studied vulnerability and resiliency in children of alcoholics and determined that there is no prototypical alcoholic family. They noted, however, that "it is within the context of the family that the development and maintenance of risk for a particular child gets played out" (p. 81). Rather than a clear hierarchy with the parents in a healthy coalition to manage the family, there are two lines of control in the alcoholic family: (1) around the alcoholic and the drinking, and (2) around the nonalcoholic spouse who tries to control the alcoholic spouse. The children are encouraged to do or not do something so that drinking will change, giving the children an illusion of power as they are delegated to do the impossible. The children also have a distorted perception of reality because of the denial of the problem of alcoholism by both the alcoholic and the spouse. In addition, because of their heightened impermeability to their children's experiences, the parents do not validate the children's perceptions in a highly oscillating environment. There is then a blunting of interest and curiosity because of denial and mystification.

Despite these problems, Berlin and Davis (1989) found that some children and some families protect themselves from the alcoholism. This protective factor is adaptive distancing, which is the breaking away from the centricity of the alcoholism and obsession. Adaptive distancing provides a buffer from the alcoholism and makes it possible for adolescents to develop self-esteem and to acquire constructive goals. Crucial in adolescence is the difference between defensive and adaptive distancing. Defensive distancing consists of flight, isolation, and denial of personal stress. Adolescents who choose this manner of distancing may become isolated or impulsive and delinquent, with substance-abusing groups as their most frequent contacts outside the family. Adaptive distancing involves activities and relationships that allow some breathing room for reparative work and acknowledgment of the effect of family alcoholism on the sense of self.

In a longitudinal study of a cohort of 698 children on Kauai (Werner, 1985; Werner & Smith, 1982), it was found that 59% of the 49 offspring of alcoholics had not developed problems by age 18. Of the resilient group, 79% were female, while 70% of the group with psychological problems were male. Of the children with alcoholic fathers, 50% were resilient, but only one child in the resilient group had an alcoholic mother. Werner concluded that the gender of the child and the gender of the alcoholic parent significantly affected outcome. Male offspring of alcoholic mothers were at greater risk for problems. Werner found that the mothers of resilient children were less likely to have become pregnant or given birth before the child was 20 months old and were more likely to have been gainfully and steadily employed during the child's early or middle childhood. In addition, resilient children experienced fewer family conflicts, and they had a more internal locus of control and better self-esteem than did children who developed problems. The constitutional characteristics of the child and the quality of the early care-giving environment seemed to have buffered the resilient child against the parental alcoholism.

Wilson and Orford (1978) theorized that, in cases in which children took large amounts of responsibility for household tasks, responsibility may contribute to strengths in adult life. They also found that relatives and adults outside the immediate nuclear family were sources of support. Werner said, "Evaluation of sources of strength of children of alcoholics is as important as focusing on their potential handicaps" (1985, p. 34).

Using a combination of the California Psychological Inventory, the Sixteen Personality Factors Questionnaire, and the Impact of Event Scale, Plescia-Pikus, Long-Suter, and Wilson (1988) compared 44 adult children of alcoholics with 92 control subjects to examine the relationships among achievement, well-being, intelligence, and stress reaction. They found that adult children of alcoholics, as a group, were significantly lower in well-being and achievement via conformance, with no significant correlations found for birth order or number of affiliations. A secondary analysis showed that adult children of alcoholics with high well-being scored significantly higher on achievement via conformance and achievement via independence than did the controls. Although the sample population was skewed because it did not include adult children of alcoholics who were in support groups, this study suggests that there are definitely some individuals who are able to transcend the condition of being children of alcoholics and go on to live full and productive lives.

REFERENCES

Ackerman, R.J. (1987). *Same house different homes: Why adult children of alcoholics are not all the same*. Pompano Beach, FL: Health Communications.

Ackerman, R.J. (1988, August). *Differentiating adult children of alcoholics: The effects of background and treatment on ACOA symptoms*. Paper presented at the American Sociological Association Annual Meeting, San Francisco, 1989.

Berlin, R., & Davis, R.B. (1989). Children from alcoholic families: Vulnerability and resilience. In T.J. Dugan & R. Coles (Eds.), *The child in our times: Studies in the development of resiliency* (pp. 71–82). New York: Brunner/Mazel.

Blane, H.T., & Barry, H. (1973). Birth order and alcoholism. *Quarterly Journal of Studies in Alcoholism, 34*, 837–852.

Bowen, M. (1974). Alcoholism as viewed through family systems theory and family psychotherapy. *Annals of the New York Academy of Science, 42*, 161–167.

Chafetz, M.E., Blane, H.T., & Hill, M.J. (1971). Children of alcoholics: Observations in a child guidance clinic. *Quarterly Journal of Studies in Alcoholism, 32,* 687–698.

El-Guebaly, N., & Offord, D.R. (1977). The offspring of alcoholics: A critical review. *American Journal of Psychiatry, 134*(4), 357–365.

Goodwin, D.W. (1981). Family studies of alcoholism. *Journal of Studies on Alcohol, 42*(1), 156–162.

Hecht, M. (1973). Children of alcoholics are children at risk. *American Journal of Nursing, 10,* 1764–1767.

Kaufman, E. (1984). Family system variables in alcoholism. *Alcoholism: Clinical and Experimental Research, 8*(1), 4–8.

Kaufman, E. (1985). Family systems and family therapy of substance abuse: An overview of two decades of research and clinical experience. *International Journal of the Addictions, 20*(6&7), 897–916.

Kaufman, E. (1986). The family of the alcoholic patient. *Psychosomatics, 27*(5), 347–359.

Miller, D., & Jang, M. (1977). Children of alcoholics: A 20-year longitudinal study. *Social Work Research & Abstracts, 13*(4), 23–29.

Monteiro, M.G., & Schuckit, M.A. (1988). Populations at high alcoholism risk: Recent findings. *Journal of Clinical Psychiatry, 49*(9), 3–7.

O'Sullivan, C.M. (1990). Alcoholism and abuse: The twin family secrets. In G. Lawson (Ed.), *Alcoholism and special populations* (pp. 273–303). Gaithersburg, MD: Aspen Publishers.

Pickens, R.W. (1984). *Children of alcoholics.* Minneapolis: Hazelden.

Plescia-Pikus, M., Long-Suter, E., & Wilson, J.P. (1988). Achievement, well-being, intelligence, and stress reaction in adult children of alcoholics. *Psychological Reports, 62,* 603–609.

Seixas, J. (1977). Children from alcoholic families. In *Alcoholism: Consequences and interventions* (pp. 153–161). St. Louis: C.V. Mosby.

Steinglass, P. (1980a). The impact of alcoholism on the family: Relationship between degree of alcoholism and psychiatric symptomatology. *Journal of Studies on Alcohol, 42*(3), 288–303.

Steinglass, P. (1980b). A life history model of the alcoholic family. *Family Process, 19*(3), 211–226.

Steinglass, P. (1981). The alcoholic family at home: Patterns of interaction in dry, wet, and transactional stages of alcoholism. *Archives of General Psychiatry, 38,* 578–584.

Steinglass, P. (1987). *The alcoholic family.* New York: Basic Books.

Tanner, J.M. (1971). Sequence, tempo, and individual variation in the growth and development of boys and girls twelve to sixteen. In M. Bloom (Ed.), *Life span development: Bases for preventive and interventive helping* (pp. 216–219). New York: Macmillan.

Walsh, W. (1981). *A primer in family therapy.* Springfield, IL: Charles C. Thomas.

Werner, E.E. (1985). Resilient offspring of alcoholics: A longitudinal study from birth to age 18. *Journal of Studies on Alcohol, 47*(1), 34–40.

Werner, E.E., & Smith, R.S. (1982). *Vulnerable but invincible: A study of resilient children.* New York: McGraw-Hill.

Wilson, C., & Orford, J. (1978). Children of alcoholics. *Journal of Studies on Alcohol, 39*(1), 121–142.

Woodside, M. (1982, July). *Children of alcoholics.* Report to Hugh L. Carey, Governor, State of New York, for Joseph A. Califano, Jr., Special Counselor on Alcoholism and Drug Abuse. New York: Children of Alcoholics Foundation.

Part V

Prevention

It is only logical that preventing substance abuse is a far less invasive and a more productive approach to adolescent substance abuse than trying to stop the behavior after it has started. Yet our society vacillates on this point. Funding sources swing from the position of promoting prevention as a cost effective measure to funding only treatment because it is more necessary. Proponents of both positions battle for funds, claiming that their cause is the most important. Some of the issues that feed this battle are disagreements about the etiology of substance abuse problems and the failures of previous prevention efforts.

First, we have to believe that substance abuse can be prevented. The widespread acceptance of the disease model of substance abuse confuses people and does not clearly point to a prevention strategy. We continue to fund research to find a biological or genetic "marker" that would predict which people will become substance abusers; however the chances of creating a vaccine against substance abuse are slim. If we define alcoholism and other addictions as diseases, it is important to look at the environmental variables that are part of the etiology of other diseases (e.g., heart disease and diabetes). These environmental factors include family influences, psychological states, and sociocultural factors.

Second, our attempts to prevent substance abuse in this society have not been very successful. Our biggest failure was Prohibition, which gave alcohol forbidden fruit appeal for the entire country. Other failures include scare tactics such as the movie *Reefer Madness* and giving incorrect information to adolescents about the negative effects of drugs. The next approach to prevention involved giving accurate information to adolescents about drugs and the consequences of their use and abuse. Although this seems a logical approach, research indicated it actually increased the use of drugs.

Just as a blanket approach to treatment of substance abuse is ineffective, so is a blanket approach to prevention. The chapters in this section not only provide models of prevention for various settings but include models designed for special groups of adolescents.

30

Developing a Comprehensive Health Promotion Program to Prevent Adolescent Drug Abuse

Rick Petosa

Throughout history, most societies have attempted to reduce problems related to psychoactive drug use (Aaron & Musto, 1981; Abel, 1980; Erikson, 1987). Yet, these same societies have also promoted the use of drugs. In the United States today, public concern and political response have produced a public policy of "War" on illicit drugs; while this War is being waged, however, U.S. citizens continue to consume huge quantities of alcohol, tobacco, over-the-counter remedies, and medically prescribed drugs. Despite the documented social, health, and economic costs, these drugs continue to be subsidized by the government, produced and promoted by manufacturers, and overused by citizens.

Drug use of others in the immediate social environment and society at large heavily influences personal drug use. Too often, efforts to prevent drug abuse target only illicit drugs and only adolescents. The net result is that young people receive inconsistent messages. On the one hand, carefully orchestrated prevention messages warn them of the dangers of using certain drugs; on the other hand, society continues to model and support the use of other drugs. If prevention programs are to be successful, an effort must be made to broaden the scope of drug use policy and interventions so that young people receive messages that are consistent, scientifically valid, and socially constructive.

ADOLESCENT DRUG USE IN PERSPECTIVE

Since the early 1980s, adolescent illicit drug use has been declining. Not only are fewer adolescents using most types of drugs, those who do use drugs are reporting less frequent use. One important exception to this trend is alcohol. Nearly all young people (93%) have tried alcohol by the time that they graduate from high school, and 41% report occasional binge drinking (five or more drinks in a row). Although rates of drug use are declining, 63% of adolescents experiment with an illicit drug before they finish high school. These U.S drug use figures are the highest levels of illicit drug use of any industrialized nation in the world.

Although often confused, the distinctions between the terms *drug use* and *drug abuse* should be clearly maintained. Most people who use alcohol, over-the-counter drugs, and prescribed drugs do not abuse these products. Furthermore, most young people do not habitually use illicit drugs (Donovon & Jessor, 1984; Johnston, O'Malley, & Bachman, 1986). Many of those who experiment with illegal drugs do not become regular users (Goodstadt, 1986). Use of the "gate-way" drugs (i.e., alcohol, tobacco, marijuana) rarely leads to addiction to more powerful drugs (Baumrind, 1984; Yamaguchi & Kandel, 1984).

Standards of acceptable drug use are a function of cultural and societal norms. Although drug use among young people is declining, it is still high compared to that in other industrialized nations. The growing public awareness of the health and social costs of drug abuse is likely to result in continued interest in prevention programs for adolescents.

EVOLUTION OF ADOLESCENT DRUG ABUSE PREVENTION PROGRAMS

Information-Based Prevention Programs

Most contemporary programs designed to prevent drug abuse are based on the factual/rational approach. It is assumed that most health-compromising behavior, including drug abuse, is due primarily to ignorance. Logically, it follows that knowledge would prevent drug abuse. The main tasks of this type of prevention program are (1) to communicate accurate information about the health and social consequences of substance abuse and (2) to inculcate attitudes against drug abuse. Few programs have a theoretical basis, however, and even fewer have employed evaluation methods to improve effectiveness.

The information-based approach has had disappointing results. It has increased student knowledge of the hazards, but has not changed attitudes; in fact, experimentation with drugs often increased (Bangert-Drowns, 1988; Berberian, Gross, Lovejoy, & Paparella, 1976; Hanson, 1982; Kinder, Pape, & Walfish, 1980; Stuart, 1974; Tobler, 1986; White & Biron, 1979). There are several reasons for the lack of effectiveness. First, the information presented to the students is often not consistent with their experience. For example, most adolescents experiment with alcohol. Very few, if any, intend to become alcoholic, and most feel invulnerable to the development of future health or social problems (Elkind, 1978). Indeed, most adolescents and adults who drink do not develop health problems (Jacobson & Zinberg, 1975).

From a cognitive/developmental perspective, most adolescents are beginning to develop formal operational thought capabilities. They have a strong identification with adult behavior and respond critically to inconsistencies between what they are told to do and what they see adults doing. When one-sided, persuasive appeals run contrary to their experience, the credibility of the prevention staff and the program are seriously compromised.

Most important, the information-based approach does not directly address the immediate, specific reasons that adolescents choose to use chemical substances: to cope with stress, to gain social status, to impress peers, to facilitate social interactions, to satisfy curiosity, to rebel against authority, to avoid problems, to obtain pleasure, or to explore themselves. The emotional changes characteristic of adolescence increase their susceptibility to social influences. Yet most adolescents are not skilled in realistically assessing the risk of many substance use situations.

In spite of the disappointing results of most drug education programs, many current programs are repeating the mistakes of the past. Most are based on approaches that are politically expedient, for example. Many parents and citizens support the *Just Say No!* approach. They appear to find comfort in the direct, uncomplicated message, even though there is no empirical evidence that this approach is effective. Similarly, in spite of evidence to the contrary, many believe that scare tactic approaches to prevention are effective. Scare tactics have not proved to yield enduring changes in health practices, however (Leventhal, 1972; Soames, 1988). Very often, fear-based appeals seem unrealistic to young people and undermine the credibility of the program. In contrast, many other approaches to drug prevention are complex and politically controversial. For example, decision-making curricula are unacceptable to some adults who believe that the adolescent has no right to be making decisions about drugs because drug use among minors is illegal.

The factors associated with drug abuse may differ from those associated with drug experimentation and, therefore, may be of limited usefulness in prevention efforts. Furthermore, it is not always clear whether the known correlates are causal factors or are actually the result of drug use. Finally, several correlates are not subject to modification in prevention programs. For example, there is no evidence that a classroom-based prevention program can produce meaningful, enduring changes in self-esteem (Hayes & Fors, 1990).

Theory-Based Prevention Programs

To increase the effectiveness of prevention efforts, theory and research from the behavioral and social sciences are being used to design programs. As a result, adolescent prevention programs have incorporated more realistic and effective approaches to influencing health practices.

Unfortunately, many of the theories that have evolved to explain the etiology of drug use are based on research designed to examine drug use among heavy users or "troubled" youth. In addition, most research and theory focuses on drug use instead of on the processes involved in drug experimentation and gradual adoption of regular drug use patterns. For these reasons, most theories are of limited practical use in designing effective strategies to prevent drug abuse. Two theories have been influential in the design of effective prevention programs, however—problem behavior theory and social learning theory.

Problem Behavior Theory

Adolescence is a unique developmental stage in which many behaviors (e.g., smoking, alcohol, sexual activity) that society generally considers acceptable for adults are specifically prohibited for young people (Jessor & Jessor, 1977). Because these activities are socially approved only for adults, young people consider these "problem behaviors" indicators of transition to a more mature, adult-like status. This perception, combined with adolescents' high motivation to assume adult roles, increases the appeal of problem behaviors and often overwhelms competing concerns regarding health or social consequences. Adolescents engage in problem behavior because it helps them attain their personal goals: rebel against authority, exert independence, gain entrance to a social group, achieve a degree of social status, enhance perceived maturity, or develop a sense of identity. Adolescents at greatest risk of chronic drug use are those who do not perceive themselves as capable of achieving these goals through socially acceptable means.

Adolescents who have fewer effective coping strategies, fewer skills in handling social situations, and less access to socially approved opportunities (e.g., sports, academics, jobs, valued social roles) are more vulnerable to problem behaviors. To reduce vulnerability to substance abuse, adolescents must have alternative methods of meeting these needs. Thus, it is essential to increase their social skills, expand their awareness of the variety of options available for meeting perceived needs, and ensure that the social environment provides a variety of opportunities to meet these needs.

Social Learning Theory

According to social learning theory (Bandura, 1977), young people learn many behaviors through observation of role models and the consequences of the models' behavior. Models may come from the media, peers, family, and others in the social environment. The model need not be liked or respected, but is usually perceived as holding a desired status. Models inadvertently help adolescents develop beliefs about normal and acceptable behavior, including beliefs about the social meaning of substance use. Any perceived association of substance use with popularity, maturity, success, or sophistication, for example, often influences adolescent decisions subconsciously. Ultimately, these beliefs increase adolescents' vulnerability to substance use. To reduce the chances of drug use, it is important to provide adolescents with models of desired attributes that do not rely on drugs to achieve their status. It is equally important that the young people have opportunities to attain these attributes themselves without the use of drugs.

Vulnerability to these social influences can be partially mediated by personal knowledge, skills, and goals. If young people have goals that are inconsistent with drug abuse and believe that they have real opportunities to reach their goals, they are less likely to use drugs. Adolescents often need guidance in the development of goals, reinforcement for having such goals, and reminders to define daily activities that will ultimately lead to goal attainment, however.

Social learning theory emphasizes the importance of self-regulatory processes. Students can learn skills that reduce their vulnerability to social influence. For example, if students learn to analyze critically the methods that media advertising uses to influence their beliefs, they can become psychologically inoculated and, therefore, less vulnerable. Students can learn to resist indirect or direct social pressures to use drugs with peer resistance skills.

Sample Theory-Based Prevention Projects

Several of the prevention projects that have been implemented to influence adolescent health behavior during the initiation phase of drug use reflect a sophisticated, theory-based approach to adolescent health behavior. Evans, Rozell, and Mittlemark (1978), for example, pioneered an innovative approach to adolescent cigarette use. They observed that, although most young people believe that smoking is dangerous, many still experiment or smoke regularly. They hypothesized that formidable social forces must support smoking behavior. In the belief that becoming a smoker may help adolescents feel more mature and gain acceptance by peers, Evans and his colleagues developed a social approach to prevention, often referred to as the Houston Project.

Based on social learning theory, the Houston Project trained adolescents to recognize and develop skills to cope with pressures to smoke from peers, from adult models, and from the media. In addition, the project emphasized the immediate physiological effects of smoking rather than the long-term negative health consequences. Preparing adolescents to deal with social pressures psychologically inoculated them against pressures to smoke. One-year evaluation studies of this approach suggested that this approach significantly reduces rates of smoking.

The Houston Project was a radical departure from traditional prevention approaches. Rather than the long-term disease consequences, it addressed the social forces related to the initiation of smoking behavior. This project marked an important transition from an information-based disease avoidance model to a skills-based psychosocial model. It also demonstrated the important contributions that the behavioral sciences can make to prevention efforts.

Building on the promising results of the Houston Project, Botvin and associates (Botvin, Eng, & Williams, 1980; Botvin & McAlister, 1981) sought to refine and broaden contemporary approaches to the prevention of smoking. They hypothesized that adolescent smoking is a socially learned, functional behavior that results from the interaction between an individual's attributes and environmental factors. Previous descriptive research had revealed that rebelliousness, high need to assume adult roles, high impulsivity, low self-esteem, and low social confidence are all related to early experimentation with smoking and drug use (Botvin & McAlister, 1981). Thus, while some young people may begin to use drugs in response to social forces, others may be coping with deficiencies perceived in their life situations.

Botvin and associates developed the life skills curriculum to address both the social and the psychological factors related to smoking (Botvin et al., 1980). Designed to enhance general personal competence, the program builds positive self-image, decision-making ability, assertiveness, and effective methods of dealing with peer pressures. Several evaluation studies found this curriculum to reduce the onset of smoking and the use of other drugs.

The life skills curriculum represented an important step in adolescent health promotion efforts. By focusing on both social and personal factors, it helped to initiate the development of programs to influence a wide range of forces that directly affect drug use behavior.

The social coping skills curriculum carries this trend a step farther by promoting personal, social, and environmental change simultaneously (Petosa, 1986a). During adolescence, many health compromising behaviors tend to covary, constituting a syndrome of problem behavior (Jessor & Jessor, 1977). Rapid personal development and increasing social expectations make early adolescence a period of high psychological vulnerability (Simmons, Blyth, & Van Cleave, 1979). Many adolescents view their social environment as too competitive, but hesitate to request social support, especially from adults. Overreliance on peers, poor social competence, and a defiant, impulsive approach to life style choices often circumvent responsible decision making. Therefore, it was postulated that a more generalized approach that would build personal effectiveness could be instrumental in preventing poor health practices, particularly drug use.

The social coping skills approach helps young people recognize symptoms of personal and environmental stress (Petosa, 1984). They learn specific ways that social support can help them effectively cope with stressors and reflect on their experiences. Students construct a differentiated social support network that includes peers, parents, and professionals who are available on a daily basis and who can help them define the decision to be made, generate alternatives, and examine the likely consequences for each possible course of action. Relying heavily on teacher modeling and behavioral rehearsal among the students, this approach transforms decision making into a more overt, behavioral, and social experience. An important element of the intervention is to provide systematic instruction to the parents of the students so that they can knowledgeably respond to student requests for social support. Family support is important to the success of the program.

The social coping skills approach appears simple so that the students perceive it as practical. From an organizational point of view, however, it has been designed to change personal, social, and environmental factors. On the personal level, the program enhances self-efficacy in the development of social, decision-making, and coping skills. From a social point of view, the acquisition of these skills can help prevent an overreliance on peers and create a variety of social role opportunities to give and receive assistance. Environmentally, the program builds a more supportive social milieu by establishing positive expectations and a foundation of skills among many people with whom the adolescent interacts daily. Initial evaluation efforts indicate that the social coping skills approach does help prevent the onset of smoking and alcohol use.

In general, each of these approaches has been shown to reduce the onset of smoking or experimental drug use in young adolescents by approximately 50%. In addition, these approaches have provided insights into the design of effective substance abuse prevention programs. For most adolescents, the process of experimenting with drug use has a social dimension. It is necessary to address these social pressures by helping students acquire skills that help them counteract both direct and indirect pressures. Most important, effective programs seek to influence personal, social, and environmental factors that will discourage drug use and encourage the practices of health-enhancing behavior.

COMPREHENSIVE HEALTH PROMOTION MODEL

Health promotion is defined as the organization of educational, social, and environmental resources to enable individuals to adopt and maintain behaviors that reduce risk of disease and enhance wellness (Petosa, 1986b). This definition supports multidimensional approaches to health behavior without circumventing the individual's personal responsibility. This approach is consistent with the biphasic approach to health education, which focuses first on helping individuals make informed decisions and second on developing specific strategies to support desired behavior (Kolbe, Iverson, & Kreuter, 1981). It also clearly encourages professionals to go beyond the prevention of health problems and examine opportunities for health enhancement. The multidimensional model of health promotion focuses specifically on personal, interpersonal, and community factors that influence the development and maintenance of health-related practices (Table 30-1). It broadens both the goals and methods of traditional disease prevention practice.

Table 30-1 Model for Adolescent Health Promotion Interventions

Personal Factors	Interpersonal Factors	Community Factors
Health knowledge acquisition skills	Health behavior/status norms	Adequate health behavior resources
Health-related values	Peer models of health practices	Policies that support health-enhancing behavior
Health-related attitudes	Adult models of health practices	Policies that prohibit health-damaging behavior
Health locus of control	Social role opportunities	Democratic processes of empowerment
Decision-making skills	Effective family functioning	
Coping skills	Differentiated social support	
Social skills		
Behavior self-regulation skills		

Personal Factors

Although the personal factors that influence health actions are somewhat stable, they are amenable to change in educational settings and are, therefore, potentially valuable health promotion targets.

Health Knowledge Acquisition Skills

Even though health knowledge is rarely sufficient to promote long-term health behavior change, it is the foundation of informed decision making. The health information presented must be not only scientifically accurate, but also persuasive, balanced, and relevant to the "street scene," otherwise, program credibility could be seriously compromised. The information should also address the motives, needs, and abilities of the students. This information-processing perspective focuses on students' "images" of drug use, such as a belief that drug use will help them gain popularity (Cvetkovich, Earle, & Schinke, 1987). Classroom discussion could focus on the source of such images, challenge their validity, and explore more effective alternatives to meeting students' needs.

Because health information changes rapidly and health claims are often conflicting, it is essential to teach students the skills that will enable them to identify quality sources of reliable information. Critical thinking skills, for example, enable students to determine the scientific credibility of a claim.

Health-Related Values and Attitudes

Recent health education research suggests that attitudes and values related to health are more resistant to change than are health knowledge and practices (Connell, Turner, & Mason, 1986). Specific efforts must be directed toward fostering the development of health supportive attitudes and values. Respected peer and adult models who openly express and act on health-enhancing values can influence attitudes and values significantly. The models tend to carry more influence if the adolescent believes that they share some common values.

Health Locus of Control

In a comprehensive review of the research literature, Wallston and Wallston (1978) found that the health locus of control (i.e., the generalized belief that actions under personal control influence personal health status) promotes health-enhancing behavior. Because adolescents believe that they are invulnerable or are personally exempt from negative health consequences, it is difficult to strengthen their health locus of control (Elkind, 1975). Classroom demonstrations of the immediate effects of specific actions on health can be helpful. For example, it is possible to detect immediate differences in heart rate, blood pressure, and carbon monoxide levels in response to cigarette smoking. As a project, students can change specific behaviors and monitor the subsequent changes in health status; the changes in health status should occur in a short time and be clearly measurable. These strategies help students directly experience the behavior–health status link and strengthen their health locus of control. Developmentally, adolescents are not capable of cognitively or emotionally acknowledging long-term health consequences in a way that leads to consistent motivation.

Decision-Making Skills

A comprehensive substance abuse prevention program must include some emphasis on decision-making skills (Schaps, Moskowitz, Condon, & Malvin, 1982). Many young people do not simultaneously consider health knowledge, values, and attitudes in order to generate alternative courses of action and to determine the probable consequences of those alternatives. There are a variety of decision-making models, but most have four crucial components: (1) identifying the decision to be made, (2) listing a set of alternatives, (3) considering the consequences of each alternative, and (4) formulating a plan for acting on the alternative chosen. Adolescents harbor many competing motivations, only some of which focus on health protection. Adolescents also face many social pressures to experiment with risk behavior. In a supportive classroom environment, students' decisions can be tested and refined through feedback from teachers and peers. This process can be repeated often during the academic year to build students' skill and confidence in their own decision-making abilities. When adolescents become sufficiently skilled to anticipate decisions that are likely to be necessary in the future, they increase their ability to act independently of social influences.

Coping Skills

Students must learn to recognize the symptoms of stress, anticipate stressful situations, and recognize the impact of stress on their behavior. For example, most young people find socially expected drug use and peer confrontations stressful. Students who rehearse responses to these situations are less likely to comply with social pressures. Some adolescents abuse drugs as a stress-coping mechanism. If adolescents learn effective stress reduction strategies, they should be less susceptible both to pressures to experiment with drugs and to drug use as a coping response (Volpe, 1977).

Social Skills

Several types of social skills are currently used to prevent drug abuse. Peer resistance training focuses on building student skills and confidence in confronting direct pressures to use drugs (Duryea, Mohr, & Newman, 1984). Assertiveness training emphasizes students' rights and reveals ways in which others typically violate these rights (Dupont & Jason, 1984). Teaching these skills involves extensive role playing of realistic situations in which the students develop responses that they find acceptable. Often, students initially need help in creating effective responses, but practice rapidly builds their confidence.

Self-Regulation Skills

Evidence suggests that individuals who can carry out decisions successfully possess a set of identifiable self-regulation skills (Perri & Richards, 1977). Thus, students who learn these self-regulation skills, such as stimulus control and contingency reinforcement, are more likely to meet their behavioral goals. Experience has revealed that many adolescents have trouble accurately monitoring their own actions (Petosa, 1986b). They also need help in identifying appropriate behavioral goals and in learning to use behavioral cues and habit association techniques to prompt desirable behavior. Establishing contingencies to reinforce behavior also can be useful. The central goal of instruction in self-regulation is to enable adolescents to approach behavior change from a systematic, skills-based perspective.

Self-Efficacy: Foundational Concepts

Before students can effectively use the cognitive and behavioral skills that they have learned, they must be able to generalize the application of these skills to actual situations. They must also develop self-efficacy, which is confidence in their ability to use the skills (Bandura, 1986). Self-efficacy gradually increases in a supportive setting in which students experience considerable success. With constructive feedback and extensive practice, students can refine their skills. Then, the emphasis shifts to generalizing the skills to the specific situations in which this skill will reduce the risk of drug use. For example, assignments can be arranged in which students use peer resistance skills with their peer group in real situations. Back in the classroom, they can discuss their performance and ways to refine their skills. If individuals are motivated to act, their belief in their own capacity to engage in the behavior increases the probability that they will act. In addition, their effective functioning in a variety of environments enhances their self-esteem.

Beyond the Focus on Individual Behavior Change

Recent public health policy has focused heavily on the individual life style approach to risk reduction. This emphasis on changing the behaviors of individuals to prevent health problems has two major shortcomings, however. First, a complex array of social, organizational, and environmental factors that are often beyond the control of the individual influence the behavior of the individual. Second, it has been estimated that approximately 52% of health problems in the United States result from personal life style. According to Powell, Spain, Christenson, and Mollenkamp (1986), the remaining 48% of health problems are caused by human biology (16%), environment (22%), and deficiencies in the medical care system (10%). Although the focus on life style is warranted, it is professionally irresponsible to ignore the other important factors that influence health status and behavior.

For not addressing factors beyond the individual's control, substance abuse prevention specialists have been accused of "blaming the victim" and of recommending health-related practices to people who do not have the resources or opportunity to carry them out (Allegrante & Green, 1981; Crawford, 1977). Hochbaum (1976) and Freudenberg (1979) have urged prevention specialists to become more actively involved in social, organizational, and political change that would support health practices. In addition, they should encourage the lay public to work for social change (Freire, 1975).

Interpersonal Factors

As social beings, humans are influenced by values, beliefs, and social norms acquired through relationships with others. By addressing interpersonal factors, the model expands prevention efforts into the social environment of the adolescent. The goal is to affect the health practices of large groups who have a high degree of social interaction. This approach works to change social norms, which in turn can help provide a "critical mass" of social influence that reinforces health-protecting practices and prohibits health-compromising behavior. Diffusion of innovations research has clearly illustrated the importance of direct social contact on personal behavior (Rogers, 1983).

Popular conceptions of peer pressure to use drugs imply direct, coercive ploys designed to force individuals to comply with group norms, but peer pressure to use drugs is generally more subtle (Newman, 1984). The peer group appears to influence the social meaning of drug use by associating drug use with images of social recognition, independence, maturity, fun, and a variety of other desirable payoffs. Thus, drug use often occurs in peer groups because the young people reinforce each other's beliefs in these images. This type of peer "compliance to images" is different from traditionally recognized peer pressure and suggests different prevention strategies.

Health Behavior/Status Norms

Adolescents develop powerful images of behaviors that are normative or desirable. Research has revealed that adolescents often develop beliefs about normative behavior that are inaccurate, however. For example, adolescents consistently overestimate the percentage of their peers, older adolescents, and teachers who smoke (Duryea & Martin, 1981). This distortion in perceived norms can influence students' motivations to use drugs. Because they tend to think in exaggerated terms (i.e., "everybody does it"), providing them with accurate information about the rates of drug use will reduce perceived pressure to comply with the norm. Conducting local school surveys of drug use is an effective way of persuading students that actual use is lower than perceived use and that the majority of students do not use drugs.

Peer/Adult Models of Health Practices

Modeling is an important means of demonstrating beliefs, skills, and new behaviors. Bandura (1969) postulated that modeling may promote the acquisition of new behaviors through the observation of the functional value of these behaviors, may strengthen or weaken inhibitions, or may provoke the performance of previously learned behavior (cueing). Observed consequences of modeled actions can promote the development of outcome expectations. Images of drug use, for example, are often a result of outcome expectations derived from observation of models.

Models of positive health behavior can be used intentionally in prevention programs, but a variety of factors must be considered if the modeling is to be effective. The attributes of the models must appeal to the intended audience; adolescents consider status, success, popularity, independence, and maturity desirable attributes and are likely to emulate a model with these attributes. If the model and audience have similar backgrounds, the audience is likely to feel capable of emulating the model. If the model is perceived as too different (e.g., too competent, too successful), however, the adolescent may perceive the behavior or rewards as personally unattainable. Careful observation and direct questions can determine whom adolescents perceive as desirable models.

The use of modeling is most effective when the students can observe the specific actions that lead to the desired outcomes. Having a high status model condemn drug use is not an effective use of modeling. If the same model demonstrates the decision-making skills used to achieve goals, however, new behaviors and outcome expectations can be learned. In addition, students should have opportunities to practice and receive feedback on skills. At first, students should practice in small, highly structured groups. Once students have developed competence, demonstration of modeled skills in front of an audience can improve retention.

Social Role Opportunities

Adolescents can direct many of their desired images toward positive, growth-enhancing goals if they are provided with appropriate social role opportunities. To appear mature, independent, and competent requires situations in which their responsibility can be assumed and acknowledged. Indeed, formal group affiliation does reduce the risk of drug use considerably among teens (Selnow & Crano, 1986). In organized groups, the adolescent develops a sense of goal orientation and learns to appreciate the benefits of cooperation. Organized groups also provide formal, structured surroundings, such as the school, and adult supervision—both factors that implicitly prohibit drug use. Unfortunately, many existing organizations that provide these opportunities for young people (e.g., sports teams) are competitive and, thus, meet the needs of only a small percentage of adolescents.

Johnson (1980) has proposed that trust, perspective taking, and meaningful interdependence can reduce the risk of drug use. He criticized schools for overemphasizing competition with peers and individualistic efforts in which students work alone to meet set criteria. By means of cooperative methods, classroom learning processes can promote social competence. Students can interact with peers, share ideas and resources, and help each other achieve goals. This type of learning promotes the adoption of social roles within the context of completing a task. Through these experiences, students learn communication, conflict management, leadership, and trust as basic academic skills.

Effective Family Functioning

Many studies have established the link between parent-adolescent drug use (Huba & Bentler, 1980; Huba, Wingard, & Bentler, 1979; Kandel, Kessler, & Marguilies, 1978). Adolescents from families in which one or both parents smoke, drink, or take recreational drugs are more likely to use these substances than are adolescents with parents who do not. This observation underscores the importance of prevention program efforts to educate parents about this potential modeling effect. Although the hypothesis is still untested, it has been proposed that instructing adolescents about the parental modeling effect may help "psychologically inoculate" them. Exposing young people to a variety of adult role models also may help reduce the direct influence of any particular substance-abusing adult.

Family effectiveness training is one type of direct intervention designed to change family interaction styles in order to reduce adolescent risk of drug abuse (Szapocznik, Rio, Vidal, Santiseban, & Kurtines, 1989). In 13 lessons offered to them simultaneously, parents and children learn to communicate better and to take responsibility for their behavior. Adolescents are encouraged to participate in family decision making to encourage democratic relationships. The goal is to help parents change from forceful and directive authority figures to skillful and influential leaders. These leadership skills can reduce rebelliousness and encourage adolescents to internalize mature values.

Differentiated Social Support Network

Empirical studies have established that those with access to supportive social ties are more likely to avoid negative health consequences under stress (Cassel, 1976; Cobb, 1976). For adolescents, the health consequences of stress include both an increased risk of disease and the development of maladaptive coping patterns, such as drug abuse. Social support can mitigate the effects of stress through the sharing of emotional burdens, instruction on specific strategies to deal with stressors, prohibitions on maladaptive coping strategies, and direct instrumental support (e.g., money, resources). Given their developmental needs, adolescents may need social support from a variety of sources, including both peers and adults. Research on social networks has shown that adolescents who belong to multiple, heterogeneous groups tend to be less influenced by any particular group and consequently develop fewer social problems (Gottfredson, 1987).

The social coping skills approach was developed to teach adolescents about the physical and behavioral effects of stress, as well as ways to use social support resources to cope with stress effectively (Petosa, 1984). Students construct a differentiated social support network that includes peers, family members, and adults from their social environment. Specific skills in providing and receiving social support are identified. Through the use of modeling and videotaped feedback, students develop competence in these skill areas. This approach has been useful in helping young adolescents recognize the benefits of social support and reduce stress-related health-compromising behavior.

Community Factors

For the purposes of the model, community factors include societal, environmental, and institutional sources of influence on changing health practices. These macrolevel approaches complement personal and interpersonal efforts by enabling and reinforcing health-promoting behaviors. The model is grounded in the ecological perspective that implies reciprocal causation between the individual and the environment. Although the environment clearly exerts a directional influence on health practices, it is equally important that individuals are capable of collectively changing these environmental forces.

Health-Promoting Environment

The design of physical environments should provide readily accessible opportunities to demonstrate health-promoting behavior or should clearly establish barriers to health-compromising behavior. Providing students with facilities and equipment to participate in extracurricular activities enriches the environment and encourages health-promoting behavior, for example. In contrast, not providing students with a physical space on the school grounds to smoke cigarettes poses a clear barrier to health-compromising behavior. Designing health-promoting environments also can involve providing access to health resources. For example, more students may use drug counseling services if they are easily accessible.

Health Promotion Policy

Historically, one of the most effective tools to protect the health of communities has been the informed use of regulatory policies and laws. In fact, it has been estimated that most of the improvement in health realized by U.S. citizens in the past century has been attributable to effective public health policies (McKinlay & McKinlay, 1977). Success in reducing infectious disease mortality rates has lead to similar efforts in the area of drug abuse.

Policies and laws can be formulated to restrict behaviors (e.g., prohibitions on smoking in public buildings and on airplane flights, age restrictions on alcohol sales, driver intoxication laws, and the criminalization of selected psychoactive drugs). Policies can also provide negative or positive incentives. Negative incentives include, for example, increased taxes for alcohol and cigarettes; a positive incentive is a reduced insurance premium for individuals who do not smoke.

Resource allocation policies may be used to support access to program services, particularly for those without the means to afford such treatment.

Democratic Processes of Empowerment

Given the effective/coercive influence that community factors can exert on an individual's behavior, it may be tempting to rely on these approaches alone to prevent adolescent substance abuse. Policies, laws, and environments designed to regulate human behavior impose limits on personal choice, however. Therefore, it is important that a democratic society maintain procedures by which the constructive use of these community strategies reflects the collective will of citizens.

Prevention specialists can encourage citizens to become involved in policy development, policy advocacy, and policy analysis. Education is vital to increase public participation in the policy development process. Citizens can participate in public advocacy by voting, lobbying, organizing coalitions, and monitoring policy implementation on important health issues. Citizens can take an active role in policy analysis by providing policy makers, the general public, and target populations with a variety of policy options to consider. The intent is to encourage maximum public participation in the policy-making process. Active participation at the policy level enhances community empowerment, enabling communities to take control over their environments. Most important, active participation can galvanize commitment to improving the health of the public through collective actions.

REFERENCES

Aaron, P., & Musto, D. (1981). Temperance and prohibition in America: A historical overview. In M. Moore & F. Gerstein (Eds.), *Alcohol and public policy: Beyond the shadow of prohibition.* Washington, DC: National Academy Press.

Abel, E. (1980). *Marihuana: The first twelve thousand years.* New York: Plenum Press.

Allegrante, J., & Green, L. (1981). When health policy becomes victim blaming. *New England Journal of Medicine, 305,* 1528.

Bandura, A. (1969). *Principles of behavior modification.* New York: Holt, Rinehart & Winston.

Bandura, A. (1977). *Social learning theory.* Englewood Cliffs, NJ: Prentice-Hall.

Bandura, A. (1986). *Social foundations of thought and action: A social cognitive theory.* Englewood Cliffs, NJ: Prentice-Hall.

Bangert-Drowns, R. (1988). The effects of school based substance abuse education—A meta-analysis. *Journal of Drug Education, 18,* 243–263.

Baumrind, D. (1984). Specious causal attributions in the social sciences: The reformulated stepping stone theory of heroin use as exemplar. *Journal of Personality and Social Psychology, 45,* 1289–1298.

Berberian, R., Gross, C., Lovejoy, J., & Paparella, S. (1976). The effectiveness of drug education programs: A critical review. *Health Education Monographs, 4,* 377–398.

Botvin, G., Eng, A., & Williams, C. (1980). Preventing the onset of cigarette smoking through life skills training. *Preventive Medicine, 9,* 135–143.

Botvin, G., & McAlister, A. (1981). Smoking among children and adolescents: Causes and prevention. In C. Arnold (Ed.), *Annual review of disease prevention.*New York: Springer.

Cassel, J. (1976). The contribution of the social environment to host resistance. *American Journal of Epidemiology, 104,* 107–123.

Cobb, S. (1976). Social support as a moderator of life stress. *Psychosomatic Medicine, 38,* 300–314.

Connell, D., Turner, R., & Mason, E. (1986). Summary findings of the school health education evaluation: Health promotion effectiveness, implementation, and costs. *Journal of School Health, 55,* 316–323.

Crawford, R. (1977). You are dangerous to your health: The ideology and politics of victim blaming. *International Journal of Health Services, 4,* 663–680.

Cvetkovich, G., Earle, T., & Schinke, S. (1987). Child and adolescent drug use: A judgment and information processing perspective to health behavior interventions. *Journal of Drug Education, 17,* 295–312.

Donovon, J., & Jessor, R. (1984). Problem drinking and the dimension of involvement with drugs: A Guttman scalogram analysis of adolescent drug use. *American Journal of Public Health, 14,* 543–551.

Dupont, P., & Jason, L. (1984). Assertiveness training in a preventive drug education program. *Journal of Drug Education, 14,* 369–378.

Duryea, E., & Martin, G. (1981). The distortion effect in student perceptions of smoking prevalence. *Journal of School Health, 51,* 115–118.

Duryea, E., Mohr, P., & Newman, I. (1984). Six-month follow-up results of a preventive alcohol education intervention. *Journal of Drug Education, 14,* 97–104.

Elkind, D. (1975). Recent research on cognitive development in adolescence. In S. Dragastin & G. Elder (Eds.), *Adolescence in the life cycle: Psychological change and social context* (pp. 49–61).Washington, DC: Hemisphere Publishing.

Elkind, D. (1978). Understanding the young adolescent. *Adolescence, 13,* 127–134.

Erikson, P. (1987). *The steel drug: Cocaine in perspective.* Lexington, MA: Lexington Books.

Evans, R., Rozell, R., & Mittlemark, M. (1978). Deterring the onset of smoking in children: Knowledge of immediate physiological effects and coping with peer pressures, media pressures, and parent modeling. *Journal of Applied Social Psychology, 18,* 126–136.

Freire, P. (1975). *Pedagogy of the oppressed.* Middlesex, Harmondsworth, England: Penguin.

Freudenberg, N. (1979). Shaping the future of health education: From behavior change to social change. *Health Education Quarterly, 4,* 372–377.

Goodstadt, M. (1986). Factors associated with cannabis nonuse and cessation of use: Between and within survey replication of findings. *Addictive Behaviors, 11,* 275–286.

Gottfredson, G. (1987). Peer group interventions to reduce the risk of delinquent behavior: A selective review and a new evaluation. *Criminology, 25,* 223–246.

Hanson, D. (1982). The effectiveness of alcohol and drug education. *Journal of Alcohol and Drug Education, 27,* 1–12.

Hayes, D., & Fors, S. (1990). Self-esteem and health instruction: Challenges and curriculum development. *Journal of School Health, 60,* 208–211.

Hochbaum, G. (1976, July). At the threshold of a new era. *Health Education,* 2–4.

Huba, G., & Bentler, P. (1980). The role of peer and adult models for drug taking at different stages in adolescence. *Journal of Youth and Adolescence, 9,* 449–465.

Huba, G., Wingard, J., & Bentler, P. (1979). Beginning adolescent drug use and adult interaction patterns. *Journal of Consulting and Clinical Psychology, 47,* 265–276.

Jacobson, R., & Zinberg, N. (1975). *The social basis of drug abuse prevention.* Washington, DC: Drug Abuse Council.

Jessor, R., & Jessor, S. (1977). *Problem behavior and psychosocial development: A longitudinal study of youth.* New York: Academic Press.

Johnson, D. (1980). Constructive peer relationships, social development, and cooperative learning experiences: Implications for the prevention of drug abuse. *Journal of Drug Education, 10,* 7–24.

Johnston, L., O'Malley, P., & Bachman, J. (1986). *Drug use among high school students, college students and other young adults: National trends through 1985.* Rockville, MD: National Institute on Drug Abuse.

Kandel, D., Kessler, R., & Marguilies, R. (1978). Antecedents of adolescent initiation into stages of drug use: A developmental analysis. In D. Kandel (Ed.), *Longitudinal research on drug use: Empirical findings and methodological issues.* Halstead: New York.

Kinder, B., Pape, N., & Walfish, S. (1980). Drug and alcohol education: A review of outcome studies. *International Journal of the Addictions, 15,* 1035–1080.

Kolbe, L., Iverson, D., & Kreuter, M. (1981). Propositions for an alternate and complementary health education paradigm. *Health Education, 3,* 24–30.

Leventhal, H. (1972). Experimental studies on fear. In G. Zaltman, P. Kotler, & I. Kaufman (Eds.), *Creating social change.* New York: Holt, Rinehart & Winston.

McKinlay, J., & McKinlay, S. (1977, Summer). Medical measures and the decline of mortality. *Milbank Memorial Fund Quarterly, 405–428.*

Newman, I. (1984). Capturing the energy of peer pressure: Insights from a longitudinal study of adolescent cigarette smoking. *Journal of School Health, 54,* 146–148.

Perri, M., & Richards, C. (1977). Investigation of normally occurring episodes of self-controlled behavior. *Journal of Counseling Psychology, 34,* 178–183.

Petosa, R. (1984). *Evaluation of the social coping skills approach to adolescent health behavior: Progress report.* W.T. Grant Foundation.

Petosa, R. (1986a). Emerging trends in adolescent health promotion. *Health Values, 10,* 22–28.

Petosa, R. (1986b). Enhancing the health competence of school-age children through behavioral self-management skills. *Journal of School Health, 56,* 211–214.

Powell, K., Spain, G., Christenson, G., & Mollenkamp, M. (1986). The status of the 1990 objective for physical fitness and exercise. *Public Health Reports, 101,* 17–20.

Rogers, E. (1983). *Diffusion of innovations* (3rd ed.). New York: Free Press.

Schaps, E., Moskowitz, J., Condon, J., & Malvin, J. (1982). Process and outcome evaluation of a drug education course. *Journal of Drug Education, 12,* 353–364.

Selnow, G., & Crano, W. (1986). Formal vs. informal group affiliations: Implications for alcohol and drug use among adolescents. *Journal of Studies on Alcohol, 47,* 48–52.

Simmons, R., Blyth, R., & Van Cleave, E. (1979). Entry into adolescence: The impact of school structure, puberty, and early dating on self-esteem. *American Sociological Review, 44,* 948–962.

Soames, R. (1988). Effective and ineffective use of fear in health promotion campaigns. *American Journal of Public Health, 78,* 163–167.

Stuart, R. (1974). Teaching facts about drugs: Pushing or preventing. *Journal of Educational Psychology, 66,* 189–201.

Szapocznik, J., Rio, A., Vidal, A., Santiseban, D., & Kurtines, W. (1989). Family effectiveness training: An intervention to prevent drug abuse and problem behavior in Hispanic adolescents. *Hispanic Journal of Behavioral Sciences, 11,* 4–27.

Tobler, N. (1986). Meta-analysis of 143 adolescent drug prevention programs: Quantitative outcome results of program participants compared to a control or comparison group. *Journal of Drug Issues, 16,* 537–567.

Volpe, R. (1977). Feedback facilitated relaxation training as primary prevention of drug abuse in early adolescence. *Journal of Drug Education, 7,* 179–193.

Wallston, K., & Wallston, B. (1978). Locus of control and health. *Health Education Monographs, 6,* 107–117.

White, R., & Biron, R. (1979). *A study of the psychological and behavioral effects of the decisions about drinking curriculum* (Evaluation Report No. 9). Washington, DC: National Institute on Alcohol Abuse and Alcoholism.

Yamaguchi, K., & Kandel, D. (1984). Patterns of drug use from adolescence to young adulthood: Sequences of progression, predictors of progression. *American Journal of Public Health, 74,* 668–681.

31

Primary Prevention of Alcoholism: Public School Programs

Merriel F. Mandell

Primary prevention programs designed to educate students on the dangers of drug and alcohol use have not proved effective in reducing substance use, abuse, or addiction (Cooper & Sobell, 1979; Freeman & Scott, 1966; Hanson, 1982; Mauss, Hopkins, Weisheit, & Kearney, 1988; Polich, Ellickson, Reuter, & Kahan, 1984). Traditionally, these programs have been part of public school curricula and have involved only the classroom teacher and the students. With an understanding of the reasons that these programs have consistently failed, efforts can be directed toward developing primary prevention programs that stand a better chance of success.

SOCIALIZATION THROUGH EDUCATION

The public school system was organized in the United States in the 1830s to offer an equal and free education to all. The idea that public education could provide solutions to social problems was an outgrowth of the basic philosophical tenets on which the state public school systems were founded: that a democratic nation is best served and maintained through education of the populace; that the quality of community life rests on the quality of the education provided; and that education fosters the ability to make intelligent political, economic, and social choices. This set of beliefs is predicated on the ancient Greek idea that education transforms a person into a rational, civilized being whose behavior will henceforth serve the best interests of his or her community, country, and fellow citizens (*World Book Encyclopedia,* 1972). Thus, if education helps a person recognize the danger or evil of some behavior, it can be expected that the person will cease to engage in that behavior.

ALCOHOL AS A SOCIAL PROBLEM

At the same time that public education was taking shape for the benefit of the general population, the use of alcohol was becoming a social problem. During colonial times, drinking was confined primarily to the consumption of beer and small amounts of wine that had been manufactured either locally or at home. For the most part, alcoholic beverages were consumed at home with meals and during religious ceremonies.

Prior to 1840, beer accounted for 90% of all alcoholic beverages consumed; wine, for another 5%. During the late 18th and early 19th centuries, however, the drinking habits of the U.S. public changed. The popularity of distilled spirits increased considerably. After 1840, hard liquor accounted for 90% of all the alcohol consumed. This change resulted from a production increase and a price decrease. It became cheaper and more profitable for farmers to turn grain into whiskey than to ship it in bulk over bad roads (*World Book Encyclopedia,* 1972).

Because of the higher alcohol content per volume in distilled spirits, it took far fewer drinks and much less time to become inebriated. Dropping by a saloon, a man could rationalize that he would be there only a short while and have just one little drink. Saloons became a flourishing business, and men began to spend their drinking time away from home. Public drunkenness became a matter of civic concern. It was this environment that gave birth to the Temperance Movement (Bacon, 1967).

RISE OF THE TEMPERANCE MOVEMENT

At first, those in the Temperance Movement were concerned with combating the abuse of distilled spirits. In part, their hopes for effectiveness rested on education. They believed that young people could be taught never to begin drinking whiskey and to use other alcoholic beverages in moderation.

This early reform group gave way to one with a much broader goal—total abstinence from the use of all alcoholic beverages. The new group believed that all alcoholic beverages were evil; that they were the cause of evil; that the use of alcohol was immoral, unpatriotic, and criminal; and that any use would result in disease, degradation, and death (Bacon, 1967). The focus of their educational program shifted from one that stressed moderation to one that stressed the "evils" of alcohol.

Founded in 1874, the Women's Christian Temperance Union (WCTU) focused on the evil effects of alcohol, tobacco, and narcotics. In 1879, Frances Willard, a noted educator, became the second president of the WCTU. She designed the campaign that led to prohibition. As part of this campaign, the WCTU made a concerted effort to have legislation passed that mandated the inclusion of hygiene and physiology in the public school curriculum. Materials on the "evils of alcohol" were to be part of each course. In 1884, Frances Willard spoke before the National Education Association on the success of the movement.

> It is to that proposition that one branch of our temperance work is dedicated, and in five States of our nation, already New York, Michigan, New Hampshire, Vermont, and Rhode Island, by the effects of our society, the State has declared that a part of the curriculum in the public schools shall be that of hygiene with special reference to this curse of drink, with special reference to alcoholic stimulants upon the tissues of the body and the temper of the soul. (Means, 1962, p. 52)

EARLY YEARS OF PREVENTION EDUCATION

The WCTU was so effective in lobbying for its educational program that, between 1880 and 1890, 38 states and territories passed laws to require alcohol education in the schools. Material for the classes was provided by the WCTU, whose members were allowed in several states to present the temperance lectures (Hirsh, 1947).

The material was designed to inspire total abstinence by convincing the students that any use of alcohol would result in dire moral failings and imminent physical destruction. The distinction between occasional use and chronic drunkenness was blurred so that conditions that might be associated with advanced alcoholism were described as the ramifications of even the most minor use. The combination of factual knowledge and myths presented also slanted the course material to encourage total abstinence. All the material was presented as "scientific fact" and aimed at reinforcing the student's fears, although little was known at the time about the actual effects of alcohol addiction (Bacon, 1967).

As education to prevent alcohol use became more institutionalized in the public schools, some attempts were made to provide adequate preparation for the teachers responsible for presenting this material. In some teacher-training programs, certification was dependent on passing an examination on alcohol and alcoholism. Most teachers, however, were allowed to base their teaching on their own personal knowledge of the subject. This knowledge was gained either through personal exposure to an alcoholic parent, relative, or neighbor, or through the teaching of the WCTU (Means, 1962).

In 1915 when he made an early evaluation of the success of the campaign for abstinence through education, Rapeer (cited in Means, 1962) noted the mix of myth and science in the material presented and the attempt to instill abstinence through fear. Rapeer stated,

The increased per-capita consumption of both alcohol and tobacco in the generation during which "scientific temperance instruction" has had a place in the schools is sufficient proof of the failure of the specific aim of the movement. (cited in Means, 1962, p. 55)

As the influence of those in the Temperance Movement grew, the campaign turned increasingly political. Impetus for a Constitutional amendment gathered steam, and two other groups came into play. One was a countermovement made up of the distillery owners and others who strongly disagreed with any attempt to control the supply of alcoholic beverages. The other group was much larger than either of the first two and consisted of those who supported neither movement and wished the issues would go away altogether. This group, though having no formal organization, has been the source of an attitude of avoidance whose impact can still be felt today (Bacon, 1967).

Although the WCTU was effective in getting legislation passed that required schools to teach their students about alcohol and alcoholism, there was a gradual reduction in the amount of formal teaching materials published. The percentage of elementary school health textbook space devoted to alcohol declined from 13.4% in 1885, to 12.9% in 1910, to 2.7% in 1935 (Thompkins, cited in Milgram, 1976). Apparently, because textbook publishers were leery of providing material that would offend either the Temperance Movement or the distillery industry, they tried to avoid the topic as much as possible. In general, interest in education to prevent alcoholism decreased after the passage of the Prohibition Amendment to the Constitution in 1919. In the minds of a large segment of the population, passage of the amendment ended alcoholism as a social problem (Bacon, 1967).

TRANSITIONAL PERIOD

Following the repeal of Prohibition in 1933, interest in education programs to prevent alcohol abuse slowly increased. During the late 1930s and the 1940s, alternative approaches were based on a variety of attitudes: the original concept that alcohol is evil and total abstinence can be achieved through fear; the more moderate idea that responsible use should be emphasized; the philosophy that onset of use can be delayed by teaching children that they should not drink until they are adults; and the permissive stance of presenting the facts and letting everyone make up his or her own mind (Milgram, 1976).

In surveying the field, Singerman (1941) noted the conflicting philosophies, the inadequate text material, and the lack of government-funded research to provide factual information about the effects of alcohol. He stressed the futility of trying to teach adolescents about the "evil" effects of alcohol when they and their drinking friends did not come to evil ends. These wasted attempts to impose adult myth on adolescent reality stemmed from a refusal to recognize that an ever increasing segment of the adolescent population was already drinking (Bacon, 1967).

Researchers and educators struggled to find effective ways to prevent adolescent alcohol abuse. Singerman (1941) suggested that more attention should be paid to the healthy emotional adjustment of the adolescent and the societal ills that were related to alcoholism. In an attempt to make the consequences of drunkenness more immediate, Weber (1941) suggested the use of significant events, such as traffic accidents, to make course material relevant and provide a format for the inclusion of extended information about the use and abuse of alcohol.

During the 1950s, the extent of adolescent alcohol use was finally recognized. Studies showed that a fairly large percentage of adolescents drank on a regular basis and that only very few totally abstained (Baur & McCluggage, 1958; Chappell, 1953). These early epidemiological studies helped renew interest in education on alcohol and alcoholism. The Joint Committee on Health Problems in Education (1954) noted that education in schools played a vital role in prevention, sharing the task with home and church.

The "evils of alcohol" approach continued to dominate the field during the 1950s. Journal commentaries on the state of education to prevent alcohol abuse called for a more reasoned approach, however. Milich, Potter, & Monnier (1951) stressed that adolescents need to understand alcoholism as an illness and called for teaching teen-agers to distinguish between acceptable social drinking and alcoholism. Linden (1959) noted a general shift in the perceived purpose of education from the transmission of past knowledge to the younger generation to the development of problem-solving techniques for dealing with current life situations. He supported the application of these ideas to alcohol education. He also commented on the lack of good teaching materials and the need for better teacher training. McCarthy (1960) stressed that past programs had been put together to satisfy adult goals (i.e., total abstinence) and that, until materials were made relevant to student goals, results would be seen mostly in the students' ability to answer questions on quizzes. He called for teaching the concept of moderate use, as the vast majority of adults use alcohol and most children learn to drink in the home.

By the 1960s, the second generation since the repeal of Prohibition was coming of age. The use of alcohol was a socially acceptable means of relaxing among adults and a frequent means of expressing rebellion among adolescents. The "evils of alcohol," total abstinence approach was no longer considered a realistic foundation for education to prevent alcohol abuse. Teaching responsible use through the objective presentation of factual material was accepted as a more enlightened alternative. Instead of leading to an improved and more effective curricula, however, this change led to programs that incorporated divergent goals. In their textbook, for example, Brownell, Evans, and Hobson (1961) began one chapter objectively by stressing the distinction between use and abuse, but ended by warning young people against drinking at all. "Alcohol seems to have a particularly devastating effect on young people's morals. . . . Each time a person drinks, he runs the risk of a dangerous temporary breakdown of his morals or his judgment" (pp. 283–284).

During the 1960s, the education curriculum for the prevention of alcohol abuse was expanded to include marijuana and other drugs, but attempts to associate moral decay with the use of marijuana met the same fate as attempts to associate evil with the use of alcohol. Few data on the long-term effects of marijuana or drug use were available. Observing marijuana use among their peers and adults, teen-agers saw no immediate negative consequences; therefore, those who attempted to scare them into abstinence lost credibility (Bacon, 1969). The expanded focus only increased the already considerable problems of executing an effective prevention program, such as the variety of attitudes prevailing in the culture toward the use of alcohol and drugs, the diversity and ambiguity of course objectives, and the lack of research in the areas of methodology and outcome effectiveness.

INTRODUCTION OF THEORY-BASED MODELS

In 1964, Gerald Caplan introduced the idea of primary prevention to the field of mental health (Caplan, 1964). This concept, borrowed from the public health field, originated in the assumption that the incidence of mental disorders in a community could be reduced by counteracting the contributing circumstances before they had an opportunity to produce illness. Caplan's model was based on the principle that individuals' resistance to mental disorders rested on their ability to get their needs met in healthy interpersonal relationships. According to the model, the educational system is one of the prime agents of socialization and, thus, is an appropriate arena for instruction in shaping relationships. The influence of Caplan's ideas can be seen in many school programs, including those designed to prevent alcohol abuse (Rappaport, 1977).

Types of Programs

Several models of prevention education were developed in the 1970s. Moskowitz (1983, 1989) has categorized these into three different domains: knowledge/attitudes, values/decision making, and social competency. A theoretical base supports each of these programs types (Fishbein & Ajzen, 1975), and the learning achieved is assumed to have a substantial impact on the incidence of personal substance use and abuse. Most programs currently in vogue use some combination of the three.

Knowledge/Attitudes Approach

The goal of knowledge/attitudes programs for the prevention of alcohol abuse is to inculcate students with attitudes and beliefs that support either abstinence or moderate use, depending on the particular course objectives. Such programs focus on the negative effects and consequences of the use and abuse of alcohol. Information may be presented in didactic form by teachers or outside "experts" (Williams, Ward, & Gray, 1985); through teacher-led discussion groups (Williams, DiCicco, & Unterberger, 1968); by computer-aided instruction (Meier & Sampson, 1989; Moncher, Parms, Orlandi, & Schinke, 1989); or in games (Wodarski & Hoffman, 1984). This approach involves two assumptions: (1) adolescents lack this information, and (2) adolescents possess either positive or neutral attitudes that foster use. Programs cover such topics as the effects of drugs on the body and behavior, physical and social hazards of using, school and community norms, and legal regulations. This method is reminiscent of the old "evils of alcohol" approach with the "evil" part removed.

Values/Decision-Making Approach

Based on Caplan's primary prevention model, the values/decision-making approach focuses on individual improvement. This approach aims to increase the adolescent's inner strength through recognition of needs, clarification of values, improved self-concept, and improved self-worth. The underlying concept is that drug and alcohol use and abuse are outcomes of poor social adjustment, unclear values, and poor problem-solving skills. Adolescents who are interpersonally and intrapersonally competent, it is theorized, form healthy peer relationships that focus on sharing activities other than substance use.

Programs that use this approach teach decision-making and problem-solving skills, include exercises in values clarification and communication processes, and work on the development of a positive self-concept and increased awareness of emotions. Among the methods used are discussion groups, peer counseling, and intervention techniques. Programs designed to improve self-concept, self-esteem, and emotional awareness have generally been addressed to elementary school-aged children (Kim, McLeod, & Palmgren, 1989), while programs designed to work with problem-solving skills and values have been more widely applied to adolescents (Goodstadt & Sheppard, 1983; Mooney, Roberts, Fitzmahan, & Gregory, 1979; Teichman, Rahav, & Barnea, 1988).

Social Competency Approach

The primary goal of the social competency approach is to change the adolescent's behavior. Consistent with the theories of social learning and self-efficacy developed by Bandura (1977, 1986), the model is based on the hypothesis that individuals create their actual social environments from a global potential environment by their choices and their behavior. According to this model, adolescents use and abuse drugs and alcohol because they lack the psychosocial skills necessary to establish a social environment that helps them to resist peer pressure and provides rewards unrelated to drug and alcohol involvement. Programs based on this approach teach health-promoting skills, as well as skills for coping with social situations and stress (Baer, McLaughlin, Burnside, & Pokorny, 1988; Hansen et al., 1988; McGuire, 1961; Rohrbach, Graham, Hansen, & Flay, 1987).

Effectiveness of Current Programs

Evaluations of the programs now being implemented have shown them to be no more effective than were those in any previous era. In reviewing the literature of prevention program outcome studies, for example, Bukoski (1985) noted that most of the programs designed to delay or prevent the onset of drug or alcohol use or abuse have been ineffective. He pointed out that approximately one third of graduating high school seniors have not received any education on substance use. Others have pointed to the continued ambivalence about alcohol in the community (Ritson, 1981) and the lack of community support (Lohrmann & Fors, 1986) as the reasons for the absence of any clear plan to prevent alcohol problems.

In 1984, Polich and associates reviewed the literature relating to law enforcement, treatment, and prevention as methods of controlling adolescent drug abuse. They concluded that school-based prevention programs have the most potential for effectiveness, even though such programs have not been successful in the past. Careful reading of the report indicates that their conclusions do not apply to alcohol, however. "Because alcohol is so much more commonly used by adolescents and adults, and because its use is so widely accepted, we doubt that the prevention approaches we have identified will work against adolescent drinking" (Polich et al., 1984, p. xvi). Moskowitz (1989), in a review of the literature on education to prevent alcohol abuse, concluded that educational programs have been, for the most part, ineffective; that methodological weaknesses undermine the internal validity of most studies and the ability to infer program effectiveness; and that few evaluation reports provide enough descriptive information to allow for adequate generalizability.

CONCLUSION

The goal of primary prevention is to reduce the incidence of a problem by counteracting the factors that contribute to its onset through a learning/socialization process. The first step in designing a primary prevention program is to identify the problem and decide whether it is, in fact, subject to reduced incidence through a learning/socialization process.

Polich and associates (1984) made clear the need for differentiation in approaches to prevent abuse for different drugs and different aspects of drug usage. Methods for preventing the abuse of alcohol should be differentiated from those for preventing the abuse of other drugs, because using alcohol in some ways is an accepted part of our culture. It is used in the home, in the community, and in business operations to relax, to ease social relationships, and to celebrate certain religious ceremonies. Illicit experimentation by those under the legal drinking age, when confined to alcohol use, is not legally sanctioned but is often socially condoned. Children receive different messages about the use of alcohol than they do about the use of other drugs.

Alcohol use can be differentiated into three types.

1. Use is the ingestion of an amount of alcohol less then would have adverse consequences on the environment, on the drinker's physical well-being, on the drinker's self-concept, and/or on the drinker's interpersonal relationships. This definition encompasses the *DSM III-R* (American Psychiatric Association, 1987) diagnosis of alcohol use without intoxication, but expands the definition to include a nonbehavioral component.
2. Abuse is the ingestion of an amount of alcohol that is sufficient to result in the adverse consequences noted. It corresponds to the *DSM III-R* diagnosis of alcohol intoxication.
3. Addiction or dependence corresponds with the *DSM III-R* diagnosis of psychoactive substance dependence.

Although primary prevention has traditionally sought to prevent or delay the onset of use in the hope of reducing abuse and addiction, alcohol use should not be made a target of primary prevention programs in the schools. Research carried out during the last decade has suggested that public education does not affect the factors most relevant to the onset of alcohol use and abuse. These factors include religious upbringing, positive attitudes toward use prior to onset, peer influence, and family members' use of alcohol (Polich et al., 1984).

By 7th grade, a substantial minority of children have begun to use alcohol (Polich et al., 1984). Therefore, if programs to prevent alcohol abuse are to have an impact prior to onset, they must begin while children are in elementary school. Polich and associates indicated that the information most likely to inhibit the initial use of a drug emphasizes immediate dangers associated with the initial use. The potential danger of the initial use of alcohol is the rapid onset of addiction. Although it is thought that some people become addicted to alcohol quite rapidly, too little is known at this time about the factors involved to present this information to elementary or junior high school students in a way that will convince them of the danger.

Even if this were possible, it seems unlikely that it would have a significant effect in terms of preventing alcohol use. Among the children at highest risk for inappropriate use of alcohol are those from families with a history of alcoholism. Members of such families frequently deny that the use of alcohol has any relevance to any problems involving any members of the family. It would be difficult to influence these children to act differently from their dysfunctional families at an age when they are still primarily attached to and dependent on their families.

For more than a century, society has burdened the schools with a responsibility for which they are ill-suited. Decade after decade of evaluation, critique, and renewed effort in the schools have failed to reduce the incidence of adolescent alcohol use, abuse, and addiction. Although schools can provide accurate, up-to-date, factual information about alcohol and other drugs, they should not be assigned the responsibility for primary prevention of any socially maladaptive behavior. Schools can be used to teach social skills, however. Teaching assertiveness, stress management, conflict resolution, negotiation, decision-making skills, and problem-solving skills would enhance all children's ability to function in the community and strengthen the likelihood that they will make prosocial choices.

REFERENCES

American Psychiatric Association. (1987). *Diagnostic and statistical manual of mental disorders* (3rd rev. ed.). Washington, DC: Author.

Bacon, S.D. (1967). The classic temperance movement of the U.S.A.: Impact today on attitudes, action and research. *British Journal of Addictions, 62,* 5–18.

Bacon, S.D. (1969). Relevance of social problems of alcohol for coping with problems of drugs. In J.R. Wittenborn, H. Brill, J.P. Smith, & S.A. Wittenborn (Eds.), *Drugs and youth: Proceedings of the Rutgers Symposium on Drug Abuse* (pp. 44–51). Springfield, IL: Charles C. Thomas.

Baer, P.E., McLaughlin, R.J., Burnside, M.A., & Pokorny, A.D. (1988). Alcohol use and psychosocial outcome of two preventive classroom programs with seventh and tenth graders. *Journal of Drug Education, 18,* 171–184.

Bandura, A. (1977). *Social learning theory.* Englewood Cliffs, NJ: Prentice-Hall.

Bandura A. (1986). *The social foundations of thought and action: A social cognitive theory.* Englewood Cliffs, NJ: Prentice-Hall.

Baur, E.J., & McCluggage, M.M. (1958). Drinking patterns of Kansas high school students. *Social Problems, 5,* 317–326.

Brownell, C.L., Evans, R., & Hobson, L.B. (1961). *High school health science* (chap. 20). New York: American Book Company.

Bukoski, W.J. (1985). School-based substance abuse prevention: A review of program research. *Journal of Childhood in Contemporary Society, 18*(1–2), 95–115.

Caplan, G. (1964). *Principles of preventive psychiatry.* New York: Basic Books.

Chappell, M.M. (1953). *Use of alcoholic beverages among high school students.* Hempstead, NY: Hofstra Research Bureau.

Cooper, A.M., & Sobell, M.B. (1979). Does alcohol education prevent alcohol problems? Need for evaluation. *Journal of Alcohol and Drug Education, 25,* 54–63.

Fishbein, M., & Ajzen, I. (1975). *Belief, attitude, intention and behavior: An introduction to theory and research.* Reading, MA: Addison-Wesley.

Freeman, H.E., & Scott, J.F. (1966). A critical review of alcohol education for adolescents. *Community Mental Health, 2,* 220–230.

Goodstadt, M.S., & Sheppard, M.A. (1983). Three approaches to alcohol education. *Journal of Studies on Alcohol, 44,* 362–380.

Hansen, W.B., Graham, J.W., Wolkenstein, B.H., Lundy, B.Z., Pearson, J., Flay, B.R., & Johnson, C.A. (1988). Differential impact of three alcohol prevention curricula on hypothesized mediating variables. *Journal of Drug Education, 18,* 143–153.

Hanson, D.J. (1982). The effectiveness of alcohol and drug education. *Journal of Alcohol and Drug Education, 27,* 1–13.

Hirsh, J. (1947). Alcohol education—Its needs and challenges. *American Journal of Public Health, 37,* 1574–1577.

Joint Committee on Health Problems in Education. (1954). *Journal of the American Medical Association, 155,* 40–42.

Kim, S., McLeod, J., & Palmgren, C.L. (1989). The impact of the "I'm special" program on student substance abuse and other related student problem behavior. *Journal of Drug Education, 19,* 83–95.

Linden, A.V. (1959). Some random thoughts on alcohol education. *Journal of School Health, 29,* 3–11.

Lohrmann, D.K., & Fors, S.W. (1986). Can school-based educational programs really be expected to solve the adolescent drug abuse problem? *Journal of Drug Education, 16*(4), 327–339.

Mauss, A.L., Hopkins, R.H., Weisheit, R.A., & Kearney, K.A. (1988). The problematic prospects for prevention in the classroom: Should alcohol education programs be expected to reduce drinking by youth? *Journal of Studies on Alcohol, 49,* 51–61.

McCarthy, R. (1960). Alcohol and the adolescent. *Journal of School Health, 30,* 99–106.

McGuire, W. (1961). The relative efficacy of various types of prior belief-defense in producing immunization against persuasion. *Journal of Abnormal Psychology, 62,* 327–337.

Means, R.K. (1962). *A history of health education in the United States.* Philadelphia: Lea & Febiger.

Meier, S.T., & Sampson, J.P. (1989). Use of computer-assisted instruction in the prevention of alcohol abuse. *Journal of Drug Education, 19,* 245–256.

Milgram, G. (1976). A historical review of alcohol education research and comments. *Journal of Alcohol and Drug Education, 2*(2), 1–16.

Milich, O., Potter, M.G., & Monnier, D.C. (1951). Problems of alcoholism as related to health education in the secondary schools. *Quarterly Journal of Studies on Alcohol, 12*(3), 495–516.

Moncher, M.S., Parms, C.A., Orlandi, M.A., & Schinke, S.P. (1989). Microcomputer-based approaches for preventing drug and alcohol abuse among adolescents from ethnic-racial minority backgrounds. *Computers in Human Behavior, 5,* 79–93.

Mooney, C., Roberts, C., Fitzmahan, D., & Gregory, L. (1979). Here's looking at you: A school-based alcohol education project. *Health Education: Washington, 10,* 18–41.

Moskowitz, J. (1983). *Preventing adolescent substance abuse through drug education.* (Research Monograph Series No. 47, pp. 233–249). Rockville, MD: National Institute on Drug Abuse.

Moskowitz, J. (1989). The primary prevention of alcohol problems: A critical review of the research literature. *Journal of Studies on Alcohol, 50,* 54–88.

Polich, J.M., Ellickson, P.L., Reuter, P., & Kahan, J.P. (1984). *Strategies for controlling adolescent drug use.* Santa Monica, CA: Rand Corporation.

Rappaport, J. (1977). *Community psychology—Values, research, and action.* New York: Holt, Rinehart & Winston.

Ritson, B. (1981). Alcohol and young people. *Journal of Adolescence, 4*(1), 93–100.

Rohrbach, L.A., Graham, J.W., Hansen, W.B., & Flay, B.R. (1987). Evaluation of resistance skills training using multitrait-multimethod role play skill assessments. *Health Education Research, 2,* 401–407.

Singerman, J. (1941). Teaching the alcohol problem. *Science Teacher, 8,* 122–123.

Teichman, M., Rahav, G., & Barnea, Z. (1988). A comprehensive substance prevention program: An Israeli experiment. *Journal of Alcohol and Drug Education, 33,* 1–10.

Weber, L. (1941). Making alcohol education meaningful. *Journal of School Health, 11,* 17–18.

Williams, A.F., DiCicco, L.M., & Unterberger, H. (1968). Philosophy and evaluation of an alcohol education program. *Quarterly Journal of Studies on Alcohol, 29*(3), 685–702.

Williams, R.E., Ward, D.A., & Gray, L.N. (1985). The persistence of experimentally induced cognitive change: A neglected dimension in the assessment of drug prevention programs. *Journal of Drug Education, 15,* 33–42.

Wodarski, J.S., & Hoffman, S.D. (1984). Alcohol education for adolescents. *Social Work in Education, 6,* 69–92.

World Book Encyclopedia. (1972). Chicago: Field Enterprises Educational Corporation.

32

Designing Effective AIDS Prevention Programs for Adolescents

Rick Petosa

It has been estimated that the number of active cases of acquired immunodeficiency syndrome (AIDS) in the United States will reach 1 million by the year 2000 (Burke, Brundage, & Goldenbaum, 1990). The dramatic rise in morbidity and mortality rates associated with human immunodeficiency virus (HIV) infection has created an urgent need for prevention programs. The development of sound prevention strategies requires the systematic identification of behaviors that increase risk followed by the careful study of factors that reduce risk behavior in the target population.

RISK OF HIV INFECTION AMONG YOUTH

Although AIDS is not "exploding" into the general population as once projected, the number of heterosexual cases doubles every 14 to 16 months (Haverkos & Edellman, 1988). As the number of HIV carriers increases, the life style practices of adolescents will place them at a significantly increased risk of infection. Approximately 21% of diagnosed cases of AIDS occur in patients between the ages of 20 and 29 years. Because the incubation period for AIDS can exceed 6 years, it is believed that a number of these cases were contracted during adolescence.

Rates of sexual intercourse among young people appear to be increasing. By the time they complete high school, 50% to 79% of adolescent girls have had sexual intercourse (Hofferth, Kahn, & Baldwin, 1987; Zabin, Hirsh, Smith, Street, & Hardy, 1986). A national survey of adolescent boys revealed that 86% had engaged in intercourse by age 19 (Sonenstein, Pleck, & Ku, 1989). In each of these studies, the rates of sexual activity were increasing most rapidly among those under the age of 14. In a study of young adolescents living in rural areas, 61% of the boys and 47% of the girls had engaged in intercourse by eighth grade

(Alexander et al., 1989). In another national survey, 12.7% of white women and 8% of black women reported involuntary sexual intercourse by age 20 (Moore, Nord, & Peterson, 1989). There has also been an increase in the number of sexual partners among teens. Of the high school girls surveyed in one study, 16% reported four or more sex partners (Hass, 1979). It is not surprising that more than 1 million (3,000 daily) teen-aged pregnancies occur annually (Hayes, 1987).

The most direct indication of HIV risk can be inferred from the current rates of sexually transmitted diseases (STDs) among adolescents. The prevalence of gonorrhea, syphilis, and chlamydiosis is highest among adolescents (Bell & Hein, 1984). Rates of STDs drop off sharply after the age of 19. Still, 75% of all cases of STDs occur in individuals between the ages of 15 and 24 (Bell & Holmes, 1984). Clearly, adolescents are at risk of HIV infection.

HIV/AIDS EDUCATION NEEDS OF ADOLESCENTS

Several surveys have been conducted to determine adolescents' knowledge and beliefs about HIV infection and AIDS. In the first published study on AIDS knowledge among adolescents, Price, Desmond, and Kukulka (1986) reported that high school students in Ohio had many misconceptions and that most of their information about AIDS came from the mass media. Perceived susceptibility to AIDS was low; 73% were not worried about getting AIDS. DiClemente, Zorn, and Temoshok (1986), who conducted a similar survey in a high AIDS prevalence area (i.e., San Francisco) 1 year later, also found unacceptably high levels of misconceptions, but their subjects' knowledge scores were improved. Roughly 60% to 80% of those surveyed were aware of the different modes of HIV transmission. Approximately 40% of those surveyed had serious misconceptions about casual contact and the spread of HIV. Most surprising, 78% were afraid of getting AIDS.

Helgerson and Peterson (1988) found that many students were misinformed about high-risk groups and methods to avoid HIV infection. Most students did not recognize the existence of an HIV carrier state. Importantly, 74% of the students said they wanted to learn more about AIDS. Using in-depth interviews, Warwick, Aggleton, and Homans (1988) found that mainstream medical explanations of HIV infection and AIDS did not reduce adolescents' fears and did not give them realistic perceptions of risk. Heterosexual respondents were not very skilled in describing the clear steps that they could take to minimize their risk of HIV infection.

These studies focused on knowledge and perceptions, but did not address the adolescents' actual risk behaviors. Strunin and Hingson (1987) found that the majority of high school students in their sample knew of the relationship between HIV infection and blood, but had only limited knowledge of the mode of HIV transmission. Most did not know what sexual or drug precautions are necessary to prevent infection. The sexual practices of respondents were particularly resistant to change. Only 10% reported that they would avoid sexual contact or use condoms to prevent HIV infection; only 3% indicated a willingness to become monogamous or to ask questions about a potential sex partner's history.

The surveys demonstrate a simplistic, facts-oriented conceptualization of the educational needs of adolescents. Research on the health practices of adolescents has consistently indicated that it is necessary to address factors beyond knowledge, however. Providing adolescents with scientifically sound information is important, but it is rarely sufficient to substantially change their health-related practices. Perceived social norms and a deep motivation to assume adult roles influence adolescent health practices.

IDENTIFICATION OF BEHAVIORAL GOALS

The prevention of AIDS requires the systematic identification of effective means of breaking the chain of HIV transmission. Emphasis is placed on a set of sex and drug behaviors in which a continuum of options is available. Because most communities consist of heterogeneous populations with a variety of norms regarding sex and drug behavior, the long-term effectiveness of AIDS prevention programs ultimately requires the identification of a broad spectrum of behavioral norms.

The model outlined in Figure 32-1 illustrates the functional relationships between a public health goal, a causal agent, behavioral factors, and health promotion targets. In this case, an examination of the epidemiological and biomedical literature reveals a set of behavioral factors that can reduce the risk of HIV infection. The generation of a comprehensive list of behaviors for the target population as a whole often results in a continuum of behavior options, each of which is relevant for a segment of the target population. For example, promoting abstinence from sexual activity is highly effective in preventing HIV transmission, but only a minority of older adolescents will follow this option. Delaying the onset of sexual activity in teen-agers is likely not only to reduce the number of sex partners for each sexually active adolescent, but also to increase the probability of more mature and responsible preventive actions, such as the use of condoms. Because the majority of older adolescents are sexually active, reducing the number of sexual partners and using condoms will considerably reduce the risk of HIV infection.

Fundamental to the effective use of health promotion strategies is an in-depth knowledge of the community. The beliefs and behavioral norms of the target population must be clearly understood before relevant goals and strategies can be developed. For example, if a given population of adolescents has a high rate of sexual activity (e.g., 80% to 90%), programs designed to promote abstinence are

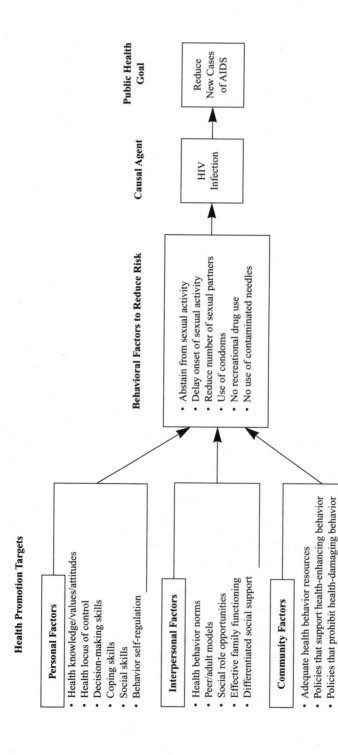

Figure 32–1 Health Promotion Planning To Prevent AIDS

unlikely to be effective (Soames-Job, 1988). A program that focuses on proper condom use will be more effective. Each of the behavioral risk factors should be carefully ranked for relevance and potential for change in the target population.

In the past, health care professionals often relied on community leaders to provide expert opinion about the health practices of community members. Owing to the highly stigmatized (and often illegal) nature of adolescent drug and sexual behavior, however, community leaders frequently have unrealistic and exaggerated views that are based only on anecdotal experiences. It is highly recommended that an anonymous survey be conducted to determine

1. extent of AIDS risk behavior in the community
2. the age of onset of drug and sex behavior
3. factors that support or reduce AIDS risk behavior

The cost and effort required to conduct such a survey is considerable, yet the results are well worth the effort. They can determine decisions regarding the timing, content, and target of interventions to prevent AIDS and, thus, the ultimate effectiveness of the interventions.

THEORY-BASED AIDS EDUCATION NEEDS ASSESSMENT

In the spring of 1988, a team of public health professionals was organized to conduct a statewide AIDS education needs assessment for adolescents in South Carolina. The purpose of the survey was to determine the onset and extent of AIDS risk behavior and to identify the factors that would encourage adolescents to adopt actions to reduce their risk of HIV infection. To this end, Health Belief Model (HBM) concepts were employed to predict adolescents' intentions to adopt safer sex actions.

The HBM has generally been effective in identifying the factors that lead to the adoption of preventive actions in a variety of different populations. The components of the HBM are derived from value expectancy theory, in which it is hypothesized that behavior is a function of (1) the value that an individual places on a goal and (2) the individual's belief that a specific action will achieve that goal. As applied in this study, safer sex actions (i.e., the goal) are influenced by beliefs regarding personal susceptibility to AIDS, the severity of the health consequences of contracting AIDS, and the possibility of reducing susceptibility and/ or severity of the disease through safer sex practices. Additionally, according to the HBM, the perceived efficacy of safer sex actions are "weighed against" perceived social, physical, or psychological barriers or benefits. Finally, a specific stimulus is often necessary to trigger the decision-making process. This "cue to action" may be conceptualized as educational or mass media messages designed to raise awareness of a health threat.

The HBM is useful as an organizing framework for explaining illness, sick roles, and many preventive health actions (Becker, 1974, 1979a, 1979b; Kegeles, 1980). Janz and Becker (1984) found the HBM valuable in understanding preventive actions and recommended its use in health education program planning. Nathanson and Becker (1983) developed a conceptual framework based on the HBM to promote contraception among young unmarried women. A pilot study based on this framework showed improvements in HBM-based contraceptive perceptions, sexual knowledge, and effective contraceptive behavior among adolescents participating in a 15-hour educational program (Eisen, Zellman, & McAlister, 1985). Simon and Das (1984) recommended the use of the HBM in assessments of the need for STD education; however, they cautioned against the use of simple, single-item measures of HBM concepts, suggesting instead the use of multiple items to measure each dimension of the model.

A strength of using the HBM in an educational needs assessment is its direct implications for intervention design. Each component of the HBM should be modifiable by means of traditional health promotion strategies. For example, presenting several realistic strategies that a young woman may employ to encourage condom use during sexual intercourse may substantially reduce a perceived barrier. Explaining the specific mechanisms by which condoms prevent HIV transmission may reinforce the perceived benefit of condom use. Using the HBM to assess HIV education needs can provide a profile of student beliefs that will be helpful in designing relevant and efficient interventions.

Instrument

The HBM was used as a conceptual framework for the development of an instrument to assess adolescent knowledge, beliefs, and preventive actions in regard to AIDS. Subscales were developed to measure perceived susceptibility to AIDS, perceived seriousness of AIDS, barriers to action, general knowledge of AIDS, knowledge of HIV transmission, and cues. An expert panel of three health educators and an epidemiologist who were members of the faculty in a school of public health generated the original pool of 67 items. The panel conducted three reviews of the instrument to ensure conceptual clarity, factual accuracy, and readability.

The original instrument was tested on 70 seventh grade students to determine the readability and comprehension of items. Based on the comments of teachers and students, minor revisions were made to the wording of items. For the knowledge items, a Chronbach alpha reliability coefficient of .73 was judged adequate. Factor analysis was used to verify empirically the subscales designed to measure the HBM variables. A factor-loading coefficient of .35 was used as the criterion for inclusion of an item; several items were dropped from the instrument because they did not sufficiently load on the intended subscale. After this revision, the subscales yielded the following Chronbach alpha reliability coefficients: perceived susceptibility (.78), perceived severity (.81), cues to preventive actions (.58), barriers to preventive actions (.76), and safer sex intentions (.64). The revised instrument contained 42 items (Exhibit 32-1).

Sample

A stratified, random sampling technique was employed to generate a sample of seventh, ninth, and eleventh grade students representative of South Carolina. Schools were stratified based on urban/rural, racial, and geographical distinctions. Urban areas were defined as those with a population density of at least 50,000 residents. Approximately one third of the state population is black; schools were stratified to ensure that the sample contained similar racial representation. Finally, an effort was made to represent the three main geographical regions of the state (i.e., Midlands, Coastal, and Piedmont areas). Initially, 12 schools were invited to participate in the study; 2 declined and were replaced with similar schools. The resultant sample included 232 seventh graders, 225 ninth graders, and 222 eleventh graders. The age range was 12 to 18 years old, and 33% of the sample was black.

Data were collected in a 3-week period during the spring of 1988. A trained health educator with classroom experience administered the instrument. School districts required that the instrument be administered to intact classes of health, biology, or science. The students were read a standardized set of instructions explaining the purpose of the survey and informing them that participation was voluntary. Thirty-three (5%) students declined to participate or turned in uninterpretable surveys, resulting in a 95% response rate.

Results

General Knowledge of AIDS

Levels of knowledge about AIDS appeared to have improved modestly since earlier surveys. Table 32-1 shows the percentage of students who correctly answered the knowledge questions. On 6 of the 14 items, the older students had a higher percentage of correct responses. There were serious gaps in knowledge, however. More than 50% of the students believed that almost all homosexuals carry HIV. A majority believed that it is possible to get AIDS from donating blood. Approximately 20% to 30% did not understand that a person can contract AIDS from an asymptomatic carrier. A large percentage believed that a vaccine is available to prevent AIDS. A very serious misconception was revealed by the

Exhibit 32-1 Items Used To Measure HBM Concepts

AIDS KNOWLEDGE
1. Women with AIDS can infect men.
2. Men with AIDS can infect women.
3. You can get AIDS from kissing.
4. You can get AIDS from oral sex.
5. A person can be infected with the AIDS virus and not have any symptoms of the disease.
6. You can get AIDS from a blood transfusion.
7. Almost all homosexual men have the AIDS virus.
8. You can get AIDS from someone who is infected but doesn't have any symptoms.
9. You can get AIDS by donating blood.
10. You can tell if people have the AIDS virus by looking at them.
11. Any person with the AIDS virus can pass it on to someone else during sexual intercourse.
12. A pregnant woman who has the AIDS virus can give AIDS to her baby.
13. A man who has sex only with women cannot get the AIDS virus.
14. You can get AIDS from kissing someone on the mouth who has AIDS.
15. You can get AIDS from shaking hands or hugging someone who has AIDS.
16. You can get AIDS from sharing plates, forks, or glasses with someone who has AIDS.
17. There is a vaccine available to protect you from getting AIDS.

KNOWLEDGE OF PREVENTIVE ACTIONS
18. One way to decrease the chance of getting AIDS is to avoid sex with many people.
19. Using a condom during sex can lower the risk of getting AIDS.
20. You can get AIDS by sharing a needle with a drug user who has the disease.
21. Not having sex reduces your chances of getting AIDS.

PERCEIVED SUSCEPTIBILITY
22. I am afraid of getting AIDS.
23. I am less likely than most people to get AIDS.
24. I know enough to protect myself from the AIDS virus.
25. Someone I know is likely to get AIDS.
26. The number of people getting AIDS is increasing.
27. I would feel fearful of getting AIDS from students who have the disease if they were in any of my classes at school.

PERCEIVED SEVERITY
28. People with AIDS usually get cancer.
29. AIDS can be cured.
30. People with AIDS die within ten years.
31. AIDS can be cured if treated early.

CUES TO PREVENTIVE ACTIONS
32. I have discussed AIDS with my friends.
33. I have discussed AIDS with my parents.
34. I have learned about AIDS in school.

Exhibit 32-1 continued

BARRIERS TO PREVENTIVE ACTIONS
35. Condoms are difficult to get.
36. Condoms are embarrassing to use.
37. It is hard to ask someone if they have had sex with several people.
38. I feel pressure from my friends to have sex.

SAFER SEX INTENTIONS
39. I would always make sure a condom was used when having sex.
40. I would not have sex with several people.
41. I would not have sex with someone who had sex with other people.
42. I do not plan on having sex until I graduate from high school.

Table 32-1 AIDS Knowledge Levels of 7th, 9th, and 11th Graders

		Grade Level		
	Key	7	9	11
Women with AIDS can infect men.	T	93%	93%	93%
A man who has sex only with women cannot get AIDS.	F	70%	80%	84%*
You can get AIDS from a blood transfusion.	T	90%	90%	90%
You can get AIDS from donating blood.	F	63%	65%	76%*
Almost all homosexuals have the AIDS virus.	F	38%	37%	50%*
You can get AIDS from a person who is infected, but has no symptoms.	T	68%	70%	84%*
You can be infected with AIDS and not have symptoms.	T	67%	64%	82%*
You can tell if people have the AIDS virus by looking at them.	F	85%	82%	83%
A woman can infect her baby with AIDS during pregnancy.	T	86%	85%	82%
You can get AIDS from shaking hands or hugging a person with AIDS.	F	88%	90%	88%
You can get AIDS from sharing forks or glasses with a person who has AIDS.	F	59%	60%	63%
You can get AIDS from kissing.	F	58%	73%	72%
You can get AIDS from oral sex.	T	66%	64%	74%
A vaccine is available to prevent AIDS.	F	61%	67%	76%

*$p = .01$

16% to 30% who believed that men whose only sex partners are women cannot get AIDS. Students also revealed an inaccurate understanding of kissing and oral sex as modes of HIV transmission. If not corrected, many of these misconceptions could lead to behaviors that increase risk of HIV infection.

Knowledge of Preventive Actions

The majority of adolescents had a clear understanding of the preventive actions that have been recommended to reduce risk of HIV infection (Table 32-2). There remained a small but important group (10% to 15%) who appeared to be "hard to reach" and needed additional information regarding preventive actions, however.

Perceived Susceptibility to AIDS

Clearly, the young people were frightened of AIDS (Table 32-3). Almost 80% indicated that they were afraid of contracting AIDS, and only approximately half believed that they were less likely than most people to get AIDS. In spite of their knowledge about casual contact and HIV transmission, almost half would worry about getting AIDS if a classmate had the disease. Apparently, these fears were not mitigated by the 70% who believed that they knew enough about AIDS to protect themselves.

Perceived Severity of AIDS

Students do not seem to fully understand the severity of AIDS (Table 32-4). Very few knew that AIDS often leads to cancer. Only about 40% realized that AIDS is fatal, and about 50% believed that AIDS can be cured if treated early.

Perceived Barriers to Preventive Actions

Older students tended to report lower rates of barriers to preventive actions (Table 32-5). Still, 15% to 20% reported that condoms are embarrassing to use. About half reported that it is difficult to discuss sexual histories with a partner.

Perceived Pressures To Increase Risk Behavior

Peer pressure to engage in risk behavior appeared to be age-related (Table 32-6). The seventh grade students reported higher levels, but peer influence was a reported factor in both sex and drug decisions for all age groups.

Safer Sex Intentions

Crucial to the prevention of HIV infection is for adolescents actually to change their risk behavior. As shown in Table 32-7, approximately 70% of the students across grade levels reported an intention to use condoms. There were important

Table 32-2 Knowledge of Preventive Actions

	Grade Level		
	7	*9*	*11*
One way of reducing risk of AIDS is			
To avoid sex with many people	86%	87%	89%
To use a condom during sex	86%	90%	92%
Not to share needles with drug users	95%	92%	94%
Not to have sex	85%	82%	90%

Table 32-3 Perceived Susceptibility to AIDS

	Grade Level		
	7	*9*	*11*
I am afraid of getting AIDS.	78%	78%	72%
I am less likely than most people to get AIDS.	46%	48%	58%
I know enough to protect myself from AIDS.	75%	70%	70%
Someone I know is likely to get AIDS.	51%	52%	57%
The number of people with AIDS is increasing.	81%	81%	91%*
I would be fearful of getting AIDS if someone in my class had AIDS.	44%	39%	45%

*$p = .001$

Table 32-4 Perceived Severity of AIDS

	Grade Level		
	7	*9*	*11*
People with AIDS usually get cancer.	14%	11%	10%
People with AIDS die within 10 years.	33%	43%	41%
AIDS can be cured if treated early.	54%	44%	35 %*

*$p = .05$

Table 32-5 Perceived Barriers to Preventive Actions

	Grade Level		
	7	9	11
Condoms are hard to get.	21%	9%	9%*
Condoms are embarrassing to use.	19%	15%	15%
It is hard to ask if someone has had sex with several people.	53%	47%	40%*

*p = .01

Table 32-6 Perceived Pressures To Increase Risk Behavior

	Grade Level		
	7	9	11
I feel pressure from friends to have sex.	28%	24%	14%*
I feel pressure to use needles to inject drugs.	21%	15%	14%

*p = .001

Table 32-7 Safer Sex Intentions by Gender and Grade

		Grade Level		
		7	9	11
I would always use a condom when having sex.	Males	68%	65%	73%
	Females	74%	75%	66%
I would not have sex with several people.	Males	63%	51%	54%
	Females	77%	49%	46%
I would not have sex with someone who had had sex with others.	Males	45%	20%	26%
	Females	51%	28%	38%
I do not plan on having sex until I graduate from high school.	Males	30%	18%	18%
	Females	53%	32%	37%
I would not have sex until I had a long-term relationship with one person.	Males	62%	46%	40%
	Females	75%	81%	80%

gender differences for intentions regarding monogamy and abstinence. In the seventh grade, 63% of the males and 77% of the females reported monogamous intentions. A sharp drop in monogamous intentions was reported by ninth and eleventh grade males (slightly more than 50%) and females (slightly below 50%). By the eleventh grade, the percentage of females (38%) who intended to abstain from sex until after high school was more than twice the percentage of males (18%). Similarly, the percentage of eleventh grade females who regarded sexual activity as contingent on a long-term relationship was double (80% vs. 40%) the percentage of males.

The other findings on intentions revealed a consistent trend of lower percentages for the older students. Only 42% of the seventh graders reported a willingness to abstain from sex during high school years. This percentage dropped to 27% by the eleventh grade. The data indicated that a majority of the students did not intend to abstain from sex or practice monogamy.

Prediction of Safer Sexual Behavior

A main purpose of this needs assessment was to determine if HBM variables were useful in predicting safer sexual behavior among teens and, therefore, if addressing the HBM factors in programs would promote successful behavior change. Figure 32-2 presents the HBM variables order of entry into the model and the hierarchical addition to model R^2 for the three grade levels. For the seventh grade, 43% of the variance in safer sex intentions could be explained by the HBM variables. For the ninth grade cohort, only gender, cues, and perceived susceptibility were significant, and 27% of the variance was explained. This trend continued with an explained variance of 17% for the eleventh graders, with gender the only significant predictor. Thus, the HBM variables were effective predictors of seventh grade safer sexual behavior, but were no longer effective predictors in the older grade levels.

Discussion

Clearly, there is a need for educational programs to provide in-depth instruction about the complex etiology of HIV infection. Without comprehensive instruction on the biological aspects of communicable diseases in general and HIV transmission in particular, serious misconceptions are likely to persist. These false beliefs may result in many students' placing themselves at risk unintentionally.

The lack of consistency between knowledge and intention is well documented in the health behavior literature. Sexual behavior can be considered age-related, and many adolescents are highly motivated to adopt adult patterns of behavior. In addition, sexual activity is related to important biological, social, and personal

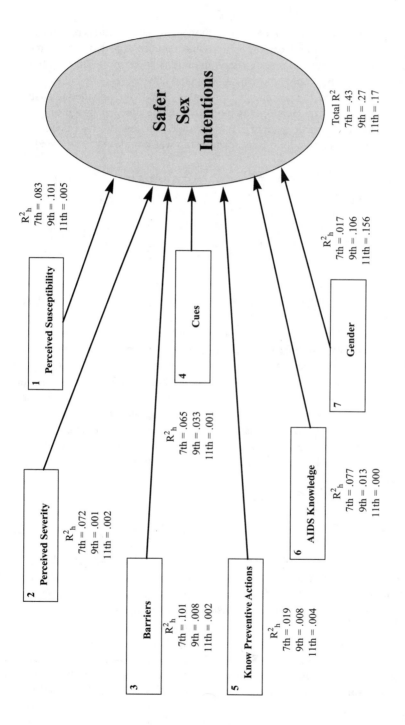

Figure 32-2 Multiple Regression Using the Health Belief Model To Predict Intentions, 7th, 9th, 11th Grade Sample, R^2_h = Hierarchical Addition to R^2

needs. Programs designed to promote the adoption of preventive actions must go beyond health motivations to address the complex set of needs and social forces that shape adolescent behavior.

The survey revealed a high degree of perceived susceptibility in the sample. Approximately 75% of the students surveyed were afraid of getting AIDS. High levels of fear can produce ironic results, particularly among adolescents (Soames-Job, 1988). Young people often mobilize defense mechanisms (e.g., denial) to avoid fear, rather than change behaviors to reduce risk. Complicating this issue further was the students' poor understanding of the severity of AIDS. Students need a better understanding of the health effects of HIV infection. Program efforts should emphasize the knowledge and skills necessary for students to feel confident that they can reduce risk of HIV infection. Enabling students to deal proactively with social influences has proved to be an effective education approach (Petosa, 1986). Instructional time should be devoted to specifically identifying perceived barriers and helping students develop skills to overcome these barriers.

It is likely that actual risk behavior may be greater than these figures suggest. Although previous research has suggested that the use of intention measures is a sound research approach, caution is warranted when interpreting safer sex intentions reported by adolescents. Sexual behavior among adolescents is influenced by situational and social factors that are often independent of and sometimes contrary to personal intention. In addition, the intention-performance relationship usually diminishes as the time period between declaration of intention and actual behavior lengthens; thus, expressed intentions may be good predictors of behavior in the immediate future, but are generally unreliable predictors as time passes. This intention-behavior decay effect is particularly important during adolescence when sexual maturation and social role expectations rapidly evolve. These considerations suggest that the safer sex intentions reported in this study are likely to become progressively more conservative when used to infer actual sexual behavior as these adolescents mature.

Most striking were the results of the regression analysis between the three grade levels. The HBM variables were quite useful in explaining safer sex intentions among seventh grade students, accounting for 43% of the variance, but there was a definite deterioration in these relationships among the ninth and eleventh grade students. Clearly, health-related motivations are important to seventh grade students' safer sex intentions. These same motivations appear to diminish in importance in higher grade levels, however. The most obvious interpretation is that forces other than health concerns (e.g., needs for acceptance, esteem, affection, and recognition as an adult) influence older adolescents' sexual intentions. The HBM focus on specific health-related motivations does not address these motivations. It is recommended, therefore, that future studies of adolescent health behavior incorporate a broader theoretical model that builds and expands on the HBM.

Interpreting the results from a cognitive/developmental perspective is also useful. Elkind (1975) noted that many adolescents tend to believe in a "personal fable" that they are "invulnerable" to negative health consequences. The denial of risk assessments to which they are exposed often maintains this sense of invulnerability. It is possible that many older adolescents have had sexual experiences and have not detected any negative health consequences. This sexual experience may reinforce beliefs of personal invulnerability and reduce older adolescents' responsiveness to health-related concerns.

IMPLICATIONS FOR THE PREVENTION OF AIDS AMONG ADOLESCENTS

The practical importance of HBM variables is that health education efforts can often influence them. Based on the results of this study, it is recommended that educational programs designed to promote safer sexual behavior should focus on health-related motivations up to the seventh grade. Older students are knowledgeable about AIDS and report high levels of health-related motivation, but these factors lose influence over safer sex intentions. For these older adolescents, educational efforts not only should reinforce health knowledge and health motives, but also should establish linkages between health knowledge/motivations and safer sexual behaviors. As part of this effort, adolescents can be exposed to models of desired attributes (e.g., maturity, popularity, sophistication) who do not rely on sexual activity for this status. Particular attention should be placed on the skills necessary for achieving desired status.

Educational programs should also address the motivational schema under which older adolescents are operating. For example, compliance with perceptions of normative sexual behavior, adoption of adult roles, and need for peer support and affection may be highly salient for adolescents. Students should be encouraged to consider carefully how these factors may influence their behavior. Students also can be encouraged to explore a variety of alternatives to meeting their perceived needs in ways that do not increase their health risk. Specific efforts should be made to ensure that young people have the skills to act on health-related motivations. For example, decision-making skills and peer resistance skills have consistently been found useful in health interventions (Botvin, Eng, & Williams, 1980).

To be effective, HIV education should begin prior to the onset of experimentation. Yet many communities are reluctant to begin sex and drug education efforts until high school. It is recommended that communities conduct anonymous surveys of students to determine the onset of risk behaviors. The use of sophisticated, theory-based surveys can yield a wealth of information about adolescents' knowledge, beliefs, and behavior. This information is particularly important when dealing with controversial topics, such as education about safer sex practices. Collecting quality needs assessment data can assist teachers, parents, administrators, and politicians make informed decisions regarding health promotion policy.

REFERENCES

Alexander, C., Ensminger, M., Kim, Y., Smith, J., Johnson, K., & Dolan, L. (1989). Early sexual activity among adolescents in small towns and rural areas: Race and gender patterns. *Family Planning Perspectives, 21,* 261–266.

Becker, M. (1974). The health belief model and personal health behavior. *Health Education Monograph, 2,* 236–473.

Becker, M. (1979a). Psychosocial aspects of health-related behavior. In H. Freeman, S. Levine, & I. Reeder (Eds.), *Handbook of medical sociology.* Englewood Cliffs, NJ: Prentice-Hall.

Becker, M. (1979b). Understanding patient compliance: The contributions of attitudes and other psychosocial factors. In S. Cohen (Ed.), *New directions in patient compliance* (pp. 1–31). Lexington, MA: DC Heath.

Bell, T., & Hein, K. (1984). The adolescent and sexually transmitted disease. In K. Holmes (Ed.), *Sexually transmitted diseases* (pp. 73–84). New York: McGraw-Hill.

Bell, T., & Holmes, K. (1984). Age specific risks of syphilis, gonorrhea and hospitalized pelvic inflammatory disease in sexually experienced U.S. women. *Sexually Transmitted Disease, 11,* 291–295.

Botvin, G., Eng, A., & Williams, C. (1980). Preventing the onset of cigarette smoking through life skills training. *Preventive Medicine, 9,* 135–143.

Burke, D., Brundage, J., & Goldenbaum, M. (1990). Human immunodeficiency virus infections in teenagers: Seroprevalence among applicants for U.S. military service. *Journal of the American Medical Association, 263*(15), 2074–2077.

DiClemente, R., Zorn, J., & Temoshok, L. (1986). Adolescents and AIDS: A survey of knowledge, attitudes and beliefs about AIDS in San Francisco. *American Journal of Public Health, 12,* 1443–1445.

Eisen, M., Zellman, G., & McAlister, A. (1985). A health belief model approach to adolescents' fertility control: Some pilot program findings. *Health Education Quarterly, 12,* 185–210.

Elkind, D. (1975). Recent research on cognitive development in adolescence. In S. Dragastin & G. Elder (Eds.), *Adolescence in the life cycle: Psychological change and social context* (pp. 49–61). Washington, DC: Hemisphere Publishing.

Hass, A. (1979). *Teenage sexuality: A survey of teenage sexual behavior.* New York: Macmillan.

Haverkos, H., & Edellman, R. (1988). The epidemiology of acquired immunodeficiency syndrome among heterosexuals. *Journal of the American Public Health Association, 13,* 1922–1929.

Hayes, C. (Ed.). (1987). *Risking the future: Adolescent sexuality, pregnancy, and childbearing.* Washington, DC: National Academy Press.

Helgerson, S., & Peterson, L. (1988). Acquired immunodeficiency syndrome and secondary students: Their knowledge is limited and they want to know more. *Pediatrics, 3,* 350–355.

Hofferth, S., Kahn, J., & Baldwin, W. (1987). Premarital sexual activity among U.S. teenage women over the past three decades. *Family Planning Perspectives, 19,* 46–53.

Janz, N., & Becker, M. (1984). The health belief model: A decade later. *Health Education Quarterly, 11,* 1–47.

Kegeles, S. (1980). The health belief model and personal health behavior. *Social Science Medicine, 146,* 227–229.

Moore, K., Nord, C., & Peterson, J. (1989). Nonvoluntary sexual activity among adolescents. *Family Planning Perspectives, 21,* 110–114.

Nathanson, C., & Becker, M. (1983). Contraceptive behavior among unmarried young women: A theoretical framework for research. *Population and the Environment, 6,* 39–59.

Petosa, R. (1986). Emerging trends in adolescent health promotion. *Health Values, 3,* 22–28.

Price, J., Desmond, S., & Kukulka, G. (1986). High school students' perceptions and misperceptions of AIDS. *Journal of School Health, 3,* 107–109.

Simon, K., & Das, A. (1984). An application of the health belief model toward educational diagnosis for VD education. *Health Education Quarterly, 11,* 403–418.

Soames-Job, R. (1988). Effective and ineffective use of fear in health promotion campaigns. *American Journal of Public Health, 2,* 163–167.

Sonenstein, F., Pleck, J., & Ku, L. (1989). Sexual activity, condom use and AIDS awareness among adolescent males. *Family Planning Perspectives, 21,* 152–158.

Strunin, L., & Hingson, R. (1987). Acquired immunodeficiency syndrome and adolescents: Knowledge, beliefs, attitudes and behaviors. *Pediatrics, 5,* 825–828.

Warwick, I., Aggleton, P., & Homans, H. (1988). Constructing commonsense: Young people's beliefs about AIDS. *Sociology of Health and Illness, 3,* 213–233.

Zabin, L., Hirsh, M., Smith, E., Street, R., & Hardy, J. (1986). Evaluation of a pregnancy prevention program for urban teenagers. *Family Planning Perspectives, 18,* 119–126.

33

New Skills for Parents of Teens

Thomas F. Brock

The goal of successful parenting is to assist the youth into independent adulthood. While providing shelter and sustenance, parents must also provide the skills necessary for the teen-ager to achieve incremental independence. The task of parenting, in short, is to help the young person to grow up. Parents must learn to distinguish between succoring and nurturing. Succoring means aiding the children, coming to their aid in times of distress, rescuing them; parents who do this may help their children into helplessness. Nurturing means to train, to help develop. It is the parents' job to be the catalyst for their children's development, to train them to independence. Karamigios (1987) stated that the goal of adolescent psychiatry is to help youngsters to become taxpayers. That is a succinct description of the role of parenthood.

DEVELOPMENTAL TASKS OF ADOLESCENCE

Sometime between the ages of 10 and 18, youngsters must make career decisions, decide the level of their sexual behavior, and develop age-appropriate independence. These events do not take place overnight, nor are they finalized during the teen years—if ever. They are incremental processes. The parental goal is for the child to be at an age-appropriate point along this incremental continuum.

Career Decisions

The first task of the teen years is for the youngster to make age-appropriate decisions regarding a career. For instance, it may be appropriate for a 13-year-old to decide that she has the intellectual capacity and the self-discipline to pursue a career in science. That same young person may be 16 or 17 years old before she decides on a specific range of colleges or universities that she may want to attend, and she may be 20 before she decides on the type of graduate school. Nevertheless, she has made and re-made a conscious, determined, career decision as she traveled through her adolescence. A 15-year-old may decide that the university does not offer an appropriate education for him, that he wants to work in the general field of automotive repair, and that he needs to develop mechanical skills rather than precollegiate university skills during his high school years. The teenager must develop a clear concept that he or she will one day be involved in a meaningful career and will be economically self-supporting.

Decisions About Sex

Teen-agers must come to terms with their own sexuality. This task, like the others, is accomplished in an uneven, incremental fashion. Teen-agers must decide in a general way their own sexual orientation, begin to feel comfortable and integrated with that decision, and decide whether their own sexual expression is going to be a meaningful part of a relationship or simply a physical conquest or activity. They must begin to determine for themselves their own values regarding sexual responsibility.

Age-Appropriate Individuation

At each stage of development, adolescents must decide to what degree and when they are separate from their mothers and fathers. Therapists who work with teen-agers are frequently privy to moments of insight when young people realize that they are not entirely limited by the personalities or achievements of Mom or Dad. Younger children believe that nearly all facets of their lives are genetically predetermined or imposed upon them by their parents. Adolescents must begin to separate self-regulation and self-determination from parentally imposed behaviors and attitudes. Although the individuation continuum may seem to be highlighted by moments of insight, it also is a gradual, incremental process.

PARENTING SKILL AREAS

It is said that adolescents learn primarily in three ways: by example, by example, and by example. If it is the goal of parents to assist their teen-agers with the tasks of adolescence, the parents must master the skill of providing an appropriate example. Parents will become more proficient at providing a good model as they continue to articulate and reinforce with each other the goal of nurturing their children to independence.

Recognizing parents' need to improve their skills, school districts all over the United States are providing lectures on parenting. Parents need an organizational framework to help them integrate and utilize specific skills and approaches to the problems and challenges of raising teen-agers. The Teen ´ Life Connection program in the mental health center of a large regional hospital in Southern California offers a four-step parenting class. The four steps are intended to be devoid of psychobabble and course-specific vocabulary. Parents can quickly grasp the concepts of the four general skill areas and over time increase their skill in each of the areas.

1. how to tell who needs the help at this moment
2. what to do if the teen-ager needs help
3. what to do if the parent needs help
4. what to do when the relationship needs help

One of the benefits of this organizational approach is that parents can begin using the four-step approach after their first introduction to the program. Every problematic interaction with their child becomes an exercise in the use of this framework. New skills and new methods can be appropriately placed within the framework and are instantly available for parents to use.

Who Needs Taking Care Of

Parents often confuse their needs with those of their child. The very first lesson that parents must learn is to separate their needs, values, desires, and goals from those of their children. They must ask themselves the following questions:

- Who is feeling the pain in the current situation? Is it the parent, or is it the child?
- Who is feeling uncomfortable? Is it Mom, Dad, or the youngster?

Sometimes the answer is obvious. If the child comes home from school crying, the child clearly has a problem. The situation is also clear-cut when the child comes home well after curfew and the parents are quite upset. It is important for parents to ask in each interaction with their child, "Is there discomfort here, and whose discomfort is it?" The answers are very individual and depend on the particular parent and child. In similar situations, even among siblings, the answers are different. This is an important first step, however, because the skills that the parents must use are dependent on the answers. The skills required to nurture a person to independence are different from the skills required to protect the parents' own needs and aspirations. (Of course, the parent who is successfully assertive sets an extremely good example for the young person and in that way contributes to the young person's individuation and eventual independence.)

When the Child Needs Taking Care Of

When the parents have been able to determine that an issue is clearly the child's problem and offers the child an opportunity to grow, the parents must use active listening, problem-solving, and confidence-building skills. The Los Angeles County Superintendent of Schools sponsors an expansive program, called Teacher Expectancy and Student Achievement (TESA), that has shown school teachers and administrators the importance of the self-fulfilling prophecy. The teacher in the classroom who expects all the students to pass certain tests, or to receive an A or a B, and who treats every student as capable of doing so has taken the most critical step toward accomplishing that goal. Similarly, the principal who sets high standards for teachers and conveys the message both verbally and nonverbally that the staff is capable increases the productivity of the staff. Parents must likewise take advantage of the self-fulfilling prophecy and, in their own words and in their own way, continue to give the message to the youngster in need of nurturance.

- "I have confidence in you and in your ability to handle the situation."
- "I trust your ability to learn from the situation and your ability to solve the problem for the very best outcome."

In addition to sending messages of confidence in the child's problem-solving ability, the parents must, in their own words, repeat the message.

- "I have confidence in your decision-making ability."
- "I believe that what you do is done for the very best of your own personal reasons."
- "I trust your decision in this regard, and I know that you make good decisions for yourself for your own reasons."
- "I support you, whatever your decision is."

Parents find such statements very difficult to make at first, but they soon recognize that their desire to control the child's life and to make decisions for the child interferes with the higher task of leading the child toward independence in situations that are within the child's realm and do not threaten the parents' values or the parents' self-respect. For example, Brian comes home from school complaining that he received an unfair detention for being late, that the principal is friendlier to all the other students than she is to Brian, and that the principal is really quite a stupid woman. Brian wants Mom and Dad to call the principal and help him avoid after school detention. The parents determine that there is some pain, discomfort, or unhappiness and that there is some opportunity for growth in this interaction. Someone is invested enough to want to take some action. The parents have asked themselves, "Whose issue is this?" and have decided that this is their son's concern. Brian was late to school, not his parents, and the adults have no great pain or discomfort about the issue of this isolated tardiness and its consequence. The parents see the situation as an opportunity for Brian to take one small step on the incremental continuum to maturity. Therefore, the parents give messages with a self-fulfilling prophecy such as, "You are normal; you are mature; you are capable; you will make a good decision." The parents' responses can be anything that conveys those messages. Some possible responses are

- "I'm not sure what you are going to do about your detention, but I'll bet you do what you think is the right thing."
- "It must be awful feeling that the principal doesn't like you. How will you overcome that?"
- "I'm interested in knowing how you are going to take care of the detention issue."

It is the parents' job to put that issue back in the hands of the child, offering parental support and parental encouragement, but definitely not allowing the child to abdicate his or her responsibility.

When the Parents Need Taking Care Of

Parents need to know what to do when it is they who feel the pain, who are uncomfortable, or whose values are threatened. When Heather comes home after midnight despite an 11 p.m. curfew and the parents are unhappy, for example, they must use their skills of assertion and limit setting to take care of themselves. They need make no pretense that what they are doing is good for the child or that they are doing it because of their love for the child, although clear boundaries are indeed helpful to the child. They are taking steps to meet their own needs. When parents reinforce legitimate boundaries, they are helping the child individuate, helping the child understand that he or she is separate from the parents, and providing a good model for self-care. Parents must state their own needs and their own expectations.

- "I want and need my sleep."
- "I want you in by 11:00."
- "I worry about you when you are gone, and I don't want to worry past curfew."
- "I'm afraid my insurance rates will go up if you have an accident. I believe accidents are more frequent late at night. You must be home by 11:00."

Parents can use whatever statement correctly reflects their needs and desires—not their need for control, but their need for comfort and self-protection.

Parents must recognize that, as the child grows older, more autonomous, and more independent, the nature of the parental limits changes. For the younger, more immature child, the limits are usually physical. Parents allow their 3-year-old to play in the back yard, but not the front yard. The 5-year-old may be allowed to ride her tricycle around the block, but not across the street.

When the child is older, temporal limits replace physical limits. The 10- or 11-year-old may be allowed to ride his bicycle to his friend's house, but must be home at 4:30 p.m. to get ready for dinner. The 14- or 15-year-old may be allowed to be with his friends unsupervised in the evening, but must be home by 9:00 p.m. to get ready for bed.

Older teen-agers, like adults, are not given physical or temporal limits, but functional limits.

- "We will not tell you when to do your homework, but you must be getting A's or B's."
- "We will not tell you what time to go to bed, but you must get yourself up each morning and off to school on time."
- "We will not tell you what clothes you must buy, but you must live within the clothes budget or earn your own money to supplement the clothes budget."

The rule of functional limits extends, of course, to postadolescents.

- "You may live in our house as long as you are working full-time and paying rent, or going to school full-time and maintaining good grades."

Parents may have to go up and down the ladder of limits as the situation and the day-to-day maturity of the child require. The child who has been operating on functional limits may regress, for example, making temporal restraints necessary until he or she demonstrates the ability to profit from functional limits once again. Parents need to keep in mind that adolescence is a time of rapidly changing behaviors, and it may be necessary to adjust limits on a weekly or sometimes daily basis. The child's behavior, not the whim or will of the parents, determines the type of limits that are appropriate. Again, the focus of limits is the parents' goal of raising independent children and assisting their teen-agers to age-appropriate individuation.

When the Relationship Needs Taking Care Of

Parents and teen-agers can learn to resolve conflicts in their relationship by means of the three-step strategy developed by the Lennox School District in 1970. The steps are for each party to identify

1. this is what you did
2. this is how it made me feel
3. that is what I want you to do

This three-step method has been used successfully to help peers avoid physical conflicts, as well as to solve real and potential conflicts between students and teachers, teachers and administrators. An abbreviated, easy-to-remember version of the three steps is

1. "I see."
2. "I feel."
3. "I want."

POWER AND AUTHORITY

Parents want their children to follow their direction; they want to retain some power over their children. To most parents, power means getting their children to follow their will in spite of the children's disinclination to do so. Authority is dependent on the willingness of the children to follow the parents' will and is based on the children's giving legitimacy to the adult authority figure. Power (especially brute force) is a rather short-lived tool, except when used with authority.

Parents' (teachers') authority requires some cooperation from the child. Parents can frequently think of many methods (or reasons for cooperation) that some people with authority use to get others to follow their will.

- charismatic approach. Charisma is based on respect for some outstanding power in the leader. Some parents and teachers seem naturally charismatic. Most are not, but there are authority figures who are perhaps good-looking or athletic, or simply have some natural vitality that makes children just automatically want to do their bidding.

- traditional approach. Tradition bases the legitimacy of authority on established custom: "Do it because I say, and I'm the parent." There is nothing inherently wrong or immoral with this approach, but it seldom works.

- rational legal approach. Rules rest on a belief in their legitimacy and on the supremacy of laws: "Do it this way because that is the rule in the house." This is not a bad thing to say, but it seems to work seldom, if at all.

- expert approach. Using expertise for authority depends on strong respect for demonstrated ability and technical resources. It is hard for parents always to be experts, but this approach seems to work well. The child in woodshop follows the teacher's direction because he or she wants to make a new skateboard that looks really sharp and the teacher is an expert on making sharp-looking skateboards.

Parents must recognize the kinds of power available to them, build on their strengths, and ignore their weaknesses. Most parents are comfortable developing a combination of the charismatic approach and the expert approach. Parents develop charisma with their children when they nurture them. They become exciting, interesting people to be around; after all, nothing is more interesting to teen-agers than themselves. Parents have great power when they nurture their children, actively encouraging the development necessary for age-appropriate individuation and independence. Properly nurturing children gives them what they most deeply want and need—confidence, self-assurance, self-respect, high self-esteem. The more successfully the parents nurture, the more charisma they will have with their children. Parents may choose not to become technical experts on matters of special interest to the children, but, as they become experts in helping their children help themselves, the teen-agers will more and more follow their parents' direction, will not have to rebel for the sake of rebellion, and can take advice and guidance when needed.

SUGGESTED READING

Armstrong, H., Morris, R., Amerongen, M., & Kernaghan, P. (1983). Group therapy for parents of delinquent children. *International Journal of Group Psychotherapy, 33*(1), 85–97.

Bernal, M.E., Klinnert, M.D., & Schultz, L.A. (1980). Outcome evaluation of behavioral parent training and client-centered parent counseling for children with conduct problems. *Journal of Applied Behavior Analysis, 13,* 677–690.

Box, S. (1986). Some thoughts about therapeutic change in families at adolescence. *Journal of Adolescence, 9,* 186–198.

Bryce, S., & Baird, D. (1986). Precipitating a crisis: Family therapy and adolescent school refusers. *Journal of Adolescence, 9,* 199–213.

Cunningham, C. (1985). Training and education approaches for parents of children with special needs. *British Journal of Medical Psychology, 58,* 285–305.

Forehand, R., & McCombs, A. (1988). Unraveling the antecent-consequence conditions in maternal depression and adolescent functioning. *Behav. Res. Ther., 26*(5), 399–405.

Helm, D.T., & Kozloff, M.A. (1986). Research on parent training: Shortcomings and remedies. *Journal of Autism and Developmental Disorders, 16*(1), 1–22.

Huberty, D.J., Huberty, C.E., Flanagan-Hobday, K., & Blackmore, G. (1987). Family issues in working with chemically dependent adolescents. *Pediatric Clinics of North America, 34*(2), 507–521.

Kazdin, A.E., Esveldt-Dawson, K., French, N.H., & Unis, A.S. (1987). Effects of parent management training and problem-solving skills training combined in the treatment of antisocial child behavior. *Journal of the American Academy of Child and Adolescent Psychiatry, 5/87,* 416–442.

Kraemer, S. (1987). Working with parents: Casework or psychotherapy? *Journal of Child Psychology and Psychiatry, 28*(2), 207–211.

Patterson, G.R. (1974). Interventions for boys with conduct problems: Multiple settings, treatments, and criteria. *Journal of Consulting and Clinical Psychology, 42*(4), 471–481.

Will, D. (1983). Some techniques for working with resistant families of adolescents. *Journal of Adolescence, 6,* 13–26.

Will, D. (1986). Family therapy and systems work with adolescents. *Journal of Adolescence, 9.*

34

Substance Abuse Prevention Programs for American Indian Youth

Audrey Hill and Virginia Hill

Although American Indians inhabited the North American continent before its European "discovery," the U.S. government has consistently attempted to assimilate and then acculturate them into "mainstream society." As early as the 1800s, restrictions mandated by U.S. law forced the Indians to specific territories and utilized institutional conformity to alter their cultural life styles. Churches were built on reservations to implement Western Christianity, for example. Although culturally diverse and geographically dispersed, the American Indians resisted complete assimilation, acculturation, and loss of a distinct cultural identity. Since the period between the 1930s and the 1950s, however, when Indians were encouraged to relocate from reservations to urban areas, the deterioration of traditional Indian culture within some tribal communities has accelerated. Some of these tribal communities also host the highest rates of substance abuse among their youth (Beauvais & Oetting, 1987).

Today, the American Indian population is one of the smallest and youngest ethnic populations. Of the 1.4 million living in the Reservation States, an estimated 32% are under the age of 15 years. Furthermore, according to the 1980 U.S. Census, American Indians have become increasingly urbanized. Of the 1.4 million American Indians, 24% to 37% reside on reservations, with the remaining living in urban communities, usually within one of the 32 Reservation States in the western portions of the United States and often within the vicinity of their reservations (LaFromboise, 1988; May, 1987). Because 80% of reservation Indian youth and 52% of urban Indian youth engage in moderate to heavy substance use (U.S. Senate Select Committee on Indian Affairs, 1985), there is a critical need for effective prevention programs designed especially for American Indian youth (National Institute on Drug Abuse, 1987). Current data on substance abuse among Indian youth indicate that there are important cultural considerations in the development of such programs.

SUBSTANCE ABUSE AMONG AMERICAN INDIAN YOUTH

Since 1975, researchers who are conducting an epidemiological study of substance abuse among Indian youth have surveyed more than 15,000 youth in Grades 7 through 12. They found that this segment of the population most commonly uses alcohol, marijuana, stimulants, and cocaine and that there was increased use between the years 1975 and 1981. A comparison of substance use among Indian and non–Indian youth revealed that 21% more of the Indian youth had tried alcohol, 35% more had tried marijuana, 16% more had tried inhalants, 14% more had tried stimulants, and 3% more had tried cocaine. Although a similar decrease in substance use is evident in the years 1981 to 1985, the rate of substance use and abuse, particularly with the four most commonly used drugs among Indian youth, remains disproportionately high when compared to that among the general population (Beauvais & Oetting, 1987; Harras, 1987).

There were 28.2 drug- and alcohol-related deaths per 100,000 Indian youth, compared to 16.4 per 100,000 in the general population. A summary of studies examined in a report on substance abuse among Indian youth revealed that the high rates of use and mortality are associated with an age of first use between 11 and 13 years (National Institute on Drug Abuse, 1987). The report also determined that the factors leading to substance abuse are firmly in place by the age of 13 years.

PROBLEMS OF INDIAN YOUTH

Chronic unemployment, poverty, and low education levels, combined with substandard housing, malnutrition, inadequate health care, lack of community resources (i.e., social, economic, and recreational), and acculturational pressures toward urbanization, are among the problems of Indian youth. Unemployment among Indian youth is consistently and extremely high, ranging from more than 70% on some reservations to a low of 20% in the more prosperous tribal communities (U.S. Senate Select Committee on Indian Affairs, 1985). The unemployment rate of the American Indian is 2 times higher than the national rate, while the average income level is approximately 25% lower than the national average. May (1987) reported that the income of approximately 30% of the Indian population was below the poverty level. Dropout rates range from 48% to 85% between the eighth and ninth grades and approach 50% in Bureau of Indian Affairs boarding schools and elementary schools on reservations. Only 16% of the American Indian students who enter a college or university earn an undergraduate degree, compared to 34% of their non–Indian counterparts. The segment of the American Indian population that is 25 years of age or older has an average of 9.6 years of formal education, which is below the national mean of 10.9 years and is the lowest of any ethnic group in the United States (LaFromboise, 1988).

Rates of criminal arrests and juvenile delinquency among American Indian youth are the highest of any ethnic group in the nation; the number of offenses committed under the influence of substances is 4 times that of black youth and 10 times that of white youth (Beauvais & Oetting, 1987; LaFromboise, 1988).

Cultural epidemiologists have claimed that forced acculturation through urbanization; failure to form a traditional frame of reference; and early exposure to ceremonies, rituals, and life style has increased the developing Indian youth's vulnerability to psychological disturbance. Numerous studies (e.g., Barter & Barter, 1974; Kemnitzer, 1973; Spindler & Spindler, 1978) have shown the extreme stress experienced by the American Indian in adapting to the aggressive and rapidly changing Western society. Despite the major stresses of interaction with a dominant culture (e.g., introduction to technology, the government assimilation policies, subsequent forced relocation to reservations), the American Indian has continually strived to retain a distinct cultural identity. The later modification of assimilation policies to acculturation policies has lessened the stress of adapting to the dominant society, but continued interaction within an ethnically diverse society has introduced new stressful challenges.

At the community level, forced urbanization heightens the stress by making it necessary to relinquish sovereign rights to health care, education, the traditional supports of extended family, and tribal ritual and ceremony. For example, a young Indian family that relocates to an urban area in search of adequate housing and income not only relinquishes its rights to health care, educational benefits, tax exemption, and the supports of extended family members and friends, but also reduces the availability of tribal rights and privileges. The successful adaptation to an urban life style often requires the supports that the young family has relinquished, however. The young family may turn to substance abuse as an inadequate means of coping with these stresses or may return to the reservation where the experience of failure predisposes one or more family members toward unsatisfactory adjustment, dependence on the welfare system for subsistence, and substance abuse.

Not surprisingly, depression and adjustment disorders are common among American Indians. Manson, Shore, and Bloom (1985) reported that the prevalence of depression is 4 to 6 times higher than had been reported earlier. National concern for the incidence of suicide among Indian youth has led to an examination of this problem, and it has been found that the annual suicide rate in some tribal communities has increased by 200% in the past 20 years to a current rate of 18 per 100,000 (Harras, 1987).

CULTURAL CONSIDERATIONS

Given the prolonged social problems and the high rates of psychological dysfunctions, there is a high probability that many substance-abusing Indian youth will have a dual clinical diagnosis. With this awareness, LaFromboise (1988) pointed out that current studies have focused on the psychopathological disorders of American Indians to the neglect of further research on the family and sociocultural factors associated with the disorders. The effective coping strategies employed by American Indians in coping with numerous social and psychological stressors require further examination in relation to the etiology and prevention of substance abuse among Indian youth, however.

In a population that is culturally heterogeneous, young, and geographically dispersed, a diverse range of approaches to the prevention of substance abuse should be available on a short-term and long-term basis. The family may provide the best arena for preventing and combating substance use and abuse. Indian youth need strong family supports if they are to develop and remain rooted in a strong sense of cultural identity, self-esteem, and values that seem to be lacking in their peers who are prone to substance use and abuse. Thus, although external factors may have initiated and maintained the high rates of substance abuse, internal factors within tribal communities and Indian families may make it possible to curb these high rates among the youth. The well-being of Indian youth is inseparable from the well-being of their familial, social, cultural, and environmental context. Therefore, the development of effective prevention programs requires the integration of current data on substance abuse, its specific impact on Indian youth, and the identification of cultural factors that will enhance the acquisition of culturally appropriate coping skills.

Types of Indian Families

As a result of the U.S. government's historical relocation policy and urbanization, four types of Indian families have developed: reservation, bicultural, migratory, and transitional (Red Horse, Lewis, Feit, & Decker, 1978; Spindler & Spindler, 1978). Their impact on developing Indian youth and substance abuse problems, as well as their potential value in the development of effective prevention programs, has gone unrecognized in the past. Current trends in substance abuse research have led to an integration of cross-cultural psychology, family systems theory, and a biopsychosocial framework that will promote the development of prevention approaches based on these data and knowledge in the future, however.

Reservation Families

Traditionally, adults and elders have the role of providing cultural, tribal, and familial information to the young. The reservation and tribal elders remain the source of cultural knowledge, and their accessibility continues to allow reservation Indian families to retain more cultural knowledge than do their urban counterparts. Although faced with severe poverty, unemployment, poor health, and high rates of substance abuse, many Indian families prefer to remain on reservations where they can be in close contact with the extended family members and can retain sovereign rights to health care, education, tax exemption, and customary tribal sources of support (e.g., elders, medicine societies, and sacred ceremonial sites).

Substance abuse has played a major role in denying Indian youth the opportunity to acquire the strengths and survival strategies inherent in the oral traditions, ceremonies, and rituals. The loss of traditional, culturally specific means of coping has affected each generation of Indian youth and varies from tribe to tribe, from reservation to urban community (Barter & Barter, 1974; Kemnitzer, 1973; LaFromboise, 1988). Indian youth will continue to bear the burden of cultural alienation with the passing of each generation that does not assume the responsibility for revitalizing the strengths of traditional culture.

With exposure to high rates of substance abuse and lack of exposure to inherent strengths of traditional culture, Indian youth exist in an acculturation gap. Reservation families have access to the resources for bridging that gap by means of the coping strategies inherent in the culture, tribe, and family. Empowerment through positive cultural identity and self-esteem, social adjustment within the community, and psychological development as a family and as tribal members underlie the necessary coping skills for avoiding dysfunctional behavior and substance abuse. Functional family living is associated with lower rates of substance abuse in various stages of personal and family development (Lawson, Peterson, & Lawson, 1983). According to Red Horse and associates (1978), reservation Indian families that demonstrate cultural knowledge do indeed appear to have effective coping strategies.

Bicultural Families

American Indian bicultural families are often at least second-generation urban, are characterized by higher levels of educational attainment and middle-class income levels, and have generally remained in a particular urban community. They seem to have consciously chosen to remain in urban areas and have been able to adapt successfully to an urban life style, functioning socially and occupationally without the supports of the traditional extended Indian family. They maintain a strong sense of cultural identity, however, and visit their reservation and tribe of origin often unless the physical distance is prohibitive. Although rates of substance abuse among urban Indian youth are high, the youth from these particular families appear to have acquired the coping skills and strategies necessary to retain their cultural identity and live within the dominant culture, in effect, becoming bicultural.

Migratory Families

Characterized by frequent relocations from reservation to urban communities, migratory families appear to be searching constantly for a means of subsistence. Inadequate housing, unemployment, accessibility of transportation, or eligibility for services and education are common reasons for these frequent moves. The instability of this life style, the break from the traditional family supports, and the lack of urban supports create psychosocial stressors that increase the migratory families' difficulty in adapting to urban life. They seek relief in a return to the reservation, only to repeat the process in a few months or weeks. These families usually remain in close proximity to their reservations and extended family systems. Substance abuse may occur as a dysfunctional means of coping with instability in the family environment (Lawson et al., 1983).

Transitional Families

Indian families in transition may have adjusted to an urban style of living, but they are alienated from both the traditional extended Indian family system and dominant society. Their closed social system allows for interaction with other urban Indians, but only infrequent social interaction with members of the dominant society. As a result, family members have little opportunity to acquire cultural knowledge and maintain a low level of acculturation with the dominant society. Often a vast distance away from their reservations and tribes of origin, these families are commonly second- or third-generation urban. Although they appear to be bicultural, their lack of positive cultural identity indicates maladjustment. They also lack the social skills, as well as the higher levels of income and education, that characterize the functional, bicultural Indian families.

Migratory and transitional Indian families appear to have the highest rates of substance abuse and associated psychological and social problems. They may be the least functional socially and occupationally, and both are alienated from cultural and familial supports. Efforts to prevent substance abuse should take into account the levels of acculturation and adaptation found in these four types of Indian families and their influence in the development of effective coping strategies in Indian youth.

American Indian Value System

Despite their great diversity, American Indians share a cultural value system that provides the basis for socialization in the family and tribal units (Table 34-1). Socialization of the young adheres to these cultural values, as well as to sociopolitical customs and ceremonial beliefs.

Table 34-1 American Indian Values vs. Dominant Western Values

Indian Values	Dominant Western Values
Cooperation/group concern	Competition/self-concern
Interdependence	Independence
Permissiveness	Coercion
Spiritual attainment	Material acquisition
Humility/modesty	Egoism/confidence
Harmony-nature, others	Domination-nature, others

Source: From "Family Behavior of Urban Americans" by J. Red Horse, R. Lewis, M. Feit and J. Decker, 1978, *Social Casework, 59,* pp. 67–72. Family Service America.

The American Indian principles of interpersonal relations include the following:

- noninterference. Most American Indian groups and families consider interference in another's behavior to be disrespectful. The philosophy of "live and let live" allows others to make mistakes, to learn from them, and to alter their own behavior. Social conformity is subtly enforced with silence. The provision of support and assistance that have been requested is not considered interference, however.

- self-reliance. Most Indians hesitate to ask for assistance. This is often perceived by non–Indians as ignorance, stubbornness, or belligerence.

- non-confrontation. Indians usually prefer not to confront an antagonist and will often avoid interpersonal contact instead. Noncompliance with perceived aggression is often interpreted as defiance or belligerence, however.

- diversity. Indian families and groups understand and respect diversity, despite societal stereotypes. The tendency to generalize on the basis of these stereotyped images has been a major problem in the development of culturally sensitive services and programs for American Indians.

- respect for elders. Traditionally, Indians tribal elders are symbols of wisdom and traditional teachers, especially those who have demonstrated tribally appropriate behaviors and relations throughout their life span. These behaviors are interpreted as applications of cultural knowledge and the attainment of spiritual wisdom. Other tribal members recognize the promotion of cultural values and tribal custom and reward it with social respect, shown during an honoring ceremony hosted by other tribal members.

- extended Indian family. Kinship extends beyond the nuclear family system to include grandparents, parents, aunts, uncles, siblings, and cousins. In most groups, kinship extends to blood relatives on both parental sides, as well as to other members of the clan or tribal unit.

Essentially, Indian family structure is based on tribal origin and the philosophy of interdependence. Descendant patterns, matriarchal or patriarchal, have resulted in the development of complex ideologies concerning psychosocial well-being. Based on cultural values, a family's life style has a strong community aspect that promotes the development of an interdependent support network and curbs the need to seek outside help. This system is extremely effective for child-rearing and parenting. Indian parents are not expected to raise their young alone or even in a nuclear family system; all adult family members function in the parental role. Although there are clear gender roles in the American Indian society, the boundaries of these roles are less rigid in child-rearing practices. Furthermore, it is not considered abandonment if a child or children are left in the care of family members for an extended period of time.

Indian children represent the renewal of life and the perpetuation of cultural identity; they are central to the tribal community. Indian children are allowed more independence earlier in life and encouraged toward self-reliance. Mistakes, poor judgment, and misconduct are considered opportunities for a child to learn, make good decisions, and develop good interpersonal skills take precedence over individual task accomplishment, although the latter is likely to emphasize survival and craftsmanship.

The importance of learning social responsibility is clear in early child-rearing practices. In contrast to Western society, the American Indian tribal community gives a child many opportunities to interact with adults and elders. In their primary role of passing on cultural values, customs, and beliefs to the child, the elders help to develop cultural and tribal identity in the young. The socialization process is an educational one, taught through the many opportunities to observe, interact, and copy behavior of peers, older siblings, parents, adults, and elders. Traditional rituals and ceremonies enable the young to acquire the values of a communal system that promotes psychosocial adjustment and to develop effective coping skills that prevent maladjustive behavior such as substance abuse.

Strengths of the American Indian Family

The primary sources of strength in the American Indian family are interdependence, group affiliation, and social respect. Interdependence provides a network of supports and opportunities both to provide and to receive assistance in mutually satisfying and diverse relationships and experiences. Group affiliation and the sense of belonging promote a sense of role fulfillment and selfless purpose toward the psychosocial development of Indian youth. Social respect is acquired and maintained through self-restraint and conduct within the recognized parameters of family and tribal custom.

Family members' independent and interdependent actions and interactions with peers and of the larger group maintain the sources of family strengths. Each member carries an equal share of group responsibility in discovering his or her unique role in the family and community. The development of these strengths is based on the transmission of cultural values to each generation of young. Understanding the source and development of the inherent strengths of the Indian family is essential to the improvement of Indian family functioning, the development of socially and occupationally healthy Indian youth, and the development of programs aimed at decreasing the high rates of substance abuse among Indian youth.

PREVENTION PROGRAMS FOR INDIAN YOUTH

The School/Community Based Alcoholism/Substance Abuse Prevention Survey (National Institute on Drug Abuse, 1987) indicated an urgent need for early intervention efforts among Indian youth, with a strong emphasis on self-determination and recognition of the Indian family as the "bulwark to prevent and/or reduce the incidence of alcohol and substance abuse among Indian youths" (p. 51). Beginning Alcohol and Addictions Basic Education Studies (BABES), for example, is a primary prevention program for children aged 3 to 8 years; it is based on the concept that learning interdependent living skills, coupled with facts about substance abuse, is essential to healthy growth and development. TRAILS is a youth program for early and late adolescents.

Social and recreational activities offer health promotion and disease prevention while providing opportunities for drug and alcohol-free interaction with peers and positive adult role models. These and other programs aimed at the prevention of substance use and abuse among American Indian youth require a continuing course of action in the areas of research, design, implementation, and evaluation, as well as a creative application of cultural considerations. Primary importance must be given to the Indian family as a resource for cultural identity, motivation, and support for preventing the early use of substances. Further examination is necessary to identify the characteristics and development of culturally adapted coping skills that have been demonstrated by reservation and bicultural families and tribal communities.

It is necessary to promote the retention of a positive Indian identity, curb cultural alienation, and utilize the psychosocial strengths inherent in a family and tribal community that is structured and supported by cultural values, rituals, and custom if prevention services are to achieve the goal of decreasing substance abuse levels in the American Indian population. In addition, understanding the acculturation factors in Indian family dynamics is essential in developing prevention programs that promote a positive, mature identity within the familial and cultural context of American Indian youth.

REFERENCES

Barter, R.E., & Barter, J.T. (1974). Urban Indians and mental health problems. *Psychiatric Annals, 4,* 37–43.

Beauvais, F., & Oetting, E.R. (1987). High rate of drug use among Native American youth. *NIDA Notes, 2*(2), 14.

Harras, A. (1987). *Issues in adolescent Indian health: Suicide.* Washington, DC: U.S. Department of Health and Human Services.

Kemnitzer, L.S. (1973). Adjustment and value conflict in urbanizing Dakota Indians measured by Q-sort technique. *American Anthropologist, 75,* 687–707.

LaFromboise, T. (1988, May). American Indian mental health policy. *American Psychologist.*

Lawson, G.W., Peterson, J.S., & Lawson, A.W. (1983). *Alcoholism and the family: A guide to treatment and prevention.* Gaithersburg, MD: Aspen Publishers.

Manson, S., Shore, J., & Bloom, J. (1985). The depressive experience in American Indian communities: A challenge for psychiatric theory and diagnosis. In A. Kleinman & B. Good (Eds.), *Culture and depression: Studies in the anthropology and cross-cultural psychiatry of affect and disorder.* (pp. 331–368). Berkeley, CA: University of California.

May, P. (1987). Suicide and self-destruction among American Indian youth. *Journal of the National Center. American Indian and Alaskan Native Mental Health Research, 1*(1), 67–69.

National Institute on Drug Abuse. (1987). *School/community based alcoholism/substance abuse prevention survey.* Washington, DC: U.S. Government Printing Office.

Red Horse, J., Lewis, R., Feit, M., & Decker, J. (1978). Family behavior of urban American Indians. *Social Casework, 59,* 67–72.

Spindler, G., & Spindler, L. (1978). Identity, militance and cultural congruence: The Menominee and Kainai. *Annals of American Academy, 436,* 73–85.

U.S. Senate Select Committee on Indian Affairs. (1985). *Indian juvenile alcoholism and eligibility for BIA schools* (Senate Hearing 99-286). Washington, DC: U.S. Government Printing Office.

35

Brain Lateralization and Implications for Substance Abuse Prevention Among Indian Youth

The new body of knowledge on brain lateralization has important implications within the field of child development because it extends the range of individual learning in ways that are likely to maximize the potential of all children. In the field of substance abuse this new perspective has implications for prevention through education strategies. Combined with the development of a learning model that is culturally relevant, for example, this approach may become the basis of effective prevention services and become a central concept in the treatment of American Indian youth who abuse substances.

BRAIN LATERALIZATION AND LEARNING

The left and right hemispheres of the brain function separately in terms of thought processes. The left hemisphere is focused for detail and specific thought processing, while the right tends to be spatially oriented for generalized and abstract thinking. Thus, it appears that the cerebral hemispheres have a complementary dominance for various tasks. Evidence to support this theory was obtained from case studies of lateralized lesions and from testing of patients with cerebral commissurotomy (Fadely & Hunley, 1983).

For the field of psychology and education, this split brain research has provided several basic principles that seem to apply directly to working with children.

- At birth, the brain is plastic and able to form neurological structures appropriate to the demands of its environment.

- Brain adaptation and the development of behavioral responses to the environment are founded first in genetics and second in the environment.

- The brain tends to assign certain functions to the left or right hemisphere, although both receive the same sensory input.
- The left hemisphere is anatomically structured to process and develop language functions, although the right hemisphere has the ability. (With normal development, language specialization occurs in the left hemisphere and spatial integration develops in the right.)
- The corpus callosum is an interhemispheric route for sensory data exchange and a communication link for the function of associative thought.
- Lateralization (i.e., specialization of function in each hemisphere) is accomplished by degree and sex, resulting in wide variations in individual processing of information.
- The concept of mature intelligence can be generalized into intellectual competencies in verbal and spatial areas and understood by the WISC-R IQ Test.
- Such a test score is a measure of the child's ability (from genetic and environmental influences) to use such competencies (i.e., environment affects the increase or decrease of competency in function).
- Competence is a measure of hemispheric efficiency in function, and wide disparities between the competence levels in the left and right hemispheres can alter the learning and behavioral style of the child.
- The development of personality can be directly related to hemispheric function and competence in the same process whereby mental health states affect hemispheric competence.
- There is a greater potentiality in competence with the integration of hemispheric functions.
- Consciousness, in quality and quantity, is dependent on the development of the ability to learn and process information in an integrated way, facilitating self-awareness and perception of subjective and objective experiences.
- Rational consciousness is developed with functions of the left hemisphere competence, while intuition and transcendental thought is achieved with the holistic function to right hemispheric competence.
- Naturalistic thought is universal to humans and is linked to self-consciousness through right hemispheric thinking first; through eventual abstracting functions of a socialized and competent left hemisphere, dominance is achieved in the left hemisphere.
- Naturalistic thinking tends to be nondirectional, but has a tendency toward right-left organization, as in left-handed children, because of sensory orientation of right hemispheric organization.
- Socialized thought tends to be nondirectional, but has a tendency toward right-left organization and produces the orientation typical of right-handed people.

- There is a natural tendency for left hemispheric dominance and language superiority over naturalistic organization.

- Cerebral dominance and its relationship to hand, eye, ear, and foot dominance tends to be one lateral organization (i.e., left hemispheric dominance is indicated by right ear and eye dominance and right-handedness and footedness).

- Either hemisphere can control either motor side, although the hand is normally controlled by the opposite hemisphere.

- Poor establishment of cerebral dominance, hand dominance, or eye-hand dominance can create disorganization in the spatial functions of the developing child (Fadely & Hunley, 1983).

These general constructs demonstrate the complexity of left and right hemispheric dominance. Further research is necessary to understand the specific educational and emotional needs of children and to develop practical techniques for teaching children from this perspective. In short, the theory of brain lateralization requires an examination of the general integrative functions in child development and learning with the application of knowledge in the fields of psychology and education.

LEARNING MODELS TO PREVENT SUBSTANCE ABUSE

According to Bell and Battjes (1985), there are six approaches to school-based substance abuse prevention programs: (1) educational modes (cognitive and affective), (2) alternative programs, (3) psychosocial programs, (4) intrapersonal skills training, (5) interpersonal skills training, and (6) cognitive-developmental training that focuses on physiological reaction and user perception. May (1986) provided the following rationale for emphasizing educational programs for American Indian youth:

- Today's Indian youth are more socialized than are their parents toward educational concepts.

- In all tribes, 50% are school-aged or younger and easily accessible.

- Prevention of drug and alcohol misuse will begin with new patterns of behavior.

- The number of drug- and alcohol-related deaths is greatest in those aged 15 to 40 years; therefore, these individuals must be reached before or early in this age range.

Based on this rationale, May recommended that prevention programs for Indian youth should emphasize a "learning model that builds self-esteem and coping skills in individuals and their peer groups while imparting alcohol and drug information" (p. 86).

The Indian Health Service (1987) reported that prevention programs aimed at Indian youth are making progress, although slowly. Early intervention is critical, as evidenced by the high mortality rates among Indian youth due to drug- and alcohol-related accidents and suicide. The framework for action requires a diversity of prevention strategies that address tribal heterogeneity and variance of the drug and alcohol problem from tribe to tribe.

The recommendation for an effective learning model stimulates further inquiry into the implications of brain lateralization and the basic principles that apply directly to adolescents. Currently, there are two programs that involve the application of these principles: the whole brained approach of learning (Vitale, 1986) and new choices, a life style course in balanced living (Marshall, 1986).

Whole Brained Approach to Learning

When research on brain lateralization began to appear, Vitale (1986) realized that many learning-disabled children are more competent in those functions associated with the right side of the brain. She decided to develop right brain techniques to enhance learning. After outlining and contrasting the left and right brain modes of consciousness (thinking) and the resulting behaviors in each hemisphere, Vitale developed activities that used colors, shapes, imagery, music, and touch to help students of all ages learn to read, spell, tell time, subtract, and add. Students have been able to progress from a first-year reader to a fourth-year reader with a few hours of instruction with this method.

New Choices

Marshall (1986) expanded on Vitale's right brain technique by developing a program that emphasizes the integration of left and right brain techniques to achieve a balance of brain power. Balance is the basis for an educational model that uses group process, exercises, visualization, role playing, body work, creative expression, stress reduction techniques, and physiological awareness of the shift from the left to right hemisphere of the brain. According to Marshall (1986), the shift in brain dominance has important implications for the field of substance abuse.

It is clear that brain dominance shifts as the direct result of alcohol. By anesthetizing the higher brain functions (rational thought) first, low levels of alcohol release the baser personality. The loss of logic and judgment is followed by the loss of time, language, and organized thought processes associated with the left hemisphere of the brain. Relaxation, emotional expression, creativity, imagination, sensuality, singing, and dancing are enhanced, demonstrating the shift from left to right brain dominance. Continued ingestation of alcohol intoxicates the individual, however, and impairs the right brain functions as well. When the user becomes dependent on alcohol to experience this shift, there is a risk of addiction unless the user incorporates alternatives for achieving such a shift into his or her life style.

Cultural Relevance for American Indian Youth

Bogen (1975) conducted a study with the Hopi tribe that revealed a definite right brain dominance in the traditional cultural values of harmony, respect, and nature. Bogen found a life style based on a spiritual philosophy maintained through tribal customs, ceremonial rituals, and creative forms of expression that clearly indicated right brain dominance throughout the life cycle. In view of the implications of the left and right brain dominance described by Vitale (1986) and Marshall (1986), Bogen's finding of right brain dominance should be further investigated before it is generalized to the Indian population as a whole. If support is obtained, however, the development of right brain techniques based on the concept of balance would provide a valuable educational model for learning among the American Indian population. According to Bogen's study, a learning model that emphasizes right brain dominance would be culturally relevant and, most likely, more effective than are current models of learning that are based on left brain dominance. Therefore, the right brain techniques developed should incorporate aspects of cultural heritage and tribal tradition. The spiritual balance of total health must outweigh the attraction of drug and alcohol use in the individual, family, and tribal community (Marshall, 1986).

CONCLUSION

In the field of educational psychology, the 1980s has witnessed increasing concern for the individual child. Current issues in cross-cultural research indicate that the minority child may need an individual learning style that is culturally oriented (Fadely & Hunley, 1983). Socioeconomic pressures for accountability and a multitude of other factors make it difficult to address such concerns. Newer theories in learning and child development may be valuable in regard to the increasing problem of drug and alcohol abuse in the American Indian population, however. The application of new knowledge needed by an ethnic population restricted by the duality of poor socioeconomic factors and an extremely high rate of substance abuse among its youth should lead to the development of prevention techniques that are culturally relevant, use the principles of brain lateralization, and fulfill May's (1986) recommendations for an effective learning model for prevention programs.

REFERENCES

Bell, C., & Battjes, R. (1985). *Prevention research: Deterring drug abuse among children and adolescents* (NIDA Research Monograph No. 63; DHHS Publication No. ADM 85-1334). Washington, DC: U.S. Government Printing Office.

Bogen, J.E. (1975). Some educational aspects of hemispheric specialization. *UCLA Educator, 17*(2), 27–30.

Fadely, J. & Hunley, V. (1983). *Case studies in left and right hemispheric functioning.* Springfield, IL: Charles C. Thomas.

Indian Health Service. (1987). *School/community based alcoholism/substance abuse prevention study.* Washington, DC: U.S. Government Printing Office.

Marshall, J.A. (1986). *Right on—Prevention power.* Glendale, CA: American Safeteen.

May, P.A. (1986). Alcohol and drug misuse prevention programs for American Indians: Needs and opportunities. *Journal of Studies on Alcohol, 47*(3).

Vitale, B.M. (1986). *Unicorns are real: A right brained approach to learning.* Miami, FL: Jalmar Press.

36

Prevention of Alcoholism in Black Youth

Patricia Copeland

With approximately 29.9 million people, Black America represents the largest ethnic minority group in the United States. The black community is about 12.1% of the U.S. population (U.S. Department of Commerce, 1991), but remains over-represented among the health statistics for life-threatening illnesses. Moreover, alcoholism is the largest health problem in the black community (King, 1982).

A look at several of the leading causes of "excess deaths" among blacks (i.e., deaths above and beyond mortality rates expected for a given population) strongly suggests a correlation with alcohol and other drug abuse. One major cause of death directly attributable to alcohol, cirrhosis of the liver, is twice as common among black males as it is among white males. Murder, accidents of all kinds, and some cancers are also correlated with substance abuse. Alcohol is being pinpointed as a factor in several cancers, for example. The evidence of a direct causal relationship is strongest with cancer of the esophagus, and the rate among black men who are 35 to 49 years old is 10 times that of white males.

The identical factors that seem to result in a high level of violence in Black America also produce high rates of drug and alcohol abuse: low income; physical deterioration of the neighborhood; welfare dependency; disrupted families; lack of social support; low levels of education and vocational skills; high unemployment; a high proportion of young, single males; overcrowed, substandard housing; mixed land use; and high population density. Marshall (1989) asserted that 50% to 75% of the violent episodes involving blacks are in some way drug-related. One need only to know that the murder rate among blacks is 3 times the national average in some inner city neighborhoods to begin to understand the dimension of the problems.

It is necessary to develop a stronger sense of community and a clear consensus on acceptable and unacceptable behavior according to Afro-centric values that are based on a profound sense of collective responsibility for the mental, ethical, spiritual, and material well-being of the black community. Because the treatment prognosis for black people is currently very bad, more emphasis and effort should be placed on prevention. It appears that the focus should be directed toward the youth.

HISTORICAL ANTECEDENTS

Alcohol use among American blacks began during slavery. Slaves were commonly given alcohol by their owners on holidays as a reward for obedience and hard work. Drunkenness became an acceptable norm for holiday celebrations and was viewed as a means for preventing insurrection. However, fear of mass drunkenness and potential revolt was heightened following Nat Turner's rebellion in 1830. Laws were subsequently enacted placing tighter controls on drinking. Most even prevented blacks from owning stills. While these laws were virtually unenforceable during the Civil War, southern states again prevented blacks from possessing alcoholic beverages or firearms after the Civil War (Franklin, 1980).

"Political, social and economic conditions for Blacks worsened during Reconstruction. Political gains were quickly lost. In 1883, the Supreme Court outlawed the Civil Rights Act of 1875 and the doctrine of 'separate but equal' was instuted" (Brown & Tooley, 1988, p. 186). By 1910, most southern states had constitutionally disenfranchised free blacks (Frankin, 1980). The failure to gain political and economic reform in the South, along with maltreatment, resulted in a mass migration of blacks into northern industrial cities. In Philadelphia alone, the number of blacks rose from 84,000 in 1910 to 250,000 in 1940 (Ballard, 1984).

The great majority of the migrants were forced into slum ghettoes because of racial discrimination, a lack of marketable skills, and the country's economic instability. Moreover, family structure and relationships were disrupted and often dissolved as black men left their families behind in the agrarian South and went to find work and housing in the industrial North. Davis (1984) postulated that, for some, drinking became one means of coping with an environment devoid of support.

The conditions during that time were chronicled in the *Public Ledger* of June 24, 1925: "A slum can be found strongly entrenced in this North Philadelphia neighborhood. Ignorance, dirt, over crowding, disease, sloth, wine, drunkenness, corruption of youth; all have their strangle hold" (Ballard, 1984, p. 188). As the migration continued, blacks were still using alcohol for ceremonial celebrations—weddings, funerals, wakes, christenings, and holidays.

Black taverns grew up along the route to the North and, together with the churches, became centers for activities and social gatherings. These were the focal points of black social life partly because the housing situation was cramped and did not provide opportunities to gather and socialize. In addition, the laws that discriminated against blacks restricted them to using alcohol in restaurants and public bars.

Even today, many members of the black community see alcohol as a form of enslavement that is used to control the black community. Any kind of substance abuse, be it drug or alcohol, is destructive to black society because it interferes with the overall progress of blacks, numbs the frustration of discrimination, and decreases the chance that corrective action will be taken.

THE BLACK CHURCH

From the time that the first black church was founded in 1773, black churches have played a critically important role in sustaining the black family. They have served as both spiritual haven and extended family, providing a beleaguered people with vital material and human resources for survival. In addition to offering pastoral counseling, the churches have raised funds within their congregations to help friends and neighbors in need; they have taught reading and writing; they have established black colleges, burial societies, and other institutions in the black community; they have provided soup kitchens, nutritional education, housing, day care, and health care for the sick and elderly, among other services. The black church was a welfare agency for blacks long before the federal Department of Health and Human Services existed.

In the early decades of the 20th century, black churches became more secularized and began to lose what Frazier (1964) called "their other-worldly outlook" (p. 51). They became more interested in the affairs of the community and contributed to the work of the National Association for the Advancement of Colored People (NAACP) and the National Urban League. As mass migrations brought blacks from the South to northern cities, the black churches served as important way stations. The churches found that they had to respond to more transient populations and more families under stress. Furthermore, during the Civil Rights Movements, much of the organization and training in the tactics of nonviolence took place in the black churches.

Presently, the churches not only continue to respond to spiritual needs, but also are paying more attention to economic and social development within black communities. The majority offer services to one or more of the following groups: the elderly, children, teen-agers, the handicapped, substance abusers, run-aways, ex-offenders, and the families of the terminally ill.

Religion has also been a tool for controlling alcohol use. Historically, black churches have been conservative, Protestant, and against alcohol. This religiously motivated view of drinking has been changed in recent years, however.

YOUTH DRINKING BEHAVIOR

Research shows that young people from a background of abstinence drink and tend to drink heavily. The reason seems to be that these young people have no role models who drink moderately. The lack of ground rules for moderate drinking presents distinct challenges for those concerned with black youth and alcohol abuse prevention. Problem drinking among teen-agers is a growing concern in most black communities. Substance abuse prevention is the way of the future.

The appeal for abstinence is likely to fall upon deaf ears, because drinking is a behavior valued by teen-agers. Efforts to alleviate drinking problems and misuse are better accepted by teenagers than are attempts to stop their drinking. Today, prevention programs stress the right of teen-agers to make their own decisions and then focus on helping them set guidelines. This approach to prevention rests in a belief that individuals will make right and healthy choices about their own behavior.

A major concern of many black communities is the extent to which culture is infused into prevention projects. Because ethnic background, culture, and customs influence drinking behavior, they must be a part of any prevention program.

PREVENTION OF PROBLEM DRINKING

Research information on alcohol and blacks is limited. Experts on alcoholism generally agree, however, that youngsters need positive adult role models. Models come from many sources—the street, the home, the church, the school, the social services agencies, the media, and others. Because some are negative, especially those from television, youth must be exposed to positive role models for counterbalance.

Media messages on television, in magazines, and on billboards associate alcohol with glamour, sophistication, and maturity. With the use of very attractive models, ads create the illusion that liquor brings success, strength, wealth, and sexual conquest. Prime time television programs often portray drunkenness as humorous. All these say that alcohol use is an acceptable part of a modern way of life.

Other images significantly affect the way in which black youth see themselves: the unemployed gathered on the street corner, the abundance of liquor stores in black neighborhoods, the "drunk" at the bus stop. Drug and alcohol abuse in black lower income communities is a method of coping with unemployment, poverty, and all the accompanying social and economic derivatives. "Hanging out on the street corners" and drinking or abusing drugs gives black youth something to do.

Wilson (1987) noted that youth who graduate from high school are eager to find jobs and work at improving their marketable skills. Constant disappointments created by a lack of job opportunities over a period of 2 or 3 years cause black youth to develop an unemployed life style, however. They become accustomed to not working and, after some months or years, stop looking for work. According to Hare and Hare (1986), drinking among these adolescents is often associated with low self-esteem, a sense of powerlessness, poor interpersonal and social skills, poor academic or vocational performance, negative peer pressure, and poor family relationships.

In the black community, strategies to minimize alcohol abuse must directly counteract negative influences, such as the numerous alcohol ads, the presence of bars adjacent to schools and churches, and the availability of alcohol in grocery stores (Wilson, 1987).

Strategies may or may not be alcohol-specific. Those that are alcohol-specific deal directly with alcohol. They may include

- providing alcohol education in schools and churches
- encouraging responsible role models by parents and others who drink
- conducting alcohol-related film showings and conferences
- organizing community efforts to counter media glamorization of alcohol consumption
- sponsoring peer education programs
- training bartenders to expand their role
- developing public awareness campaigns to limit the number of alcohol ads on billboards in the community

All alcohol-specific strategies should provide clear and concise information on the debilitating effects that alcohol use and abuse have on the individual and on the community. This information should cover the psychological and physical aspects of alcohol use, as well as myths and misconceptions about alcohol. If youth are to relate to the information, it should be written in language that they can understand. Black culture and the history of alcohol use and abuse among blacks as a whole are also important. Information on the availability and accessibility of alcohol locally is also needed for planning ways to influence youthful drinking positively.

Non–alcohol-specific strategies focus on drinking patterns and behavior only indirectly; they deal with the broader aspects of living. They offer alternatives to drinking and facilitate interpersonal relations. For example, they may include

- job finding and job training skills
- assertiveness training classes

- alternative methods for relaxing (e.g., sports/recreation)
- opportunities for social interaction that do not involve alcohol
- peer counselor programs to assist young people with personal problems
- enhancement of skills that youth already have
- efforts to make the educational system more responsive to the students' needs

Regardless of what strategies are chosen, two factors should always be kept in mind:

1. Involvement of youth is crucial in all stages of program planning, implementation, and evaluation. Serious input by young people not only lends credibility to a program, but also adds fresh thinking and creativity.
2. Prevention strategies should be designed to influence as much of the total environment as possible.

Because alcohol use and abuse are interwined with so many aspects of life—home, school, advertising, law, media, economy, and the community—any strategy limited to a single aspect can achieve only limited objectives. The most meaningful strategy is one that promotes responsible behavior around the use or nonuse of alcohol and reduces the personal and social damage associated with inappropriate usage.

Potential Strategies

A communitywide master plan should be instituted to educate parents and community leaders about substance abuse and to establish standards of acceptable behavior in relation to adolescent drinking. Such a project is likely to require a long-term campaign supported by local media, the schools, fraternal organizations, the local philanthropic community, churches, and others to disseminate information creatively and through a variety of means. The community can no longer look the other way or give direct or indirect support to the alcohol and drug dealers and users: pimps, prostitutes, thieves, and drunks. No more buying and selling of stolen goods; no more bootlegging; and no more hiding, ennobling, or enabling of criminals. A network of school, church, and social services agencies should be established to demand and promote change. Schools should be resource centers to help promote this change.

A nationally sponsored media blitz, paid for by media outlets/networks, is needed to educate parents on the importance of their role in their children's decisions about drugs. Such programs should focus specifically on blacks in order to be effective with black families. They should be positive and upbeat, with the emphasis on establishing family traditions that do not include the use of alcohol or other drugs.

A uniform drug abuse prevention program for kindergarten through Grade 12 should be established in all states. A national board should monitor implementation. Community leaders should review the disciplinary policies of local school systems concerning drugs and alcohol. Intervention and education programs are needed to combat fetal alcohol syndrome and to provide postnatal education, as well as to assist pregnant teens.

Adolescents who have not used chemicals or who have begun to use chemicals, but have not yet experienced any problems, should have a support group. Social workers, counselors, or anyone who is trained in chemical dependency could lead such groups. These groups should be encouraged to implement community service projects for prevention.

Culturally specific services for children of alcoholics, including early intervention and reporting of symptomatic behavior by school personnel, are needed. A training program with cultural sensitivity should be developed around successful peer modeling. Black social fraternities and sororities can play a role in the development of alternative rites of passage for black children.

A media campaign featuring black actors and actresses who promote good health and wellness can be effective. Community leaders should lobby for free public service announcements on television, radio, cable television, and free cable resources. Black-owned media should take responsibility for disseminating information on health promotion and on the abuse of alcohol and other drugs through health fairs, editorials, public service announcements, and special promotions. A national campaign should be started to reduce and eventually eliminate alcohol advertising. Schools should organize student peer groups that discourage sexual acting out and substance abuse by exploring the health risks.

Black Values System Approach

Katrenga (1978), in cooperation with the Institute for Positive Education, has developed a black values system approach that can serve as a foundation for a black alcohol abuse prevention program. The principles may be used in a number of ways in educational programs for black youth. It can be adapted to meet special needs; it is culturally specific, as well as youth- and community-oriented.

1. *umoja* (unity): to strive for and maintain unity in the family, community, nation, and race
2. *kujichahulia* (self-determination): to define ourselves, name ourselves, and speak for ourselves instead of being defined and spoken for by others

3. *ujimma* (collective work responsibility): to build and maintain our community together and to make our brothers' and sisters' problems our problems and to solve them together
4. *uama* (cooperative economics): to build and own stores, shops, and other business, and to profit together from them
5. *nea* (purpose): to make as our collective vocation the building and developing of our community in order to restore our people to their traditional greatness
6. *kuumba* (creativity): to do always as much as we can, in order to leave our community more beautiful and beneficial than when we inherited it
7. *imani* (faith): to believe in our parents, our teachers, our leaders, our people, and ourselves, and the righteousness and victory of our struggle (Katrenga, 1978, p. 48)

CONCLUSION

The most effective programs to prevent alcohol abuse among black adolescents have adapted a culture-specific alcohol-specific educational model that focuses on the individual and his or her environment. Black history, self awareness, and values are all integrated into a broader framework focused on the adolescents as citizens in a multicultural pluralistic society. Cultural identity is an important aspect of society and of an alcohol abuse prevention program. There is and there should be sensitivity toward the language and terminology used to connote a racial or cultural heritage, religion, or color.

An alcohol education program for black youth must provide opportunities for these youngsters to discard negativism. Many of them have been hardened by the reality of their life styles, but it is possible to help them see beyond the present and set positive goals for the future. It is important to change their attitudes about themselves and to teach them survival skills, such as problem solving, decision making, and valuing. Black youth should learn that everyone has problems. The issue is not the number of big problems, but ways to find solutions.

Because black youth are often confined to their communities, they may lack knowledge or exposure to the majority community; this can make any contact frustrating, intimidating, or frightening. Low-income youth, however, have a cadre of skills that they have developed through necessity. Many of these youngsters assumed adult responsibilities when they were very young. Some have complete charge of younger brothers and sisters, do economical grocery shopping with food stamps, and manage households while their mothers work or are absent from the home. Many youngsters take on this responsibility as early as age 6. Thus, black youth do have a base knowledge for learning coping and survival skills.

Because drinking is part of U.S. society and black culture as well, youth alcohol abuse prevention efforts should focus on teaching responsible decision making about alcohol use. The study of other cultures provides an opportunity for black youth to gain new knowledge to help them establish their own ground rules. An awareness that fundamentalist Christians, for example, have low alcohol consumption rates may stimulate discussions on transferring certain aspects of these cultures to black communities.

An understanding of the reasons that youth drink, the influence of role models and value systems, and the significance of black culture are important considerations when designing behavioral change programs. Planners should incorporate culturally specific strategies into their program plans, learning from similar ongoing black community efforts when possible. Traditional prevention strategies that have successfully served other youth populations can be adapted and made relevant to black youngsters, provided that new programs are philosophically committed to recognizing the importance of cultural differences.

REFERENCES

Ballard, A.B. (1984). *One more day's journey.* New York: McGraw-Hill.

Brown, F., & Tooley, J. (1988). *Alcoholism in the black community* (pp. 185–212). Paper presented to Dr. Gary Lawson. Spring Quarter, United States International University.

Davis, F. (1984). Alcoholism among American blacks. *Addiction, 3,* 8–16.

Franklin, J.H. (1980). *From slavery to freedom: A history of Negro Americans.* New York: Knopf.

Frazier, E.F. (1964). *The Negro church in America.* New York: Schocken Books.

Hare, N., & Hare, J. (1986). *The endangered black family.* San Francisco: Black Think Tank.

Katrenga, R.M. (1978). *Essay on struggle: Position and analysis.* San Diego: Kawaida Publications.

King, L.M. (1982). Alcoholism: Studies regarding black Americans, 1977–1980 (*Alcohol and Health* Monograph No. 4). *Special Population Issues,* 385–407.

Marshall, O.A. (1989). Speaker at Conference on *Chemical dependency and the black community.* Paper presented at conference of Morehouses' Cork Institute on Black Alcohol and Drug Abuse.

U.S. Department of Commerce, Economics and Statistics Administration. (1991). *Statistical abstract of the United States.* Washington, DC: U.S. Government Printing Office.

Wilson, W.J. (1987). *The truly disadvantaged.* Chicago: University of Chicago Press.

Summary and Conclusions

Adolescents have always faced problems growing into adulthood. However, rarely in human history have there been so many obstacles between childhood and adulthood and so many expectations for our youth. At the same time, the resources available for a struggling adolescent seem to be dwindling.

Nuclear and extended families are not as available as they once were; for a variety of reasons, both parents work, parents are separated, grandparents live across the country. Classes in schools are often large and impersonal. Teachers have little personal time for individual students. School counselors are overworked and are often assigned many additional duties that do not include helping troubled students. Social services offered by the federal, state, and local governments are limited by budget cuts, and, when programs are available, they are crowded with a waiting list for services. Adolescents are reluctant to take advantage of the services they offer. Churches, due to their conservative and often dogmatic nature, are often unappealing to the young.

Adolescent substance abuse is not a problem that will go away on its own. It is not a problem that can be solved with less than a Trojan effort on the part of everyone including parents, extended families, mental health professionals, schools, churches, the government, private agencies, and perhaps most of all, adolescents themselves.

Yet there are forces that work against solutions to substance abuse. There are strong economic and social factors that must be overcome. As the "haves" have more and the "have nots" have less, it becomes less and less likely that we can expect drug abuse to go away. In fact, as it becomes less likely that a young person from a ghetto or poor neighborhood will have a legitimate and equal opportunity to achieve a reasonable social and economic status, it becomes more likely that he or she will turn to drugs to achieve economic independence or to escape the reality of the situation by dulling the senses with drugs.

On the other end of the continuum, those adolescents who are economically advantaged and grow up wanting for little, lacking direction and purpose in life, are equally victims of their circumstances. It is perhaps easier to blame them or their drug use for their problems, than to blame their situation in life. We are all totally responsible for our own behavior and our fate, yet not responsible at all, unless we know the relationship between the behavior and fate. Adolescents are dependent on the adults around them to provide knowledge and guidance while they seek answers to questions that may not have answers and as they find answers that don't fit the questions. For all too many adolescents, drugs seem to be the only answer.

It is up to responsible adults to provide new answers and new questions for these troubled adolescents. It is our hope that this book will help provide some of the answers and perhaps some new questions that will ultimately assist in finding the solutions to these most pressing problems of our young.

Appendix A

Suggested Readings

Alexander, J.F. (1974). Behavior modification and delinquent youth. In J.C. Cull & R.E. Hardy (Eds.), *Behavior modification in rehabilitation settings*. Springfield, IL: Charles C. Thomas.

Friedman, A.S., Tomoka, L.A., & Utada, A. (1991). Client and family characteristics that predict better family therapy outcome for adolescent drug abusers. *Family Dynamics of Addiction Quarterly, 1*(1), 77–93.

Lewis, R.A., Piercy, F.P., Sprenkle, D.H, & Trepper, T.S. (1991). The Purdue brief family therapy model for adolescent substance abusers. In T. Todd & M. Selekman (Eds.), *Family therapy approaches with adolescent substance abusers*. Needham Heights, MA: Allyn & Bacon.

Lewis, R.A. (1991). Testimony before the House Select Committee on Children, Families, Drugs and Alcoholism. *Hearing on adolescent substance abuse: Barriers to treatment*. 101st Congress of the United States, Washington, DC.

Liddle, H. & Diamond, G. (1991). Adolescent substance abusers in family therapy: The critical initial phase of treatment. *Family Dynamics of Addiction Quarterly, 1*(1), 55–68.

Minuchin, S., Rosman, B., & Baker, L. (1978). *Psychosomatic families: Anorexia nervosa in context*. Cambridge, MA: Harvard University Press.

Piercy, F.F., & Frankel, B.R. (1989). The evolution of an integrative family therapy for substance-abusing adolescents: Toward the mutual enhancement of research and practice. *Journal of Family Psychology, 3*(1), 5–25.

Quinn, W.H., Kuehl, B.P., Thomas, F.N., & Joanning, H. (1988). Families of adolescent drug abusers: Systemic interventions to attain drug-free behavior. *American Journal of Drug and Alcohol Abuse, 14*(1), 65–87.

Stanton, M.D., & Todd, T.C. (1982). *The family therapy of drug abuse and addiction*. New York: Guilford Press.

Szapocznik, J., & Kurtines, W.M. (1989). *Breakthroughs in family therapy with drug-abusing problem youth*. New York: Springer.

Szapocznik, J., Kurtines, W.M., Foot, F., Perez-Vidal, A., & Hervis, O. (1983). Conjoint versus one person family therapy: Some evidence for the effectiveness of conducting family therapy through one person. *Journal of Consulting and Clinical Psychology, 51,* 889–899.

Szapocznik, J., Kurtines, W.M., Foot, F., Perez-Vidal, A., & Hervis, O. (1986). Conjoint versus one person family therapy: Further evidence for the effectiveness of conducting family therapy through one person with drug abusing adolescents. *Journal of Consulting and Clinical Psychology, 54*(3), 395–397.

Szapocznik, J., Perez-Vidal, A., Brickman, A.L., Foote, F.H., Santisteban, D., & Hervis, O. (1988). Engaging adolescent drug abusers and their families in treatment: A strategic structural systems approach. *Journal of Consulting and Clinical Psychology, 56*(4), 552–557.

Szapocznik, J., Rio, A., Perez-Vidal, A., Santisteban, D., & Kurtines, W. (1989). Family effectiveness training: An intervention to prevent drug abuse and problem behavior in Hispanic adolescents. *Hispanic Journal of Behavioral Sciences, 11*(4), 4–27.

Index _____